ISSN 0043-8243

Volume 8 No 1
June 1976

World Archaeology

This issue
Archaeology and linguistics

World Archaeology

Volume 8 No. 1 June 1976

Published thrice yearly by the proprietors
Routledge & Kegan Paul Ltd
68–74 Carter Lane, London EC4V 5EL

Single copies £3 ($8.00)
Annual subscription £7·50 ($20.00)

ISSN 0043-8243

Printed in Great Britain by
The Camelot Press Ltd, Southampton

Issues of *World Archaeology* now in preparation cover the themes:
'Climatic Change' (October 1976. Editor: W.M.B.)
'Bioarchaeology' (February 1977. Editor: D.R.)
'Island Archaeology' (June 1977. Editor: I.C.G.)
'Architecture and Archaeology' (October 1977. Editor: M.B.)

The editors welcome suggestions for contributions to any of the projected issues, and would be glad at all times to consider important new work for immediate publication, whether or not it coincides with an announced theme.

It is not current editorial policy to publish reviews as a regular feature of the journal. Review articles will cover literature in particular fields, and a list of books received will be printed from time to time.

Archaeology and linguistics

Contents

page

5 Linguistic evidence and its correlation with archaeology
Christopher Ehret

19 Austronesian culture history: some linguistic inferences and their relations to the archaeological record
Robert Blust

44 Time perspective and proto-Indo-European culture
J. P. Mallory

57 Loanwords and Roman expansion in north-west Europe
John Peter Wild

65 Archaeology and Bantu linguistics
D. W. Phillipson

83 Language and the prehistory of North America
M. Dale Kinkade and J. V. Powell

101 Archaeological and linguistic correlations in Mayaland and associated areas of Meso-America
Terrence Kaufman

Cover: The Rosetta stone (by courtesy of the Trustees of the British Museum).

Theme titles of past issues of *World Archaeology*

Volume	Number	Theme
1	1	Recent work and new approaches
1	2	Techniques of chronology and excavation
1	3	Analysis
2	1	Early man
2	2	Urban archaeology
2	3	Subsistence
3	1	Technological innovations
3	2	Archaeology and ethnography
3	3	Art and design
4	1	Population
4	2	Nomads
4	3	Theories and assumptions
5	1	Colonization
5	2	Trade
5	3	Stone Age studies
6	1	Political systems
6	2	Miscellany
6	3	Currency
7	1	Burial
7	2	Dating
7	3	Archaeology and history

Linguistic evidence and its correlation with archaeology

Christopher Ehret

Introduction

Historical reconstruction from linguistic evidence alone or from the correlation of linguistic with archaeological findings is in neither case a new enterprise. A whole field of Indo-European studies arose around the investigation of linguistic relationships of the Indo-European family of languages and has for many decades included, as a major component, the search for the archaeological correlates of the groupings postulated by linguistics. The attribution of particular archaeological traditions to particular Indo-European language groups began first to be firmly established for the Classical period in the Mediterranean and the contemporary eras in central Europe, but more recent work is beginning to push the frontier of effective archaeological linguistic correlation in European history back to the third millennium B.C. (e.g. Gimbutas 1963; Mellaart 1970). An extensive literature of correlation has been developed also in the field of pre-contact American history – as copious in quantity as for Indo-European studies, but more uneven in coverage, perhaps because of the greater area and complexity of societies to be studied.

But despite its respectable pedigree, historical reconstruction from language evidence has never been used to the full, and hence archaeological correlations have had to be made from less detailed and therefore less solid evidence than might have been desirable. The linguistic emphasis has been placed on just one level of potential argumentation for history, namely on those sorts of historical inferences which derive from the establishment of the common ancestry of languages and on the shared elements which go to make up that common ancestry. Extensive use has also been made of toponymy, the study of place names. Some scholars, to be sure, have sought out the elements in particular languages which were not derivable from the ancestry of the language and which might therefore have been adopted into the language from another nearby speech. Especially this approach has been applied in the attempt to discover which languages might have been spoken in a region before the present language came into use there. But such investigations have been so often vaguely defined in conception, and so unsystematically pursued, that this kind of research has become suspect.

It is understandable that European studies tend to pursue the first line of investigation, since most of Europe is covered, and has been covered for two thousand to three thousand years, by languages of a single family. The evidence for earlier languages is difficult to pick out because of the lack of any extant versions of such languages (except perhaps Basque) with which to compare possible pre-Indo-European elements in Indo-European languages; and the potential of word-borrowing patterns among more recent languages for historical studies has never been followed up because of the frequency of documentary sources for European history. The failure to pursue all lines of linguistic argument in New World studies is less understandable, unless perhaps it is because anthropologists rather than historians have been prominent in archaeological endeavours and so may not have been interested in all the sorts of historical questions which would have encouraged the expansion of linguistic methodology for history.

It is, instead, in African historical studies where documentary sources rapidly thin out as we go back in time, where a complexity of language families persist often side by side, and where archaeology is in the Old World rather than the New World mould – that the full potential of linguistic evidence as a historical source is beginning to emerge. This emergence will in turn make Africa a laboratory for study of correlation between archaeology and linguistics in understanding the past.

Inference from the evidence of relationship

The underlying foundation of all historical inference from linguistic evidence, whether in Africa or elsewhere, is the establishment of the relationships of all the languages in and about the region of historical investigation. The methods of establishing relationship are too complex to discuss here, but at base they revolve around the concept that languages, as systems of communication, go through systematic phonological changes as a simple consequence of the necessity of preserving intelligibility. Related languages, 'related' because they derive from a common ancestral language, will share in a common fund of cognate words which go back to their common ancestor. These cognates will no longer be pronounced exactly the same, but they will differ phonologically in regularly predictable ways. The rules governing the sound changes can then be worked out by a linguist, and the relative chronological order of the rules in the history of the languages can for the most part be reconstructed.

As the whole last fifty to sixty years of linguistic research have shown, each language has a single line of descent. There seems to be no such creature as a true *Mischsprache*, a language formed from the merging of two or more languages. Every language consists of a fundamental inherited core, plus differing degrees of admixture, sometimes extensive, of elements adopted from other languages with which that language has interacted during its history.

The genetic metaphor for linguistic relationships turns out to be a quite precise fit for linguistic reality if it is clearly understood that mitotic descent is meant (Welmers 1973: 2–9; for a misunderstanding of the genetic metaphor and a resulting somewhat quixotic defence of *Mischsprachen*, see Dalby 1966). A language may diverge over a period of centuries, into two or more daughter languages, even as a mother cell splits by mitosis, but over a period of minutes, into daughter cells. As in mitosis there is a period when the elements of two separate bodies have appeared, but the parent body has not yet broken into two distinct offspring. In linguistic terms the mother language begins first to diverge into dialects but remains none the less one language. As differentiation proceeds the dialects gradually become no longer mutually intelligible, and so finally become separate daughter languages. As also with mitotic division, the mother persists only in its daughters, so that it is absurd to speak of one language as older than another, except perhaps in the case of a dead language such as church Latin, which has been preserved by the fossilization we call writing. Daughter languages can become mother languages themselves, and their daughters in turn mother languages, and so on through history. Whether a particular language will diverge in such a manner or continue as a single, though continually changing, language through a particular period of time depends, of course, on the particular historical circumstances of the language and the society which speaks it.

The past historical existence of a society

This inference is a simple direct one: If the former existence of a language (the mother language of some modern languages) must be postulated, then there must also have been a community or set of communities speaking that language. The usual picture of relationships will imply the existence of a whole array of societies existing at different relative periods in the past. Consider the Southern Cushitic languages of East Africa. Ancestral Southern Cushitic, or proto-Southern Cushitic, diverged into three daughter languages, proto-Rift, proto-Mbuguan, and proto-Dahaloan. The latter two each today have only a single extant descendant language, so their histories between the proto-Southern Cushitic period and the present cannot be followed on the basis of relationship evidence alone. But proto-Rift, on the other hand, diverged into two daughter languages, which are called proto-West Rift and proto-East Rift. Proto-East Rift has two modern daughter languages, Asa and Kw'adza, whilst proto-West Rift split into three languages, Iraqw, Burunge and Alagwa, which are still spoken today (Ehret *forthcoming* a). This history can be diagrammed as follows:

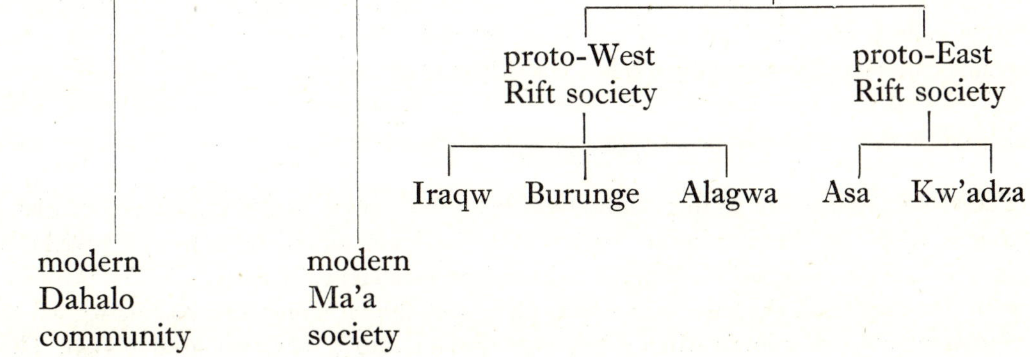

For linguistic continuity there must also be parallel social continuities of some kind. So the second inference that must be made is that between the historical nodes of the diagram there continuously existed societies speaking Southern Cushitic languages. Each line on the diagram represents a line of cultural-historical, as well as linguistic, descent. It does not always have to have been an unbroken descent. Dahaloan began apparently as the language of a food-producing community. Then, at some point probably two or three thousand years ago, a hunter-gatherer community speaking a Khoisan language came under the economic and political domination of the Dahaloans. In time, the hunter-gatherers gave up their Khoisan language in favour of Dahaloan while still maintaining their hunter-gatherer pursuits. Other dominant food-producing societies subsequently displaced and absorbed the Dahaloan food-producers; but the Dahalo language continued to be used by the hunter-gatherer community, and it was through this new line of social descent that the Dahalo speech has come down to us in its modern form (Ehret 1974a: 9–12).

Inference of culture from reconstructed vocabulary

For each mother language on a diagram of relationship, such as that shown above for Southern Cushitic languages, it is possible to reconstruct, on the basis of cognate forms in daughter languages, a goodly portion of the mother language's vocabulary, including words for cultural items and ideas. The existence of a word for something requires at least the acquaintance of the people speaking the language with the thing named, and the reconstructibility of a whole set of words dealing with a particular set of practices or ideas would show not only the bare knowledge but the practical importance of the set in the culture. Proto-Southern Cushitic roots, among others, for two species of grains, gruel, porridge, flour, 'to cultivate', 'to harvest', and 'to pound grain' make an irrefutable case for cultivation of grain crops by the proto-Southern Cushitic society. An equally complex reconstructible herding vocabulary, including verbs for 'to milk' and 'to bleed cattle', shows a similar practical importance of livestock raising in proto-Southern Cushitic economy (Ehret *forthcoming* a: table I; 1974a: 7–9).

The proto-Nilotes, who resided in the south-eastern Middle Nile Basin in (very approximately) the third millennium B.C., were sharply different in economy from the roughly contemporary proto-Southern Cushites (Ehret 1971: 26–31). While a complex herding vocabulary attests proto-Nilotic pastoralism, the presence of only three proto-Nilotic grain terms at most and no other cultivation terms suggests only a peripheral acquaintance with cultivation of any kind, possibly through the trade of livestock for grains cultivated by neighbouring peoples (Ehret *et al.* 1974).

Location of proto-communities from vocabulary evidence

The classic application of this method has been in the case of the Indo-European languages, where the distribution of beech trees and salmon, among other things, have been used to locate the proto-Indo-European homeland (see Heller 1972: 33–5). The problem with this method is the ease with which plant and animal names can be re-assigned to similar plants and animals when a language spreads into a new ecological region. The beech tree reconstruction in proto-Indo-European may be semantically certain, but then beech trees occur all over Europe, in patches as far south as the Mediterranean regions and as far east as the Caucasus zone. And the root with the supposed meaning 'salmon' could have referred to another similar fish found in the Caspian and Black Sea watersheds. This method is thus most useful in eliminating areas as the possible homeland, but not particularly effective in pinpointing locations.

Location of proto-communities on distributional grounds

This method is essentially an application of the rule of Occam's razor. The proposed location of the proto-language which requires the fewest and least complex population movements to explain the present-day distribution of daughter languages is the most probable solution. In many cases a very close determination of high probability can be made on the basis of this criterion. The Kalenjin language, for instance, consists of five very distinct dialects. Four of these are spoken in a compact region of western Kenya, while the fifth, South Kalenjin, occurs several hundred kilometres away in central Tanzania. It is so immensely improbable that four peoples should spread out of some third area, or for that matter out of central Tanzania, and all by mere chance end up tightly clustered in another place altogether that no solution can reasonably be entertained other than that proto-Kalenjin was spoken somewhere in the area of western Kenya defined by the four clustered dialects, and that the South Kalenjin spread via population movements from there. More complex applications of the same basic principle have been made in plotting the spread of the Bantu peoples (Ehret 1973), Ubangian speaking peoples (Ehret *et al.* 1974), and the Austronesians (Dyen 1965). Other important applications have been made in Native American history (e.g. Sapir 1916; Lamb 1958).

The preceding four types of inference have accounted for most of the use made so far of linguistic evidence to reconstruct history. The first three have been particularly important in Indo-European studies; the last has been most widely applied in Amerindian studies. But at least two additonal categories of inference can be based on the evidence of linguistic relationships.

Shifts in semantic categorization as indicators of cultural change

Some sort of system seems always present in human perceptions of a set of items, and that system can be determined by eliciting the folk taxonomy of the words dealing with the items. One level of historical inference from such evidence is internal to a language. Ambiguities and semantic overlap in a taxonomy would tend to show up where significant changes had occurred in the content and organization of knowledge in the sphere indicated by the taxonomy. Also, the etymologies of particular words could reveal underlying metaphors or conceptual associations once, but no longer, present in the language or not in keeping with the taxonomy into which the particular words were now fitted. But the most productive enterprise should be the comparative study of taxonomies in daughter languages with a view towards reconstructing the organization and significance of different kinds of knowledge in their mother language, and therefore in the society which spoke that language (Ehret 1972). The method has special value in deciphering intangibles of past cultures, things rarely amenable to archaeology's ministrations. But material culture as well is part of knowledge and equally suited to taxonomic analysis. The relatively late (first millennium A.D.) and separate developments of extensive livestock raising by different Eastern Bantu peoples shows up quite clearly in their various replacements of the proto-Eastern three-part classification of livestock – category ('cow', 'goat') with subdivisions of 'male domestic animal' and 'female domestic animal' – by several much more complex systems of classification according to age and sex, with a separate taxonomy for each kind of domestic animal eaten, of which there were now not just two but as many as five (Ehret 1974b).

Dialect networks as a stage in linguistic differentiation

As a mother language begins to differentiate into daughters, an intermediate period ensues during which the language consists of dialects each eventually to give rise to a daughter language but still not so different from each other as to be considered separate languages. If speakers of different dialects do not move off to settle in distant areas, and if no inruptive movements of other peoples break up the continuity of the language area, then the dialects will continue to be spoken by contiguous communities each able to understand each other's speech, i.e. the communities will form a dialect network or chain. In such a network of related but diverging communities, a tendency will exist for changes, such as lexical innovations, which arise in one dialect to spread to one or more of its neighbouring dialects. The long-term result with respect to vocabulary will be that daughter languages which arose out of neighbouring dialects of the mother language will share a somewhat greater proportion of apparent inherited vocabulary than will dialects further removed from each other in the dialect continuum. The original geography of dialects in the mother language can thus often be inferred from the variations in the percentages of cognation between the various daughter languages (Ehret *et al.* 1972).

Historical inference from adopted elements in languages

The potentialities of using adopted, in linguistic terms 'borrowed', elements as a guide to the historical interactions between societies have for the most part been given scant appreciation. But they seem in fact to be the most useful kind of linguistic evidence of all. While all parts of a language – lexicon, morphology, and syntax – can in theory absorb adopted elements, in practice it is only borrowings in the lexicon (loanwords) which provide a sufficient body of data with specific historical content.

While loanwords may provide the single most important source of linguistic evidence for history, their usefulness depends on establishment first of the relationships of the languages in which they occur. The evidence of language relationship is essential to the distinguishing of loanwords from inherited vocabulary and to the determination of direction of word-borrowing. Moreover, it is the framework of language relationships which acts as the relative time scale of the linguistic and the related historical developments.

The less certain technique for dating a loanword is to determine when earliest it can be said with certainty to appear of a linguistic time scale. If the word can be reconstructed for a particular former language but not located in a still earlier language ancestral to that one, then it must have been borrowed no later than the period when the more recent of the two was spoken. A Khoisan loanword for honey, *-dʌn-, is known only in the West Rift languages of Southern Cushitic and so was certainly borrowed as early as the proto-West Rift period. The problem is that there is no way of eliminating the possibility that the root belongs in fact to the set of Khoisan loanwords which date to proto-Southern Cushitic (Ehret *forthcoming* a), but just happens to have persisted down to the present only in West Rift languages while dropping out of use elsewhere in the language family.

The better method, where applicable, is to locate the time of word-borrowing relative to the historically ordered rules of sound change in the languages involved. If a loanword in a language shows an expected sound change, then it must have been borrowed before the governing rule came into effect; if it fails to show the expected change, then it was borrowed after the rule ceased to operate. In similar fashion a loanword can be dated with respect to sound-shifts in the language from which it was borrowed. An unusual rule reversing tones in words occurred at some point in the history of the Luba language during the last thousand years. The Luba word for tribute *musònkò* turns in Nyanja in a form without the tone reversal, thus reflecting political influences spreading from the Luba area prior to the sound-shift – influences presumably identifiable with the appearance of Luban chiefly houses in Malawi ascribed by tradition to approximately the thirteenth or fourteenth century. In contrast, the same noun occurs *with* tone reversal through most of eastern Zambia, thus reflecting a later wave of Luba influence, dating after the sound change. Eastern Zambian oral traditions, which place the spread of Luba political influence there in the sixteenth to eighteenth centuries, confirm the linguistic inference.

Once loanword data have been thus processed and grouped by source and relative date of borrowing, it becomes possible to assess the kinds of situations in which they were adopted and the sorts of history that account for their being borrowed.

Identification of the ethnic neighbourhood

Before the development of specialized intellectual traditions, words were normally only borrowed in situations of direct contact between peoples. Hence the borrowing of words during a particular period implies that people speaking the borrowing language lived nearby or adjoining the people from whose language the words came. In a regional study, where the relationships and word-borrowing patterns of each language of the region are taken into account, a complex interlocking picture of relative linguistic, and therefore societal, distributions through time can be constructed (Ehret *forthcoming* b). Transferred to a real map, it can allow correlations with archaeology of far greater confidence than the study, however sophisticated, of a single language family, can ever hope to attain.

Location of communities through loanword-attested contacts

Loanword evidence can also be used to corroborate and expand on the inferences of location from language relationship. For instance, the South Kalenjin dialect, as discussed previously, is spoken today by a small community in central Tanzania, while the rest of the Kalenjin dialects are spoken hundreds of kilometres away in western Kenya. For reasons of distribution, South Kalenjin must be argued to have spread through population movements from western Kenya to its present location. But the form and paths of spread remain unclear. Loanword evidence fills in the missing data. South Kalenjin loanwords were borrowed by the Asa language of central Masailand in Tanzania before the spread of the Masai across that area in the eighteenth century; South Kalenjin loans also occur in Masai in a set which must have been adopted by that language during the first stage of Masai expansion. That stage, according to the oral record, took place across central south Kenya during roughly the sixteenth and seventeenth centuries; hence South Kalenjin speakers must have lived that far north, adjoining the rest of the Kalenjin, as late as the sixteenth century (Ehret 1971: 63–71). Loanword evidence thus confirms the South Kalenjin expansion out of western Kenya and shows in addition the geography of that expansion and, in conjunction with the Masai data, the subsequent decline of the South Kalenjin before the advance of the Masai since mid-millennium.

Identifying no longer existing societies

Frequently in history languages have become entirely extinct with not even a remnant of speakers left. Almost universally some sort of loanword evidence of a language's former existence persists in its successor language, but the identification of the loanword remnant requires the continued existence somewhere of a language clearly related to the extinct one. The unique West Germanic root seen in English *sheep*, though presumably of non-Indo-European provenance, will probably always remain unattributed because of the complete extinction of the pre-Indo-European languages of north-western Europe. In contrast, a heavy general loanword set in the Thagicu languages of central Kenya can be shown to come from a language related to, but quite distinct from, modern Ma'a (Southern Cushitic). So many words passed from the now extinct language into its successor, proto-Thagicu, that even many of its sound-change rules can be indirectly discerned in its loanwords; and from these rules the language can be seen to have belonged originally to the same Mbuguan branch of Southern Cushitic as Ma'a, but to have later split from Ma'a and gone off on its own course of linguistic change. Hence the loanword evidence not only shows the manner of shift of people from Mbuguan to Thagicu speech and the kinds and degrees of culture change through the period of language shift, but also reveals important facets of the history of the region before the language shift.

Inferring the general nature of interethnic relations

The frequency of word-borrowing and kinds of words borrowed correlate with the kinds of relations which obtained between people during the period of borrowing.

Investigations in modern East African history suggest the tentative defining of five categories of word-borrowing (for the first four categories, see Ehret 1971: 10–25). The categories need refinement and testing against the experience of linguists elsewhere, but give every indication of wider applicability, as some of the examples which follow suggest.

A category of *intensive word-borrowing*, characterized by heavy word-borrowing generally through the culture vocabulary plus the borrowing even of a number of core vocabulary[1] words, seems to result from a situation in which the people adopting the words have been, usually for a few centuries, under the political and economic domination of the people from whose language the words come. The extreme examples in East Africa are provided by the situations of numerically small hunter-gatherer groups surrounded by not only dominant, but much more numerous Masai pastoralists. In the languages of some such communities as much as 10% of the items on the Swadesh 100-word list of core vocabulary – an extraordinary proportion – have been borrowed over the past three to four hundred years from Masai (e.g. Kamelilo in Ehret 1971: 94). A less intense dominance, perhaps because the conquered far outnumbered the conquerors, is reflected in the medieval French loanword set in English, which consists of numerous borrowings in the culture vocabulary but only a very few, such as *mountain*, in the core vocabulary.

A second category, *heavy general word-borrowing*, is characterized by numerous borrowings throughout the culture vocabulary but little or no borrowing in core lexicon. The East African examples suggest that this pattern generally results from the dying out of the language from which the loanwords came and its replacement by the language which borrowed the set, but with considerable cultural carry-over despite the shift in language.

The third category, *light general word-borrowing*, is characterized by the presence of loanwords in many parts of cultural vocabulary but nowhere in great numbers. It may reflect either the replacement of one language by another, accompanied by almost complete eclipse of the previous culture, or extensive and important cultural and/or economic relations between peoples without language replacement. The non-religious loanwords from Latin in early Anglo-Saxon conform to this pattern and support the argument that the language of lowland Britain which gave way before Anglo-Saxon expansion was in fact Latin, not Celtic. The light general set of Middle Dutch and Low German loanwords in English reflects, on the other hand, the extensiveness and deep importance of Medieval English relations with Flemish, and to a lesser extent, Hanseatic areas.

To this can be added a fourth category, *sporadic word-borrowing*, reflective of the presence of the people speaking the donor language of the loans as neighbours of the people borrowing the words, but without notable cultural, political, economic, or demographic influence on the word-borrowers. Portuguese loanwords in Swahili fit this category, as do Celtic loanwords in Anglo-Saxon and Welsh loans, such as *flimsy*, in later English. The Celtic evidence thus further supports the argument above that Celtic speakers were western neighbours of the early Anglo-Saxons, but that it was Latin-speaking Britons who were actually absorbed by Anglo-Saxon expansion in lowland Britain.

[1] The concept of core vocabulary encompasses the terminology of universally recognized, everyday things and actions, such as 'eye', 'nose', 'rain', 'to eat', 'to fly' etc.

The final category, *specific cultural borrowing*, includes both the borrowing of a set of words restricted in reference to one area of culture and the borrowing of a single word for a single culture item. Such borrowing indicates that the people speaking the source language of the loanwords were viewed as especially knowledgeable or gifted in the specific cultural area of the loans or, when a single word was involved, that the people speaking the source language were the immediate source of the item or trait indicated by the word.

Inferring the specific content of culture influence

This area of historical inference is in essence an extended application of the category of specific cultural borrowing. Every general loanword set, intensive, heavy, or light, can be seen to consist of many specific cultural subsets. To the extent that loanwords are scattered randomly through the culture vocabulary they cannot be argued to show more than the general fact of interaction. But where randomness breaks down, specific kinds of cultural influence can be demonstrated. In Dahalo, for instance, intensive word-borrowing sets from Galla and coastal Bantu languages turn up and can be followed throughout the vocabulary with the exception of one area of non-overlap in subsistence terminology: loanwords for livestock in Dahalo come from Galla, while loanwords dealing with cultivation all come from Bantu, a division entirely in keeping with what we know of the subsistence emphases of the two dominant societies.

Tracing the diffusion of things and ideas

Another sort of extended application of the evidence of specific cultural borrowing is used in tracing the diffusion of cultural materials. Simplistically speaking, the sequence of borrowing of terms for an item from language to language traces the diffusion of the item from people to people. The spread of knowledge of the banana to the English from West Africa can be followed in the borrowing of the term for the fruit, *banana*, first by Portuguese from a Guinea coast language and then by English from the Portuguese language. The German term shows a slightly different transmission, entering the language from French which had in turn adopted its form of the word from Portuguese, probably via Spanish. Many, if not most, applications of this technique turn out to be more difficult and complex than the example of the banana, however; but the basic idea, at least, can be seen in the example (for other discussions and applications relevant to African history, see Knappert 1970; also Ehret 1974b).

Other kinds of historical inference from linguistic evidence

Toponymy

The study of place names is an additional type of linguistic study for history that has venerable standing. There are two particular uses for toponymic evidence. One is the identification of earlier languages spoken, and hence societies resident, in a region through the preservation of their place names into later times when other languages had come to be spoken in their place. While extensive place-name studies have been made all over Europe, the possibilities of African place-name evidence in historical reconstruction have remained untapped. For example, systematic place-name investigations in present Masai territory in East Africa should corroborate the history of the South Kalenjin people discernible in other types of linguistic evidence. Indeed, there are preliminary indications that such is the case. In central south Kenya the name of a stream *Pinyiny* has no meaning in Masai, but means 'leeches' in Kalenjin; and leeches indeed occur in the stream. Further south in central Masailand there is a hilly area called simply *Ol-lekemet*. *Ol-* is the Masai article, but the stem of the word is the South Kalenjin word for 'hill' (Akie *lekeme*, from earlier *lekemet).

The second use of toponymy is an etymological one. Place names all originally had some specific reference either to a feature of the place, or to an event that occurred thereabout, or to a person or thing associated with the place. If the meaning of a place-name can be discovered, that meaning therefore frequently has some historical reference of which the archaeologist or historian may be able to make use. If a stream, for instance, is called 'Pine River', and there are no pines about, then we have learned something about the past ecology of the area and about its past potential usefulness to people. The fact that there are no pines there today is probably because people have cut them all down. The historian is then able to ask, what caused so great a demand for wood or need to clear the trees and where was the wood taken? And if a hill bears the name 'King's Capital', as another example, and yet no one lives there today, the archaeologist will not be long in surveying the area for sites.

Absolute dating

What linguistic data can do of itself is set up a relative chronology of linguistic developments and, by extension, a relative chronology of the historical developments congruent with the linguistic events. The diagram of relationship, such as that shown for the Southern Cushitic languages, together with the ordered rules of sound change that can be fitted into such a diagram, provides the relative historical order. There are two ways of trying to attach absolute dates to points on the relative scale, neither usually leading to very precise results but at least to rough estimates.

One method is to correlate particular sound changes with historical events which are datable on other grounds. In African situations it is frequently difficult to date a shift more closely than the already described instance in Luba, where tonal reversal appears to have taken place between the thirteenth and sixteenth centuries. A closer correlation, but so recent in date that other historical evidence is available, would be the Dahalo shift of *a to /i/ in certain contexts; the change occurred since the end of Galla influence on the Dahalo, *c.* 1830, because Galla loans show the shift, and before the first recordings of Dahalo some years prior to 1950.

The second method involves a lexicostatistical technique, the counting of rates of cognation in core vocabulary between related languages. A variation of this method, called glottochronology, attempted to set up a universal formula to calculate time depth of linguistic differentiation on the basis of vocabulary retention in a standard list of core vocabulary. But even if randomness of attrition in noncultural vocabulary is accepted, and there seems some empirical basis for the idea, the formula developed did not deal with the problem that the individual words in the standard list, in any standard list for that matter, clearly have differing resistances to replacement. Moreover, the standard vocabularies, the Swadesh 100-word and 200-word lists, do not fit all languages as well as they suited the European languages for which they were first developed. As well, there is the occasional problem that some taint of culture touches probably all vocabulary, and so can potentially interfere with the hypothesized randomness of attrition. (For thoroughgoing discussions of the possibilities of, and the problems with, glottochronology, see Hymes 1960; Bergland and Vogt 1962.)

It seems none the less useful to use versions of the Swadesh lists modified for the particular linguistic family to calculate patterns of cognation within that family, for the simple reason that, time and again, relationships within a family of languages determined on other grounds are corroborated in cognate counts. Vocabulary change thus does seem to show some rough regularity over time, even if that tendency towards regularity cannot be given universal formulation. If the more recent time spans on the diagram of relationship can then be correlated with events attested and datable from other kinds of historical evidence, the length of earlier periods on the time chart can be roughly estimated. As one goes further back in time, the estimates become more and more approximate, till one is talking about developments that took place sometime during a period of several centuries or even a millennium (e.g. Ehret 1971: 26–31; 1974a: 47–55). Despite the roughness and uncertainty of such dating, the effort must be undertaken, for the correlation of the cultures and cultural developments that appear in the linguistic record with archaeological findings can be effective only if their locations and chronology can both be approximated.

Conclusions

What should now be apparent is that the potential for linguistic and archaeological correlation is much greater than has generally been supposed. By traditional expectations scholars would be able to establish proto-languages, aspects of the cultures of peoples speaking such languages, and the approximate regions in which such languages might have been spoken, and then would seek to correlate these data with archaeological evidence for cultures having approximately the same characteristics. Left aside were whole periods of historical development between the time an ancestral language was spoken and some later era where its descendants could be recognized. Archaeology on its own resources alone had to argue for historical continuities or their lack. But fuller use of linguistic resources allows reconstructions of patterns of change in culture all along the line of linguistic and societal descent – with obvious potential for correlations with the patterns of ongoing change which archaeology reveals. Linguistic evidence, in the form of loanwords, can show the appearance of new ideas and things in the course of history of a society and indicate their sources; and if preservable material culture is involved, the same things and their directions of spread will show up in the archaeological record as well. Furthermore, because we can argue also from linguistic evidence whether a particular language shift accompanied a situation of major cultural break or one of considerable cultural continuity, linguistics also allow us to deal with the most difficult problem of correlation – whether a significant break or the lack of it should appear in the archaeological sequence correlatable with the particular historical sequence suggested by the linguistic evidence. Moreover, relative geographies of ethnicities through time can be built up from the combining of relationship and loanword evidence, and the fitting of such linguistic mappings over archaeological maps will eventually yield correlations of near certainty of correctness. Finally, linguistic evidence can confirm whole dimensions of culture history which are only occasionally, or not at all, inferable from the material remains.

15.vii.1975

University of California
Los Angeles

References

Bergland, K. and Vogt, H. 1962. On the validity of glottochronology. *Current Anthropology*. 3:115–53.

Dalby, D. 1966. Levels of relationship in the comparative study of African languages. *African Language Studies*. VII:171–9.

Dyen, I. 1965. *A Lexicostatistical Classification of the Austronesian Languages*. Indiana University Publications in Anthropology and Linguistics, 19.

Ehret, C. 1971. *Southern Nilotic History: Linguistic Approaches to the Study of the Past*. Evanston: Northwestern University Press.

Ehret, C. 1972. Language evidence and religious history. *The Historical Study of African Religions*, pp. 45–9 (eds T. O. Ranger and I. N. Kimambo). London: Heinemann.

Ehret, C. 1973. Patterns of Bantu and Central Sudanic settlement in central and southern Africa. *Transafrican Journal of History*. 3:1–71.

Ehret, C. 1974a. *Ethiopians and East Africans: the Problem of Contacts*. Nairobi: East African Publishing House.

Ehret, C. 1974b. Agricultural history in central and southern Africa, *c*. 1000 B.C. to A.D. 500. *Transafrican Journal of History*. 4:1–25.

Ehret, C. (*Forthcoming*, a). *Comparative Southern Cushitic: Phonological Aspects.*

Ehret, C. (*Forthcoming*, b). Aspects of social and economic change in western Kenya, 500–1800. In B. A. Ogot (ed.), *Aspects of the Precolonial History of Kenya.*

Ehret, C. *et al.* 1972. Outlining southern African history, a reconsideration, A.D. 100–1500. *Ufahamu*. 3:9–27.

Ehret, C. *et al.* 1974. Some thoughts on the early history of the Nile-Congo watershed. *Ufahamu*. 5, 2.

Gimbutas, M. 1963. The Indo-Europeans: archaeological problems. *American Anthropologist*. 65:815–36.

Heller, L. 1972. *Communisational Analysis and Methodology for Historians.* New York.

Hymes, D. 1960. Lexicostatistics so far. *Current Anthropology.* 1:3–44.

Knappert, J. 1970. Contribution from the study of loan words to the cultural history of Africa. *Language and History in Africa*, pp. 78–88 (ed. D. Dalby). London: Cass.

Lamb, S. 1958. Linguistic prehistory in the Great Basin. *International Journal of American Linguistics.* 24:

Mellaart, J. 1970. Anatolia, *c.* 4000–2300 B.C. Chapter 18 in *Cambridge Ancient History*, 3rd ed. I, 2.

Sapir, E. 1916. *Time Perspective in Aboriginal American Culture.* Ottawa.

Welmers, W. E. 1973. *African Language Structures.* Berkeley.

Abstract

Ehret, C.

Linguistic evidence and its correlation with archaeology

Linguistic evidence has long been applied to problems of historical reconstruction; and, in particular, considerable effort has been expended in the search for correlations between archeological and linguistic sources for history. Nevertheless, linguistic sources have remained, for the most part, insufficiently utilized. Historical inferences can be made from the kinds of evidence which inhere in the data of language relationships and from toponymy; and both these kinds of data have received extensive use. But historical inferences, of much more detailed and more complex kinds, can be made from the diachronic analysis of adopted elements, specifically word-borrowings, in languages; and this sort of study has only too frequently not been undertaken. Applied in conjunction, the two categories of linguistic evidence reveal the probable approximate locations through time of, the relative historical sequence of interactions between, and the sequence of developments within, the groups of societies from whose languages the data is drawn. Finally, the estimation of absolute dating, however approximate and tenuous, of events on the linguistically-attested scheme must be made in order to guide the culminating correlation of archaeological and linguistic findings.

Austronesian culture history: some linguistic inferences and their relations to the archaeological record[1]

Robert Blust

Austronesian subgrouping

There is no generally accepted subgrouping of the 600 or more Austronesian (AN) languages, though some linguists (Dempwolff 1934–38; Milke 1938, and subsequent works; Grace 1955 and subsequent works; Biggs 1965; Pawley 1972; Blust 1972a) have recognized the existence of a large subgroup, now called 'Oceanic' (OC), which includes all the AN languages east of a north–south line running through Teluk Sarera (formerly Geelvink Bay) in Irian Jaya except Palauan, Chamorro and possibly Yapese. Others (Dyen 1963; Ferrell 1969; Dahl 1973) have observed that the languages of Formosa are internally quite diverse (falling into three remotely related groups), and that some of these diverge considerably from all other members of the AN family. In the present state of uncertainty, reconstructed forms will be assigned to Proto-Austronesian (PAN) only if reflected in at least two of the following partly geographical groups: 1. Oceanic, 2. Western, 3. Formosan. In 1–2 comparisons 2 will be defined as including Sumbawa-Sumba, Sulawesi and the Philippines, but excluding islands further to the east; in 2–3 comparisons 2 will be defined as including all non-OC languages south of the Philippines. There is some evidence that the OC group is part of a larger genetic unit extending into eastern Indonesia (Blust 1974a). It is therefore possible that the comparison of words in languages of western Indonesia or the Philippines with cognate forms in eastern Indonesia is equivalent to comparison with cognates in OC languages. This assumption will be maintained here only where the languages compared are not contiguous or near-contiguous, and the probability of borrowing as an alternative explanation can thus be kept to a minimum.

The major purpose of this paper is to demonstrate the application of the Comparative method to the reconstruction of culture history in the AN-speaking world and to illustrate some of the ways in which this tool may complement, corroborate or contradict the independent testimony of archaeology. Because it is still imperfectly understood and in many ways constitutes a self-contained problem, the reconstruction of the PAN kinship system will not be undertaken here. Similarly, no attempt is made to deal with features of the natural environment, since these relate more directly to the problem of the AN homeland – a question that I hope to take up in a separate paper.

[1] Introductory matter already covered in the first paper has been omitted.

The linguistic evidence

Limitations of space prevent citation of the full evidence for many of the linguistic inferences set out below. Most of the supporting data can be found in Dempwolff (1920; 1925; 1934–8) or Blust (1970; 1972a; 1972b; 1973).

The following reconstructions (table 1) are intended simply as a guide to that part of the published material that can be assigned to Proto-Austronesian and which is relevant to the reconstruction of AN culture history. The material is organized into partly arbitrary semantic groups, and each reconstruction followed by at least two of the symbols W, N or E to indicate that a reflex is known in a western, northern (Formosan) or eastern (Oceanic; eastern Indonesian) AN language.

Abbreviations of language names in the following sections, geographical locations and sources of material are shown in table 2. Linguistic symbols are: *: reconstruction, >: becomes, <: is derived from, ø: zero; parentheses mark a choice between the enclosed segments which is not further specifiable on available evidence; square brackets mark the possible presence of an additional segment; hyphens mark the boundary between analyzable elements within a word. The orthography of sources has generally been modified in accordance with conventions adopted in Blust (1970). Unless otherwise noted, Proto-Oceanic reconstructions follow Grace (1969).

Complementary inferences

Complementary inferences can be divided into two types: (1) those in which linguistic evidence permits an inference which is practically closed to archaeology, and (2) those in which archaeology is the exclusively illuminating discipline.

Perishable referents

The material in table 1 provides a basis for numerous inferences of the first type. Thus, while archaeological evidence may enable us to determine the general floorplan of an ancient living structure, it is unlikely – given the combination of materials and physical environment in the tropical world – to shed light on such features as form of the roof (A2, 4, 6), or on any structure which does not leave traces in the soil (A5, 9). This is true of virtually the entire canoe complex (G), and of many utensils, weapons and so forth. As illustrating the need for interdisciplinary co-operation in prehistoric research, the importance of this observation cannot be emphasized too strongly: despite the improbability of ever recovering archaeological correlates, we can be virtually certain that Proto-Austronesian speakers used the bow, bamboo trail or pitfall spikes, the bamboo basket trap for fish etc., and carried these into the Pacific by about 3000 B.C. (Pawley and Green 1973).

Terminological non-distinctness

A second type of complementary inference involves discrete or semi-discrete stylistic traditions (prehistoric or modern) for which there are no known corresponding

TABLE 1

A *The house and its contents*
1 *balay 'public building' (WE)
2 *bu(qS)uŋ bu(qS)uŋ 'ridgepole' (WE)
3 *dapuR 'hearth' (WE)
4 *kasaw 'rafter' (WE)
5 *paRa 'storage rack above the hearth' (WE)
6 *qatep 'thatch (usually sago leaf)' (WE)
7 *Rumaq 'house, family dwelling' (NWE)
8 *SaDiRi 'housepost' (WE)
9 *SaReZaSan 'notched log ladder' (WE)

B *Tools, utensils, weapons*
1 *buli(Ct) 'putty, caulking substance' (WE)
2 *busuR 'bow' (NWE)
3 *(cs)aRu 'comb' (WE)
4 *(CtT)ambuRi 'conch shell trumpet' (WE)
5 *kuDen 'cooking pot' (WE)
6 *paku 'nail' (WE)
7 *panaq 'shoot an arrow' (NWE)
8 *quluŋa 'pillow, wooden headrest' (WE)
9 *sual 'digging stick' (WE)
10 *suja 'bamboo trail or pitfall spikes' (WE)
11 *suluq 'torch' (WE)
12 *taliS 'rope, cord' (NWE)
13 *(tT)aRaq 'hew, plane' (WE)

C *Arts*
1 *añam 'plait, weave' (WE)
2 *ba(CtT)u(lØ) 'plait, make with the hands' (WE)
3 *bari[ ] 'iron, metal' (NW)
4 *(CtT)u(cs)i 'draw, write' (WE)
5 *malat 'parang, machete' (NW)
6 *surat 'write' (NW)
7 *Sasaq 'whet, sharpen' (WE)
8 *tinequn 'weave (cloth)', *tinequn-an 'loom' (NW)
9 *zaqit 'sew' (WE)
10 *ZaRum 'needle' (NWE)

D *Adornment*
1 *beCik 'tattoo' (NW)

E *Refreshment*
1 *apuR 'lime (for betel quid)' (WE)
2 *buqaq 'betel nut' (WE)
3 *ma-buSek 'drunk' (NW)

F *Hunting and fishing*
1 *baŋi 'bait' (WE)
2 *buqu buqu 'bamboo basket trap for fish' (WE)
3 *(cs)a(Dlr)uk 'kind of fishnet' (WE)
4 *kawil 'fish-hook' (WE)
5 *kebu(rR) 'fish drive' (WE)
6 *puket 'dragnet' (WE)
7 *pulut 'bird lime' (WE)
8 *qaNup 'hunt, go hunting' (NW)
9 *tuba 'derris root fish poison' (WE)
10 *zariʏ 'snare' (WE)

G *The canoe*
1 *baŋkaq 'canoe' (WE)
2 *be-R-say 'canoe paddle' (WE)
3 *(cs)a-R-man 'outrigger' (WE)
4 *laŋe(nN) 'rollers for beaching a canoe' (WE)
5 *layaR 'sail' (WE)
6 *limas 'canoe bailer' (WE)
7 *paluja 'to paddle' (WE)
8 *qabaŋ 'canoe, boat' (NW)
9 *quliŋ 'rudder; steer' (WE)
10 *Rakit 'raft' (WE)
11 *seŋkar 'cross-seat in a boat' (WE)
12 *teken 'punting pole' (WE)
13 *waŋkaŋ 'canoe' (WE)

H *Domesticated animals*
1 *beRek 'domesticated pig' (NWE)
2 *laluʏ 'cock, rooster' (WE)
3 *Wasu[ ] 'dog' (NWE)

I *Garden and field*
1 *babaw 'to weed' (WE)
2 *beRas 'husked rice' (NW)
3 *biRaq 'giant arum, Alocasia spp.' (WE)
4 *kulu(rR) 'breadfruit' (WE)

TABLE 1—*cont.*

5 *laqia 'ginger' (WE)
6 *lesuŋ 'mortar' (NW)
7 *limaw 'citrus fruit' (WE)
8 *pajay 'riceplant, paddy' (NWE)
9 *pun(tT)i 'banana' (WE)
10 *qaSelu 'pestle' (NWE)
11 *qubi 'yam' (WE)
12 *qumaH 'garden; cultivated field' (NWE)
13 *rampia 'sago' (WE)
14 *Semay 'cooked rice' (NW)
15 *tales 'taro' (WE)
16 *talun 'fallow land' (WE)
17 *tanem 'to plant' (WE)
18 *tapeS 'winnow' (NW)
19 *tebuS(u) 'sugarcane' (NWE)
20 *timun 'melon' (WE)
21 *zawa 'millet' (NW)
22 *ZaRami 'rice straw' (NW)

J *General foodstuffs and food preparation*
1 *Capa 'to smoke meat or fish' (NWE)
2 *qasiRaq 'salt' (NW)

K *Sociopolitical organization*
1 *datu 'chief, headman' (WE)
2 *pe(nñN)e(dDj) 'official gathering' (WE)

L *Pathology*
1 *bulaR 'cataract of the eye' (WE)
2 *bu(nñ)i 'ringworm' (WE)
3 *kurap 'scaly skin disease' (NW)
4 *panaw 'skin disease leaving white patches' (WE)

TABLE 2

AA	'Āre 'Āre, southern Malaita (Geerts 1970)
Akl	Aklanon, central Philippines (Zorc 1969)
Am	Amis, eastern Formosa (Ferrell 1969)
Ar	Arosi, northern San Cristoval (Fox 1970)
AtC	Ci'uli Atayal, north-central Formosa (Ferrell 1969)
AtSq	Squliq Atayal, north-central Formosa (Ferrell 1969)
Bar	Bare'e, central Sulawesi (Adriani 1928)
Bim	Bimanese, eastern Sumbawa (Blust n.d.)
BM	Bolaang Mongondow, eastern Sulawesi (Dunnebier 1951)
Btk	Batak, north-eastern Palawan (Warren 1959)
Buli	Buli, eastern Halmahera (Maan 1940)
Bun	Bunun, central Formosa (Jeng 1972)
Caj	Cajeli, Buru (Wallace 1869)
CB	Cebuano Bisayan, central Philippines (Wolff 1972)
Chm	Chamorro, Marianas islands (von Preissig 1918)
Fi	Fijian (Dempwolff 1934–8)
Ib	Iban, south-western Sarawak (Scott 1956)
Ilc	Ilocano, north-western Luzon (Carro 1956)
Isg	Isneg, northern Luzon (Vanoverbergh 1972)
Jv	Javanese, Java (Dempwolff 1934–38)
Kad	Kadazan, western Sabah (Antonissen 1958)
Kan	Kankanay, northern Luzon (Vanoverbergh 1933)
Kei	Kei islands, between Ceram and the Aru group (Geurtjens 1921)

TABLE 2—*cont.*

Kel	Kelabit, northern Sarawak, north-western Kalimantan (Blust, n.d.)
Kn	Kanakanabu, south-central Formosa (Ferrell 1969)
Kuv	Kuvalan, north-western Formosa (Ferrell 1969)
LA	Long Anap, northern Sarawak (Blust n.d.)
Li'o	Li'o, central Flores (Arndt 1933)
Mal	Maloh, south-western Kalimantan (Ray 1913)
Mar	Maranao, southern Mindanao (McKaughan and Macaraya 1967)
MbT	Tigwa Manobo, eastern Mindanao (Reid 1971)
Mer	Merina (=Hova), Malagasy Republic (Dempwolff 1934–8)
Ml	Malay, Malay peninsula; plus widespread regional dialects (Dempwolff 1934–8, Wilkinson 1957)
Mor	Morella, Ambon (Wallace 1869)
Mys	Mysol, Mysol island, between Ceram and the Vogelkop peninsula of New Guinea (Wallace 1869)
Nf	Numfor, Numfor and Biak islands, Teluk Sarera (van Hasselt and van Hasselt 1947)
Ngadha	Ngadha, western Flores (Arndt 1962)
NgD	Ngaju Dayak, south-eastern Borneo (Dempwolff 1934–8)
Nias	Nias island, west of Sumatra (Sundermann 1905)
PAM	Proto-Ambon, southern Moluccas (Stresemann 1927)
PMA	Proto-Manus, Admiralty islands (Blust n.d.)
Pn	Pangasinan, north-central Luzon (Benton 1971)
Pul	Puluwat, western Carolines (Elbert 1972)
PuyT	Puyuma (Tippon dialect), south-eastern Formosa (Ferrell 1969)
Pw	Paiwan, southern Formosa (Ferrell 1970)
Pz	Pazeh, west-central Formosa (Ferrell 1969)
Se	Sediq, north-central Formosa (Ferrell 1969)
Sich	Sichule, Simalur island, west of Sumatra (Kähler 1959)
Sim	Simalur, Simalur island (Kähler 1961)
Sm	Samoan (Dempwolff 1934–8)
Ss	Saisiat, north-western Formosa (Ferrell 1969)
SubS	Siocon Subanun, western Mindanao (Reid 1971)
TB	Toba Batak, northern Sumatra (Dempwolff 1934–8)
Tbl	Tagabili, southern Mindanao (Forsberg and Lindquist 1955)
Tel	Teluti, Ceram (Wallace 1869)
Teor	Watubela archipelago, between Ceram and Kei (Wallace 1869)
Tg	Tagalog, central Luzon (Dempwolff 1934–8, Panganiban 1966)
Th	Thao, central Formosa (Ferrell 1969)
Tim	Timorese, western Timor (Blust n.d.)
To	Tongan (Dempwolff 1934–8)
Ts	Tsou, south-central Formosa (Ferrell 1969)
UJ	Uma Juman, central Sarawak (Blust n.d.)
Uma	Uma, west-central Sulawesi (Esser 1964)
Way	Wayapo, Buru (Wallace 1869)
WBM	Western Bukidnon Manobo, central Mindanao (Elkins 1968)

terminological distinctions. Thus, a number of prehistoric ceramic traditions have been reported for areas that were probably AN-speaking at the time of manufacture and use (Solheim 1964; Chang 1964; Bellwood 1975). Yet reflexes of *kuDen 'clay cooking pot' are distributed from at least the central Philippines (CB *kúlun*) through Borneo (Kad *kuon*, LA *kuden*) to Sumatra (TB *hudon*), Sulawesi (Bar *kura*), the Moluccas (PAM (64) *kudĕn, Buli *ulan*), the Admiralties (PMA *kur(o)) and eastward as far as Fiji (*kuro*) and even western Polynesia (To *kulo*, Sm *qulo*), where pottery has not been made in historic times. From the linguistic evidence it thus seems clear that there has been an unbroken tradition of pottery manufacture and use in the AN-speaking world for well over 5000 years. Although functional differences are often labelled linguistically (PMA *kur(o) 'cooking pot', but *p^w(ei)n(V)taŋ(V) 'water jar'), the waves of manufacturing and decorative innovations that have swept various parts of this ever-expanding territory during the period in question, providing the archaeologist with much valuable material for tracing past culture contacts, are simply not known to be reflected in linguistic usage. To take one specific example, the Pacific pottery tradition known as Lapita is fairly discrete and appears to correlate with the ancestral community of identifiable contemporary groups (Golson 1971) – conclusions which are of considerable interest to Pacific prehistory – but the existence of such a tradition certainly would not be inferable from the available linguistic evidence.

Corroboratory inferences

From a somewhat more general point of view the preceding discussion can be taken as illustrative of a corroboratory inference – that pottery was known to speakers of Proto-Austronesian. Indeed, wherever the members of a cognate set refer to non-perishable material, the potential exists for linguistic and archaeological evidence to lead investigators independently to the same conclusion. Ideally this is what should happen in all cases, and where significant discrepancies exist one is led to suspect the presence of one or more erroneous assumptions.

The pig

A particularly striking example of partial agreement between linguistic and archaeological inferences involves the pig. To account for the agreement of Tg *báboy*, TB, Jv, Ml *babi*, NgD *bawoi* 'pig' Dempwolff (1934–8) posited PAN *babuy 'pig'. Reflexes of this word are in fact considerably more widespread than Dempwolff indicated, occurring as well in all major Formosan subgroups (Se *bábui* 'domesticated pig'; Kn *baburu*, Pw *vavui* 'wild pig'), Sulawesi (Bar *wawu*) the Lesser Sundas (Tim *fafi*) and the southern Moluccas (Way *fafu*, Mor, Tel *hahu*, Teor *faf*, Kei *wāv* 'pig'). It is thus noteworthy that a cognate form has been reported in no AN language east of the Moluccas except Palauan, Chamorro and Yapese, in all of which phonological irregularities suggest that the item is a loan.

Somewhat later Capell (1943: 38) called attention to the frequent appearance of words

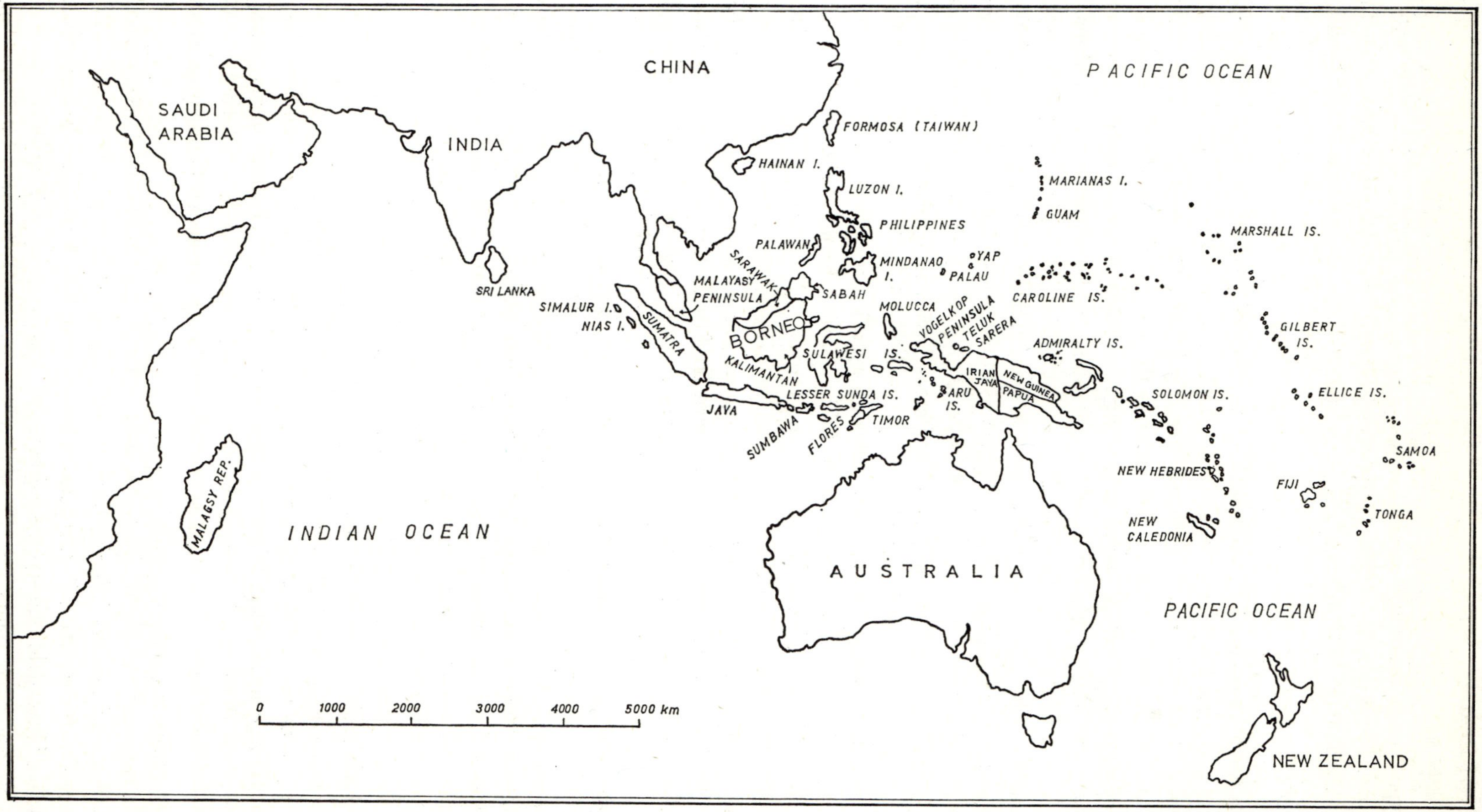
CHINA
PACIFIC OCEAN
SAUDI ARABIA
INDIA
FORMOSA (TAIWAN)
HAINAN I.
LUZON I.
MARIANAS I.
GUAM
MARSHALL IS.
PHILIPPINES
PALAWAN
YAP
MINDANAO I.
PALAU
SARAWAK
MALAYASY PENINSULA
SABAH
CAROLINE IS.
SRI LANKA
SIMALUR I.
NIAS I.
SUMATRA
BORNEO
MOLUCCA IS.
VOGELKOP PENINSULA
TELUK SARERA
GILBERT IS.
ADMIRALTY IS.
SULAWESI
KALIMANTAN
IRIAN JAYA
NEW GUINEA
PAPUA
LESSER SUNDA IS.
ARU IS.
SOLOMON IS.
ELLICE IS.
JAVA
SUMBAWA
FLORES
TIMOR
SAMOA
NEW HEBRIDES
FIJI
TONGA
NEW CALEDONIA
MALAGSY REP.
INDIAN OCEAN
AUSTRALIA
PACIFIC OCEAN
0
1000
2000
3000
4000
5000 km
NEW ZEALAND

Figure I

of the type Nemea *boro* 'pig' in south-eastern Papua, but hesitated to admit their AN provenance. More recently Milke (1968) demonstrated the assignability of such forms to Proto-Oceanic (POC) *mpoRo 'pig'; and slightly later the present writer found that cognates are also widespread in the west, extending from Formosa (PuyT *verék* 'domesticated pig') through the Philippines (Pn *belék* 'piglet, suckling pig', Tg *biik* 'suckling pig', Tbl *bʌlʌk* 'male pig') to Borneo (Kad *vogok* 'pig', Kel *berek* 'domesticated pig'). A cognate (*wök*) has since been recognized in Old Javanese (Prentice 1974). Based on the distribution of attested meanings it was suggested that Dempwolff's *babuy originally meant 'wild pig', and that forms belonging to the second set could be attributed to a PAN reconstruction *beRek 'domesticated pig'. Two sets of facts unknown to me at the time now appear highly relevant to an understanding of the foregoing observations.

First, words for 'pig' which strikingly resemble Milke's *mpoRo are widespread in New Guinea – often far from the coast – in *non-Austronesian* languages belonging to several posited genetic groupings not known to be related to one another. Thus Wurm, Voorhoeve and McElhanon (1975: 318–19) cite Gadsup (East New Guinea Highlands stock) *po*, Moni (Wissel Lakes-Kemandoga stock, western highlands, Irian Jaya) *woro*, Sentani (Sentani stock, north-eastern Irian Jaya) *bo* and Afoa (Goilala stock-level family, central mountain range, Papua) *polu*. D. C. Laycock has called my attention to the following additional examples: Boiken (Ndu family, Sepik-Ramu phylum) *bwale*, Elepi (Torricelli phylum) *mbalə*, mountain Arapesh (Torricelli phylum; reported in Fortune, 1942: 34) *mbul* 'pig'.

Second, radiocarbon dates obtained by Bulmer (1966) for pig bone from the Kiowa rock shelter (near Chuave patrol post, Eastern Highlands District) suggest that the pig was present in the eastern highlands by 2890 ± 140 B.C. Slightly earlier dates have been obtained by White (1967) from Kafiavana, in the eastern highlands. Since it is generally agreed that the pig is not native to New Guinea (Darlington 1957), its present distribution would seem to imply human introduction. The assumption that this introduction accompanied the AN penetration of the western Pacific provides a natural explanation both for the widespread occurrence of words resembling POC *mpoRo in non-AN languages, and for the absence of reflexes of *babuy east of the Moluccas, since it is clearly the domesticated, not the wild, pig that would be transported. Strengthening this impression is the close agreement of archaeological chronology as reported by Bulmer, and by White, with the date (3000 B.C.) suggested by Pawley and Green (1973) for the dispersal of the POC speech community.

Against this body of observations is the more recent C^{14} dating of a single pig incisor from the Kiowa rock shelter at 10350 B.P. (Bulmer 1974), and a second, similar find from the Yuku rock shelter, Western Highlands District (R. Bulmer, *pers. comm.*). To the extent that these two independent pieces of evidence cannot be explained as intrusive, they pose a serious problem to the interpretation advanced here. Since Bulmer's dates are earlier than the formation of Torres Strait, however, her claim fails to account for the absence of the pig in Australia. Moreover, at least three superficially unrelated facts (absence of directly inherited reflexes of *babuy in New Guinea and the Pacific, presence of a form of POC *mpoRo in many non-AN New Guinea languages, the agreement of linguistic time-depth estimates for the break-up of Proto-Oceanic with the earliest well-attested dates for the pig in the highlands) become intelligible on the assumption of an AN introduction of the pig into New Guinea, and any adequate theory of Pacific prehistory must ultimately account for this agreement.

Polynesia

There is at least one portion of the AN world in which the evidence of linguistics and archaeology appears to be leading overwhelmingly towards the same conclusions: Polynesia. Thus Pawley (1966) first explicitly challenged the traditional theory of Western and Eastern first-order Polynesian (PN) subgroups, suggesting instead that the split-up of the PPN speech community produced one language (Proto-Tongic) ancestral to Tongan, Niue and possibly Uvean, and another (Proto-Nuclear PN) ancestral to all remaining PN languages. The implications of this scheme were considerable: the settlement of eastern Polynesia and New Zealand could not have been effected from Tonga; since a western PN source was ultimately required in any case, this left Samoa as the most likely homeland of the Nuclear PN group, and Tonga as the likely homeland of the Tongic group and possibly of the entire PN family. Archaeological evidence not available at the time of its original formulation now appears to offer strong support for the view that Tonga was the first PN island group to be settled (by at least the late second millennium B.C.), and that Samoa was probably peopled from Tonga (by about 700–600 B.C.) in the second major PN movement (Pawley and Green 1973; Pawley, *pers. comm.*; Bellwood 1975 and *pers. comm.*). More recently, Pawley and Green (1971) have shown that lexical inferences about the PN homeland are not incompatible with such a hypothesis.

Contradictory inferences

Like *kuDen 'clay cooking pot', *beRek 'domesticated pig' involves relationships that can be construed on different levels as examples now of one type of inference and now of another. Thus, if we wished to emphasize the difficulty of reconciling the abovementioned chronologically anomalous pigs' teeth with the other facts considered, we could regard the linguistic and archaeological evidence for the presence of the pig in New Guinea as essentially contradictory. In contrast to this case, an apparent contradiction may often result simply from gaps in our knowledge – the lack to date of known support from one line of evidence for an inference based on the other.

Iron

Such gaps may underlie a growing discrepancy between the linguistic and archaeological evidence for early use of iron in the AN-speaking world. To account for the agreement of Ml *bĕsi*, TB *bosi*, Jv *wĕsi*, Mer *vi* (*s > ø unexpl.) 'iron', Fi *vesi* 'name of a spear', Dempwolff (1934–8) reconstructed *besi 'iron'. Dyen (1971) has observed that the Fijian word probably is not cognate with the other forms, and argues (8) that '. . . there is no fundamental evidence for the early knowledge of iron among Austronesians'. While Dyen's doubts regarding Fi *vesi* are shared by others, and the phrase 'early knowledge' is safely non-specific, the above remark was apparently made without awareness of a growing body of linguistic evidence for knowledge of iron in the AN world which would seem to predate the available archaeological evidence by several millennia.

Consider the following comparisons:

C3 *bari [ ] 'iron'.

Ib *bari* 'steel', Btk *baribari* 'iron, metal', AtSq *baliq*, AtC *bali*, Th *baliθ*, Kuv *balis* 'iron/metal'.

C5 *malat 'parang, machete'.

Ib *malat* 'short sword', UJ *malat* 'parang, machete', Ss *malat* 'knife/sword'.

There are three possible explanations for the formal resemblances between members of these sets:

1 the resemblance is due to chance
2 the resemblance is due to borrowing
3 the resemblance is due to common origin

Similarly, the agreement of attested meanings for directly inherited forms of common origin (category 3) would seem to have two possible sources:

3(a) the agreement is due to the retention of an original meaning
3(b) the agreement is due to semantic convergence

It now appears possible to account for reflexes of *besi in terms of fairly recent borrowing (if Mer *vi*, which exhibits irregularities, is regarded as non-cognate), or of common inheritance from a relatively low-order proto-language (ancestral to at least Malay and Javanese), or both. Such explanations, however, are considerably more difficult to maintain for cps. C3 and C5.

C3. Apart from the minor matter of reduplication, Iban *bari* 'steel' (gloss apparently overspecific) shows completely regular correspondences with Palawan Batak *baribari* 'iron, metal'. Given the number of segments compared, the probability that the resemblance of these forms is due to chance (1) must be regarded as quite small. Neither can borrowing (2) offer a compelling alternative. The Batak are described as an isolated hunting and gathering group of 800–1,000 persons wandering the forested mountains of north-eastern Palawan (Warren 1959). Although the source of their knowledge of iron remains unclear, and a cognate word could occur in coastal Palawan, a reflex of *bari [ ] has not yet been noted for any other language in Indonesia or the Philippines. If this comparatively wide and broken distribution is taken as minimizing the plausibility of (2), the same can be said to apply *a fortiori* to the similar forms in Formosan languages.

In including the latter languages in C3, however, we are seriously confronted with alternative (1). It has not been established that *r > AtSq, AtC, Th, Kuv *l*, and the final consonant correspondence is difficult to account for under any known formula. None the less, there is no reported counter-evidence to the first assumption, and weakly attested correspondences similar to the final of C3 (corresponding to zero in extra-Formosan non-suffixed forms) appear to be relatively common among Formosan languages (Dyen 1965a).

There is thus a fairly high probability that the Iban and Palawan Batak forms are cognate with some or all of the Formosan material. If so, the determinable time depth for a knowledge of iron in the AN-speaking world, not presently datable from the archaeological record to earlier than 600 B.C. (Fontaine 1972), is vastly extended. Dyen's (1963) citation of lexicostatistical percentages for Formosan languages shows a maximum agreement for an Atayalic with a non-Atayalic list (Sediq with Paiwan) of 15·8%, indicating a most proximate common ancestor some 4,500 years in the past. However, Ferrell (1969: 32) has pointed out that the percentages of Sediq with Paiwanic are probably inflated, and estimates (p. 73) a minimum separation time for Atayalic from all other AN languages of 5,000 to 6,000 years. The highest percentage cited for Atayal proper with a non-Atayalic language (9·3% with Paiwan) supports a date of nearly 6000 B.P., yet may itself be inflated by borrowing. Finally, in view of the vacillating glosses given for the Batak and Formosan items, it is possible that *bari[ ] did not mean iron', but carried the general meaning 'metal'. Such a view is more nearly compatible, with the emerging archaeological picture for mainland South-East Asia, where Solheim (1968) has reported a well-developed bronze industry prior to 2300 B.C. All carefully described AN languages that had a precontact term, however, apparently used distinct roots to refer to iron, copper, bronze, gold and silver. For this reason chances are great that the Batak and Formosan words refer specifically to iron, and the probability that *bari[ ] meant 'iron' must accordingly be regarded as higher than any currently conceivable alternative.

C5. The comparison Iban *malat* 'short sword', Kayan *malat* 'parang, machete', Saisiat *malat* 'knife/sword' shows a distribution similar to that of *bari [ ]. The likelihood of borrowing is equally low, and the implied time depth nearly as great (Ferrell 1969). Furthermore, if (1) cannot be considered a serious explanation for the non-Formosan members of C3, its value is smaller still in the case of C5.

It seems likely then, that a word *malat referring to a knife-like or sword-like cutting implement was found in a language ancestral to most if not all members of the AN family. But there are difficulties associated (3b) with using this item as evidence for early knowledge of iron. In both Iban and Kayan (which probably count as a single witness) the *malat* is an iron parang or machete. Saisiat *malat*, on the other hand, is cited in a comparative word-list under the general gloss 'knife/sword', and the exact meaning remains unclear. Yet even if the attested referents prove to be similar there is a significant chance, given only two independent witnesses, that the original was of some other material (as bamboo) or some other form (as a knife). C5 thus adds some thrust to the argument for early knowledge of iron, but its force must be tempered by due recognition of the potential role of semantic convergence.

Even if the Formosan members of C3 are assumed to be chance resemblances, however, and C5 is dismissed as not necessarily implying iron, the assignable time-depth for *bari [ ] would be considerable. Thus basic vocabulary cognate percentages calculated by the author (1974b) for a number of the languages of Borneo and the southern and central Philippines yield an average figure of about 28·5% (separation time = 3,000 years) for North Sarawak languages with Palawan Batak. Implied separation times for North Sarawak languages with subgroup relatives of Palawan Batak, however, are considerably greater (Western Bukidnon Manobo, Tiruray 3,800 years), suggesting that the

Batak percentages reflect a lower than average rate of lexical replacement. Figures are not available for Iban, but there is no reason to believe that Batak would score higher with it than with North Sarawak languages, and a minimum separation time of 3,500 years can probably safely be assumed.

More evidence for early iron

Several other comparisons support this general picture, as follows:

(a) *(cs)al(cs)al 'blacksmithing'

NgD *tasal* 'hammer', Kel *aar* (*l > *r* unexpl.) 'bellows', n-*aar* 'the process of making iron tools, blacksmithing', WBM *salsal* 'to blacksmith, work in metal, forge', CB *salsal* 'forge into shape, of making metal tools; blacksmithing'.

(b) *lanDas-an 'anvil.

Mer *landaiznăa* (*s > ø unexpl.), Jv *landĕsan* (*ĕ* for expected *a*), TB, Ml, CB *landasan*, Kad. *handasan* 'anvil'.

(c) *kara(Ct) 'rust'.

Ml, Btk *karat* 'rust'.

(a) It is conceivable that *(cs)al(cs)al is a loan of no great antiquity, but the likelihood of this possibility is reduced by two observations: (1) if the word spread into the Philippines from a source to the south, the source language remains unidentified; if the opposite direction of diffusion is assumed, it is difficult to account for the apparent absence of cognate forms in northern Borneo or Sarawak coastal languages. Although Ngaju has been subject to external contact influences for an appreciable period (Dyen 1956), Kelabit has not; and it is difficult in any case to imagine a contact situation of such obvious benefit which would have left no linguistic traces elsewhere (2) Kel *aar* shows regular loss of *s. Since this change has occurred in all Kelabit dialects and Kelabit has *s* from an unknown source in some items, *s* would presumably be retained in a recent borrowing of a form like *salsal.*

It might be argued that even if Kel *aar* is not a recent loan, it could be an ancient loan. But the question of chronology again intrudes itself, since it is precisely this that we wish to determine.

(b) Although recent borrowing may be partially responsible for the distribution of reflexes of *lanDas-an (the western Indonesian and Philippine forms could be Malay loans), this hypothesis can effectively be ruled out in the case of the Merina cognate. Likewise, despite an unexplained phonological irregularity in the latter item (parallel to the change assumed by Dempwolff in *vi* < *besi 'iron'), the number of comparable segments greatly weakens chance as an alternative explanation. Since it is now generally agreed that the ancestral Malagasy speech community departed from south-eastern Borneo at least 1,500 years ago (Dahl 1951, Dyen 1953, where a date of A.D. 400 is proposed and accepted; Vérin, Kottak and Gorlin 1969, where a date some 500 years earlier is suggested), it is difficult to argue that the anvil, and hence presumably iron, was not already known in western Indonesia by that time.

(c) All of the objections that might be raised against *kara(Ct) 'rust' have already been met. The distribution is partially similar to C3; chance and borrowing do not appear to offer strong alternatives, and although convergent development may lie behind the observed semantic agreement, comparative evidence that would suggest a differing earlier meaning is unknown.

There is a remote possibility that some other explanation will ultimately be found for all of the above observations that seem to point to early knowledge of iron in the AN-speaking world. Because of their number and mutual independence, however, the probability is small that a collection of unrelated hypotheses will provide a more plausible explanation of these facts than the single hypothesis that iron was known and worked at an early date, perhaps as early as Proto-Austronesian times.

Additional problems

The foregoing example can be taken as an instance of a major disconformity between present archaeological and linguistic evidence. There are in addition a number of problems connected with inferences that may be complementary or contradictory. The most important of these involve the history of (1) rice (2) millet/barley (3) systems of writing (4) the loom (5) headhunting and (6) the blowpipe. Limitations of space require that the discussion be kept brief.

Rice

Based on the comparison

I8 Tg *pálay* 'riceplant', TB *pa*-l-*ge* 'especially fine rice grains' NgD *parei* 'rice in the field'

Dempwolff (1934–8) reconstructed *pajay 'riceplant, rice in the field'. Reflexes of this term are actually much more widely distributed, including all major Formosan subgroups (AtSq *pagai*, Ts *páì*, Pw *padai*), all parts of the Philippines (Kan *págey*, Tbl *halay*), the Marianas (Chm *faqe*), Borneo (Kad *paai*, UJ *pare*, Mal *ase*), the Barrier islands west of Sumatra (Sim *axae*, Nias *fache*), Madagascar (Mer tsimpari-*fari* 'wild rice'), Sulawesi (BM *pajoi*, Bar *pae*), the Lesser Sundas (Li'o *pare*, Tim *ane*), the southern Moluccas (Caj *hálai*, Tel *fála*, Mys *fās*) and northern New Guinea (Nf *fas*).

The above items clearly are cognate, and are assignable to Proto-Austronesian at the highest level. The nearly universal and exclusive meaning 'riceplant, rice in the field, unhusked rice' leaves little choice but to attribute a similar meaning to the reconstructed form. One might argue, however, that rice could be a secondary introduction. It is noteworthy that a number of investigators not familiar with the linguistic evidence have found it unnecessary to assume early knowledge of rice in the AN world. Such a position is adopted by the Harrissons (1971: 253, n. 2) for Borneo, and according to Ferrell (1969: 10), who rejects it, was long the dominant point of view regarding the prehistory of Formosa. Let us call the theory of secondary acquisition T1 and the opposing view T2.

In earlier examples the problem of borrowing was decided in part by distributional characteristics of the proposed cognate set. In particular, a wide and scattered distribution was not considered compatible with the assumption of recent borrowing. The converse proposition – that distributional continuity is compatible with such an assumption – might, then, be taken as support for T1.

Several observations, however, are difficult to reconcile with the theory of secondary acquisition. First, if *pajay was a loanword acquired within the past two or three millennia one would expect some evidence for a source language on the Asian mainland. To date no one has suggested a candidate. Second, because of the great phonemic range of its reflexes, *j must have been phonetically unusual and highly unstable. T1 thus assumes a rather remarkable coincidence – that the medial consonant in the word for 'riceplant' was quite similar to *j even though from an unrelated language.

Either of these objections could be met by an *ad hoc* argument allowing the relatively recent existence of an appropriate source language, that then disappeared without leaving any trace besides those for which it was posited. Apart from the logical shortcomings of such an alternative, however, it can be shown by a somewhat technical linguistic argument that the wide attestation of *pajay is more likely to represent the persistent retention of a term that has been of central importance throughout the reconstructible period of AN culture history.

In each of the languages cited above the medial reflex of *pajay is the expected development of PAN *j. Moreover, *j has merged with some other PAN phoneme (usually *d, *D, *g, *r, *s, *y, *z or *Z) in every reported AN language. This regularity of historical development is compatible with T1 only on the assumption that the word for 'riceplant' was borrowed before *j had ceased to be distinct from all other PAN phonemes. There seem to be two choices: either we accept the improbable conclusion that there has been a massive late merger of *j throughout the AN family, or we assign the putative loan for all practical purposes to Proto-Austronesian itself. But then the question of borrowing ceases to be significant, since in any case the antiquity of rice in the AN world would be admitted.

The difficulty of accounting for reflexes of *pajay with T1 is further increased when we consider that this item is a single point in a constellation of terms relating to rice. Thus, terms for 'husked rice' and 'cooked rice' have a distribution nearly as wide as that for *pajay, and similarly contain reconstructed segments (*R and *S respectively) of considerable diagnostic value in ruling out late borrowing;

I2 *beRas 'husked rice'

AtSq *buax* (?), Ts *fúesə*, Puy *vərás*, Tg *bigás*, CB *bugas*, Chm *pugas*, UJ *bahah*, BM *bogat*, MI *bĕras*, Jv *wos* 'husked rice'.

I14 *Semay 'cooked rice'

Pz *sumái*, Am *həmái*, Akl *humáy*, MbT *himiy*, Subs *glmay*, Ml *imai* (*e > *i* unexpl.) 'cooked rice'.

In addition various other terms which can be assigned to Proto-Austronesian on present subgrouping assumptions (I6, I10, I22), and certain items of more problematic chronological status (Isg *báyo*, Bim *mbaju* < *bayu 'pound rice'), clearly imply early knowledge of rice or some other cereal crop.

Millet/Barley

To account for the agreement of

I21 Tg *dáwa*, NgD *jawe̱* 'millet',

Dempwolff (1934–8) proposed *zawa 'millet'. This comparison can now be extended as follows: Puy *dáwa*ʔ, CB *dáwa* 'millet', Ml *jawa* 'millet, barley'. Wilkinson (1957) marks Ml *jawa* as a Sanskrit loan, an identification confirmed by Gonda (1952) who regards the AN forms as derived from Sanskrit *yawa*. It is curious that this interpretation should be adopted. Wilkinson himself points out that Java is described by early Indian writers as rich in millet and gold, and may have been named from the former. Similarly, Ferrell (1969: 10) notes that millet is universally grown by modern Formosan aboriginal groups, and it is around the growing cycle of this crop that the native religious calendars are constructed. There is, moreover, a distinct possibility that millet was already known in Formosa by the Lungshanoid Horizon (beginning *c.* 2500 B.C.). Since the probability is small that a word of Sanskrit origin would be adopted for a culture-complex present in Java at Indian contact, and then spread as far as Formosa, where millet has evidently long been of central importance, there appear to be grounds for questioning the traditional view of the history of this item.

Systems of writing

Based on the resemblance of

C6 Tg *súlat*, TB, Jv, Ml, NgD *surat*, Mer *suratră* 'write, writing'

Dempwolff (1934–8) posited *surat 'write'. This comparison can now be extended to languages representing at least two of the three major Formosan subgroups: Sa *sulatə* 'paper', s-um-a-*sulatə* 'write', Sir *soulat* 'book, letter', *s*-m-*oulat* 'write', Kuv *s*-əm-*ulál* 'write'. Given its often modern meanings one is tempted to explain away C6 as a recent loan. The occurrence of Mer *suratră*, however, makes it virtually certain that reflexes of *surat were present in western Indonesia by the time of the Malagasy migration. Since all reported 'indigenous' scripts in Indonesia and the Philippines (Harrisson 1966, Jaspan 1964, Postma 1972) appear to be based on Indian originals, there is no known physical reason to suppose a pre-Indian tradition of 'bamboo literacy'. *surat is not a Sanskrit loanword, however, invariably and exclusively refers to writing, and must have existed in western Indonesia only slightly later than the earliest inscriptions in an Indian-based script. It therefore seems unlikely that writing was introduced to Indonesia entirely as a result of direct or stimulus diffusion from India.

A second term, *(CtT)u(cs)i (Tim *tuis* 'picture, writing, tattoo', Sm *tusi* 'write'), sometimes associated with writing, is not sufficiently well-attested to permit secure semantic reconstruction.

The loom

To account for the similarity of

C8 TB *tonun*, Jv, Ml *tĕnun*, Mer *tenuna* 'weave'

Dempwolff (1934–8) proposed *tenun 'weave'. This comparison can now be extended and refined as follows: Pw *tj*-m-*enun* 'to weave (cloth)', *tjenun*-an 'loom', Ml *tĕnun* 'weaving (of cloth from cotton, silk or fibre)', *tĕnunan* (Sumatra) 'loom', Tim *teun* 'weave' (cloth).

All of these items refer specifically to the weaving of cloth (forms in some other languages, as B̲un *tinʔun* 'weave' may also refer to the weaving of baskets etc.), and in the case of Paiwan and Malay the addition of the locative suffix -an forms the word for 'loom' (possibly a convergent development). There thus appears to be a significant probability that the loom was known by AN speakers at an early time.

This probability is further strengthened by the comparison *balija: Ilc *balíga* 'flat wooden bar inserted in the shed of the warp to facilitate insertion of the stick used to hold the threads in place', Ml *belĕra*~*bĕlira* 'weaver's "sword" or beater-in', Tg *balila*, TB *baliga* 'stick used in weaving'. Once again we can rely upon the diagnostic value of *j to rule out recent borrowing. The conclusion seems inescapable that the loom was known to speakers of a language ancestral to at least Malay, the Batak languages and various languages of northern Luzon. A minimum time depth of 4,000 years would seem to be implied.

Headhunting

To account for the agreement of Ml, NgD *kayaw* Dempwolff (1934–8) proposed *kayaw 'go headhunting'. This comparison can now be extended as follows: Ilc, Isg *kayaw* 'hunt heads'.

Dempwolff's comparison could be explained as a local innovation in Borneo, with Malay borrowing of the Dayak term. In a similar vein Middelkoop (1963, 1: 37) has argued for a secondary introduction in Timor. But the occurrence of a cognate form among some of the relatively remote mountain peoples of northern Luzon clearly attests to the antiquity of headhunting (and presumably of various associated religious ideas) in the AN world. On present linguistic evidence this term cannot be assigned to Proto-Austronesian, but the assumption of a minimum time depth comparable to that for the loom seems warranted.

The blowpipe

To account for the comparison Tg *sumpit* TB *suppit* 'blowpipe', Ml *sumpit* 'shooting with a blowpipe; blowpipe' Dempwolff (1934–8) posited *sumpit 'blowpipe'. This comparison can now be extended by the addition of Ngadha, Li'o *supi* 'blowpipe'.

In addition we can cite a second semantically similar comparison: UJ *heput*~*hemput*, Uma *hopu* < *(cs)empu(Ct) 'blowpipe'.

In some cases it is possible that the meaning 'blowpipe' is a secondary development.

Thus, Tombatu *seput* 'blow' may more faithfully reflect the original meaning of *(cs)empu(Ct) than do the forms cited above. This possibility is strengthened by isolation of the monosyllabic root *pu(Ct) 'puff', reflected also in Tim *fufut* 'blowpipe', presumably < *pu(Ct)pu(Ct) 'puff, blow suddenly'.

Since the Tagalog, Toba Batak and Florinese forms could be Malay loans, and the semantic agreement of the Uma Juman and Uma words could be a convergent development, the antiquity of the blowpipe – sometimes cited as one of the more striking examples of independent invention (in Indonesia and South America) – remains indeterminate.

Overview

Fit of the evidence

For various reasons the foregoing attempt to co-ordinate archaeological and linguistic evidence has only partially succeeded in yielding a consistent picture of AN culture history. In addition to a few areas in which the two disciplines appear to point to similar conclusions, we have discovered a major disconformity between archaeological and linguistic inferences relating to iron, and possibly similar contradictions with respect to other features of material culture.

To some extent this lack of fit is undoubtedly a product of the complex human history of much of the AN-speaking world (the Philippines, Indonesia, New Guinea), coupled with the fragmentary state of current prehistoric knowledge. In historically simpler areas, as Polynesia, the dovetailing of linguistic and archaeological inferences in recent years, in relation both to sequence and to chronology, has been impressive.

Culture-historical reconstruction

In a paper remarkably resourceful for its time, Hendrik Kern (1889) presented lexical evidence that the original AN speech community must have inhabited an environment in which sugarcane, the coconut, various kinds of bamboo, rattan, the cucumber, stinging nettle, derris root, taro, banana, pandanus, yam and such animals as the dark-haired langur were found. Kern argued further that the AN homeland must have been insular or littoral, as many far-flung cognates relating to the sea, marine life and maritime technology would otherwise be unexplained. In addition he attributed to PAN speakers domestication of the dog, pig and fowl, a knowledge of rice and of iron; in this way he was able to limit the class of possible homelands to the coastal zone of the South-East Asian mainland. As a consequence of his reconstructional inferences, Kern concluded that certain original cultural possessions (as iron-working) must have been lost as AN-speaking groups moved east.

A strikingly different view is developed by Murdock (1964). Basing himself on Dyen's (1963; 1965b) claim that the highest index of (lexicostatistically-defined) diversity within the AN family, and hence the probable earliest centre of dispersal is in the New Guinea-Bismarck archipelago area, Murdock proceeds to sketch an imaginative picture of AN culture history. It is argued (p. 124) that the assumed westward expansion of AN speakers would 'almost certainly antedate the spread of South-East Asian agriculture and its major crops (bananas, breadfruit, taro and yams) into Indonesia'. As a consequence, the conclusion is reached that these plants, together with the pig and fowl, and later iron, rice, the water buffalo and writing were borrowed from 'peoples of a different language and superior culture' on the South-East Asian mainland. Murdock's paper is quite extraordinary in its disregard for well-established linguistic evidence (known at least since Kern) which requires – on almost any conceivable subgrouping assumptions – the assignment to Proto-Austronesian of many of the very culture items he proposes to introduce through borrowing. No attempt is made to identify a possible source language for any of these putative loans, nor to explain why many of them (at least banana, breadfruit, taro, yam, pig and rice) show regular correspondences between widely divergent members of the AN family.

Given the items in table 1, the broad outlines of AN culture history can be summarized as follows: PAN speakers occupied settled villages which contained both dwelling units (*Rumaq: Bun *lumaq* 'family, house, home', Ml *rumah* 'house, specifically a dwelling-house in contrast to a mosque or to a *balai*, or meeting-house open to all', Ar *ruma* 'house, family') and some kind of public building (*balay: Ml *balai* 'public building, in contrast to a private house; an unwalled or low-walled building where people met, public business was transacted, and strangers spent the night', Pul *fáál* 'boat house', AA *hare* 'house of retirement for women during menstruation and after childbirth', Ar *hare* 'shed for yams; house with one side of roof only, made in gardens; shrine, small house on poles'). Dwelling units were evidently raised on posts (A8) and entered by a (probably notched log) ladder (A9). The roof (which was, therefore, gabled) contained a ridgepole (A2), possibly covered by an inverted log or bamboo rain shield (Pn *kolób* 'bamboo used to cover ridge of roof', Kel *kulub*, UJ *kulum* 'hollowed log laid inverted over the ridge of the roof to shed water') and was thatched, probably with sago leaf (A6). A hearth (A3) was built on the floor (probably in one corner) and one or more storage shelves for pots, firewood etc., above it (A5). The inhabitants slept using a wooden pillow or headrest (B8). They possessed the pig (H1), fowl (H2) and dog (H3), but also hunted (F7, F8, F10); made pottery (B5), plaited (presumably) mats and baskets (C1), but also wove true fabrics on a (probably simple back) loom (C8); mended torn materials with needle and thread (C9, C10), tattooed themselves (D1), chewed betel (E1, E2) and evidently had a form of intoxicating drink (E3). The known linguistic evidence for the presence of bark cloth is restricted to eastern languages (Bul *māl*, POC *malo 'the paper mulberry: Broussonetia papyrifera; cloth of same'), but it is likely that bark cloth has an older history. Iron was apparently known (C3, C5?), though its uses remain unclear. In addition, some form of native script may have been invented, and used on perishable materials (C4?, C6).

There is persuasive evidence that PAN speakers possessed a well-developed maritime technology (G1–13), cultivated a variety of root and tree crops (I3, I4, I5, I7, I9, I11, I12, I13, I15, I17, I19, I20) rice (I2, I8, I14, I22) and possibly millet (I21). Cereal crops were hulled by pounding in a wooden mortar (I6, I10).

The bow (B2, B7), and sharpened bamboo trail or pitfall spikes (B10) were used (probably both in hunting and in warfare), and headhunting with its associated complex of religious ideas must certainly have existed as early as 2000 B.C. It seems likely that there was a high degree of social stratification (Gad *qaripan*, NgD *jipen* 'slave' suggest the presence of slavery at a time level comparable to that for headhunting), but the available linguistic data for social organization are sparse and difficult to interpret. Various tropical skin diseases were evidently prevalent (L).

In summary, the somewhat mixed picture that emerges from these interpretations (with stone tools next to iron, probable bark cloth next to textiles, root crops next to grain) suggests a polymorphous economic base incompatible with the somewhat rigid notion of 'progress' from one exclusive level to the next.

Culture loss

Given the culture-historical reconstruction suggested above, a major question arises concerning the metamorphosis of the proposed PAN culture type into the substantially different immediate post-contact Oceanic culture type lacking grain crops, iron, writing and (except for Micronesia) the loom. It is sometimes argued that nothing of real importance has ever been lost in human history (Wissler 1923). While this claim may be true for the human species as a whole (as Wissler evidently meant), contrary cases among particular groups can easily be cited. Thus, pottery evidently disappeared altogether in Micronesia and eastern Polynesia, and survived in western Polynesia only long enough to leave archaeological traces of its former presence (but was reacquired by Tonga from Fiji in precontact times).

Some of the people of eastern Indonesia (as of Ceram) rely primarily on sago (Wallace 1869), yet plant some rice and refer to it by terms that appear to be directly inherited. A similar partial or complete transition to sago by earlier rice-growing populations is found in the Melanau coastal area of Sarawak (Morris 1953). It seems likely then that the early AN settlers of the Pacific took rice with them (simultaneously exploiting sago), but that rice did not succeed under Oceanic conditions and sooner or later passed away altogether. A consideration of this possibility in future archaeological work on early AN sites in the western Pacific may prove worthwhile.

It is conceivable that some iron was similarly carried into the western Pacific during the earliest period of AN settlement but that the absence of replenishment led to eventual loss of familiarity with it. The astonishing assertion of Cook (Lloyd 1949: 309) that the Hawaiians had heard of iron and were aware of its superior properties at first contact is difficult to place in a coherent context. Since no metal was actually observed this report is perhaps best attributed to misunderstanding.

The Micronesian loom is sometimes described (Howells 1973: 28) as of 'Indonesian type'. Because reflexes of *tinequn or *balija are unknown in Micronesia there are no linguistic grounds for assuming transportation by speakers of Proto-Oceanic. Independent invention is a logical possibility, but the close formal similarity to the Indonesian back-loom is suggestive of common origin. Whether the loom was part of the POC cultural equipment, or was lost during the initial AN penetration of the Pacific and only later reacquired in Micronesia by chance contact and borrowing is indeterminate on present evidence.

Acknowledgements

Much appreciation goes to F. J. Allen, Peter Bellwood, Jack Golson, Jenny Hope and Andrew Pawley for information and useful criticism of an earlier version of this paper. None of these persons, of course, shares any responsibility for inadequacies in the final product.

25.vii.1975 *The Australian National University*

References

Adriani, N. 1928. *Bare'e-Nederlandsch Woordenboek met Nederlandsch-Bare'e Register*. Leiden: Brill.

Antonissen, A. 1958. *Kadazan-English and English-Kadazan Dictionary*. Canberra: Government Printing Office.

Arndt, P. 1933. *Li'onesisch-Deutsches Wörterbuch*. Ende.

Arndt, P. 1962. *Wörterbuch der Ngadha-Sprache*. Studia Instituti Anthropos 1.

Bellwood, P. 1975. The prehistory of Oceania. *Current Anthropology*. 16.1:9–28.

Benton, R. A. 1971. *Pangasinan Dictionary*. Pali language texts: Philippines. Honolulu: University of Hawaii Press.

Biggs, B. 1965. Direct and indirect inheritance in Rotuman. *Lingua*. 14:383–415.

Blust, R. A. 1970. Proto-Austronesian addenda. *Oceanic Linguistics*. 9.2:104–62.

Blust, R. A. 1972a. Proto-Oceanic addenda with cognates in non-Oceanic Austronesian languages: a preliminary list. *University of Hawaii Working Papers in Linguistics*. 4.1:1–43.

Blust, R. A. 1972b. Additions to 'Proto-Austronesian addenda' and 'Proto-Oceanic addenda with cognates in non-Oceanic Austronesian languages'. *University of Hawaii Working Papers in Linguistics*. 4.8:1–17.

Blust, R. A. 1973. Additions to 'Proto-Austronesian addenda' and 'Proto-Oceanic addenda with cognates in non-Oceanic Austronesian languages' – II. *University of Hawaii Working Papers in Linguistics*. 5.3:33–61.

Blust, R. A. 1974a. Eastern Austronesian: a note. *University of Hawaii Working Papers in Linguistics*. 6.4:101–7.

Blust, R. A. 1974b. The Proto-North Sarawak vowel deletion hypothesis. Unpublished Ph.D. dissertation, University of Hawaii, Honolulu.

Blust, R. A. n.d. Personal field-notes.

Bulmer, S. 1966. Pig bone from two archaeological sites in the New Guinea highlands. *Journal of the Polynesian Society*. 75.4:504–5.

Bulmer, S. 1974. Settlement and economy in prehistoric Papua New Guinea. *Department of Anthropology, University of Auckland, Working Paper* 30.

Capell, A. 1941. *A New Fijian Dictionary*, Sydney: Australasian Medical Publishing Co.

Capell, A. 1943. *The Linguistic Position of South-Eastern Papua.* Sydney: Australasian Medical Publishing Co.

Carro, A. 1956. *Iloko-English Dictionary.* (Translated, augmented and revised by Morice Vanoverbergh.) Manila.

Chang, K-C. 1964. Prehistoric and early historic culture horizons and traditions in south China. In K-C. Chang, G. W. Grace and W. G. Solheim II, Movement of the Malayo-Polynesians: 1500 B.C. to A.D. 500. *Current Anthropology.* 5.5:359–406.

Dahl, O. C. 1951. *Malgache et Maanjan: une comparaison linguistique.* Oslo: Studies of the Egede Institute, 3.

Dahl, O. C. 1973. *Proto-Austronesian.* Lund: Scandinavian Institute of Asian Studies monograph series, 15.

Darlington, P. J., Jr. 1957. *Zoogeography: the Geographical Distribution of Animals.* New York: Wiley & Sons.

Dempwolff, O. 1920. Die Lautentsprechungen der indonesischen Lippenlaute in einigen anderen austronesischen Südseesprachen. *Zeitschrift für Eingeborenen-Sprachen,* Supplement 2. Berlin: Dietrich Reimer.

Dempwolff, O. 1925. Die L-, R- und D-Laute in austronesischen Sprachen. *Zeitschrift für Eingeborenen-Sprachen.* 15:19–50, 116–38, 223–38, 273–319.

Dempwolff, O. 1934–8. Vergleichende Lautlehre des austronesischen Wortschatzes. *Zeitschrift für Eingeborenen-Sprachen.* 1. Induktiver Aufbau einer indonesischen Ursprache, Supplement 15 (1934); 2. Deduktive Anwendung des Urindonesischen auf austronesische Einzelsprachen, Supplement 17 (1937); 3. Austronesisches Wörterverzeichnis, Supplement 19 (1938). Berlin: Dietrich Reimer.

Dunnebier, W. 1951. *Bolaang-Mongondowsch-Nederlandsch Woordenboek.* 's-Gravenhage: Nijhoff.

Dyen, I. 1953. Review of *Malgache et Maanjan: une comparaison linguistique,* by O. C. Dahl. *Language.* 29:577–90.

Dyen, I. 1956. The Ngaju-Dayak 'old speech stratum'. *Language.* 32:183–7.

Dyen, I. 1963. The position of the Malayo-Polynesian languages of Formosa. *Asian Perspectives.* 7:261–71.

Dyen, I. 1965a. Formosan evidence for some new Proto-Austronesian phonemes. *Lingua.* 14:285–305.

Dyen, I. 1965b. A lexicostatistical classification of the Austronesian languages. *International Journal of American Linguistics.* 31.1, Memoir 19.

Dyen, I. 1971. The Austronesian languages and Proto-Austronesian. *Current Trends in Linguistics,* 8, pp. 5–54 (ed. T. Sebeok). The Hague: Mouton.

Elbert, S. H. 1972. *Puluwat Dictionary.* Pacific Linguistics Series C, no. 24. Canberra: Australian National University.

Elkins, R. E. 1968. *Manobo-English Dictionary.* Oceanic Linguistics Special Publication no. 3. Honolulu: University of Hawaii Press.

Esser, S. J. 1964. De Uma-taal. *Verhandelingen van het koninklijk Instituut voor taal-, land- en volkenkunde*, 43. 's-Gravenhage: Nijhoff.

Ferrell, R. 1969. *Taiwan Aboriginal Groups: Problems in Cultural and Linguistic Classification.* Institute of Ethnology, Academia Sinica. Monograph no. 17.

Ferrell, R. 1970. Paiwan stem vocabulary (draft).

Fontaine, H. 1972. Nouveau champ de jarres dans la province de Long-Khanh. *Bulletin de la Société des études Indo-chinoises.* 47:399–446.

Forsberg, V. and A. Lindquist. 1955. *Tagabili vocabulary.* Manila: Summer Institute of Linguistics.

Fortune, R. F. 1942. *Arapesh.* New York: J. J. Augustin.

Fox, C. E. 1970. *Arosi-English Dictionary.* Pacific Linguistics Series C, No. 11. Canberra: Australian National University.

Geerts, P. 1970. *'Āre 'Āre Dictionary.* Pacific Linguistics Series C, No. 14. Canberra: Australian National University.

Geurtjens, H. 1921. *Woordenlijst der Keieesche Taal.* Verhandelingen van het Bataviaasch Genootschap van Kunsten en Wetenschappen. 63.3.

Golson, J. 1971. Lapita ware and its transformations. *Studies in Oceanic culture history* (*2*), *Pacific Anthropological Records*, no. 12, pp. 67–76 (eds R. C. Green and M. Kelly). Honolulu: Bishop Museum.

Gonda, J. 1952. *Sanskrit in Indonesia.* Sarasvati Vihara Series, 28. Nagpur.

Grace, G. W. 1955. Subgrouping of Malayo-Polynesian: a report of tentative findings. *American Anthropologist.* 57:337–9.

Grace, G. W. 1969. A Proto-Oceanic finder list. *University of Hawaii Working Papers in Linguistics.* 1.2:39–84.

Harrisson, T. (ed.) 1966. *Borneo Writing and Related Matters.* Sarawak Museum Journal Special Monograph no. 1.

Harrisson, T. and B. 1971. *The Prehistory of Sabah.* Sabah Society Journal Special Monograph no. 1.

Howells, W. W. 1973. *The Pacific Islanders.* New York: Scribner's; London: Weidenfeld and Nicolson.

Jasapan, M. 1964. *Folk Literature of South Sumatra.* (Rejang ka-ga-nga texts). Canberra: Australian National University Press.

Jeng, H. 1972. *A Bunun-English Dictionary.* Taipei.

Kähler, H. 1959. *Vergleichendes Wörterverzeichnis der Sichule-Sprache auf der Insel Simalur an der Westküste von Sumatra.* Veröffentlichungen des Seminars für Indonesische und Südseesprachen der Universität Hamburg, 1.

Kähler, H. 1961. *Simalur-Deutsches Wörterbuch mit Deutsch-Simaluresischem Wörterverzeichnis* Veröffentlichungen des Seminars für Indonesische und Südseesprachen der Universität Hamburg, 3.

Kern, H. 1889. Taalkundige gegevens ter bepaling van het stamland der Maleisch-Polynesische volken. *Verslagen en Mededeelingen der Koninklijke Akademie van Wetenschappen, afdeeling Letterkunde*. 3de reeks, 6:270–87 (reprinted in *Verspreide geschriften*. 6:105–20. '-Gravenhage, 1917.

Lloyd, C. (ed.) 1949. *The Voyages of Captain James Cook around the World, selected from his Journals*. London: Cresset Press.

Mann, G. 1940. *Boelisch-Nederlandsche Woordenlijst*. Verhandelingen van het Bataviaasch Genootschap van Kunsten en Wetenschappen 74.3.

McKaughan, H. P. and Macaraya, B. A. 1967. *A Maranao Dictionary*. Honolulu: University of Hawaii Press.

Middelkoop, P. 1963. *Head Hunting in Timor and its Historical Implications*. Oceania Linguistic Monographs, 8a, b, c.

Milke, W. 1938. Die Benennungen der Geschwister in den austronesischen Sprachen ozeaniens. *Zeitschrift für Ethnologie*. 70:51–66.

Milke, W. 1968. Proto-Oceanic addenda. *Oceanic Linguistics*. 7.2:147–71.

Morris, H. S. 1953. *Report on a Melanau Sago-Producing Community in Sarawak* (Colonial Research Studies, 9). London: Her Majesty's Stationery Office, for the Colonial Office.

Murdock, G. P. 1964. Genetic classification of the Austronesian languages: a key to Oceanic culture history. *Ethnology*. 3.2.117–26.

Panganiban, J. V. 1966. *Talahuluganang Pilipino-Ingles*. Manila: Government Printing Office.

Pawley, A. K. 1966. Polynesian languages: a subgrouping based on shared innovations in morphology. *Journal of the Polynesian Society*. 75:39–64.

Pawley, A. K. 1972. On the Internal Relationships of Eastern Oceanic Languages. *Studies in Oceanic culture history*, (3) Pacific Anthropological Records, no. 13. Honolulu: Bishop Museum.

Pawley, A. K. and Green, K. 1971. Lexical evidence for the Proto-Polynesian homeland. *Te Reo*. 14:1–35.

Pawley, A. K. and Green, R. C. 1973. Dating the dispersal of the Oceanic languages. To appear in *Proceedings of the First International Conference on Comparative Austronesian Linguistics* 1: Oceanic languages. Honolulu: University of Hawaii Press.

Postma, A. 1971. Contemporary Mangyan scripts. *The Philippine Journal of Linguistics*. 2.1:1–12.

Prentice, D. J. 1974. Yet another Proto-Austronesian phoneme? To appear in *Proceedings of the First International Conference on Comparative Austronesian Linguistics*, 2: Western Austronesian languages. Honolulu: University of Hawaii Press.

Ray, S. H. 1913. The languages of Borneo. *Sarawak Museum Journal*. 1.4:1–196.

Reid, L. A. (ed.) 1971. *Philippine Minor Languages: word lists and phonologies*. Oceanic Linguistics Special Publication no. 8. Honolulu: University of Hawaii Press.

Scott, N. C. 1956. *A Dictionary of Sea Dayak*. London: School of Oriental and African Studies, University of London.

Solheim, W. G., II 1964. Pottery and the Malayo-Polynesians. In K-C. Chang, G. W. Grace and W. G. Solheim II, Movement of the Malayo-Polynesians: 1500 B.C. to A.D. 500 *Current Anthropology*. 5.5:359–406.

Solheim, W. G., II 1968. Early bronze in north-eastern Thailand. *Current Anthropology*. 9:59–62.

Stresemann, E. 1927. Die Lauterscheinungen in den ambonischen Sprachen. *Zeitschrift für Eingeborenen-Sprachen*, Supplement 10. Berlin: Dietrich Reimer.

Sundermann, H. 1905. *Niassisch-Deutsches Wörterbuch*. Moers: J. W. Spaarmann.

Van Hasselt, J. L. and F. J. F. 1947. *Noemforsch Woordenboek*. Amsterdam: J. H. de Bussy.

Vanoverbergh, M. 1933. *A Dictionary of Lepanto Igorot or Kankanay*. Anthropos Linguistic Monograph, 12.

Vanoverbergh, M. 1972. *Isneg-English Vocabulary*. Oceanic Linguistics Special Publication no. 11. Honolulu: University Press of Hawaii.

Vérin, P., C. P. Kottak and P. Gorlin. 1969. The glottochronology of Malagasy speech communities. *Oceanic Linguistics*. 8.1:26–83.

Von Preissing, E. R. 1918. *Dictionary and Grammar of the Chamorro Language of the Island of Guam*. Washington: Government Printing Office.

Wallace, A. 1869. *The Malay Archipelago*. London: Macmillan.

Warren, C. P. 1959. *A Vocabulary of the Batak of Palawan*. Transcript no. 7, Philippine Studies Program, University of Chicago.

White, J. P. 1967. *Taim bilong bipo. Investigations towards a prehistory of the Papua New Guinea Highlands*. Unpublished Ph.D. dissertation, Australian National University, Canberra.

Wilkinson, R. J. 1957. *A Malay-English Dictionary (romanised)*. London: Macmillan & Co.

Wissler, C. 1923. *Man and Culture*. New York: T. Y. Crowell.

Wolff, J. U. 1972. *A Dictionary of Cebuano Visayan*. Philippine Journal of Linguistics Special Monograph no. 4.

Wurm, S. A., C. L. Voorhoeve and K. McElhanon. 1975. The Trans-New Guinea phylum in general. *New Guinea Area Languages and Language Study*, 1: *Papuan Languages and the New Guinea Linguistic Scene*, pp. 229–322. Pacific Linguistics Series C, no. 38. Canberra: Australian National University.

Zorc, R. D. 1969. *A Study of the Aklanon Dialect, vol. 2: Dictionary*. Kalibo, Aklan.

Abstract

Blust, R.

Austronesian culture history: some linguistic inferences and their relations to the archaeological record

Although subject to limitations of its own, historical linguistics can illuminate fragments of the human cultural past that are often irrecoverable from the archaeological record. Where both lines of evidence bear on a common referent they may be mutually corroboratory or contradictory. A number of inferences of all three types are considered, and certain conclusions reached which differ markedly from recent word-based reconstructions of Austronesian culture history, but lend support to the early ideas of Kern (1889). In particular, it is argued that the original Austronesian speakers (circa 4,000 B.C.) were sedentary villagers who possessed (in addition to a universally acknowledged sophisticated maritime technology) root and grain crops, the pig, dog and fowl, pottery, apparently some knowledge of iron, probably the loom and possibly an indigenous syllabary. To account for a variety of observations it is simplest to assume that this community was located west of the Wallace Line, and that Austronesian culture history in its eastern efflorescence was to a significant extent a history of (material) culture loss.

Time perspective and proto-Indo-European culture

J. P. Mallory

Introduction

The use of linguistic palaeontology to reconstruct the culture of the prehistoric speakers of the Indo-European (IE) language family is now well over a century old, and its basic methodology is generally known. A comparison of cognate words among the IE languages affords one the possibility of reconstructing the earlier phonetic shape and meaning of their proto-form. For example, the series of cognates evidenced by Sanskrit *áviḥ* 'sheep', Greek *ó(w)is* 'sheep', Latin *ovis* 'sheep', Lithuanian *avìs* 'sheep' etc., permits one to posit a Proto-Indo-European (PIE) **owis* 'sheep' and assign this item to the cultural universe of the PIE speakers. Optimistically, many scholars hoped to correlate the linguistically reconstructed culture traits with archaeological evidence of the Late Neolithic-Early Bronze Age in order to delimit the prehistoric distribution of the PIE language. In actuality, even the most spatially restricted PIE faunal, floral and technological items have proved so extensive that they accommodate nearly all of the conflicting solutions to the IE 'homeland' problem independently proposed by archaeologists. Moreover, the numerous instances of egregious overinterpretation of the linguistic data and the very real methodological problems involved in producing a reasonably convincing reconstruction of PIE culture have cast a good deal of suspicion on the results of linguistic palaeontology. Among the numerous methodological issues, the problem of co-ordinating the time depths of the reconstructed cultural items with each other and with the archaeological evidence has been of constant interest to prehistorians. This brief review of the time depth problem will attempt to sample the possibilities and pitfalls of linguistic palaeontology in that language family where it has been most extensively applied.

The problem of synchrony

Even before the twentieth century it was argued that linguistic palaeontology did not provide a valid cultural picture of the speakers of the IE proto-language since there was no guarantee that the reconstructed proto-forms were synchronic with one another. According to Paul Kretschmer, the theoretical basis of linguistic palaeontology rested on the fallacious equation of two distinct concepts: the real PIE language from which the attested IE languages must have been genetically derived, and a Common-Indo-European (CIE) representing the linguistic reconstructions generated by the comparative method. There was no certainty that each proto-form appearing in CIE was actually inherited from the time of the real PIE language rather than the result of inter-language borrowing after the expansion/diversification of the PIE language. One could only determine the relative order of the phonetic changes which a word underwent before emerging in the historically attested IE languages. For example, PIE **gʷōus* 'cow' is reconstructed from Sanskrit *gáuḥ*, Old High German *chuo*, Greek *boũs*, Umbrian **bōs* Old Irish *bó* etc. One might then conclude that a word **gʷōus* 'cow' had spread among the prehistoric speakers of the IE language family before the **gʷ* of **gʷōus* had become *b* in Greek, Umbrian and Old Irish. There was no certain evidence that a real PIE community at the unknown time of its existence was familiar with this word or the cultural item to which it referred. Kretschmer contended that 'the diffusion of the individual words which one was accustomed to lump under the term "PIE" not only could but no doubt did fall in quite different periods of IE linguistic history' (Kretschmer 1896: 22).

Kretschmer's criticism has been echoed throughout the twentieth century. J. Fraser argued that linguistic palaeontology could only offer a misleading 'composite photograph' of the culture of the IE speakers through time. There was no certainty, for example, that the IE speakers acquired their word for 'beech' in the same area or at the same time as their word for 'horse'. Fraser offered a cautionary tale based on a linguistic reconstruction of 'Proto-Romance' culture from the Romance languages wherein we should be able to retrieve words for 'king', 'priest', 'bishop', 'coffee' and 'tobacco', and thereby produce a quite ludicrous image of Roman culture (Fraser 1926: 268). More recently, Ernst Pulgram has warned that the application of linguistic palaeontology 'can only result in illusory findings' since it confuses the reconstructed language with a real PIE language 'which is not actually placeable in time and place' (Pulgram 1959: 424). The criticism that the culture attributed to the speakers of the IE proto-language may be an erroneous compilation of chronologically different culture traits has not so much undermined linguistic palaeontology as prompted attempts to seriate the reconstructed lexicon. Indo-Europeanists have employed three different approaches for stratifying the lexicon of the IE proto-language:

1. an approach based on the morphological complexity of the reconstructed words,
2. one founded on the semantic development of commonly inherited words in the IE daughter languages, and
3. a method founded on the geographic distribution of the cognate words themselves.

Morphology and lexical-cultural seriation

The employment of morphological (grammatical) evidence to lexical data in order to recover a relative chronology is a familiar approach to lexical-cultural seriation. The relative antiquity of stockbreeding among English speakers, for example, is linguistically supported by the irregular (archaic) plural formations of such terms as *ox/oxen*, *cow/kine*, *sheep/sheep* etc., and is contrastive with more recent cultural pursuits which consistently display the more regular *s*-plural formation (Anttila 1972: 573). A similar approach has been extended to the prehistoric IE vocabulary, especially by A. Nehring (1936), F. Specht (1944), and H. Kuhn (1953).

A. Nehring proposed that the nouns of the reconstructed PIE lexicon could be assigned to three general linguistic periods. The earliest of these periods was linguistically marked by nouns that formed their nominative case with one stem suffix but employed a different stem for the other cases. Nouns so formed were believed archaic since such irregular formations (heteroclitics) were not active in the IE daughter languages. The antiquity suggested by the linguistic evidence was supported by the semantic field of the heteroclitics since they designated only the most basic cultural terms, *e.g.* 'light', 'day', 'year', 'water', 'fire', the seasons, parts of the body etc. (Nehring 1936: 149). The second period was marked by all other stem formations except the *o* and *ā*-stems, and was thus defined as the period mediating the oldest and most recent formations. The final period was linked to the *o* and *ā*-stems which were quite productive in most IE languages and filled out a culturally more recent semantic field. For example, a root stem PIE **sūs* 'wild pig' was assigned to the second period and was followed by PIE **porḱos* 'domesticated pig', an *o*-stem which was both morphologically and culturally later than PIE **sūs*. Similarly, PIE **eḱwos* 'domesticated horse' was assigned to a more recent stage of the PIE language on both morphological and cultural grounds (also Wagner 1958: 64).

Co-ordinating archaeological data and his scheme of lexical-cultural seriation, Nehring went on to draw a number of inferences about the location and development of the IE language family. For example, since PIE **ḱwon* 'dog' was not a heteroclitic formation of the earliest period, this argued against setting the IE homeland in Northern Europe where dog remains had been known dating from the Mesolithic (Nehring 1936: 68). Since PIE **bhereǵh-os* 'birch' was an *o*-stem, it was incongruent with a homeland in Central Europe where the birch had been known from the earliest times (1936: 211–12). Among the IE languages there are a number of cognate sets for 'goat' which usually appear in no more than three daughter languages. Of these, the *o* and *ā*-stems clearly dominated and this indicated that the domestic goat was a very late cultural acquisition of the IE speakers (1936: 110–11).

F. Specht employed a somewhat more cautious and less precise seriation by placing the heteroclitics along with the other stem formations except the *o* and *ā*-stems into the 'irregular' or archaic category. The *o* and *ā*-stems were naturally the repositories of the later cultural items. For example, the words for copper, gold and silver all exhibited archaic stem formatives as opposed to those words in the IE languages for the later metals, e.g. Greek *sídēros* 'iron', Latin *ferrum* (<**fersom*) 'iron', Gothic *eisarn* (<**īsarno-*) 'iron', all of which were *o*-stems. Where the evidence of Specht's archaeologically determined IE homeland in Northern Europe contradicted the morphologically seriated lexicon, special pleading was introduced. For example, PIE **eḱwos* 'horse', **wḷk^{w}os* 'wolf' and **r̥tkos* 'bear' were all *o*-stems although one might expect them to have been morphologically more archaic since the latter two items were known from the Palaeolithic and the wild horse was known in Northern Europe since the Mesolithic. Therefore, Specht explained **eḱwos* as an old *u*-stem, ***eku-*, that had been re-formed as an *o*-stem during the later period. The particular root vocalism in the two wild animal names was aberrant for verb-derived nouns, *e.g.* **wḷk^{w}os* 'the ripper', and thus they too might be considered archaic (Specht 1944: 37). Like Nehring, Specht designated the goat as a late cultural acquisition since it was not reconstructible from more than three IE subgroups. This was believed to accord well with the archaeological evidence that the Corded Ware culture (IE speakers) had expanded southwards and only gained the goat from the Balkan agriculturalists who had been practising goat breeding throughout the Neolithic (Specht 1939: 13).

The most recent attempt at lexical-cultural seriation on morphological grounds has been made by Hans Kuhn (1954) who disregarded stem suffixes as chronological diacritics and proposed that the mechanism of vowel alternation (ablaut) and the appearance of an *a*-vocalism in the root were the most distinctive markers of time depth in PIE. Kuhn advanced the theory that the names of the domesticated animals and the terms for agriculture and metallurgy all sprang from a period when ablaut ceased to be an active mechanism in PIE and the *a*-vocalism, an aberrant vowel in the reconstructed IE phonetic system, was introduced. According to Kuhn, none of the names of the domestic animals indicated that they were formed when ablaut was still active, i.e. the evidence of the cognates uniformly reconstructed the same root vocalism. Even the wild animals such as PIE **wl̥kʷos* 'wolf' were also post-ablaut and culturally more recent terms. Kuhn argued that the wolf would not have gained cultural significance until it had become a threat to the IE domestic livestock, therefore, it would lexically date to the same period as the domestic animals. The agricultural terminology was also entirely post-ablaut and was frequently characterized by an *a*-vocalism in the root, e.g. PIE **dam-* 'to tame', **ar-* 'to plough', and **aǵ-* 'to drive cattle'. Like Nehring and Specht, Kuhn also regarded the domestic goat as a later cultural item since there was no evidence for ablaut in the six cognate sets. The occurrence of this *a*-vocalism in the names of the earlier metals, e.g. **ayes* 'bronze' (?), Latin *aurum* 'gold', *argentum* 'silver' in contrast to the different root vocalisms of the later metals, e.g. Greek *sídēros* 'iron', Latin *ferrum* 'iron' etc., all indicated that the period of the *a*-vocalism flourished from the Neolithic to the Bronze Age and had ended by the Iron Age (Kuhn 1954: 158–9). Kuhn associated the *a*-vocalism agricultural terms with the expansion of the PIE speakers out of the east into the Balkan and Central European Neolithic communities where there was also evidence for a system of allegedly non-IE river and place names in which the *a*-vocalism dominated.

Semantics and lexical-cultural seriation

W. Brandenstein contended that it was not morphological complexity but rather the semantic development underlying the common roots inherited in the individual daughter languages that provided the most sensitive indices of time depth (Brandenstein 1936a, 1936b, 1957). He reasoned:

> The various IE peoples became independent at various moments in the semantic developments [of the inherited PIE words] and have either maintained this moment of development or have gone on from there on their own course. Because of this, the various phases of semantic change have been collected by us. Moreover, it happens that we are able to order these phases chronologically . . . (Brandenstein 1936a: 25).

Brandenstein observed, for example, that several reconstructed meanings could be assigned to the root **sē(y)-*: 'to throw', 'to throw dice', and 'to sow'. Indo-Iranian evidence indicated only the first two meanings whereas the European IE languages all evidenced the sememe 'to sow'. Although the phonetic shape of the root was the same, there appeared to be a semantic break between Indo-Iranian and European. The division was consistent with a cultural break between the two language areas which indicated different periods of IE cultural development. The first was one in which all of the IE languages shared common meanings for the same roots and exhibited an economy based on pastoral nomadism. The second period occurred after the separation of the Indo-Iranian speakers from the ancestors of the European languages who went on to develop an economy based on settled agriculture. For example, PIE **aǵros* found its meaning petrified in Indo-Iranian as 'meadow, plain', while in European it had further developed to mean 'cultivated field'; **mel-* meant 'to soften, to weaken' from the Indo-Iranian evidence, while the European speakers had extended it to mean 'to mill, to grind grain' etc. This caesura was augmented by differences in other semantic spheres. The early period, for example, was replete with terms for hills, cliffs, running water and warm weather, while the second period was marked by the further semantic development or even the creation of new terms in the European languages indicating a moister climate, marshlands etc. Brandestein concluded that the IE languages had been formed in the area of the Kirghiz steppe near the original stockbreeding centre of the Near East. The second period reflected the economic and environmental shift to Eastern Europe, captured in the common semantic developments of the European languages.

Geolinguistics and lexical-cultural seriation

Attempts to seriate the cultural development of the IE languages on spatial criteria are associated with the norms arising from the geolinguistic (or neolinguistic) school of M. Bartoli, who advanced several norms for determining the age of a linguistic feature by the geographic distribution of different cognate words (the age and area hypothesis). This approach has been extended to IE cultural words, especially in the works of G. Devoto (1931, 1941, 1962) and G. Bonfante (1934, 1939).

Devoto illustrated the method by which a relative chronological ordering of lexical-cultural terms might be accomplished through geolinguistics. A PIE **egnis* 'fire' is found in a number of non-contiguous IE languages, e.g. Latin *ignis*, Lithuanian *ugnìs*, Sanskrit *agniḥ*. On the other hand, PIE **pūr* 'fire' is found in a more central group of languages, e.g. Greek, Umbrian, Germanic, Old Prussian. Since the independent development of **egnis* in the peripheral languages can be *a priori* excluded, one then assumes that this word was once spread among all of the IE dialects but has since been left in the outer periphery with the more recent **pūr* replacing it throughout the more central area (Devoto 1962: 187–88). There was even an underlying semantic distinction between the two words that indicated a cultural shift among the IE speakers. PIE **egnis* falls in the animate gender and was deified by the ancient Indians as a 'mysterious vital force' whereas its later replacement, PIE **pūr*, was a neuter connotating fire only as a material instrument (Devoto 1931: 91). This downgrading of its religious connotations was part of one of the favourite concepts of the geolinguistic approach to the IE lexicon – the 'democratic revolution' of the centre.

G. Bonfante argued that the presence or absence of a word such as PIE **rēǵs* 'king' among the different IE subgroups could not be due to chance since the term was too full of socio-political import. IE cognates for this word only occur in the marginal languages: Celtic, Italic and Indic, and not in those languages constituting the geographic centre of the IE speaking world. The geolinguistic norm that marginal areas tend to preserve archaisms while the central zone is more innovative suggested that the IE peoples were earlier under a strong authoritative system, evidenced by **rēǵs*, which was later displaced – still in prehistoric times – by a revolution 'which destroyed the politico-religious edifice of the ancient Indo-Europeans' (Bonfante 1934: 269). This central area, approximating to that of the present-day Slavic languages, shared a number of such aristocratic losses or the social downgrading of previously upper class words; for example, PIE **ner-* 'aristocratic warrior' or **pəter* 'father' (with important juridical connotations) were both lost in Baltic and Slavic but retained on the IE periphery (also Devoto 1931; 1941).

The geolinguistic approach did not distinguish a relative chronology for the names of the domesticated animals except for the goat, which was again interpreted as a late acquisition because of its weak overall attestation (Devoto 1962: 259).

Observations

Even ignoring the validity of the methodological approaches, one may dispute many of the lexical-cultural conclusions so far presented on purely substantive grounds. For example, most Indo-Europeanists would agree with E. Benveniste (1949) that the distinction between PIE **sūs* and **porḱos* was not between a wild and a domesticated pig as suggested by Nehring but rather between the adult and young domesticated pig. Kuhn's proposition that the names of the domesticated animals postdated PIE ablaut is directly contradicted by PIE **gʷōus* 'cow' in both declension and composition (Thieme 1954: 62–63) as well as by other examples. Brandenstein's conclusions were frequently supported by invalid evidence, e.g. PIE **mel-* does underlie Sanskrit *mṛṇtā́i* 'to mill, to grind grain' (Thieme 1939; Mayrhofer 1956: 672–3), which contradicts the conclusion that Sanskrit did not inherit a sememe of the agricultural sphere with this root. Rather than discussing these and similar issues of more limited philological interest, I shall confine my remarks to the more general problems of time depth and the IE proto-language.

At the very best, linguistic palaeontology reconstructs the cultural vocabulary of prehistoric communities immediately prior to the diversification of the attested IE languages. Indo-Europeanists have been rather consistent at estimating this period – the 'real' PIE of Kretschmer and Pulgram – to *c.* 3000 B.C. ± 500 years. Attempts to apply glottochronology to dating PIE (for those who believe in its efficacy) have generally found major language separations by 3500 B.C. (Swadesh 1960: 245–52; Wittmann 1969: 5; Tischler 1973: 100, but note that Tischler rejects the method altogether). The problem of setting a *terminus ante quem* on linguistic evidence can only be answered with the first historical attestations of already individualized IE languages. Hittite appears *c.* 2000 B.C. while Indic (already separate from Iranian) and Greek are known from *c.* 1500 to 1300 B.C. Employing the minimum extrapolation, we should imagine that major language splits occurred at least by the period 2500 to 2000 B.C. (cf. Crossland 1972).

If one wishes to employ archaeological correlations with the PIE vocabulary to set a *terminus ante quem* for the maintenance of linguistic unity, then the wheeled vehicle and associated terms are temporally most diagnostic, i.e. the most recent technological concept solidly reconstructed from most of the IE languages. Wagon remains are known in Transcaucasia for the Kura-Araxes culture (Piggott 1968) which may fall *c.* 3700 to 3400 B.C. in the recalibrated radiocarbon chronology (Gimbutas 1973: 171–5). The wagon may be known in the North Pontic as early as Gimbutas' Kurgan II period, *c.* 4000 to 3500 B.C. (Gimbutas 1974: 298), and it appears in south-eastern Europe as clay models in the Baden culture, which would set it to *c.* 3400 to 2850 B.C. (Neustupný 1969: 805), and later throughout the rest of Europe. If the first appearance of the wagon in all of these areas is proximate to the dates cited, the relative linguistic uniformity of the dialects ancestral to those historically attested in the IE family should have existed up to at least *c.* 4000 B.C. if not considerably later, depending on the location of the homeland area.

Deciding the chronology of PIE purely on archaeological evidence seems to be the most dubious approach to the time depth problem. One might assume, for example, a general homeland region such as the North Pontic-Volga steppe region proposed by M. Gimbutas (most recently, 1974) and supported by many others, and then argue a chronology of linguistic differentiation from the evidence of cultural expansion. The expansion of the Kurgan (PIE?) tradition from the North Pontic into Romania occurred by *c.* 4000 to 3500 B.C.; and if one should further assume that it would take a millennium for a linguistic split to occur between the home and colonial area, then we might expect linguistic differentiation by 3000 B.C. Also, one would need to assume that the colonial area was invaded by immigrants speaking a language directly ancestral to historically attested languages and not some pre-PIE language which plays no part in the PIE diachrony as we perceive it by the comparative method. All of this discussion requires appeals to general norms for the temporal and spatial vectors that would affect linguistic divergence of a particular language occupying a particular geographic area with specific variables of social organization and communication systems – none of which have been yet established with empirical data. Finally, we might attempt to set a *terminus ante quem* with the dates of the Battle-Axe and Bell Beaker cultures of Central and Eastern Europe which fall *c.* 2900 to 2400 B.C., since they are generally held to be ancestral to already differentiated IE speaking groups. Given the questionable theoretical foundations of these archaeological approaches to chronology, I doubt that they can provide specific chronological diacritics. It would seem then that PIE, the linguistic phenomenon immediately prior to the differentiation of the IE daughter languages, can only be very loosely confined to a diachrony of *c.* 4000 to 2500 B.C.

The reconstructed PIE language should also be envisioned as a diachronic phenomenon. To be sure, Kretschmer's reduction of the comparative method to the simple ordering of phonetic changes has rightly been refuted by P. Thieme, who found in the comparative evidence an ancestral linguistic system that could only have existed when 'we project the scattered examples in all the individual languages back to a common period in which they were all associatively combined with one another' (Thieme 1954:

63). Whether it is a century or a millennium that might accommodate this 'common period' seems impossible to determine; and I believe that we must reckon with lexical reconstructions that may not be wholly synchronic. This is in part due to the gradually created language splits between the different communities. A solid PIE reconstruction normally requires cognates in most of the IE languages, cognates in geographically non-contiguous languages, e.g. Celtic, Greek, and Indic, or cognates of such considerable morphological complexity that borrowing may be reasonably excluded. Since every reconstruction is not based on identical criteria, it is possible that we may reconstruct to PIE terms that are not wholly synchronic. For example, neither of the two common PIE terms for 'wheel' (*$k^w ek^w los$* and **roto-*) are known from Hittite texts, but rather we find *ḫurki-*, a word of IE derivation but unconnected with the reconstructed PIE wagon nomenclature. Possibly the common PIE forms have merely been replaced; possibly the dialects ancestral to Hittite already separated from the other IE dialects before *$k^w ek^w los$* and **roto-* were current throughout the remaining PIE-speaking area. There might then be a chronological difference between *$k^w ek^w los$* and, for example, **ṛtḱos* 'bear' which is attested in Hittite and the other IE languages.

The whole problem of erroneously assigning late lexical borrowings to the PIE period should be approached along the lines suggested by W. Dressler: we should only accept as PIE inheritances those words for which there is sufficient linguistic evidence to argue against late inter-language borrowing (Dressler 1965: 36–48). It would seem unlikely that after *c.* 2500 B.C., the period by which considerable linguistic differentiation should have been under way, many loan words would be mistakenly interpreted as *solidly* reconstructed to PIE. Again we must reckon with a loose diachrony for the lexically reconstructed proto-culture of the IE language family.

The lexical-cultural picture gained by linguistic palaeontology does provide a 'composite photograph' of the cultural accumulations of the IE speakers up through the period of the PIE diachrony. This is natural since culture itself is cumulative. That PIE might have contained archaisms as Fraser warned is, of course, possible, but it seems unlikely that we should be able to provide a solid reconstruction for a proto-word which had lost its referent in the proto-culture, since this would involve the retention of a linguistic archaism in different subgroups and its parallel reapplication to the same cultural item.

Lexical-cultural seriation founded on morphological evidence assumes that we may treat reconstructed PIE on a synchronic plane and argue chronology from internal evidence. In an absolute sense this is probably false since we have no way of confining the linguistic evidence to anything less than a time plane of a millennium and a half. Whether this is too great a period to assume a heuristic synchrony or is not so great as to affect the validity of the morphological approach seems impossible to assess.

The internal reconstruction employed in morphological seriation can at best order the flexional type, not the root morphemes. For example, the inherited English reflex of PIE *$g^w \bar{o}us$* 'cow' appeared in Old English as *cū/cȳ*, in Middle English as *cou/kine*, and is now *cow/cows*. Although there have been three different plural formations in the last 1,500 years, the root morpheme signalling the meaning 'cow' has continued through this entire period. It would be preposterous to assume that, given only the contemporary evidence, the lexical item *cow* is only as old as its *s*-plural period. Equally specious are any conclusions regarding the age of the root morpheme in **ek̂wos*, **wl̥kʷos* etc., as discussed by the scholars reviewed above. Neither the root morpheme nor its referent are necessarily tied to the age of the flexional type (cf. Arumaa 1949).

It is also erroneous to assume that inherited inflexional types or root morphemes need reflect the 'original' word for a given cultural item. To imagine, for example, that PIE **wl̥kʷos* 'wolf' need be somehow correlated with the IE speakers' first acquaintance with the wolf is to assume that the proto-language existed at a time proximate to the origin of speech itself. To paraphrase N. Collinge's study of linguistic palaeontology (1970), PIE is simply 'post-wolf IE', and the linguist can say little of its earlier lexical-cultural existence. Even among the domesticated animals we have reason to expect a considerable time lag between their first appearance among the pre-PIE speakers and the proto-language diachrony from which we inherit the lexical forms. The IE speakers were likely to have known the domesticated cow by *c.* 5000 B.C.; perhaps they referred to it under a form similar to **gʷōus*; perhaps a root morpheme **gu-* existed with a flexional type we have not inherited or cannot reconstruct since it was remodelled by the PIE period; or perhaps they called the object a **moo* and only replaced it with the form we reconstruct *c.* 3500 B.C. The only possible aid here is an archaeological correlation where we might assess the distance between when an item may have been known and the projected dates for the proto-language itself. For example, since wheeled vehicles among the IE speakers would seem to be a quite late development, it is less likely that there has been considerable change from the initial referent to the inherited form. In any event, discussion begins with archaeological parameters for potential time depths of items, and chronological conclusions can never be safely drawn from the linguistic evidence alone.

One must be cautious in utilizing archaeological parameters since linguistic referents are not necessarily direct correlates of prehistoric items. For example, the word for goat in seriation studies has been frequently judged very recent and the item assigned to late PIE or post-PIE. As a prehistoric item, however, the domestic goat is known throughout the proximate IE homelands from the same time as the other well reconstructed animal names (cf. Murray 1970; Bökөny 1974). There are thus no archaeological grounds to believe that the goat itself was not known to the IE speakers at the same time as the other basic domesticates. To account for its lexical treatment one can suggest several hypotheses: (1) the goat is well anchored in the PIE diachrony (Thieme 1954: 42–7); (2) the attested forms for goat are later replacements for an earlier name, e.g. Germanic *horse* replaced the PIE **ek̂wos*, Old English *eoh* in our own language; (3) the ancient PIE speakers did know the goat but did not classify it lexically under a separate word from **owis* 'sheep' until the latter term became wholly attracted to the wool bearing animal during the Late Neolithic, thus prompting the creation of new terms for the non-sheep, i.e. goat. The last hypothesis is purely conjectural and is merely intended to emphasize that an archaeologist deals with his own sets of cultural categories and that these need not be equivalent to those of the language whose cultural remains he is studying.

Chronological judgement can only be made from morphological evidence when we have a root morpheme associated with a non-productive flexional type, and we can date when it ceased to be productive. In reconstructed PIE this borders on the impossible. Although the heteroclitics constitute the best case for non-productivity in IE, even they continue on into Hittite in some ostensibly late semantic concepts, e.g. *ašuwar* 'pen, fold'. And even if we can determine the loss of productivity, we can say no more than that the root morpheme was probably as old as the flexional type; we cannot say that root morphemes associated with this type are necessarily older than those associated with later flexional types since we can generally expect considerable remodelling of non-productive types, e.g. *oxen* is not older than *cows* in a cultural sense (cf. Sapir 1949: 442).

Brandenstein's lexical-cultural seriation of the IE language family on semantic grounds was theoretically founded on a dubious 'law of the irreversible semantic shift'. While criticism of Brandenstein's handling of evidence is considerable in itself (e.g. Pisani 1937; Specht 1939), the major theoretical objection should concern his one-way semantic change. In an illustration of the simple clarity of this concept, Brandenstein offered the following short example: 'When Germanic **fehu* "livestock" (= Latin *pecu* "livestock") has the meaning "wealth" in Gothic *faíhu*,, then the semantic shift in question is only possible in this direction: "livestock">"livestock possessions">"possessions">"monetary possessions">"wealth", just as Latin *pecunia* means first of all "livestock possessions" and only secondarily "possessions" and "wealth" ' (Brandenstein 1957: 24). In a more recent study of this word from PIE on into Indo-Iranian, E. Beveniste has attractively argued that the original meaning was actually 'movable personal property' and was later attracted into increasingly tighter semantic classes: 'livestock'>'small livestock'>'sheep' (Benveniste 1970). Without going into the details of Benveniste's exegesis of this word, it should be enough to observe that one can make an excellent case for reversing the 'irreversible semantic shift' proposed by Brandenstein. The use of semantic criteria to establish a lexical-cultural seriation – at least by W. Brandenstein – appears to have been founded on a method too arbitrary to produce convincing results.

Lexical-cultural seriation founded on geolinguistics has frequently made invalid use of negative evidence. The 'democratic revolution' of the central area, for example, rests on the non-attestation of certain political terms such as **rēǵs* 'king' among languages that are only themselves attested in comparatively late times. One cannot project back into the late PIE period conclusions founded on the non-attestation of words in Slavic which is not recorded until the ninth century A.D. and in Baltic which does not emerge until the fourteenth century. Even if all the norms of geolinguistics were true (and there is good reason to reject this assumption, cf. Hall 1946), the evidence employed should be synchronic and chronologically proximate to the period of one's reconstructions.

In addition, lexical-cultural seriation based on geolinguistics often creates lexical isoglosses of supposedly temporal value that contradict the morphological isoglosses of the IE languages. Sanskrit shares a number of supposedly late morphological features with Greek although it retains the 'older' word for fire (**egnis*). On the other hand, two peripheral languages which are frequently considered archaic show different words for this concept, i.e., Latin *ignis* but Hittite *paḫḫuwar*, which is supposedly more recent although it is a heteroclitic. Even the area where the religio-centric **egnis* should have been first replaced exhibits both reflexes for the word for fire, i.e. Lithuanian *ugnìs* but Old Prussian *panni*. It seems more logical then to assume that there were two PIE words for fire of indeterminate chronological origin, possibly with a semantic distinction, but where they have been attested is due more to fortuitous factors than reflecting anything of the lexico-cultural development of the PIE language.

Conclusions

Linguistic and archaeological evidence has not as yet suggested any greater temporal precision for dating the IE proto-language than its inclusion within a diachrony of *c.* 4000 to 2500 B.C. All attempts to effect archaeological correlations with the linguistically reconstructed culture traits should take this diachrony as their field of inquiry. The PIE diachrony should also be conceived as a somewhat arbitrary segment of the linguistic and cultural development of Eurasia. Attempts to achieve greater chronological control of the lexical-cultural development through the PIE diachrony appear unconvincing with respect to methodology as well as their handling of the empirical data. Finally, the conclusion that PIE is a diachronic phenomenon would seem to frustrate any attempts to propose static borders for a PIE culture or homeland defined by the boundaries of a single archaeological culture at a particular time. The spatial delimination of PIE cannot be expected to be more precise than its temporal definition.

Acknowledgements

I wish to thank Joan Puhvel for a number of useful corrections, R. A. Crossland and Marija Gimbutas for providing me with bibliographical assistance, and J. Jones and E. J. Stern for comments on an earlier draft of this paper.

27.vi.1975 *Topanga, California*

References

Anttila, R. 1972. *An Introduction to Historical and Comparative Linguistics*. New York. Macmillan.

Arumaa, P. 1949. Semantics and age of declension. *Apophoreta Tartuensia*, pp. 73–8. Stockholm.

Benveniste, E. 1949. Noms d'animaux en indo-européen. *Bulletin de la Société de linguistique de Paris*. 130:74–103.

Benveniste, E. 1970. Les valeurs économiques dans le vocabulaire indo-européen. *Indo-European and Indo-Europeans*, pp. 307–20 (eds G. Cardona, H. Hoenigswald and A. Senn). Philadelphia: University of Pennsylvania Press.

Bököny, S. 1974. *History of domestic mammals in Central and Eastern Europe*. Budapest: Akadémiai Kiadó.

Bonfante, G. 1934. Notas sobre el vocabulario céltico y latino. *Emeritas*. 2:263–306.

Bonfante, G. 1939. Civilisation indo-européenne et civilisation hittite. *Archiv Orientáni*. 11:84–90.

Brandenstein, W. 1936a. *Die erste 'indogermanische' Wanderung*. Vienna: Gerold.

Brandenstein, W. 1936b. Die Lebensformen der 'Indogermanen'. *Die Indogermanen- und Germanenfrage: Neue Wege zu ihrer Lösung*, pp. 231–77. [=*Wiener Beiträge zur Kulturgeschichte und Linguistik*, 4]. Salzburg-Leipzig.

Brandenstein, W. 1957. Etymologica. *Studies presented to Joshua Whatmough on his sixtieth birthday*, pp. 23–7 (ed. E. Pulgram). 's-Gravenhage: Mouton.

Collinge, N. S. 1970. Prehistory via language: some guidelines. *Collectanea Linguistica*, pp. 49–66. The Hague: Mouton.

Crossland, R. A. 1972. Recent re-appraisal of evidence for the chronology of the differentiation of Indo-European. *Acta of the 2nd International Colloquium on Aegean prehistory*, pp. 46–55. Athens: Ministry of Culture and Sciences.

Devoto, G. 1931. Preistoria di lingue e di cultura. *La Cultura*. 10:1–14.

Devoto, G. 1941. Il problema indeuropeo come problema storico. *Romana*. 5:360–8.

Devoto, G. 1962. *Origini indeuropee*. Firenze: Sansoni.

Dressler, W. 1965. Methodische Vorfragen bei der Bestimmung der 'Urheimat'. *Die Sprache*. 11:25–60.

Fraser, J. 1926. Linguistic evidence and archaeological and ethnological facts. *Proceedings of the British Academy*. 12:257–72.

Gimbutas, M. 1973. The Beginning of the Bronze Age in Europe and the Indo-Europeans: 3500–2500 B.C. *Journal of Indo-European Studies*. 1:163–214.

Gimbutas, M. 1974. An archaeologist's view of PIE in 1975. *Journal of Indo-European Studies*. 2:289–307.

Hall, R. 1946. Bartoli's 'Neolinguistica'. *Language*. 22:273–83.

Kretschmer, P. 1896. *Einleitung in die Geschichte der griechischen Sprache*. Göttingen: Vandenhoeck and Ruprecht.

Kuhn, H. 1954. Ablaut, *a* und Altertumskunde. *Zeitschrift für vergleichende Sprachforschung*. 71:129–61.

Mayrhofer, M. 1956–. *Kurzgefasstes etymologisches Wörterbuch des Altindischen*. Heidelberg: Carl Winter.

Murray, J. 1970. *The first European agriculture: A study of the osteological and botanical evidence until two thousand B.C.* Edinburgh: Edinburgh University Press.

Nehring, A. 1936. Studien zur indogermanischen Kultur und Urheimat. *Die Indogermanen- und Germanenfrage: Neue Wege zu ihrer Lösung*, pp. 7–229 (ed. W. Koppers). [= *Wiener Beiträge zur Kulturgeschichte und Linguistik* 4]. Salzburg-Leipzig.

Neustupný, E. 1969. Absolute chronology of the neolithic and aeneolithic periods in Central and South-East Europe II. *Archeologické rozhledy*. 21:783–810.

Piggott, S. 1968. The earliest wheeled vehicles and the Caucasian evidence. *Proceedings of the Prehistoric Society*. 34:266–318.

Pisani, V. 1937. Re. Wilhelm Brandenstein. Die erste 'indogermanische' Wanderung. *Annali della R. Scuola Normale Superiore di Pisa*. Ser. II, 6:177–83.

Pulgram, E. 1959. Proto-Indo-European reality and reconstruction. *Language*. 35:421–6.

Sapir, E. 1949. Time perspective in Aboriginal American culture: A study in method (1912), *Selected Writings of Edward Sapir in Language, Culture and Personality*, pp. 389–462 (ed. D. G. Mandelbaum). Berkeley and Los Angeles: University of California Press.

Specht, F. 1939. Sprachliches zur Urheimat der Indogermanen. *Zeitschrift für vergleichende Sprachforschung*. 66:1–74.

Specht, F. 1944. *Der Ursprung der indogermanischen Deklination.* Göttingen: Vandenhoeck and Ruprecht.

Swadesh, M. 1960. Unas correlaciones de arqueología y lingüística. *El problema indoeuropeo*, pp. 343–52 (ed. P. Bosch–Gimpera). Mexico: Universidad Nacional Autónoma de México.

Thieme, P. 1939. Drei altindische Wurzeln mit Tiefstufemr. *Zeitschrift für vergleichende Sprachforschung.* 66:232–37.

Thieme, P. 1954. Die Heimat der indogermanischen Gemeinsprache. [=*Akademie der Wissenschaften und der Literatur: Abhandlungen der Geistes- und Sozialwissenschaftlichen Klasse*, 11]. Wiesbaden.

Tischler, J. 1973. *Glottochronologie und Lexikostatistik* [=*Innsbrucker Beiträge zur Sprachwissenschaft*, 11]. Innsbruck.

Wagner, H. 1958. Indogermanisch-Vorderasiatisch-Mediterranes. *Zeitschrift für vergleichende Sprachforschung.* 75:58–75.

Wittmann, H. 1969. A lexico-statistical inquiry into the diachrony of Hittite. *Indogermanische Forschungen.* 74:1–10.

Abstract

Mallory, J. P.

Time perspective and Proto-Indo-European culture

The problem of reconstructing a synchronic Proto-Indo-European culture from the linguistic evidence is introduced. Some of the major attempts to effect a cultural seriation from the lexical development of the Proto-Indo-European language are briefly examined and criticized. It is concluded that Proto-Indo-European as both a linguistic and cultural phenomenon can only be confined to a loose diachrony dating *c.* 4000 to 2500 B.C.

Loanwards and Roman expansion in north-west Europe

John Peter Wild

In his classic account of 'languages in contact' Uriel Weinreich (1953: 5) drew attention to the fact that, while the methodologies of anthropology and comparative linguistics are distinct from one another, there are 'certain inescapable parallels in the two domains'. If we substitute 'archaeology' for 'anthropology', the observation still holds good.

Scholars concerned with the older languages of the Indo-European family in western Europe have sometimes sought to interpret linguistic developments there in terms of the archaeological views current at the time (Pokorny 1935: 315ff; 1936: 489ff; 1938: 55ff; Schrader 1907). The difficulties of achieving a lasting result are considerable; for not only has the archaeological dating of the earlier phases of European prehistory changed radically in recent years, but the realization that remains of early substrate languages survived as late as the Roman conquest makes the linguistic panorama more confused (Weisgerber 1953: 269, 274; 1954: 47). Collaboration between scholars from different backgrounds, such as is exemplified by the work of Hachmann, Kossack and Kuhn (1962) is the exception rather than the rule.

In the comparatively well documented period of Roman rule in Europe, loanwords are a fruitful source of cultural information. In 1970 I tried to demonstrate in the context of Roman Britain that a loanword which denotes a concrete object may with fair probability be taken as evidence in itself that the object, too, was borrowed (Wild 1970). I sought there, not merely to repeat a linguistic truism, but to establish the *degree of probability* of parallel borrowing of noun and object, so that the archaeologist seeking information from this source might appreciate its limitations.

At its simplest, 'lexical interference', which gives rise to most loanwords of interest to an archaeologist, involves the straightforward transfer of a phonemic sequence (the complete word) into a new language. This was prevalent in the western Roman provinces, where the vocabulary of an advanced society made an impact on the languages of less advanced peoples. But where Roman met Greek on the same plane, subtler forms of lexical interference, as defined by Weinreich (1953: 51), are found. The use of a Greek word might be extended to conform with the Latin model (e.g. πρεσβευτής for *legatus*, a senior officer) or loan-translations of various types might be preferred by the Greek purist to a straight borrowing (ὕπατοι for *consules* rather than κωνσούλες) (Hahn 1906: 116, 126).

The thesis that loanword implies loan-object is untenable for a small proportion of loanwords. Terminology for parts of the body is a case in point (Wild 1970: 127;

Haarmann 1973: 52; von Wartburg 1952: 30; Gamillscheg 1970: 344). Such borrowings may be explained in a variety of ways. Foreign words *per se* often had a social cachet – or were used for sheer force of expression in cursing and swearing (Weinreich 1953: 56ff.).

Britain provides a good starting-point for a review of how loanwords supplement the historical and archaeological evidence for the impact of Rome on its north-western provinces (Jackson 1953: 76ff; Haarmann 1970); for contact between Latin and the insular Celtic British can be set within comparatively close chronological and geographical limits (*c.* 55 B.C. to *c.* A.D. 450). After the relaxation of Roman political control in the early fifth century, the Latin of the Church was the main fount of new loanwords for Celtic speakers, and these are not difficult to isolate.

The character of British Latin was conservative, as can be seen in its phonology (Greene 1968: 77; Jackson 1953: 105ff.). Conservatism is a normal phenomenon on the margins of a linguistic province (Palmer 1954: 23ff.), heightened in this case by the relative backwardness of Romano-British society. Latin was the only language for writing and communicating Roman culture. It was probably spoken mainly by the rural and urban upper classes and by those in official circles, including the army. Evidence for Vulgar Latin, the colloquial speech from which the European Romance languages grew, can be found in Roman Britain, as Greene (1968) has argued; but its currency was restricted. Mann (1971) has shown that some of those who cut the inscriptions in Britain spoke Vulgar Latin. I cannot follow Greene (1968: 76) in accepting that there was a considerable bilingual population in Roman Britain. The borrowing of Latin vocabulary could take place without the medium of bilinguals (Weinreich 1953:56).

Latin never ousted the British language; but nearly 600 words, mostly nouns, were borrowed by British speakers during the Roman occupation (Lewis 1943; Jackson 1953: 76ff.). Once borrowed, they followed the regular grammatical and phonological development of British into Old and Middle Welsh – or, in the case of the British emigrants to Armorica in the fifth and sixth centuries, into Old and Middle Breton (Haarmann 1973). Welsh and Breton have about 370 Latin loanwords in common, but about a quarter of the loanwords in Old Breton must have been adopted after the emigrants left Briton and reflect the influence of Gallic Vulgar Latin (Haarmann 1973: 30–1).

In 1953 Jackson drew attention to the detailed picture of life in Roman Britain which the Latin loanwords give. A brief review of this will indicate the scope of the linguistic evidence.

Roman technology is as apparent on the linguistic as on the archaeological side. Mining and metallurgy (*aurum*, 'gold'; *plumbum*, 'lead'; *durus*, 'steel'), the building industry (*pontem* (acc.), 'bridge'; *parietem*, 'house wall'; *fenestra*, 'window'), glassworking (*vitrum*) and industrial milling (*molina*, 'millstone') are attested. The textile industry, too, which was already flourishing in the Iron Age, learnt new techniques of cloth finishing (*pexa*, 'soft-finished cloth'; *lixivium*, 'urine (for fulling)'; *pannus*, 'web of cloth'). The improved agricultural techniques introduced on the villa-estates of Lowland Britain account for at least 30 loan words. By comparing borrowed plant-names with Godwin's list of British flora (1956) I indicated in 1970 the proven and the likely Roman introductions, mostly fruit and vegetables (Wild 1970).

The Roman kitchen and table made some impression on the British. Olive oil (*oleum*) and wine (*vinum*) are not unexpected among the loanwords; for the inscriptions on imported amphorae – and their sheer quantity – prove a brisk trade in Mediterranean oil, wine and sauces (Callender 1965) which stretched back into the Iron Age (Peacock 1971). The famous sauces, *garum* and *liquamen*, the *sine qua non* of the Roman cuisine and the ubiquitous *mortarium*, 'mixing bowl', are not attested in British. This is curious; for even in the fifth and sixth centuries the kitchen of the lord of Dinas Powys was the most Roman part of his household (Alcock 1963). At least the British took lunch (*prandium*) and dinner (*cena*).

Archaeological evidence for the eagerness with which the British accepted the Roman economic order is plentiful. Their vocabulary was enriched, for example, by new terms for market (*mercatus*), weights and measures (*sextarius*, *modius*) and coin denominations (*denarius*, *solidus*). Roman military organization and equipment is reflected in such basic concepts as weapons (*arma*), fort (*castra*, *castellum*), soldier (*miles*) as well as tent (*papilio*), breastplate (*lorica*) and infantry (*pedites*).

While most of the aspects of provincial-Roman life mentioned above can be studied by archaeological means, there is an imbalance between the rates of survival of organic and inorganic archaeological material. Loanwords help to correct this. In technology, to quote one example, we know little of Roman cloth-finishing methods in Britain; but the loanwords, some of which are noted above, suggest that the industrial processes revealed in Pompeii, Herculaneum and Ostia were widely practised in Britain (Wild 1970a: 79ff.). Loanwords also shed light on fields where historical rather than archaeological sources are normally informative. The Roman calendar, Roman legal and administrative practices and the whole spectrum of education and cultural life are reflected in at least seventy loanwords in British.

Haarman (1970; 1973) has arranged the Latin loanwords in Welsh and Breton according to Dornseiff's (1970) semantic classification. It is thus possible to discover those spheres of human life where Latin made *no* impact on British, namely the human emotions and thought processes. While the Romans moulded the environment of the British, it is evident that they did not win their hearts and minds.

The situation in the continental Roman provinces was quite different. When Julius Caesar arrived, Celtic dialects were spoken throughout Gaul (Whatmough 1970). In the north-west remains of a pre-Celtic language or languages could still be traced (Hachmann, Kossack, Kuhn 1962), while in the south Greek loanwords revealed the extent of Greek commercial penetration inland from their coastal colonies (von Wartburg 1952: 1ff.). Vulgar Latin, however, ultimately replaced continental Celtic, and the regional dialects in Gaul prove its vigour (Jud 1917). There is still some doubt about how quickly this happened (Whatmough 1944; Weisgerber 1939: 27), but an observation by Jerome (Migne 1845: col. 382), probably based on Lactantius, suggests that Celtic speakers were a small minority by the later fourth century. The few Celtic words which appear in the Romance language of Gaul pertain, suggestively, to rural life (Thurneysen 1884). The Celtic-speaking refugees in Brittany, an intrusive linguistic entity, serve to highlight the cultural differences between Gaul and Britain at the end of the Roman period.

The Latin language was in contact on the Rhine frontier with another major linguistic group, the Germanic dialects. Soon after Caesar's campaigns the Ubian tribe was moved by the Romans from east to west of the Rhine, and linguistic pointers to their Germanic origin persisted in the epigraphic record for three centuries (Weisgerber 1968: 143ff.). The main contact, however, between Rome and the Germanic peoples came in the third and fourth centuries, when increasing numbers of Germans from across the Rhine were recruited into the Roman army, settled on unoccupied Roman territory or employed as federate troops. The rise of the independent Frankish kingdoms was a natural result of this policy.

The Lower Rhine was the principal contact-zone, but the city of Trier, the leading political, economic and ecclesiastical centre of the hinterland, played a prominent role, too. Four hundred Latin loanwords (almost all from Vulgar Latin) have been claimed for the Germanic dialects and Old English (Eggers 1963: 103ff.; Frings 1966: 85ff.; Betz 1959). The Anglo-Saxon migration to Britain in the fifth and sixth centuries gives a *terminus ante quem* for the borrowing of many of these (Frings 1966: 85ff.). Other dating criteria are discussed by Gamillscheg (1970: 9ff.). Loanwords which were subject to the second, Old High German, soundshift were probably assimilated by A.D. 500 (Gamillscheg 1970: 13).

The semantic range of Latin or Vulgar Latin loanwords in the western Germanic dialects is similar to the range which we have seen in the British of Roman Britain, as Jud noted (1917: 65). There are some interesting points of contrast, however.

The Germans borrowed surprisingly few Roman military expressions (*pilum*, *petraria*, *campus*), considering how many of them served with the Roman army – or fought against it! Gamillscheg (1970: 18) believed that the Latin loanwords were adopted, not by soldiers, but by the 'great mass of the Germanic people' in daily contact with the provincial-Roman population. It is hard to find historical or archaeological evidence for such mass contact before A.D. 400, and I am sceptical about his conclusion.

The country between the Rhine and the Elbe was in Roman hands for only a brief spell (12 B.C. to A.D. 9); but for over 400 years the Germanic inhabitants of North Germany and Scandinavia received Roman imported goods. Glass, pottery, metal vessels and coins were among the multifarious items in transit (Eggers 1951). *Aquarium*, 'pail', may have been the term borrowed by the Germans for the bronze or brass buckets manufactured in the Aachen district and distributed far and wide in Free Germany (Minis 1972: 45ff.). Roman customs dues (*teloneum*) were also familiar to the Germans according to Gamillscheg (1970: 17). It is no surprise that the Latin for shopkeeper (*caupo*) and 'dubious salesman' (*mango*) were widely borrowed by Germanic speakers. *Caupo* is not found in the Romance languages, and *mango* rarely so (Frings 1968: 175, 314); for they gave way to *mercator*, 'trader', in Gaul. *Caupo* therefore must be an early loanword.

While viticulture was known in Roman Britain (Frere 1967: 293), the two associated loanwords *cupa*, 'barrel', and *vinum*, 'wine', suggest consumers rather than producers. Some of the barrels may have arrived from the important wine-growing area of the Mosel Valley (Cüppers 1970), whence a number of technical terms entered the Germanic dialects (Frings 1948: 15). *Calcatorium*, 'wine-press' (Frings 1966: 71; 1968: 136ff.), (*vinea*) *camerata*, a form of 'vine trellis' (Frings 1968: 143), *lorea*, 'after-wine' (second pressing), (Frings 1968: 310), *mustum*, 'new wine' (Gamillscheg 1970: 11), *vindemia*, 'grape harvest' and **aequare*, 'to gauge' (Frings 1966: 71; 1968: 238) come from the vocabulary of the Gallo-Roman vintner.

Anglo-Saxon (Old English) is an integral part of the Germanic group of languages centred geographically on the Lower Rhine. The Latin loanwords in Anglo-Saxon are potentially of considerable interest to the archaeologist attempting to assess Pagan Saxon society (Frings 1968: 522f.). Many of them, perhaps the majority, were borrowed before the Völkerwanderung from North Germany and the Frisian coast was completed in the sixth century. They show most of the characteristics of the Latin loanwords in the other early Germanic languages – which is not necessarily what one might have expected. Frings (1966: 85, 94) has pointed out that a considerable proportion of the loanwords must have been derived from the Vulgar Latin of Gaul. Here we come upon the difficulty of distinguishing the pre-migration from the post-migration 'layers'; for comparative linguists can offer a relative, but not an absolute, chronology (Luick 1921: 192ff.). All too often they rely on out-of-date archaeological publications to supply the context. Some words may be most naturally taken as evidence for Roman trade with villages like Feddersen Wierde before the migrations from the homeland (Frings 1966: 94f.; Luick 1921: 63). Contact between the wealthy Anglo-Saxon kingdom of Kent and the Franks of the Rhineland and North Gaul may have been the vehicle for later linguistic borrowings (Evison 1965). The Church, too, played a role in these. The full political, social and economic implications of the loanwords, however, will only become evident after a thorough sifting of the dating criteria and a close examination of the meanings of the words. *Mortarium*, for example, may not have meant a 'mixing bowl' to the Anglo-Saxons, but a marshy hollow (Frings 1968: 330).

Horticultural terminology has a regular place in the interchange of vocabulary in early Europe, and it can be cited here as an example of Anglo-Saxon borrowing from the Romans. While the gardener of Roman Britain was planting cabbages (*brassica*) and beans (*faba*), his Anglo-Saxon successor preferred peas (*pisum*), turnips (*napus*) and perhaps radishes (**radica*) (Wild 1970: 128; Frings 1968: 397, 338; Luick 1921: 197; Godwin 1956). Onions seem to have been particularly popular in Pagan Saxon England; for two forms (*unio, cepa*) are proven early loanwords (Frings 1966: 89, 99). Mulberries (*morus*) and pear-trees (*pirum*) were already grown in Roman Britain (Wild 1970: 128), and the Anglo-Saxons introduced, or intensified the cultivation of, the sorb-apple (*sorbum*) and perhaps the peach (*persicum*) (Frings 1968: 466, 381). Plants with medicinal or aromatic properties familiar to the Anglo-Saxons included cat-mint (*nepeta*), elecampane (*inula*) and lovage (*ligusticum*) (Frings 1968: 339, 288, 304). Other terms of later date can be attributed to the spread of Anglo-Saxon monasticism.

Finally, it should be noted that there was two-way traffic in loanwords in the Roman period. There are remarkably few Germanic loanwords in Latin attested by Roman authors. Among them *ganta* (goose), *sapo* (soap), *reno* (hides) and *glaesum* (amber) reveal the reverse side of Roman trade with Free Germany (Gamillscheg 1970: 23).

Celtic loanwords – or loanwords entering Latin through the medium of Celtic – are more numerous (about 150), and informative. Rome's first contact with the Celts dates to the fifth century B.C. when the latter were at their military peak. They conquered North Italy and sacked Rome itself. By the end of the third century B.C. Rome's expansion at their expense had begun, but was not complete until the first century A.D.

Schmidt (1967) has drawn attention to the problems of establishing a Celtic etymology and of dating the successive 'layers' of loan-vocabulary, but it is the meanings of the loanwords and their cultural implications which concern us here.

Roman terminology for wheeled vehicles is completely dominated by Celtic loanwords, as Dottin (1918) and Schmidt (1967) have demonstrated. Twelve terms have a clear or likely Celtic etymology (Schmidt 1967: 168f.) and they are so well integrated into Latin that they form the basis for Latin lexical development (e.g. *essedum*, 'wagon (with a seat)' to *essedarius*, 'waggoner'). Only their etymologies give any hint of their precise meaning, and that may have been submerged after borrowing. Archaeological sources confirm the importance of wagons and chariots in the Celtic world (Joffroy 1958), but do not yet indicate in what respect the Celtic wheelwright and cartwright was technically so inventive.

A number of clothing terms – and probably the articles themselves – entered the Roman world through Celtic. Two cloaks (*mantos*) (Wild 1966), (*sagum*) and four capes (*cucullus*, *bardocucullus*, *byrrus* and *caracallus* (Wild 1963; 1964)) may be cited. In addition, the Germanic loanwords *braca* (trousers) and *camisia* (shirt) may have reached Italy through the Celts. Roman fashion was wide open to foreign influence and ultimately the older Italic forms of dress were displaced by Gallic and Partho-Persian modes (Wild 1968).

Only the wagon terms stand out as unusual in the list of Celtic loanwords in Latin if we compare it with the list of words borrowed from Latin in the insular Celtic and the Germanic dialects. Schmidt (1967) has given grounds for believing that most of the Celtic loanwords were borrowed into Latin at a time when the Celts were still formidable enemies of the Romans. Celtic cultural influence upon Rome was followed by Roman influence upon the Celts to a point where the continental Celtic culture was practically obliterated.

This brief review may indicate the nature of linguistic contact and linguistic borrowing in Roman Europe, as seen from an archaeological standpoint. Much research remains to be done, ideally by a comparative philologist and an archaeologist working in tandem. More precise dating may be sought for the borrowing of words, and more attention paid to the linguistic geography of loanwords. Closer comparison between the semantic ranges of loanwords in each language would also be fruitful.

3.vii.1975

University of Manchester

References

Alcock, L. A. 1963. *Dinas Powys: an Iron Age, Dark Age and Early Medieval Settlement in Glamorgan.* Cardiff.

Betz, W. 1959. Lehnwörter und Lehnprägungen im Vor- und Frühdeutschen. *Deutsche Wortgeschichte* (eds F. Maurer and F. Stroh). Berlin.

Callender, M. H. 1965. *Roman Amphorae.* London.

Cüppers, H. 1970. Wein und Weinbau zur Römerzeit im Rheinland. *Gymnasium.* Beiheft 7:138ff. Heidelberg.

Dornseiff, F. 1970. *Der deutsche Wortschatz nach Sachgruppen.* Berlin.

Dottin, G. 1918. *La Langue Gauloise.* Paris.

Eggers, H. 1963. *Deutsche Sprachgeschichte.* I. Hamburg.

Eggers, H-J. 1951. *Der römische Import im Freien Germanien.* Hamburg.

Evison, V. I. 1965. *The Fifth Century Invasions South of the Thames.* London.

Frere, S. S. 1967. *Britannia.* London.

Frings, T. 1948. *Grundlegung einer Geschichte der deutschen Sprache.* Halle.

Frings, T. 1966. *Germania Romana* (ed. G. Müller). *Mitteldeutsche Studien.* 19.1. Halle.

Frings, T. 1968. *Germania Romana* (ed. G. Müller) *Mitteldeutsche Studien.* 19.2. Halle.

Godwin, H. 1956. *The History of the British Flora.* Cambridge.

Greene, D. 1968. Some linguistic evidence relating to the British Church. *Christianity in Britain, 300–700,* p. 75ff. (eds M. Barley and R. P. C. Hanson). Leicester.

Haarmann, H. 1970. *Der lateinische Lehnwortschatz im Kymrischen. Romanistische Versuche und Vorarbeiten.* 36. Bonn.

Haarmann, H. 1973. *Der lateinische Lehnwortschatz im Bretonischen.* Hamburg.

Hachmann, R., Kossack, G. and Kuhn, H. 1962. *Völker zwischen Germanen und Kelten.* Neumünster.

Hahn, L. 1906. *Rom und Romanismus im griechisch-römischen Osten.* Leipzig.

Jackson, K. H. 1953. *Language and History in Early Britain.* Edinburgh.

Joffroy, R. 1958. *Les Sépultures à Char du Premier Âge du Fer en France.* Paris.

Jud, J. 1917. Probleme der altromanischen Wortgeographie. *Zeitschrift für romanische Philologie.* 38:1ff.

Lewis, H. 1943. *Yr Elfen Ladin yn yr Iaith Gymraeg.* Cardiff.

Luick, K. 1921. *Historische Grammatik der englischen Sprache.* I. Leipzig (reprint Oxford, 1964).

Mann, J. C. 1971. Spoken Latin in Britain as evidenced in the inscriptions. *Britannia.* 2:218ff.

Migne, J. P. 1945. Patrologia Latina. 26. Paris.

Minis, C. 1972. Der Niederrhein in der Germania Romana. *Festschrift für H. Eggers* (ed. H. Backes). Tübingen.

Palmer, L. R. 1954. *The Latin Language.* London.

Peacock, D. P. S. 1971. Roman Amphorae in Pre-Roman Britain. *The Iron Age and its Hill-Forts,* pp. 161ff. (eds D. Hill and M. Jesson). Southampton.

Pokorny, J. 1935. Zur Urgeschichte der Kelten und Illyrier. *Zeitschrift für celtische Philologie.* 20:315ff.

Pokorny, J. 1936. Zur Urgeschichte der Kelten und Illyrier. *Zeitschrift für celtische Philologie.* 20:489ff.

Porkorny, J. 1938. Zur Urgeschichte der Kelten und Illyrier. *Zeitschrift für celtische Philologie.* 21:55ff.

Schmidt, K. H. 1967. Keltisches Wortgut im Lateinischen. *Glotta*. 44:151ff.

Schrader, O. 1907. *Sprachvergleichung und Urgeschichte*. 3rd ed. Jena.

Thurneysen, R. 1884. *Keltoromanisches*. Halle.

Wartburg, W. von 1952. Die griechische Kolonisation in Südgallien und ihre sprachlichen Zeugen im Westromanischen. *Zeitschrift für romanische Philologie*. 68:1ff.

Weinreich, U. 1953. *Languages in Contact*. New York.

Weisgerber, J. L. 1939. Zur Sprachkarte Mitteleuropas im frühen Mittelalter. *Rheinische Vierteljahrsblätter*. 9:23ff.

Weisgerber, J. L. 1953. Die sprachliche Schichtung der Mediomatrikernamen. *Rheinische Vierteljahrsblätter*. 18:249ff.

Weisgerber, J. L. 1954. Das Namengut der Germani Cisrhenani. *Annalen des historischen Vereins für den Niederrhein*. 155–6:35ff.

Weisgerber, J. L. 1968. *Die Namen der Ubier*. Köln.

Whatmough, J. 1944. κελτικα. *Harvard Studies in Classical Philology*. 55:1ff.

Whatmough, J. 1970. *The Dialects of Ancient Gaul*. Cambridge, Mass.

Wild, J. P. 1963. The *Byrrus Britannicus*. *Antiquity*. 37:193ff.

Wild, J. P. 1964. The Caracallus. *Latomus*. 23:532ff.

Wild, J. P. 1966. Mantus. *Zeitschrift für vergleichende Sprachforschung*. 80:247ff.

Wild, J. P. 1968. Clothing in the north-west provinces of the Roman Empire. *Bonner Jahrbücher*. 168:166ff.

Wild, J. P. 1970. Borrowed names for borrowed things? *Antiquity*. 44:125ff.

Wild, J. P. 1970a. *Textile Manufacture in the Northern Roman Provinces*. Cambridge.

Abstract

Wild, John Peter

Loanwords and Roman expansion in north-west Europe

In this article the author reviews the evidence which loanwords supply for the character of cultural contact in north-west Europe during the Roman period. After some brief comments on the general position of borrowed vocabulary, Latin loanwords in British Celtic and in the Germanic dialects are discussed. Words borrowed by the Anglo-Saxons from the Romans are also considered. Loanwords passing in the opposite direction, from Germanic and Celtic into Latin, are examined in their historical context. Attention is drawn throughout to the value of language as an independent source of information on economic, social, political and administrative conditions.

Archaeology and Bantu linguistics

D. W. Phillipson

This paper presents an attempted inter-disciplinary reconstruction of the Iron Age history of those parts of eastern and southern Africa which are today occupied by peoples speaking Bantu languages. Traditionally, most of these people are mixed farmers growing a variety of cereal and other food crops, and herding – wherever the natural environment permits – domestic animals, principally cattle, sheep and goats. In many areas they are skilled potters and workers of iron and copper. Their traditional settlement pattern is one of villages of small thatched houses built of mud applied over a wooden framework, although in parts of southern Africa an indigenous stone architecture was also developed.

The correlation has frequently been made and, on occasion, somewhat acritically accepted, between the spread of Iron Age culture into eastern and southern sub-equatorial Africa and the dispersal of the Bantu-speakers (e.g. Huffman 1970; Oliver 1966). This correlation is largely based on circumstantial evidence, the main arguments being, firstly, that in those parts of Africa now occupied by Bantu-speaking peoples, the distributions of Iron Age culture and of the Bantu languages have been (both today and in the recent past) broadly conterminous, there being strong indications that indigenous non-Bantu speakers here never possessed a full Iron Age culture. Secondly, the close degree of linguistic similarity which exists between Bantu languages spread over an enormous area of the subcontinent indicates that they are probably derived from a common ancestor within the comparatively recent past; a similarly brief antiquity and common ancestry are attributed to the Iron Age industries on the basis of archaeological evidence and radiocarbon dating. Reconstructions of 'proto-Bantu' languages include vocabulary relating to many items known to have been familiar to the Early Iron Age populations. Although general correlation between the spread of the Bantu languages and that of Iron Age culture in what is now Bantu Africa is almost certainly an over-simplification, it seems to be holding up reasonably well to the more detailed information which is becoming available through current archaeological and linguistic research. The purpose of this paper is to stimulate discussion on the possibility of making more detailed correlations between individual phases of the two spreads than has previously been attempted. The current states of research in the archaeological and linguistic fields will be considered separately; the inter-relationship of the two lines of evidence will then be considered. Finally, a provisional historical outline will be presented, based on both archaeological and linguistic data.

It is appreciated that there is no *a priori* reason why linguistic and archaeological data should be expected to correlate closely, in so far as language and material culture may be (not *are*, but *may be*) independent variables. On the other hand, it is not unreasonable to expect that some at least of the major demographic developments which are indicated by archaeology will be reflected to some degree or another in past patterns of linguistic distribution. Furthermore, some historical linguists have used their data to propose hypotheses relating to phenomena, such as the spread of domestic animals, which are also illustrated in the archaeological record. When the same processes are being investigated by two distinct disciplines, comparison of the results obtained provides a useful check on the methodologies employed by each.

The archaeological background

In a recent paper (Phillipson 1975), I have reviewed the evidence for the chronology of the Iron Age in Bantu Africa provided by the over 400 radiocarbon dates which have now been processed. The conclusions of this survey are summarized below.

The Early Iron Age Industrial Complex

A detailed account of the Early Iron Age in eastern and southern Africa cannot be included in the present paper; the reader is referred to the surveys by Soper (1971) and the present writer (Phillipson 1976). Suffice it to say that this Industrial Complex shows a remarkable degree of uniformity throughout its area of distribution which, as at present known, is illustrated in fig. 2. It appears to have been introduced by means of a rapid and coherent movement of people (who may, however, have been relatively few in number) who took with them a fully fledged but largely alien culture, the formative processes of which had taken place elsewhere. These people seem to have been responsible for the inception of metallurgy throughout this part of the sub-continent and also, in the regions lying to the south of what is now central Tanzania, for the introduction of techniques of food production and pottery manufacture.

The spread of the Early Iron Age Industrial Complex is now seen not to have been quite so rapid or so simple as was previously supposed. Its earliest known manifestation is around Lake Victoria, where it is represented by the pottery known as Urewe ware. The ancestry of Urewe ware is to be sought further to the west, north of the equatorial forests. The inception of Early Iron Age settlement in the Lake Victoria basin may be placed in the second half of the first millennium B.C., most probably around 300 B.C. if not before, at least in the areas west and south-west of the Lake. Possibly its spread to the Winam (Kavirondo) Gulf area of south-western Kenya was rather later.

In the spread of the Early Iron Age to other regions, two distinct streams may be recognized (fig. 2). These were first distinguished on the basis of pottery typology. They are now seen also to be differentiated chronologically and by their differential possession of some metallurgical techniques and domestic animals. The eastern stream, as I have called it, appears to be the earlier of the two. It is almost certainly best derived – directly or indirectly – from the Urewe group.

The earliest known manifestations of the eastern stream are the Kwale ware sites

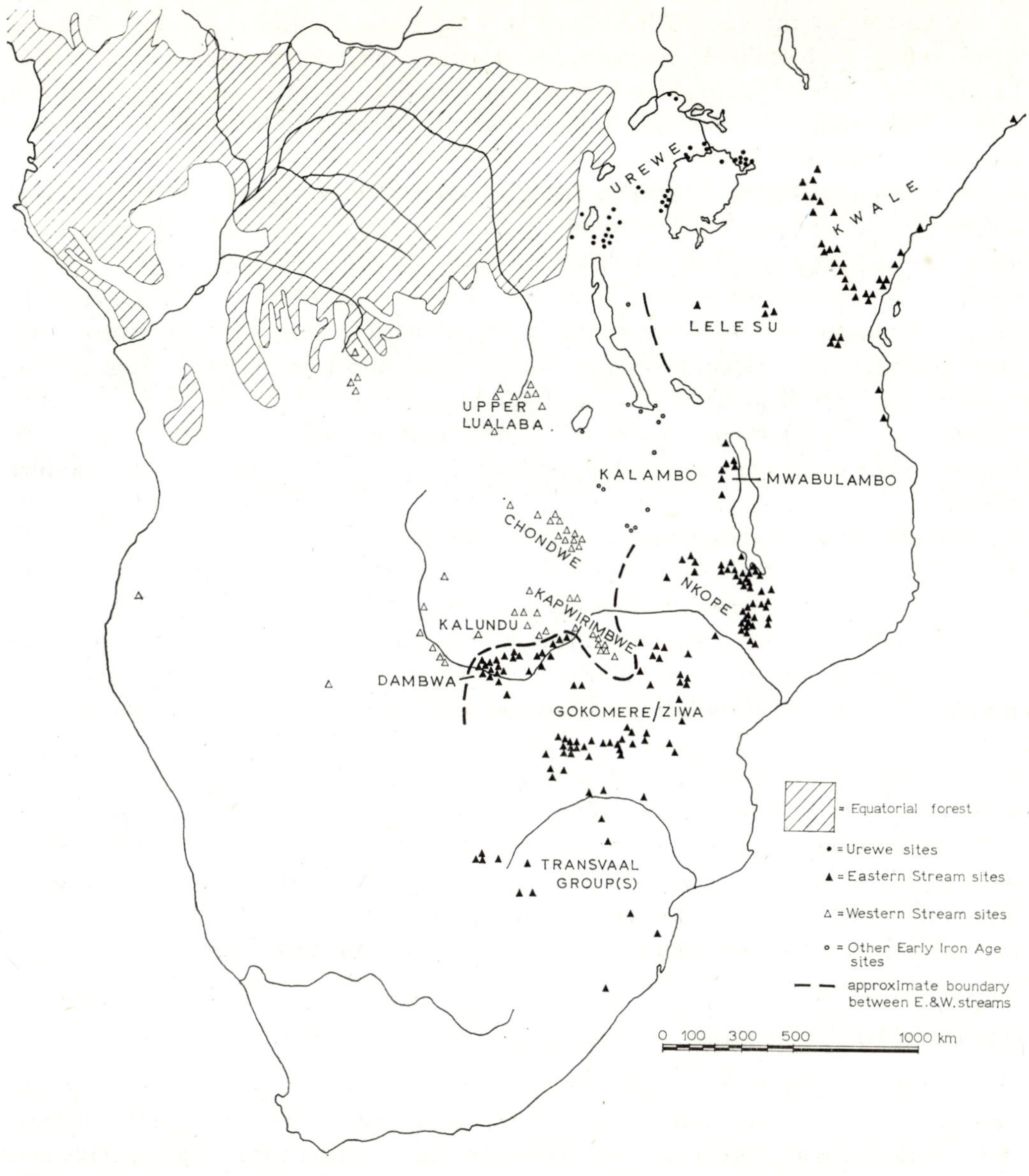

Figure 2 Distribution of the early Iron Age industrial complex in eastern and southern Africa, showing the groups and streams currently recognised (Phillipson 1976).

centred on south-eastern Kenya, but extending also along the Indian Ocean coast northwards into Somalia and southwards to the neighbourhood of Dar-es-Salaam. The inception of this Kwale occupation appears to date from the second century A.D. Elsewhere in the territory of the eastern stream, i.e. in Malawi and eastern Zambia, in Rhodesia and in the Transvaal, the *floruit* of the Early Iron Age appears to have begun in the fourth century A.D., indicating an extremely rapid north-to-south penetration. There are indications that, whereas the Early Iron Age in Rhodesia (represented by Gokomere/Ziwa ware) was derived from that of the region between Lake Malawi and the Luangwa, its counterpart in the eastern Transvaal may be more directly descended from the Kwale settlements, probably via the archaeologically unexplored regions to the east of Lake Malawi (Klapwijk 1974). A final extension of the eastern stream, from Rhodesia north-westwards into the Victoria Falls region of southern Zambia, took place around the sixth century A.D.

The archaeology of the Early Iron Age's western stream is less well known, except in central Zambia. There, it is represented by what I have named the Chondwe, Kapwirimbwe and Kalundu groups (Phillipson 1968). The *floruit* of the Early Iron Age did not begin in this area before the fifth century. The cemeteries of Sanga and Katoto on the upper Lualaba are likewise attributed to the western stream, as are the sparse Early Iron Age sites known from the upper Zambezi area and from northern Angola. It is interesting to note that the Early Iron Age occupation of north-western Mashonaland – Huffman's (1971) Sinoia tradition – unlike that elsewhere in Rhodesia, clearly belongs to the western stream, and can probably be subsumed within my Kapwirimbwe group.

Although sheep and goats were herded by members of at least some groups of both Early Iron Age streams, bones of domestic cattle are only found on western stream sites and on those of later phases of the eastern stream. It thus seems highly probable that cattle did not spread to the eastern stream until a relatively late date, after contact had been established with the western stream. The view that small stock were herded in Rhodesia before the introduction of cattle receives some confirmation from rock art studies (Willcox 1971). The presence of domestic cattle bones at the (apparently eastern stream) fifth-century Iron Age site at Broederstroom in the Transvaal (Mason 1974; Welbourne 1973) is anomalous and is further discussed below.

There are indications that certain metal-working techniques, notably that of flange-welding, were – at least initially – restricted to the western stream. The more advanced economy and technology of the western stream may tentatively be attributed, at least in part, to its later derivation from the common ancestor of the two streams.

The later Iron Age industries

The Early Iron Age pottery traditions were, in most areas of Bantu Africa, replaced around 1,000 years ago by more heterogeneous industries which most archaeologists now group informally under the term 'later Iron Age' (Sutton 1972: 10). The only area where there are convincing indications of continuity of pottery traditions from the Early Iron Age into recent times is in north-western Zambia and adjacent regions of Angola (Phillipson 1974). My recent analyses of the radiocarbon dates show that, despite the greater heterogeneity of the later Iron Age wares in contrast with those of the Early Iron Age, the inception of the later Iron Age took place at virtually the same time over an enormous area.

In a recent article in the *Journal of African History* (1974) I drew attention to the abrupt and pronounced discontinuity which took place in the archaeological sequence of the Zambian Iron Age early in the present millennium, and offered some suggestions as to how and why this break took place. By analogy with relatively well documented nineteenth-century events, it was suggested that a linguistic change might reasonably be expected to have accompanied this pronounced discontinuity in the archaeological record.

It now appears that the pottery style which made its appearance over a large area of Zambia at that time, and which I have named the Luangwa tradition, is intimately related to that which marks the advent of the later Iron Age in most of Rhodesia, the Transvaal and adjacent regions. My observations concerning the sharp discontinuity between the Luangwa tradition and the various Early Iron Age wares (both eastern and western stream) which it displaced have been confirmed by Robinson (1973) in Malawi and in Rhodesia by Huffman (1974). The Uitkomst industry of the Transvaal should also be subsumed into the later Iron Age and not into the Early Iron Age as has previously been assumed (*pace* Mason 1962; Soper 1971).

Further to the north, beyond the Tanganyika/Malawi divide, different and more varied later Iron Age traditions held sway. The nature of the interface or transition between the Early Iron Age and the later Iron Age is not yet so clearly illustrated archaeologically in East Africa as it is in more southerly regions; but most if not all of the East African later Iron Age pottery traditions appear to be markedly distinct from those of the Early Iron Age Industrial Complex. Unlike those in the south, by no means all the later Iron Age Industries of East Africa fall within the known past or present distribution of the Bantu languages. Fig. 3 shows the present northern margin of the Bantu area. There are indications that speakers of non-Bantu languages may, within the relatively recent past, have been more widespread to the south of this line than they are today. In East Africa, the archaeologically best known non-Bantu later Iron Age peoples are those of the Kenyan western highlands (Sutton 1973), who most probably spoke a Nilotic language closely ancestral to modern Kalenjin. Unfortunately, the chronology of these and other non-Bantu Iron Age peoples of East Africa remains poorly understood; we do not know whether the more northerly parts of the region were host to Iron Age folk during the first millennium B.C. – peoples who would then have been contemporaries and counterparts of the practitioners of the Early Iron Age Industrial Complex further to the south.

The *floruit* of the later Iron Age commenced – throughout the regions of eastern, central and southern Africa for which relevant radiocarbon dates are available – around the eleventh century A.D. In no region is any overlap indicated between the *floruit* of the Early Iron Age Industrial Complex and that of the later Iron Age. This is in keeping with the archaeological evidence for the sharp discontinuity between the respective traditions.

The linguistic background

The various ways in which the Bantu languages have been classified present a confusing and often contradictory picture to the non-specialist. It appears that, whilst it is commonly realized that the languages of neighbouring peoples who live for some generations in close contact with one another may be expected to show many points in common, little allowance has been made for this in the phyletic classifications which have been drawn up. The linguistically closer the languages are to begin with, the more such

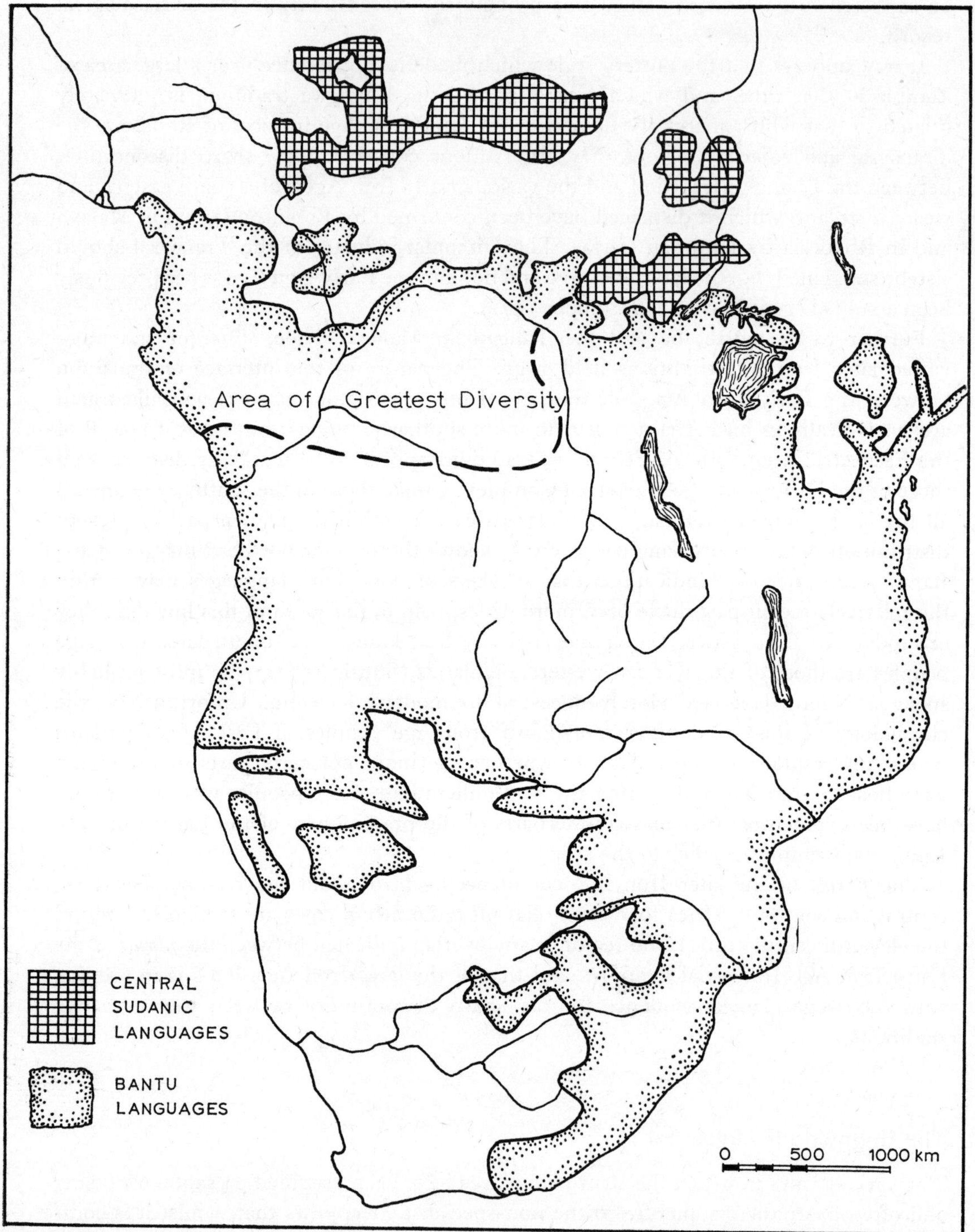

Figure 3 Present distribution of Bantu and Central Sudanic languages (after Greenberg and Guthrie).

interchange is to be expected, and the more difficult it will be for the linguist to recognize it as such. Thus, it is only to be expected that the lexical variation within a closely related group of languages such as Bantu will show a close correlation with geographical distribution, as Henrici (1973) and Ehret (1972) have demonstrated on practical and theoretical grounds respectively. It is noteworthy that almost all studies of the interrelationships of Bantu languages have concentrated their attentions on vocabulary. Comparatively little work has been done on comparison of grammatical constructions or of morphotonological characteristics (but see Carter 1973). The preparation of dendrograms based on lexical similarity, even if only general roots are taken into consideration, can only show the extent of such similarities between languages – similarities which may have developed over an unknown period of time. It is arguable that greater significance should be attached to the presence or absence of loanwords or sets of loanwords which can be traced back to a distant or unrelated linguistic souce (Ehret 1971).

For the archaeologist, one of the most severe limitations of linguistic studies as a basis for historical reconstructions in the context of eastern and southern sub-equatorial Africa is the absence of an accurate absolute chronology. Ancestral forms may be reconstructed, but there is at present no firm foundation for ascertaining the time-depth to which they relate. Linguistic data may, on occasion, be made to supply a relative chronology showing postulated sequential stages of language development and – much less certainly – their progressive areas of distribution; but linguistic evidence for the absolute time-scale against which these developments took place is generally exceedingly tenuous. Our views on the speed of long-term linguistic development are, of necessity, based on languages which have a long written history; yet writing may, in many cases, have a retardative effect on the rate of developmental linguistic change. It is thus possible that some conventional views on the lengths of time necessary for the evolution of recent African languages from their reconstructed ancestral forms may prove to be substantial over-estimates. Application of glottochronometrical techniques to Bantu languages has not yet yielded meaningful results: see Sharman 1972; 1973 for discussions of some of the problems involved. In the final resort, the best approximation to an absolute chronology for the development of an unwritten language must come from the correlation between the stages of its linguistically determined developmental processes and a dated archaeological succession.

Concerning the area of ultimate origin of the Bantu languages, the majority would now subscribe – at least in basic outline – to the views of Greenberg (1955; 1972), who places their homeland close to the north-western limit of their present distribution. Not only is this the area where there is found the greatest diversity among the modern Bantu languages (fig. 3); there is also a marked degree of similarity – both in vocabulary and in grammatical form – between the Bantu languages and other (non Bantu) tongues spoken in this particular area.

A significantly different reconstruction of the origin and early development of the Bantu languages was proposed by Guthrie (1962; 1967). His argument involved the recognition of certain linguistic roots common to at least a minimum proportion of modern Bantu dialects, and the calculation of the percentage of such roots present in each language tested. It was found that the highest occurrence of these common roots was in the centre of the savannah belt lying to the south of the equatorial forests, and that in general the rate of retention showed a constant decrease with increased distance from this central area. (The lowest occurrence of the common roots was in fact found in the north-western area, which Greenberg had seen as the Bantu homeland.) Guthrie tentatively proposed that the area of highest retention represented the 'nucleus area' from which the speakers of the Bantu languages had dispersed, and that the decreasing rates of retention found in more peripheral areas (including the north-west) were indicative of successive phases of spread from the nucleus area.

The model thus tentatively proposed by Guthrie was at first somewhat acritically accepted by historians, partly – it appears – because of its apparent concurrence with some prevailing interpretations of the archaeological data. It was pointed out by Oliver (1966) that the views of both Greenberg and Guthrie could be combined into a single model, Guthrie's 'Bantu nucleus' being regarded as a secondary centre of dispersal. It was suggested that the spread of the Bantu languages from this 'nucleus' could be paralleled by the dispersal of Early Iron Age culture as illustrated by the interpretations of the archaeological record which were then current. A contradiction in this hypothesis was that it took little account of Guthrie's own division of the Bantu languages into eastern and western groups.

More recently, Greenberg (1972), Ehret (1972) and Henrici (1973) have all, using independent arguments, argued that Guthrie's data cannot, in this case, logically support his conclusion. They also consider, however, that Guthrie's Eastern and Western Bantu divisions have little validity at the time-depth originally proposed. Oliver's (1966) suggestion that Iron Age culture could be seen as concomitantly spreading from a similarly situated nucleus is also less convincing in view of the evidence summarized above for the chronology of Early Iron Age spread. This shows that the Early Iron Age was not established in the supposed nucleus area until a relatively late date.

In fact, however, it seems that the widely accepted correlation between the spread of the Bantu languages and that of the Early Iron Age Industrial Complex can still be sustained, and that the more recent interpretations of the linguistic spread are in keeping with those now indicated by archaeology. I shall later present more detailed supporting evidence for this statement.

As noted, above, the greatest diversity of Bantu languages is today found in the north-western corner of their area of distribution (in Guthrie's zones A–C). The languages of the remaining zones are now widely regarded as belonging to a single subbranch which encompasses all the Bantu languages spoken to the south and east of the equatorial forests. Ehret's (1973: 4) proposed term for this subbranch – 'Savannah Bantu' – is a convenient one.

There is now wide agreement that the validity of Guthrie's (1967) Western Bantu/ Eastern Bantu division (if indeed it has any validity) is at this level only: they are at best subbranches of the Savannah Bantu subgroup. The dichotomy is certainly much less marked than was at one time thought; nevertheless, Henrici's recent analysis (1973) does suggest that the modern Bantu languages of the eastern half of subequatorial Africa show a slightly greater degree of homogeneity than do those further to the west. This is also borne out by loanword studies cited by Ehret (1973), on which the following three paragraphs are based. (The present writer is not qualified to pass judgement on the linguistic quality of Ehret's work, which has not yet received detailed critical evaluation, in print, from his colleagues in the field of Bantu linguistics. It is, however, clear that most of the historical reconstructions and chronologies which he postulates are not in keeping with the archaeological evidence. However, it seems that the linguistic framework constructed by Ehret can be used to support a historical reconstruction which is in remarkably close agreement with that now indicated by the archaeology.)

On the basis of loanwords, most of which he believes to be of Central and/or Eastern Sudanic origin, Ehret (*op. cit.*) has attempted a subclassification of these eastern languages. (It may be noted in passing that he offers no very clear definition of what he considers to be an eastern Bantu language, and whether or not his usage of the term is synonymous with that of Guthrie.) He recognizes one particular loanword set which is very widespread in the eastern Bantu languages and which is seen as dating back to a time when a 'proto-eastern Bantu' dialect was spoken in a single restricted area. On linguistic grounds he places this dialect somewhere in the broad region of south-eastern Zaire. Words included in this loanword set include those for cow (**-gombe*), hoe, sorghum, eleusine, porridge and millet beer. Three groups of successors to 'proto-eastern Bantu' are recognized on the basis of further loanword sets; one of these eventually gave rise to the two major linguistic subdivisions which Ehret names 'Pela' and 'Pembele'. These are by far the most widespread clusters among the eastern Bantu languages; the geographical division between them roughly follows the line from the south end of Lake Tanganyika to the northern extremity of Lake Malawi. 'Pela' seems to have given rise to all the modern Bantu languages of Kenya and most of those of Tanganyika as far to the south as the areas now occupied by the Yao and the Makonde. 'Pembele' is seen as ancestral to the languages of northern and eastern Zambia, Malawi, Rhodesia and much of Mozambique, as well as to the South-East Bantu languages.

Within the 'Pembele'-derived languages, Ehret recognizes seven subgroups. Six of these (the exception being the South-East Bantu dialect cluster) he sees as each possessing a different loanword set of Sudanic origin. He suggests that these in turn permit the recognition of at least three pre-Pembele Sudanic-speaking populations, located respectively west of Lake Malawi, in northern Zambia and on the southern Zambian plateau. A small set of putatively Sudanic loanwords, incorporating – it seems – exclusively words connected with food production, has also been recognized in the Khoikhoi languages. South-East Bantu contains a substantial number of Khoisan loanwords, including several which may be ultimately of Sudanic origin. Of prime importance among these is the word for cattle (**-koma*).

The South-East Bantu dialects spoken south of the Limpopo are seen to form a single interlocking dialect network which is believed to have developed within the area of its present distribution. Shona, despite its strong affinity with Venda, is not a part of this network. The implication of recent studies (Ehret *et al.* 1972) is that the South-East Bantu languages separated from the rest of the eastern languages at a relatively early date, and that since that time they have developed in close contact with each other but isolated from the related languages spoken further to the north, the main exception to this being the Shona/Venda influences already noted.

On the basis of his loanword evidence discussed above, Ehret (1967) sees the spread of cattle into subequatorial Africa as having been initiated, prior to the Bantu expansion into eastern and southern Africa, by a single group of people who may have been speakers of a (Central) Sudanic language. He attributes the spread of cattle in western parts of central and southern Africa to Bantu-speakers, but considers that cattle were subsequently passed on to some at least of the South-East Bantu by an intermediate source, which was probably Khoisan. Whereas cattle had been milked from the early days of their presence in southern Kenya and northern Tanzania (i.e. by the 'Late Stone Age' pastoralists of these regions during the first millennium B.C.), the practice of milking probably spread to more southerly latitudes long after the introduction of cattle themselves. Ehret also considers that the words for 'sheep' found in much of eastern and southern Africa may be traced back to a Sudanic source (Ehret 1968). Of the various roots one, *-*bil*- 'sheep', is of particular interest, being distributed 'west of Lake Malawi, southwards into Rhodesia and even into parts of South Africa, and west up the Zambezi' (*op cit.*: 219).

Ehret's interpretation of the evidence cited above is that Sudanic languages were once spoken over a very much wider area, extending southward as far as the modern Rhodesia; and that it was the Sudanic speakers who were responsible for the introduction into this wide region of domestic cattle and sheep (Ehret 1968; 1973). In view of the strong archaeological indications that these animals were introduced into south-central Africa through the medium of the Early Iron Age, these linguistic interpretations must be regarded as antithetical to the common supposition that the spread of the Early Iron Age is to be correlated with that of the Bantu languages.

Interpretations and correlations

It is now appropriate to attempt to proceed beyond broad archaeological/linguistic correlations based on general similarities between patterns of dispersal, to more detailed considerations of the evidence for the distribution of specific cultural traits as illustrated by the two lines of enquiry.

It has often been assumed, for reasons not specifically stated, that the Early Iron Age dispersal was concomitant with that of the Eastern Bantu languages (e.g. Huffman 1970). The place of the Western Bantu languages in this model does not appear to have been considered. It is, however, important to note that, while the Early Iron Age Industrial Complex was widespread in regions where both western and eastern Bantu languages are now spoken, the distinctive later Iron Age industries, in so far as they are now known, were largely restricted to the eastern part of the subcontinent. It is probable that the establishment of the closely inter-related eastern language subgroup in its present area was associated with the inception of the later Iron Age rather than with any earlier event. This would attribute to these languages an antiquity of approximately one thousand years instead of the two millennia which have conventionally been allocated.

Excellent support for this hypothesis is available from Ehret's view of the developmental processes of the eastern languages. The linguistic evidence for placing the original ancestral dialect (his 'proto-Eastern Bantu') in eastern or south-eastern Zaire accords with archaeological data, which suggests that the Luangwa tradition and related later Iron Age industries may have developed from an Early Iron Age predecessor in broadly this same general area (Phillipson 1972: 119). The presence of the root *-*gombe* 'cow' in the loanword set which serves to characterise Ehret's 'proto-Eastern Bantu' is surely significant in view of the archaeological evidence that cattle were originally restricted to the western stream of the Early Iron Age, which was located in that same area which Ehret sees as the homeland of his 'proto-Eastern Bantu'. The spread of 'proto-eastern Bantu' may provisionally be correlated with the expansion of the Early Iron Age's *western* stream, an expansion which ultimately brought it into contact with the eastern stream and resulted in the transfer of cattle to the latter population. A date around the third quarter of the first millennium A.D. is indicated on archaeological grounds for this contact, and is – I submit – not unacceptable linguistically.

It is with the emergence of the language groups dubbed 'Pela' and 'Pembele' that the later Iron Age correlation becomes clearest. As noted above, the geographical division between the two linguistic groups runs roughly from the south end of Lake Tanganyika to the north end of Lake Malawi and thence south-eastward. This is in remarkable agreement with the archaeologically known division in the distribution of the later Iron Age pottery traditions. To the south of the Tanganyika–Malawi line, in the territory of the 'Pembele' languages, are found a series of closely interrelated later Iron Age ceramic industries, notably those of the Luangwa tradition in northern, central and eastern Zambia and in neighbouring countries, together with the related wares in Rhodesia, Mozambique, Botswana and South Africa. The appearance of these industries is securely dated to around the eleventh century A.D. The rapidity of these processes is attested both by archaeology and by linguistic studies, one view being that the spread of the ancestral Shona and South-East Bantu-speakers south of the Zambezi and 'the development of two centres of spread of Bantu speech and ideas in the north and south respectively of that span of country must have been accomplished within a very short time, perhaps only two or three centuries' (Ehret *et al.* 1972: 15).

Were we to accept the conventional attribution of the early eastern Bantu languages to the bearers of Early Iron Age culture, we should be forced to concede that the almost equally widespread and rapid inception of the later Iron Age industries has left no significant mark on the pattern of linguistic distribution in eastern and southern Africa. Nowhere are the complications raised by such a concession clearer than in the regions south of the Zambezi. Here, several writers have proposed correlations between the Rhodesian later Iron Age and speakers of Shona, and between the makers of the Uitkomst pottery and early Sotho-speakers (Fagan 1965; Ehret *et al.* 1972; Huffman 1974). The relative isolation of South-East Bantu from the time of its inception south of the Limpopo, which has been postulated on linguistic grounds, is an archaeologically acceptable hypothesis only if we concede the later Iron Age correlation. Isolation since the time of the arrival of the Early Iron Age population is highly improbable in view of the broad later Iron Age continuity which has been noted above. The linguistic evidence for some degree of contact and interaction between early speakers of Shona and those of Venda is supported by the archaeological affinities of the Bambandyanalo material to that of Rhodesian sites of the Leopard's Kopje II industry (Huffman 1975).

Turning now to eastern Africa north of the Tanganyika–Malawi corridor, the picture is far more complex. Basically, there is no objection to correlating many of the later Iron Age wares of this region, which display a much greater heterogeneity than do those in the south, with the speakers of Ehret's 'Pela' linguistic subbranch. The typology and chronology of the several distinct later Iron Age pottery traditions in this region are much less clearly understood than is the case in the south, although the inception of the later Iron Age appears in both regions to have been very closely contemporaneous. There are indications that some of these East African pottery traditions may be derived ultimately from the north, from speakers of Nilotic or Cushitic languages, from which sources they were subsequently adopted by the Bantu-speaking peoples in whose dialects Nilotic or Cushitic loanword sets are likewise apparent (Ehret 1973). As noted above, the later Iron Age Industries of East Africa are by no means restricted to speakers of Bantu languages; and there is no clear typological distinction between those industries practised to the south of the 'Bantu line' and those found further to the north. The local linguistic pattern is also complicated both by the apparent survival, notably in the interlacustrine region, of Bantu languages which originally developed from the ancestral stock before the appearance of the 'Pela' subbranch, and by the possible retention of pre-eastern Bantu forms in some coastal languages.

There is thus good evidence to link the spread of the eastern Bantu languages with that of the later Iron Age. This may best be demonstrated in areas to the south of southern Tanzania but, in view both of the basic homogeneity of the eastern languages and of the chronological evidence outlined above, is most probably true of more northerly regions also. This correlation, however, leaves two important questions unanswered: firstly, it does not tell us what language or even what sort of language was spoken by the practitioners of the Early Iron Age Industrial Complex; secondly, it throws little or no light on the identity of the hypothetical Sudanic-speaking populations with whom, according to Ehret, some Bantu-speakers came into contact at various stages of their spread. It will be convenient to examine these problems in reverse order.

The interpretation which has been placed (by Ehret) upon the loanword evidence outlined above is that it was from Sudanic-speakers *within eastern and south-central Africa* that the early Bantu-speakers adopted many aspects of their food-producing metallurgical economy, together with much of the relevant vocabulary, and that these Sudanic-speaking peoples were actually present – indeed remarkably widespread (although archaeologically invisible) – in many widely scattered regions of eastern and south-central Africa, at least as far south as the Zambezi, at the time of the arrival there of the first Bantu-speaking folk. Ehret (1973: 10) concedes that 'the loanword sets in Bantu are the only evidence that remains of the existence of these particular Central Sudanic languages and peoples'. In view of their supposed impact on the sub-continent's economic and linguistic history at a comparatively shallow time-depth, the absence of any clearly defined evidence for these Central Sudanic-speakers in the archaeological record is, to say the least, surprising.

It should logically follow from this that the cultural traits which are diagnostic of what the archaeologists have termed the Iron Age were initially introduced into the greater part of eastern and southern Africa by speakers of Sudanic languages. However, in the light of the unambiguous archaeological evidence that these traits were introduced into much of the subcontinent as part of the Early Iron Age Industrial Complex, this hypothesis must be seen as incompatible with the widely accepted correlation between the spread of Iron Age culture and that of the Bantu languages.

Attention has already been drawn to the distribution of the **-bil-* root, meaning 'sheep'. This closely follows the route which I have postulated (Phillipson 1975) for the introduction into Malawi and Rhodesia of the eastern stream of the Early Iron Age Industrial Complex, with which remains of sheep are indubitably associated. The distribution of the *-*bil*- root thus coincides with that of the Mwabulambo, Nkope and Gokomere/Ziwa groups of the Early Iron Age, together with the phase 2 extension of the last, which gave rise to the Dambwa group settlements of the Victoria Falls region (fig. 2). The concordance should also be observed with Cooke's (1965) interpretation of the distribution of rock paintings depicting fat-tailed sheep. Many of the other cultural traits indicated by the putatively Sudanic loanwords are represented in the archaeological record of the Early Iron Age Industrial Complex. These loanwords appear to have been absorbed into the eastern Bantu languages at the time of their initial spread. If we accept the eastern Bantu/later Iron Age correlation proposed above, the source of the loanwords can only have been the language or languages which were spoken by the Early Iron Age folk.

In three cases Ehret has felt able to propose approximate locations for the donor-populations of the Sudanic loanwords. These are the populations which he has named Nyasa, Inter-Lake and Batoka (map in Ehret 1973: 23). Their locations enable tentative correlations to be made respectively with the Mwabulambo, Kalambo and Kalundu groups of the Early Iron Age. The general fit or coextension of these archaeological groups with the three populations postulated on purely linguistic grounds is a further confirmation of the hypothesis that the Sudanic loanwords recognized in eastern Bantu were derived from an Early Iron Age source. Of the three groups concerned, Nkope is clearly attributed to the eastern stream of the Early Iron Age and Kalundu to the western stream, while the position of the Kalambo group is undetermined. Words of Sudanic origin must therefore have been present in the languages of both streams, as is implied in the attribution of *-*gombe* to a western stream source.

We are thus left with two distinct possibilities; either the Early Iron Age folk spoke Sudanic languages, or else they spoke languages which belonged to another family, but in which Sudanic loanwords formed an important element. There are several lines of argument which strongly indicate that the second alternative is more probable.

In the first place, if the speakers of the eastern Bantu languages had come into extensive contact only one thousand years ago with peoples who spoke a full-fledged Sudanic language, and given the archaeological indications for basic continuity of population between the Early Iron Age and the later Iron Age, one would expect to find far stronger indications of Sudanic influences on the eastern Bantu languages than is in fact the case. Secondly, one would expect these influences to be apparent throughout the known distribution of the Early Iron Age Industrial Complex. In fact, however, such influences appear to be virtually absent south of the Limpopo, in the territory where the languages of the South-East Bantu dialect network are now spoken (Ehret 1973; Ehret *et al.* 1972). They are also weak in Rhodesia, but Early Iron Age settlement of both areas is well attested.

The most plausible and economical theory as to the nature of the language spoken by the Early Iron Age folk is that it was a Bantu language of the Savannah subbranch. This is in keeping with the linguistic evidence for the relative antiquity of eastern Bantu itself and of Savannah Bantu (of which eastern Bantu is a subgroup). It postulates a linguistic relationship between the Early and later Iron Age languages which parallels the connection which is indicated on archaeological grounds. The areas, such as western Zambia and adjacent regions of Angola, where the modern pottery traditions show signs of direct continuity from those of the Early Iron Age are those areas where (western) Savannah Bantu languages are now spoken (Phillipson 1974). The possible survival of western linguistic forms on the east coast accords with the view that such languages were widespread throughout the region before the inception of the later Iron Age. These may be regarded as remnants of a previous continuum of Early Iron Age language, subsequently interrupted by the later Iron Age spread of the eastern Bantu languages.

It is, of course, an essential part of this theory that Sudanic loanwords must have been an integral part of these early Savannah Bantu languages. There is nothing inherently improbable in this. The cultural traits indicated by this vocabulary are known to have been present in the Early Iron Age Industrial Complex. Indeed, many of them are believed to have been derived, so far as the Early Iron Age is concerned, from broadly those same regions where the Central Sudanic languages are now spoken. Despite our as yet scanty knowledge of the archaeology of the central part of the Sudanic belt, the accumulated evidence is now very strong that it was somewhere within this general region that was located the population which ultimately gave rise to the Early Iron Age Industrial Complex.

This central Sudanic region is known to have been one which saw an early establishment of mixed farming and of metallurgy. By the first millennium B.C. it may reasonably be assumed that domesticates which originated in the western and the eastern Sudan were generally distributed through much of the zone (Clark 1970; Phillipson in press). Being adjacent to the north-western part of the present Bantu language distribution, now widely accepted as the area where such languages have been established for the longest time, it is not unreasonable to suppose that it was here that some of the early Bantu-speakers obtained from their Sudanic-speaking neighbours a variety of cultural items, including domestic sheep and cattle, as well as metal-working techniques (together with the words used to name them) which they in turn rapidly spread through eastern, central and southern Africa. Goats, being known by a name common to almost all the Bantu languages, may be regarded as having been in the possession of the Bantu-speakers for a longer time (Ehret 1972: 7).

The linguistic variation among the Sudanic words later incorporated into Bantu languages is best explained by sound-shifts within Sudanic rather than in Bantu languages. This implies a prolonged process of contact and borrowing between Sudanic- and Bantu-speaking groups, which may have occupied many centuries, perhaps most of the first millennium B.C. The cultural differentiation within the Early Iron Age, reflected both in the pottery tradition and in the various groups' differential possession of domestic animals, may be attributed partly to distinctions within the early Bantu-speakng population and partly to environmental and other factors determined in the course of their subsequent dispersal.

The important point which emerges from the present enquiry is that this borrowing took place at an early stage in the dispersal of the Bantu-speaking peoples, largely in areas adjacent to those where Central Sudanic languages are now spoken. There is no need to postulate, as Ehret does, a vastly widespread Sudanic-speaking population in eastern and central Africa.

Summary and conclusions

We may now summarize the conclusions which have been drawn concerning the development and spread of the Bantu languages in the light of the Iron Age archaeological succession.

1 The early development of the Bantu languages took place, in or near the north-western area of their present distribution, among a 'Late Stone Age' population which, at a relatively early date, obtained domestic goats and adopted some form of agriculture.
2 Later, as these early Bantu-speakers began to disperse eastwards through the savannah which lay to the north of the equatorial forests – most probably during the first half of the first millennium B.C. – they came into contact with speakers of various Central and/or Eastern Sudanic languages and from these, during a prolonged period of contact, they adopted the cultivation of certain cereal crops, notably sorghum, as well as the herding of domestic sheep and (in some cases) cattle. It was almost certainly at this time also that knowledge of metallurgy came to the Bantu-speaking people.
3 Most probably by this period the two main cultural divisions of the Bantu-speakers, which gave rise to the eastern and western streams of the Early Iron Age Industrial Complex, were already at least partially differentiated: it appears that only the latter became at this stage herders of cattle. Both divisions spoke similar languages akin and ancestral to the modern Savannah Bantu subgroup. By about the fourth century B.C. such an Early Iron Age population had penetrated south-eastwards and settled in the interlacustrine region.
4 Several centuries later a rapid spread of the eastern stream introduced Early Iron Age culture and Savannah Bantu languages to eastern and southern Africa as far south as the Transvaal. Almost certainly the numbers of people involved in these initial movements were small and in many areas their impact on the 'Late Stone Age' folk with whom they came into contact must have been minimal.
5 It is probable, though not yet demonstrated archaeologically, that while the spread of the eastern Early Iron Age stream was in progress, a parallel movement was under way around the flank of the equatorial forests to the southern savannah, thus introducing the ancestral Savannah Bantu dialects to the area of their descendants' greatest modern distribution. This movement of cattle-herders gave rise, around the fifth century A.D., to the western stream of the Early Iron Age, which at that time penetrated what is now central and southern Zambia.
6 By this time, if not before, domestic cattle and other stock had passed from these ancestral western stream Bantu-speakers to some of the Khoisan-speaking 'Late Stone Age' folk of southern Africa. It was from this latter, Khoisan, source that cattle passed at a still relatively early date to the eastern stream Early Iron Age inhabitants of the Transvaal. The other eastern stream groups appear to have obtained their cattle directly from western stream contacts at a date not earlier than the eighth

century, by which time a proto-eastern Bantu dialect was emerging within Savannah Bantu, most probably in what is now south-eastern or eastern Zaire.

7 Around the eleventh century the speakers of this early form of eastern Bantu initiated a rapid dispersal which introduced to wide areas (coinciding closely with the modern distribution of the eastern Bantu languages) the industrial manifestations known to archaeologists as the later Iron Age. Their pottery traditions, some of which were derived ultimately from that of the western stream of the Early Iron Age, rapidly and completely displaced that of their predecessors. The linguistic contribution of the eastern stream of the Early Iron Age was probably greater than appears from this account, but it is difficult to recognize, except in the form of the old Sudanic loan-words.

Acceptance of the chronology of linguistic and cultural development outlined above will enable us to make greater use of linguistic evidence for the elucidation of Iron Age history than has previously been practicable. Great, perhaps undue, emphasis has been placed in the preceding pages on the spread of domestic animals in eastern and southern Africa because this is one of the relatively few cultural traits whose history is reflected both in the archaeological and in the linguistic record. Many other traits, however, which may be traced on linguistic grounds, cannot be distinguished at all by archaeological methods and it will be useful to be able to utilize the linguistic evidence for these against the framework of the archaeologically based chronology.

17.vii.1975

British Institute in Eastern Africa

References

Carter, H. 1973. Tonal data in '*Comparative Bantu*'. *African Language Studies.* 14:36–52.

Clark, J. D. 1970. *The Prehistory of Africa.* London: Thames and Hudson.

Cooke, C. K. 1965. Evidence of human migration from the rock art of Southern Rhodesia. *Africa.* 35:263–85.

Ehret, C. 1967. Cattle-keeping and milking in eastern and southern African history: the linguistic evidence. *Journal of African History.* 8:1–17.

Ehret, C. 1968. Sheep and Central Sudanic peoples in southern Africa. *Journal of African History.* 9:213–21.

Ehret, C. 1971. *Southern Nilotic History.* Evanston: Northwestern University Press.

Ehret, C. 1972. Bantu origins and history: critique and interpretation. *Transafrican Journal of History.* 2:1–9.

Ehret, C. *et al.* 1972. Outlining southern African history: a re-evaluation A.D. 100–1500. *Ufahamu.* 3:9–27.

Ehret, C. 1973. Patterns of Bantu and Central Sudanic settlement in central and southern Africa. *Transafrican Journal of History.* 3:1–71.

Fagan, B. M. 1965. *Southern Africa in the Iron Age.* London: Thames and Hudson.

Greenberg, J. 1955. *Studies in African Linguistic Classification.* New Haven: Yale University Press.

Greenberg, J. 1972. Linguistic evidence regarding Bantu origins. *Journal of African History.* 13:189–216.

Guthrie, M. 1962. Some developments in the prehistory of the Bantu languages. *Journal of African History.* 3:273–82.

Guthrie, M. 1967. *Comparative Bantu*, I. Farnborough: Gregg.

Henrici, A. 1973. Numerical classification of Bantu languages. *African Language Studies.* 14:82–104.

Huffman, T. N. 1970. The Early Iron Age and the spread of the Bantu. *South African Archaeological Bulletin.* 25:3–21.

Huffman, T. N. 1971. A guide to the Iron Age of Mashonaland. *Occasional Papers, National Museum of Rhodesia.* 4(1):20–44.

Huffman, T. N. 1974. The linguistic affinities of the Iron Age in Rhodesia. *Arnoldia* (*Rhodesia*). 7, 7.

Huffman, T. N. 1975. *The Leopard's Kopje Tradition.* Salisbury: National Museums of Rhodesia.

Klapwijk, M. 1974. A preliminary report on pottery from the north-eastern Transvaal, South Africa. *South African Archaeological Bulletin.* 29:19–23.

Mason, R. J. 1962. *Prehistory of the Transvaal.* Johannesburg: Witwatersrand University Press.

Mason, R. J. 1974. Background to the Transvaal Iron Age – discoveries at Olifantspoort and Broederstroon. *Journal South African Institute of Mining and Metallurgy.* 74:211–16.

Oliver, R. 1966. The problem of the Bantu expansion. *Journal of African History.* 7:361–76.

Phillipson, D. W. 1968. The early Iron Age in Zambia – regional variants and some tentative conclusions. *Journal of African History.* 9:191–211.

Phillipson, D. W. 1972. Early Iron Age sites on the Zambian Copperbelt. *Azania.* 7:93–128.

Phillipson D. W. 1974. Iron Age history and archaeology in Zambia. *Journal of African History.* 15:1–25.

Phillipson, D. W. 1975. The chronology of the Iron Age in Bantu Africa. *Journal of African History.* 16: 321–42.

Phillipson, D. W. 1976. The Early Iron in eastern and southern Africa: a critical reappraisal. *Azania.* 11: in press.

Phillipson, D. W. in press. Early food production in sub-Saharan Africa. *Cambridge History of Africa*, I (ed. J. D. Clark). Cambridge: Cambridge University Press.

Robinson, K. R. 1973. The pottery sequence of Malawi briefly compared with that already established south of the Zambezi. *Arnoldia* (*Rhodesia*). 6, 18.

Sharman, J. C. 1972. Glottochronometry: some critical considerations in general and for sub-Saharan Africa in particular. *Mila.* 3:27–42.

Sharman, J. C. 1973. Glottochronometry and lexicostatistics: a possible step forward. *Journal of East African Research and Development*. 3:89–93.

Soper, R. C. 1971. A general review of the Early Iron Age in the southern half of Africa. *Azania*. 6:5–37.

Sutton, J. E. G. 1972. New radiocarbon dates for eastern and southern Africa. *Journal of African History*. 13:1–24.

Sutton, J. E. G. 1973. *The Archaeology of the Western Highlands of Kenya*. Nairobi: British Institute in Eastern Africa.

Welbourne, R. G. 1973. Identification of animal remains from the Broederstroom 24/73 Early Iron Age site. *South African Journal of Science*. 69:325.

Willcox, A. R. 1971. Domestic cattle in Africa, and a rock art mystery. *South African Journal of Science*, special issue. 2:44–8.

Abstract

Phillipson, D. W.

Archaeology and Bantu linguistics

The archaeological evidence for the spread and development of the Iron Age in eastern and southern Africa is re-examined, and two distinct streams are recognized in the Early Iron Age Industrial Complex. The inception of the later Iron Age in most of this region is shown to have taken place around the eleventh century A.D., and a marked degree of similarity is noted in the later Iron Age industries from northern Zambia southwards. This picture is compatible in many respects with that of the spread and development of the Bantu languages, particularly as described by C. Ehret. It is suggested, however, that Ehret is mistaken in several important points, notably with regard to chronology and the part played by speakers of Sudanic languages in the spread of Iron Age culture to south-central Africa. In conclusion, archaeological and linguistic evidence is used to produce a provisional outline of the Iron Age history of eastern and southern Africa.

Language and the prehistory of North America

M. Dale Kinkade and J. V. Powell

Introduction

In this paper we will discuss some of the problems involved in correlating a language spoken in the past with a particular geographical location or with a given archaeological site. This problem will be treated in the context of North America (exclusive of Eskimo-Aleut). Speculations on language movements, spread, and replacement, and on the influence of one language on another will be cited to point up the difficulty of assigning a language to a particular location in prehistoric times. We will mention briefly some of the problems in dating reconstructed forms of languages and in quantifying the time periods involved in linguistic divergence. Although most of our discussion will be negative in demonstrating specific site-language correlations, we will note some points of contact between the findings of archaeology and of historical linguistics. A specific instance of such interdisciplinary contact will constitute the last part of this paper.

Because no North American language was written down before European contact, and because languages leave no other tangible remains, it is virtually impossible to make a direct and definite correlation between a prehistoric archaeological site and a specific language. Nevertheless, a number of speculations can and have been made about what language was spoken at a specific site, and about where an ancestral form of a specific language or of a language family might have been spoken. Such educated guesses are probably the most that can be expected at the present stage of our knowledge of archaeology and historical linguistics. Both deal with the past, and both can reconstruct culture to a degree. Archaeological sites and artefacts can be dated by a variety of techniques with varying degrees of accuracy (for a useful summary of available techniques, see Michels 1972), but no reliable method has yet been devised to date reconstructed languages (except where written documentation exists), nor can the provenance of a reconstructed language be ascertained. Thus only the largely random similarity between cultural features of a vaguely located reconstructed language and the reconstructed culture of an archaeological site provide a tenuous point of contact – tenuous because of all the indeterminate quantities involved. More interesting however, are speculations on the locations of language groups in the past.

Attempts at specific site-language correlations based on proto-language locations have been frustrated by the need for a reliable linguistic method to date reconstructed languages or establish the divergence dates of related tongues. The dating procedures available to archaeologists have no reliable counterparts in the methodology of historical linguistics – there are no means for applying radiocarbon, archaeomagnetic, thermoluminescence, potassium-argon or fission-track dating procedures to a reconstructed lexicon. The most notable attempt to devise a procedure for dating linguistic prehistory is lexicostatistics. Developed in the 1950s by Swadesh and others, lexicostatistics is based on three assumptions, all of which are, unfortunately, invalid. These premisses are:

1 A basic core vocabulary of 200 (or 100) words are less subject to change than other parts of the language, these words including terms for the same items in all languages.
2 The rate of retention of vocabulary items in the basic core vocabulary is constant through time.
3 The rate of loss is the same in all languages.

These generalizations obstruct the most basic intuitions of historical linguistics. Thus, the generalization based on these assumptions – that, knowing the percentage of cognates, one can compute the time depth of divergent languages – must also be emphatically rejected. Many linguists have used lexicostatistics in the absence of any other dating procedure; however, we feel that it is improper to use the methods of lexicostatistics when it suits our purposes, in view of our misgivings about all of its premisses.

Admitting this inability to devise precise chronologies of language prehistory which could then be related to datable archaeological sites, is it still possible to maintain that linguistic data are of value to the prehistorian? In the absence of all other indications, *any* evidence of prehistory becomes invaluable, and numerous aspects of linguistically-transmitted culture can be effectively used by archaeologists in deliberations regarding the identity of the prehistoric inhabitants of a site.

A number of procedures are available to the linguist to determine the earlier residence of a linguistic group or something about the earlier residents of an area:

1 *Language distribution:* Related languages which are geographically separated must have been adjacent at some time in the past (e.g. Cherokee within Iroquoian, the separation of Comanche from a larger Shoshone-speaking group); the location of related languages scattered around the periphery of an unrelated language or family of languages suggests that the unrelated language is intrusive, and that the related languages were once neighbours (e.g. Hokan languages around California Penutian).
2 *Original homeland:* By finding the common geographical denominator of the distributions of flora and fauna for which words exist in the languages of a family, an original homeland (Urheimat) for the proto-language of that family may be localizable. Another method often used is to assume that the area within the family where there is the greatest diversity of languages, or where the major divisions within the family occur, was the original homeland where divisions began to take place.
3 *Intra-family indications of movements:* Similarities between less closely related members of a family may suggest earlier locations nearer to each other, and sharp differences between neighbouring languages suggest geographical movement towards each other, with the possible absorption of dialects or languages in between.
4 *Loan word Patterns:* The distribution of words within a restricted region which have apparently replaced earlier words (still found beyond this region) suggests that the dispersion centre was an area of prestige, capable of causing modification of the

language of neighbours; loan-words from one language to another may suggest that one or the other language intruded into the area and borrowed terms for local flora or fauna from the indigenous group.

5 *Cultural reconstruction via language:* Comparison and reconstruction of lexical items suggest aspects and implements present in the ancestral culture; sometimes these reconstructed terms may represent something that can be localized, indicating earlier residence in a particular place, or movement from there.

6 *Place-names:* Place-names which are unanalysable in the language of the group living where they occur suggest either that they are names given by earlier, unrelated occupants, or that they are native but very old, and their meaning is no longer recognizable in the present language because of phonological and semantic changes; a corollary of this is that easily analysable place-names often suggest recency of occupation of the territory.

7 *Legends:* Occasionally legends suggest that a group migrated from another region, but the accuracy of these legends diminishes as one goes back in time.

Areal similarities found in unrelated languages (as in the Northwest) complicate many of these speculations. Such areal features include aspects of language that would not normally be expected to diffuse across language family boundaries, or that can be reconstructed for more than one family in the area, but which are sufficiently unusual that they would not be expected in more than one family. It is difficult in these cases to determine which family was donor, which borrower, and any relevance to geographical location is thereby made indeterminate.

In what follows, we will refer primarily to procedures 1 and 2 above, with occasional reference to 3 and 5, in summarizing speculations which have been made about original homelands of various American Indian groups. We will then refer briefly to attempts at correlating archaeological sites and language families, followed by a more detailed study of a specific attempt at such correlation in the Northwest, using primarily procedures 6 and 7.

Distribution and homelands of North American languages

Implicit in the notion of a reconstructed language is the assumption that this language was spoken by a single group of people in a restricted and unified territory. But in North America, modern daughter-languages of such proto-languages are often as not found in scattered, separated locations, suggesting either migrations of parts (or all) of the earlier group, or invasion by an outside group and replacement or pushing out of the language originally spoken at the place in question. An examination of a map of North American Indian languages (fig. 4) should make this point clear. Only the Muskogean, Wakashan (and Eskimo-Aleut) families were spoken in uninterrupted areas (language isolates will be considered later; as isolates they are usually found in self-contained areas). We will review the other families (touching on possible more remote relationships), beginning in the east. All locations cited are those at first white contact or earliest information about the group in question.

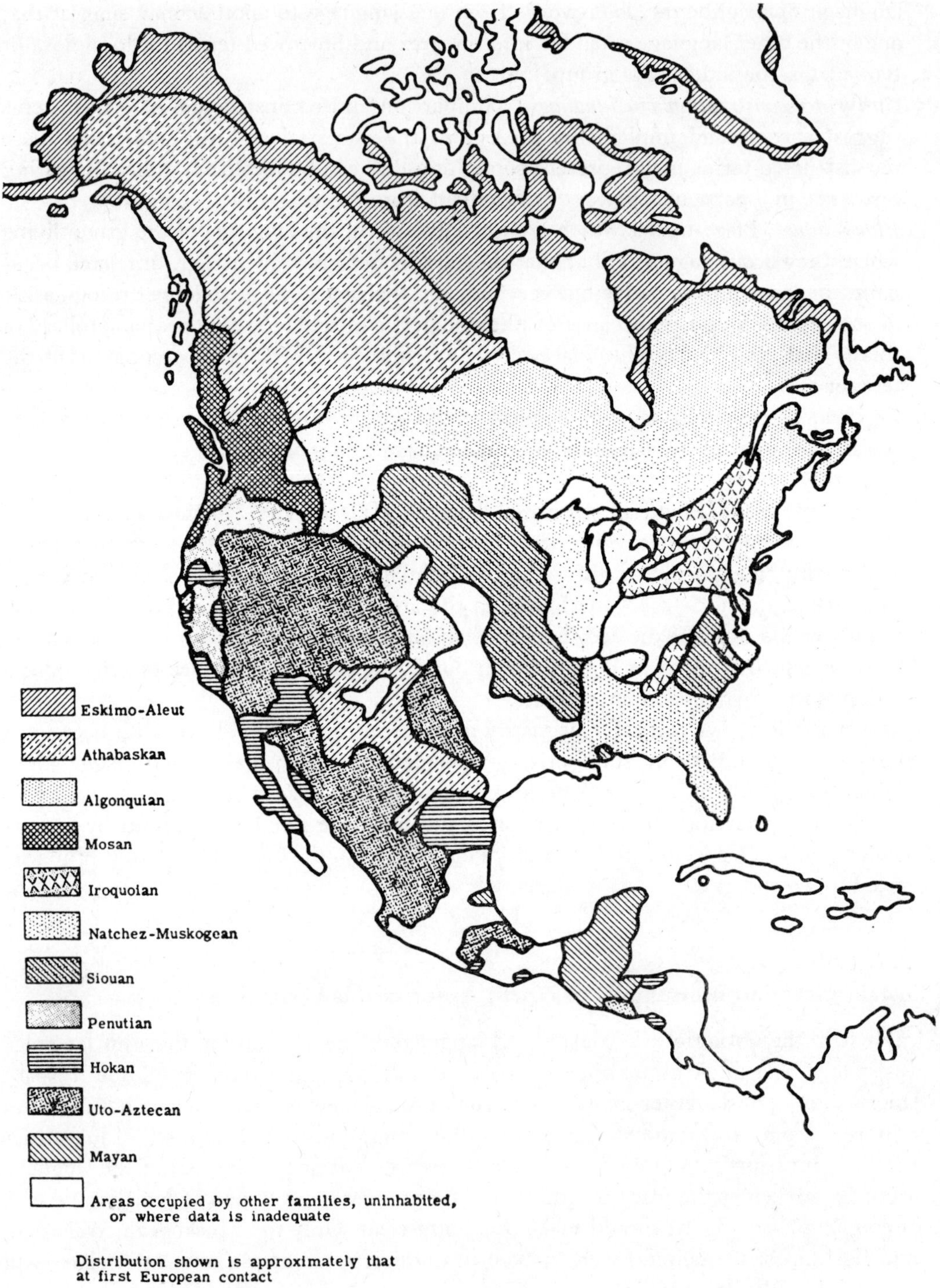

Figure 4 North American Indian languages: published by permission of Holt, Rinehart and Winston.

Iroquoian

Iroquoian languages were spoken in three distinct areas: along the St Lawrence River and Lakes Erie and Ontario, coastal Virginia and North Carolina, and in the Appalachian foothills of North Carolina and Tennessee and surrounding areas. The first two groups of languages are classified together as Northern Iroquoian, and the third (Cherokee) as Southern Iroquoian. There were, earlier, other Northern Iroquoian languages spoken in western New York. Pennsylvania, and Maryland, and these likely adjoined the Iroquoian groups along the St Lawrence. A further link through them to the two more southern groups is not difficult to imagine, but not known in historical times. Chafe (1973: 1169) asserts that 'the degree of difference between these two branches is only a little less than that between the most divergent languages of the Indo-European family'. Clearly, Cherokee began diverging from the other Iroquoian languages long ago, and its degree of difference today from Northern Iroquoian languages suggests a long period of geographical discontiguity between the two branches. As to an original homeland for the Iroquois, Crawford, in a recent survey of south-eastern Indian languages (1975: 18), accepts Powell's observation that 'a tradition of the Iroquois points to the St Lawrence region as the early home of the Iroquoian tribes, whence they gradually moved down to the south-west along the shores of the Great Lakes' (Powell 1891: 77). This does not seem to account for the location of the Cherokee, however.

Siouan

Siouan languages were also spoken in three distinct areas. Most of them were originally at the eastern edge of the Great Plains, along the Mississippi, Missouri, and (perhaps) Ohio Rivers, with three groups established further out in the Plains, but still on the Missouri or its tributaries. A second cluster of Siouan languages was spoken east of the Appalachians in Virginia, North and South Carolina. The third group consisted of two languages spoken on the lower Mississippi River, surrounded by various Gulf languages. The accepted internal classification of Siouan languages is that of Voegelin (1941) into at least four groups: (1) Catawba (in the Carolinas); (2) Ofo and Biloxi (southern Mississippi Valley) and Tutelo (in Virginia); (3) Hidatsa and Crow (upper Missouri River); (4) Chiwere, Winnebago, Dhegiha, Dakota (western Plains, Missouri and Mississippi River valleys); and with Mandan (upper Missouri River) as a possible fifth group. A great deal of shifting about is known to have occurred among various Siouan groups, some of it in historical times. Thus the Dakota were first encountered in the Upper Mississippi River area and, under pressure from Indian groups to the east, spread westwards into the upper Missouri River drainage in the eighteenth century. According to Chafe, 'in prehistoric times the ancestors of the Dhegiha speakers may have lived farther to the east (according to tradition, near the junction of the Wabash and Ohio Rivers), but earliest European contact found them in the central plains' (Chafe 1973: 1182–3). The Biloxi moved westwards from where they were first contacted in southern Mississippi in the early eighteenth century, and subsequently largely died out while living in Louisiana and eastern Texas (Crawford 1975: 51). We know of no speculations about an original homeland for Siouan speakers, but given what is known about eighteenth- and nineteenth-century locations of these groups, and their own migration legends, a region along the central Mississippi River, the lower Missouri River, and the lower Ohio River seems like a reasonable location from which dispersal occurred north, east, south and west along major river valleys.

Caddoan

Caddoan languages are usually shown on maps as occurring in three separate locations, all on the Great Plains. The northernmost of these is the Arikara, which is an offshoot of the Pawnee who had moved northward along the Missouri River, and ended up in the midst of Siouan groups. The Pawnees themselves were in central Nebraska and northern Kansas. The southern Caddoan area was occupied by speakers of at least three languages, but they may not always have been contiguous. In the sixteenth century, 'the Wichita were probably located in central Kansas. After moving into what is now Oklahoma, where they were found by Frenchmen in the early eighteenth century, they were gradually forced further south into Texas before the end of that century' (Chafe 1973: 1166), and 'the Kitsai may have been located prehistorically in Oklahoma, but Europeans first found them living in what is now Texas between the Red River and the upper Trinity' (Chafe 1973: 1166). This suggests that the Pawnee, Wichita, and Kitsai may earlier have formed a continuum or chain of dialects (later diverging into distinct languages), with Caddo separated and to the south-east. Such an arrangement would agree with the present relationships among Caddoan languages, among which Caddo is the most divergent. A southern plains origin for Caddoan is thus suggested.

Algonquian-Ritwan

The Algonquian languages were spoken in a large, mostly continuous area in eastern North America, along the Atlantic coast from North Carolina north, across Canada north of the Great Lakes, and in the United States south and just east of the Great Lakes. They later expanded into the western Canadian plains as far as the Rocky Mountains, and from there southward into the western plains in the United States. In a careful study employing the 'technique of using natural history terms that can be reconstructed in a proto-language in an attempt to locate the original home' (Siebert 1967: 13) of the Proto-Algonquian people by locating the common territory occupied by various types of flora and fauna, Siebert 'arrives at a center of diffusion in the eastern upper Great Lakes region' (Teeter 1973: 1154). Siebert further gives 'an educated guess as to the dates for latest Algonquian unity, which he finds from 1200–900 B.C.' (Teeter 1973: 1154). Algonquian languages are relatively close to one another, the most divergent being the three western-most languages, Blackfoot, Cheyenne and Arapaho. The two Ritwan languages, Yurok and Wiyot, are sister languages of the Algonquian family spoken on the northern California coast; no explanation has yet been advanced for the very distant and very ancient separation of these two languages from Algonquian.

Athapaskan

Athapaskan languages are widely spread over western North America. The largest group is in central Alaska and north-western Canada; those in the American south-west

(Apachean) are a closely-knit group; the third major cluster consists of a few languages spoken along the northern California and southern Oregon coast (the Pacific coast group). One or two languages were spoken in north-western Oregon and south-western Washington, and one (Nicola) was spoken in south-central British Columbia; these are all now extinct. The Pacific coast group is more divergent from northern Athapaskan than are the Apachean languages of the Southwest. Hoijer (1960) and Krauss (1973) consider Kwalhioqua and Tlatskanai (near the lower Columbia River) as a branch of the family distinct from the Pacific coast languages, and not clearly identifiable with any northern language. Nicola is apparently linguistically part of the northern group. Sapir long ago (1936) demonstrated that the south-western Athapaskans originated in the north, by showing that Navajo contains words which can be reconstructed in Athapaskan as referring to items not found in the Southwest ('sleeplessness' from 'travel by canoe'), or which can be shown to have taken on a meaning applicable to the Southwest but not the sub-arctic ('gourd' from 'horn', 'seed lies' from 'snow on the ground', and 'corn' from 'food'); and they are generally believed to have been in the Southwest for only a few centuries. Krauss states that Alaska includes 'the original home of the Athapaskans and is the sector longest inhabited by Athapaskans. This history is clearly reflected in the fact that far greater variety and divergence in Athapaskan is found within Alaska than anywhere else' (1973: 904). Because of their greater divergence from the northern languages, the Pacific coast language speakers must have migrated southwards earlier than the south-western Athapaskans. Eyak is a sister language to Athapaskan as a whole, and its location in Alaska adds support to Krauss' claim to an Alaskan homeland for the family.

Uto-Aztecan

Uto-Aztecan languages range from southern Idaho to southern Mexico and beyond (through Aztec colonization). The major break in this expanse of languages is along the Colorado River, where Yuman speakers separate Piman from several northern Uto-Aztecan languages, and in New Mexico and eastern Arizona, where Athapaskans intrude. The other separate group of Uto-Aztecans is a group of Comanches who migrated recently into the southern Plains from the northern desert region; their language is merely a dialect of Shoshoni. Since these languages are spoken in a nearly continuous stretch, a simple expansion theory might be expected here. But in fact there is considerable controversy about an original Uto-Aztecan homeland. Linguists largely favour a homeland along the Arizona–Sonora border (Goss 1968), basing their hypotheses on linguistic evidence; several archaeologists, however, favour a more northerly homeland, e.g. north of the Great Basin (as Taylor 1961). There was considerable discussion of this question at a symposium held in 1966, the results of which were published as *Utaztekan Prehistory* (Swanson 1968). Since Uto-Aztecan homeland and dispersal is intimately tied up with the origin and spread of other languages in the Southwest, this question will be dealt with further below.

Kiowa-Tanoan

Kiowa-Tanoan has four divisions, and three of them (Tanoan) are at present found within a relatively confined area along the upper Rio Grande (allied Tanoan groups were earlier found further south). The fourth, Kiowa, is located in the Plains. The culture of the Kiowa is utterly different from that of the pueblo-dwelling Tanoans, although the Kiowa language does not differ more greatly from any of the Tanoan languages than the latter do from each other. This cultural and geographical distance between Kiowa and Tanoan poses a problem, particularly since the Tanoans have apparently been in their present location for a very long time: where was the original Kiowa-Tanoan homeland, and did both or only one division move from it and adopt a different culture? The Kiowa have left no recognizable archaeological traces, but are reported to have been 'in or beyond the mountains at the extreme sources of the Yellowstone and the Missouri, in what is now western Montana' (Mooney 1898: 153) at about A.D. 1650. A reasonable argument can be made that the Kiowas moved out of the south-west via the Panhandle Aspect culture (in north-eastern New Mexico and the Texas and Oklahoma Panhandles) and into the Plains; they would then have had to move northwards and later southwards again into the central and southern Plains. Trager, however, prefers a radically different origin: 'the Kiowa-Tanoans had come down from the northern plains to what is now eastern Colorado or perhaps eastern New Mexico. Some of them – the Tanoans – went west over the mountains' (Trager 1967: 348) and thence down the Rio Grande. Such a theory could leave the Kiowas in the north-western Plains where they were first encountered. Other hypotheses that the Tanoans are the descendants of the Anasazi culture will be discussed below.

Hokan

Hokan is a large, fragmented, and highly divergent group of languages in northern and western California and from western Arizona through southern California into Baja California. Coahuiltecan, Karankawa, and Tonkawa in eastern Texas and north-eastern Mexico have been posited as further extensions of this family (as a Hokan-Coahuiltecan family), and affinities have been suggested in Central American languages. As noted, the diversity within Hokan is great, and the groups involved are small (except for Yuman). These languages are located largely on the peripheries of California, surrounding the California Penutian languages. Such an arrangement suggests that the Penutian languages in California are intrusive, and drove the various Hokan groups in all directions. Such a dispersal would account for the diversity among these languages and for their discontinuous locations. As to a homeland for Hokan-Coahuiltecan, Kroeber (1955) and other linguists favour California (although no particular part of this large state is specified); Taylor (1961), an archaeologist, would have them move from the Great Basin westward into California and 'southward through the Southwest and into Northern Mexico' (Langdon 1974: 75).

Penutian

Penutian languages are the most scattered and diversified languages in North America. It is not even certain that all languages currently classified as Penutian are indeed related, and little comparative work has been done to demonstrate their overall relationship. Granting for present purposes that they are related, they range from Zuni in New Mexico to Tsimshian in northern British Columbia. They occur in four distinct geographical areas, and are often divided into five groups. The Tsimshian and Zuni are isolated linguistically within Penutian, as well as geographically. The California Penutians occupied the central valleys of California, reaching the Pacific coast in the San Francisco Bay region. Plateau Penutian occupied the eastern flanks of the Cascades in southern Oregon, all of north-eastern Oregon, south-eastern Washington and adjacent regions of Idaho. The very diverse group of languages to the west of Plateau Penutian are lumped together as Oregon Penutian, and occupied the Willamette Valley, the lower Columbia Valley, and much of the Oregon coast. Given this diversity and the lack of comparative studies, it is difficult to suggest a homeland for Penutian, although Swadesh (1956) has suggested Oregon, and other writers have accepted this as a working hypothesis. If Hokan speakers occupied California, Oregon would be a reasonable source for the group that disrupted them. Suttles and Elmendorf (following Cressman 1960) hypothesize a Great Basin origin for the Penutians, from whence they spread into the Plateau; then the Salish began moving into the Plateau, gaining 'territory at the expense of the Penutians. Ultimately a Penutian wedge (the Chinook) was driven down the Columbia, and another fragment (the Tsimshian) was pushed northward' (Suttles and Elmendorf 1963: 49). The Zuni remain difficult to account for in such terms.

Salishan

The Salishan language family is located in mostly adjacent territory in the north-west, from eastern Montana to the Pacific coast, and from central British Columbia to the Columbia River. This large area is usually divided into two branches, Coast Salish and Interior Salish. Two languages are separated from the rest, however: Bella Coola in the north, and Tillamook in the south. Bella Coola seems to be linguistically equidistant from either Coast or Interior Salish, and is best considered a separate branch of the family; no adequate explanation of its location to the north of the rest of the family has been offered. Tillamook has also usually been considered a separate branch of Salishan, but more recent studies suggest that it belongs with the Coast Salish continuum. The Olympic Salish languages, however, are not as close to the other Coast Salish languages, and may have been diverging from that group even before Tillamook split off. The Olympic languages also show a number of lexical similarities to Interior languages, suggesting that Olympic may have been further east or north-east at an earlier period. Suttles and Elmendorf have suggested that the Salish were originally in the riverine valleys west of the Cascade Mountains, 'perhaps from the southern end of Puget Sound north to the Fraser River' (1963: 45). This would be an appropriate place for the major divisions within the language to have taken place, with one group crossing the Cascades (perhaps via the Fraser River), and another moving north (Bella Coola). Various linguistic considerations make it possible to suggest other aspects of the spread of Salishan languages, particularly in the Interior. There, a northern group occupied the Fraser and Thompson River valleys and the upper Columbia drainage. A southern group moved down the Okanogan and Columbia Rivers into central Washington and eastwards up the Spokane River valley to Lake Coeur d'Alene. Another division of this group subsequently moved around the then eastern-most Coeur d'Alenes into the Flathead valley of Montana. The Interior Salishan languages are all quite closely related, suggesting that these eastern expansions occurred only a few centuries ago.

Isolates and smaller families

A few other language families in North America occupied undivided territories, and their immediate reconstructible points of origin are usually assumed to have been within those territories. The largest of these is the Gulf stock of the south-east, comprising the Muskogean languages and Natchez, Tunica, Chitmacha and Atakapa. The greatest diversity within Gulf is around the lower Mississippi River, and that might be a reasonable point of dispersal of this group. The Yuchi are an isolate in the south-east, but may be remotely connected with Siouan. The Keresan are another pueblo group in western New Mexico, and are sometimes thought to have been the original residents of that area. In northern California is the Yuki family (Yuki and Wappo); this family remains an isolate in spite of numerous attempts to connect it with other North American languages. The Kutenai are located on the western flanks of the Rocky Mountains in British Columbia and northern Montana, but apparently were earlier on the eastern side, moving west because of other westward-moving groups. The other isolates are all on the peripheries of the continent: Timucua is southern Florida, Beothuk on Newfoundland, Tlingit in southern Alaska, Haida on the nearby Queen Charlotte Islands, Wakashan on the British Columbia coast, and Chimakuan on the Olympic Peninsula of Washington. The Wakashans occupy a fairly long stretch of territory, with the main division in the family occurring on northern Vancouver Island, leading Suttles and Elmendorf (1963: 47) to suggest that that was where they lived when the split took place.

Remoter connections

A number of deeper-level connections between language families have been suggested. Most of these are tenuous, and the classifications are changed periodically, according to the indications of new research. Eyak-Athapaskan, Tlingit, and Haida have been linked in a Na-Dene phylum, but more recently Haida has been withdrawn from that group, and a connection between the other two is by no means universally accepted. Algonquian and Gulf languages are now linked into one phylum, largely due to the work of Mary Haas; but again, the relationship (if real) is quite remote. Siouan, Caddoan, Iroquoian, and Yuchi are also classified as constituting one phylum, but little evidence has been offered to substantiate such a group (but see Chafe 1973). Uto-Aztecan and Kiowa-Tanoan have been linked at the phylum level at least since the 1930s.

If homelands of the proto-languages are anything like what has been suggested (fig. 5), connections between Gulf and Algonquian, Siouan-Caddoan-Iroquoian-Yuchi, and Uto-Aztecan-Kiowa-Tanoan seem less easy to defend; obviously, elaborate migrations would have to be proposed. In fact, suggesting relatively small homelands for

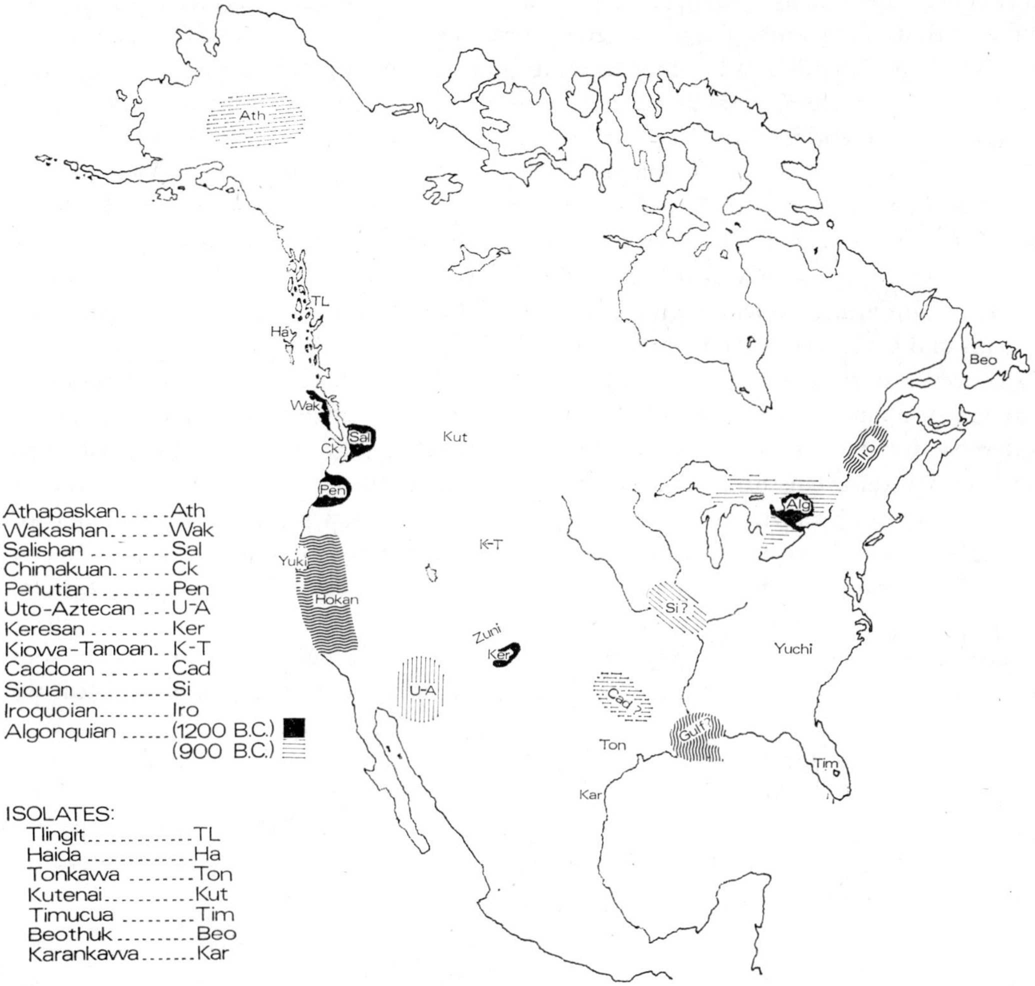

Figure 5 Hypothesized language homelands.

language families raises a number of problems. Even including the known isolates, and assigning them homelands in their present locations, much of the North American continent is left unaccounted for. However, archaeological sites show that most of the continent was indeed inhabited at various early prehistoric times. It is reasonable to assume, of course, that many other languages were spoken in North America at earlier periods, and that many of them became extinct as they were absorbed or destroyed by other groups (indeed, the present isolates may be remnants of such groups).

Archaeological-language correlations

What correlations have been made between the various hypothesized language homelands and prehistoric archaeological sites? There seem to be few attempts at such correlations specifically, although in some areas there have been suggestions based on cultural traits as to which linguistic groups occupied a given site. According to Spencer and Jennings, 'linguistic and other tribal diagnostic traits cannot be identified, but the archaeologic ancestors, so far as material traits are concerned, for a surprising number of tribes can be identified with reasonable assurance' (1965: 99). They then list several language groups and the archaeological culture with which they identify these tribes: the Pima and Papago with Hohokam; the Zuni and Keres with Mogollon; the Hopi and Taos with Anasazi; Southern Paiute and Gosiute with Desert Culture; Lipan-Apache with Dismal River; Pawnee with Lower Loup; Oto, Missouri, Iowa, and Peoria with Oneota; Wichita with Great Bend; Eskimo with Thule; and various Gulf groups and Caddo with Plaquemine/Late Mississippian.

However, in spite of Spencer and Jennings' confidence, there is a large amount of disagreement about the group that actually occupied any particular site. There is a considerable literature on relationships between existing language groups in the Southwest and the several prehistoric cultures there; a useful summary with pertinent references can be found in Swanson (1968), although the points of view presented there (by Goss, Epstein, *et al.*) are disputed by others and cannot be taken as definitive. The presence of such diverse groups in the south-west as Zuni, Keresan, Tanoan, Uto-Aztecan, Yuman, and Apachean – most of which can be shown to have been in the area for many centuries – makes such association of languages and the prehistoric cultures of particular sites extremely difficult. As an example of the different conclusions that can be reached, we note that Spencer and Jennings assign the Hopi and Taos to Anasazi, Trager postulates 'that the Anasazi cultural tradition was developed by the ancestors of the Zuni' (1967: 347), and Goss (1968) would make the Anasazi specifically the ancestors of the Hopi. The best case of association of site and language seems to be that of Hohokam with the ancestors of the Pima, since the Pima continue several significant cultural traits associated with Hohokam.

The Ozettes of Cape Alava: a type case

The remainder of this paper will be devoted to an example of the language data available to archaeologists currently involved in the excavation of a particular archaeological site in North America. The site under consideration is one of the most interesting excavations on the continent, the Ozette dig underway at Cape Alava, located 15 miles south of Cape Flattery on the Olympic coast of Washington state.

The original inhabitants of the Cape Alava area, known as the Ozettes, are extinct. Extant neighbouring tribes on the Olympic Peninsula are the Makah, a Wakashan (Nootkan) group located at Neah Bay to the north, and the Quileute, a Chimakuan tribe settled south of Cape Alava at La Push. The Clallam and Quinault, Salishan groups, are more distant neighbours and were not contiguous with the Ozettes. A common cultural pattern relates the Quileute and Makah, including secret ceremonial societies, material culture and economic practices including whaling and sealing. The Makah appear to have emphasized the halibut as a primary staple, while the Quileute exploited salmon runs as well as the halibut grounds around Tatoosh Island; but despite a few such distinctions the cultures of the Quileute and Makah were remarkably homogeneous. This culture is usually referred to as 'Nootkan', an unfortunate appellation, since it suggests the prejudice that the culture was totally of Nootkan origin and was simply adopted later by the Quileutes. Indeed, the elaboration of some cultural motifs among the Nootka and the use of various Makah loanwords in Quileute would suggest Nootkan groups as the diffusion point for certain aspects of the common Quileute and Makah culture. However, the issue is of interest to us only in suggesting the homogeneity of the cultural patterns of the two groups and what appears to be a considerable period of interaction between Quileute and Makah. It is this common Nootkan culture which is reflected in the remarkable artefacts continuing to be found at the Ozette site: basketry, ceremonial items, and tools and implements known to characterize this central area of the Northwest coast.

At the establishment of regular European contact (1850s), the Ozettes were considered a band of the Makah. Both Quileute and Makah tradition support this conclusion, although intermarriage had apparently resulted in some admixture of Quileute speakers among Ozettes. This may have been responsible for including the Cape Alava area in the Quileute cession to the United States (*BAE* Report, 1896–7: 800), a fact at odds with Makah claims. The village at Cape Alava (ˀoseˀiƛ) was considered one of the five original Makah villages (Colson 1953: 75) and was among the landmarks claimed to have belonged to them in pre-treaty days in a formal list prepared by Makah elders in 1941 (Colson 1953: 43). Some substance thus relates to the claim that the village at Cape Alava was a Makah community at the time of contact and that recent deposits at the Cape Alava site derive from a Wakashan-speaking Nootkan-culture group.

Can language data be presented which shed light on the populations responsible for the deeper, earlier strata at Cape Alava? A great deal of evidence suggests that the entire northern Olympic Peninsula was originally controlled by Chimakuan peoples. The time depth of Nootkan occupation of the north-west tip of the peninsula cannot be determined with accuracy, but an estimate based on linguistic evidence places it at approximately a millennium. The language evidence bearing importantly on the issue of Nootkan settlement relates to place-names, the mythic corpora of the Makah and Quileute, and Chimakuan comparative linguistics. Although we necessarily speak of estimates, data of several types complement each other in suggesting this figure.

Place-names

The place-names on the north-west tip of the Olympic Peninsula provide us with a crucial insight into the prehistory of the area. A number of significant features of the littoral included within traditional Makah territory have Chimakuan place names which are used by both the Quileute and Makah. We consider a place-name to be of Chimakuan origin if it can be shown to be composed of morphological components which are demonstrably Chimakuan, whether or not they are recognized as such by Quileute speakers (although in only two cases presented below are the names changed to such a degree that they are no longer recognizable). The following Chimakuan place names can be cited within Makah territory (numbers relate to fig. 6):

Place name	*Meaning*	*Current name*
1 hokʷóˀwa·	‘drifting place’	Hoko River mouth
2 hač̇á·wat	‘good beach’	Archawat Beach
3 ˀaƛá·biɬ	‘Ears point’	
4 q̓ʷi·ƛa	‘(rocks) falling off’	near Kydikkabit Point
5 kití·dit	‘different’	Duncan Rock
6 wá·ˀač	‘It’s not there’	Waatch River
7 taˀóqʷat	‘overlapping, pleated spot’	Strawberry Rock
8 c̀isciyapó·sa	‘having hats on’	Mushroom Rock

Number six must be reconstructed to be seen as acceptable Chimakuan, for Quileute has generalized a morpheme (-x) making the 3rd person non-present suffix (-xač). This place name maintains the earlier (*-ač) suffix. The last form derives from the Chinook Jargon term (ciyápos, meaning ‘hat’, from French *chapeau*). It is considered Chimakuan because it reduplicates and contains the Quileute suffix (-a) meaning ‘having, wearing’.

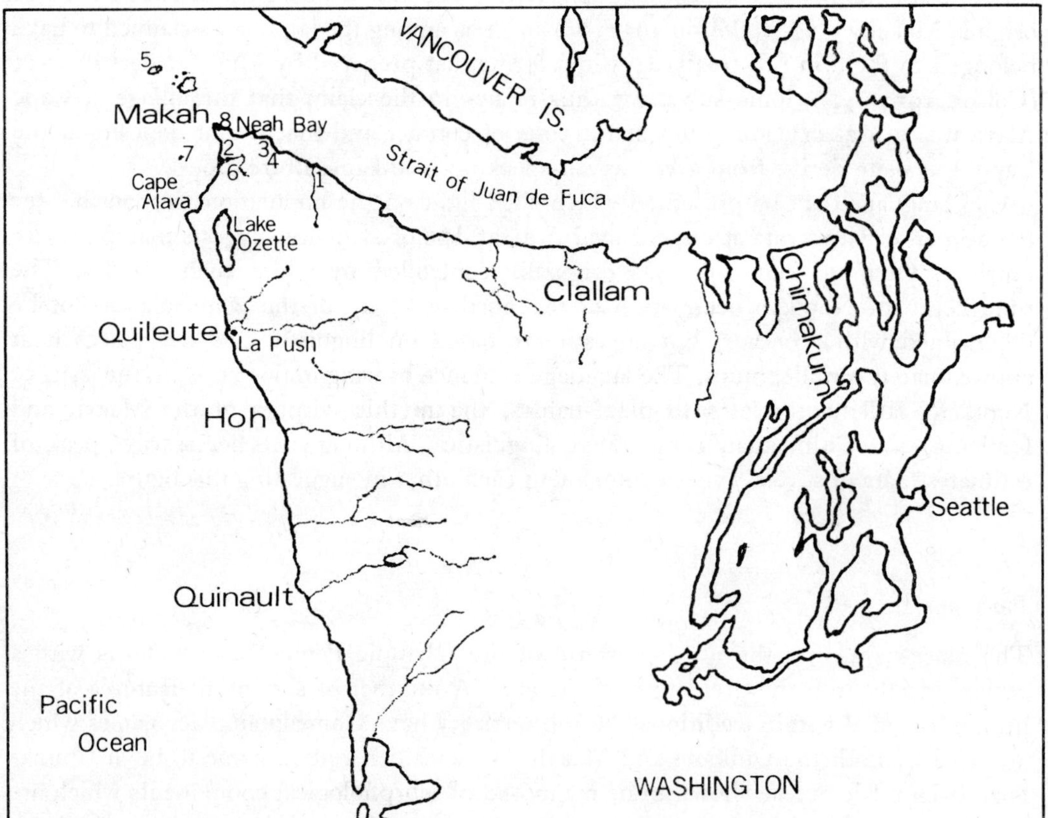

Figure 6 Olympic peninsula.

The explanation for the existence of Chimakuan place-names for such important features of the Makah landscape appears to be prior Chimakuan occupation, with their names continuing in use among the Nootkan community which displaced them. We refer to these prior inhabitants as Chimakuans, rather than specifically as ancestors of the Quileute. These original Chimakuan-speakers may have comprised part of a continuum of Chimakuan bands which were replaced by the arriving Nootkans. They may also have been the early Chimakums, who would have been displaced eastward by the Nootkans, and then later pushed further to the east (into the Port Townsend area) by the immigrating Clallams. This would also explain the separation of the Quileute and Chimakum.

Mythic and legendary corpora

A second aspect of the linguistic case for Olympic prehistory is the mythic and legendary tradition of the Makah and Quileute. Reconstructing folk movements on the basis of legend and folkloric memory is notoriously problematic beyond a time depth of a few centuries. However, it can be used to augment other data in an important and effective way if considered with care.

The Quileute creation myth suggests that the tribe was created on the Peninsula where they continue to live.

> Then ḳʷá·ti went on and reached the Quileute land. He saw two wolves. There were no people here. Then ḳ̇ʷá·ti transformed the wolves into people. Then he instructed the people saying: 'The common man shall have only one wife. Only a chief may have four or eight wives. For this reason you Quileute shall be brave, because you come from wolves.' Said ḳ́ʷá·ti, 'In every manner you shall be strong.' (Andrade 1931: 85.)

No such certainty of origin is reflected in Makah tradition. Although Swan states that the Makah believe they were 'created on the Cape' (Swan 1870: 56), Colson elicited some uncertainty and contradiction:

> These things happened before history or before the Makah themselves existed. They distinguish a historic time of events through which they believe their own ancestors lived. These too are localized within the Cape region. Some say that the Makah have always lived here, created in the region by the Transformer when he came. Others think that an ancient flood, whose traces they still find in the shells and sand dug up away from the beaches, brought them drifting down from Vancouver Island. (Colson, 1953: 47.)

This confusion as to origin is also noted in the literature in a story of how the Makah came to control Neah Bay, told by D. Irvine (1921). According to the legend, Neah Bay was first owned (i.e. claimed, not necessarily settled) by the Nitinat, along with Tatoosh Island and several camp-sites. A Makah engaged in a hair pulling contest with one of the Nitinat and was killed. This so enraged the Makah that they went to war against the Nitinat and captured the present site of Neah Bay and Tatoosh Island.

Another account of the migration of the Makahs to Neah Bay, which is told among the Clallam and Quileute, suggests that a Nitinat princess gave birth to a litter of dog-children and was forced to leave Vancouver Island. Arriving at Neah Bay, she discovered that the puppies were really normal children in dog suits. Commandeering the dog costumes, she hid them and the Makah have been people ever since. The story has numerous versions, but implies that among the neighbours of the Makah as well, they are considered newcomers to the Neah Bay area. Such mythic evidence suggests that the Makah moved to the Cape Flattery area and that this migration occurred long enough ago to have become factually dim, but has not been eroded completely from folkloric memory.

Chimakuan comparative linguistics

A comparison of Quileute with its only documented sister language, Chimakum (formerly spoken near Port Townsend, but extinct since the 1930s), reveals that the two languages had been separated long enough for phonological, grammatical, and lexical innovations to appear. Under the influence of the Clallam (who apparently arrived on the Peninsula in late prehistoric times), Chimakum developed phonologically as follows:

*k	>	č	<	*y	*č	>	c	<	*c
*k̓	>	č̓			*č̓	>	c̓	<	*c̓
*x	>	š			*š	>	s	<	*s
*w	>	k^w	<	*k^w					

Quileute and Makah influenced each other, changing nasals to voiced stops:

*m	>	b
*n	>	d

This change apparently developed first in Quileute (some uncertainty as to the actual origin of this sound change on the Coast exists), and was adopted by Makah, and to some extent by Nitinat. Makah, on the other hand, has influenced Quileute. Makah loanwords into Quileute containing /ƛ/ have resulted in [ƛ] arising as a new phonemic unit in Quileute.

A reconstruction of the Proto-Chimakuan grammatical morphology indicates innovations on the part of both Quileute and Chimakum. Unfortunately, the extant Chimakum lexicon is insufficient to determine exactly how much lexical innovation had occurred in the two tongues. It is possible, however, to conclude that the languages remained mutually intelligible to some extent, a conclusion upheld by Quileute elders who recall speaking to Chimakums. Thus, comparative linguistics, while providing us no specifiable timetable of divergence for Quileute and Chimakum, allows us to decide that the two languages could have separated approximately one to two millennia ago, but little more than that. A time depth greater than that would make such mutual intelligibility highly improbable. Furthermore, it is altogether possible that the Chimakuans split long before the arrival of the Nootkans, with Quileute and Chimakum representing the ends of a continuum of Chimakuan communities or neighbours who were forced further apart when the newcomers settled between them.

Thus, three types of language data allow us to conclude that Chimakuan peoples originally controlled the northern end of the Olympic Peninsula, including the area around Cape Alava. Additional evidence deriving from Wakashan historical linguistics might further confirm the recent split of Makah from Nitinat, but these data are not available. No exact chronology of settlement can be provided; nonetheless the evidence suggests that settlement of the area by the Makah could easily have happened approximately 1,000 years ago. Admitting the necessarily tentative nature of the date, the conclusion seems quite defensible that habitation in the Cape Alava area previous to the commencement of the second millennium A.D. could represent Chimakuan-speaking communities.

30.vi.1975 *University of British Columbia*

References

Andrade, M. J. 1931. Quileute texts. *Columbia University Contributions to Anthropology*. 12.

Bureau of American Ethnology Annual Report, 1896–97 (ed. J. W. Powell). Washington.

Chafe, W. L. 1973. Siouan, Iroquoian and Caddoan. *Current Trends in Linguistics, 10: Linguistics in North America*, pp. 1164–1209 (ed. T. A. Sebeok). The Hague.

Colson, E. 1953. *The Makah Indians*. Minneapolis.

Crawford, J. M. 1975. Southeastern Indian languages. *Studies in Southeastern Indian Languages*, pp. 1–120 (ed. J. M. Crawford). Athens, Georgia.

Cressman, L. S. 1960. Cultural sequences at The Dalles, Oregon. *Transactions of the American Philosophical Society*, 50. 10:1–108.

Goss, J. A. 1968. Culture-historical inference from Utaztekan linguistic evidence. Utaztekan Prehistory, pp. 1–42 (ed. E. H. Swanson). *Occasional Papers of the Idaho State University Museum, 22.*

Hoijer, H. 1960. Athapaskan languages of the Pacific coast. *Culture in History*, pp. 960–76 (ed. S. Diamond). New York.

Irvine, D. 1921. How the Makah obtained possession of Cape Flattery. *Indian Notes and Monographs*. 6:5–11.

Krauss, M. E. 1973. Na-Dene. *Current Trends in Linguists*, 10: *Linguistics in North America*, pp. 903–78 (ed. T. A. Seboek). The Hague.

Kroeber, A. L. 1955. Linguistic time depth results so far and their meaning. *International Journal of American Linguistics*. 21:91–104.

Langdon, M. 1974. *Comparative Hokan-Coahuiltecan Studies*. The Hague.

Michels, J. W. 1972. Dating methods. *Annual Review of Anthropology*, I:113–26 (ed. B. J. Siegel). Palo Alto.

Mooney, J. 1898. Calendar history of the Kiowa Indians. *Bureau of American Ethnology Annual Report*, 17:129–445.

Powell, J. W. 1891. Indian linguistic families north of Mexico. *Bureau of American Ethnology Annual Report*. 7:1–142.

Sapir, E. 1936. Internal linguistic evidence suggestive of the northern origin of the Navaho. *American Anthropologist*. 38:224–35.

Siebert, F. T., Jr. 1967. The original home of the Proto-Algonquian people. (Contributions to Anthropology: Linguistics I – Algonquian.) *National Museum of Canada Bulletin*, 214, *Anthropological Series*. 78:13–47.

Spencer, R. F. and Jennings, J. D., *et al.* 1965. *The Native Americans*. New York.

Suttles, W. and Elmendorf, W. W. 1963. Linguistic evidence for Salish prehistory. *Symposium on Language and Culture: Proceedings of the 1962 Annual Spring Meeting of the American Ethnological Society*, pp. 41–52 (ed. V. E. Garfield). Seattle.

Swadesh, M. 1956. Problems of long-range comparison in Penutian. *Language*. 32:17–41.

Swan, J. G. 1870. The Indians of Cape Flattery. *Smithsonian Institution Contributions to Knowledge*. 16.220:1–108.

Swanson, E. H., Jr. (ed.) 1968. *Utaztekan Prehistory. Occasional Papers of the Idaho State University Museum*, 22.

Taylor, W. W. 1961. Archaeology and language in western North America. *American Antiquity*. 27:71–81.

Teeter, C. V. 1973. Algonquian. *Current Trends in Linguistics, 10: Linguistics in North America*, pp. 1143–63 (ed. T. A. Sebeok). The Hague.

Trager, G. L. 1967. The Tanoan settlement of the Rio Grande area: a possible chronology. *Studies in Southwestern Ethnolinguistics*, pp. 335–50 (eds D. H. Hymes and W. E. Bittle). The Hague.

Voegelin, C. F. 1941. Internal relationships of Siouan languages. *American Anthropologist*. 43:246–9.

Abstract

Kinkade, M. Dale and Powell, J. V.

Language and the prehistory of North America

This paper addresses some of the problems involved in correlating a language spoken in the past with a particular archaeological site or geographical location, within the context of North America. It discusses both the values and limitations of linguistic data in attempting to assign a language to a particular location in prehistoric times or arrive at archaeological site/language correlations. Speculations regarding the area in which the ancestral forms of specific languages or language families were spoken, and procedures available to linguists and archaeologists in determining earlier residence of a linguistic group, are presented and discussed. The presentation and analysis of evidence bearing on the language group inhabiting a specific North American archaeological site, the Cape Alava or Ozette site in the state of Washington, concludes the paper.

Archaeological and linguistic correlations in Mayaland and associated areas of Meso-America

Terrence Kaufman

Methodological introduction

The purpose of this article is to describe some of the ways in which historical-comparative linguistic, archaeological, and ethnohistorical studies may be integrated to provide a fuller reconstruction of the culture history of a particular area than each could independently. Implicit in all studies of this nature is a knowledge of the ecology – historical if possible – of the region. The area focused on here is that of Mayan speech in southern Meso-America, with some reference to other parts of Meso-America which have had contacts with the Mayan area. It will be assumed that the reader can familiarize himself with the main cultural and ecological features of Meso-America, and with the outline archaeological succession. For details of the classification and distributions of the non-Mayan languages mentioned here I must refer the reader to my article 'Meso-American Indian Languages' in the 15th edition of the *Encyclopaedia Britannica* (Kaufman 1974).

The historical-comparative linguist, in his comparison and reconstruction within language families, can set himself a number of fairly restricted tasks – the discovery of all the valid phonological correspondences; the establishment of the phonological system of the proto-language; the exhaustive comparison of the morphological and syntactic systems of the related languages and the reconstruction of a major part of proto-grammar therefrom; the establishment of many etymologies, and the attempt from ethnosemantic and other viewpoints to delineate the original meanings of the reconstructed lexical items. Each of these tasks (and there are others) can be tackled more or less separately (though some presuppose others) and can bring much satisfaction to the mind of the linguist involved and, occasionally, to the minds of the linguist's audience.

But there is a larger framework into which details of the kind just mentioned fit. All that we know about language change and language contact leads us to realize that when we recognize language families we necessarily postulate, usually correctly, proto-languages (perhaps at several levels) which were spoken by real people, mirroring particular cultures, in particular places, with a realistic amount of internal linguistic variation, and probably in contact with other languages. Thus, workers in the historical development of a particular genetic group of languages, it seems to me, must inevitably be led to the realization that their contribution has to be fitted into a broad historical framework involving places, objects, time, and all the kinds of inferences of which historical disciplines are capable.

A linguistic classification and reconstruction is nothing less than a theory or history of the diversification of a group of languages. It should be as elaborate as possible. A family tree, or a listing by groups, over-simplified as it is, though it can sometimes be a useful summary of results, can be no substitute for a discursive, data-filled, and minutely detailed treatment of everything that is comparable. The archaeologist's aim with his material is similar in many ways to that of the comparative linguist, and neither can ignore the work of the other when the data are there.

Archaeological framework for Meso-America

The archaeological phases of Meso-America are conventionally grouped into several periods:

1 The Archaic (8000–1500 B.C.) – in which plant domestication took place and early agriculture began;
2 A Formative or Pre-Classic period (1500–0 B.C.) – at the beginning of which ceramics, highly productive agriculture, public buildings and clearly marked regional differentiation of culture patterns all make their appearance;
3 The Proto-, Full and Post-Classic (A.D. 0–1500). Here writing, a calendar, irrigation and state systems appear, although naturally all have their roots in the previous period.

The Mayan languages and their diversification

Comparative linguistic studies show that most Meso-American languages (and families) have been in Meso-America since considerably before the beginning of the Formative Period. It would be bad strategy to expect to find it necessary to identify particular Meso-American cultures as being borne by speakers of languages currently outside Meso-America or of unknown extinct languages. Since A.D. 900 we must not assume much population displacement in Meso-America.

There are today about thirty Mayan languages, spoken in Guatemala, Chiapas, and the Yucatan peninsula, by about two million people. One Mayan language, Huastec, is spoken in north-eastern Mexico. The following chart (table 1) lists the languages by genetic grouping within the family. Specified are number of centuries of separation for the languages of groups at various levels, and kind of habitat of speakers.

Although Zimmermann (1955) has claimed that the common Spanish name for the language commonly known as Chicomuceltec was Cotoque, evidence given in the same article shows that Motozintlec-Tuzantec, whose self-name is/qatoˀk'/ ('our language') was spoken in 1775 in the region of Chicomucelo. I therefore usurp the name Cotoque and apply it in the sense of Motozintlec-Tuzantec. I hope to justify this act in print at a later time.

TABLE I

The Mayan language family

Mayan Family (42 centuries)
- I Huastecan (9 centuries) – Lowland
  - a Huastec
  - b Chicomuceltec
- II Yucatecan (10 centuries) – Lowland
  - a Yucatec
  - b Lacandón
  - c Itzá
  - d Mopán

Western Mayan (30 centuries)
- III Greater Tzeltalan (19 centuries)
  - III A Cholan (14 centuries) – Lowland
    - a Chortí
    - b Chol
    - c Chontal
  - III B Tzeltalan Proper (14 centuries) – Highland
    - a Tzotzil
    - b Tzeltal
- IV Greater Kanjobalan (21 centuries)
  - IV A Chujean (16 centuries)
    - a Tojolabal – Lowland
    - b Chuj – Highland
  - IV B Kanjobalan Proper (15 centuries)
    - 1 Kanjobal complex (7 centuries) – Highland
      - a Kanjobal
      - b Acatec
      - c Jacaltec
    - 2 Cotoque complex (6 centuries)
      - a Motozintlec – Highland
      - b Tuzantec – Lowland

Eastern Mayan (34 centuries) – Highland
- V Greater Mamean (26 centuries)
  - V A Mamean Proper (15 centuries)
    - a Teco
    - b Mam
  - V B Ixilan (14 centuries)
    - a Aguacatec
    - b Ixil
- VI Greater Quichéan (26 centuries)
  - VI A Uspantec
  - VI B Quichéan Proper (10 centuries)
    - a Sipacapa
    - b Sacapultec
    - c Quiché
    - d Tzutujil
    - e Cakchiquel
  - VI C Pocom (10 centuries)
    - a Pocomam
    - b Pocomchí
  - VI D Kekchí

I will here present a sketch of the temporal and geographical diversification of the Mayan languages based on the following evidence:

1 the reconstructed order of separation of the languages;
2 the mutual influences after split of the languages, and their contacts with non-Mayan languages;
3 all the places where the languages are known to have been spoken;
4 approximate dates derived from glottochronological calculations done by the author;
5 any cultural information that can be gleaned from the as yet small and never complete vocabulary of proto-Mayan and major Mayan subgroups. (It has not been possible to include maps in this article; the map in Miles 1965: 277 can serve as a rough guide – it omits Teco, Sacapultec, Sipacapa, Kanjobal, and Acatec.)

I would like to lay out a number of preliminary working principles specific to the Mayan languages and area:

1 In general I use a 'least moves' model, unless convincing evidence points in a different direction.
2 Proto-Mayan has terms for both highland and lowland flora and fauna. In this area, lowland people are ignorant of highland products, but highland people are aware of lowland products. Therefore, the proto-Mayan homeland was in a highland area not far from the lowlands.
3 In broken highlands, river valleys would facilitate population movements. It is easier to move downstream than upstream.
4 There is one highland area in the Mayan region that is both fairly near the lowlands and near rivers flowing north, east and west. This area is *Soloma* (including Santa Eulalia, Barillas, and San Juan Ixcoy).

Proto-Mayan must have begun to break up by 2200 B.C. Our ignorance of the nature of occupation, if any, of the Soloma region before *c.* 300 B.C., must not deter us from following out subgrouping, geographical, and glottochronological data as far as it will take us. There are very few parts of the Chiapas and Guatemala highlands and Pacific Coast that are well known archaeologically. In the Soloma area are several small rivers which unite to form the Ixcán, which flows north into the Lacantún. Parallel to the Ixcán and to the east the Xacbal also flows north. A little way to the south-east of Soloma are the headwaters of the eastward-flowing Río Negro and of the northward-heading Chixoy and Salinas; the confluence of the Salinas and the Lacantún forms the Usumacinta, which heads north-west. In the same area that contains the headwaters of the Río Negro are the headwaters of two other large rivers, the Selegua and the Cuilco, which flow west and unite to form the Grijalva. Mayans do not seem to have migrated down the Cuilco and Selegua into the Grijalva, if at all, until fairly late – Late Classic – times. This suggests that the presence of non-Mayan peoples in the area may have blocked expansion in that direction.

With the exceptions of:

(a) the Cholan, Yucatecan, and Huastecan groups, and Tojolabal, which are spoken largely in hot country;

(b) the Tzeltalan group which is found in an area uninhabited by Mayans before A.D. 200;
(c) Cotoque which is spoken in an area inhabited only in the Late Classic period;
(d) Tzutujil and Cakchiquel – southern outliers of Quichéan Proper which has a time depth of about 1000 years;
(e) Pocomam – separate from more northerly Pocomchí by about 1000 years' time depth;

all the Mayan languages are spoken in a fairly compact highland zone along or near the jagged line Jacaltenango – Soloma – Huehuetenango – Aguacatán – Sacapulas – Cunén – Uspantán – San Cristóbal Verapaz – Cobán. The western end of this string of towns falls within the Cuchumatán highlands.

Summary of proto-Mayan habitat and culture

Besides having a considerable number of terms for plants and animals of cold country or highlands, proto-Mayan also has terms for exclusive hot country or lowland plants and animals – e.g. * ʔahi:n 'alligator'; *ma(:)p 'coyol'; * ʔinu:p 'ceiba'; *¢'ihn 'cassava'. In the Mayan area at least, there are exclusively lowland peoples ignorant of the highland zone; there are, however, no primarily highland peoples ignorant of the lowland zone. Since proto-Mayan vocabulary conforms to the latter specification, I suppose proto-Mayan was spoken in a highland zone bordering on the lowlands.

Proto-Mayan names for other domesticated plants do not point to any particular area or epoch within Meso-America: avocado, chile, chicozapote, anona, palm (two kinds), yellow squash (ayote), sweet potato, bean, achiote (*bixa*), greens, cotton, maguey, corn (=maize), corncob, ear of corn (mazorca), roasting ear (elote), tobacco, cigarette (originally cigar?), atole; to sow. Other plant names are: nettle, fern, wild grape, vine, willow, cork tree, oak, cypress, pine, soaproot.

Domestic animals in proto-Mayan are: dog, turkey, pet. Other animals are: jaguar, possum, rat, gopher, armadillo, cougar, squirrel, deer, weasel, coyote, agouti, skunk, fox, bird, crow, buzzard, hummingbird, owl, bat, hawk, flea, bee =honey, fly, gnat, ant, spider, louse, tick, butterfly, bumblebee, scorpion, toad, fish, turtle, worm, shake, snail.

Further examples of proto-Mayan vocabulary may be classified as follows:

Food preparation: metate, to grind, to roast.
Containers: water-gourd, trough.
Constructions and Tools: bench, cord, mat, road, house (2 words), whetstone, axe, bed.
Entertainment: drum, toy, rattle, to jump ~ dance ~ sing.
Commerce and Social organization: to pay, writing, paper, tribe, to lose, sale, lord.

It is noteworthy that there are no proto-Mayan words for *comal* or *tortilla*; both were absent in southern Meso-America at least until the Classic period. There seems to be a proto-Mayan word for *hammock* (* ʔa:b') but the word may either be diffused or else may have meant something else in proto-Mayan times.

Here follows a sketch of the diversification of the Mayan family using all the information at my disposal (but not citing all of it). It is based on standard subgrouping techniques, geographical considerations, cultural analysis of reconstructed vocabulary, and glottochronological calculations by the author. It should be emphasized that the glottochronological calculations are still tentative, this apart from the fact that such calculations, even when not tentative and when fully controlled, yield approximate (and minimal) and not absolute dates of separation. Reconstructed vocabulary is incomplete since we still lack a Mayan etymological dictionary based on full dictionaries for most, at least, of the languages.

My current view, held since 1970, of the phonological system of proto-Mayan is as follows:

consonants								*vowels*			*root shapes*
p	t	t̯	¢	č	k	q	ʔ	i		u	CVC
b′	t′	t̯′	¢′	č′	k′	q′		e		o	CV:C
			s	š		x	h		a		CVʔC
m	n				ŋ						CV:ʔC or CVʔV_iC
	l			r							CVhC
w				y							CVSV (S =s, š, x)

Stage I Proto-Mayan spoken in Soloma area of Cuchumatán highlands for at least some generations prior to 2200 B.C.

Stage II Around 2200 B.C., Huastecan separates from its homeland, migrating northwards down the Ixcán and Lacantún or Xacbal Rivers to the Usumacinta River, and eventually making its way west and then north along the Gulf coast to the Huasteca – probably before 1500 B.C. and surely before 1000 B.C. Huastecan has no known special relations with any other group in the Mayan family. Two phonological changes in Huastecan found also in other Mayan languages (*r→y and *q→k) I consider to be independently motivated. The language left in the homeland can be called Late proto-Mayan. Stage II lasted some 600 years – until *c.* 1600 B.C. No archaeological correlations, except in the Huasteca, are yet possible.

Stage III *c.* 1600 B.C., Eastern Mayan moves south and east along the Río Negro and strings out along the line Aguacatán–Chiantla–Sacapulas–Cunén–Uspantán. Over the next 200 years, Eastern Mayan develops two dialect regions, one in Aguacatán–Chiantla (later Greater Mamean) another in Sacapulas–Cunén–Upsantán (later Greater Quichéan). The language left in the homeland can be called Remnant Mayan. Two phonological (phonetic !) changes correlate with the separation of Eastern Mayan (*t̯→ć;*ŋ→h̯). Stage III continued until *c.* 1400 B.C., having a duration of some two centuries. No archaeological correlations can be proposed. Around 1600 B.C. the Mixe-Zoque languages begin to diversify, probably by spreading north, east and south-east from a homeland in the middle of the Isthmus of Tehuantepec. There may earlier have been stimulating contact in the Mixe-Zoquan homeland between Mixe-Zoque-speakers and pre-Huastecans, on the latter's northward movement.

Stage IV (A) About 1400 B.C., Eastern Mayan separates into Greater Mamean (Chiantla–Aguacatán) and Greater Quichéan (Sacapulas–Cunén–Uspantán). I offer no speculation as to the mechanism of separation, nor any archaeological correlations. (B) Sometime between 1400 and 1000 B.C., Yucatecan separates from Remnant Mayan and moves off, probably along the same route as Huastecan; instead of turning west, it goes north and east and arrives in the Yucatán peninsula perhaps as early as 1000 B.C. A possible archaeological correlation with earliest Dzibilchaltun may be proposed. The language remaining in the homeland can be called Western Mayan, but is defined by no special innovations. Stage IV continued for some 400 years – until *c.* 1000 B.C.

The following archaeological-ethnic identifications may be proposed for the neighbouring regions:

Kaminaljuyú (Arévalo): Mixe-Zoqueans or other non-Mayans
Chiapa (Cotorra): Mixeans
Soconusco (Ocós): Tapachultec
Southern Gulf Coast (San Lorenzo, La Venta pre-Complex A): Zoquean.

Some culture-words which are Eastern Mayan innovations are as follows:

anona, cornshuck, tamale, thing owned, money, rich, to buy, sweathouse, obsidian, lime (calx), star.

Comparable Greater Quichéa innovations are:

cornfield, atole, skirt, blouse, to borrow, comal, net, tumpline, arrow, coati, pig, youngest offspring, lady, to help, prayer, to dance, guilt.

Stage V At 1000 B.C., or thereabouts, Greater Tzeltalan separates from Western Mayan, moves off northwards downriver, stops somewhere past the beginning of the Usumacinta River and settles on both sides of the river. The language remaining in the homeland can be called Greater Kanjobalan. Stage V continued until *c.* 600 B.C. An archaeological correlation for Greater Tzeltalan is Mamom. Between 1400 and 600 B.C. there occur, in Huehuetenango, several phonological changes common to all Greater Mamean languages, some of which are shared with Greater Kanjobalan: (1) *š→ṣ and *č→ç̣ (shared); (2) some *¢→ç̣ (shared); (3) **ć→¢; (4) *t→č (shared); (5) *r→t; (6) **[ḥ]→x; (7) *‡‡h→ˀ. Somewhere between 1400 and 600 B.C. occurs one phonological innovation in Greater Quichéan: **ć→č.

Since Greater Kanjobalan and Greater Tzeltalan did not separate until 1000 B.C., the period of changes 2–5 should be located within the time span 1000 to 600 B.C. Change 1 is only a phonetic change until change 4 makes it contrastive; it could have been shared by Greater Tzeltalan and later reverted. Changes 6 and 7 are not shared by Greater Kanjobalan languages and have no natural ordering with respect to rules 1–5. The numerical order given for changes 1–5 is the only possible temporal sequence.

Archaeological-ethnic identifications for this period are:

Yucatán (Maní, Xtampac): Yucatecans
Kaminaljuyú (Las Charcas, Majadas): non-Mayans
Chiapa (Dili, Escalera): Mixeans
Soconusco (Conchas): Tapachultecs
South Gulf Coast (La Venta): Zoqueans

Stage VI Around 600 B.C. two sets of splits occur

(A) Greater Quichéan splits up into Uspantec, Quichéan Proper, Pocom, and Kekchí. I postulate that Uspantec stays put; that Kekchían moves into the Cobán region and the two are effectively separated from each other; and that both Quichéan Proper and Pocom move south, the former keeping some contact with Uspantec, Pocom keeping some contact with Kekchí, and Quichéan Proper and Pocom some mutual contact. I suppose that Quichéan Proper moved into the Guatemalan departments of Quiché, Chimaltenango, and possibly Totonicapán; also that Pocom moved into the departments of Sacatepéquez, Guatemala, and Baja Verapaz.

The glottochronological figures suggest an even more detailed statement:

1 *c.* 600 B.C. Kekchí separates from Greater Quichéan, going to Cobán.
2 The rest of Greater Quichéan occupies the regions already named.
3 By 200 B.C. the rest of Greater Quichéan is differentiated into Uspantec, Quichéan Proper, and Pocom (Kaminaljuyú: Miraflores).

Although the evidence is by no means clear, I would prefer to believe that Pocoms moved into Kaminaljuyú at the Majadas stage and that previously the occupants were Mixe-Zoque speakers, or speakers of some now unknown language; at this time there is a striking influence from highland Guatemala in Chiapa, and I take the influence to derive from refugees from Kaminaljuyú.

(B) Greater Mamean splits up into Ixilan and Mamean Proper. I postulate that Mamean Proper moved off to the south and west into the Guatemalan departments of Huehuetenango (Huehuetenango, Malacatán, Sipacapa, Santa Bárbara) and San Marcos (Tejutla, Tajumulco). Ixilan would have occupied Aguacatán and the present day Ixil area. Stage VI continued for 400 years, until *c.* 100 B.C.

Archaeological-ethnic identifications are proposed as follows:

Kaminaljuyu (Providencia, Miraflores): Pocom
Zacualpa, Utatlán: Quichéan
Chiapa (Francesa, Guanacaste): Mixean
Soconusco (Izapa): Tapachultec
South Gulf Coast (Tres Zapotes-Izapa style): Zoquean
Yucatán (Yaxuná): Yucatecan
Petén (Chicanel), Copán: Greater Tzeltalan

Before Stage VII, Greater Tzeltalan occupied most of the southern Mayan lowlands, including the Copan region.

Stage VII Around 100 B.C., Chujean separated from Kanjobalan Proper by moving northwards across country and occupying the Ixatán, Coatán and Nentón regions. Kanjobalan Proper expanded southward and westward into the regions of Jacaltenango, Acatán, Ixtahuacán, Cuilco, Necta, and Chimaltenango (down to the river Selegua). The last four named places I assume to constitute the zone in which Cotoque (Motozintlec and Tuzantec of the presentday) developed. This stage lasted for two centuries, until about A.D. 100.

Archaeological-ethnic identifications are:

Kaminaljuyú (Arenal, Santa Clara): Pocom
Chiapa (Horcones, Istmo): Mixean
Soconusco: Tapachultec
Southern Gulf Coast (Tres Zapotes-Izapa style): Zoquean
Yucatán (Yaxuná): Yucatecan
Petén (Holmul I, Matzanel): Greater Tzeltalan.

Stage VIII About A.D. 100, Cholan separated from Tzeltalan Proper, perhaps by crossing the Usumacinta and crowding Tzeltalan Proper westward. Within 100 or 200 years the Tzeltalans moved into the Chiapas highlands near Teopisca (Kan phase). During this stage Kaminaljuyú (Santa Clara) goes into decline and is in ruins by A.D. 300. Stage VIII continued until *c.* A.D. 400.

The following set of sound changes marks off Greater Tzeltalan from the rest of the family: some *ă→ə; some *b'→p'; some *k→č; *q→k; *ŋ→n; *r→y; *t̯→t; *CVʔC→CV:C. They can be dated within the period 1000 B.C. to A.D. 100. The following changes mark off Cholan from Greater Tzeltalan: some *e:→i(:); some *o:→u(:); *V:→V̆; *x→h. They can be dated within the period 100 to 600 A.D. Many of these changes are found in other non-Eastern Mayan languages but they can be explained by two kinds of contact situations, and the sharing of certain of these changes does not help define any subgroup in the family. Only the total set of changes defines a particular group, namely Greater Tzeltalan. They include: (a) Changes probably induced by imitating the accent of Greater Tzeltalan or Cholan speakers, who, after the sound changes listed above, would have had difficulty with several of the phonemic contrasts still preserved in highland languages (*q→k, *t̯→t, *ŋ→n, *r→y). These changes would have spread from Cholan languages to Yucatecan and to the highland languages in Huehuetenango (i.e. Greater Kanjobalan languages) after the beginning of the Proto-Classic in the lowlands, probably long after they actually occurred in Greater Tzeltalan or Cholan. These kinds of influence by Cholan do not imply any high degree of bilingualism on the part of either Cholans or Kanjobalans. (b) Simplifications brought about by contact with non-Mayan speaking peoples – the only likely cases being Huastec and Yucatec (maize pollen was found from 2000 B.C. at Lake Petenxil in the Petén), e.g. *r→y and *q→k, since /r/ and /q/ are rare in Meso-American languages. The specific range of each change of type (a) is shown in table 2.

There is a number of words found only in Cholan and randomly in languages in contact with Cholan languages, which I call Classic Maya culture words. Among them are words (usually displacing a proto-Mayan word) for: moon, debt, numeral classifier for persons, rabbit, trap, 400, 8000, star, eleven, female relative, cornfield, bean, word, atole, heart, name.

From this point, in the Early Classic, things become complex. I will merely sketch in some important linguistic facts, reserving a fuller treatment to a later study.

TABLE 2

Sound changes in Yucatecan, Greater Tzeltalan and Greater Kanjobalan

	Yucatecan	Greater Tzeltalan	Greater Kanjobalan
1	+	*ă→ə	
2	+	*b′→b′, p′	
3	(+)	*k→k, č	Chuj, Tojolabal (Kanjobal–Acatec–Jacaltec)
4	+	*q→k	Chuj, Tojalabal
5	+	*ŋ→n	Tojolabal, Kanjobal, Acatec
6	+	*r→y	all but Motozintlec–Tuzantec
7		*t̯→t	all
8		*CV ʔC→CVC	Jacaltec, Kanjobal
9		*V:→V	all but Motozintlec–Tuzantec

Change 3 must be ordered to precede change 4, and *t→č occurring in Huehuetenango must precede *t̯→t; otherwise the changes have no inherent order. However, lexical borrowings from Greater Tzeltalan in highland languages show that (a) *k→č precedes *ŋ→n in the Greater Tzeltalan languages and (b) Greater Tzeltalan *k→č precedes *t→č in Huehuetenango.

Proto–Mayan	gloss	Yucatecan	Cholan	Greater Kanjobalan	Ixil
*koŋ	'to sell'	kon	čon	cọŋ (Jacaltec, Cotoque)	
*kitam	'pig'	♮ kitam	čiəam	či:ta:m (Cotoque)	çičam
*kar	'fish'	kay	čəy	çay (Kanjobal)	çay

Jacaltec and Cotoque çoŋ is borrowed from an intermediate Greater Tzeltalan form **čoŋ.

About A.D. 400 Tojolabal separates from Chujean by moving westwards into the region of Las Margaritas in Chiapas.

About A.D. 500 (a) Cotoque separates from Kanjobal–Acatec–Jacaltec by moving westwards and southwards into Motozintla, Tuzantán, and Chicomucelo. Dialect mixture in Cotoque suggests to me that speakers of several original Cotoque dialects were mixed up together in the presentday Cotoque region, perhaps as refugees from their Huehuetenango home. (b) Teco and Mam separate. At this time, I assume, Mam begins to expand to its present or an even larger size. I expect Mams pushed Cotoque out of its present location and Teco became an isolated outpost without renewed contact. Up to this time Mayans had not moved westward into the Grijalva Valley, which is close to the postulated Mayan homeland; I suppose it was because until this time the Chiapa culture had been too strong. Chiapa was abandoned about A.D. 600.

About A.D. 600, at the end of the Early Classic, (a) Cholan breaks up into Chortí and

Chol-Chontal. The date of separation of latter two is possibly after A.D. 600. (b) Tzeltalan Proper breaks up into Tzeltal and Tzotzil. (c) Ixilan breaks up into Aguacatec and Ixil. These three events correspond to the end of the Early Classic and general disorder in Meso-America.

Cholan influence on highland languages directly to the south, which has already been mentioned, probably began in the Early Classic or even the Proto-Classic. Additional cases of Cholan influence are such items as /čakalte ʔ/ 'cedar' or /k'anti ʔ/ 'cantil (poisonous snake)' which are widespread in highland languages but can only be etymologized in Cholan (the former ='red tree', the latter ='yellow mouth').

So far we can place no linguistic events for Mayan in the Late Classic; this correlates with the condition of general peace and picking up of the pieces in Meso-America.

In the Early Post-Classic the following linguistic events occurred in Mayan:

1 About A.D. 1000: (a) common Yucatecan broke up into four languages; (b) common Pocom broke up into two languages; common Quichéan broke up into five languages. This correlates with Toltec and Pipil intrusions in the area. The fact that Yucatecan does not diversify from *c.* 1000 B.C. – when it split off from proto-Mayan – until A.D. 1000, suggests a high degree of cohesion and efficiency of communication within the Yucatecan-speaking region until the area's fragmentation on the arrival of the Toltecs. Of course, we can suppose gratuitously that languages have peeled off from Yucatecan in the past and simply not survived.
2 About A.D. 1100 Chicomuceltec migrated from north-east Mexico to south-east Chiapas, splitting off from Huastec. The glottochronological calculation is highly approximate, since a complete Chicomuceltec list is unobtainable: I do not wish to speculate on the motives for their migrating; there is no question, however, that Chicomuceltec *did* migrate from the Huastec area – it shares many phonological, lexical, and grammatical peculiarities uniquely with Huastec.

In the Late Post-Classic (a) the Kanjobal complex broke up into Kanjobal, Acatec, and Jacaltec – if these are really separate languages; (b) Cotoque broke up into Motozintlec and Tuzantec – though these may be only dialects.

A longer, but more primitive version of the above sketch appears in Kaufman 1969. Other scholars have dealt in part with the diversification, linguistic and geographic, of the Mayan family: Diebold 1960, Swadesh 1960, McQuown 1971, Manrique (oral presentation 1968), and Josserand 1974. They will not be analysed here. Only Josserand's and McQuown's are in partial agreement with the scheme outlined in this article. Although I naturally feel that I am in the end more likely to be right on more points, the variety of opinions that have been expressed shows that the whole attempt is really premature.

The kind of sketch presented here must, however, be done for other areas and the results integrated and balanced. When Mayan is reduced to a small proto-area and the rest of the Meso-American families as well, we may see that there is a lot of unoccupied space, linguistically speaking. Was it really unoccupied? The homeland of a language family's protolanguage is not necessarily within the area where the descendant languages are now spoken.

Internal diffusion, cultural and linguistic, in the Mayan region

Into the Late Pre-Classic (say until 250 B.C.) highland Guatemala was more highly developed than the lowland Mayan region; highland Guatemala even developed writing which, however, we are unable to read. Thereafter the lowland Mayan region caught up with and surpassed the highland region in complexity and wealth. There is evidence for fairly steady trade between the regions. Linguistic geography and ethnohistory make it almost inescapable that the central Mayan area was occupied by Cholan speakers. All the highland languages in regions in contact with the lowland area, and Yucatecan as well, have lexical borrowings from Cholan languages, and further, have here and there participated in sound changes of a simple merger type with Cholan, presumably by imitating the phonetic characteristics of Cholan languages. Other kinds of internal borrowing, of a more prosaic nature, have occurred. The proto-Mayan word for 'fish' was *kar, but in some areas of the Guatemala highlands the native word for 'fish' has been lost and the word has been borrowed from some other Mayan language. In Mam, where the word should be /kat*/ it is /kiy/ or /kiš/, from a pronunciation like [kəy] which is found, for example, in Jacaltec /kay/. In Kanjobalan, where it would be /kay*/ and in Ixil where it would be /kat*/, the form is /çay/, probably borrowed from Cholan where it is /čəy/ (or Chuj where it is /čay/). The highlands of Guatemala have few rivers and streams and some groups must have obtained what fish they used from other areas. Fish is not an important item of consumption in the highland Mayan region except around Lake Atitlán. To summarize: besides the usual kind of lexical borrowing between adjacent languages, in the Mayan region there is one language group which has had vastly more lexical and phonetic influence than any other – Cholan.

Some cultures and languages that have influenced Mayans

The Valley of Oaxaca

The valley of Oaxaca had an unbroken local development since at least 1350 B.C. (K. Flannery, pers. comm.), though Monte Albán was not built until *c.* 600 B.C. During the late Post-Classic there was a Mixtec overlay which has since virtually disappeared. We assume that the speech of this area was common Zapotec until *c.* 400 B.C. when Chatino broke off to the south-west, and thereafter Zapotec which shows 1,400 years of internal divergence. During the Late Pre-Classic there was Monte Albán influence on or contact with lowland Mayans and also influence on central Veracruz. This may have been the time when Yucatecan borrowed some lexical items (e.g. /pè:k'/ 'dog') and calendrical terms (e.g. ꜩ manik' 'deer' (day-name)) from Zapotec. The Huastecans may at this time have been in central Veracruz as well as further north, and thus borrowed several Zapotec words (petate, coati, deer, dog). By 100 B.C. there were as many as sixty towns outside the Valley of Oaxaca which were tributary to Monte Albán. During part of the Proto-Classic there was an intrusive aristocratic superstrate minority of rulers or priests whose influence later disappeared. During the Early Pre-Classic there was Teotihuacán contact or influence but no conquest. By Early Classic B the Mixteca began to differ culturally from the Valley of Oaxaca. During the Late

Classic there was no outside influence at all. By the end of that period Monte Albán was abandoned. During the Early Post-Classic there was Toltec influence.

Central Mexico

Through time, Central Mexico has had at least four focal areas, not all of which were culturally separate, or even in existence at any one time – the Valley of Mexico, Cholula (Puebla), Xochicalco (Morelos), and Tula (Hidalgo). Since at least the beginning of the Late Pre-Classic the cultural tradition leading to Teotihuacán civilization was unbroken – though in Late Pre-Classic B there was foreign influence from the North (Chupícurao) and the South (Cholula) which was either rejected or incorporated into the synthesis that produced Proto-Classic and Early Classic Teotihuacán. The area contains Oto-Mangue languages of the Oto-Pamean family: Matlazinca-Ocuiltec and Otomí-Mazahua. Totonacs claimed to have built Teotihuacán (Carrasco 1971: 472–3; Coe 1962: 121).

Nahuas, who were there later, are intrusive. The presence of other Oto-Pamean languages – North Pame, South Pame, and Jonaz (Chichimec) – to the north of this area make it virtually certain that some Oto–Pamean languages have always been spoken in the area in question. Teotihuacán declined and was destroyed in Late Classic A. The culture pattern was maintained in Cholula and Xochicalco in different ways. A new pattern, apparently started by the squatters on the ruins of Teotihuacán was begun at Tula (Coe 1962: 141).

Since Toltecs were undoubtedly Nahua speakers, we can be fairly confident that at least some of the destroyers of Teotihuacán spoke Nahua. The Xochicalco culture occupied more or less the region of presentday Matlatzinca and Ocuiltec, and the former were independent even of later Tenochtitlán. The area of Cholula was Nahuatized in the Late Post-Classic; in the Early Post-Classic the Cholula area had close ties with the Mixteca; even if Cholula originally had the same language as Teotihuacán, it may have been replaced by a Oaxacan Oto-Mangue language before its being in turn replaced by Nahua. Some students of the Mixtec codices believe that the traditions of the Mixteca-Puebla peoples extend back to the time of Teotihuacán's power. Likely languages for Teotihuacán are then: Matlatzinca-Ocuilteco, Otomí-Mazahua, Totonac, Tepehua, possibly even common Chochoan or Mixtec. Teotihuacán and the Huasteca had little mutual contact, and Michoacán (where Tarasco is spoken) was outside Meso-America at the time. In the Early Classic there was Teotihuacán influence on Monte Albán, central Veracruz, the Grijalva Valley, and Pacific coast Guatemala, and infiltration in the lowland Maya region and the southern Gulf coast. Several scholars have suggested that this was motivated by a desire to control the production of and trade in cacao in Meso-America. Whatever language(s) were spoken by the Teotihuacanos, they should have left some traces in the languages spoken in those areas at the time, if we can figure out what they were and if they are still spoken. I have already suggested that in the Late Pre-Classic Huastec may have been spoken in central Veracruz as well as in the Huasteca. By Tajín I times this may not have been so likely. On the other hand sure occupation of central Veracruz by Totonacs is only Late Post-Classic. Totonac and Tepehua seem to have separated by 600 B.C. or the beginning of the Late Pre-Classic. Totonac is well documented: Tepehua is not. I have identified about ten possible cases of lexical items found only in highland Guatemalan languages and Totonac. Otomí is fairly well documented, but I can find nothing in any Mayan language that looks like anything in Otomí or Mazahua. Matlatzinca is not well documented. It is also possible that Kaminaljuyú was not occupied by Mayan speakers in the Arenales phase; if so, that language is extinct – unless it was Xinca, which seems unlikely. The known vocabulary of Xinca, which is moribund, is about 2,000 morphemes and will probably not be amplified. The vocabularies of Otomí, Mazahua, Matlatzinca, Ocuiltec, Tepehua, Totonac, maybe Popoloc and Mixtec, should be searched for common words that would reflect borrowing, as should Nahua, since it has much non-Uto-Aztecan vocabulary which it must have picked up in Meso-America from the survivors of Teotihuacán culture. Nahua has some clear Mixe-Zoque borrowings: petate, cacao, metal, sandals. Is it possible that there were Mixe-Zoque speakers in central Mexico in A.D. 600? Is it possible that the Teotihuacanos spoke a Mixe-Zoque language? Is it possible that Nahuas were already in Meso-America at the time of Olmec influence on central Mexico (800–400 B.C.)? Or were the Nahuas merely on the north-western borders of Meso-America? In the latter case, which is the only one I consider possible, Nahua could have picked up Meso-American words not only from Olmecs but also from Teotihuacanos before moving into Meso-America.

The Cotzumalhuapa Culture

On the Pacific coast of Guatemala, at least by Early Classic B, appears a new cultural pattern typified from Bilbao, El Baúl, and Cotzumalhuapa. The art and its symbols has its closest connection with central Veracruz. It is not clear whether the culture is the result of immigration and settlement from central Veracruz, or conquest, or simply superimposed influence (see Ruz 1971: 215).

The distinctive style persists to the end of the Classic. There must have been local contacts with highland Guatemala and the Soconusco. Parts of this area show Teotihuacán influence (while Kaminaljuyú Esperanza shows outright take-over). If central Veracruz was Totonacan at the time, and if Cotzumalhuapa is an immigrant culture, then the presumed borrowings into highland Guatemalan languages from Totonac would lose their value as clear indications of Teotihuacán influence, even if central Veracruz and Teotihuacán spoke related languages. The Guatemala coast was later settled by Pipils during the Toltec (Early Post-Classic) period, so the language of the Cotzumalhuapa culture is gone. The non-Mixe-Zoque element in Tapachultec could be a relic of Cotzumalhuapa contact or it could be a substratum from the language of the Soconusco before the arrival of Tapachultec, which must have been near the beginning of the Pre-Classic.

Where archaeologists go astray

There has been a good deal of idle speculation by archaeologists as to the possible role of Nahua speakers in the history of Meso-America – idle because done in ignorance of certain basic linguistic facts about Nahua.

1 The only culture that we *know* was Nahua-speaking was the Aztec.
2 There are two languages in the Aztecan group, Pochutec and Nahua. Glottochronologically both Swadesh (1962) and Hale (1958–9) have independently calculated that Pochutec separated from Nahua about A.D. 500. Nahua began diversifying internally about A.D. 900. The term Nahua covers what are probably three or four languages at the present time: Western, Central and Northern, Eastern, and Pipil.
3 All loans in Meso-American languages from Uto-Aztecan are from Nahua *as we know it* historically, therefore not going back much earlier than about A.D. 900 to 1000.
4 Aztecan is most closely related to Coran, though already separate from it in times B.C.
5 Aztecan, as the only Uto-Aztecan group in Meso-America, has great numbers of words of non-Aztecan origin. These correlate with the rapid culture-change which the speakers underwent, probably beginning around A.D. 500.
6 We know that Meso-American languages which were Toltec-influenced but not Mexico-influenced had Nahua loanwords.

In the light of all these linguistic facts, we can draw the following historical conclusions:

1 The Toltecs probably spoke Nahua (point 6).
2 The Teotihuacanos can hardly have spoken Nahua (points 2, 3) – despite Coe's (1962: 115–16) speculation.
3 The Cotzumalhuapa culture, even if only Late Classic (though I expect Parsons' C14 dates placing it in Early Classic as well are correct), can also hardly have been Nahua-speaking (point 2, despite the speculation of Willey (1971: 166, 182–3) and Coe (1966: 87–90).
4 The earliest Meso-American culture that *may* have spoken Nahua is probably the Coyotlatelco culture in the valley of Mexico (Coe 1962: 141).

As for the linguistic affiliations of the Olmecs: most Meso-American languages from Oaxaca to Honduras (Nahua and Huastec too) have loans from Mixe-Zoque languages; the converse is not true. The loans refer to typical Meso-America cultural phenomena – cultigens, kinship, and symbols – which the Olmec probably had first, at least in the area mentioned. Adding the fact that the Olmec heartland is inside the territory of the Mixe-Zoque languages, the identification of Olmecs with Mixe-Zoque speakers is almost conclusive.

Here are a few typical Mixe-Zoque loans in Meso-American languages: *kakawa (cacao), *¢ima (gourd), *¢iʔwa (squash), *koya (tomato), *sək (bean), *mənE (camote), *kəh (chayote), *sapani (plantain), *kaʔwak (zapote), *pisi (manioc), *way (to grind corn for pozole), *pi¢i (nixtamal), *poʔt (to grind corn for pinole), *hə¢ (to grind), *po·mV (incense), *may (count), *ʔukA (dog), *pus (to cut), *pusan (metal), *naʔwa(y) (old man), *pata (petate), *toto (paper), *tuʔnuk (turkey), *ʔa·kaw (wasp), *kəak (sandal), *ʔoH (pulque), *¢uk (mouse), *¢a·m (good), *wa·s (fox), *nas-oʔna (fog), *ʔu·ma (deaf mute), *ʔuspi(n) (alligator), *koya (rabbit), *(hah)¢ukuʔ (ant) – and several others.

In Meso-America the actual distributions and relationships of most languages suggest that large-scale migrations have not been typical historically. The clearest cases of actual migration are:

1 Huastecan from Mayan area (*c.* 2200 B.C.).
2 Tapachultec from Isthmus of Tehuantepec (*c.* 1600 B.C.)
3 Yucatecan from farther south (before *c.* 1000 B.C.)
4 Pochutec from north-western Mexico (*c.* A.D. 500)
5 Chiapanec and Mangue from somewhere west (*c.* A.D. 700)
6 Pipil from central Mexico (*c.* A.D. 900)
7 Chicomuceltec from Huastec area (*c.* A.D. 1100)
8 Subtiaba from Guerrero (*c.* A.D. 1200)

This suggests that culture patterns and complexes probably migrate much more commonly than nations, although substantial numbers of individuals may move about as contact men. Where the archaeological record is clear as to conquest by people from a particular region, it must of course be accepted, even in the (hopefully temporary) absence of linguistic corroboration.

Concluding remarks

The statements made in this article are those of a historical-comparative linguist with an interest in the results arrived at by archaeologists. I hope that I have not been so uncritical in the handling of archaeological data as I have blamed some archaeologists of being in the handling of linguistic speculations.

Here I wish to sum up my ethnic-linguistic identifications for Meso-American archaeological horizons, at the times when they had important outside contacts. Many attributions of culture = language have been stated before by other scholars. I hope I may be forgiven for having failed to note in certain cases that the attribution has already been mentioned in print. A correct guess in the absence of linguistic data is little better than a wrong guess under the same conditions; since others are unable to test the hypothesis, it remains in limbo. I have, however, attacked attributions which are in my view impossible and which have been repeated in the literature. All the identifications I have ventured here have a linguistic basis of at least the following kinds of knowledge: how the languages are related; at what approximate time-depths; where they are spoken; if immigration is to be assumed, how it could most easily have been done. In most cases the occurrence of linguistic borrowing has made it possible to establish which languages were donors and which receivers at various periods.

The identifications I offer here without question marks or other qualifications are made with 75% or greater confidence. (The letters E and L alongside the culture names mean *expansionist* and *localized* respectively.)

Middle Pre-Classic

(E) Olmec: Zoquean (common ancestor of Sierra Popoluca, Texistepec Popoluca, and Zoque)
(L) Chiapa: Mixean (common ancestor of Sayula, Oluta, Mixe A, Mixe B)

Late Pre-Classic

(E?) Izapan: Tapachultec (and Zoquean in South Gulf coast)

(L) Kaminaljuyú Miraflores: Pocom (no more than 60% confidence; equally good alternative hypotheses could be entertained; if Kaminaljuyú is not Mayan, an absence of Teotihuacán words in highland Guatemalan languages would be explained)

(L) Monte Albán: Zapotecan

Classic (Early and Late)

(E) Teotihuacán (Early) and (L) Cholula (Late) } Matlatzincan ?; Otomían ?; Totonac ?; Tepehua ?; Mixtec ?; Chochoan?

(L) Xochicalco (Late): Matlatzincan ?; Language of Teotihuacán ?

(L) Kaminaljuyú Esperanza (Early): language of Teotihuacán as superstrate on local Mayan language.

(L/E?) Tajín: Totonac ?; Huastecan ?; Sport Mayan ? (see Kaufman 1970)

(L) Cotzumalhuapa: language of Tajín ?; Tapachultec ?; Xinca ?

(L) Petén Maya: Cholan

(L) Yucatán Maya: Yucatecan

Post-classic

(E) Toltec: Nahua

(E) Mixteca-Puebla: Mixtec; also Chochoan ?

(L) Chiapa: Zoque and Chiapanec

7.vii.1975

University of Pittsburgh

References

Carrasco, P. 1971. The people of Central Mexico and their historical traditions. *Handbook of Middle American Indians*, 10, 2.19, pp. 459–73 (ed. R. Wauchope). Austin: University of Texas Press.

Coe, M. D. 1962. *Mexico*. London: Thames and Hudson.

Coe, M. D. 1966. *The Maya*. London: Thames and Hudson.

Diebold, A. R. 1960. Determining the centers of dispersal of language groups. *International Journal of American Linguistics*. 26:1–10.

Hale, K. 1958–9. Internal diversity in Uto Aztecan. *International Journal of American Linguistics*. 24:101–7; 25:114–21.

Josserand, J. K. 1974. Archaeological and linguistic correlations for Mayan prehistory. MS.

Kaufman, T. 1969. *Some recent hypotheses on Mayan diversification*. Berkeley: Language-Behaviour Research Laboratory (Working Paper 26).

Kaufman, T. 1970. Pre-Columbian borrowing into and out of Huastec. MS.

Kaufman, T. 1974. Meso-American Indian languages. *Encyclopaedia Britannica*, 15th ed.

McQuown, N. 1971. Los orígenes y la diferenciación de los Mayas segun se infiere del estudio comparativo de las lenguas mayanas. *Desarollo Cultural de los Mayas*, 2nd ed., pp. 49–80 (eds E. Z. Vogt and A. Ruz). Mexico: Centro de Estudios Mayas.

Miles, S. W. 1965. Summary of pre-conquest ethnology of the Guatemala-Chiapas highlands and Pacific slopes. *Handbook of Middle American Indians*, 2, 1.11, pp. 276–87 (ed. R. Wauchope). Austin: University of Texas Press.

Ruz Lhuillier, A. 1971. Influencias mexicanas sobre los mayas. *Desarollo Cultural de los Mayas*, 2nd ed., pp. 203–35 (eds E. Z. Vogt and A. Ruz). Mexico: Centro de Estudios Mayas.

Swadesh, M. 1960. Interrelaciones de las lenguas mayenses. *Anales Instituto Nacional de Antropologia e Historia (Mexico)*. 11:231–67.

Swadesh, M. 1962. Nuevo ensayo de glotocronologia yutonahua. *Anales Instituto Nacional de Antropologia e Historia (Mexico)*. 15:263–302.

Willey, G. R. 1971. An archaeological frame of reference for Maya culture history. *Desarollo Cultural de los Mayas*, 2nd ed., pp. 136–86 (eds E. Z. Vogt and A. Ruz). Mexico: Centro de Estudios Mayas.

Zimmermann, G. 1955. Das Cotoque: Die Mayasprache von Chicomucelco. *Zeitschrift für Ethnologie*. 80:59–87.

Abstract

Kaufman, Terrence

Archaeological and linguistic correlations in Mayaland and associated areas of Meso-America

A sketch of the linguistic, geographic and temporal diversification of the Mayan language-family is offered, and correlations with archaeological discoveries are suggested in many cases. Linguistic contacts of Mayan with non-Mayan languages and cultures are discussed, and a number of archaeological-linguistic correlations are suggested. Reference is made to some common linguistic misconceptions often voiced by Meso-American archaeologists. Some of the more important claims (oversimplified) made here are that Classic Mayans were Cholans, Olmecs and Izapans were Mixe-Zoqueans, and that there were no Nahuas in Meso-America before the fall of Teotihuacán.

Contributors

Robert Blust received his doctorate in linguistics at the University of Hawaii in 1974, and presently holds a two-year post-doctoral fellowship at the Australian National University, Canberra. His major research interest is in the comparative study of the Austronesian languages.

Christopher Ehret was educated at the California Institute of Technology and the University of Redlands, before entering Northwestern University where he studied linguistics and history and was awarded a Ph.D. in African history in 1969. He has written two books and contributed a number of articles and reviews to a variety of journals.

Terrence Kaufman studied at the University of Chicago and at the University of California, Berkeley (Ph.D.). He has specialized in historical linguistics, language planning, pidgin and creole languages, Mayan, Meso-American, and Amerindian languages, and Romani, and has taught at the University of Pittsburgh since 1971.

M. Dale Kinkade is Professor of Linguistics and has been at the University of British Columbia since 1973. He was previously associated with Central Washington State College and the University of Kansas. His Ph.D. is from Indiana University. He has done research on several Salishan languages (Upper Chehalis, Lower Chehalis, Cowlitz, Twana and Columbian), and has worked on comparative Salishan.

J. P. Mallory received his Ph.D. in Indo-European Studies from the University of California, Los Angeles. His main interests are in East European prehistory and Indo-European cultural reconstruction. Currently he is preparing a new English edition of Otto Schrader's *Sprachvergleichung und Urgeschichte*.

D. W. Phillipson, a graduate of Cambridge University, ran the Zambia National Monuments Commission from 1964 to 1972. He is now Assistant Director of the British Institute in Eastern Africa.

J. V. Powell is Assistant Professor of Anthropology at the University of British Columbia. His Ph.D. is from the University of Hawaii. He has done research on the Quileute language and has worked on comparative Chemakuan.

John Peter Wild, M.A., Ph.D., F.S.A., is a lecturer in Archaeology and Ancient History at the University of Manchester, and is a former Classical scholar. His main research interest is in ancient textiles.

Notes to contributors

Manuscripts should not normally exceed 5,000 words in length. They should be typed on good quality A4 paper (i.e. approx. $11\frac{3}{4}$ in. × $8\frac{1}{4}$ in., or 30 cm. × 21 cm.), using double pacing throughout. Two copies of the manuscript should be submitted, the author retaining another. Unsolicited contributions and related correspondence should be addressed to the Executive Editor – Professor Barry Cunliffe, Institute of Archaeology, Oxford.

Referencing should follow the modern scientific convention. Footnotes, wherever possible, should be avoided. Bibliographic references, to be included in the text, should list the author's last name, date of publication, and number of page, e.g. (Clark 1952: 211). Where an author's name has been cited already in the text, references need only be made to the date of publication and page, e.g. (1952: 211). Extended references should be listed alphabetically at the end of the paper, e.g.

Bouard, M. de 1965. La mesure de la résistivité électrique des sols en archéologie. *Annales de Normandie*. 15:461–77.
Clark, J. G. D. 1952. *Prehistoric Europe: the economic basis*. London: Methuen.
Wace, A. J. B. 1958. Aegean prehistory: a review. *Antiquity*. 32:30–4.
Woodburn, J. 1968. An introduction to Hazda ecology. *Man the hunter*, pp. 49–55 (eds R. B. Lee and I. DeVore). Chicago: Aldine Publishing Company.

Text figures, site plans and distribution maps should be drawn on strong paper, white card, or good quality tracing film. The lettering on diagrams should be in the type face Univers (medium weight). This is obtainable on transfer sheets (e.g. 'Letraset'). They should measure approximately twice the intended final size (i.e. a published full-page illustration may not exceed 8 in. × $5\frac{15}{16}$ in., or 20·5 cm. × 15·5 cm.). Plates should be printed on glossy paper and should be mounted on thin card. Figures, maps and plates should be titled and numbered; originals should be numbered in pencil only. A list of captions to figures and plates must be provided on a separate sheet.

Each contribution should be accompanied by a brief abstract (100–150 words) summarizing its contents. A short note on individual contributors should also be supplied.

It is important that authors should submit accurate, well-prepared copy ready for the printer. Re-drawing of maps or figures cannot be undertaken by the editors, who may return sub-standard work to contributors for re-presentation in an improved form. Galley proofs of all articles will be sent to authors, who are reminded that these are intended for checking, not re-writing. Failure to return proofs by the required date may lead to the editor of the issue sending his own corrected proofs to the printer without further reference to the author.

Twenty-five free offprints and a voucher copy of the journal will be supplied to authors on publication of a paper. Additional offprints may be purchased at cost price, and should be ordered not later than on the return of corrected proofs. The free allocation must be shared between joint authors.

ISSN 0043-8243

Volume 8 No 2
October 1976

World Archaeology

This issue: Climatic change

World Archaeology

Volume 8 No. 2 October 1976

Published thrice yearly by the proprietors
Routledge & Kegan Paul Ltd
Newtown Road, Henley-on-Thames, Oxon RG9 1EN

Single copies £3 ($8.00)
Annual subscription £7·50 ($20.00)

ISSN 0043–8243

Printed in Great Britain by
The Camelot Press Ltd, Southampton

Issues of *World Archaeology* now in preparation cover the themes:

'Human biogeography' (February 1977. Editor: D.R.)
'Island archaeology' (June 1977. Editor: I.C.G.)
'Architecture and archaeology' (October 1977. Editor: M.B.)
'Landscape archaeology' (February 1978. Editor: B.W.C.)
'Field techniques' (June 1978. Editor: I.H.L.)
'Archaeology and religion' (October 1978. Editor: C.P.S.P.)

The editors welcome suggestions for contributions to any of the projected issues, and would be glad at all times to consider important new work for immediate publication, whether or not it coincides with an announced theme.

It is not current editorial policy to publish reviews as a regular feature of the journal. Review articles will cover literature in particular fields, and a list of books received will be printed from time to time.

Climatic change

Contents

page

121 Environment and empire: climatic factors in prehistoric Andean culture change
Allison C. Paulsen

133 Climate, environment and prehistory in the Sahara
Brent D. Shaw

150 Evidence from the insects of climatic variation during the Flandrian period: a preliminary note
P. J. Osborne

159 Crops and climate in prehistoric Europe
R. N. L. B. Hubbard

169 Near Eastern alloying and some textual evidence for the early use of arsenical copper
E. R. Eaton and Hugh McKerrell

192 Comparison of column and whole unit samples for recovering fish remains
Richard W. Casteel

197 The effects of climatic change on settlement in Eastern Lesotho during the Middle and Later Stone Age
P. L. Carter

207 Valleys and settlement: some new evidence
T. W. Potter

220 Palaeoclimate in urban environmental archaeology at York, England: problems and potential
P. V. Addyman, J. S. R. Hood, H. K. Kenward, A. MacGregor and D. Williams

Cover The Sehonghong river valley, a tributary of the Upper Orange in Eastern Lesotho. Excavations at the rock shelters of Sehonghong and Melikane have yielded a complex, but well-dated, sequence of artefactual and faunal evidence as well as information on climatic change.

Theme titles of past issues of *World Archaeology*

Volume 1	Number 1	Recent work and new approaches
1	2	Techniques of chronology and excavation
1	3	Analysis
2	1	Early man
2	2	Urban archaeology
2	3	Subsistence
3	1	Technological innovations
3	2	Archaeology and ethnography
3	3	Art and design
4	1	Population
4	2	Nomads
4	3	Theories and assumptions
5	1	Colonization
5	2	Trade
5	3	Stone Age studies
6	1	Political systems
6	2	Miscellany
6	3	Currency
7	1	Burial
7	2	Dating
7	3	Archaeology and history
8	1	Archaeology and linguistics

Environment and empire: climatic factors in prehistoric Andean culture change

Allison C. Paulsen

In any given year, the rainfall and temperature of a specific area are governed by a world-wide system of atmospheric circulation whose patterns are determined by the world budget of energy. Hence every local episode of climatic change great enough to leave archaeological evidence of its economic effect in the form of alteration of ground water conditions, of vegetation, and, ultimately, of fauna, indicates some modulation in the total world climatic system. Although the details of these global climatic arrangements are still poorly understood, it is already clear that they are riddled with apparent contradictions and anomalies and that the direction of simultaneous climatic changes is not uniform for all parts of the world, or even in all parts of one continent. For example, rainfall may increase in one region simultaneously with a marked decrease of rain in another area (Bryson, Baerreis and Wendland 1970).

The effects of a sudden modification of climate are particularly noticeable in an ecotone – a zone of transition between two diverse biotic communities – where an abrupt shift from one climate pattern to another is especially obvious. Such an area always responds to meteorological fluctuations with a series of relatively rapid, step-like transformations from one specific quasi-stable climate to another. Over a period of centuries, the climatic history of an ecotone consists of repeated configurations of episodes of climatic change which create a sequence of similar dynamic profiles (Baerreis and Bryson 1965: 203–5).

Since climate is a fundamental and independent variable of human existence, any major climatic shift will reverberate through the whole cultural system of the area affected in ways that are recognizable to the archaeologist as change of subsistence, population size and density, settlement location, trade, and artefact assemblage. These visible prehistoric changes in sociocultural behaviour may be taken to imply commensurate dislocations in prehistoric economy, social organization and ideology.

Each of these general statements about climate change is exemplified in the Santa Elena Peninsula in south-west coastal Ecuador, a coastal ecotone where the evidence for prehistoric interrelations between climate and culture is particularly clear. In this article I will first briefly describe socio-environmental relations in this area for the period between 500 B.C. and A.D. 1532. Next I will summarize a contemporary archaeological sequence for the south coast of Peru which is a standard of reference for the prehistory of the central Andes. Comparisons between the Ecuadorian and the Peruvian sequences reveal such detailed specific correspondences between the two areas that they must be attributed to a factor common to both parts of the Andean coast. Finally I propose a hypothesis: successive horizons of climatic deterioration were a major factor underlying the sudden rise of pan-Andean highland empires during the Middle and Late Horizons.

Climate of the Santa Elena Peninsula

The climate of any area of coastal Ecuador or Peru is determined by one of two powerful, contrasting oceanographic currents of the Pacific Ocean. The cold Peru, or Humboldt, Current that sweeps north from Chile to Ecuador, effectively lowers the offshore temperature and thereby drastically lowers precipitation on the adjacent coast which, under this influence, is exceptionally desiccated. On the other hand, the warm Equatorial Countercurrent that flows south along the Colombian coast to Ecuador has the opposite effect on the climate of the coastal areas it passes, which are tropically warm and humid. There is a significant climatic boundary on the coast at the spot where these two currents meet offshore and head westward. North of this boundary lie the tropics; south of it lies a strip of coastal desert that stretches south as far as Chile. Obviously a shift in the location of this boundary would have far-reaching consequences for the local coastal inhabitants.

In recent times this border lies just to the north of the Santa Elena Peninsula. However, there is considerable evidence to indicate that the relative position of the Peru Current is inherently unstable, and that its northern margin has made northward advances and southward retreats which have been responsible for local cycles of climatic change of varying length, regularity and magnitude.

The shortest and most regular of these cycles is the yearly alternation of wet and dry seasons which is based on moderate withdrawals and advances of the Peru Current. After the September equinox, the Peru Current and its accompanying south-west winds retreat south, in response to which the Equatorial Countercurrent and the Zone of Intertropical Convergence move south. As this Zone moves south, it becomes an Intertropical Front with greatly increased precipitation (Fig. 1), a combination of circumstances that brings rain to the Peninsula in December, January and February. This sequence is reversed at the end of the rainy season, when the border between desert and tropics, advancing north, returns to its position north of the Peninsula, which then reverts to semidesert during the rest of the year (Lanning 1968).

Since the end of the Pleistocene, or about 6500 B.C., the Peninsula has also undergone other changes of climate of longer duration than the yearly seasonal cycle (McDougle n.d.). First, under the influence of a gradual northward advance of the Peru Current from its original Pleistocene position off the north coast of Peru to its present location somewhat to the north of the Peninsula, in the Ecuadorean province of Manabi, the northern border of the Andean coastal desert has crept correspondingly far to the north. During the Pleistocene, mangroves and other tropical vegetation and fauna flourished on the north-west coast of Peru, an area which is today one of the world's driest deserts (Richardson 1973).

Second, the slow drying up of the peninsular climate has been punctuated by intervals

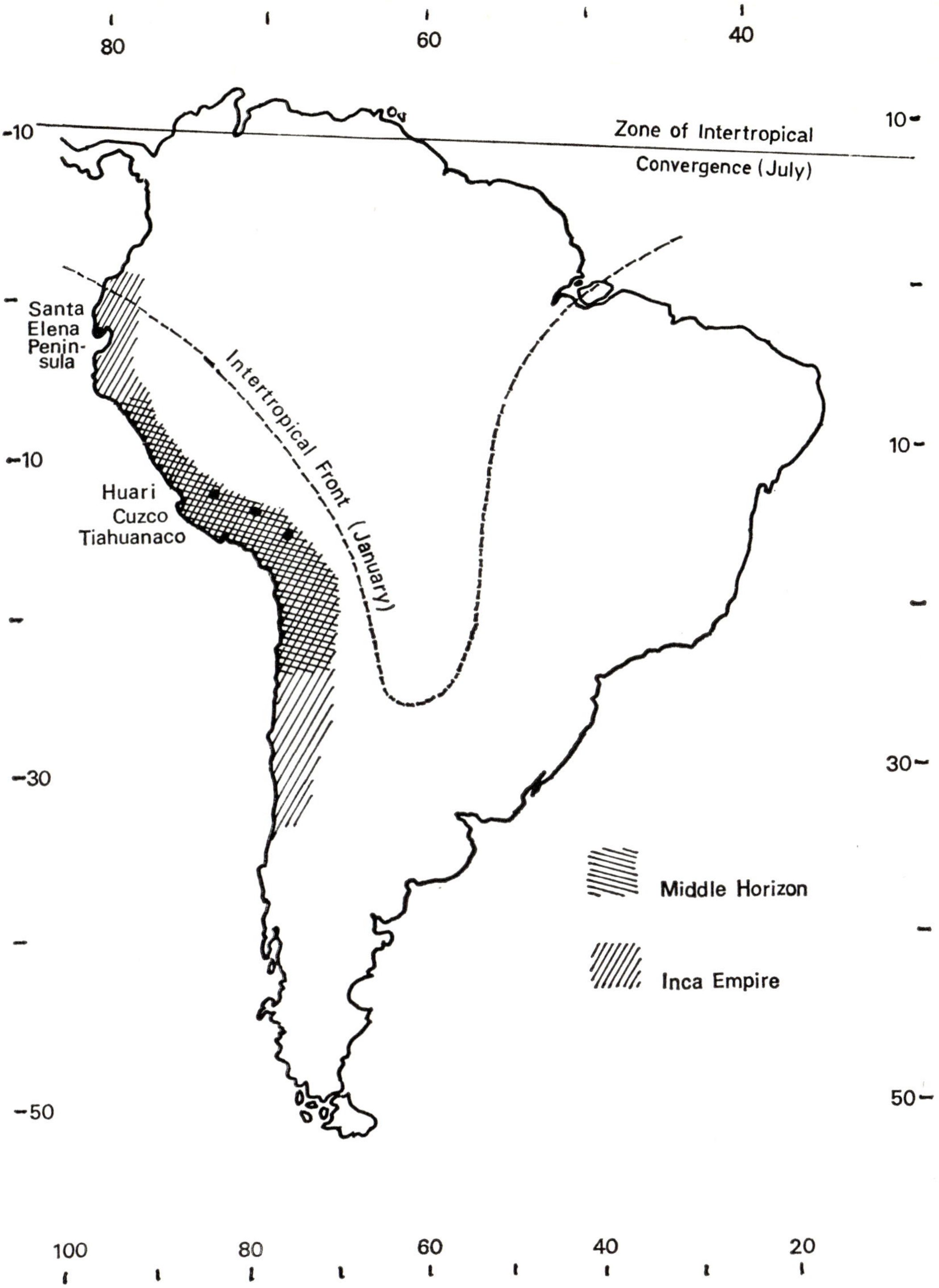

Figure 1 Map of South America: extent of Middle Horizon and Inca empires and seasonal positions of Intertropical Front

of relatively heavy and reliable rainfall according to an Andean pluvial-interpluvial pattern that is apparently determined by shifts in world temperature. These pluvial episodes on the Peninsula can be most easily understood as an exaggerated version of the yearly cycle of advances and retreats of the Peru Current. These major shifts of climate of the Santa Elena Peninsula form part of a pluvial pattern that reflects regional Andean adjustments to world-wide modifications within the global atmospheric system (Sarma n.d.).

Recent events confirm this reconstruction of the Peninsula's climatic history. In the twentieth century, the local climate became progressively drier, attaining an annual average rainfall of 50 to 80 mm. By the 1960s, the drought was so severe that all water had to be hauled by truck to La Libertad, where it was sold by the barrel. Obviously a prehistoric society could not have existed under such conditions.

Beginning about 1970 this climatic deterioration was suddenly reversed. Annual rainfall increased dramatically, with an immediate effect on the local inhabitants, although one report (Sarma 1974: 122) exaggerates this effect, perhaps for the sake of emphasis. This striking improvement of the peninsular climate during the present decade occurred simultaneously with a diminution of the Peru Current, which caused anchovies to disappear from the fishing grounds off the Peruvian coast, an event which in turn reduced the world supply of fishmeal fertilizer. At the same time severe droughts developed in sub-Saharan Africa, India and Russia, with far-reaching effects on the world's food supply. This global pattern of drastic simultaneous climatic changes (1) supports the theory that a pluvial period on the Santa Elena Peninsula is contemporary with shifts in the Peru Current and is thus probably determined by factors connected with climatic changes on the Peruvian coast; (2) suggests very strongly that sudden marked change of climate on the Andean coast signifies systemic changes in world atmospheric circulation; and (3) confirms a view that present configurations of climatic change repeat those of the past.

Climate and culture on the Santa Elena Peninsula, 500 B.C.–A.D. 1532

A detailed ceramic chronology of the Santa Elena Peninsula (Lanning 1968; Paulsen n.d.a; Paulsen and McDougle 1974) permits us to date with some exactitude the periods of climatic reversal between 500 B.C. and A.D. 1532. These climatic episodes are unusually easy to recognize, for during these twenty centuries the prehistoric inhabitants of the region alternately used and abandoned a series of walk-in wells or catch basins that were probably employed in connection with some method of intensified agriculture, possibly similar to the 'riego a brazo' described for prehistoric Oaxaca (Flannery *et al.* 1967: 450). The dates of use and abandonment of these earthworks can be determined by the age of the sherds buried in their walls during regular prehistoric cleaning and maintenance of the basins (McDougle n.d.).

Two of these basins were constructed about 500 B.C., at a time when the Engoroy population expanded enough to require the establishment of several new Engoroy settlements (Paulsen and McDougle 1974). At the end of Guangala 5, about A.D. 600, all the basins and nearly all the established Guangala sites were abandoned. The

Guangala people moved to smaller sites on the edge of the sea, where the middens of Guangala 6, 7, and 8 are relatively small and shallow, indicating commensurately short periods of occupation. This wholesale desertion of long-established settlements and water resources can only be interpreted to mean that lack of rainfall had forced a dwindling population to abandon agriculture and to rely on the sea for subsistence.

At the very time when these cultural changes were taking place, Guangala pottery styles underwent a profound stylistic devolution and simplification, suggesting a halt in the introduction and assimilation of stylistic innovations from outside the Peninsula. These changes imply that the local Guangala culture had been cut off from foreign contact, isolating local potters from access to sources of ceramic invention that had enriched Guangala pottery from its inception (Paulsen n.d.a).

One can only conclude that these changes of demography, subsistence, settlement location and artefact style were brought about primarily by climatic deterioration. The culturally impoverished Guangala people survived for two centuries longer on the Peninsula until, in A.D. 800, the area was abandoned, presumably because rainfall was now too scanty to support human existence. It was completely uninhabited for 200 years.

About A.D. 1000, the Peninsula was reoccupied by people who made Libertad pottery. The developmental profile of the Libertad occupation parallels that of Guangala in nearly every respect. The large town at La Libertad was reoccupied; the old water basins were revived and many new ones dug; and many small new Libertad sites were established between phases 1 and 4.

After Libertad 4, however, or around A.D. 1400, the basins and the sites were again abandoned. Sites of terminal Libertad phases 5 and 6 are found only on the seashore – suggestively near or actually on the sites of terminal Guangala settlements – with even thinner middens and shorter periods of occupation than those of terminal Guangala. The Libertad people deserted the Peninsula shortly after A.D. 1400. From then until the Spanish conquest in A.D. 1532, the area was practically uninhabited, a conclusion confirmed by early Spanish chroniclers who, at first contact, found the region virtually empty (McDougle n.d.).

There is thus abundant evidence to show that from 500 B.C. until A.D. 600, and again from A.D. 1000 to 1400, the peninsular climate permitted the construction and use of large water basins and the expansion of population. Conversely, two episodes of severe drought from A.D. 600 to 1000, and again from 1400 until 1532, forced first the Guangala and later the Libertad people to shift their subsistence from agriculture to the resources of the sea, and finally to leave the area entirely. It is, in fact, difficult to propose an alternative interpretation of all the evidence that includes change of subsistence, abandonment of water resources, dislocation of settlement pattern, reduced population, devolution of pottery style, and final abandonment.

In summary, the prehistory of the Santa Elena Peninsula from late Engoroy to the historic era can be divided into four major successive periods:

I 500 B.C. to A.D. 600, reasonably heavy rainfall, with expanding population and use of water basins;

II A.D. 600 to 1000, divided into two parts:

(a) 600 to 800, when drought caused fundamental displacements in Guangala culture;

(b) 800 to 1000, when the Peninsula was deserted;

III A.D. 1000 to 1400, when Libertad people reoccupied old sites and wells and built new ones;

IV A.D. 1400 to 1532, when a deteriorated climate caused a shrinking Libertad population to abandon the Peninsula (see fig. 2).

Local culture during each of these four periods was determined by the amount of rainfall which, shifting suddenly in a series of climatic fluctuations, produced rapid changes first to drought, and later back again to more hospitable pluvial conditions. Climatic change was a principal factor in the direction of cultural change on the Peninsula between 500 B.C. and the Spanish conquest. Note that the dynamic profiles of the Guangala and the Libertad occupations and abandonments reproduce each other with striking fidelity. The climate history of the region consists of two successive sets of analogous repetitions.

The prehistory of the South Coast of Peru 500 B.C.–A.D. 1532

A ceramic chronology based on the succession of pottery styles in the Ica Valley in south coastal Peru has become a standard of reference for the archaeology of the central Andes. It may be summarized as follows:

I 500 B.C. to A.D. 600, the *Early Intermediate Period*, when regional centres of coastal culture flourished in a number of Peruvian coastal valleys;

II A.D. 600 to 1000, the *Middle Horizon*, when the pottery of coastal settlements was dominated by influences centred in the highlands, a situation which reflected the rise and establishment of one, two, or more highland empires. This period is subdivided into:

(a) A.D. 600 to 800, when Huari, near Ayacucho, was the centre of a highland empire;

(b) A.D. 800, when the Huari centre collapsed, although the Middle Horizon continued until A.D. 1000.

III 1000 to 1476, the *Late Intermediate Period*, an 'interregnum' (Lanning 1967: 141) between the Middle and Late Horizons, when there were again a number of centres of regional culture on the Peruvian coast;

IV 1476 to 1532, the *Late Horizon*, when the quickly established Inca empire effectively controlled the Andes from Quito to northern Chile (Rowe 1967a: 8–9; Rowe 1967b: 25).

The Ecuadorean and Peruvian sequences correlate closely in a surprisingly specific fashion:

I The Late Engoroy-Guangala 1–5 occupation of the Santa Elena Peninsula, during a pluvial interval, coincides almost exactly with the Early Intermediate Period in coastal Peru;

II The Ecuadorian drought that followed, lasting from A.D. 600 to 1000, is coeval with the Peruvian Middle Horizon, a period of highland Andean empires.

Moreover, terminal Guangala phases 6, 7 and 8 are contemporary with the Huari empire; while the post-Huari Middle Horizon, A.D. 800 to 1000, is precisely coterminous with the period between terminal Guangala 8 and initial Libertad 1 when the Peninsula was deserted;

III The Libertad reoccupation of the Peninsula which took place between A.D. 1000 and 1400 is the chronological equivalent of the Peruvian Late Intermediate Period;

IV A drought that forced the Libertad abandonment of the Peninsula began at the time when the Inca empire arose in the Peruvian sierra.

The date of the beginning and end of each of the four major periods is practically identical in both Ecuador and Peru. This synchronism is astounding in view of the fact that each sequence was developed entirely independently.

The similarity of number and the regularity of alternation of the four segments of the two coastal sequences are also very curious and striking. Each sequence consists of four major sections in a series of regular alternations. In each area the third segment repeats the first; while the fourth repeats the second. In south-west Ecuador, the periods alternate between pluviality and drought. In Peru, the same periods alternate geographically with respect to the locus of political power and cultural vigour, which moves from coast to highlands (see fig. 2).

It is difficult to attribute the number, regularity and chronology of these parallels in Ecuador and in Peru to simple coincidence or chance. They must have been produced by a factor common to both regions. Since we can show that climatic change was the underlying cause of cultural changes on the Santa Elena Peninsula, and since we also know that the climate of the south-west coast of Ecuador and the climate of the south coast of Peru are determined by meteorological and oceanographic systems common to both areas, we may conclude that climatic change accompanied cultural change both in Ecuador and in Peru; and hence must have played an equally important role in the cultural dynamics of each part of the Andes. We may postulate, therefore, that an Andean interpluvial that began about A.D. 600 was a factor in the rise of the Huari-Tiahuanaco empires of the Middle Horizon; and that another such Andean interpluvial, beginning about A.D. 1400, was of similar importance for the establishment of the Inca empire of the Late Horizon. This proposition is elegantly parsimonious, for it uses a minimum of assumptions to subsume and explain a number of previously unrelated facts. It is also a hypothesis eminently testable by future research. In fact, there is already a substantial body of information to support this theory.

The Early Intermediate Period was a period of expanding population on the south coast of Peru (Lanning 1974: 80). The Early Intermediate Period in the Peruvian sierra is not yet as well known as that of the coast. Nevertheless, it has been stated that 'sometime between 100 B.C. and A.D. 600 there is a complete change of ceramic tradition . . . as evidence of a major population expansion along the eastern edge of the central Andean highlands' (Lathrap 1970: 173), as a result of the introduction of terrace farming during this period, and that 'it was precisely the shifts in population density caused by an increasing use of slope-farming techniques which underlay the upheavals known as Middle Horizon and the Inca Empire' (Lathrap 1969: 344).

Santa Elena Peninsula					Central & South Coastal Peru	
Date	Culture		Climate	Wells		Date
1900						1900
	Historic		Dry	Not used	Historic	
1500						1500
	None				Inca Empire	
1400						1400
	Libertad	6 5 4 3 2 1	Humid	In use	Late Intermediate Period	
1000						1000
	None		Dry	Not used	Middle Horizon	
800						800
		8 7 6				
600						600
	Guangala	5 4 3 2 1	Humid	In use	Early Intermediate Period	
100 A D B C 100						100 A D B C 100
	Engoroy	6 5 4	Humid	In use		
500						500

Figure 2 The chronological, cultural and climatic sequence of the Santa Elena Peninsula, South Coastal Ecuador, and the chronological and cultural sequence of Central and South Coastal Peru

This Malthusian speculation, that intensification of agricultural methods leads to population expansion, contrasts sharply with a contradictory but equally persuasive theory that regards the development of increasingly productive forms of intensified agriculture as a response to increased population density (Boserup 1965). In fact, an association between Peruvian highland terrace farming and highland population growth can be explained equally plausibly by suggesting that a long Andean pluvial between

500 B.C. and A.D. 600, led to population expansion in the highlands and created demographic pressures that demanded innovational measures to increase agricultural yield. Terracing would have been particularly feasible in a period of consistently heavier rainfall, for increased precipitation would have permitted the highlanders to open up to cultivation those areas previously not well enough watered to be worth exploiting. Thus, slope-farming may be seen not a reason for, but a reaction to, an expansion of the highland population during the Early Intermediate Period. While favourable climatic conditions remained unchanged in the Sierra, the pressures of population and the increasing use of terrace farming would have spiralled in multiple reinforcement of mutual systemic adaptations.

Although the relation of agricultural techniques to sociocultural change is beyond the scope of this article, I must note that there is some reason to believe that innovational methods of intensive cultivation appear to have been practised, and may have been first introduced in the Andes during pluvial periods. A series of ridged fields used in connection with annual, or seasonal, flooding is associated with the Milagro occupation of the Ecuadorean Guayas Basin, which was contemporary with the Libertad occupation of the Santa Elena Peninsula and thus dates from the pluvial between A.D. 1000 and 1400 (Paulsen n.d.a). In this connection, note that this system of ridged fields was no longer in use at the time of the arrival of the Spanish in A.D. 1532 (Parsons 1969: 79). Thus neither the walk-in water basins on the Santa Elena Peninsula nor the ridged fields in the neighbouring Guayas Basin were in operation for some time before A.D. 1532, a period when, according to our hypothesis, an Andean interpluvial drought existed, and supporting our theory that ridged fields may be associated primarily with heavy rainfall.

There is also evidence indicating that the Middle Horizon was a time of climatic deterioration on the south and central coast of Peru. After about A.D. 500, the total land under cultivation on the South Peruvian coast began to diminish, and many crops grown then were of varieties well adapted to dry conditions (Patterson 1973: 100). Again, the fog vegetation that had largely disappeared on the central coast made a partial return during the Middle Horizon, in response to increased fog precipitation resulting from a higher evaporation rate brought about by the higher temperatures of an interpluvial regimen. There are also Middle Horizon sites in the fog meadows themselves: radiocarbon dates pinpoint the time of this re-establishment of the lomas (Edward P. Lanning, pers. comm.). What is more, Middle Horizon sites are so infrequent on the central coast as to suggest that coastal population was significantly reduced (Edward P. Lanning, pers. comm.).

If the Middle Horizon was a time of coastal decline, however, it began with a period of intense political activity and expansion in the highlands when, we learn, many peoples of the Sierra lived in highly fortified cities (Isbell 1968: 110). Under the pressures of a deteriorating climate, the size of the expanded highland population fostered aggravated conditions of endemic warfare that helped set up a volatile, intrinsically unstable series of political interactions that were the forerunners of an explosion of empire building.

The Middle Horizon interpluvial drought provided the extra subsistence pressures that triggered a series of military conquests which in a comparatively short time extended the Huari empire from Chicama to south Peru. About A.D. 800, the Huari centre collapsed, perhaps because the economic surplus necessary to underwrite the apparatus of empire could not be maintained in the face of a worsening Andean climate. Note that the Guangala people also abandoned the Santa Elena Peninsula in A.D. 800. The two events may have occurred simultaneously at two widely separated parts of the Andes as the independent results of increased environmental pressure generated by Andean climatic change.

During the Late Intermediate Period in Peru – the time of the Libertad reoccupation of the Santa Elena Peninsula – an ameliorated coastal climate fostered the revival of coastal centres. This pluvial interval came to an end about A.D. 1400, a time when the Incas were beginning the series of highland military successes that established the Inca empire from Quito to Chile in a matter of decades.

This last prehistoric Peruvian empire bore so many specific linguistic and other cultural resemblances to the earlier Huari hegemony, that it has been suggested that many of the Inca patterns, including language (Torero 1964) and specific religious and cosmological symbols, represented 'points of view rooted in the Huari empire [which] . . . helped make it possible for the Incas to create another highly centralized empire in their time' (Menzel 1968: 94). If the Huari empire was established when an expanded population was subjected to environmental pressure, we may reasonably suppose that similar pressures helped evoke the Inca state. In fact, Inca rule may be considered a continuation of the earlier Huari empire, brought into being by similar situations, including a shift from pluviality to desiccation.

Extrapolating from this hypothesis, it is interesting to contemplate the possibility that Chavin – an early (possibly the earliest) New World state (Paulsen 1974, n.d.b), and certainly the first pan-Andean centre of highland influence – also took the final quantum leap towards civilization during an Andean interpluvial. The Chavin phenomenon emerged sometime between 1700 and 1100 B.C., an interval when the Santa Elena Peninsula was occupied by people making Machalilla pottery (Paulsen and McDougle 1974). We do not yet have very complete or well defined information about Machalilla, but there is some evidence that the Machalilla occupation of south coastal Ecuador took place in an Andean interpluvial drought (Zevallos 1970; McDougle n.d). There are also multiple lines of cultural continuity linking Chavin through Huari to the Inca empire (Patterson 1971: 45–6; Paulsen 1974). When Chavin's environmental and economic antecedents are more clearly delineated, it will not be surprising to discover that there were also climatic factors in the Chavin emergence.

Acknowledgements

This article is a revised version of a paper originally presented at the 36th Annual Meeting of the Society for American Archaeology, in Norman, Oklahoma, 7 May 1971.

30.xii.1975

361 Forest Avenue
Rye, New York 10580

References

Baerreis, David A. and Bryson, Reid A. 1965. Climatic episodes and the dating of the Mississippian cultures. *The Wisconsin Archaeologist.* New Series, December 1965: 203–20.

Boserup, Ester 1965. *The Conditions of Agricultural Growth.* Chicago: Aldine.

Bryson, Reid A., Baerreis, David A. and Wendland, Wayne M. 1970. The character of Late-Glacial and Post-Glacial climatic changes. In *Pleistocene and Recent Environments of the Central Great Plains.* Department of Geology, University of Kansas, Special Publication 3: 53–74. The University Press of Kansas.

Flannery, Kent V., Kirkby, Anne V. T., Kirkby, Michael J. and Williams, Aubrey W. Jr. 1967. Farming systems and political growth in ancient Oaxaca. *Science.* 158:445–54.

Isbell, William H. 1968. New discoveries in the Montana of southeastern Peru. *Archaeology,* vol. 21, no. 2, pp. 108–14. Brattleboro, Vermont.

Lanning, Edward P. 1967. *Peru Before the Incas.* Englewood Cliffs, New Jersey: Prentice-Hall.

Lanning, Edward P. 1968. *Informe Preliminar a la Casa de la Cultura Ecuadoriana, Nucleo de Guayas.* Mimeographed.

Lanning, Edward P. 1974. Western South America. In *Prehispanic America,* ed. Shirley Gorenstein: 65–86. New York: St. Martin's Press.

Lathrap, Donald W. 1969. Review of 'Peru Before the Incas', *American Antiquity.* 34 (3):341–5.

Lathrap, Donald W., 1970. *The Upper Amazon.* New York: Praeger.

McDougle, Eugene J. n.d. *Water Use and Settlements in the Changing Environments of the Southern Ecuadorian Coast.* Masters Essay, Columbia University, New York.

Menzel, Dorothy 1968. New data on the Huari Empire in Middle Horizon Epoch 2A. *Ñawpa Pacha.* 6:47–114.

Parsons, James J. 1969. Ridged fields in the Rio Guayas Valley, Ecuador. *American Antiquity.* 34:76–80.

Patterson, Thomas C. 1971. Chavin: An interpretation of its spread and influence. In *Dumbarton Oaks Conference on Chavin,* ed. by Elizabeth P. Benson: 29–48. Washington, D. C.: Dumbarton Oaks Research Library.

Patterson, Thomas C. 1973. *America's Past: A New World Archaeology.* Glenview, Illinois: Scott, Foresman.

Paulsen, Allison C. 1974. The thorny oyster and the voice of God: *Spondylus* and *Strombus* in Andean prehistory. *American Antiquity.* 39 (4):597–607.

Paulsen, Allison C. n.d.a. *A Chronology of Guangala and Libertad Ceramics of the Santa Elena Peninsula in South Coastal Ecuador.* Doctoral dissertation, Columbia University, New York.

Paulsen, Allison C. n.d.b. *Patterns of Prehistoric Maritime Trade Between Southwest Coastal Ecuador and Mesoamerica, 1400 BC–AD 600.* Paper read at conference, 'The Cult of the Sea', Dumbarton Oaks, Washington, D.C., 26–27 October 1974 (in press).

Paulsen, Allison C. and McDougle, Eugene J. 1974. *The Machalilla and Engoroy Occupations of the Santa Elena Peninsula in South Coastal Ecuador.* Paper read at 39th annual meeting, Society for American Archaeology, Washington, D.C., May 1974.

Richardson, James B., III 1973. The Preceramic Sequence and the Pleistocene and Post-Pleistocene climate of Northwest Peru. In *Variations in Anthropology:* essays in honor of John C. McGregor, eds. Donald W. Lathrap and Jody Douglas: 199–211.

Rowe, John H. 1967a. Stages and periods in archaeological interpretation. In *Peruvian Archaeology: selected readings*, eds. John H. Rowe and Dorothy Menzel: 1–15 Peek Publications, 164 East Dana Street, Mountain View, California.

Rowe, John H. 1967b. An interpretation of radiocarbon measurements on archaeological samples from Peru. In *Peruvian Archaeology: selected readings*, eds John H. Rowe and Dorothy Menzel: 16–30 Peek Publications, 164 East Dana Street, Mountain View, California.

Sarma, A. V. N. 1974. Holocene paleoecology of south coastal Ecuador. *Proceedings of the American Philosophical Society*, 118(1):93–134.

Sarma, A. V. N. n.d. *The Cultural Implications of the Upper Pleistocene and Holocene Ecology of the Santa Elena Peninsula.* Doctoral dissertation, Columbia University, New York.

Torero, A. 1964. Los Dialectos Quechuas. *Anales Cientificos de la Universidad Agraria* (Lima, Peru). 2:446–78.

Zevallos Menendez, Carlos 1970. *La Agricultura en el Formativo Temprano del Ecuador* (*Cultura Valdivia*). Guayaquil: Casa de la Cultura Ecuatoriana, Nucleo de Guayas.

Abstract

Paulsen, Allison C.

Environment and empire: climatic factors in prehistoric Andean culture change

Since the end of the Pleistocene, the Santa Elena Peninsula in south-west coastal Ecuador has undergone a series of climatic fluctuations that are the local manifestation of an Andean pattern of climatic change. The local archaeological record shows that in A.D. 600, and again in A.D. 1400, this region was struck by drought of such severity that the area was abandoned by its inhabitants. A number of specific details of this Ecuadorean sequence of marked climatic and sociocultural vicissitudes correlate with a contemporary archaeological sequence from the south coast of Peru. A hypothesis is proposed: climatic changes were factors underlying the rise and establishment of two prehistoric pan-Andean highland states, the Huari-Tiahuanaco empire about A.D. 600, and the later Inca empire about A.D. 1400.

Climate, environment and prehistory in the Sahara

Brent D. Shaw

Pioneer explorers and *voyageurs* in the Great Desert were often deeply impressed by evidence, principally the rock art, which indicated to them that the Saharan environment had once been radically different from the utter desolation about them. The impression was so profound that the idea of a veritable garden paradise in the Sahara remained one of the most persistent myths of the nineteenth century. The metamorphosis of the desert was simply attributed to climatic change. Although subsequent scientific research considerably scaled down the concept of a once verdant Sahara, the fixation with climate and climatic change remains with us to this day. Once the supposition of a dramatic climatic fluctuation had become rooted in men's minds as the cause of the arid environment, it became difficult to place any limit on the conclusions drawn *ex hypothesi*, and then applied to other problems such as the environmental conditions at the time of the Saharan Neolithic. The imprecise character of the data encouraged all manner of subjective interpretations. However, within the last decade or so, more sophisticated techniques of measurement have enabled prehistorians to assess more accurately than ever before both the scale and chronology of the desiccation of the Sahara.

The millennia immediately following the close of the last African Pluvial (*c.* 9000 B.C.) were an especially important epoch in Saharan prehistory, since this period witnessed the shift from an economy based on hunting and gathering to a Neolithic way of life based on the exploitation of large herds of domestic cattle, sheep and goats. In evaluating the principal factors involved in this economic evolution, scholars have continued to be mesmerized by the hypothetical effects wrought by possible climatic changes. An evaluation of the degree of *environmental* deterioration from the optimum conditions of the last Pluvial is, of course, all important to an understanding of the physical milieu in which the Saharan Neolithic flourished. But, to what extent *were* climatic conditions of the Neolithic significantly different from those of the period immediately preceding it – or indeed, from those of the present day? Did climatic change create a sudden resurgence of more humid conditions – a 'Neolithic Humid' phase as some have maintained (e.g. Butzer 1961: 39; 1966: 75, 79; Conrad 1969a: 275, 457–460) – or does the record reveal a different pattern in the evolution of the climate and environment? The former view seems to be based on the *a priori* assumption that a positive event such as the dawn of the Neolithic in the Sahara must have had an equally 'positive' cause – that is, optimum climatic and environmental conditions. But does the one development entail the other, or is this a simple *non sequitur*; is the assumption even logically necessary? From what sort of data are conclusions about palaeo-climatic regimes in the Sahara deduced, and are such inferences valid? always Would it not be preferable to concentrate on the immediately ascertainable environmental variables rather than attempting to grapple with the much more problematic climatic hypotheses?

The following survey attempts to elucidate the types of data employed to decide such questions; it cannot, however, claim to be comprehensive in a field where new research, discovery, and publication are adding almost daily to our fund of knowledge. The data selected to illustrate the climatic or environmental changes are representative only of the more important and well-documented prehistoric sites, bearing in mind the principal interest in the development of Neolithic pastoralism in the Sahara.

Geological studies

The major climatic fluctuations have left indelible traces on the geomorphology of the Great Desert. During the periods when the European and North American landscapes were being reshaped by the advance of glacial masses, North Africa and the Sahara were passing through a succession of damp 'pluvial' and dry 'inter-pluvial' phases. Our concern, however, is not with the geological evidence relating to the last Pluvial, but rather is with the sedimentation, deposition and erosion reflecting environmental change since the end of that period. Specifically, we shall concentrate on evidence which has been adduced to support the case for a significantly more humid period coterminous with the development of the Neolithic economy in the Sahara. The principal weaknesses of the data assembled by the geologists, however, are apparent at once. Although C^{14} techniques have enabled a much more accurate dating of the geological formations claimed as characteristic of more humid conditions, it is still very difficult to connect them to a specific set of climatic variables. Equally daunting is any attempt to establish whether or not the humid conditions reflected in the geological record signalled any real change in the life-support potential of a given region. An examination of the evidence from the Saoura region of the north-western Sahara, for example, would suggest that these data may be *geologically* significant, but of rather limited interest to prehistorians.

Geological evidence for 'more humid' phases in the Sahara since the last Pluvial is supposedly reflected in the geological morphology of wadis Saoura and Guir, on the north-western periphery of the desert. Several terraces along these wadi valleys suggest successive oscillations of 'humidity' and 'aridity' in the hydrology of the region of Beni-Abbès and Erg Shesh. Since the earlier deposits are of Pluvial times, only the most recent terrace system, the Guirian, need concern us here. These terraces, composed of several layers of black paleosols, are capped by a travertine formation, the late date of which is confirmed by the frequent discoveries of Neolithic tools within it (Beucher 1963: 2205–6; Chavaillon 1964: 245–72; Conrad 1969a: 275–7). The wadi sediments are contemporaneous with a number of similar lacustrine beds in this region and along the western periphery of the Grand Erg Occidental (Conrad 1969a: 278 ff.). Both types of alluvial fills indicate a run-off from the Ksūr highlands which was continuous enough to produce shallow lakes and marshes in lowlying depressions near the wadis. Radiocarbon dates reveal that the main period of wadi aggradation and sedimentation extended over several millennia from *c*. 7000 to 3500 B.C. (N.B. Most of the C^{14} dates reported in this article are rather early determinations, and therefore only the most recent – e.g. Pachur 1975; Geyh and Jäkel 1974 – have been adjusted according to standard calibration tables.) Dates from Neolithic sites overlying these earlier soil horizons, however, are of a later time, yielding dates from *c*. 2980 to 990 B.C. (Chavaillon 1964: 259–68; Conrad 1969a: 279–81; 1970). Similar sedimentary deposition has been found throughout the Erg Shesh region, along the western borders of the great Erg Occidental, and in the Mouydir. The lacustrine deposits in these lowland regions, often associated with marsh soils and tufa formations, indicate the same humid conditions marked by the terracing along wadis Guir and Saoura. The lacustrine strata, principally limestones and tufas, have provided a series of C^{14} dates from *c*. 8150 to 4210 B.C. (Conrad 1969a: 277 ff.).

A similar pattern of sedimentary deposition is found in the wadi valleys and enclosed basins of the rugged Atakor massif, the main peak of the Hoggar in the central Sahara. The basins contain layers of grey-white travertine horizons some tens of centimetres thick. In the wadi valleys the existence of this 'more humid' phase is marked by the same sort of alluvial terracing already discussed for the Saoura region. The difference in scale between this so-called 'humid' phase and the genuinely damp conditions of the last Pluvial can be assessed from the dimensions of the terracing systems produced during each period. The earlier Pluvial sedimentation is composed of large grain deposits some five to ten metres in thickness whereas the terracing attributed to the 'Neolithic humid' phase is only a metre in depth (Rognon 1962: 58,; 1967b). The range of C^{14} dates yielded by analysis of the carbonates in the lacustrine deposits extends from *c*. 9400 to 6400 B.C. (Delibrias and Dutil 1966: 57). It is claimed that the deposition of these calcium-laden strata was the result of erosional effects which could only have occurred under a markedly more humid climate with rainfall levels high enough to form small lakes or swamps in the lowlands about the Hoggar and with a greater seasonal water flow in the wadis (Rognon 1967a: 522 ff.; 1967b). In addition, analysis of these Neolithic paleosols from the central Hoggar suggests a climatic regime much like that of the present day sub-humid regions along the southern periphery of the Sahara (Dutil and Juste 1965).

To the record of the stratigraphy from the central and north-western Sahara may be added data concerning the fluctuation of water levels in the Lake Chad Basin and surrounding regions. The relevance of this evidence from the south-eastern periphery of the Sahara to the prehistoric environments of the northern desert might be questioned on the basis that the Sahelian frontier may have been under a different climatic system (i.e. intrusions of the Monsoon Belt from the Gulf of Guinea). Although the remarkable physical and chronological similarity between the stratigraphy of the wadis and basins of the northern Sahara and the lacustrine deposits of the southern lake basins may tell against this hypercritical view (Conrad 1963), there still remain important contradictions between the two sets of data.

Analysis of the lacustrine deposits and raised beaches shows that the Fashi, Bilma, Bodélé, and Chad depressions were filled by rather extensive lakes at least until *c*. 20,000 B.P. (Faure 1966; Faure and Servant 1970: 5–8). The very humid conditions which permitted the existence of these large lakes were related to the last Pluvial, though they seem to have been terminated within it. The onset of arid conditions was marked by the recession of the lake levels and by the formation of aeolian sand deposits along their borders. A renewed period of humid conditions began *c.* 9000–8000 B.C. This favourable environment was interrupted by another arid phase as the lake levels began to fall rapidly after *c.* 5000 B.C. until they reached the 320 m. level *c.* 3450 B.C. The dry conditions of this period are marked in the shallow zones of the lakes by a horizon of rich organic ooze and, in deeper zones, by the formation of sandy clays. The retreat of the lakes was halted by damper conditions which are reflected in the lake beds by distinct clay horizons. During the period, which lasted until *c.* 1260 B.C., the lakes maintained their water volume at the 260 m. level (Servant, Servant and Delibrias 1969; Dupont 1970; Servant 1970). This phase was succeeded by yet another retreat of the lake levels. The termination of this more arid period is fixed to the end of the fifteenth century A.D. by a C^{14} date obtained from a sedimentary core taken near Bol in the north Lake Chad archipelago (Dupont and Delibrias 1970: 43–7).

From this time until very recently, however, the lakes appear to have experienced a period of stability when their water levels remained relatively constant. In fact, sediments containing bones of elephant and hippopotami from the now utterly desolate Bahr al-Ghazal trough were dated by C^{14} to *c.* A.D. 1800! (Servant, Servant and Delibrias 1969: 1605). This record of late desiccation accords well with the indigenous traditions reported by the Tilho Expedition (1906–9) to the effect that the Chad Basin had once been a great lake which extended as far as the plains of Bornou, and that until the end of the seventeenth century native fishermen from Lake Chad could reach Borkou, over 500 km. distant, by way of the Bahr al-Ghazal (Dupont and Delibrias 1970: 47). The geological evidence and the oral tradition are in agreement that there has been extensive desiccation since the mid-nineteenth century, and that the process has accelerated since the turn of the present century.

Other lacustrine beds characterized by diatomites have been discovered in regions between Lake Chad and the highlands to the northwest: the Aïr and the Hoggar. Such lake beds were found at Borkou (Quézel and Martinez 1958) and further to the west, in an enclosed basin, bordered on the west by the escarpment of Adrar Bous and on the east by the ring of sand dunes of the Ténéré. The range of bones (cattle, horses, antelope, hippopotami, crocodile, and two species of fish) clearly indicates a more humid environment than that of the present. At Adrar Bous there were two distinct lacustrine beds. The lower, earlier formation, a very thick diatomite stratum, appears to have been deposited during the same period as the lacustrine stability of the Chad lakes, that is, from *c.* 7500 to 5000 B.C. A range of dates within this period was obtained from lake carbonates in diatomite horizons from Agadem (Delibrias and Dutil 1966: 57; Rognon 1967a: 527). Analysis of pollen grains from the earlier calcium-laden formations at Adrar Bous revealed a distribution of half arboreal and half non-arboreal species, with juniper, cypress and pine dominating the former. The thick diatomite formation and the remains of a 'Mediterranean' type vegetation are suggestive of a permanent lake environment at Adrar Bous during this period. The upper, more recent horizon, firmly dated by C^{14} to *c.* 3200 to 3100 B.C. (Delibrias and Hugot 1962: 71) reveals a progressive desiccation along the lake borders. The sedimentary deposits are characteristic of swamp rather than lake beds, and the pollen recovered from this level reveals a shift in the vegetal cover to a more Sahelian type dominated by non-arboreal xerophytes, that is arid-zone plant species (Quézel and Martinez 1962: 319–20, cf. Rognon 1967b: 119). Samples collected by the teams of the Mission Berliet (1959–60) throughout the region of the Ténéré desert, the Bahr al-Ghazal towards Koro-Toro, and from the rock shelters at Mounts Gautier and Mosseï on the western slopes of the Tibesti, revealed the presence of these same typical lacustrine sediments dated by finds of Atero-Mousterian and Neolithic tool assemblages (Quézel and Martinez 1962: 322–7).

Recently, a very thorough survey in the Tibesti mountains produced 227 C^{14} dates which relate to late Pleistocene and Holocene geological strata and to various materials (mollusca, charcoals, bones etc.) associated with these strata. The correlation between this large body of C^{14} data and that of the geological strata has provided the most extensive range of absolute dates for the effects of climate on geomorphology yet available for the Sahara (Geyh and Jäkel 1974: 92–5). To Geyh and Jäkel, the concentration of dated strata within set chronological periods suggests a succession of humid and dry phases in the massif. Rather damp conditions existed from *c.* 8350 to 6750 B.C., after which conditions remained humid until *c.* 5150 B.C., though markedly less so than in the earlier part of the phase. These conditions reached a plateau, then tapered off to rather more arid conditions which lasted approximately a millennium before the resumption of another humid phase which extended from *c.* 4150 until 2800 B.C. A final dry interval, again about a millennium in duration, occurred before the return to marginally more humid conditions after 1350 B.C. Pachur in his survey of the northern slopes of the Tibesti, however, suggests that the arid intervals postulated by Geyh and Jäkel were not significantly different from the preceding humid phases (Pachur 1975: 38 ff.). This tends to argue for a *step-like progression* through successively drier humid phases via periods of climatic deterioration rather than for any real oscillation between arid and dry phases. Considering that the origins of the Saharan Neolithic are placed slightly before 6000 B.C., we can see that, although the Neolithic coincided with the presence of a humid phase in the Tibesti, it came precisely at the time when the more humid conditions of the earlier millennia were becoming markedly less favourable.

The general import of the stratigraphical survey for the environment in the post-Würm may be briefly summarized. In the highlands and basins of the central and north-western Sahara the end of the last Pluvial was marked by a considerable worsening of climatic conditions. The succeeding millennia were characterized by conditions which were decidedly more humid than those of the present day, especially in the mountain highlands, due to the factor of altitude, but there is no indication that the period between the close of the Würm and the beginning of the Neolithic was any more arid than the Neolithic phase itself. Indeed, the evidence suggests a rather continuous degradation in environmental conditions reaching a terminal stage at the end of the third millennium when the hydrological effects of run-off were no longer measurably different from those of the present day. The only indication of oscillations in the climatic regime is the periodic rise and fall of lake levels along the south-eastern desert frontier, but the precise significance of these variations is difficult to decipher or to relate to the evidence from the north-western and central Sahara. Despite Conrad's confidence that the two areas were under similar climatic influences, it would perhaps be worth re-examining the case for disparate climatic zones (e.g. Rognon 1967b: 115). Certainly, the existence of an arid phase during the fifth to mid-fourth millennium, indicated by the oscillations of the Saharan lake levels, seems to be contradicted by the humid phases reflected in the stratigraphy of the northern Sahara (see fig. 3).

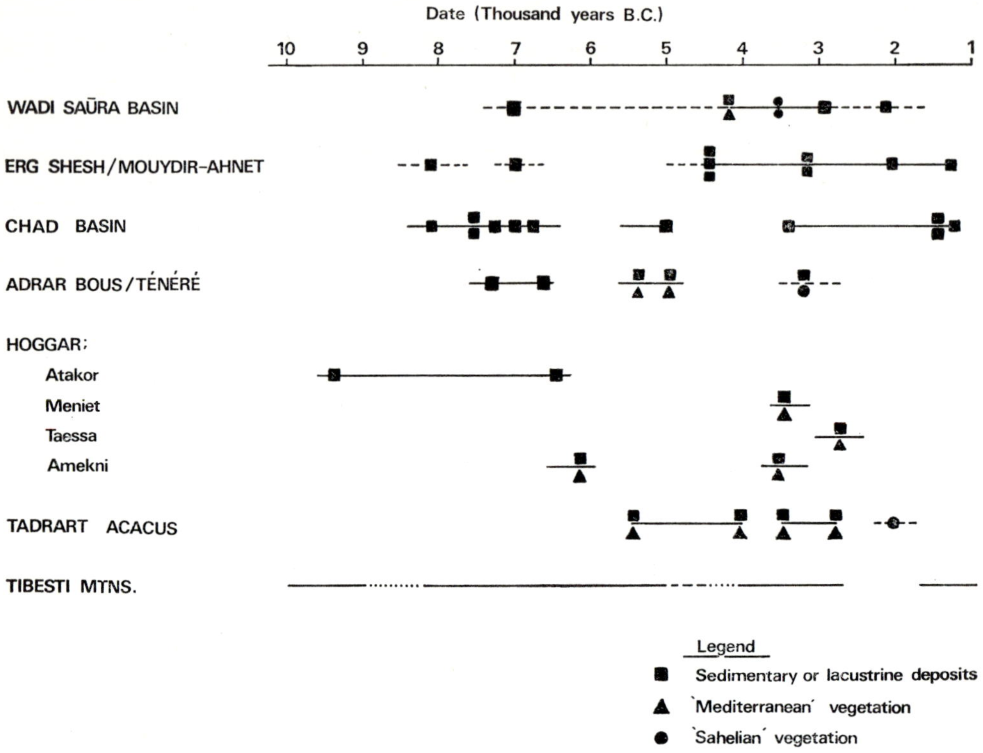

Figure 3 Dated humid phases in Saharan prehistory

Botanical studies

The record of 'more humid' phases in Saharan prehistory which emerges from the stratigraphical studies can be made more precise by correlating it with the analyses of palaeo-pollens collected not only from these same sedimentary strata, but also from Neolithic habitation sites dating to the later period of sedimentary deposition in the Sahara. Despite the more exact limits provided by pollen analyses, a degree of caution must be exercised on three counts. Firstly, there still persist fundamental objections to the uncorroborated evidence of palaeo-pollen, since possible contamination by pollen grains foreign to a site is not unknown. It is not always clear, especially in earlier field reports, whether adequate precautions were taken to prevent misinterpretation of the data. Secondly, only a few sites have yielded samples large enough to make statistical analysis valid. Lastly, as at Meniet (see below), there sometimes arises a contradiction between the range of flora indicated by the pollen and the range suggested by the actual plant remains which have been preserved, a fact which clearly implies that the pollen may not always be a representative sample of the flora which once existed. As the corpus of Saharan palynological data builds up, however, the results are extremely encouraging. They bear a striking internal consistency (that is, agreement within a range of widely separated sites of the same time period) which lends them credibility. Moreover, the absolute number and range of pollens which have been collected *in situ* are far from negligible and they indicate a more substantial and varied vegetation than is present in these same regions today (Quézel and Martinez 1958–9: 217–18).

Analysis of the pollen from the later Guirian horizons of the Saoura region reveals a small, though significant, contrast between the earlier paleosol strata and the later Neolithic travertine cap. Pollen from the black paleosols indicates that the environment was only marginally more humid than the present semi-arid conditions of the region. Aleppo pine, Acacia, oak, and a few grasses appear to have characterized the vegetation. The range of plant species in the travertine cap, however, is not radically different. A somewhat cooler and more humid environment has been claimed for this period on the basis of the coexistence of a Mediterranean flora alongside the more xerophytic Sahelian vegetation of the preceding phase. The northern species represented include birch, alder and hornbeam. Even so, this 'Neolithic humid phase' was very arid by comparison with the standards of the Tellian environment of the Maghrib (Beucher 1963; Beucher and Conrad 1963). Though it is true that the alder and birch can still be found in coastal regions of the Maghrib such as the Rif, and that other species like the beech, hornbeam and linden have completely disappeared from North Africa, the poor preservation of the pollen samples does not inspire confidence in the validity of any quantification of the shift in range of flora as suggested by Beucher; indeed, xerophytes were found in abundance, which indicates that any change in the environment was rather marginal. If the Neolithic period was humid, it was still arid in comparison with the milieu of the last Pluvial, and the vegetal cover was not so different from the 'Acacia forest' typical of the Saoura region today (Quézel and Simonneau 1963: 118–19).

An important pollen sample was obtained by Hugot during his excavations of the Neolithic rock shelter at Meniet (fig. 4, no. 1). Half the pollen sample was composed of arboreal species: Atlas cedar, Duprez's cypress, Aleppo pine, Montpellier maple, lentisk, walnut, evergreen oak, elder, ash and the hackberry. The pollen, however, is at variance with the macro-botanical finds preserved in the rock shelter which suggests that an arid zone vegetation consisting of grasses, sedges, and Artemisia (*herba-alba*) was equally dominant (Pons and Quézel 1956: 1656–7; Quézel and Hugot 1957; Hugot 1963: 154–66). This level at Meniet was dated by C^{14} to *c.* 3450 B.C. (Delibrias, Hugot and Quézel 1957: 268; Camps, Delibrias and Thommeret 1968: 28).

At Taessa, a highland site in the western Hoggar (fig. 4, no. 3), the fossil guano of an extinct Daman (*Procavia rufipes* or hyrax) was discovered and dated by C^{14} to 2730 B.C. (Delibrias, Hugot and Quézel 1957: 268). The Daman was a herbivore, and as such the pollens recovered from its guano might be expected to reflect the range of plants in its environment. The palaeo-pollens once again revealed a typical Mediterranean vegetal cover with the same arboreal species noted at Meniet (except for the lime tree), as well as numerous herbaceous plants (Pons and Quézel 1958; Quézel 1958).

Pollen studies made in connection with Camps' excavation of the Neolithic site at Amekni (fig. 4, no. 2) confirmed the presence of a Mediterranean forest cover during this period, with the Judas Tree, the hackberry, and the oak being the dominant arboreal

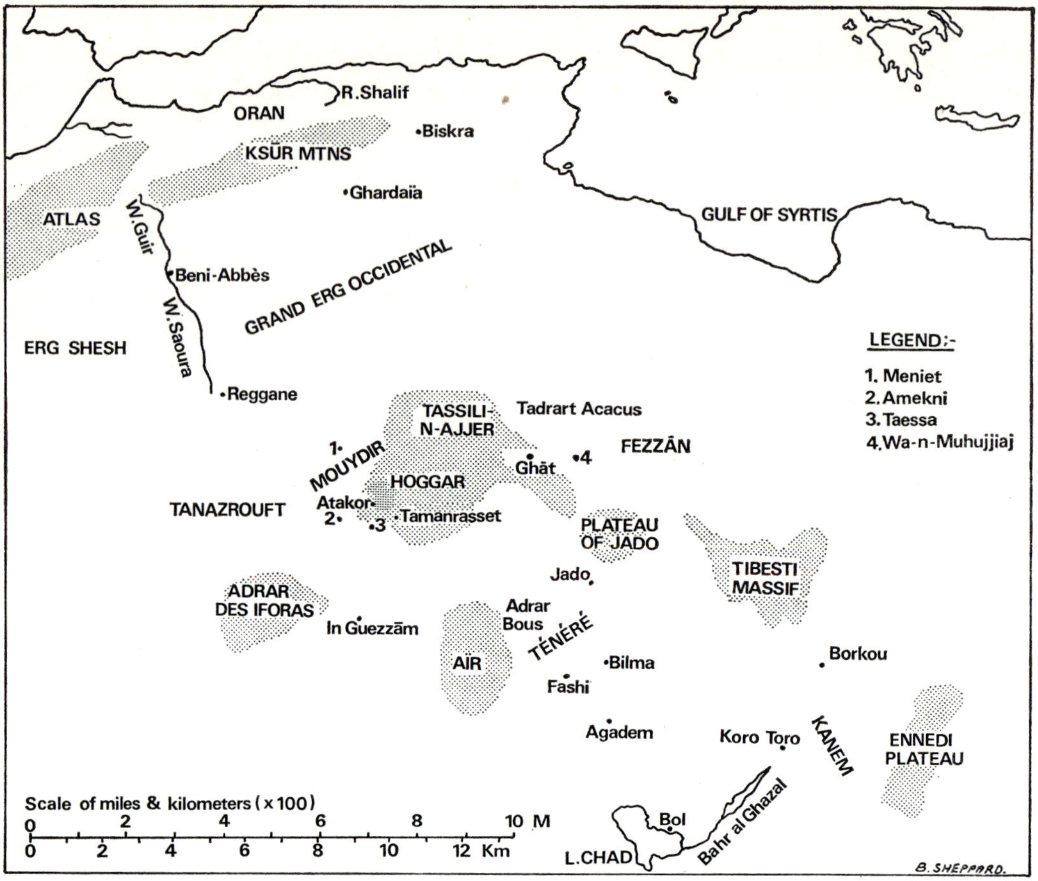

Figure 4 The Sahara: sites mentioned in the text

species. Especially striking, however, is the presence of the typha, a swamp plant now found only in the extremely humid conditions of lakes or swamps in the Maghrib. Its growth at Amekni almost certainly indicates the presence of a year-round supply of water. Such a view would be entirely consistent with the large number of fish remains discovered at Amekni, as well as at Meniet, In Guezzām, and Tiwiyne (Camps 1969: 179 ff., 186 ff.). Probably the surface run-off from the Hoggar highlands was sufficiently continuous during the Neolithic to support small lakes and swamps along the western periphery of the massif. In the Tanazrouft and Mouydir this run-off fed the lowland basins, just as the drainage from the Aïr mountains and the Jado Plateau filled the depressions in the Ténéré. The terminal dates for the two horizons at Amekni containing this predominantly humid flora are *c.* 6100 and 3550 B.C. (Camps, Delibrias and Thommeret 1968: 28).

Perhaps the most impressive and exciting evidence of more humid phases in the prehistoric environment of the Sahara has emerged from the pollen analyses made in connection with Mori's excavations in the Acacus foothills in the far south-western Fezzān (Libya). The earliest levels (*Focolai inferiori*) of the Neolithic rock shelter at Wa-n-Muhujjiāj (fig. 4, no. 4) contained bones of domestic sheep and cattle, as well as various wild species including the ostrich and the tortoise. The pollen analysis revealed a dominance in the lower levels (9–10) of typha which only subsided slightly in the subsequent strata (7–8). In the latter levels the typha still represented the majority of the pollen grains (60%) with smaller percentages of Aristida and Artemisia dominating the remainder. The homogeneity and fineness of the sediments in which these pollens were found is a strong indication of a permanent, though perhaps stagnant, water level. The macro-botanical finds from this first period were also dominated by the swamp plant typha, though xerophytic species including *Acacia albida* and *Balanites Aegyptiaca* were also found. Certainly, the level of precipitation and surface hydrology required for this sort of environment would be quite different from the present regime; the mean annual rainfall of 10–15 mm. in the Tadrart Acacus today supports virtually no vegetal cover of any sort (Dubief 1955: 57; Mori 1965: 227). From the lower levels (7–10) of the *Focolai inferiori* were obtained C^{14} dates which indicate a time span of *c.* 5500 to 4000 B.C. (Mori 1965: 215 ff., 241).

A brief arid interval (level 6) was followed by a second habitation period, the so-called *Focolai medi* (levels 1–5). Although the same bone assemblage as in the earlier period was found, the pollen revealed that the environment had become considerably more arid. The ground cover now consisted totally of xerophytes. The typha, though still managing to survive in the earlier levels (2–4), completely disappeared during the course of the most recent stratum (1). This range of ground cover indicates the persistence of small, isolated pools or marshes in a few low-lying basins, but that in the rapidly desiccating environment the number of potential habitation sites was being severely reduced. The range of C^{14} dates for this arid environment of the *Focolai medi* phase extends from *c.* 3500 to 2700 B.C. (Mori 1965: 241). The middle occupation period was succeeded by a brief span of aeolian activity that was marked by the formation of sterile sand dunes. The final damp phase at Wa-n-Muhujjiāj is identified by strata containing palaeo-pollens which would suggest even more arid conditions than in any previous 'humid' phase. The typha has utterly disappeared, and even grassland varieties such as the Artemisia and Aristida were found more rarely. The xerophytes now totally dominate the vegetal cover. Such an environment would appear to be only a marginal improvement on the present total desert of the Acacus. The fact that no signs of any human habitation were found is a clear indication that the advance of aridity had now reached very serious proportions.

The principal factor contributing to the survival of the Mediterranean vegetation which once flourished in the Sahara during the last Pluvial was the altitude of the highlands – regions favoured with lower temperatures and higher levels of precipitation. The highlands thus formed artificial *impluvia* which fed the lowlands about their bases. Typical cover for high mountain zones (over 1500 m.) was a Mediterranean flora marked by sparse stands of conifers; the lower zones (*c.* 700–1500 m.) harboured a few coniferous species, especially the Aleppo pine, but were characterized by xerophytes such as the juniper, cypress, jujube, and wild olive (Quézel and Martinez 1958–9; Quézel 1960; Rognon 1967b: 125). Evidence for the survival of this range of vegetation, even in these highly favoured mountain retreats, does not extend much beyond the mid-third millennium B.C. The process and rate of the degradation of the Saharan vegetation characteristic of the last Pluvial is difficult to assess. The mere presence of some arboreal species is particularly significant. For example, today the hackberry is found only in the sub-humid regions of the Mediterranean Basin where precipitation is well above 300 mm. per annum. The jujube no longer grows in the central Sahara: its extreme southern limit is the latitude of Ghardaïa, but it is ordinarily found further north in regions with annual rainfall levels of at least 100 mm. Yet, the degradation of the Pluvial vegetation may have been very slow and may have lagged considerably behind any shift in the climate, especially in regions where the topography favoured the entrapment of water. The basic division between the unfavoured lowland regions and the more humid highlands still persists in the present day, as does the altitudinal gradation of vegetation within the highland massifs (Quézel 1960). Many isolated valleys or basins in these highlands continue to harbour Mediterranean species which are clearly relicts of the last Pluvial (Bruneau de Miré and Quézel 1959; Gillet 1959).

To sum up, pollen analyses and macro-botanical finds add a valuable dimension to the rather sparse record provided by the geological strata. Whereas the latter mark more humid phases in the past which favoured the formation of wadi and lake sediments, they do not reveal the range of flora and fauna which those humid conditions were actually able to support. Considering the highly erratic rainfall patterns typical of arid zone climates, the question is of more than passing importance. Periodic downpours of very brief duration *could* lead to the formation of distinct sedimentary deposition and yet might be so seasonally concentrated as to make little real difference in the potential for life-support. The entirety of the evidence from the Saoura Basin, for example, would tend to suggest that the import of the geological evidence is in danger of being exaggerated unless carefully checked against the range of plant life indicated by the pollen. The overall indications of a more humid climate should be correlated with the regional peculiarities of geomorphology and topography which permitted the accumulation and storage of water in basin areas about the peripheries of the highlands, thus providing the milieu for Neolithic habitation sites and favoured zones of relict Mediterranean vegetal cover from the last Pluvial.

Faunal studies

The presence of a range of fauna remarkably different from that of today, as attested in the rock art of the Sahara, has been one of the more dramatic proofs cited in favour of a marked climatic change over the desert. Unfortunately, due to the various classificatory systems employed to date the successive stages of the rock art, the corpus of data has been misused to prove varied interpretations of climatic change.

The fact that some wildlife species important to these arguments have been able to survive in remote regions of the Sahara until quite recently should caution against overplaying theories based on faunal distribution. For example, dwarf crocodiles have been captured in this century in isolated pools along Wadi Mihero (Hoggar), Wadi Ahrir (Tassili-n-Ajjer) as well as in Arsheï Lake on the Ennedi Plateau. So too the widespread discovery of harpoons and fishhooks in Neolithic tool assemblages is not proof of a radically altered environment. Many species of fish are still commonly found in small Saharan lakes and ponds; and, of all forms of wildlife still present in the desert, fish are actually extending their domain and increasing in numbers (Pellegrin 1919; Daget 1959; Hugot 1963: 152–4). In most cases it can be demonstrated that the extinction of many large mammalian species was due to the predatory activities of the common enemy of all animal life especially after the introduction of firearms (Mauny 1956: 258, 270). Many subtropical species once common to the peripheral regions of the Sahara, such as the ostrich, have been exterminated by man within living memory (Camps-Fabrer 1963). The faunal evidence, therefore, must be treated with considerable caution; only certain species are reliable indicators of desiccation and even then (mollusca and gastropods excepted) it seems better to use such data in a supporting role to the more readily measurable record of the stratigraphy and the pollens.

By far the greatest proportion of evidence relevant to Holocene fauna in the Sahara comes from the large corpus of prehistoric rock art. Apart from residual doubts about chronology, to check these data against the actual osteological remains of the animals concerned is still extremely difficult (Butzer 1966: 73). A series of recently obtained C^{14} dates from horizons overlying the typical stylistic phases of rock art has finally confirmed in broad outline Lhote's assignation of the art styles to successive chronological periods: the 'Bubalus-Round Head' style to the Palaeolithic, the 'Bovidian' phase to the Neolithic, and the so-called 'Horse' or 'Libyco-Berber' style to the proto-historic period (Delibrias, Hugot and Quézel 1957: 268; Lhote 1964: 208; 1965: 89–91; Mori 1965: 234, 239; Camps, Delibrias and Thommeret 1968: 28). Mauny chose four large mammalian species depicted in the rock art that require large amounts of daily water and fodder, and correlated this evidence with bone finds of these same species to demonstrate the rather rapid desiccation of the Sahara. He claimed that the hippopotamus and elephant were limited to very few favoured highland retreats by the beginning of the Neolithic, and that the rhinoceros and giraffe had completely disappeared by the 'Libyco-Berber' period of rock art (Mauny 1956).

On this rather shaky basis, some scholars even ventured, by extrapolation, to draw hypothetical isohyets to reflect the higher levels of rainfall in the Sahara during the Neolithic (e.g. Butzer 1961: 40). Surveys of this sort, however, are subject to serious objections: their assignment of any given piece of rock art to a particular phase and their general schema (i.e. dating of the phases) is often at variance with the pattern now established by absolute dating and the more accurate classification of the styles. Aside from being incomplete in coverage, this leads to a rather artificial conflation of the fauna into predetermined humid phases in which they are supposed to have lived. In fact, a careful catalogue of all known rock art representations of these large African mammals has shown that in certain highlands (e.g. the Tassili-n-Ajjer) the hippopotamus survived into the Neolithic, while in others (the Aïr and Adrar des Iforas) the elephant persisted until the proto-historic period (Lhote 1965: 92–9, 108–10). The restriction of these animals to a narrower time period than this has created a misleading impression of the length of time that it took these species to disappear from the Sahara.

Based on a particularly clear case of superimposition of several rock art styles at the site of Ti-n-Ascigh in the Fezzān, Mori has cogently argued that the earliest phases of rock art date to the Upper Pleistocene. If this is accepted, it only serves to underscore the extent to which many of the great mammalian species were common to the Sahara at the end of the last Pluvial and later constituted a residual fauna of that period (Mori

1974). Naturally, the choice of subject matter by the artist, as well as the mere availability of a rock face to work, must have been important factors in determining the range of animal species depicted. With the shift to an economy based on domesticated animals, the herders would have been less concerned with wild fauna (the object of the hunt) than with the animals – principally cattle – upon which their livelihood depended. If attention is paid to factors such as these, as well as to nuances of style and regional peculiarities, a rather different emphasis emerges. Certain species were *never* found in particular regions of the Sahara: for example, the *Bubalus antiquus* and rhinoceros *never* ranged the Tibesti or the Hoggar – they were limited to rather precise ecological niches. The distribution of rock art also reveals that the hippopotamus was not found in the mountains of southern Oran province (Algeria), whereas the elephant flourished and the rhinoceros was fairly numerous in these same highlands.

In order not to distort the perspective that faunal studies are able to give us, regional differences in environment must be taken into account, as well as hypothetical climatic influences. The Saharan Atlas of southern Oran did not have the same massive, monolithic geomorphology characteristic of some of the central Saharan massifs which favoured the entrapment of permanent pools of water ideal for the hippopotamus; but, their narrow winding valleys and small inter-mountain plains were ideally suited to the migratory elephant and rhinoceros (Lhote 1965: 95–6; Lemaître 1972: 130–1, 136).

Taking all these factors into account, the decline in the great mammalian species is neither as dramatic nor abrupt as is usually claimed; rather, these large species were able to inhabit a specific type of Saharan environment created by the favourable conditions of the last Pluvial and remained in it as long as the residual environment was able to harbour them. At the other end of the spectrum, however, it seems probable that comparably minute species – the snails and molluscs – will furnish a more accurate and detailed measure of ground humidity (e.g. Llabador 1962), so that dependence on rock art representations of mammalian wildlife for a direct indication of environmental conditions will no longer be as great as in the past.

Concluding remarks

What does the sum of the data from the Sahara suggest about the scale and chronology of climatic change? Firstly, it indicates that the conditions of the last Pluvial created a marginally more humid environment in the desert which lasted until the close of the Würm, *c.* 9000 B.C. By the time of the Neolithic (*c.* 6000–2500 B.C.) the environment had become considerably more arid, though it was sufficiently humid to permit the survival of vestigial flora and fauna characteristic of the Pluvial. The contention that this period was significantly more humid than the millennia immediately preceding it, however, does not appear to be substantiated in any way by the evidence at our disposal. Similar conditions, perhaps even slightly more humid, were typical of the intervening period (9000–6000 B.C.); there was no arid hiatus by comparison with which the Neolithic was 'more humid'. The trend in the northern Sahara appears to have been a relatively constant degradation following the end of the last Pluvial.

There is no need, therefore, to hypothesize, *a priori*, a more humid upswing in the climate to coincide with the occurrence of the Neolithic. In fact, the shift to a pastoral nomadic economy based on the herding of domesticated animals appears to have taken place in an environment which was becoming increasingly more arid. This process in itself – that is the enforced contact between men and animals in an ecological system which was becoming increasingly restricted – may have led directly to the Neolithic economy as an adaptation to the advancing desiccation. The deterioration in environmental conditions appears to have reached a level by the proto-historic period (2000–1000 B.C.) when the measurable elements of the environment were not significantly different from those of the present day. The most economical hypothesis, therefore, seems to be a continuous and uninterrupted deterioration in climate following the close of the Pluvial, which produced a maximum effect on the environment by the end of the third millennium. Only the oscillations in the lake levels of the southern Saharan periphery could be argued to support climatic shifts of recognizable magnitude, but the case for connecting the climatic regime of this region to that of the northern Sahara is far from convincing.

The main problem inhibiting the reconstruction of palaeo-climatic regimes for the prehistoric Sahara is the lack of any unitary model within which the existing data, which pertain to *environmental* rather than climatic factors, can be made to produce valid results. The plain fact is that past climates can only be measured *indirectly* through extrapolation from environmental data. Since the ultimate concern for the prehistorian is to establish the latter, it would seem best for him to be satisfied with measuring the environment directly rather than in a round-about fashion through hypothetically reconstructed climatic regimes. Environment is of direct interest to the prehistorian – the climate only in so far as it ultimately affects the environment. The former is directly ascertainable, the latter is not.

To posit a given run-off, evaporation rate, atmospheric current, temperature, or precipitation level from the record left on the ground is still a very difficult task. The faunal record illustrates only some of the problems involved. The faunal evidence has often been treated as though it was a homogeneous body of data, with little attention being paid to regional peculiarities which permitted one species to survive but militated against the continued existence of another. The result has required that a number of unwarranted logical leaps be made. Extrapolations about past climates have led scholars to infer causal connections between the disappearance of animal species and changes in atmospheric conditions which never existed in the first place. The fact is that between climate and our present corpus of data lie an unknown number of variables; as yet there exists no comprehensive theoretical framework in which the faunal, geological, and botanical evidence can be fitted and connected to a given climatic regime.

It would perhaps not be out of place to suggest that a more profitable course would be to avoid the red herring of climatic change and to concentrate on the environment. Since environmental conditions are directly measurable in a way in which climatic conditions are not, there is some hope that by analysing the former we might, *as a result*, be able to make some reasonable hypotheses about the evolution of the Saharan climate. If, on the other hand, the problem is approached by *beginning* with hypothetical climatic regimes of the past, the prehistorian would still have to translate the results into environmental terms, a process which might pose insoluble theoretical problems. The case of climate, environment, and prehistory in the Sahara suggests that our priorities in this matter may have been reversed.

29.x.1975

Churchill College
Cambridge

References

Beucher, F. 1963. Flores quaternaires au Sahara nord-occidental, d'après l'analyse pollinique de sédiments prélevés à Hassi-Zguilma (Saoura). *Comptes rendus de l'Académie des sciences.* 256:2205–8.

Beucher, F. and Conrad, G. 1963. L'âge du dernier pluvial saharien. Essai sur la flore d'un épisode lacustre. *Comptes rendus de l'Académie des sciences.* 256:4465–8.

Bruneau de Miré, P. and Quézel, P. 1959. Sur la présence de la Bruyère en arbre (*Erica arborea* L.) sur les sommets de l'Emi Koussi (Tibesti). *Compte rendu sommaire des séances de la Société de biogéographie.* 315:66–70.

Butzer, K. W. 1961. Climatic change in arid regions since the Pliocene. *UNESCO, Arid Zone Research XVII: A History of Land Use in Arid Regions*, pp. 31–56 (ed. L. D. Stamp). Paris: UNESCO.

Butzer, K. W. 1963. The last pluvial phase of the Eurafrican subtropics. *UNESCO, Arid Zone Research XX: Les Changements de Climat.* pp. 211–21. Paris-Bruxelles: UNESCO.

Butzer, K. W. 1966. Climatic changes in the arid regions of Africa during early to mid-Holocene times. *World Climate from 8000 to 0 B.C.* Proceedings of the International Symposium, pp. 72–83. London: Royal Meteorological Society.

Camps, G. 1969. *Amekni: Néolithique ancien du Hoggar.* Paris: CNRS. (Centre de Recherches Anthropologiques, Préhistoriques et Ethnographiques, Mémoire X.)

Camps, G., Delibrias, G. and Thommeret, J. 1968. Chronologie absolue et succession des civilisations préhistoriques dans le Nord de l'Afrique. *Libyca* (Anthropologie-Préhistoire-Ethnographie). 16:9–28.

Camps-Fabrer, H. 1963. *La disparition de l'autruche en Afrique du Nord.* Alger: Travaux du Centre de Recherche d'Anthropologie, Préhistoire, et Ethnologie.

Chavaillon, J. 1964. *Etude stratigraphique des formations quaternaires du Sahara nord-occidentale* (*Colomb-Bechar à Reggane*). Paris: CNRS. (Centre de Recherches sur les Zones Arides, Série Géologie no. 5.)

Conrad, G. 1963. Synchronisme du dernier Pluvial dans le Sahara septentrional et le Sahara méridional. *Comptes rendus de l'Académie des sciences.* 253:2506–9.

Conrad, G. 1969a. *L'évolution continentale post-hercynienne au Sahara algérien* (*Saoura, Erg Chech-Tanezrouft, Ahnet-Mouydir*). Paris: CNRS. (Centre de Recherches sur les Zones Arides, Série Géologie no. 10.)

Daget, J. 1959. Note sur les poissons du Borkou-Ennedi-Tibesti. *Travaux de I'Institut de Recherches Sahariennes.* 18:173–81.

Delibrias, G. and Dutil, P. 1966. Formations calcaires lacustres du Quaternaire supérieure dans le massif central saharien (Hoggar) et datations absolues. *Comptes rendus de l'Académie des sciences.* 262:55–8.

Delibrias, G. and Hugot, H. 1962. Datation par la méthode dite 'du C 14' du néolithique de l'Adrar Bous (Ténéréen). *Missions Berliet Ténéré-Tchad,* pp. 71–2. Paris: Arts et Métiers graphiques.

Delibrias, G., Hugot, H. and Quézel, P. 1957. Trois datations de sédiments sahariens récents par le radio-carbone. *Libyca* (Anthropologie-Préhistoire-Ethnographie). 5:266–70.

Dubief, J. 1955. *Essai sur l'hydrologie superficielle au Sahara.* Alger: Gouvernement Général de l'Algérie, Direction du Service de la Colonisation et de l'Hydraulique Service des études scientifiques.

Dupont, B. 1970. Distribution et nature des fonds du lac Tchad (Nouvelles Données). *Cahiers O.R.S.T.O.M.* (Série Géologie). 2:9–27.

Dupont, B. and Delibrias, G. 1970. Datation par le carbone 14 d'un niveau sédimentaire de l'Archipel du lac Tchad. *Cahiers O.R.S.T.O.M.* (Série Géologie). 2:43–7.

Dutil, P. and Juste, C. 1965. Etude de la composition de la matière organique de paléosols sahariens: organique des sols. *Comptes rendus de l'Académie des sciences.* 261:4791–4.

Faure, H. 1966. Evolution des grands lacs sahariens à l'Holocène. *Quaternaria.* 8:167–75.

Faure, H. and Servant, M. 1970. Evolution récente d'un bassin continental: le Tchad. *Cahiers O.R.S.T.O.M.* (Série Géologie). 2:5–8.

Geyh, M. and Jäkel, D. 1974. Spätpleistozäne und holozäne Klimageschichte der Sahara aufgrund zugänglicher ^{14}C daten. *Zeitschrift für Geomorphologie.* 18:82–98.

Gillet, H. 1959. Découverte de nouvelles plantes relictes dans le massif de l'Ennedi (Nord-Tchad). *Compte rendu sommaire des séances de la Société de biogéographie.* 312:27–34.

Hugot, H. 1963. *Recherches préhistoriques dans l'Ahaggar Nord-Occidental (1950–1957).* Paris: CNRS. (Centre de Recherches Anthropologiques, Préhistoriques et Ethnographiques, Mémoire I.)

Lemaître, J. P. 1972. Notes sur deux conceptions traditionnelles du néolithique Saharien. *Libyca* (Anthropologie-Préhistoire-Ethnographie). 20:125–36.

Lhote, H. 1964. Faits nouveaux concernant la chronologie relative et absolue des gravures et peintures pariétales du sud Oranais et du Sahara. *Prehistoric Art of the Western Mediterranean and Sahara* (eds L. P. Garcia and E. R. Perello). *Viking Fund Publications in Anthropology.* 39:191–214.

Lhote, H. 1965. L'évolution de la faune dans les gravures et les peintures rupestres du Sahara et ses relations avec l'évolution climatique. *Miscelánea en Homenaje al Abate Henri Breuil, 1877–1961,* pp. 83–118. Barcelona: Diputación Provincial de Barcelona, Instituto de Prehistoria y Arqueologia.

Llabador, F. 1962. Résultats malacologiques de la Mission scientifique du Ténéré. *Missions Berliet Ténéré-Tchad,* pp. 235–9. Paris: Arts et Métiers graphiques.

Mauny, R. 1956. Préhistoire et zoologie: la grande 'faune éthiopienne' du nord-ouest africain du paléolithique à nos jours. *Bulletin de l'Institut français d'Afrique noire* (Série A). 18:246–79.

Mori, F. 1965. *Tadrart Acacus. Arte rupestre e culture de Saharo preistorico.* Torino: Giulio Einaudi Editore.

Mori, F. 1974. The earliest Saharan rock-engravings. *Antiquity.* 48:87–92.

Pachur, H. J. 1975. Zur spätpleistozänen und holozänen Formung auf der Nordabdachung des Tibestigebirges. *Die Erde.* 106:21–46.

Pellegrin, J. 1919. Poissons du Tibesti, du Borkou et de l'Ennedi, récoltes par la mission Tilho. *Bulletin de la Société zoologique de France.* 44:148–53.

Pons, A. and Quézel, P. 1956. Premiers résultats de l'analyse palynologique de quelques paléosols sahariens. *Comptes rendus de l'Académie des sciences.* 243:1656–8.

Pons, A. and Quézel, P. 1958. Premières remarques sur l'étude palynologique d'un guano fossile du Hoggar. *Comptes rendus de l'Académie des sciences.* 244:2290–2.

Quézel, P. 1958. Guano de Daman de l'Atakor. *Bulletin de la Société de l'histoire naturelle de l'Afrique du Nord.* 49:19–20.

Quézel, P. 1960. Flore et palynologique sahariennes: quelques aspects de leur signification biogéographique et paléoclimatique. *Bulletin de l'Institut fondamental d'Afrique noire* (Série A). 22:353–60.

Quézel, P. and Hugot, H. 1957. A propos de quelques grains fossiles du gisement préhistorique de Meniet. *Bulletin de la Société de l'histoire naturelle de l'Afrique du Nord.* 48:370–72.

Quézel, P. and Martinez, C. 1958. Etude palynologique de deux diatomites du Borkou (Tchad). *Bulletin de la Société de l'histoire naturelle de l'Afrique du Nord.* 49:230–44.

Quézel, P. and Martinez, C. 1958–9. Le dernier interpluvial au Sahara central – essai de chronologie palynologique et paléoclimatique. *Libyca* (Anthropologie-Préhistoire-Ethnographie). 6–7:211–27.

Quézel, P. and Martinez, C. 1962. Premiers résultats de l'analyse palynologique de sédiments recueillies au Sahara méridional à l'occasion de la mission Berliet – Tchad. *Missions Berliet Ténéré-Tchad*, pp. 313–27. Paris: Arts et Métiers graphiques.

Quézel, P. and Simonneau, P. 1963. Les peuplements d'Acacia du Sahara nord-occidental: étude phytosociologique. *Travaux de l'Institut de Recherches Sahariennes.* 22:79–121.

Rognon, P. 1962. Observations sur le quaternaire du Hoggar. *Travuax de l'Institut de Recherches Sahariennes.* 21:57–80.

Rognon, P. 1967a. *Le Massif de l'Atakor et ses bordures (Sahara central): Etude géomorphologique.* Paris: CNRS. (Centre de Recherches sur les Zones Arides, Série Géologie no. 9.)

Rognon, P. 1967b. Climatic influences on the African Hoggar during tbe Quaternary, based on geomorphologic observations. *Association of American Geographers (Annals).* 57:115–27.

Servant, M. 1970. Données stratigraphiques sur le quaternaire supérieur et récent au nord du lac Tchad. *Cahiers O.R.S.T.O.M.* (Série Géologie). 2:95–114.

Servant, M., Servant, S. and Delibrias, G. 1969. Chronologie du Quaternaire récent des brasses des régions du Tchad. *Comptes rendus de l'Académie des sciences.* 269:1603–6.

Abstract

Shaw, Brent D.

Climate, environment and prehistory in the Sahara

The issue of climatic fluctuation in the Sahara during the early Holocene is of considerable importance because of tbe supposedly 'more humid' phase during which the Saharan Neolithic flourished. An analysis of the evidence, however, seems to indicate the reverse, that is, that the Neolithic had its genesis and development in an environment which was becoming *increasingly arid*. In fact, the termination of the more favourable humid conditions of the pre-Neolithic marked the departure from an economy primarily dependent on hunting/gathering, and incited the shift to the herding of domestic animals. Further, the methodological assumptions which underlie the interpretation of the evidence for climatic change are examined and questioned, especially the assumption that *climatic* as opposed to *environmental* variables can be deduced from the data at our disposal.

Evidence from the insects of climatic variation during the Flandrian period: a preliminary note

P. J. Osborne

Over the last two decades investigations, mainly at Birmingham University, of many sites of Pleistocene age have shown that insects respond rapidly to climatic changes and that they are particularly useful as indicators of the timing and magnitude of these events. Several factors in combination are responsible for this high degree of utility. The most important of these are: (1) In certain types of deposit, insects (and especially beetles) preserve particularly well, so that assemblages comprising thousands of individuals representing perhaps hundreds of species can be examined, ensuring that deductions need not be made from insufficient evidence. (2) During the late Pleistocene no indication of morphological evolution has so far been detected, so that all beetles identified are referable to species still living; and furthermore, careful cross-checking within the faunal assemblages and the evidence provided by associated disciplines, e.g. Botany, has suggested that, by and large, the environmental requirements of the majority have not significantly altered either. This means that (3) the large volume of ecological and distributional information which has been accumulated by modern entomologists over the last two hundred years may be used to interpret the fossil data.

Using this beetle evidence, more particularly present day geographical distributions, it has been possible to demonstrate gross fluctuations in summer temperatures and also, to some extent, changes in continentality/oceanicity during the last 200,000 years (see for example Coope 1968; Morgan 1973; Osborne and Shotton 1968; Shotton and Osborne 1965). The latest of these major oscillations appears to have taken place during the Devensian Late-glacial (*c.* 11,000 years ago) when the insect evidence showed a swing from temperatures as high as or higher than those of the present to a rigorous arctic regime within the space of some 3,000 years (Coope and Brophy 1972; Osborne 1972). This final cold episode effectively removed from Britain all traces of the preceding thermophilous fauna, leaving the country colonized by a group of species typical of northern latitudes or high ground today. This fauna, which is typified by such species as *Helophorus sibiricus* Motsch., *H. glacialis* Villa, *Olophrum boreale* Pk., *Boreaphilus henningianus* Sahlb. and *Pycnoglypta lurida* Gyll., none of which is found living in Britain now, and by *Elaphrus lapponicus* Gyll., *Nebria nivalis* Pk. and *Arpedium brachypterum* (Gr.), all confined to high ground in the north of this country today, was widespread in Britain between 11,000 and 10,000 years ago.

That the disappearance of this group of insects occurred fairly close to 10,000 years ago is shown by radiocarbon dates on the deposits from which the assemblage has been recovered. Ashworth (1973) records it from Rodbaston, Staffordshire, prior to a layer dated 10,300±170 years b.p. and Buckland (pers. comm.) has described a similar assemblage from Messingham, Lincolnshire, with a C^{14} date of 10,250±120 b.p. A deposit as far south as Croydon, Surrey, again containing this fauna, was dated 10,130±120 years b.p. (Osborne 1971a), while in a serially sampled deposit at West Bromwich, Staffordshire, the topmost level from which the cold beetle fauna was recorded provided a date of 10,025 ± 100 b.c., whilst the next layer up, dated less than a hundred years later, contained no trace of any species indicative of a cold climatic regime (Osborne, in prep.). When this arctic episode came to an end the contemporary fauna disappeared, leaving nothing behind except a few relict species now more or less confined to the Scottish mountains. The history of the present day British insect fauna begins effectively at this time.

The climate of the Post-glacial may be investigated by the same methods as those employed with the earlier sites. This study is, however, bedevilled by a number of factors which do not afflict investigators of the Pleistocene. The climatic oscillations which may have taken place during the Flandrian are unlikely to have been anything like so great in amplitude as those of the Late-glacial and earlier times, and would therefore not be expected to leave such conspicuous traces. Furthermore, the cutting of the English Channel about 7,000 years ago must have severely curtailed immigration or re-entry of species kept out or displaced by unfavourable conditions. Finally, the latter half of Flandrian time is the period during which the impact of man on the environment has made itself felt. It is inescapable that man's destruction of certain types of habitat, notably primeval forest, in the interests of agriculture has contributed largely to the contraction in range, or to the actual extinction from this country, of a number of beetle species since the Neolithic. At one time it was the author's view that this was the major, if not the only, factor to which these effects could be attributed. It now appears likely that climatic variation was at least partly responsible. It is, however, at present debatable how much influence to assign to one factor or the other, or whether at times they were working in conjunction.

In the face of these obstacles, and in view of the slight amount of work so far accomplished on the beetle faunas of the last 10,000 years, any hypotheses must be tentative and advanced with some diffidence. Nevertheless, hints of climatic change are to be seen, and it is hoped that a great deal more work on the subject will help to paint the picture in as much detail as that of the Late-glacial. It is partly in an effort to provide some stimulus towards this end that the present paper is submitted.

Temperatures during the Post-glacial were at one time thought to have risen only slowly on a smooth curve which reached its peak at the 'climatic optimum' around 5,000 years ago. Indications from the beetles living at the time, however, suggest that this was not so but that the 'warm up' was quite early, sudden and dramatic. A site at Lea Marston, Warwickshire, whose combined C^{14} dates centred around 9,500 years b.c. contained an extensive fauna quite devoid of any cold elements, and which would have been completely at home in deciduous woodland in southern England today (Osborne 1974). As almost all the members of this fauna are found living in Fennoscandia, their distributions in that area were compared with a map of the vegetation zones. It was seen that virtually the entire assemblage was to be found in the *Fagus* (beech) zone in the southern tip of Sweden, numbers falling off northwards until in the Alpine and Arctic zones a mere 10% of the Lea Marston fauna is to be found living today. A rather more subjective comparison with the modern British fauna confirmed this assessment, as only three species on the Lea Marston list are not now found in southern England and these all have a more southerly distribution on the continent today. A large proportion of the beetles recorded are associated at present with deciduous woodland in which oak and beech are dominant elements. The radiocarbon dates, however, suggest that these trees would not have been available in the English midlands when the deposit was being laid down, and this is borne out by their complete absence from the pollen spectrum. It can be seen, moreover, that although many of the beetles listed live in this type of habitat for one reason or another, there is not a single species which depends specifically on one of the more thermophilous, broad-leaved trees for food. It was concluded, therefore, that, due to their great mobility, and given favourable temperatures, the insects had moved in well in advance of the more slowly migrating trees and that the woodland was composed of *Betula* (birch) and *Salix* (willow), both of which were abundantly represented by their pollen. The fauna suggests that the trees of temperate woodland, such as oak and beech, could well have lived in Warwickshire at this time had they had time to arrive.

The deposit of roughly similar age from West Bromwich, mentioned above, has also supplied evidence supporting the conclusions from Lea Marston. It has already been stated that in this deposit a typical zone III cold assemblage occurred at the level dated 10,025 years b.p. and that this was followed by a completely different fauna from which all the exotic cold elements had disappeared, having been replaced by temperate species, and which was dated 9,970±110 years b.p. The next layer to be dated did not contain a numerically large fauna but did indicate temperate conditions and an environment similar to that at Lea Marston. The C^{14} age of this level was 9,640±100 years b.p. From here on, the trend towards temperate woodland faunas continued up to the horizon dated 9,080±455 years b.p. and this layer contained a number of species associated with wood, some of them with conifers.

Thus, in the first 1,000 years of the Flandrian, a rapid initial rise in temperature is suggested, followed by a period during which no perceptible fluctuations, either up or down, occurred.

The next millennium is not well known entomologically although it has provided, from Little Stretton, Shropshire, the earliest record known to the author of a species, *Rhynchaenus quercus* (L.), which is attached to oak as a foodplant (Osborne 1972). Again, the following thousand-year period has been insufficiently investigated to give more than a glimpse of the environment of the time. At Little Stretton more wood-boring species appeared during this period, most of these being associated with deciduous trees but a few with conifers also. Due mostly to the small number of sites so far examined, nothing of climatic significance has been recorded from this period.

Around 7,000 years ago the English Channel was cut through, separating Britain from the continent by a barrier which, though clearly not impassable, must have made immigration from further south much more difficult. This was an important event from the point of view of climatic interpretations of insect faunas for, if there was no longer free passage of species to or from the continent in response to climatic changes, the only distributional data available would be details of movements within the British Isles or of actual extinctions. Neither of these effects is apparent in the faunal assemblages from the Little Stretton or Church Stretton sites in the succeeding 2,000 years (Osborne 1972). Despite a considerable increase in the numbers of species from both sites, no beetles were found which do not live in England today nor indeed which could not be found at the latitude of Church Stretton. On this rather slim evidence it is provisionally assumed that the climate still remained fairly steady during this time.

The first hint of climatic disturbance appeared in a collection of beetles from a deposit at Shustoke, Warwickshire, radiocarbon dated 4,830 ± 100 years b.p. (Kelly and Osborne 1964). The majority of the insects recorded from this site are still to be found in the British midlands, and the environment indicated is primarily deciduous woodland. One of the species present, *Rhysodes sulcatus* F., has since disappeared from this country, and the deposit yielded two more, *Dryophthorus corticalis* (Pk.) and *Ernoporus caucasicus* Lind., whose distributions have been reduced each to a single locality. All these insects are now found further south, and their presence at Shustoke might be construed as indicating a warmer climate than that of today. It is at least as probable, however, that the contractions in the ranges of these beetles is due to the gross destruction of their habitat, dense woodland with much undisturbed dead timber – and in the case of *E. caucasicus* of the Lime tree (*Tilia*) by man in the interests of agriculture.

On the other hand four species were present whose range in this country today is well to the north of Warwickshire. These are *Bembidion atroviolaceum* Duf., *Sphaerites glabratus* (F.), *Tropiphorus obtusus* (Bonsd.) and *Barynotus squamosus* Germ. Amongst the plants the northern clubmoss *Selaginella selaginoides* (L.) was recorded. The presence of these elements is most readily explained in terms of a deterioration in the thermal environment around 5,000 years ago. Denton and Karlén (1973) were able to show that the Post-glacial period was punctuated by intervals during which the glaciers of the northern hemisphere advanced well beyond their present-day limits and that these advances were roughly synchronous throughout the area (see fig. 5). The date of the Shustoke material falls at the end of one of these periods of glacier expansion. The sample from Shustoke was collected as a unit by means of a bucket auger so that it is not possible to say from which part of the section the northern elements came, or whether they were scattered throughout; nor is the C^{14} date precise, since it was an average one for the entire sample. Nevertheless, the occurrence of the northern species is a very broad hint of a colder period during the time of deposition. When taken in conjunction with Denton and Karlén's evidence, the presence of these species strongly suggests that further, more detailed work on deposits of this time will show, around 5,000 years b.p., the presence in southern Britain of a fauna now chiefly found in Scotland which is succeeded early in the next millennium by a group of species of much more southern aspect, many now extinct in Britain.

Throughout this period and up till Bronze Age time, deposits were being laid down at Church Stretton and Little Stretton. These contained rather nondescript faunas with nothing whose distribution was suggestive of increase or decrease in temperatures. A fauna described from the Late Bronze Age shaft at Wilsford, Wiltshire, and dated 3,330 ± 90 years b.p., however, contained an unequivocally warm fauna (Osborne 1969). Two very numerous members of this assemblage, *Onthophagus fracticornis* (Preyss.) and

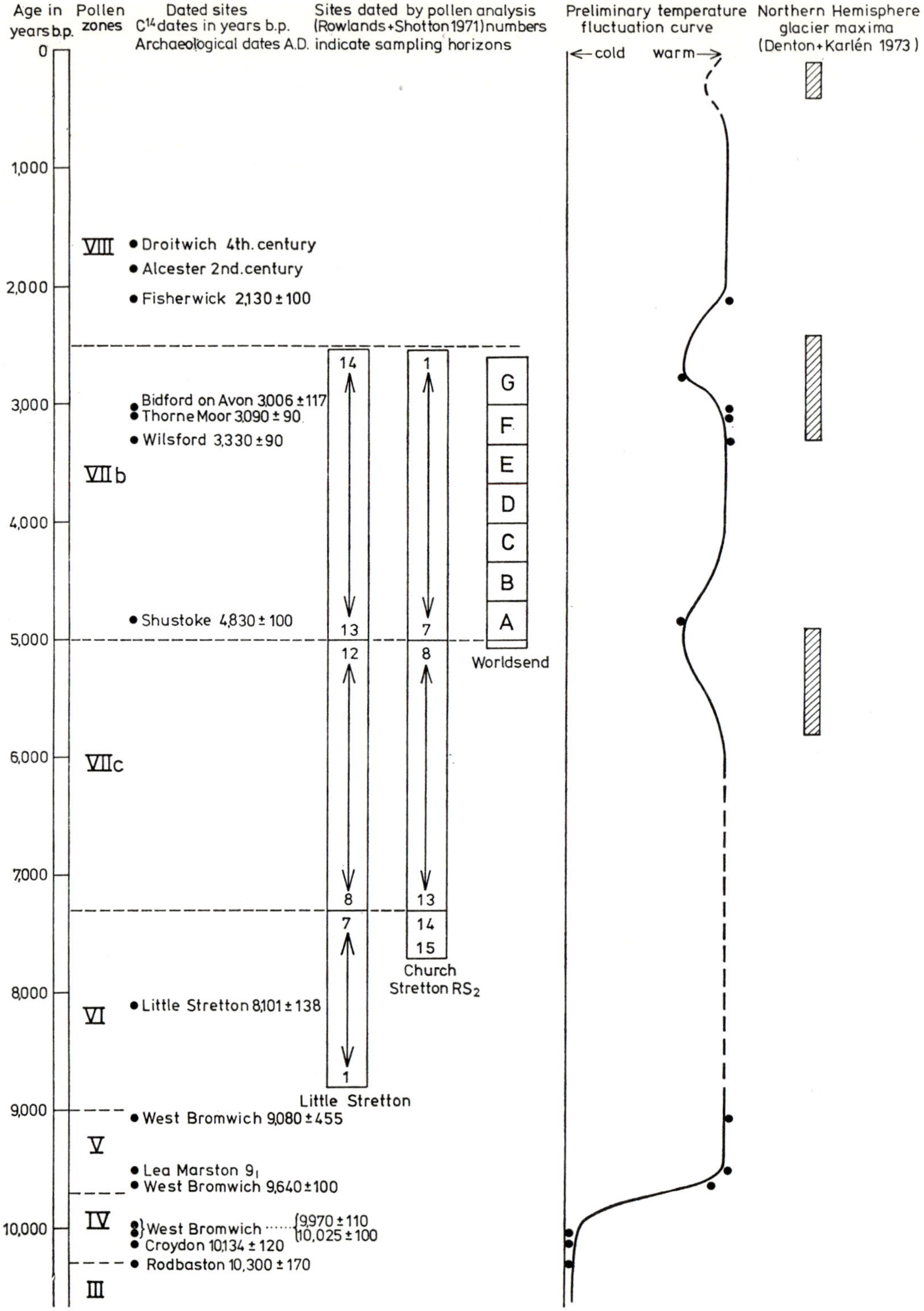

Figure 5 Climatic variation during the Flandrian period

O. nutans (F.), are probably extinct in Britain now, although both have been recorded here in the nineteenth century, *nutans* in some numbers in the south and *fracticornis* on the strength of less than a dozen examples, all lacking data. Amongst the very abundant dung beetles present was *Aphodius quadriguttatus* (Hbst.), a species which has never been on the modern British List but which is found in France and further south. The very abundance of members of the genus *Onthophagus* is suggestive of summer temperatures higher than those of Wiltshire today, and in this instance the activities of the agriculturalists in cutting down the forest can hardly be blamed for the diminution in this genus, as all its members are inhabitants of the dung of such large herbivorous mammals as cattle, horses and sheep. These beetles, one would think, would be encouraged by forest clearance rather than the reverse.

A rather similar fauna to that from Wilsford, though lacking some of the more exotic elements, has been recovered from a deposit dated $3{,}006 \pm 117$ years b.p. at Bidford on Avon, Warwickshire (Osborne, in prep.)

Yet another site in the Church Stretton area, at Worldsend (Osborne 1972) had provided only very scanty faunas from deposits of this time, i.e. between 4,000 and 3,000 years b.p., but the top two of the seven sampling horizons showed a sudden increase in insect content. The beetles here were dominated by woodland forms but, although deciduous trees were represented, a much greater proportion of the fauna was attached to coniferous woodland than in the earlier sites examined. The most notable species found was *Agabus wasastjernae* Sahlb., a water beetle which is no longer British but is now a much more northern insect. Its habitat is acid pools in coniferous forest in Scandinavia and North America. The woodborer *Hylastes brunneus* Er. lives on *Pinus* (Pine) and is exclusively northern in Britain today, whilst *Eremotes ater* (L.) and *E. elongatus* (Gyll.), though not restricted to the north, are predominantly high ground species further south on the continent. A number of beetles were found which have now retreated southwards and are extinct in Britain. These include *Porthmidius austriacus* Sch. and *Eremotes strangulatus* Perris and, from a nearby site of the same age, *Pycnomerus terebrans* Ol. All are associated with the dead wood habitat so that it is debatable whether their disappearance is attributable to forest clearance by man or to a climatic deterioration or to a combination of these factors. The whole of the Worldsend section was assigned to pollen zone VIIb by Rowlands and Shotton (1971). Provided that the deposition rate was not wildly inconstant, these two samples from the top of the deposit must have been laid down near the end of the zone. If this is so, then the Worldsend section was coming to an end just at the start of another period of glacier expansion postulated by Denton and Karlén (1973).

It is suggested, therefore, that towards the close of pollen zone VIIb a period of lowered temperatures occurred which was cold enough to bring to the midlands a fauna previously living in the north of Britain. It is also of interest to note that organic deposition at this site was terminated by a flood of angular gravel very similar to the frost shattered gravels which cut off organic deposition in pollen zone III in this area. Possibly temperatures at the altitude of the top of the Long Mynd (*c.* 550 m.) were low enough to cause shattering of exposed rocks.

This cold spell may well have been responsible, at least in part, for the extermination of many of the woodland species which are now only found further south on the continent but which survived in Britain in places at least as late as 3,090 ± 90 years b.p., the radiocarbon age of a deposit at Thorne Moor, Yorkshire (Buckland and Kenward 1973). The extensive fauna recorded from this site consisted mostly of forest dwelling insects, many well north of their present-day ranges and a large proportion now extinct in Britain. This latter group includes such species as *Rhysodes sulcatus*, already recorded from the earlier deposit at Shustoke (see above), and *Prostomis mandibularis* (F.), another inhabitant of rotting wood, both of which have much more southern distributions today. Also recorded, however, were *Zimioma grossa* (L.) and *Mycetina cruciata* Schall., both again inhabitants of rotten wood but having European ranges which Buckland and Kenward describe as boreo-montane. It is noteworthy perhaps that these authors provisionally ascribe the birch log from which *Zimioma* was taken to the Early Iron Age, rather later than the majority of the fauna and probably into the cool period tentatively suggested above.

A late Iron Age site at Fisherwick, Staffordshire, has provided a small beetle fauna quite lacking species indicative of cold conditions (Osborne, unpub.). In fact a record of *Heptaulacus* testudinarius (F.) well north of its modern British range suggests a degree of warmth at least equal to that of today. The radiocarbon age of this material, 2,130 ± 100 years b.p. is later by some 200 years than the end of Denton and Karlén's glacial advance, so it is reasonable to suppose that once again the climate had ameliorated.

Of the many beetles identified from Roman and Saxon sites few show much deviation from their present-day distributions. Most notable are *Hesperophanes fasciculatus* Fald. from the second-century Roman site at Alcester, Warwickshire (Osborne 1971b), and *Airaphilus elongatus* (Gyll.) recovered from the fourth-century well at Droitwich, Worcestershire (Osborne 1973), neither of which are found in this country today. The presence of the cerambycid *Hesperophanes* is readily explained, as the larvae of many members of this family are woodborers which sometimes take a number of years to complete their development. Consequently exotic species are often imported into this country in articles made from larva-infested wood, the adults making their appearance in due course. It is suggested that this was the case with the Alcester *Hesperophanes*.

The problem of the other species, *Airaphilus elongatus*, is not such a simple one. This insect was a common constituent of British faunas from zone II of the Late-glacial but so far there are no records of its return after zone III. To say that it has not been found, however, is not to prove that it did not exist here during the Flandrian, and it seems most probable that it did. If indeed *Airaphilus* managed to survive the vicissitudes of the latter half of the Post-glacial there should be some good reason for its apparent absence today. It may be that it is still waiting to be found by modern entomologists, a not unprecedented situation. For instance, *Ernoporus caucasicus* is now known from a number of Flandrian sites but was only recorded as living in Britain in very recent years (Allen 1970), whilst the aquatic beetle *Stenelmis canaliculatus* Gyll. was here at Bidford on Avon and other sites over 3,000 years ago but has escaped the notice of modern entomologists until recorded by Claridge and Staddon in Lake Windermere (Claridge and Staddon 1961). If we take the evidence at face value, however, and assume that, as *Airaphilus* has not been taken it does not exist in Britain, then it must have been removed by the last episode of glacial advance of Denton and Karlén, the so-called 'Little Ice Age'. It is unfortunate that so well documented an event as this cold period of *c.* 200 years ago has not been correlated as yet with accurately identified and dated insect faunas, to establish just what its effects were. It is to be hoped that this situation will be remedied in the near future.

A diagram showing the chronology of these events and the sites from which these preliminary results are derived is shown in fig. 5. Also included is a tentative first attempt at a Flandrian temperature curve from the beetle evidence. This curve is not presented as a finished article but as a starting point, either as an Aunt Sally which other investigators may knock down to clarify their own ideas or as a skeleton on which to hang the flesh of their own results.

26.iii.1976

Department of Geological Sciences
University of Birmingham

References

Allen, A. A. 1970. *Ernoporus caucasicus* Lind. and *Leperesinus orni* Fuchs (Col., Scolytidae) in Britain. *Entomologist's Monthly Magazine.* 105:245–9.

Ashworth, A. C. 1973. The climatic significance of a Late Quaternary insect fauna from Rodbaston Hall, Staffordshire, England. *Entomologica Scandinavica.* 4(3).

Buckland, P. C. and Kenward, H. K. 1973. Thorne Moor: A palaeo-ecological study of a Bronze Age site. *Nature.* 241, no. 5389:405–6.

Claridge, M. F. and Staddon, B. W. 1961. *Stenelmis canaliculata* Gyll. (Col., Elmidae), a species new to the British List. *Entomologist's Monthly Magazine.* 96:141–4.

Coope, G. R. 1968. An insect fauna from Mid-Weichselian deposits at Brandon, Warwickshire. *Philosophical Transactions of the Royal Society.* ser. B 254, no. 796:425–56.

Coope, G. R. and Brophy, J. A. 1972. Late Glacial environmental changes indicated by a coleopteran succession from North Wales. *Boreas.* 1(2):97–142.

Denton, G. H. and Karlén, W. 1973. Holocene climatic variations – their pattern and possible cause. *Quaternary Research.* 3(2):155–205.

Kelly, M. R. and Osborne, P. J. 1964. Two faunas and floras from the alluvium at Shustoke, Warwickshire. *Proceedings of the Linnaean Society of London.* 176:37–65.

Morgan, A. 1973. Late Pleistocene environmental changes indicated by fossil insect faunas of the English Midlands. *Boreas.* 2(4):173–212.

Osborne, P. J. 1969. An insect fauna of Late Bronze Age date from Wilsford, Wiltshire. *Journal of Animal Ecology.* 38:555–66.

Osborne, P. J. 1971a. The insect faunas of the organic deposits within the Wandle Gravels. *Proceedings of the Croydon Natural History and Scientific Society.* 14(7):162–75.

Osborne, P. J. 1971b. An insect fauna from the Roman site at Alcester, Warwickshire. *Brittania.* 2:156–65.

Osborne, P. J. 1972. Insect faunas of Late Devensian and Flandrian age from Church Stretton, Shropshire. *Philosophical Transactions of the Royal Society.* ser. B, 263, no. 852:327–67.

Osborne, P. J. 1973. *Airaphilus elongatus* (Gyll.) (Col., Cucujidae), present in Britain in Roman Times. *Entomologist's Monthly Magazine.* 109.

Osborne, P. J. 1974. An insect assemblage of Early Flandrian Age from Lea Marston, Warwickshire, and its bearing on the contemporary climate and ecology. *Quaternary Research.* 4:471–86.

Osborne, P. J. and Shotton, F. W. 1968. The fauna of the Channel Deposit of Early Saalian age at Brandon, Warwickshire. *Philosophical Transactions of the Royal Society.* ser. B, 796, no. 254:417–24.

Rowlands, P. H. and Shotton, F. W. 1971. Pleistocene deposits of Church Stretton, Shropshire and its neighbourhood. *Journal of the Geological Society.* 127:599–622.

Shotton, F. W. and Osborne, P. J. 1965. The fauna of the Hoxnian Deposits of Nechells, Birmingham. *Philosophical Transactions of the Royal Society.* ser. B, 248, no. 750:353–78.

Abstract

Osborne, P. J.

Evidence from the insects of climatic variation during the Flandrian period: a preliminary note

Studies over the last twenty years have demonstrated the value of fossil beetles as climatic indicators. Though entomological research on the Flandrian is still in its infancy, it is becoming possible to discern hints that, after the close of the Devensian, the thermal environment of Britain did not follow a smooth curve upwards for 5,000 years to the 'climatic optimum' and then slowly decline. Evidence is given for a rapid climatic amelioration over a very short time. The generally temperate climate prevailing thereafter appears to have been marred by intervals of considerably reduced temperatures. The times when these intervals are perceptible in the contemporary insect faunas match broadly with the times when, according to Denton and Karlén (1973), the glaciers of the northern hemisphere advanced well beyond their present-day limits.

Crops and climate in prehistoric Europe

R. N. L. B. Hubbard

It can be argued that the most important aspect of the archaeology of the Holocene period is the development of food-producing societies. For convenience we may divide their subsistence basis into three components: agriculture, stock-breeding, and manufacture, each being sensitive to climatic factors in differing degrees. In so far as the larger and better organized the society, the more capable it will be of surviving economic misfortune, one must assume that the economy would have been increasingly sensitive to climate in earlier periods. Of the three components, agriculture is the most affected by climate, as world trade still shows: unlike plants, animals are capable of moving their pastures and modifying their diet so as to accommodate short-term climatic fluctuations. Over thirty years' research has accumulated a mass of reliable information about prehistoric European and Near Eastern cultivated plants, which can be roughly quantified by presence-analysis (Hubbard 1975). Examination of the trans-continental archaeobotanical record thus created should allow us to detect the effects of climate and climatic changes upon European agriculture.

When considering what evidence we have of climatic change, it must be remembered that, although palaeoclimatic records are often interpreted in terms of temperature, other extremely important factors include the precipitation and evaporation of water, which are in turn influenced by tree-cover etc. We would appear to have a convenient botanical indicator in the numerous more-or-less continuous records from pollen-analysis all over Europe. The climatic interpretation of pollen-diagrams, however, has largely been based on the interrelationships of the woody types, and the lifetimes of even the short-lived colonist genera such as birch are to be measured in decades. Only in ivy, mistletoe, and holly (all of which are severely under-represented in peat and lake pollen-diagrams) has flowering been shown to be climatically controlled (Iversen 1944). Accordingly, at best an arboreal pollen-diagram only records climatic trends sustained over decades or centuries. The record from such analyses is, however, in reasonable accord with that from examination of sea-levels and O^{16}/O^{18} isotope records. Short-term climatic fluctuations presumably occurred, but they would only be recorded palynologically by a common annual plant, whose seeds and pollen were dispersed by wind, whose reproduction was climatically controlled, and whose pollen was identifiable specifically. Unfortunately, we know of no such plant in Europe.

Flying insects resemble this hypothetical plant in being capable of rapid movement, and in having distributions not infrequently linked to air-temperatures: in contrast, mammals, while capable of equally rapid movement, are rarely highly specific in their diet, and have a physiology that allows them a considerable degree of climatic tolerance. Insectiferous deposits are frustratingly rare, but enough work has been done to raise some doubts about the validity of the conventional picture of Holocene climate. The topic is discussed elsewhere in this volume by Osborne, and it suffices to say that at Lea Marston (Osborne 1974) he has found an insect fauna that appears to reflect temperatures higher than those of the present day, but associated with 'cold' Boreal pollen-spectra dominated by birch, willow, pine, grass and nettle, appropriate to the C^{14} dates of 9600–9200 b.p. Similarly, he has postulated the occurrence of cold-climate episodes at around 5000 b.p., and between 3000 b.p. and the present day. The divergence between the insect-based 'temperatures' and the palynological 'climate' presumably largely reflects the different rates of colonization and migration from their glacial refugia of flying insects and the thermophilous trees respectively; while the differences between the O^{16}/O^{18} isotope temperatures and those suggested by the insects reflect the time taken for ice-caps to melt and the melt-waters to mix in the oceans. Pisias *et al.* (1975) have shown that the changes in rates of silica and calcium carbonate accumulation in deep-sea cores *precede* the associated changes in O^{16}/O^{18} ratios by about 3,000 years and over 5,000 years respectively. It is possible that the insect record is over-sensitive to short-term climatic events ('weather') in comparison with the slower fundamental trends, but the air-temperatures that can be deduced from insect distributions, while important when considering human activities, are not the only factor controlling the growth of an annual crop like a cereal or pulse: rainfall is also extremely important. Dendroclimatology is producing evidence indicating localized climatic variations (e.g. Fritts 1971); but in the meanwhile the only directly relevant and abundant information in the Old World seems to be the remains of the crops themselves. Use of the crop-remains introduces further complications, since agricultural selection has produced cultivars (as in maize and soya-bean) that have unnatural climatic, photoperiodic or ecological requirements; and an over-simplified climatic interpretation might mistake the effects of irrigation for a pluvial effect. None the less, at the risk of a circular argument, could the archaeobotanical record support interpretation in climatic terms?

Before proceeding, it is necessary to describe briefly the method used to quantify the palaeo-ethnobotanical data. The numerical composition of samples of carbonized seeds and charcoal is largely accidental and usually meaningless (Hubbard 1976). Such material can be analysed quantitatively by expressing the abundance of a taxon as the proportion of the samples from the chronological or cultural group under examination in which that taxon occurs. Thus presence-values can range from 0% (absent from all samples) to 100% when ubiquitous. This method was applied by Godwin (1956) to cereal remains, and independently re-invented by Willcox (1974) for charcoal analysis. It should be noted that, as the values are not interdependent, the sum of the presences need not be 100%; and, if one assumes that a constant proportion of samples is for some reason misrepresentative or unreliable, the accuracy of the figures will not be improved by increasing the sample sum. Of course the *reliability* of the assessment of abundance will be related to the sample sum and to the richness of the samples. Equally, a taxon whose 'real' presence is 10% cannot be properly assessed with less than 10 samples. Once dubious identifications have been rejected, only two criteria need to be satisfied by samples to be used in presence-analysis: (1) the samples must be independent, and (2) they must contain more than one taxon. The first criterion poses certain archaeological problems. Samples from a pit probably cannot be treated separately, and samples from destruction levels must be treated with the greatest caution. Thus fifty-six seed samples from squares N11 and N12 at Korucutepe (van Zeist and Bakker-Heeres 1975) have been excluded from the analyses that follow because it is very unlikely that they are independent.

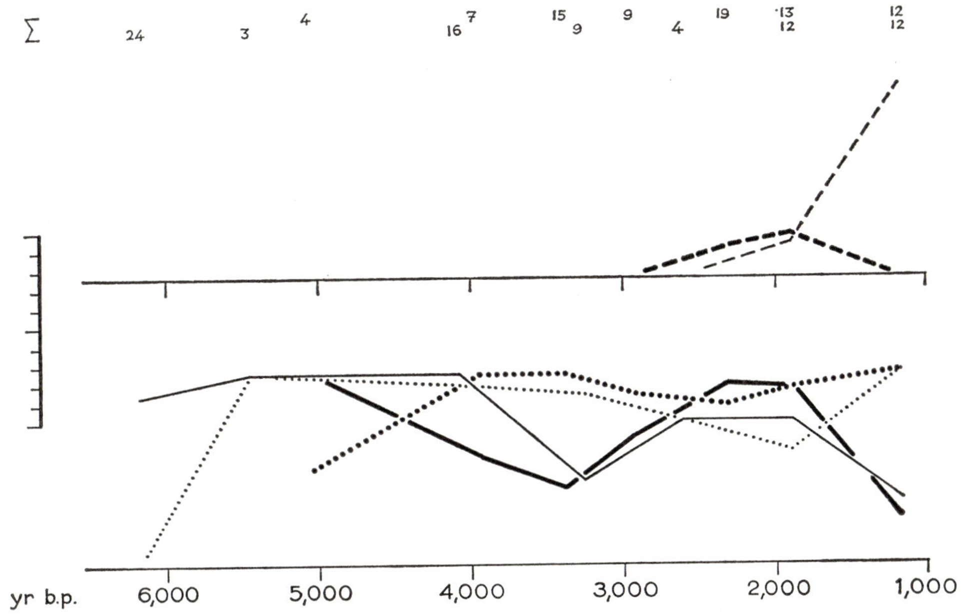

Figure 6 Presence-diagram for the occurrences of rye, wheats and barleys in Britain and NW. Europe.
Key: light curves – carbonized seeds from Holland and NW. Germany; heavy curves – pottery impressions and carbonized seeds from Britain.
Continuous lines – wheat species; dotted lines – barley species; broken lines – rye.
Upper superscript numbers: sample numbers for Britain.
Lower superscript numbers: sample numbers for continental data.
Vertical scale = 100% presence

Some of the pioneering work on climatic interpretation of archaeobotanical data was done by Godwin (1956: 264). The researches of Helbaek and Jessen (1944, 1953) had established that wheat appeared to be rarer in comparison with barley during the Bronze Age in Britain than in preceding or subsequent periods: Godwin quantified their findings by presence-analysis, and tentatively correlated the effect with the drier climate suggested by the Flandrian VIIb pollen-zone. Fig. 6 shows presence-curves for rye, and for the combined wheat and barley species and sub-species, comparing information from Britain (heavy curves) with that from Holland and NW. Germany. The calculations are on a site-by-site basis where a sample-by-sample treatment is not justifiable. The British data are from Helbaek and Jessen augmented by medieval finds from York (Buckland *et al.* 1974) and Ewen (Hubbard, unpublished), and the other sources are

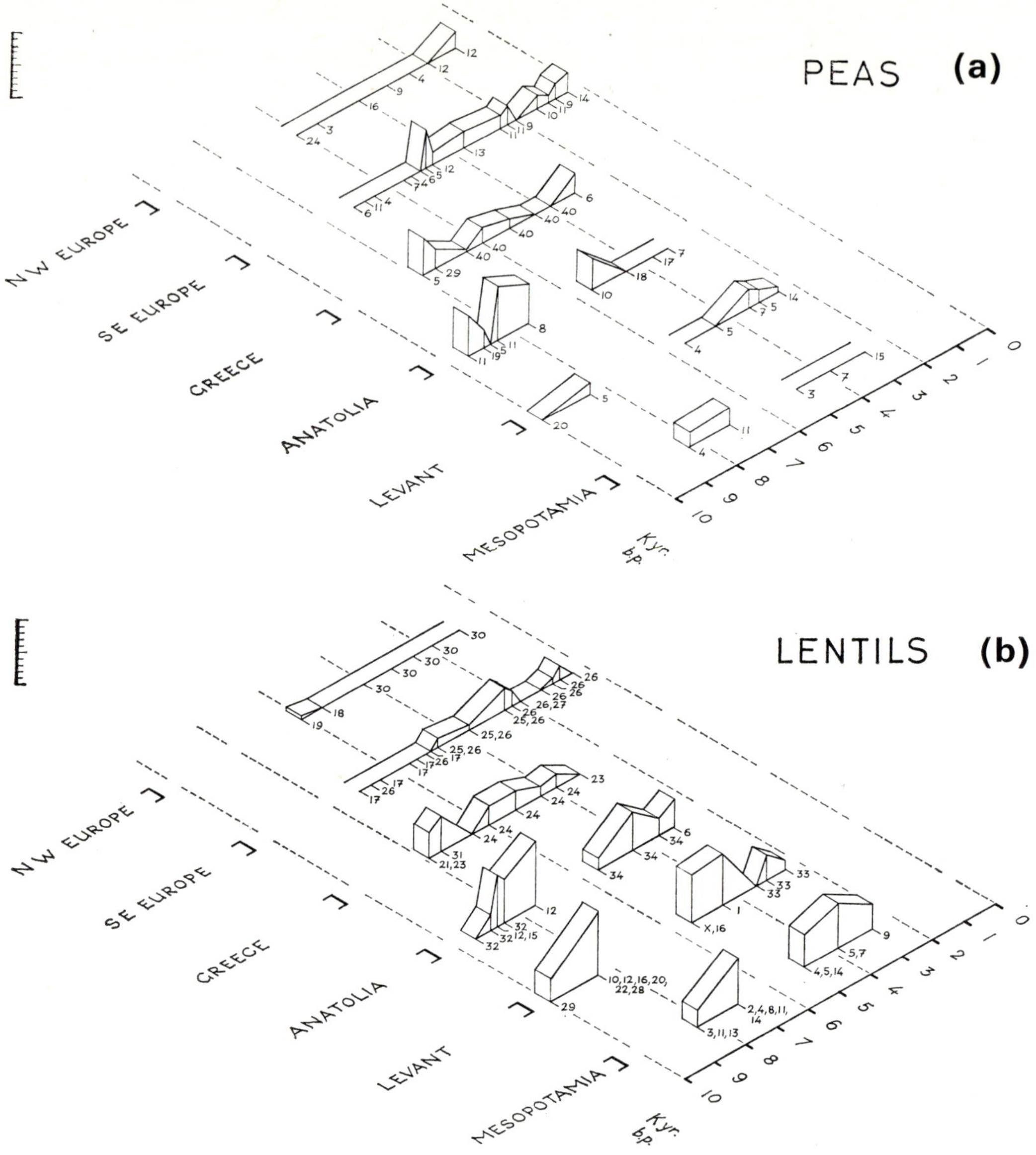

Figure 7 Block-diagrams showing the presence-values for peas (a) and lentils (b) in prehistoric Europe and the Near East.
In the pea diagram, subscript numbers give the number of samples on which the figures are calculated. In the lentil diagram, subscript numbers give references (see bibliography; X = Hubbard, unpublished).
Vertical scale = 100% presence

shown in the bibliographic annotations to fig. 7*b*. In comparing the two sets of curves, one must remember that while the continental data are all based upon carbonized remains of the crops themselves, the British record, with the exception of the Iron Age and Roman period, is almost exclusively founded upon plant impressions in pottery. It should also be noted that the curves for British cultivated plants differ from those published by Godwin, because the curves in fig. 6 are based on sites or samples yielding more then one identification. This has caused little change to the shape of the curves, but has considerably improved the correlation between the wheat curves.

The virtual or complete absence of barley seems to be a feature common to Linienbandkeramik cultures from Germany to Russia, and is in complete contrast to the earlier and contemporary cultures in the Balkan and Mediterranean regions, or to subsequent central European cultures. The correspondence between the wheat curves leaves little reason to doubt that wheats were less common in comparison with barley during the Bronze Age and Medieval periods than was the case in Neolithic, Iron Age or Roman times. The phenomenon that Godwin interpreted in climatic terms can thus be observed on both sides of the English Channel, as is essential if a climatic explanation is to be tenable; but it does not prove that such an interpretation is necessarily correct. Even if we ascribe some of the divergences between the curves in fig. 6 to misrepresentation in the record yielded by pottery impressions, the divergence between the British and continental curves for rye can hardly be attributed to the same cause. Rye has not yet been reported from early Medieval Britain, even from the four samples of carbonized seeds considered, yet appears in every Dutch sample. The dichotomy seems too drastic to be purely accidental, and it is improbable that it could be attributed entirely to climate or environmental differences. If this difference is to be ascribed to cultural factors, as presumably must be the explanation of the rarity of barley in the Bandkeramik cultures, why should not the same explanation be equally applied to the Bronze Age and Medieval wheat declines?

Examination of the trans-European archaeobotanical record by means of three-dimensional presence-diagrams might show climatic events as synchronous anomalies spanning the entire continent. Helbaek has proposed (1970: 222) that the mutations causing fertility of the lateral florets in barley, creating the six-row 'species' from the two-row *Hordeum spontaneum*, coincided with the first use of irrigation. In so far as two-row barley was largely restricted to the hotter and drier parts of the Near East in prehistoric times, while the six-row varieties were of much less importance in the two-row barley areas and were apparently the only kinds grown in prehistoric Europe, the barleys could be considered to be climatic indicators of a sort: however, the overlap between the two groups is too restricted to be easily interpreted at present and, in any case, it seems doubtful whether the distributions of the different varieties were climatically controlled.

In the process of attempting a general examination of prehistoric European and Near Eastern agriculture (Hubbard, in preparation), it transpired that the only two crops whose distribution and abundance in prehistoric times suggested climatic control were peas and lentils. The natural distributions of what are believed to be the wild ancestors of *Pisum sativum* L. and *Lens culinare* Medic. (*P. sativum* ssp. *elatius* (Bieb.) Aschers. and Graebn. and *Lens orientalis* (Boiss.) Hand.-Mazz. respectively) overlap considerably; but while the variety *pumilio* Meikle (=*P. humile* Boiss. and Noë) of *P. sativum elatius*, like *L. orientalis*, is distributed over the wetter higher altitudes in Anatolia and the Near East that were originally forested, the *elatius* variety of pea has a distribution spreading well into the north central Mediterranean (Ben-Zeev and Zohary 1973; Davis 1970; Townsend and Guest 1974; Tutin *et al.* 1968; Zohary 1972; Zohary and

Hopf 1973). Figs 7*a* and *b* are three-dimensional diagrams illustrating the presences of the wild and domestic peas and lentils respectively. It will be observed that in the Near East lentils are abundant and ubiquitous, while peas are comparatively rare or absent. The European record is more confused, since peas only became established in NW. Europe in Medieval times, possibly in the form of a more climatically tolerant cultivar. Lentils never seem to have become established in NW. Europe, and the distributions in fig. 7*b* support Helbaek's suggestion (1964a) that lentils found in Romano-British sites were imported. Combining the data from contemporary wild and feral distributions, from the ancient distributions, and from the requirements of the two genera under modern cultivation (Martin and Leonard 1967), it seems that the European distribution of lentil was controlled by the high summer temperatures of a continental climate, and the Asiatic distribution of peas by moisture in the summer months. The limits of lentil cultivation in prehistoric times seem to have been somewhere in central Europe. Our information for the other pulses is very incomplete, but the limits for bitter vetch (*Vicia ervilia*) seem to have been in SE. Europe.

Precise location of these limits is of some importance since, as Behre (1967) has pointed out, when reporting the occurrence of the Friesland and Piottino oscillations (subzones IVa and b) in NW. European pollen-diagrams, slight climatic oscillations will be most easily detected near ecological boundaries. Assuming that the prehistoric distributions of peas and lentils were subject to the climatic controls suggested, figs 7*a* and *b* show no sign that climatic changes exercised an important influence on prehistoric European agriculture. Although the eastern European abundances of lentil show fluctuations, it would be highly premature to interpret these as indicating variations in continentality of climate, particularly since they do not appear to be paralleled elsewhere. It seems possible, however, that the decline in importance of peas during the late Neolithic and early Bronze Age in Anatolia at Korucutepe and Tepecik may be correlated with a lowering of the water-table caused by forest clearance by man, for Turner and Greig (1975) have shown that in Greece deforestation has caused increased run-off from Late Neolithic times. However, the investigations of van Zeist *et al.* (1975) in south-west Turkey found no signs of large-scale forest clearance earlier than 3500 b.p.

Presence-diagrams for einkorn and emmer show an approximately synchronous decline in most parts of Europe in the later Neolithic and Bronze Age periods. Fig. 8 illustrates this interesting phenomenon, whose overall appearance strongly suggests rather severe climatic change, as exhibited by einkorn. Such an interpretation is inconsistent with the interpretation placed upon the behaviour of peas and lentils, and it fails to explain the contrasting pattern in the Near East, where emmer continues unimpaired as one of the three most important crop plants, until displaced by bread wheats in the Iron Age. A similar effect could have been caused by environmental degradation accompanying human agricultural activities but, as in the case of a climatic interpretation, it seems extremely improbable that such influences should have a less severe effect on the fragile ecological balances of the Near East than in temperate Europe. Genetic impoverishment associated with the successive sowing of a small proportion of the entire harvest in areas outside the natural range of the wild relative, where genetic replenishment through introgression could not take place, might cause a similar steady decline in productivity; but this once again fails to explain the contrasting behaviour of einkorn

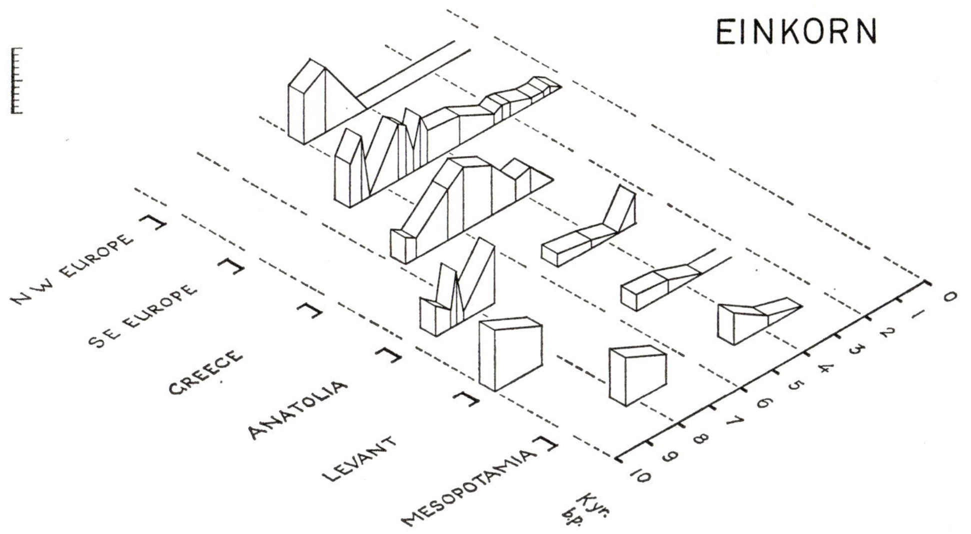

Figure 8 Block-diagram showing the history of einkorn cultivation through presence-analysis. Vertical scale = 100% presence

and emmer in the Near East, and also fails to explain why other European crop-plants of Near Eastern origin were not similarly affected. Other solutions to the enigma must be sought.

From the cases that have been examined, it seems clear that, although prehistoric agriculture must have been affected by climate and environment, in Europe at least other controls were more important – in particular, cultural preference. If this deduction is correct for prehistoric agriculture, then it seems likely that it will prove equally true of prehistoric animal husbandry. Accordingly, interpretation of prehistoric food production in local terms would appear to be futile until we understand the other more important perturbing influences better. The only exceptions to this are to be expected where environmental differences are gross, such as when comparing interglacial with glacial economies, lowlands with alpine areas, or when considering regions where man's activities have caused chronic ecological change, or those regions in which the boundary of a natural distribution is believed to lie.

Acknowledgements

I am grateful to G. W. Dimbleby, W. M. Bray and M. A.-T. Barnes for their many helpful criticisms of this paper.

1.iv.1976

Institute of Archaeology
University of London

References

(Numbers refer to annotations in fig. 7*b*)

Behre, K.-E. 1967. The late glacial and early postglacial history of vegetation and climate in North Western Germany. *Review of Palaeobotany and Palynology*. 4:149–61.

Ben-Zeev, N. and Zohary, D. 1973. Species relationship in the genus *Pisum* L. *Israel Journal of Botany*. 22:73–91.

Buckland, P. C., Greig, J. R. A. and Kenward, H. K. 1974. York: an Early Mediaeval site. *Antiquity*. 48:25–33.

Davis, P. H. (ed.) 1970. *Flora of Turkey and the Eastern Aegean Islands*, vol. 3. Edinburgh University Press.

Fritts, H. C. 1971. Dendrochronology and Dendroecology. *Quaternary Research*. 1:419–49.

Godwin, H. 1956. *The History of the British Flora*. Cambridge University Press.

Helbaek, H. 1953. Early crops in southern Britain. *Proceedings of the Prehistoric Society*. 18:194–233.

1 Helbaek, H. 1958. Plant economy in ancient Lachish. In O. Tufnell, *Lachish*, vol. 4:309–17. Oxford University Press.

2 Helbaek, H. 1959. The domestication of food plants in the Old World. *Science*. 130:365–72.

3 Helbaek, H. 1960. The palaeoethnobotany of the Near East and Europe. In R. J. Braidwood and B. Howe, Prehistoric investigations in Iraqi Kurdistan: 99–118. *Studies in Ancient Oriental Civilisation*, 31. University of Chicago Press.

4 Helbaek, H. 1960. Ecological effects of irrigation in ancient Mesopotamia. *Iraq*. 22:186–96.

5 Helbaek, H. 1960. Ancient crops in the Shahzoor Valley in Iraqi Kurdistan. *Sumer*. 16:79–81.

6 Helbaek, H. 1961. Late Bronze Age and Byzantine crops at Beycesultan in Anatolia. *Anatolian Studies*. 11:77–97.

7 Helbaek, H. 1963. Isin-Larsan and Horian food remains at Tell Bazmosian in the Dokan Valley. *Sumer*. 19:27–35.

8 Helbaek, H. 1964. Early Hassunan vegetable food at es-Sawwan near Samarra. *Sumer*. 20:45–8.

Helbaek, H. 1964a. The Isca grain Roman plant introduction in Britain. *New Phytologist*. 63:158–64.

9 Helbaek, H. 1966. The plant remains from Nimrud. In M. E. L. Mallowan, *Nimrud and its Remains*, vol. 2:613–20. Collins, London.

10 Helbaek, H. 1966. Pre-pottery Neolithic farming at Beidha. *Palestine Exploration Quarterly*. 98:61–6.

11 Helbaek, H. 1969. Plant collecting, dry farming, and irrigation in prehistoric Deh Luran. In F. Hole, K. V. Flannery and J. A. Neely, Prehistory and human ecology of the Deh Luran plain: 383–426. *Memoirs of the Museum of Anthropology, University of Michigan*, No. 1. Ann Arbor.

12 Helbaek, H. 1970. The plant husbandry of Hacılar. In J. Mellaart, *Excavations at Hacılar*, vol. 1:189–244. Edinburgh University Press.

13 Helbaek, H. 1972. Traces of plants in the early ceramic site of Umm Dabaghiyah. *Iraq*. 34:17–19.

14 Helbaek, H. 1972. Samarran irrigation agriculture at Choga Mami in Iraq. *Iraq*. 34:35–48.

15 Hillman, G. C. 1972. In D. H. French, Excavations at Can Hasan III, 1969–1970. *Papers in Economic Prehistory* (ed. E. S. Higgs): 181–90. Cambridge University Press.

16 Hopf, M. 1969. Plant remains and early farming in Jericho. *The Domestication and Exploitation of Plants and Animals* (eds P. J. Ucko and G. W. Dimbleby): 355–9. Gerald Duckworth and Co., London.

Hubbard, R. N. L. B. 1975. Assessing the botanical component of human palaeoeconomies. *Bulletin of the Institute of Archaeology, London.* 12:197–205.

Hubbard, R. N. L. B. 1976. On the strength of the evidence for prehistoric crop processing activities. *Journal of Archaeological Science* (in press).

Iversen, J. 1944. *Viscum, Hedera* and *Ilex* as climatic indicators. *Geologiska Föreningens i Stockholm Förhandlingar.* 66:463–83.

17 Janouchevitch, Z. V. and Markevitch, V. I. 1971. Éspèces des plantes cultivées des stations primitives au sud-ouest de l'U.R.S.S. *VIIIième Congrès International des Sciences préhistoriques et protohistoriques.* Belgrade.

Jessen, K. and Helbaek, H. 1944. Cereals in Great Britain and Ireland in prehistoric and early historic times. *Kongelige Danske Vetenskabernes Selskab, Biologiske Skrifter.* 3 (2).

18 Knörzer, K.-H. 1971. Pflanzliche Grossreste aus der rössenerzeitlichen Siedlung bei Langweiler, Kreis Jülich. *Bonner Jahrbuch.* 171:9–33.

19 Knörzer, K.-H. 1973. Pflanzliche Grossreste. In J. P. Farrugia, R. Kuper, J. Lüning and P. Stehlin, *Der Bandkeramischer Siedlungsplatz Langweiler.* 2:133–52. Rheinland Verlag, Bonn.

20 Legge, A. J. and Dennell, R. W. 1973. In T. Noy, A. J. Legge and E. S. Higgs. Recent excavations at Nahal Oren, Israel. *Proceedings of the Prehistoric Society.* 39:75–99.

Martin, J. H. and Leonard, W. H. 1967. *Principles of Field Crop Production.* Macmillan, New York and London.

21 Milojčić, V., Boessneck, J. and Hopf, M. 1962. Die Deutschen Ausgrabungen auf der Argissa-Magula in Thessalien, vol. 1. *Beiträge zur Ur- und Frühgeschichtlichen Archäologie des Mittelmeer-Kulturraumes* 2. Rudolf Habelt; Bonn.

22 Moore, A. M. T., Hillman, G. C. and Legge, A. J. 1975. The excavation of Tell Abu-Hureyra in Syria: A preliminary report. *Proceedings of the Prehistoric Society.* 41:50–77.

Osborne, P. J. 1974. An insect assemblage of Early Flandrian age from Lea Marston, Warwickshire, and its bearing on tbe contemporary climate and ecology. *Quaternary Research.* 4:471–86.

Pisias, W. G., Heath, G. R. and Moore, T. C. 1975. Lag times for oceanic responses to climatic change. *Nature.* 256:716–17.

23 Renfrew, J. M. 1966. A report on recent findes [*sic.*] of carbonised cereal grains and seeds from prehistoric Thessaly. *Thessalika.* 5:21–36.

24 Renfrew, J. M. 1972. In A. C. Renfrew, *The Emergence of Civilisation*: 276. Methuen, London.

25 Tempír, Z. 1964. Beiträge zur ältesten Geschichte des Pflanzenbaus in Ungarn. *Acta Archaeologica Academiae Scientarum Hungaricae.* 16:65–98.

26 Tempír, Z. 1966. Výsledky paleoetnobotanického studia pěstování zemědělských rostlin na území Č.S.S.R. (Results of paleo-ethnobotanical studies on the cultivation of agricultural plants in the Č.S.S.R. *Védecké Práce Československého Zemědělského Muzea.* 27–144.

Townsend, C. C. and Guest, E. 1974. *Flora of Iraq*, vol. 3: Leguminales. Ministry of Agriculture and Agrarian Reform, Baghdad.

Turner, J. and Grieg, J. R. A. 1975. Some Holocene pollen diagrams from Greece. *Review of Palaeobotany and Palynology*. 20:171–204.

Tutin, T. G. *et al.* (eds) 1968. *Flora Europaea*, vol. 2: Rosaceae – Umbelliferae. Cambridge Unviersity Press.

Willcox, G. H. 1974. A history of deforestation as indicated by charcoal analysis of four sites in Eastern Anatolia. *Anatolian Studies*. 24:117–33.

27 Yarwood, S. M. 1975. *A Palaeoethnobotanical study of carbonised seed material from Rumania*. Unpublished M.Sc. thesis, University of Birmingham.

28 van Zeist, W. and Bottema, S. 1966. Palaeobotanical investigations at Tell Ramad. *Annales Archaeologiques Arabes Syriennes*. 16:179–80.

29 van Zeist, W. 1970. The Oriental Institute excavations at Mureybit, Syria: Preliminary report on the 1965 campaign; Part III: The Palaeobotany. *Journal of Near Eastern Studies*. 29:167–76.

30 van Zeist, W. 1970. Prehistoric and early historic food plants in the Netherlands. *Palaeohistoria*. 14:41–173.

31 van Zeist, W. and Bottema, S. 1971. Plant husbandry in Early Neolithic Nea Nikomedeia, Greece. *Acta Botanica Neerlandica*. 20:524–38.

32 van Zeist, W. 1972. Palaeobotanical results of the 1970 season at Çayönü, Turkey. *Helinium*. 12:1–19.

33 van Zeist, W. and Heeres, J. A. H. 1973. Palaeobotanical studies of Deir 'Alla, Jordan. *Paléorient*. 1:21–37.

34 van Zeist, W. and Bakker-Heeres, J. A. H. 1975. Prehistoric and early historic plant husbandry in the Altınova Plain, southeastern Turkey. In *Korucutepe I* (ed. M. N. van Loon): 224–257. Oxford, Amsterdam.

van Zeist, W., Woldring, H. and Stapert, D. 1975. Late Quaternary vegetation and climate of southwestern Turkey. *Palaeohistoria*. 17:53–143.

Zohary, D. 1972. The wild progenitor and place of origin of the cultivated lentil: *Lens culinaris*. *Economic Botany*. 26:326–32.

Zohary, D., and Hopf, M. 1973. Domestication of Pulses in the Old World. *Science*. 182:887–94.

Abstract

Hubbard, R. N. L. B.

Crops and climate in prehistoric Europe

Selected areas of the European and Near Eastern archaeobotanical record are examined in the hope of elucidating the influences of climate, culture, and other factors on prehistoric agriculture. It is concluded that the long-term effects of climate or environment are usually of little importance in comparison with those of other perturbing influences.

Near Eastern alloying and some textual evidence for the early use of arsenical copper

E. R. Eaton and Hugh McKerrell

The primary purposes of carrying out chemical analyses on early copper alloys are (1) to attempt to relate metal compositions to ore deposits and (2) to establish the type of alloy involved. We are not concerned here with the first of these aims, since to reach objective general conclusions would require perhaps a ten- or twenty-fold increase in data. Instead, we wish to examine various aspects of the early phases of alloying, a subject of somewhat greater importance than that of metal provenance both to the ancient smith and, we believe, to the modern scholar also.

As well as bringing together the widely scattered literature (and carefully correlating the variable choices of elements analysed), this paper makes use of some two thousand new analyses obtained using our portable X-ray fluorescence system (McKerrell 1974). These latter data refer only to surface compositions but are well suited to the identification of alloy types; they afford, additionally, the advantage of detection of certain kinds of ancient surface coatings that extend considerably our knowledge of early metalworking techniques. All these results, both new and old, are to be fully published elsewhere (McKerrell 1976b) and are used here in summary only. Table 1 lists the areas and chronologies involved; tables 2 to 5 summarize the analytical data. For the present purposes we divide the analyses into the two periods, *c.* 3000 to 2200 B.C. and *c.* 2200 to 1600 B.C. corresponding to, for many areas, Early Bronze Age (EB) and Middle Bronze Age (MB) respectively. Exact chronological placement is not always possible and we follow, in general, the outlines of Ehrich *et al.* (1965). It should be noted that the considerable bulk of EB analyses from Crete, Mainland Greece and the Cyclades relate only to EB2; also that there are insufficient MB analyses for the latter two areas to warrant any sensible use of relevant data.

Near Eastern EB/MB alloying

Three main metals emerge: copper (more or less pure), as well as tin bronze and arsenical copper. Alloys with significant contents of lead, antimony and zinc are almost wholly absent. Both tin and arsenic bring about important deoxidizing and hardening properties in alloys with copper; whilst the exact levels at which tin and arsenic provide useful properties have been much debated, for the purpose of simply identifying a useful working metal, we suggest that tin contents above 5%, and arsenic in the 1 to

5% range, do unquestionably fall into such a category. For alloying purposes, then, these define our tin bronze and arsenical copper.

The primary feature of interest is the relative use of tin bronze and arsenical copper for the EB and the MB. In the earlier period the alloys vary markedly from one area to another, tin bronze for example being absent or scarcely represented in Egypt, Palestine, Crete and mainland Greece, but comprising about one-quarter of all the analysed metal from northern/western Iran, central Anatolia, the Troad and the Cyclades. Syrian and Mesopotamian metalworkers apparently used sound bronze at an intermediate proportion, about one-tenth of all analysed objects. A useful level of arsenic was, however, far more widespread, and for certain areas (Syria, NW. Iran, the Cyclades, Crete and mainland Greece) arsenical copper, as defined, was used for about two-thirds of all objects analysed. Only in the Troad was more use made of bronze rather than arsenical copper in this period.

For the MB period, tin bronze was in general more widely used, averaging perhaps one-quarter of the metal of most areas – though Minoan and Mesopotamian use is significantly less, at about half of this level. Arsenical copper is, however, still the more common alloy and again the Troad is the only exception to this generalization. Typically a quarter to a half of all artefacts were made of such metal. Fig. 9 illustrates both EB and MB data.

TABLE I

Near Eastern alloying from 3000–2200 B.C. and 2200–1600 B.C.
Areas involved

A	Egypt	Archaic – Old Kingdom	(Abydos, Tarkhan)
		1st–2nd Intermediates	(Bet Khallaf, Abydos, Hu, Kerma, Sidmant)
B	Palestine	EB	(Ajjul, Megiddo, Kfar Monash, Hesi)
		IE/MB-MB	(Gaza, Ajjul, Fara, Jericho, Lachish)
C	Syria	Amuq G–I/J	(Brak, Kara Hassan)
		Amuq I/J–L	(Serrin, Tayinat, Ras Shamra, Chagar Bazar)
D	Mesopotamia	ED1-Akkadian	(Ur, Ubaid, Taya, Ashar, Khafajah)
		Post-Akkad–Old Babylonian	(Kish, Sifr, Ur, Taya, Tepe Gawar, Ashar)
E	N. & W. Iran	*c.* 3000–2200 B.C.	(Luristan, Geoy Tepe)
		c. 2200–1600 B.C.	(Anau, Luristan, Shah Tepe, Geoy Tepe)
F	C. Anatolia	EB2–3A	(Polatli, Alaga, Alishar, Ahaltlibel, Kultepe)
		EB3B–MB	(Kultepe, Mahmatlar, Alishar, Horoztepe)
G	Troad	Troy 1–2	(Troy, Thermi, Karatas, Troad)
		Troy 3–6	(Troy, Troad, Karatas)
H	Cyclades	EC1–2	(Chalandriani, Kythnos, Amorgos)
		EC3–MB	
I	Crete	EM1–2	(Koumasa, Pyrgos, Ag. Triadha, Marathokephalon)
		EM3–MM	(Platance, Mochlos, Chamaizi, Kalathiana)
J	Greece	EH1–2	(Petralona, Eutresis)
		EH3–MH	
K	Etruria	Etruscan period	
L	Cyprus	LBA to Roman	

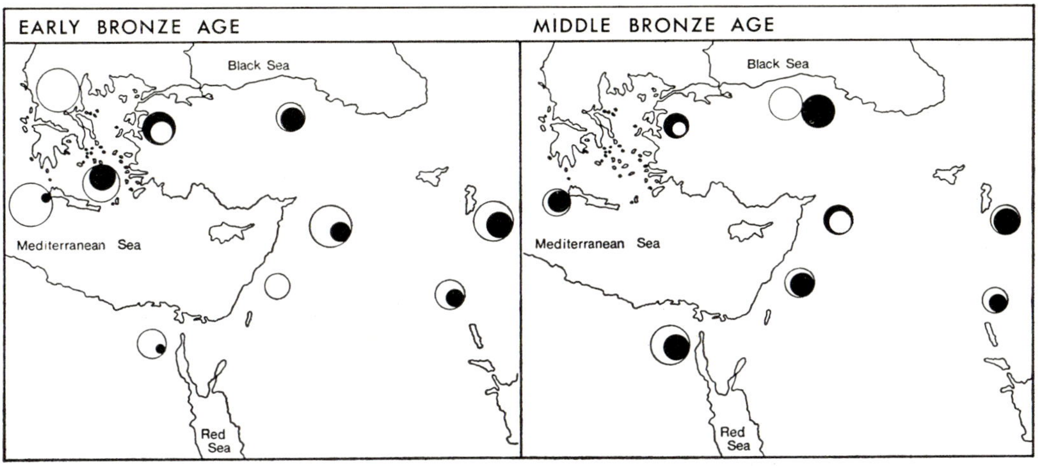

Figure 9 Early and Middle Bronze Age alloys in the Near East. Open circles represent arsenical copper, the closed circles tin bronze. Relative proportions correspond to circle areas

TABLE 2

c. 3000–2200 B.C. tin bronze data

ANALYTICAL TOTALS

Area*	A	B	C	D	E	F	G	H	I	J
Tin content										
Above 10%	1		1	9	4	3	3	3		
5–10%	3		2	6	5	24	19	7	1	
1–5%	2		2	16	8	7	5	5	10	
c. 0·5%	10	1	2	28	6	17	12	6	8	6
Below 0·1%	156	35	16	69	17	61	21	24	33	20
Totals	172	36	23	128	40	112	60	45	52	26

PERCENTAGE TOTALS

Area*	A	B	C	D	E	F	G	H	I	J
Tin content										
Above 10%	1		4	7	10	3	5	7		
5–10%	2		9	5	13	24	32	16	1	
1–5%	1		9	12	20	7	8	11	10	
c. 0·5%	6	3	9	22	15	17	20	13	8	23
Below 0·1%	91	97	70	54	43	61	35	53	33	77
Totals	100	100	100	100	100	100	100	100	100	100

ALLOYING SUMMARY. ALL ARTEFACTS. PERCENTAGE TOTALS

Area*	A	B	C	D	E	F	G	H	I	J
Tin Content										
Above 10%	1		4	7	10	3	5	7		
Above 5%	3		13	12	23	24	37	23	2	
Above 1%	4		22	24	43	31	45	34	21	
Below 1%	97	100	79	76	58	69	55	66	78	100
Below 0·1%	91	97	70	54	43	54	35	53	63	77

* A, Egypt B, Palestine C, Syria D, Mesopotamia E, NW. Iran F. C. Anatolia
G, Troad H, Cyclades I, Crete J, Greece

TABLE 3

c. 3000–2200 B.C. arsenical copper data

ANALYTICAL TOTALS

Area*	A	B	C	D	E	F	G	H	I	J
Arsenic content										
Above 10%	1									
5–10%	12							4		
1–5%	35	6	14	35	21	33	12	22	39	20
c. 0·5%	64	4	9	36	9	32	18	5	7	6
Below	60	15		40	6	42	30	11	6	
Totals	172	25	23	111	36	107	60	42	52	26

PERCENTAGE TOTALS

Area*	A	B	C	D	E	F	G	H	I	J
Arsenic content										
Above 10%	1									
5–10%	7							10		
1–5%	20	24	61	32	58	31	20	52	75	77
c. 0·5%	37	16	39	32	25	30	30	12	13	23
Below 0·1%	35	60		36	17	39	50	26	12	
Totals	100	100	100	100	100	100	100	100	100	100

ALLOYING SUMMARY. ALL ARTEFACTS. PERCENTAGE TOTALS

Area*	A	B	C	D	E	F	G	H	I	J
Arsenic content										
Above 10%	1									
Above 5%	8							10		
Above 1%	28	24	61	32	58	31	20	62	75	77
Below 1%	72	76	39	68	42	69	80	38	25	23
Below 0·1%	35	60		36	17	39	50	26	12	

* A, Egypt B, Palestine C, Syria D, Mesopotamia E, NW. Iran F, C. Anatolia
G, Troad H, Cyclades I, Crete J, Greece

TABLE 4

c. 2200–1600 B.C. tin bronze data

ANALYTICAL TOTALS

Area*	A	B	C	D	E	F	G	H	I	J
Tin content										
Above 10%	7	14	8	10	4	11				
5–10%	18	14	30	11	9	46	3	3	5	3
1–5%	10	18	18	15	8	15	4	1	5	2
c. 0·5%	22	19	16	22	8	12			7	
Below 0·1%	59	62	52	118	20	60	5	1	20	1
Totals	116	127	124	176	49	144	12	5	37	6

PERCENTAGE TOTALS

Area*	A	B	C	D	E	F	G	H	I	J
Tin content										
Above 10%	6	11	6	6	8	8				
5–10%	16	11	24	6	18	32	25		14	
1–5%	9	14	15	9	16	10	33		14	
c. 0·5%	19	15	13	13	16	8			19	
Below 0·1%	51	49	42	57	41	42	42		54	
Totals	100	100	100	100	100	100	100		100	

ALLOYING SUMMARY. ALL ARTEFACTS. PERCENTAGE TOTALS

Area*	A	B	C	D	E	F	G	H	I	J
Tin content										
Above 10%	6	11	6	6	8	8				
Above 5%	22	22	30	12	26	40	25		14	
Above 1%	31	35	45	21	42	50	58		28	
Below, 1%	70	64	55	70	57	50	42		73	
Below 0·1%	51	49	42	57	41	42	42		54	

* A, Egypt B, Palestine C, Syria D, Mesopotamia E, NW. Iran F, C. Anatolia G, Troad H, Cyclades I, Crete J, Greece

TABLE 5

c. 2200–1600 B.C. Arsenical copper data

ANALYTICAL TOTALS

Area*	A	B	C	D	E	F	G	H	I	J
Arsenic content										
Above 10%	2	1								
5–10%	13	6		3				1		
1–5%	35	31	29	33	13	56	1		18	
c. 0·5%	20	22	51	46	17	42	2	3	13	
Below 0·1%	22	60	44	90	15	37	9	1	2	1
Totals	92	120	124	172	45	135	12	5	33	1

PERCENTAGE TOTALS

Area*	A	B	C	D	E	F	G	H	I	J
Arsenic content										
Above 10%	2	1						—		—
5–10%	14	5		2				—		—
1–5%	38	26	23	19	29	41	8	—	55	—
c. 0·5%	22	18	41	27	38	31	17	—	39	—
Below 0·1%	24	50	35	52	33	27	75	—	6	—
Totals	100	100	100	100	100	100	100	—	100	—

ALLOYING SUMMARY. ALL ARTEFACTS. PERCENTAGE TOTALS

Area*	A	B	C	D	E	F	G	H	I	J
Arsenic content										
Above 10%	2	1						—		—
Above 5%	16	6		2				—	14	—
Above 1%	54	32	23	21	29	41	8	—	28	—
Below 1%	46	68	76	79	71	58	92	—	73	—
Below 0·1%	24	50	35	52	33	27	75	—	54	—

* A, Egypt B, Palestine C, Syria D, Mesopotamia E, NW. Iran F, C. Anatolia G, Troad H, Cyclades I, Crete J, Greece

It is thus quite clear that the main alloy for the Near East, during the early and middle 'Bronze' ages, is in fact not bronze but arsenical copper. Tin bronze does eventually replace arsenical copper in all areas in the Late Bronze Age, though the rate of replacement is very variable and depends upon the type of artefact involved, as well as the access of different countries to tin supplies. For ancient Egypt for example, the proportions of metal containing tin (at 1% or more) and essentially arsenic-free metal (at less than 0·1%) rise markedly from the Old Kingdom to the New Kingdom. Particularly important is the high level of technical skill involved in the use of arsenical copper, and the care and deliberate control of arsenic levels as a function of artefact use. Fig. 10 and table 6 illustrate these various points for ancient Egypt using analytical data from knives and similar blades which do have significantly high levels of that element when contrasted either with other tools or non-utilitarian artefacts. Such knives and blades would, with

TABLE 6

Relationship of various types of Ancient Egyptian metal artefacts to their arsenic contents. Figures are expressed as a percentage within each artefact type and chronological period

	Predynastic				Archaic				Old Kingdom			
Arsenic level	0·1 %	c. 0·5 %	1–5 %	75 %	0·1 %	c. 0·5 %	1–5 %	75 %	0·1 %	c. 0·5 %	1–5 %	>5 %
Daggers, knives, razors, etc.	40	20	40		33	41	8	16	20	36	36	8
Axes, adzes, etc.	66	33			100				40	60		
Pins, awls, borers, hooks, etc.	42	42	14		35	42	21		25	25		
Non-utilitarian	60	20	20		32	39	26	1	39	46	9	4

appropriate cold-working, benefit distinctly from a content of a few per cent of arsenic. Also, axes and adzes are particularly striking in their low content of arsenic, a feature paralleling that of the British and other Early Bronze Ages where tools subjected to severe blows rarely exhibit high levels of arsenic.

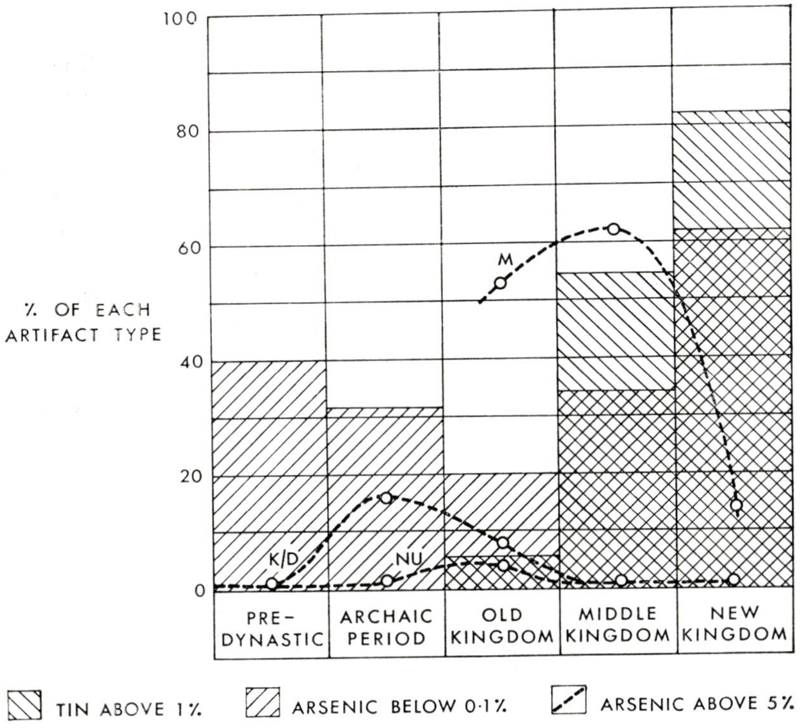

Figure 10 Proportions of various artefacts (K/D = knives, daggers; NU = non-utilitarian; M = mirrors) from Ancient Egypt containing (1) tin, (2) arsenic above 5%, (3) no arsenic. The hatched levels relate to knives and daggers only

Arsenic plating and segregation

It is, however, when we turn to those objects with the highest levels of arsenic that the skills of the early metalworkers are most clearly seen. The Ancient Egyptian artefact demonstrating the most consistent high level of arsenic is the mirror, the reason for this being due to a deliberate coating of a silver-coloured high arsenic copper alloy onto the reflecting surface.

Here, arsenical copper was not simply an alternative alloy but also a colouring technique producing in effect an artificial silver, a 'silver' which indeed tarnished less readily than silver per se. By arsenic plating or coating we are not suggesting anything akin to electroplating or gilding, or even indeed the use of metallic arsenic itself. The silver colour is in fact due to a copper-arsenic alloy containing (at least) 12% of arsenic, and there are a number of methods of effecting the required surface composition. One such simple procedure is to paint a thin paste of arsenic oxide on to the areas to be coloured, then to cover the object in charcoal powder and heat briefly until bright red. After cooling and polishing the silver colour emerges clearly.

The first recognition of such silver-coloured plating was by Fink and Kopp (1933). They believed that two Egyptian vases of fifth or sixth dynasty date had been plated with antimony, but their views were repudiated at great length by Lucas (1962). More recent work (Smith 1973) has shown, however, that the vases are indeed coated with a thin layer of metal, but that this is arsenic, not antimony. Brech and Young (1965) also demonstrated the unequivocal arsenic coating of a bronze bull from Horoztepe, and our own work has added many more examples from a number of areas.

Near Eastern examples occur in Anatolia: at Corum-Merzifon, Horoztepe, and probably with the Bayindirkoy dagger illustrated by Stronach (1957) and described as lead plated. There are also numerous examples from Caucasia where copper-arsenic technology reached a high point before 2000 B.C. In the Cyclades, also, many of the daggers from Amorgos show the same arsenic-rich surfaces; even the example from Naxos, described by Renfrew (1967) as silver plated, may be part of the same tradition. Egyptian examples with mirrors and vases have already been mentioned. Fig. 11 illustrates the distribution and, bearing in mind the relative chronologies involved, affords an interesting dispersion westwards from the East.

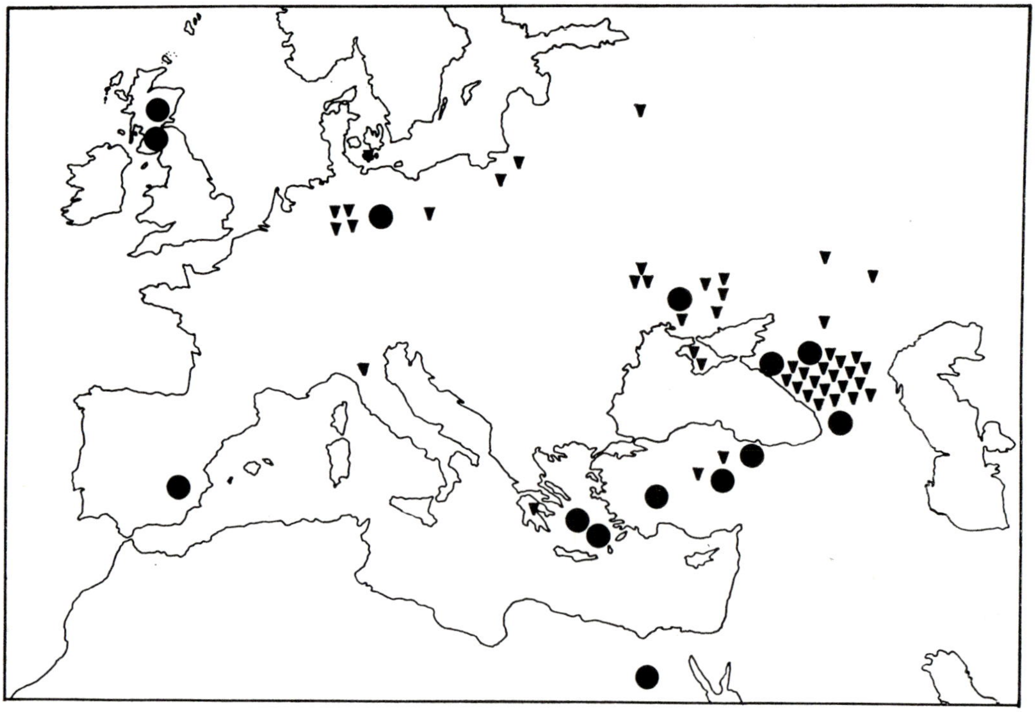

Figure 11 Distribution of silver-coloured, arsenic-rich artefacts (circles) and hammer headed pins (triangles). Latter half of the third millennium

It is with the latest examples, the halberds of central and western Europe, that the alternative to arsenic coating or plating, namely arsenic inverse casting segregation, can be most clearly demonstrated. The phenomenon involved is one of severe segregation during the casting of arsenical copper, and a small quantity of a concentrated, high (*c.* 15–20%) arsenic content copper alloy is forced to the surface to provide a complete outer skin of a silver-coloured metal. Since the low melting eutectic will contain not only a substantial level of arsenic but also the other metal impurities present in the copper, these too will be present in the surface alloy and thus provide an indication that such segregation, rather than plating, has taken place. Hunt and Ankner (1971) noted that the silver surfaces of daggers from the Gau-Bickelheim hoard (in addition to others in the Musée des Antiquités Nationales in St Germain-en-Laye) were due to their high arsenic content, without specifying a particular mechanism. Many of the halberds of Scotland, central Europe (Dieskau) and the Iberian El Argar culture have from our own analyses been shown to exhibit such surface compositions as would have rendered them silver-coloured in their original condition. Though we have not yet examined the earlier Remedello/Rinaldone blades, there is every reason (from mode of manufacture and their high arsenic contents) to believe that here too the same phenomenon would have obtained. The occasional use of soft, non-utilitarian, but solid silver rivets in certain halberds, and a distinct parallelism in the use of silver for associated objects (Siret and Siret 1887) as well as stylistically similar daggers (Branigan 1971), all fit well with the general interest in such silver-coloured artefacts. In Scotland the so-called 'tinned axes' of Early Bronze Age, thin-butted type (Smith and MacAdam 1870) also fall into the category of inverse segregation plating, though here tin is a major constituent along with the arsenic. Interestingly, one of very few Scottish halberd associations was with two of these tinned axes (at Sluie) and Coles (1969) has stressed the special nature of such axes, often found broken and in hoards.

The general dating for all the examples quoted here would be *c.* 2500–2000 B.C. The international use of copper-arsenic alloying (from Iran through to Iberia and Britain) as well as of arsenic plating, all in the third millennium, is a clear indication of the value of technology rather than typology alone in the study of the dissemination of ideas. Parallelism of the well known hammer-headed pin diffusion (Childe 1950; Gimbutas 1965; Piggott 1964) with that of silver-coloured arsenic plating is evident from fig. 11; both are absent to the East of the Caucasus and appear, chronologically, to progress westward from the Pontic region around the north and south of the Black Sea.

Correlation of the analytical and textual evidence

For the Early and Middle Bronze Ages of the Near East, we have already noted that arsenical copper was generally far more widely used than tin bronze. With the exception of the Troad, from one-quarter to three-quarters of all copper-based metal was arsenical copper. It was used skilfully and in such a manner as to suggest that, whatever its basic process of manufacture, there was clear control over the level of arsenic in the resulting alloy.

It is unlikely that alloying in any direct sense was involved, though such use of native arsenic cannot be ruled out for certain areas. In the case of Britain, and perhaps Anatolia also, we can demonstrate that the likeliest method of manufacture was by a direct co-smelting of partially roasted copper and iron-arsenic sulphide ores. Roasting is an essential prerequisite to the smelting of copper sulphide ores but, with care, leaves behind substantial (up to one-half) residues of any initial arsenic. Experimental co-smelting of almost any arsenic mineral (whether oxidized or sulphidic) with adequately roasted copper ores results in an almost complete recovery of the arsenic. Thus any arsenic remaining behind after preliminary ore-roasting would certainly transmit through to the final metal. Unless, however, the arsenic mineral was particularly pure (oxide, sulphide or the like) any related iron content would partially transmit to the copper alloy *unless* roasting had first taken place. Since in fact several per cent of iron is the exception rather than the rule in early coppers, we would in general conclude that arsenical copper would have been prepared by a smelting of partially roasted copper/iron/arsenic sulphides. Direct roasting and smelting of purer copper-arsenic sulphides, such as the grey tetrahedride ores much favoured in the Early Bronze Age of western Europe, can readily provide up to several per cent of arsenic. In general, however, we believe the mixed ore practice (whether collected from one or separate localities) to have been more prevalent for these objects with higher levels of arsenic. It seems likely to have been the procedure used in Britain. The background, plus extensive laboratory experimental verification, is dealt with fully in McKerrell (1976b).

It would have been uneconomic, distinctly tedious, and certainly quite unnecessary to have prepared a batch of arsenical copper whenever required, by direct smelting. We believe that an occasionally prepared high-arsenic metal (up to 15% arsenic) such as that published by Selimkhanov (1962) could well have served as the alloying additive to copper. Indeed, striking confirmation of this practice is provided by the ingots of high arsenic/antimony metal reported by Otto and Witter (1952: 44). Ingots such as these are likely to have been of use to the ancient metallurgist only in preparing alloys of copper. In the case of British and central Anatolian metal it is quite clear from the published analyses that basically similar copper is used for both tin bronze and arsenical copper. For certain objects tin was added to a common local copper; for others, something akin to the high-arsenic metal mentioned above was probably added to the same kind of copper, rather than using a directly smelted alloy. No confusion, such as adding tin to extant high-arsenic metal, or vice versa, takes place. The final preparation of the metal we analyse today was likely to have been a small-scale crucible process, making use of metallic tin and probably a high-arsenic copper as the alloying additives. Both metals are of course very similar in appearance though, as we have already stressed, this was not a source of confusion to the ancient smith. The parallel in the use of tin seems reasonably appropriate, and early examples of metallic tin itself are recorded from Thermi (Lamb 1936), Egypt (Lucas 1962), Odoorn (Beck and Stone 1936), Bargeroostervelt and Jutland (Butler and van der Waals 1964); possibly also Sutton Veney (Piggott 1971). Examples from the first millennium are even more common and a number have been analysed (Coghlan and Case 1957).

As well as the possibility, then, that arsenic for alloying could have been added to the melting pot in the form of a high-arsenic alloy, the surface coating techniques described above show a distinct familiarity on the part of the ancient metalworker with the chemistry and reactivity of arsenic compounds. Yet, whilst we have many third and second millennia metallurgical and commercial descriptions of tin, bronze, lead and other metals, arsenical copper and arsenic-plated copper are wholly absent from the translated versions available. It seems scarcely likely that this is due to widespread confusion on the part of the ancient scribes; the discrepancy, if any exists, must therefore lie in the translations. Some alternative possibilities may at this point be usefully considered.

(a) *Sumer*

The essential proof that Sumerian AN.NA (Akkadian *annaku*) means tin, rests upon a number of recipes describing the mixing of AN.NA with urudu (copper) to yield *zabar* (bronze) (Muhly 1973). Table 7 summarizes this evidence. The crucial point is the composition calculated from the textual recipes (four out of five suggest a bronze containing 14·2% of tin) and whether or not such a composition is regularly found with early Mesopotamian metal. Certainly Levey and Burke (1959) concluded that the aim of the early metalsmith was an alloy containing about one-sixth tin (17%) but our own data are completely at odds with such figures. Thus, for analysed artefacts of the period Early Dynastic I to Akkadian, only two objects have more than the 14% suggested by the text recipes. Similarly, for the Post-Akkadian to the Old Babylonian, only three objects have more than 14% of tin. Table 8 summarizes the figures; for both periods no more than 2% of all objects reach the text recipe levels of tin. The analytical data do not therefore support the cuneiform texts in their descriptions of tin bronze. But if not tin bronze, what else? There is only one other possibility, arsenical copper, since lead-copper alloys, or indeed any other copper alloys, are quite absent from Mesopotamia down to 1600 B.C.

TABLE 7

Sumerian bronze recipes (after Muhly 1973)

Period	Ratio of copper to tin	Tin content predicted
pre-Sargonic	80: 13·3	14·4%
Third Dynasty of Ur	6 : 1	14·4%
Third Dynasty of Ur	35 : 5	12·5%
Old Babylonian	6 : 1	14·3%
Neo-Assyrian	6 : 1	14·3%

TABLE 8

Tin bronze in Mesopotamia

	Proportion of objects analysed	
	EB	MB
Tin content above 5%	12%	12%
Tin content above 10%	7%	6%
Tin content above 14%	2%	2%

Arsenical copper, with arsenic in the range of 1 to 5%, accounts for about one-quarter to one-third of all metal from Mesopotamia over the period 3000 B.C. to 1600 B.C. – a ten-fold increase over the proportion of text recipe levels of tin bronze. Even on the unlikely possibility that all the text recipes considerably exaggerated the practice of the metalsmith, and if we take the minimal useful level of sound bronze as containing upwards of 5% of tin, such assumptions still give a two- to three-fold greater use of arsenical copper than of tin bronze. But if *zabar* could equate with arsenical copper what then of AN.NA? It is fortunately quite clear that AN.NA is a metal, and that any question of preparation of *zabar* by an ore-smelting procedure is not intended. So if *zabar* is arsenical copper, with arsenic in the optimum range of 1 to 5%, then AN.NA can only be a *high* arsenic content (and thus silver-coloured) copper-arsenic alloy. The textual support for this mode of arsenic alloying is perhaps somewhat circular but it might well fit the evidence better than the usual translations. Moreover, from laboratory experiments as well as archaeological evidence (Selimkhanov 1962; Parkinson 1956; Otto and Witter 1952: 44), it is unlikely that a *high* arsenic copper alloy would contain much more than 20% of arsenic. If such a metal is interpolated as AN.NA into the recipes described, then the calculated arsenic content for Mesopotamian arsenical copper *should* be about 3%, as is typically found. Other textual considerations come from the use of AN.NA or *annaku* in descriptions of decorative objects and jewellery; whilst almost unknown at this time in metallic tin (the Thermi bangle being the only exception), such items would quite clearly correspond well with the tint of many silver-coloured arsenic-coated artefacts. The preference for the use of real solid silver in such objects is generally well reflected in richer graves and tombs but, as an acceptable and less expensive alternative, arsenic-coated copper would have much to commend it both in terms of strength and a striking similarity to solid silver – features that are really not anything like as well displayed by metallic tin. Two bright, silver-coloured adzes from Corum-Merzifon of EB3 date (recently found in the secondary collection of the Ankara museum) illustrated this point well.

A major textual problem with *annaku* stems from its apparent point(s) of origin within the Near East. Despite many attempts to locate Near Eastern tin ore deposits, the simple facts are that no substantial deposit capable of sustaining the extensive trade recorded in the texts has ever been found. The level of this trade was truly considerable, *annaku* being transported in many tons per annum. Present knowledge of Near Eastern ore locations is well described by Crawford (1974) and Muhly (1973) whilst current rumours apparently favour both Iran and Egypt. However, until such time as an adequate source of tin is found in the Near East, it seems reasonable to consider the alternative which does unequivocally belong to the area, namely arsenic minerals, leading to a high arsenic copper. The usual preference for tin origins is north-western Iran (Muhly 1973) and it may be no coincidence that this region made considerable use of arsenical copper – between a half to two-thirds of all analysed objects for the period 3000–2200 B.C. and about one-third thereafter down to 1600 B.C. The fact that arsenic minerals are readily found nearer the Anatolian trading markets does not necessarily discredit these arguments; such minerals occur in many areas of the Aegean and the Near East. What matters is whether or not they occur in coincidence with copper ores suitable for smelting, so that a high-arsenic copper is produced from whatever local sequences of roasting and smelting were in use. The occurrence of the high-arsenic metal may well have been peculiar to particular locations with just the right combination of ore and smelting practice.

It is, however, when we consider the change in alloying patterns from the EB to MB that perhaps the most useful pointers emerge. Whether tin reached Anatolia from Assur, Mari, Larsa, Susa or the Persian Gulf, the general thrust of the textual evidence is for trade through or near Mesopotamia. North-western Iran usually, as mentioned, also figured large in such matters. Yet it is precisely these two areas which exhibit minimal changes in their use of tin bronze from the EB to the MB. Table 9 shows that tin bronze comprised only about one-tenth of all EB copper-based metal in Mesopotamia, with no increase whatsoever for the MB period. These figures are surely somewhat incompatible with any serious MB tin trade via or around Mesopotamia. Much the same situation obtains with north-western Iran, where for both the EB and MB a quarter of all metal is good bronze and there is virtually no increase from the early to the late period. The localities that do in fact show the most marked EB to MB increases in the use of tin bronze are Egypt, Palestine and Crete; all of them in the EB having virtually no supplies of tin whatsoever, but increasing by several hundred per cent in the MB. What then does this suggest in the matter of tin supplies for the MB? Certainly not an Eastern source, and even arguably a Mediterranean-based western supply.

TABLE 9

Changes in the Near Eastern use of tin bronze from EB to MB

	Tin above 5%		
	Proportion of artefacts		% Increase EB to MB
	EB	MB	
Egypt	3%	22%	+630%
Palestine	0%	22%	+200%
Syria	13%	30%	+130%
Mesopotamia	12%	12%	0%
N. & W. Iran	23%	26%	+ 13%
C. Anatolia	24%	40%	+ 67%
Troad	37%	25%	− 32%
Crete	2%	14%	+600%

Muhly (1973) has set out the extensive evidence for a later Mycenaean-inspired tin trade from Cornwall via the rivers of France to the Mediterranean. Muhly's case is distinctly more complex and persuasive than (Watkins 1976) simple extrapolation back from historical times. Is the situation we describe conceivably a Middle Bronze Age forerunner to that activity? One detail which suggests that it may well be so is the date for the onset of systematic use of tin bronze in Britian. Whilst the situation with regard to corrected C^{14} dates is far from clear in the Near East, this is not so with certain phases of the Early Bronze Age of western Europe (McKerrell 1976a). New X-ray analysis of all available British beaker-associated metalwork (McKerrell 1976b) shows that it was with Step 5 beakers (Lanting and van der Waals 1972) that tin bronze took hold in Britain. The change from copper and arsenical copper was total, and a calendar date for Step 5 commencing *c.* 2200 B.C. fits well with a similar bronze horizon for north British halberd and thin-butted axe material and its connections with the A1 Unetiče period in central Europe. It is highly probable that the first bronze age, in the sense of total use of such metal, began in Britain *c.* 2200 B.C. Could it be that this pronounced British use of tin bronze led to the situation described for the eastern Mediterranean? The evidence is certainly suggestive, and we have in hand a lengthy series of lead isotope studies which could ultimately resolve the matter.

For the moment the negative technical evidence for a substantial Near Eastern source of tin has to be set againt the detailed textual evidence of trade in such metal. But if the trade referred to in the texts is in reality in high-arsenic copper, there is virtually no support for a Near Eastern origin for tin. Indeed, turning the evidence the other way and regarding Near Eastern tin supplies in the early second millennium as essentially western in origin, the recorded and complex trading patterns in a metal suitable for alloying with copper, from within the Near East, leave little alternative to this being a high arsenic content arsenical copper. But the subtlety of *analytical* distinction between different alloys and metals, being a modern classification, was probably quite unnecessary to the ancient smith. A change, with time, in the nature of metal described as *annaku* (or even a duality involving high arsenic copper and tin) seems not at all improbable; interpreted simply as '*that silver-coloured metal which when added to copper produces a castable and hard alloy*' *annaku* might well have been both materials, used as and when available, and producing, as far as the customer was concerned, virtually the same end product.

(b) *Egypt*

The identification of the metallic substance to which the name *d*(m was applied has been a matter of much controversy among Egyptologists. The discussion, well summarized by J. R. Harris (1961), centres on the question of whether *d*(m represents a specific material, a precious metal like gold either in value or appearance, or whether it is merely a poetic name for gold with no precise meaning. Harris himself supports the translation of *d*(m as electrum. While realizing that we do not have first hand access to the texts and are here relying on Harris' presentation of the evidence, we believe that *d*(m may be better identified with arsenical copper or arsenic-coated copper, and that only later, as the use of this material became less common, could the word *d*(m be used of precious metals in general, such as gold, silver or electrum, all of which were regarded as varieties of gold.

Harris gives four cogent reasons for the identification of *d*(m as a precious metal:

1 the word is regularly determined with a sign used only for the noble metals;
2 it occurs together with nbw (i.e. gold) in captions accompanying scenes of gold working;
3 *d*(m is found replacing nbw and in parallelism with it and other terms for the precious metals;

4 the uses of *d*(m are strikingly similar to those of both nbw and h*d* (gold and silver). That *d*(m refers to a specific metal and is not simply a poetic word for gold is suggested by its appearance in offering lists and in other references where it is cited as the material of specific objects. These references show that *d*(m was used for vessels, for statues and parts of statues, for offering tables, furniture, mirrors, jewellery, as well as for plating or inlay on a variety of objects, including the famous obelisks of Heliopolis mentioned by St Ephrem and Arab writers. It also occurs in rings and as dust or lumps in bags.

In the Old and Middle Kingdoms *d*(m was considered to be a naturally occurring material, not an alloy, though during the New Kingdom it was apparently counterfeited by artificial means.

Harris' principal reason for identifying *d*(m as electrum rests on the passage in the Harris papyrus where a magnificent balance made of *d*(m is described; the materials listed as components for the balance include silver, gold, copper and various woods. Harris takes the metals in this list to be the materials of the alloy from which the balance is made, an alloy that would closely resemble naturally occurring electrum. An alternative explanation, however, is that these other materials were used for inlay or perhaps, like the woods referred to, for separate parts of the balance, since at this time there was considerable interest in the visual effects gained by displaying different metals on the same object. Moreover, one should note that this is a later reference and that by the time of the New Kingdom, *d*(m may indeed properly refer to electrum.

The translation, then, of *d*(m as a silver-coloured arsenic-plated copper does fit the descriptive facts. This material is most common in the early periods when arsenical copper was widely used everywhere in the ancient world, and it became less frequent in the later periods when largely replaced by tin bronze. Later references are also known, for example, in the recipes for whitening copper in the Leyden X papyrus. Interestingly, St Ephrem's reference is to a material described as 'white' copper. As mentioned above, we now possess objects from Egypt known to be plated with a silvery coating of arsenic: for example, the two vases of fifth or sixth dynasty date in the Metropolitan Museum, and a number of mirrors in the Ashmolean and British Museums ranging from the Old to Middle Kingdom, coated on one side only with a reflective surface of arsenic-rich copper (table 10). It is probable that other museum pieces now described as silver or silver-plated may in fact be of copper coated with arsenic. Furthermore, the extensive use of *d*(m for covering doors, columns and obelisks is reasonable, since arsenic-plated copper would have been far more readily available, as well as much more hard wearing, than electrum. Arsenic plating over copper would also fit well with the otherwise puzzling references in Arab writers to the greenish copper corrosion residues on the *d*(m obelisks of Heliopolis. The white colouring of objects of *d*(m on Middle Kingdom coffins would also be explicable, since a homogenous alloy of arsenic and copper is golden coloured, whilst either inverse arsenic segregation or deliberate arsenic coating gives a white silvery surface.

The early description of arsenical copper as a naturally occurring material would not be surprising. Brass was not always recognized to be an alloy even in the Renaissance, and it is possible that arsenic-coated copper was produced by a similar cementation process. It is also possible that in the early periods arsenical copper was not even produced in Egypt but was imported in the form of a high arsenic alloy; this high arsenic alloy

TABLE 10

Arsenic-coated ancient Egyptian mirrors

Site	Period	Ashmolean no.	Arsenic content
	Old Kingdom		
Beni Hasen		E4253	14·3%
Mostagedda		1930.514	10·3%
	First Intermediate		
Beni Hasen		E1990	24·2%
	Middle Kingdom		
El Kab		E2141	10·7%
El Kab		E2145	9·8%
Abydos		1913.400	11·7%

would then have been added to copper to produce the lower levels of arsenic (1 to 5%) commonly found in utilitarian objects of this time. During the New Kingdom it was evidently recognized that the special property of 'silvering' copper belonged to a particular earth; by this time at least, the product was seen to be artificial.

(c) *Greece*

The identification of the metal called *oreichalkos* presents many problems. There is little doubt that for Roman coinage under the Empire it did definitely mean brass, the alloy of copper and zinc. Chemical analyses confirm this in detail (Caley 1964). However, there are Greek literary references from as far back as the seventh century B.C. which would not afford such straightforward interpretation; these may, we believe, refer more plausibly to the silver-coloured metal produced by an arsenic-rich surface on copper.

Metallic zinc itself is difficult to prepare and thus remained unknown until the eighteenth century. The smelting reaction requires a temperature above 1,000° C to proceed rapidly and, as this is higher even than the boiling point of the metal, collection is very difficult. Both Dioscorides (V. 84) and Pliny (N.H. XXXXIV.10.100–3) confirm that zinc was unknown to the Romans, brass being produced not by direct alloying but from the cementation process using calamine, a technique continuing in use until the nineteenth century (Smith and Gnudi 1966). The only reliable find of metallic zinc from the period comes from the Agora excavations in Athens and is discussed in Farnsworth *et al.* (1949). The date should be no later then the second century B.C. Forbes (1964) has, however, raised objections to the find, emphasizing in particular the surprising survival under the wet conditions of burial of such a reactive metal as zinc; he believed the specimen to be zinc sheeting of a much later period.

Many hundreds of new analyses that we have recently completed of artefacts in the Ashmolean and British Museums and the London Institute of Archaeology (McKerrell 1976b) show that brass was indeed a distinct rarity before the Christina era. Table 11 summarizes all the analytical data known to us from Late Bronze Age to Roman times, and it is apparent that sound brass containing 5% or more of zinc comprises typically only 1% of all metal from any locality. The level and scatter of the zinc levels suggests

TABLE II

c. 1600–0 B.C. brass data

ANALYTICAL TOTALS

Area*	A	B	C	D	E	F	K	L
Zinc Content								
Above 10%	1	1	1	3	2			1
5–10%		2			1		1	
1–5%	1	1	2	5	5		4	1
c. 0–5%	20	1	2	7	31	2	14	4
Below 0·1%	238	139	81	313	315	65	37	92
Totals	260	144	86	328	354	67	56	98

PERCENTAGE TOTALS

Area*	A	B	C	D	E	F	K	L
Zinc content								
Above 10%		1	1	1	1			1
5–10%		1					2	
1–5%		1	2	2	1		7	1
c. 0·5%	8	1	2	2	9	3	25	4
Below 0·1%	92	97	94	95	89	97	66	94
Totals	100	100	100	100	100	100	100	100

ALLOYING SUMMARY. ALL ARTEFACTS. PERCENTAGE TOTALS

Area*	A	B	C	D	E	F	K	L
Zinc Content								
Above 10%		1	1	1	1			1
Above 5%		2	1	1	1		2	1
Above 1%		3	3	2	2		9	2
Below 1%	100	97	97	98	98	100	91	98
Below 0·1%	92	97	94	95	89	97	66	94

* A, Egypt B, Palestine C, Syria D, Mesopotamia E, Iran F, C. Anatolia K, Etruria L, Cyprus

strongly that the introduction of zinc was not from metallic alloying but rather through retention of zinc in the copper smelting process. This quite adventitious acquisition of low levels of zinc is again emphasized by the fact that so often the main alloying elements, tin or lead, are present in considerably greater proportions and would completely mask any slight advantages in the presence of the zinc. Etruscan bronzes, in which zinc impurities are regularly to be found, are a particularly appropriate example, in this respect, with often very high levels of both tin and lead. It is hard to believe that the low levels of zinc offered any practical advantages or were even known to be present in the alloy. We believe the analytical evidence to be overwhelmingly in favour of only accidental introduction of zinc into early copper alloys. The contrast with the deliberate mass production of brass coinage from the time of Augustus onwards is striking. Such conclusions do, then, suggest that the early references to *oreichalkos* do not and could not relate to brass.

There are, however, other reasons for doubting such a translation. First, the very few references to the colour of *oreichalkos* describe a metal that is white or very pale, certainly not the colour of brass. Then the relative colours of brass and bronze would themselves present certain problems. Though it is perhaps usual to regard brass as a golden-yellow metal, and bronze as not very different in colour from copper itself, this is not necessarily correct and merely reflects the level of alloying normally involved with modern metals. In fact both tin and zinc effect very similar colour changes in copper, and levels within the 10 to 15% range for either metal produce visually identical pale golden alloys. If anything, tin has the edge in effectiveness for this colouring change, and there is no visual means of distinguishing either alloy. If, then, bronze could be rendered visually indistinguishable from brass, there are distinct difficulties with the usual textual translations. For *oreichalkos* was not simply a poetic reference; it was the metal of actual objects, including temple dedications. Objects made of *oreichalkos* did exist and must thus surely have been distinguishable from bronze. Also, *oreichalkos* was generally considered to be of distinct value, certainly more precious than bronze. Quite how these facts can support the usual translation as 'brass' we cannot understand.

Oreichalkos is first mentioned in Greek poems before 600 B.C. Particularly relevant references (Halleux 1973) relate to the value of the metal; comparable to thrice refined gold (Page 1967: 282) and second only to gold (Plato, Critias). In the Inscriptiones Graecae there are three fourth-century B.C. inscriptions from Athens which preserve the word *oreichalkos*. The first (1G–1416) describes an object of *oreichalkos* in a list of copper and bronze objects believed to be from the Chalkotheke. The second inscription (1G–1517) is a catalogue of objects dedicated to Artemis Brauronia and is dated by the eponymous archon to the mid fourth century. The catalogue includes objects of gold, copper or bronze, ivory and wood as well as vestments and some miscellaneous pieces. The metal objects are largely jewellery: necklaces, rings and bracelets. On the fragment of interest (1517b col 2 183) there appear coins of silver, rings, an object (name missing) of *oreichalkos*, an object (name missing) of iron and an object (name missing) of ivory. The third inscription 1G–1533 is a catalogue of dedications to Asclepius. The portion of interest (124–5) dated to 339/8 B.C. describes two chains (in the sense of necklaces), one of copper, the other of iron and the first of *oreichalkos*.

Amongst later commentators we find the Scholia on Hesiod (122), thought to be based on the commentaries of Didymus Calcenterius of the first century A.D., wherein *oreichalkos* is defined as 'a kind of copper' (Lockwood and Browning 1970). And the Scholia on Apollonius Rhodibe us (IV.973), thought to based on the commentaries of Theon, a scholar of the first century B.C., also has an interesting description of the whiteness of *oreichalkos*: '*oreichalkos* is a kind of material, so called, which is not found now. But others say that it is an alloy of copper which *is* now to be found (this is not true) for copper cannot be made white by any technique, being ruddy by nature.' (Forbes and Browning 1970.) In the lexicon of 'Suidas' (554) written about the tenth century A.D., but important for its collection of earlier literary sources, *oreichalkos* is defined as 'the lustrous copper, the esteemed form.'

Another interesting passage comes from the pseudo-Aristotlean compilation, *On Marvellous Things Heard*, of uncertain date but thought to have been put together between the second and sixth centuries A.D. (Owen 1970). The passage may be translated as follows: 'they say that the copper of the Mossynoeci is very brilliant and very white in colour, though tin is not mixed with it, but a kind of earth which occurs on the spot is smelted with it'. The word *leukotaton* used to describe the appearance of the metal is particularly significant. It means 'very white' or 'very pale' and would not describe the golden colour of brass. It could refer, however, to the colour of high arsenic copper, and it may well be no coincidence that the Mossynoeci lived in the Pontic region, an area demonstrating the use of arsenical copper as far back as the third millennium (as discussed above) and noted in antiquity for its supplies of the arsenical minerals, orpiment and sandarack (Vitr de Arch. VIII.1.5).

There are two important technical descriptions involving *oreichalkos*. The first, in Strabo's Geography (XIII.1.56), dates to the beginning of the Christian era: 'About Andeira (a city in the Troad) is found a stone which when burned becomes iron. Then when heated in a furnace with a kind of earth, it drips down mocksilver and this, with the addition of copper, becomes the so called mixture which some name oreichalkos.' Then in the Leyden X papyrus, believed to date to the third century A.D. but representing a much older literature, *oreichalkos* is used as an ingredient for *asem*, a word used for any silvery alloy (Liddel *et al.* 1968). Recipe 85, referring to 'an exact preparation of asem, preferable to that of asem properly so-called', reads: 'take oreichalkos, one drachma for example; place it in a crucible until it melts; throw upon it four drachmas of salt of Ammon or Cappadoecian salt (in amount equal to) the weight of an Egyptian bean; remelt, add to it one drachma of decomposed sandarack, not the golden sandarack but that which whitens; then transfer to another crucible previously coated with earth of Chios; after fusion add a fourth part of asem and put into use.' This translation by Caley (1926) is based on that of Berthelot (1887).

In the earliest references *oreichalkos* is evidently considered a precious metal suitable for jewellery, decorative armour and mirrors. The characteristic property is its distinctive lustre, and both this and the value attached to it are entirely consistent with the identification 'arsenic-plated copper' or even 'arsenical copper'. The translation 'brass' is not supported, particularly on consideration of the impossibility of distinguishing the latter from tin bronze. It is important to remember that in antiquity there was no conception of metals as distinct elements in the modern sense. Metals were thought to owe their distinctive properties to varying attributes imposed on them by nature, colour being particularly important in this respect. Thus a silver-coloured metal could be equated with silver metal proper, and such an outlook has been seen as having led to a belief in the transmutation of metals, then to the rise of alchemy (Hopkins 1967). The three fourth-century B.C. inscriptions from Athens, being prosaic lists of definite objects, do show that *oreichalkos* was an actual metal, known and used at that time, and in the only inscription where the name of the article survives it is significantly an article of jewellery.

The interpretation and authority of the passage in Strabo has been much debated.

Although written at about the beginning of the Christian era, the passage apparently comes from Theopompus, a fourth-century B.C. historian whose work has survived only in fragments. Unless generously interpreted, Strabo's account is at face value a metallurgical nonsense. By his time, the manufacture of brass for coinage had begun. However, as we know from Dioscorides and Pliny, its preparation did not involve metallic zinc but rather a cementation process. Thus the equation zinc=*pseudoargyros* (mocksilver) generally followed by Leaf (1914), Michell (1955), Caley (1964) and Halleux (1973) amongst others has no sound literary backing. Nor, as we have stressed, for pre-Roman metalwork in any area of the ancient world, is true brass more than barely represented. Also, from our own direct experimentation, the concept of metallic zinc *dripping down* from an ore smelting preparation seems quite inconceivable; under such circumstances metallic zinc is evolved as a gas and rapidly follows the flue gases up and out of the furnace to collect, if at all, as a dark grey amorphous powder. We simply cannot follow the usual idea that the silver coloured molten metal is zinc. Searching for an alternative, a high arsenic copper seems distinctly more plausible. Certainly among the *asem* recipes of the Leyden X papyrus we are clearly involved with arsenic minerals in the preparation of what is, by definition, a silvery metal. And the Scholia on Hesiod quite positively describes a white colour for *oreichalkos*, as does the brilliant and very white copper ascribed to the Mossynoeci.

In sharp contrast, *orichalcum* is correctly translated as brass. That metal is described by Cicero as being like gold in colour (de Off 3.2392) and Pliny gives an account of its production using *cadima* (zinc oxide) (N.H. XXXIV 2.2). By this time arsenical copper seems to have passed out of use, except for the imitation of silver. A systematic analytical examination of jewellery surfaces (not internal metal drillings) would seem well worthwhile and need involve no damage if X-ray fluorescence be used. For the late centuries B.C. and the early centuries A.D. such investigation might add considerably to our understanding of the words for early metals as well as of their changes in meaning with time.

Summary

The extensive use of arsenic minerals for alloying and providing silver-coloured coatings on copper, as revealed by X-ray fluorescence analytical surveys, contrasts markedly with the total absence of such metal in the textual translations. It is possible that the much debated Akkadian *annaku*, Egyptian *d*(m and Greek *oreichalkos* all refer to either a high arsenic content copper or else to arsenic-coated copper, both of them silver-coloured in appearance.

Alloying patterns for the Near East, when contrasted with Early Bronze Age Britain, are suggestive of tin supplies for bronze manufacture coming from western Europe, even before the Mycenaean era and possibly from the end of the third millennium. Such contact, and that evidenced by the international use of the arsenic coating techniques from the same time, are suggestive of far more technological unity and exchange of ideas in the ancient world than is generally conceded.

Acknowledgements

Grateful thanks are due to many colleagues in museum and other departments of Belgium, Britain, the German Democratic Republic, Netherlands and Turkey, for every help and facility with the analysis of objects in their care; particularly Mr A. K. Annable, Dr R. D. Barnett, Dr H. Behrens, Mr A. M. Burchell, Mr H. Case, Dr D. French, Dr O. Harsema, Dr R. Higgins, Dr I. Longworth, Dr M. Marien, Mr T. Mitchell, Dr P. R. S. Moorey, Mrs R. Maxwell-Hyslop, Professor D. Oates, Mr A. Shore and Dr R. Temizer. Also we have greatly benefited from helpful discussion with Dr J. Butler, Mr H. Case, Dr J. Charles, Dr J. Coles, Professor C. F. C. Hawkes, Professor R. Maddin, Dr J. Muhly, Professor G. J. Toomer and Dr R. F. Tylecote. For financial support we are indebted to the British Academy, Mr D. F. O. Russell and the Russell Trust and the Society of Antiquaries of Scotland. And for painstaking care with the analytical interpretation we are grateful to Mrs E. Roger; for help with some of the museum analyses, to Mr D. Adams. The line drawings are the work of Miss H. Jackson.

25.iii.1976

National Museum of Antiquities of Scotland
Edinburgh

References

Beck, H. C. and Stone, J. F. S. 1936. Faience beads of the British Bronze Age. *Archaeologia.* 85:203–51.

Berthelot, M. 1887. *Collections des Anciens Alchemists Grecs.* 1. Paris.

Branigan, K. 1971. Halberds, daggers and culture contact. *Origini.* 5:47–58.

Brech, F. and Young, W. J. 1965. The laser microprobe and its application to the analysis of works of art. In *Application of Science in Examination of Works of Art*, ed. W. J. Young: 230–7. Boston.

Butler, J. J. and van der Waals, J. D. 1964. Bell beakers and early metalworking in the Netherlands. *Palaeohistoria.* 12:41–139.

Caley, E. R. 1926. The Leyden Papyrus X, an English translation with brief notes. *Journal of Chemical Education.* 3:1160–6.

Caley, E. R. 1964. Orichalcum and related ancient alloys: origin, composition and manufacture with special reference to the coinage of the Roman Empire. *American Numismatic Society.* 23–4.

Childe, V. G. 1950. *Prehistoric Migrations in Europe.* Oslo.

Coghlan, H. H. and Case, H. 1957. Early metallurgy of copper in Ireland and Britain. *Proceedings of the Prehistoric Society.* 23:91–123.

Coles, J. M. 1969. Scottish Early Bronze Age metalwork. *Proceedings of the Society of Antiquaries of Scotland.* 101:1–110.

Crawford, H. E. W. 1974. The problem of tin in Mesopotamian bronzes. *World Archaeology*. 6:242–7.

Ehrich, R. W. *et al.* 1965. *Chronologies in Old World Archaeology*. London.

Esin, V. 1969. *Kuantitatif Spektral Analiz Yardimiyla Anadolu da Baslangicindam Asur Kolonilesi Cagina Kadar Bakir ve Tunc Madenciligi*. Istanbul.

Farnsworth, M., Smith, C. S. and Rodda, J. L. 1949. Metallographic examination of a sample of metallic zinc from ancient Athens. *Hesperia Suppl.* VIII:126–9.

Fink, C. G. and Kopp, A. H. 1933. Ancient Egyptian plating on copper objects. *Metropolitan Museum Studies*. 4:163–7.

Forbes, P. B. R. and Browning, R. 1970. Theon of Alexandria. In *Oxford Classical Dictionary*. 1058. Oxford.

Forbes, R. J. 1964. *Studies in Ancient Technology*. VIII.

Gimbutas, M. 1965. *Bronze Age Cultures in Central and Eastern Europe*. London.

Halleux, R. 1973. L'orichalque et le laiton. *L'Antiquité Classique*. 42:64–81.

Harris, J. R. 1961. *Lexicographical Studies in Ancient Egyptian Minerals*. Berlin.

Hopkins, A. J. 1967. *Alchemy, Child of Greek Philosophy*. New York.

Hundt, H. J. and Ankner, D. 1971. Der Dolchort von Gau-Bickelheim in Rheinhessen. *Jahrbuch de Römisch Germanischen Zentralmuseums, Mainz*. 18:1–50.

Lamb, W. 1936. *Excavations at Thermi in Lesbos*. Cambridge.

Lanting, J. N. and van der Waals, J. D. 1972. British Beakers as seen from the Continent. *Helinium*. 12:20–46.

Leaf, W. 1914–15. Some problems on the Troad. *Annual of the British School at Athens*. 21:23–45.

Levey, M. and Burke, J. E. 1959. A Study of ancient Mesopotamian bronze. *Chymia*. 5:37–50.

Liddel, H. G., Scott, R. and Jones, H. S. 1968. *A Greek-English Lexicon*. Oxford: 255.

Lockwood, J. F. and Browning, R. 1970. Didymus. In *Oxford Classical Dictionary*: 340–1. Oxford.

Lucas, A. 1962. *Ancient Egyptian Materials and Industries*. London.

McKerrell, H. 1974. *The Application of Non-dispersive X-ray Fluorescence to Archaeological Material*. Edinburgh.

McKerrell, H. 1976a. Correction procedures for carbon-14 dates. In *Radiocarbon Calibration and Prehistory*, ed. T. F. Watkins: 55. Edinburgh.

McKerrell, H. 1976b. *The Alloys of the Early Bronze Age in Scotland*. Edinburgh.

Michell, H. 1955. Oreichalkos. *Classical Review*. 5:21–2.

Moorey, P. R. S. and Schweizer, F. 1972. Copper and copper alloys in ancient Turkey: some new analyses. *Archaeometry*. 16:112–15.

Muhly, J. D. 1973. Copper and tin: the distribution of mineral resources and the nature of the metals trade in the Bronze Age. *Transaction of the Connecticut Academy of Arts and Sciences*. 43:155–535.

Otto, H. and Witter, W. 1952. *Handbuch der ältesten vorgeschichtlichen Metallurgie in Mitteleuropa*. Leipzig.

Owen, G. E. L. 1970. Aristotle. In *Oxford Classical Dictionary*: 115. Oxford.

Page, D. L. 1967. *Poetae Melici Graeci.* Oxford.

Parkinson, A. E. 1956. Appendices 1 and 2. In M. G. Mellink, *A Hittite Cemetery at Gordion.* Philadelphia.

Piggott, S. 1964. *Ancient Europe.* Edinburgh.

Piggott, S. 1971. *Victoria County History, Wiltshire.* London.

Renfrew, C. 1967. Cycladic metallurgy and tbe Aegean Early Bronze Age. *American Journal of Archaeology.* 71:1–23.

Selimkhanov, I. R. 1962. The chemical composition of knives, awls and beads – from eastern Europe in the III–II millennium B.C. *Academy of Sciences U.S.S.R., Soviet Archaeology.* 1:57–65.

Selimkhanov, I. R. 1962. Spectral analyses of metal artifacts from archaeological documents of the Caucasus. *Proceedings of the Prehistoric Society.* 28:68–79.

Siret, H. and Siret, L. 1887. *Les Premiers Ages du Metal dans le sud-est de l'Espagne.* Anvers.

Smith, C. S. 1973. An examination of the arsenic-rich coating on a bronze bull from Horoztepe. In *Application of Science in the Examination of Works of Art*, ed. W. J. Young: 96–102. Boston.

Smith, C. S. and Gnudi, M. 1966. *The Pyrotechnia of Vannochio Biringuccio.* Cambridge, Mass.

Smith, J. A. and MacAdam, S. 1870. Notice of bronze celts or axe heads, which have apparently been tinned. *Proceedings of the Society of Antiquaries of Scotland.* 9:428–35.

Stronach, D. B. 1957. The development and diffusion of metal types in Early Bronze Age Anatolia. *Anatolian Studies.* 7:89–125.

Watkins, T. F. 1976. Review of J. D. Muhly, 'Copper and Tin . . .' *Antiquity.* 50:70–1.

Abstract

Eaton, E. R. and McKerrell, Hugh

Near Eastern alloying and some textual evidence for the early use of arsenical copper

The analytical background to the textual translations of words for ancient metals is considered in the light of all previously published analytical data and of several thousand new results. The possibility of alternatives to the usual translations of the metals Egyptian *d*(m, Greek *oreichalkos* and Akkadian *annaku* are discussed in the light of the analytical evidence.

Comparison of column and whole unit samples for recovering fish remains

Richard W. Casteel

Introduction

The use of column samples or small subsamples of midden material for detailed examination of micro-faunal and floral constituents is not new to archaeology. During the 1950s and 60s this type of analysis was widely discussed (see for example Meighan *et al.* 1958; Cook and Heizer 1951; Davidson 1964). Normally removed from the sidewalls of excavated units, these samples ideally have uniform volumes and provide an adequate basis for quantitative comparisons. It has also been suggested that the column sampling approach be extended to include pre-excavation faunal studies by means of the use of augering devices (Casteel 1970). This allows for a rapid recovery of column samples and eliminates the prerequisite of excavation of full-sized units prior to removal of column samples. With this approach, detailed micro-faunal study is compatible with many regional surface-survey techniques. This approach to the column sampling problem is not new and dates back, at least, to the pioneering work of Moorehead (1929), who removed borings from the Cahokia Mounds which contained molluscan remains, seeds etc.

With the growing recognition that recovery techniques have a significant effect upon the results of faunal analyses (Watson 1972; Payne 1972; Thomas 1969; Casteel 1972; Heizer and Squier 1953; Treganza and Cook 1948) and the more widespread use of wet- and fine-screening techniques in archaeology (Struever 1968; Schock 1971), significant new data are being made available for palaeo-ecological studies.

The present paper is concerned with a comparative study of the micro-faunal spectrum resulting from two different types of field and laboratory processing and analysis of midden material. Also of concern is the stability of faunal representations derived from column samples. The discussion will be restricted to a single class of faunal material – remains of marine and freshwater fishes.

Sampling locality and data acquisition

Material for this study was obtained during excavation of the Glenrose Cannery site, located on the Fraser River, just east of New Westminster, British Columbia. The excavation was conducted by the University of British Columbia, Department of Anthropology and Sociology, under the guidance of Dr R. G. Matson. A number of units had already been excavated to depths of several feet when column samples were removed for analysis. These column samples were removed from two excavation units (numbers 1 and 4). The first samples were removed 30 cm. below the soil surface from the west wall of each unit, and successive samples removed at 30 cm. intervals until the maximum depth of the excavated unit was encountered. Each sample measured $10 \times 7 \times 6$ cm. (420 cm.³). These samples were returned to the laboratory, weighed, and water-sieved through superimposed sieves of 2, 1 and 0·5 mm. mesh.

During excavation of each unit the crew had dry-screened all midden material and removed all visible faunal remains in the field. This ichthyofaunal sample from unit 1 provides a basis for comparison with the column sample from this same unit.

Since concern here is only with the relative performance of column samples with lab analysis versus field sorting, all data have been combined, without regard for stratigraphic order, in order to analyse performance of these two approaches for the site as a whole. In all, 4,874 fish bones and scales were analysed. The fauna included *Squalus acanthias* Linnaeus, *Acipenser* spp., *Clupea harengus pallasi* Valenciennes, *Oncorhynchus* spp., *O. tshawytscha* (Walbaum), *O. gorbuscha* (Walbaum), *Thaleichthys pacificus* (Richardson), Catostomidae (gen. et sp. indet.), Cyprinidae (gen. et sp. indet.), *Mylocheilus caurinus* (Richardson), *Gasterosteus aculeatus* Linnaeus, Pleuronectidae (gen. et sp. indet.), and *Platichthys stellatus* (Pallas).

Results

Of the 4,874 fish bones and scales examined, 4,418 (>90%) came from the single, field-sorted unit. As examination of table 12 and fig. 12 indicates, this tremendous expenditure of effort resulted in the discovery of but a single spine of *Squalus acanthias* and a few vertebral fragments of this or another cartilaginous fish. Otherwise the faunal spectrum is the same as that recovered in the column samples. Together these make up only about 0·1% of the identified material from this unit.

TABLE 12

Fish remains from each unit as percentage of total identified

Identification	Unit 1	Column 1	Column 4
Chondrichthys	0·00127		
Osteichthys			
Acipenser spp.	0·02145	0·01071	0·01704
Clupea harengus pallasi		0·00357	0·00568
Oncorhynchus spp.	0·94431	0·65714	0·65340
Thaleichthys pacificus		0·12142	0·11363
Cyprinidae/Catostomidae	0·01507	0·00357	
Gasterosteus aculaeatus		0·18928	0·19886
Pleuronectidae	0·01762	0·01428	0·01136
Total	0·99972	0·99997	0·99997

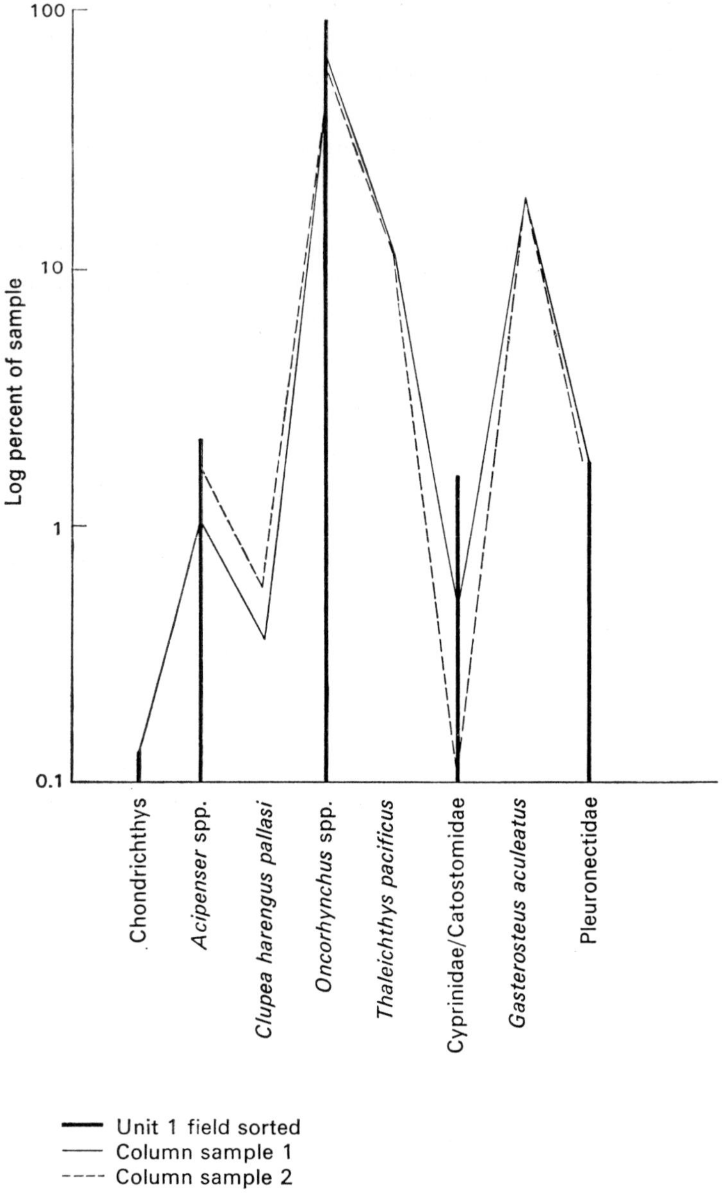

Figure 12 Fish remains from the Glenrose Cannery site

The column samples recovered all fishes represented in the field-sorted unit, with the exception of the cartilaginous remains (i.e. all species except for those with frequencies of occurrence in the field-sorted sample of <1% of the identified fish remains). In addition the column samples and laboratory analysis produced three species of smaller, but dietarily important fishes not found in the field-sorted unit (*Thaleichthys pacificus*, *Clupea harengus pallasi*, and *Gasterosteus aculeatus*).

Consideration of fig. 12 and table 12 indicates that while field-sorting of entire units is capable of identifying the major ichthyofaunal components, it is heavily biased in favour of the larger-sized animals (*Acipenser*, *Oncorhynchus*, Catostomidae, Cyprinidae,

Pleuronectidae). This phenomenon is the same as that described by Sparks (1961) in his study of non-marine molluscan faunas from archaeological sites. It also parallels the findings of Paaver (1958) in his study of faunal remains from archaeological sites in the Estonian SSR.

The column samples from units 1 and 4 provide an opportunity for comparison of the stability of the relative frequencies of the seven groups of fishes between column samples. These data are presented in table 12 and fig. 12. The ichthyofaunas appear to be internally consistent. The relative frequencies of each group were compared utilizing Spearman's rank-correlation coefficient ($r_s = 0{\cdot}84$, significant at $\alpha = 0{\cdot}05$) (Siegel 1956).

Summary and conclusion

Ichthyofaunas derived from laboratory analysis of column samples were compared with those from the same units which had been field sorted. The results indicated that laboratory analysis of column samples required only about one-tenth the effort required for analysis of whole-unit samples. In addition, this detailed study of column sample material produced an approximately 30% increase in the types of fishes identified over the number identified in the whole-unit, field sorted samples.

The results derived from column samples from different units within the site show internal consistency and relative stability in their ichthyofaunal compositions.

Although whole-unit, field analysis proved capable of identifying the major ichthyofaunal components, it proved to be highly biased in favour of larger animals. Given that (a) the analysis of field-sorted faunas from entire units proved 9 times more time consuming than the analysis of comparable column samples, (b) the field-sorted samples were highly biased against smaller individuals and species, and (c) the column samples provided a more complete representation of the ichthyofauna, it appears that column sampling is a highly accurate, efficient, and clearly justified approach for ichthyofaunal and micro-faunal sampling in archaeological sites.

Acknowledgements

This study was supported by funds from a Canada Council Research Grant. My sincere thanks to Dr R. G. Matson, University of British Columbia, and Mr W. I. Follett, California Academy of Sciences, for their assistance.

3.xi.1975

Department of Archaeology,
Simon Fraser University

References

Casteel, R. W. 1970. Core and column sampling. *American Antiquity*. 35(4):465–7.

Casteel, R. W. 1972. Some biases in the recovery of archaeological faunal remains. *Proceedings of the Prehistoric Society*. 38:382–8.

Cook, S. F. and Heizer, R. F. 1951. The physical analysis of nine Indian mounds in tbe Lower Sacramento Valley. *University of California Publications in American Archaeology and Ethnology.* 40:281–312.

Davidson, J. M. 1964. Processing and analysing midden samples. *New Zealand Archaeological Association Newsletter.* 7(3):152–63.

Heizer, R. F. and Squier, R. J. 1953. Excavations at site Nap-32 in July, 1951. *University of California Anthropological Record.* 12(6):appendix IV.

Meighan, C. W., Pendergast, D. M., Swartz, B. K. and Wissler, M. D. 1958. Ecological interpretation in archaeology: part I. *American Antiquity.* 24(1):1–23.

Moorehead, W. K. 1929. *The Cahokia Mounds.* Urbana: University of Illinois Press.

Paaver, K. L. 1958. K metodike opredeleniia otnositel'nogo znacheniia vidov i grupp mlekopitaiuschchikh v osteologicheskom materiale iz raskopok arkheologicheskikh pamiatnikov. *Izvestiia akademii nauk Estonskoi SSR, seriia biologicheskaia.* 7(4):277–90.

Payne, S. 1972. Partial recovery and sample bias: the results of some sieving experiments. In E. S. Higgs (ed.), *Papers in Economic Prehistory:* 49–64. Cambridge University Press.

Schock, J. M. 1971. Indoor flotation – a technique for the recovery of archaeological materials. *Plains Anthropologist.* 16(53):228–31.

Siegel, S. 1956. *Nonparametric Statistics.* McGraw-Hill.

Sparks, B. W. 1961. The ecological interpretation of Quaternary non-marine mollusca. *Proceedings of the Linnaean Society of London.* 172:71–80.

Struever, S. 1968. Flotation techniques for the recovery of small-scale archaeological remains. *American Antiquity.* 33(3):353–62.

Thomas, D. H. 1969. Great Basin hunting patterns: a quantitative method for treating faunal remains. *American Antiquity.* 34(4):392–401.

Treganza, A. E. and Cook, S. F. 1948. The quantitative investigation of aboriginal sites: complete excavation with physical and archaeological analysis of a single mound. *American Antiquity.* 13(4):287–97.

Watson, J. P. N. 1972. Fragmentation analysis of animal bone samples from archaeological sites. *Archaeometry.* 14(2):221–7.

Abstract

Casteel, Richard W.

Comparison of column and whole unit samples for recovering fish remains

Comparisons were made between fish faunas recovered from entire excavation units and sorted in the field by the excavators and fish faunas from column samples recovered in the same units and examined in the laboratory with the aid of a microscope. The results indicated that the smaller column samples provided adequate control for defining the number of species utilized and often surpassed the whole unit analyses by showing the presence of smaller individuals of species not recovered from the larger units. Microscopic examination of small samples appears to provide a much needed addition to the commonly utilized methods of sampling fish faunas.

Plate 1 The Belleview section after excavation. Clearly visible are the archaeological layers separated from the hill wash by a clean sand deposit. The divisions on the ranging rod are at 20 cm intervals

Plate 2 The excavated section at Sehonghong in the Orange River Valley showing the layer of roof spalls dated to between 30,900 and 32,150 b.p.

The effects of climatic change on settlement in Eastern Lesotho during the Middle and Later Stone Age

P. L. Carter

A considerable body of published data exist for changes in the climatic regime of the Northern Hemisphere during the past 50,000 years. However, the Southern Hemisphere remains less well documented, although recent work in Australia, Sub-Saharan Africa and South America is beginning to provide a tentative framework of events (Charlesworth 1963; Bakker 1972; Bowler, in press). The dangers of long-distance correlation are well known, as is the need for the establishment of detailed local sequences before any overall synthesis of climatic events can be attempted. This paper, based on fieldwork carried out in 1969, 1971 and 1974 (Carter 1969), presents evidence for changes in precipitation and temperature that have occurred in Eastern Lesotho during the past 50,000 years. The manner in which such change may have affected human settlement is discussed.

Evidence from previous authors

Van Zinderen Bakker and Butzer (1973) and Butzer (1973) have synthesized the earlier work of Sparrow (1964, 1967; Harper 1969; Hastenrath 1972; Alexandre 1962; Linton 1969) on periglacial phenomena in Southern Africa. Following Harper (1969), but bearing in mind the justified strictures of Butzer (1973) concerning imprecise geomorphological observation and reasoning, we may conclude that:

1 Evidence, based on geomorphological features, exists for two periods of lowered temperature in Lesotho. There is no stratigraphic evidence for the dating of these two cold periods but it is postulated that the younger (later) is equivalent to the maximum of the last (Würm) glacial and that the other is of an age prior to the last glacial maximum.
2 The altitude of the climatic snowline and associated periglacial features in the past, as inferred from the present distribution of solifluction features and cirque bases, can best be explained by assuming that the present wind systems and precipitation regime have not materially altered.
3 Any precipitation increase that may have occurred in Eastern Lesotho during the last period of climatic cooling would have resulted in a snow, rather than a rainfall, increase.

4 A drop of 5·5° C in temperature occurred during the maximum of the last glacial (Flint 1959).
5 A subsequent rise of 5°C occurred at around 10,000 b.p. (Vincent 1972: 45–54).

Evidence from the present fieldwork

Greater stratigraphic detail and improved radiometric precision are needed to explain the changes that have taken place in the course of the South African Quaternary (Van Zinderen Bakker 1973: 247). The data now available from Eastern Lesotho provide details of stratigraphy and dating that are relevant to an assessment of climatic change during the past 50,000 years. These data comprise a series of radiometric dates and stratigraphic observations based on excavations at five different sites (see fig. 13). Table 13 lists the relevant dates and associated climatic events.

TABLE 13

Radiocarbon analyses referred to in text; Pta = Pretoria Laboratory, Q = Cambridge Laboratory

Site	Altitude Metres	Laboratory number	Date b.p.	Evidence	Inference
Mashai	2,850	Q 1156	7,280 ± 150	Peat formation	Wetter than present
Belleview	2,260	Pta 359	8,650 ± 80	Deposition of hill wash	Wetter than present
Sehonghong	1,800	Pta 787 Pta 785	30,900 ± 550 32,150 ± 770	Intense rock spalling	Temperature decrease
Melikane	1,800	Pta 1331 Pta 1330 Pta 1534	35,830 ± 920 42,300 ± 2,100 42,000 ± 1,700	Rock spalling	Temperature decrease
Ha Soloja	2,286	Pta 741	38,800 ± 2,200	Rock spalling	Temperature decrease
		Pta 771	$42{,}450\,^{+2{,}500}_{-1{,}900}$	3·75 Metre terrace	Stream downcutting
		Pta 760	Greater than 43,000		
Moshebi's Shelter	2,286			Increased spring activity	Wetter than present

Climatic change 13,000 to 4,000 b.p.

At the site of Belleview there is good evidence for a precipitation increase within the time range 13,000 to 4,000 b.p. The deposit at the site is clearly divided in two, with a stratigraphic uncomformity between the geological and archaeological layers (plate 1). The geological layers are the result of the deposition of hill wash within the shelter consequent upon an increase in precipitation. The same pattern of deposition may be observed at present during periods of heavy rainfall such as occur during violent summer convection storms.

There is now evidence from many parts of Africa for marked precipitation increases

Figure 13 Map of Eastern Lesotho showing the location of sites referred to in the text

during the Holocene and terminal Pleistocene (Butzer *et al.* 1972: 1069–76), from which it is clear that a major period of rainfall increase occurred between 10,000 and 8,000 years before present as evidenced by the many high lake levels recorded at this time in West, East and North-East Africa. The Belleview evidence with a central date of 8,650±80 b.p. is therefore in accord with evidence from other parts of the continent. Although there are no relevant radiometric dates available from the site of Moshebi's Shelter, we can with some confidence attribute an increase in spring activity at the site to the same time period by virtue of the relative stratigraphic position of the spring deposits and the artefactual affinities between the sites of Moshebi's Shelter and Belleview which are only 6·5 km. apart. Further confirmation of changes in precipitation amount during the period 13,000 to 4,000 b.p. is provided by a stratified series of peat deposits interbedded with fluvatile material occurring in association with a spring eye at a height of 2,850 m. in the Upper Mashai River catchment. As peat is not forming at the site today, it is considered that each peat layer represents a period of local rainfall increase of which the earliest occurred at 7,280 ± 150 b.p.

Climatic change at between 30,900 and 32,150 b.p.

Throughout Southern Africa, at many sites that have yielded a Middle Stone Age sequence, the excavator reports the presence of one or more clearly marked rock falls. The origin and date of such rock falls have largely been a matter for speculation, and although a tectonic origin has been suggested, a climatic explanation is to be preferred (Sampson 1974: 246–7).

We now have, for the first time in Southern Africa, a clearly marked and well dated deposit of roof spalls, in an archaeological context, that is coeval with the beginning of the coldest part of the last glacial maximum (plate 2). The presence of this rock fall between 30,900 and 32,150 years ago at Sehonghong is strong support for Harper's suggestion (1969) that the youngest set of periglacial features in Eastern Lesotho date to the maximum of the last (Würm) glaciation.

The date for Harper's earlier set of periglacial features is still a matter of debate, but at both Sehonghong and Melikane there is evidence for roof spalling prior to 32,000 b.p. On the Sehonghong evidence, all that can be said is that the earlier spalling occurred prior to 32,000 b.p. but at Melikane a layer of roof spalls may be dated between 35,830 ± 920 and 42,000 ± 1,700 (plate 3).

Climatic change prior to 43,000 b.p.

Three dates have been obtained from the site of Ha Soloja, all of which exceed 38,800 b.p. (table 13). This series of dates is stratigraphically above layers of rock spalls in the deposit. The dates do not, of course, provide an accurate chronology of the underlying layers but at least they enable us to state that at some time prior to 43,000 b.p. there is evidence at Ha Soloja for a temperature decrease as shown by the presence of the roof spall layers. The *terminus ante quem* of this temperature decrease is a matter for speculation, but the river terrace that lies at the base of the deposits may well be significant. Since the deposition of the terrace, downcutting by the Thamathu River to the extent of 3·75 m. has taken place. This downcutting must have taken place at some time prior to 43,000 b.p. and, if the cause of downcutting was a lowering of the base level due to a lowering of sea level and not consequent upon local changes in base level, it is possible that the downcutting relates to the lowering of sea level that occurred at the beginning of the last glacial period ± 65,000 b.p. It is significant in this respect that at the site of

Nelson's Bay Cave in the Cape Province of the Republic of South Africa Butzer (1973: 98) reports the presence of a 12-m. beach at the base of an extensive Middle Stone Age sequence. This beach is correlated with a late last glacial (Eem) sea level. The stratigraphical and archaeological parallel with the Ha Soloja river terrace is not without interest but at present it must remain a matter of speculation whether or not the 12-m. beach at Nelson's Bay is coeval with the Ha Soloja river terrace.

Effect of observed climatic change on settlement patterns

From the study area we have therefore good field evidence based on excavation at six sites, which together produce more than twenty-five radiometric dates, of at least four past changes in climate:

1 A lowering of temperature at some time prior to 43,000 b.p. and possibly later than 65,000 b.p.
2 A lowering of temperature between 35,830 and 42,000 b.p.
3 A lowering of temperature between 30,900 and 32,150 b.p.
4 A rainfall increase at some time between 12,000 and 4,000 b.p. with an apparent peak at 8,650±80 b.p.

We shall now discuss the effect of temperature decrease as a factor affecting settlement patterns in Eastern Lesotho and then consider the effects of rainfall increase.

Effect of temperature decrease

The consensus of informed opinion suggests that, whatever the underlying causes may have been, during a period of glacial maximum (i.e. of lowered temperature) the world pattern of atmospheric circulation would be intensified and the climatic belts, and with them the middle latitude storm tracks, would move towards the equator (Willet 1950: 179–87; Flint 1957: 497). Acceptance of this change in storm track path has important implications for precipitation patterns in Southern Africa generally and for snowfall patterns in Lesotho in particular.

There are no quantative data on present-day snowfall in Eastern Lesotho and data are also very scanty from adjacent parts of the Republic of South Africa. It is not surprising therefore that many questions relating to snow in Southern Africa, especially depth of snow and the duration of snow cover in the mountainous areas, remain unanswered. The following comments are therefore based on personal observation over the period 1959 to 1974 and on statements collected from local inhabitants. The most striking fact to emerge is the marked difference in snow cover today between the Orange River Valley and the Sehlabathebe basin, and between the latter and the largely easterly-facing slopes of the Drakensberg escarpment. The available meteorological data clearly show that the Orange River Valley is in a rain shadow area so that it is both warmer and drier than the Sehlabathebe basin, which in turn is drier than the Drakensberg escarpment slopes. In other words, present-day snowfall and duration of snow cover are at a minimum in the Orange River Valley and a maximum on the easterly-facing Drakensberg escarpment. The snow regime in the Sehlabathebe Basin approximates far more closely to the escarpment than to the valley (table 14).

TABLE 14

Relationship between precipitation amount and earliest dated occupation sites in Eastern Lesotho

	Orange River Valley	Sehlabathebe Basin	Drakensberg Escarpment
Present rainfall	560 mm	780 mm	1,500 to 1,750 mm
Present and past snow amount	Minimal	Intermediate	Maximal
Middle Stone Age surface sites	Present	Absent	Absent
Middle Stone Age rockshelter occupation	Substantial and virtually continuous	Sporadic	Absent
Excavated sites	Sehonghong Melikane	Ha Soloja Moshebi's Shelter	Belleview Good Hope
Earliest C^{14} dates	Sehonghong 32,150 b.p. Melikane 42,000 b.p.	Ha Soloja 43,000 b.p. Moshebi's: No date available but Middle Stone Age artefacts present	Belleview 8,650 b.p. Good Hope 8,200 b.p.

Over the escarpment and basin at present the prevailing weather direction is from the east and south-east, but in the Orange River Valley the rain shadow effect is marked, regardless of the prevailing weather direction. It is precisely from the south-east that the snow-bearing winter weather comes today, and would have come in the past with an equatorial shift in the middle latitude storm tracks caused by an overall global temperature decrease. Furthermore, if we assume the distribution of snow in the past to be the same as at present, as the evidence of Harper (1969) would suggest, but allow that the amount and duration of snow cover would have increased at a time of lowered temperature, we find a very high negative correlation between the areas of high snowfall and the distribution of Middle Stone Age sites, particularly surface sites.

Effects of rainfall increase

The effect of rainfall increase on settlement pattern is difficult to assess. It is, however, indisputable that rainfall amount in the study area is highly variable, being largely dependent on local topographic features. No detailed rainfall figures are available, but survey of the Cathedral Peak area some 100 km. to the north of the Sehlabathebe Basin provides a rainfall transect of the Drakensberg escarpment that well illustrates local variation in rainfall (Killick 1963: 17). Regardless of the amount, rain falls at clearly defined times. Both daily and seasonal patterning occur.

Unlike the negative correlation between Middle Stone Age occupancy of rockshelters and snowfall amount, Later Stone Age occupancy and rainfall, taken over the whole of the survey area, appear to be independent factors. Interesting, however, is the variation between sites in the same ecological zone that are occupied in the Later Stone Age.

If we classify sites as wet and dry, we find that there are occupation gaps in the wet sites but not in the dry sites. A wet site may be defined as a site that has, or had in the past, a spring within the shelter, or as a site that is located in a situation where, at times of heavy rainfall today, hill wash is deposited within the shelter. Table 15 shows the available information from the excavated sites.

It is clear from inspection of the table that, in the Orange River Valley, dry sites such as Melikane and Sehonghong, have been occupied since the Middle Stone Age and that variation in precipitation, whether snow or rain, has apparently had little effect on rockshelter occupancy. Within the Sehlabathebe Basin the dry shelter, Ha Soloja, shows a similar picture, but at the wet site, Moshebi's Shelter, there is evidence of non-occupation during the ninth millennium b.p. In contrast, the escarpment sites of Belleview and Good Hope have only Late Stone Age occupation, but again the wet site, Belleview, has a clear indication of non-occupation during a period of increased rainfall.

The foregoing discussion of settlement patterns has been restricted to rockshelter sites that have been occupied over considerable time periods. It is equally fruitful to consider the effect of precipitation, whether in the form of rain or snow, on the distribution of surface sites of both Middle and Later Stone Age date. In the Orange River Valley (the rain shadow part of the study area, with the lowest rainfall today and the presumptively lowest snowfall in the past), surface sites of both Middle and Later Stone Age date are of common occurrence. Conversely, in the Sehlabathebe Basin and the adjacent slopes of the Drakensberg escarpment, where precipitation today and in the past has been markedly higher than in the Orange River Valley, surface sites are extremely rare and indeed are absent in many valleys.

In other words, in Eastern Lesotho and the adjacent parts of the Drakensberg escarpment, snowfall is a strong constraint on site distribution, particularly during the Middle Stone Age when the amount and duration of snow cover was in excess of today's value.

The distribution of Stone Age sites in the Natal Drakensburg is discussed by Willcox (1974) who, following Acocks (1935), suggests that during the period 14,000 to 50,000 b.p. human settlement was not possible between 1,219 and 2,100 m. because of the presence of thick *Podocarpus latifolius* forest claimed to be impenetrable to man and large game animals. Most botanical authorities would probably agree that the past distribution of *Podocarpus latifolius* was somewhat greater than today but, as Killick (1963: 99) and Edwards (1967: 177) point out, it is difficult to believe in the existence of extensive Drakensberg forest in the past for three reasons. First, the natural occurrence of fire in the area as a result of lightning strikes; secondly, the frequency of severe frosts which inhibit the development of forest, and, thirdly, the lack of forest relics at the higher levels. It is highly likely therefore that the major factor governing site distribution in Eastern Lesotho and the Drakensberg escarpment is not the presence of extensive *Podocarpus latifolius* forest but the amount and duration of snow cover.

TABLE 15

Relationship between rainfall and occupation of rockshelters in Eastern Lesotho

<table>
<tr><th></th><th colspan="2">Orange River Valley</th><th colspan="2">Sehlabathebe Basin</th><th colspan="2">Drakensberg Escarpment</th></tr>
<tr><td>Site</td><td>Melikane</td><td>Sehonghong</td><td>Moshebi's</td><td>Ha Soloja</td><td>Belleview</td><td>Good Hope</td></tr>
<tr><td>Type</td><td>Dry</td><td>Dry</td><td>Wet</td><td>Dry</td><td>Wet</td><td>Dry</td></tr>
<tr><td rowspan="4">Occupation</td><td rowspan="2">Later Stone Age</td><td rowspan="2">Later Stone Age</td><td>Later Stone Age</td><td rowspan="2">Later Stone Age</td><td>Later Stone Age</td><td rowspan="2">Later Stone Age</td></tr>
<tr><td>Sterile</td><td>Sterile</td></tr>
<tr><td colspan="4">Middle Stone Age</td><td colspan="2" rowspan="2">Bed Rock</td></tr>
<tr><td colspan="4">Bed Rock</td></tr>
</table>

Acknowledgements

The fieldwork on which this paper is based was funded by the James A. Swan fund of the University of Oxford and the Crowther Benyon fund of the Cambridge Museum of Archaeology and Ethnology. Mention must also be made of the assistance given by Patricia Vinnicombe of King's College, Cambridge, throughout all three field seasons. Dr J. C. Vogel of the Pretoria Radiocarbon Laboratory should also be thanked for his enthusiastic and willing co-operation in the analysis of most of the dating samples.

30.iii.1976

Downing College
Cambridge

References

Acocks, J. P. H. 1935. Veld types of South Africa. *Botanical Survey Memoir*. 28. Pretoria.

Alexandre, J. 1962. Phénomènes périglaciares dans le Basutoland et le Drakensberg du Natal. *Biuletyn Peryglacjalny*. 11:11–13. Lódž.

Bakker, E. M. Van Zinderen. 1972. *Palaeoecology of Africa*. 6:15–27. A. A. Balkema: Capetown.

Bakker, E. M. Van Zinderen and Butzer, K. W. 1973. Quaternary environmental changes in southern Africa. *Soil Science*. 116(3):236–48.

Bowler, J. M. *et al.* Late Quaternary climates of Australia and New Guinea. *Quaternary Research*. In press.

Butzer, K. W. *et al.* 1972. Radiocarbon dating of East African lake levels. *Science*. 175:1069–76.

Butzer, K. W. 1973. Pleistocene 'periglacial' phenomena in southern Africa. *Boreas*. 2:1–12.

Carter, P. L. 1969. Moshebi's Shelter: exploitation and excavation in Eastern Lesotho. *Lesotho*. 8:1–11.

Charlesworth, J. K. 1957. *The Quaternary Era*. London. 2 vols.

Edwards, D. 1967. A plant ecological survey of the Tugela River Basin. *Botanical Survey Memoir*. 36:176–8. Pietermaritzberg.

Flint, R. F. 1957. *Glacial and Pleistocene Geology*. 485–6. New York.

Flint, R. F. 1959. Pleistocene climates in Eastern and Southern Africa. *Bulletin of the Geological Society of America*. 70:343–74.

Harper, G. 1969. Periglacial evidence in southern Africa during the Pleistocene epoch. *Palaeoecology of Africa*. 4:71–101. Capetown.

Hastenrath, S. and Wilkinson, J. 1972. A contribution to the periglacial morphology of Lesotho, southern Africa. *Biuletyn Periglacjalny*. 22. In press. Lódž.

Killick, D. J. B. 1963. An account of the plant ecology of the Cathedral Peak area of the Natal Drakensberg. *Botanical Survey Memoir*. 34:89–100. Pretoria.

Linton, D. L. 1969. Evidences of Pleistocene cryonival landforms in the southern hemisphere. *Palaeoecology of Africa*. 5:71–89. A. A. Balkema: Capetown.

Sampson, C. G. 1974. *The Stone Age Archaeology of Southern Africa*. 246–7. London and New York.

Sparrow, G. W. A. 1964. Pleistocene periglacial landforms in the southern hemisphere. *South African Journal of Science*. 60:143–7.

Sparrow, G. W. A. 1967. South African cirques and arêtes. *Journal of Geography*. 9–11.

Vincent, E. 1972. Climatic change at the Pleistocene-Holocene boundary in the southwest Indian Ocean. *Palaeoecology of Africa*. 6:45–54. A. A. Balkema: Capetown.

Willcox, A. R. 1974. Reasons for the non-occurrence of Middle Stone Age material in the Natal Drakensberg. *South African Journal of Science*. 70:273–5.

Willett, H. C. 1950. The general circulation of the last (Würm) glacial maximum. *Geografiska Annaler*. 32:179–87.

Abstract

Carter, P. L.

The effects of climatic change on settlement in Eastern Lesotho during the Middle and Later Stone Age

Three seasons' excavation in Eastern Lesotho have produced a prehistoric sequence from a number of stratified sites that extends back in time at least 43,000 years. Data relating to precipitation increase and temperature decrease were obtained. The effect of climatic change, particularly increased snowfall, on the distribution of sites, is discussed.

Valleys and settlement: some new evidence

T. W. Potter

Introduction

One of the more conspicuous features of recent archaeological research has been the greatly increased emphasis upon field survey, as a means of reconstructing the settlement forms of older landscapes. Amongst the more extensive surveys has been the study by the British School at Rome of over 1,000 sq. km. of the fertile volcanic uplands of South Etruria (Ward-Perkins 1955, 1957, 1961, 1968; Duncan 1958; Jones 1962, 1963; Ogilvie 1965). This survey, initiated by Ward-Perkins in the early 1950s, came at the timely moment when much long-established pasture came under the modern plough for the first time. As a result, prodigious quantities of archaeological material were brought to light, yielding a clear idea both of the date and of the character of sites. In all, a total of very nearly 3,000 sites has now been recorded in this manner. They range in date from the middle Bronze Age down to the post-medieval period and furnish a most detailed picture of a series of superimposed archaeological landscapes.

One of the major problems raised by this survey concerns the valleys. Generally speaking, it was only the fringes of the valleys which were in any way productive of archaeological material: the valley floors proved almost entirely devoid of anything older than a few centuries. This might imply either that there were strong constraints against settlement on the valley floors in antiquity, or that the archaeological evidence was obscured or missing. In either case this constituted an important area of inquiry, of relevance both to archaeologists and sedimentologists, and this paper offers a conspectus of some recent evidence, primarily from central Italy but also from England.

The river valleys: general characteristics

The terrain of South Etruria is built up of successive overlays of volcanic ash, deriving principally from the Monti Sabatini, the southern part of a chain of volcanic vents which extend northwards into Central Etruria. These volcanic ridges create major watersheds and thus to a large extent shape the geography of the drainage basins of South Etruria. The water drains in two principal directions, either westwards towards the coastal flats and Tyrrhenian Sea or eastwards into the Tiber valley. The streams are numerous and fast flowing and soon erode downwards through the soft volcanic rock. As a result the terrain of South Etruria is seamed with steep-sided canyons and ravines which in many instances approach depths of 100 m. The rivers themselves normally run in deep trenches incised into a broad floodplain. Their regimes vary, but all except the minor streams maintain their flow through the summer and can rise several metres when in spate, sometimes topping their banks and spilling out over the floodplain. Standing water on the floodplain has been a rare occurrence in recent years, however.

The volcanic topography of South Etruria (and especially Etruria Tiberina) has been recently investigated by Alvarez (1972, 1973) and Mattias and Ventriglia (1970). They have shown that the drainage pattern of the region was established from the period of the earliest volcanism and that each subsequent phase of tectonic activity was followed by re-excavation through erosion of the main river valleys.

The recent stream sediments in the area have been studied in detail by Judson (1963a), with results that have far-reaching archaeological implications. The best documented site lies in the valley of the Fosso della Crescenza, near the north Rome suburb of Tomba di Nerone (fig. 14). Immediately beside the present course of the stream is a mausoleum, built in the first century A.D.; adjoining it is a building of early

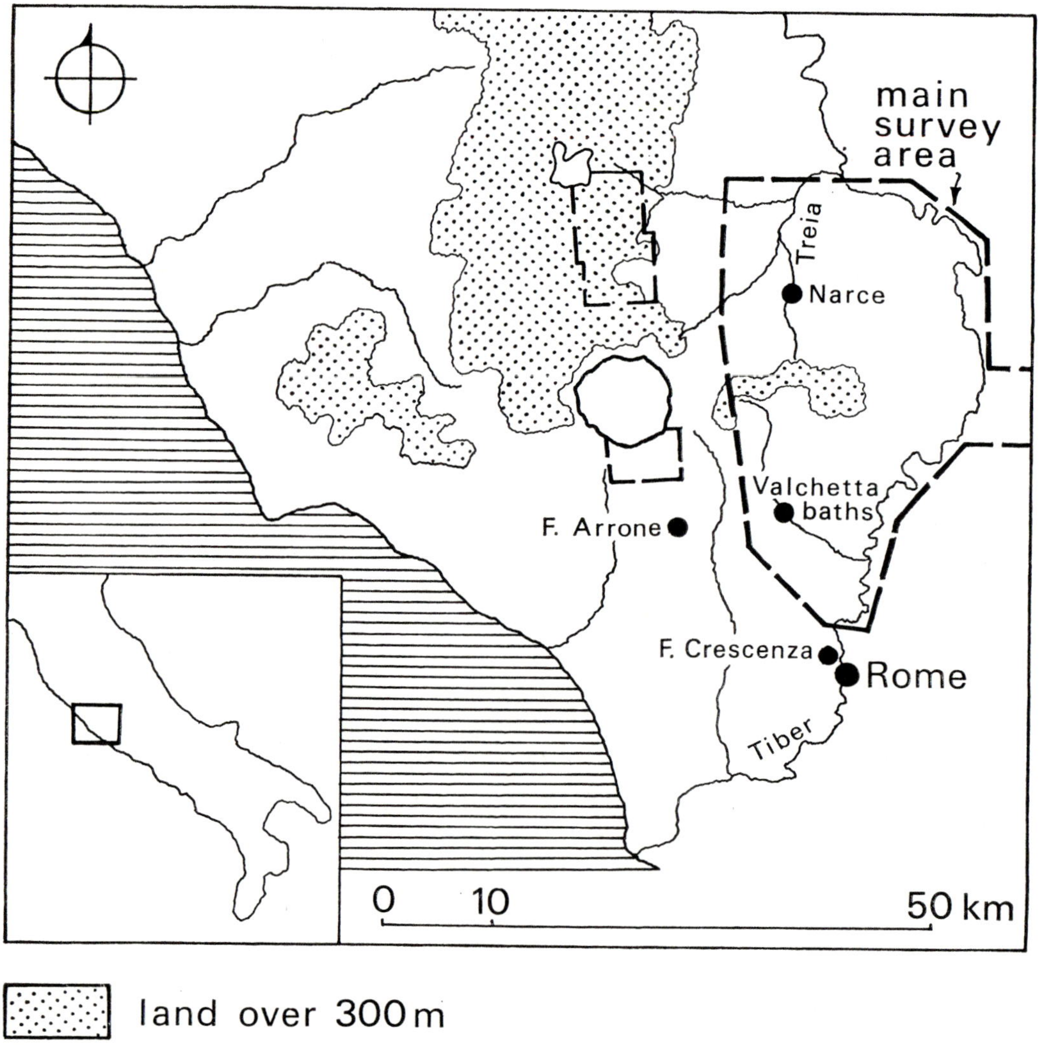

Figure 14 Location map for the South Etrurian survey and Central Italian sites discussed in the text

third century date. Both structures were found to be choked in alluvium which, as excavation demonstrated, had been laid down intermittently during the first and second centuries A.D., and more or less continuously from the mid third century onwards (Judson 1963a; Ward-Perkins 1964: 14–15). A radiocarbon date of A.D. 550±100 (I–882) showed that alluviation persisted into medieval times, while the overall depth of these silts (in places nearly 8 m.) indicates a very lengthy period of formation.

Similar results were obtained from two other sites in Etruria Tiberina. At Veii, a bath-house (the 'Bagni della Regina') situated on the floor of the Valchetta valley was partially excavated in 1959 (Jones 1960). The building appears to have been constructed during the first half of the first century A.D. and underwent major modifications sometime before the end of the second century. Its lifespan is not closely defined, but there is no third- or fourth-century pottery from the site and it would appear to have been abandoned during that time. The sections clearly show the building deeply buried beneath several metres of alluvium (Jones 1960: plate xxiia); evidently, as at the Fosso della Crescenza, the valley became liable to severe flooding in the late Roman period. Another example of a similar sequence may be cited from the Arrone valley, near the Via Clodia, some 15 km. to the north-west of Rome. Fieldwork by Judson and the writer in 1967 revealed a valley-bottom site, partly exposed in the river bank. There were two layers of archaeological material, sealed between thick deposits of alluvium (fig. 15). The archaeological finds consisted mainly of large quantities of building debris, including masonry, cement and tile, all evidently from a nearby building, as well as a large sample of unabraded pottery of the first century A.D. Silt deposits both divided and sealed this occupation debris, suggesting (as at the Fosso della Crescenza) an initial phase of intermittent flooding followed by fairly sustained inundation. Furthermore, the lower layers of archaeological material rested upon another thick deposit of silt, indicating that the valley had also been waterlogged in pre-Roman times, although there was no close dating evidence for this layer.

These three sites provide a consistent picture of recent valley-bottom history in South Etruria: that relatively short-lived occupation of the valley floors in the first and second centuries A.D. was followed by drastic and prolonged inundation which discouraged any further attempt at settlement. Moreover, as Judson (1963b) and, more recently, Vita-Finzi (1969) have shown, the phenomenon is not restricted to central Italy. Judson was able to demonstrate a very similar sequence in the Gornalunga valley of Sicily and Vita-Finzi, in a much more widely based study, cited numerous examples of late Roman and medieval alluviation throughout the Mediterranean region. In addition, he envisaged a second and older phase of major silt deposition (the 'older fill') which apparently belonged to the early Würm.

The alluvial sequence from Narce

The archaeological implications of this alluvial sequence for the understanding of landscape history are obviously considerable and it is fortunate that a further opportunity arose to study the problem more closely. In 1966, a small valley-bottom settlement, occupied from *c.* 1400–250 B.C., was located in the bank of the River Treia, below the

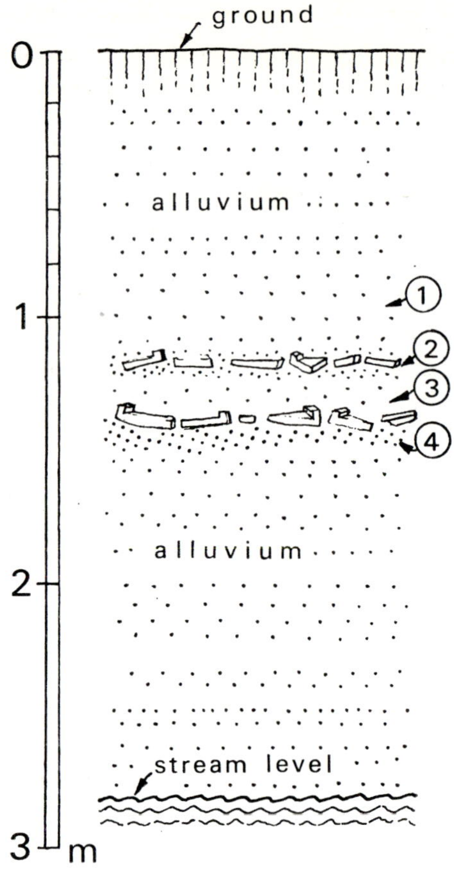

Figure 15 Section exposed in the bank of the Fosso Arrone (Central Italy), showing Roman period debris sealed between alluvial deposits.
Key to the units: 1. Yellow silt, unlaminated. 2. Layer of building debris, including *terra sigillata*. 3. Clay-silt with a little charcoal. 4. Layer of debris with tile, masonry, cement, charcoal and much pottery of the first century A.D.

well known Faliscan acropolis of Narce (Barnabei 1894; Potter 1976a). The Treia, the major river of a drainage basin covering some 350 sq. km., flows at this point in a deeply incised ravine, nearly 150 m. in width. The newly discovered site lay in the east side of this valley, adjoining the present river; indeed, it soon became clear that much of the site had been eroded away by the Treia, creating a broad floodplain over the western part of the valley (fig. 16). In 1970–1, in conjunction with the excavation of the settlement, Dr Douglas Cherkauer of Princeton University carried out extensive excavation and augering of the Treia floodplain, with the aim of defining the relationship between the river and the settlement (Cherkauer 1976). In the event, most of the pre-Roman riverine deposits proved to lie well below the maximum depth that could be achieved by trenching (*c.* 2·5 m. below the valley floor); however, the work did yield a detailed history of the river's movements from *c.* 250 B.C. down to the present day, and fairly close dating was provided by an abundance of stratified, datable pottery, representing all periods from the middle Bronze Age down to the present century. Fortunately,

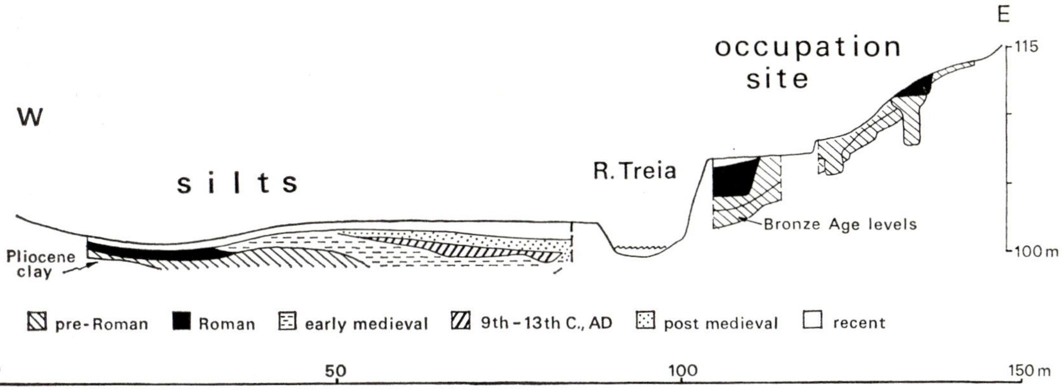

Figure 16 Section across the Treia valley at Narce (Central Italy), showing the chronology of the deposits

there were nearby Roman and medieval sites (Potter 1972) which introduced sufficient rubbish into the valley to provide dating evidence for these periods.

The trenching produced a clear and obvious distinction between deposits laid down in former river beds (generally coarse gravels but including both small and large boulders) and the clay-silt alluvium deposited as sediment upon the floodplain (plate 4). Moreover, it became evident that the course of the river bed had moved more or less continuously during the last two millennia, for there were a number of different channels, and that its regime had also varied; at some periods (as at present) the river tended to downcut through older sediments, creating a trench in the valley floor, while at others it was aggrading – i.e. flowing in a comparatively shallow channel and, when in spate, depositing large quantities of silt upon the flood plain. The sections placed these fluctuations in relative sequence and an absolute chronology was provided by the stratified potsherds: as a result the river history could be reconstructed in some detail and may usefully be summarized at this point (fig. 17).

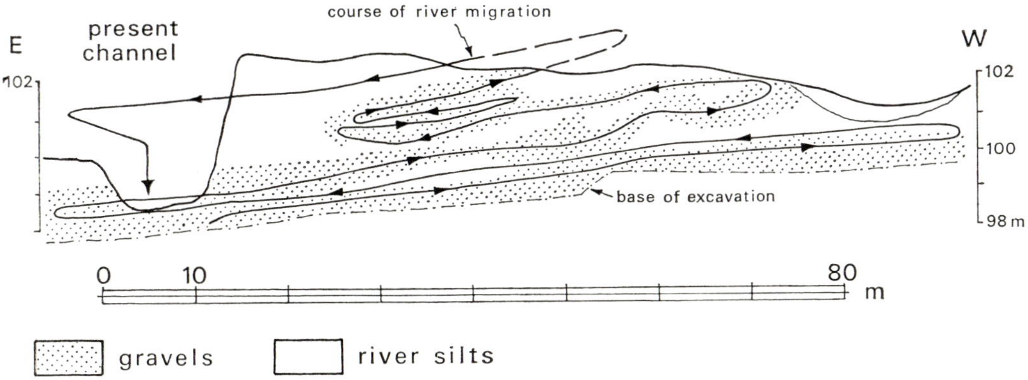

Figure 17 Schematic section through the floodplain of the River Treia, reconstructing the horizontal and vertical movements of the river between *c.* 250 B.C. and the present day. Adapted from Cherkauer 1976

During the late pre-Roman period, the river seems to have moved gradually westwards across the valley. The river was aggrading and thus built a silt bank behind it, a conclusion which is matched by the alluvial deposit which preceded the first century A.D. occupation at the Fosso Arrone site. During the period *c.* 250 B.C.–A.D. 150 the river migrated eastwards, downcutting through the older deposits and laying down comparatively little silt. This corresponds with the 'dry' periods in the valleys of the Crescenza, Valchetta and Arrone, when buildings were being constructed on the valley floor. Subsequently the river began a second westwards movement and its regime altered so that it began heavy aggradation. Excavation demonstrated the presence of several riffles, characterized by clusters of very large boulders, indicating that the volume and velocity of the water when the river was in spate must have been very considerable. The pottery from these levels included many Roman sherds and some medieval material, suggesting a synchronism with heavy alluviation attested in the other central Italian valleys. This phase was followed by a brief eastwards migration, associated with downcutting by the river and probably datable to the last part of the first millennium A.D., and then a long period of stream aggradation, extending from *c.* A.D. 1000 down into the eighteenth century. A radiocarbon date of A.D. 1490±30 (I–6110) supports the archaeological dating for this late floodplain deposit. Finally, *c.* 1750, the river began moving towards its present position near the east wall of the valley, while at the same time beginning a downcutting trend which resulted in the present deep stream channel. A post-medieval date for the downcutting of the Fosso della Crescenza has also been demonstrated (Judson 1963a).

Causes of alluviation

There are as yet no other Italian alluvial sequences which are as thoroughly documented as the river history at Narce. Nevertheless, it is clear that other valleys in central Italy demonstrate a broadly similar pattern of events (although with minor chronological differences), and the case for a late Roman-medieval period of alluviation seems to be particularly well sustained. Moreover, if Vita-Finzi (1969) is right, then a similar pattern can be also demonstrated for many other areas of the Mediterranean, including Greece, Jordan, Spain and several areas of North Africa, a conclusion which has recently been supported by the results of extensive fieldwork in Greece (Bintliff 1975).

Given that valley-bottom alluviation at certain well defined periods is not just a local phenomenon, it follows that a generalized explanation is likely for these fluctuations in the river regimes. It has been suggested that factors like deforestation and agricultural activity might have been sufficient to initiate major changes in the behaviour of rivers (Vita-Finzi 1969: 105–11) but the arguments against such an assumption are strong. In South Etruria for example it is clear both from pollen analysis (Bonatti 1963, 1970; Frank 1969) and from archaeological evidence (Ward-Perkins 1968: 14–17) that forest clearance was initiated on a substantial scale during the late Bronze Age and that by the middle of the first millennium B.C. most of the terrain was employed for agricultural purposes (Ward-Perkins 1968: 202). Thus, by the third century A.D., a period of major valley alluviation, the pattern of farming in South Etruria had been established for

Plate 3 The roof spall layer at Melikane which is dated between 35,830 and 42,000 b.p. Beneath the spall layer the rich Middle Stone Age layers are visible

Plate 4 Section through the alluvial deposits at Narce, Central Italy. A river channel, represented by coarse gravel, is sealed between floodplain silts

more than 800 years. If human activity can thus be ruled out as a primary cause of valley alluviation, then the only factor which seems to be sufficiently general is, as Vita-Finzi (1969: 112–15) and others have affirmed, climatic change. It is now clear that the Mediterranean climate in the later Roman and medieval periods was on the whole much damper than at present: the 'little Ice Age' of north Europe between *c.* A.D. 1550–1850 is a reflection of these Mediterranean conditions (Lamb 1966). The precise implications of these climatic changes remains to be worked out in detail but a correlation between increased precipitation and the aggrading tendencies of the rivers seems wholly plausible, and it is to be hoped that further more detailed correlation will prove possible.

Archaeological implications

If the alluvial sequence outlined above applies to all Mediterranean valleys, then it is clear that most low-lying sites of pre-medieval date must be blanketed by deep deposits of recent alluvium: as a consequence distribution maps are in some respects likely to be misleading, especially in dissected areas like South Etruria where valleys account for a considerable proportion of the land (nearly 20% in the Faliscan area). However, it is also evident that there must have been major constraints upon valley-bottom settlement in some periods. Due significance must be given to the fact that there is not one known late Roman or medieval site in a valley-bottom context in any surveyed area of Etruria Tiberina. Similarly there is also an absence of valley settlement in South Etruria during the period between the sixth and first centuries B.C.; significantly, domestic riverside settlements like the Treia site at Narce were generally evacuated in the seventh century B.C. and the area abandoned or turned over to other purposes. At Narce, a tile manufacturing complex was established, an activity which, by analogy with contemporary practice, is restricted to the summer months (Potter 1976a). Indeed, it may be relevant to recall that it was in this period that the underground drainage channels known as *cuniculi* were developed and, furthermore, that they were sometimes used to create dry valleys (Judson and Kahane 1963); this may well have been a measure taken to reclaim waterlogged land in a period when, as field survey work has clearly shown, there was a fast increasing population (Potter 1976a), and hence much greater pressure on resources. In the Faliscan area of Etruria Tiberina the number of sites in occupation increased by nearly 40% between the seventh and five centuries B.C. (fig. 18) and the figures for adjoining areas like the Ager Capenas (Jones 1962, 1963) and the Ager Veientanus (Ward-Perkins 1968) are similar. A reduction in the available land for settlement and agriculture must have had serious consequences. Equally, it is important to note the strong evidence, outlined above, for extensive exploitation of the valleys in the first–second centuries A.D., a period when settlement density reached a peak only equalled in the present century (fig. 18; Ward-Perkins 1968: 149–50). It may be no more than coincidence that this seems to correspond with a minor climatic optimum and that the number of sites in occupation began to fall sharply as the climate deteriorated; but the correlation is close and was arguably an additional factor in the complex model describing the decline in rural settlement under the mid-late Empire (Potter 1975).

GWA

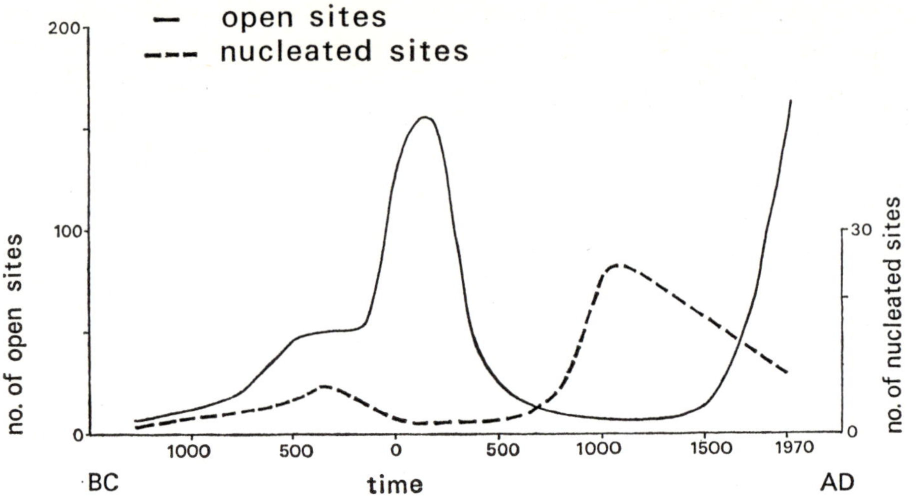

Figure 18 Graph illustrating the fluctuations in the number of open and nucleated sites (which generally occupy fortified positions) in the Ager Faliscus. The total sample amounts to 476 sites

Wider implications

Alluvial sequences have frequently been compared through the Mediterranean but there has been little attempt to correlate them with recent river histories in northern Europe. The problem of Vita-Finzi's 'older fill' (1969: 92–100) lies beyond the scope of this paper but it is worth drawing attention to the increasing number of sites in Britain where late Roman and medieval flooding has been demonstrated. Some of the best documented evidence comes from the Cambridgeshire Fenland (Phillips 1970). Here there is a clearly attested phase of alluviation between *c.* A.D. 220–75 which affected both riverside sites like Welney (Phillips 1951: 269–70; Churchill 1970: 135–8) as well as settlements on low-lying ground bordering the peat fen, as at Hockwold (Salway 1967), Stonea (Potter 1976b) and Willingham-Cottenham (Bromwich 1970). Moreover, this was followed towards the end of the fourth century by drastic inundation, resulting in the deposition of many metres of silt, especially on the seaward side of the Fens. In a recent and authoritative survey (Phillips 1970), the consensus favoured a breakdown of drainage systems in a period of political instability as the best explanation for this flooding (Salway 1970: 15–16; Bromwich 1970: 122–5); but it is now very clear that other sites elsewhere in Britain were also troubled by flooding in the same period. A rather similar sequence has been demonstrated in the Somerset Fens (Cunliffe 1966) and excavation has shown that the low-lying parts of both York (Ramm 1971: 181–3) and Brough-on-Humber (Wacher 1969: 78–81) became waterlogged in the later Roman period. Two recent excavations afford an opportunity to examine the problem more closely. At a Roman settlement at Braughing in Hertfordshire an extensive area of low-lying buildings lining the Ermine Street was examined in 1971–2. There were hints of first century flooding, which caused the level of Ermine Street to be raised substantially, and a nearby bath-house, situated on the valley floor of the River Rib, was found to be choked in flood silt and had apparently been abandoned by the early third century (Partridge 1975). Other low-lying parts of the site were sealed beneath more than a metre of alluvium apparently laid down by a minor stream early in medieval times (fig. 19). This evidence for a deterioration in conditions in the late Roman and medieval

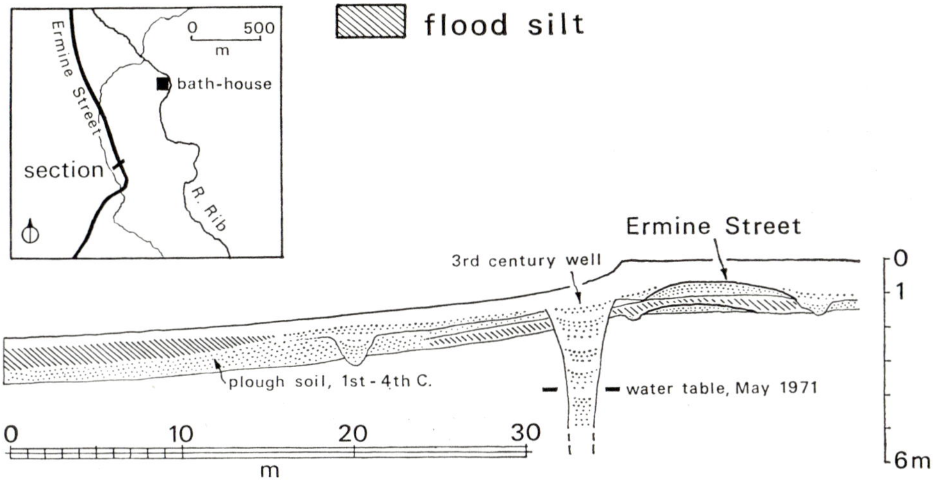

Figure 19 Section across part of the Roman site at Braughing, Hertfordshire (England), excavated 1971–2. The section illustrates flood levels both of the mid-first century A.D. and the medieval period

periods is matched by results from recent excavations of a small Roman fort at Watercrook near Kendal, Cumbria. The fort was sited in a loop of the River Kent, on a platform built at a height of *c.* 3m. above the present-day river level (fig. 20). Extensive excavations in 1974–5 (Potter 1976c) showed that the fort was intermittently garrisoned from *c.* A.D. 90–220 and that the final evacuation came in the period A.D. 270–80, a surprising conclusion in view of the fact that most of the north-western fort sites maintained garrisons throughout the fourth century. The likely explanation for this premature abandonment of the site came from a series of trenches cut between the fort and the river (fig. 20). These showed that this area was built up entirely of alternate beds of gravel and silt, closely resembling the sections from Narce. These alluvial deposits yielded large quantities of reworked Roman material, sherds occurring to a depth of over 2 m. below the present-day ground surface, the maximum depth of the excavation. These show that the silts are of late Roman or medieval creation and imply that the peripheral land around the fort must have become subject to periodic inundation at this time. On analogy with other British sites, the late Roman period provides the likeliest context, probably explaining the final evacaution of the fort site.

These examples (which could be easily multiplied) must suffice to show that in Britain, as in the Mediterranean, sites in low-lying positions were troubled by flooding in the late Roman period and that this was followed by the sustained deposition of alluvium in medieval times. There is thus close comparability with the Mediterranean sequences described above, a conclusion which suggests that both phenomena may be attributable to the same cause, that of climatic fluctuation.

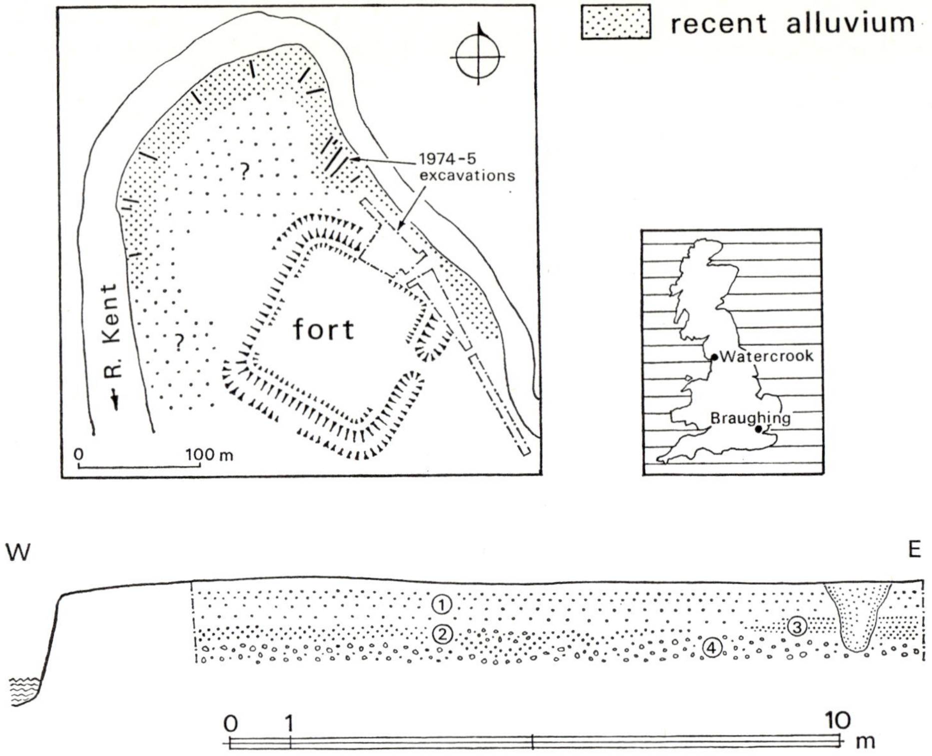

Figure 20 Plan and section of the Roman fort at Watercrook near Kendal, Cumbria (England), excavated 1974–5. The plan illustrates the known extent of the late Roman-medieval silt, while the section shows the nature of the alluvial deposits in the north-east part of the site. Key to the units: 1. Unlaminated brown silt. 2. Grey-orange silt with some laminate. 3. Laminated grey silt. 4. Fine gravel with average grit size of 1 mm., giving way to pebbles and cobbles (up to 300 mm. in size)

Conclusions

Evidence has been offered which sustains Vita-Finzi's case (1969) for a period of major valley alluviation in the late Roman and medieval periods in the Mediterranean. A similar pattern of river behaviour can also be demonstrated for Britain and there are hints in both areas of an earlier phase of valley-bottom alluviation, in the second half of the first millennium B.C. These geomorphological changes are best explained by climatic fluctuations. From an archaeological point of view it is clear both that many pre-Roman sites are blanketed beneath recent alluvium and, furthermore, that in some periods, flooding must have ruled out much of the lower ground as potential settlement areas. The extent to which these geomorphological fluctuations may have affected the shape of settlement patterns is a matter which requires further detailed study: but undoubtedly any definition of ancient landscapes needs to take account of this phenomenon.

Acknowledgements

This paper has its genesis in a number of field trips with Professor Sheldon Judson in 1966–7, and I owe him a very great debt of gratitude. My thanks are due to Dr Douglas Cherkauer who has allowed me to cite his conclusions about the history of the Treia river in advance of detailed publication, and to Mr J. B. Ward-Perkins, mentor of so much research into the archaeology of central Italy.

16.iii.1976

Dept. of Classics and Archaeology
University of Lancaster

References

Alvarez, W. 1972. The Treia valley north of Rome: volcanic stratigraphy, topographic evolution and geological influences on human settlement. *Geologica Romana.* 11:153–76.

Alvarez, W. 1973. The ancient course of the Tiber river near Rome: an introduction to the middle Pleistocene volcanic stratigraphy of Central Italy. *Bulletin of the Geological Society of America.* 84:749–58.

Barnabei, F. (with Gamurrini, G. F., Cozza, A., Pasqui, A.) 1894. Antichità del territorio Falisco esposte nel Museo Nazionale Romano a Valle Giulia. *Monumenti Antichi.* 4.

Bintliff, J. L. 1975. Mediterranean alluviation. *Proceedings of the Prehistoric Society.* 41:78–84.

Bonatti, E. 1963. Stratigrafia pollinica dei sedimenti postglaciale di Baccano, lago craterico del Lazio. *Atti della Società Toscana di Scienze naturali.* 40:40–8.

Bonatti, E. 1970. Pollen sequence in the lake sediments. *Ianula – an account of the history and development of the Lago di Monterosi, Latium, Italy* (ed. G. E. Hutchinson). *Transactions of the American Philosophical Society.* 40(4):26–31.

Bromwich, J. 1970. Freshwater flooding along the Fen margins south of the Isle of Ely during the Roman period. *The Fenland in Roman Times.* Royal Geographical Society Research Memoir no. 5 (ed. C. W. Phillips). 114–26.

Cherkauer, D. 1976. Site K: tbe alluvial deposits at Narce. In T. W. Potter, *A Faliscan town in South Etruria. Excavations at Narce 1966–71.* British School at Rome. In press.

Churchill, D. M. 1970. Post-Neolithic to Romano-British sedimentation in the southern Fenlands of Cambridgeshire and Norfolk. *The Fenland in Roman Times.* Royal Geographical Research Memoir no. 5 (ed. C. W. Phillips). 132–46.

Cunliffe, B. W. 1966. The Somcrsct Lcvcls in the Roman period. *Rural Settlement in Roman Britain.* Council of British Archaeological Research Report, no. 7. (ed. C. Thomas). 68–73.

Duncan, G. C. 1958. Sutri (Sutrium). *Papers of the British School at Rome.* 26:63–134.

Frank, A. H. E. 1969. Pollen stratigraphy of tbe Lake of Vico (Central Italy). *Palaeogeography, Palaeoclimatology, Palaeoecology.* 6(1):67–85.

Jones, G. D. B. 1960. Veii: the Valchetta Baths. *Papers of the British School at Rome.* 28:55–69.

Jones, G. D. B. 1962. Capena and the Ager Capenas. Pt I. *Papers of the British School at Rome.* 30:116–207.

Jones, G. D. B. 1963. Capena and the Ager Capenas. Pt II. *Papers of the British School at Rome.* 31:100–58.

Judson, S. 1963a. Erosion and deposition of Italian stream valleys during historic time. *Science.* 140(3569):898–9.

Judson, S. 1963b. Stream changes during historic time in east-central Sicily. *American Journal of Archaeology.* 67:287–9.

Judson, S. and Kahane, A. 1963. Underground drainageways in southern Etruria and northern Latium. *Papers of the British School at Rome.* 31:74–99.

Lamb, H. H. 1966. *The Changing Climate.* London.

Mattias, P. P. and Ventriglia, U. 1970. La regione vulcanica dei Monti Sabatini e Cimini. *Memorie della Società Geologica Italiana.* 9:331–84.

Ogilvie, R. M. 1965. Eretum. *Papers of the British School at Rome.* 33:70–112.

Partridge, C. R. 1975. Braughing. *Small Towns of Roman Britain.* British Archaeological Reports, no. 15 (eds W. Rodwell, and T. Rowley). 139–57.

Phillips, C. W. 1951. The Fenland Research Committee, its past achievements and future prospects. *Aspects of Archaeology* (ed. W. F. Grimes). 258–73.

Phillips, C. W. 1970. *The Fenland in Roman Times.* Royal Geographical Society Research Memoir no. 5.

Potter, T. W. 1972. Excavations in the medieval centre of Mazzano Romano. *Papers of the British School at Rome.* 40:135–45.

Potter, T. W. 1975. Recenti ricerche in Etruria meridionale: problemi della transizione dal tardo antico all'alto medioevo. *Archeologia Medievale.* 2:215–36.

Potter, T. W. 1976a. *A Faliscan town in South Etruria. Excavations at Narce* 1966–71. British School at Rome.

Potter, T. W. 1976b. Excavations at Stonea, Cambs. *Proceedings of the Cambridge Antiquarian Society.* 66. In press.

Potter, T. W. 1976c. Excavations at Watercrook: an interim report. *Transactions of the Cumberland and Westmorland Archaeological Society.* 76. In press.

Ramm, H. G. 1971. The end of Roman York. *Soldier and Civilian in Roman Yorkshire* (ed. R. M. Butler). 179–200.

Salway, P. 1967. Excavations at Hockwold-cum-Wilton, Norfolk, 1961–2. *Proceedings of the Cambridge Antiquarian Society.* 60:39–80.

Salway, P. 1970. The Roman Fenland. *The Fenland in Roman Times.* Royal Geographical Society Research Memoir no. 5 (ed. C. W. Phillips). 1–21.

Vita-Finzi, C. 1969. *The Mediterranean Valleys.* Cambridge University Press.

Wacher, J. S. 1969. *Excavations at Brough-on-Humber 1958–1961.* Society of Antiquaries of London Research Report. 25.

Ward-Perkins, J. B. 1955. Notes on Southern Etruria and the Ager Veientanus. *Papers of the British School at Rome.* 23:44–72.

Ward-Perkins, J. B. (with Frederiksen, M. W.) 1957. The ancient road systems of the central and northern Ager Faliscus. *Papers of the British School at Rome.* 25:67–208.

Ward-Perkins, J. B. 1961. Veii. The historical topography of the ancient city. *Papers of the British School at Rome*. 29:1–123.

Ward-Perkins, J. B. 1964. *Landscape and History in Central Italy*. Second J. L. Myers Memorial Lecture. Oxford.

Ward-Perkins, J. B. (with Kahane, A. and Murray-Threipland, L.) 1968. The Ager Veientanus north and east of Veii. *Papers of the British School at Rome*. 36:1–218.

Abstract

Potter, T. W.

Valleys and settlement: some new evidence

Extensive field survey in South Etruria (central Italy) has revealed little evidence for valley-bottom settlement. This is partly explained by an overlay of recent silt but was caused principally by periodic valley flooding, for which a climatic explanation is likely. Settlement evidence is mainly restricted to the period before the sixth century B.C. and the first and second centuries A.D. A number of low-lying English sites in valley and fenland contexts also demonstrate a similar sequence.

Palaeoclimate in urban environmental archaeology at York, England: problems and potential

P. V. Addyman, J. S. R. Hood, H. K. Kenward, A. MacGregor and D. Williams

Introduction

Medieval walled cities are by their nature large and permanent settlements where occupation has been intensive rather than extensive. Many have much earlier origins, in England often in Roman or Anglo-Saxon settlements on the same site. These factors sometimes combine to produce remarkably complete series of archaeological deposits from which data can be drawn to provide a full and continuous settlement history over a long period. In recent years the opportunity has increasingly been taken in towns throughout the British Isles to obtain such information, as new urban renewal projects have made large, and often critically important, parts of the ancient settlements available for excavation before new buildings either reoccupy the site, or destroy the accumulated archaeological layers for ever (Heighway 1972). Though few of the results have yet been published it is evident that many of these excavations are encountering ground conditions favourable to the preservation of a wider range of evidence than is usual. In particular the riverside situation of many towns, combined with alterations to the water-table caused by man's activities, have resulted in the waterlogging of deposits and the laying down of materials which promote anaerobic conditions. Such deposits contain not only organic artefacts but also very complete assemblages of biological remains which can be used to reconstruct environmental conditions in and around the buildings of the town. By this means it is possible to show both man's impact on the natural environment of the area, and also the actions which may have been forced on the town population at various times by changes in the environmental conditions. This paper explores the possibilities resulting from excavations in York, England, where good conditions of preservation are commonly found, and where a major campaign of rescue excavations has been in progress continuously since 1972 in advance of new building projects. Fuller accounts of the evidence for York's past environment will be published elsewhere. The aim of the present paper is to consider whether evidence of climatic change may be obtained from these studies, and to what extent climatic factors may have had a part to play in the various environmental changes observed.

York owes its origin to the establishment in the first century A.D. of a 21 hectare (53 acre) Roman legionary fortress on a spit of land between the rivers Foss and Ouse, which were at that time tidal. The fortress, located at a natural route centre where the slightly elevated York moraine crosses the low-lying Vale of York, here about 32 km (20 miles) wide, soon formed the nucleus of a more extensive civil settlement. By the third century this had gained the status of *colonia*. At this time a major civil town, probably walled, faced the fortress across the river Ouse. The banks of the two rivers provided wharfage, and there were sprawling extra-mural settlements and cemeteries along the several approach roads.

The fate of the Roman settlement in the fifth century, at the time of germanic invasions in other parts of Britain, is unknown, though there is a good *prima facie* case for continuity of occupation. So-called 'lacustrine' clays, observed at various times in the past overlying Roman levels, have suggested to one scholar that periodic flooding must have restricted the area available for occupation (Ramm 1971; RCHM 1975 xxvi f.) though the suggestion has yet satisfactorily to be proved.

By the eighth century, occupation of the city is again well-attested through documentary sources, and it provided a centre of defence against Viking attack. Later, because of its political status and economic importance, it proved a strong attraction for Anglo-Scandinavian trade. In 876 it became the capital of an Anglo-Scandinavian kingdom and its prosperity increased until, by the time of the Norman conquest, it had approximately doubled in size since the Roman period and was pre-eminent in the north of England. Deposits relating to this period are commonly found in excavations in the city. They are frequently dark, are retentive of water, and contain abundant organic matter. Such deposits accord well with a contemporary description of York in Anglo-Scandinavian times as 'the damp domain'. The reasons for the build-up of such deposits, which contrast often with the better-drained Roman deposits below them, is clearly of importance in understanding the character of the town at the time (Buckland 1974).

York retained its importance as a political, military and economic centre for the North throughout the Middle Ages, though there was a later relative decline as Hull supplanted it as a port, and the cloth industry shifted to the emergent towns of the West Riding of Yorkshire. The city's ecclesiastical pre-eminence, however, continues to the present. Numerous later medieval buildings survive in York, and on almost all excavation sites archaeological deposits of this period are encountered. Only in a minority of cases are these later deposits completely waterlogged. More usually organic remains and evidence of the environment in the later medieval period have to be recovered from wells, rubbish pits, latrines and industrial pits, which often penetrate to the water-table.

Archaeological conditions vary from place to place and period to period in the city, but it should be possible to build up a series of samples for biological and pedological research covering much of York's area and most of its history. In places, particularly near the rivers, archaeological deposits can reach a depth of 10 m., and in these situations they are for the most part waterlogged. The rich potential of these deposits as a source of archaeological information is now being exploited by a permanently constituted excavation unit of York Archaeological Trust (Addyman 1975 and n.d.) and an Environmental Archaeology Unit has been set up at the University of York to recover the biological evidence.

Problems of interpretation

The natural environment of York over the past two millennia has been altered by numerous agencies, of which climatic change is by no means the most important. However, no systematic attempt has yet been made to investigate climatic changes on the basis of material from York. It is only with the large volume of information now becoming available in York and the multidisciplinary approach of the Unit that we are in a position to hope to find convincing evidence of climatic changes. The method for the most part will be through recognition in ancient deposits of species whose modern distribution does not extend to York, or conceivably in certain periods through the consistent absence of species which are abundant at other times and known to be intolerant of slightly colder conditions than those of the present day.

The task is not easy, for the urban environment is essentially an artificial one, and the problem, at York at least, is one of separating the climatic from a multiplicity of other factors. This can only be undertaken when the various parameters affecting the urban environment are known and when the volume of information is large enough to give a reasonable degree of probability to each aspect of the evidence. Nevertheless, the task seems worth undertaking, for the amount of environmental information is probably greater from urban excavations than from rural ones, and the spate of urban rescue work provides particular opportunities at present throughout the country. If such work can be undertaken for other towns, general trends are more likely to become apparent.

Before such opportunities can be taken, various fundamental problems concerning urban environmental archaeology and climatic studies must be considered. The existence of a town itself creates a local climate. Nowadays temperatures may be 5° C higher than in a surrounding rural area. A richly organic Viking or medieval town, with clustered houses, may well have had a similarly higher temperature. Insects and plants could well have survived under these conditions further north than they would have done in a non-urban situation. To judge from present distributions, the range of some plants and insects may be seriously affected by a change of only 1° or 2° C. This is significant in view of the fact that the mean summer temperature of the early medieval climatic optimum is estimated as having been about 1° C higher than at present. The response of plants and animals to minor climatic fluctuations is, however, not known; locally favourable conditions may well enable some species to linger on in an area generally unsuitable for their continuance.

Edaphic factors may affect species more than climatic ones and mask the climatic effect (Lamb 1964). Changes in the environment brought about by differing agricultural practices, for example drainage or soil erosion, may limit a habitat sufficiently for it to be no longer able to support a viable population. A northward extension of a species' range may be impossible if no suitable habitats exist or are created, or if they are too far apart. The effect of human activity can confuse matters further. The introduction of crops, interbreeding and cultivation lead to unnatural plant distributions. Deliberate cultivation in locally favourable or artificial conditions, such as south-facing slopes, walled gardens, or by mulching, may contribute further 'southern' elements to the flora and fauna. Changes in the physiology and genetics could also result in misleading interpretations where the ancient and modern records of species are compared.

Imported non-perishable foods such as figs, grapes and cereals will be difficult to distinguish from locally grown ones. Grape-seeds, for example, have been found in ancient deposits in York and, while they might have been grown in the area, they could equally well have been imported as dried fruit for eating. The point is of some importance since vineyards have often been cited as an indication of the climatic optimum. However, the social and economic aspects have not always been adequately stressed. Taxes on imported wine might have encouraged viticulture in Britain although it was hardly favourable for grape cultivation. Changes in economic circumstances, for example taxation to favour better imported wines, would lead to a decrease and possible cessation of viticulture which might be incorrectly interpreted as a climatic change. The dangers apply as much to the interpretation of documentary sources as to the conclusions drawn from grape seeds. The monastic tradition of viticulture, together with political events like the dissolution of the monasteries, might also have affected the duration and distribution of vineyards (Manley 1962; Lamb 1965b). Similar problems affect the interpretation of certain elements of the fauna. Insects associated with materials used by man and stored product pests may also be introduced and may even survive and breed in artificial conditions. The climatic changes believed to have occurred during the past two millennia are small in scale, a matter of a degree or two. This makes their detection extremely difficult, even allowing for the sensitivity of some organisms to temperature. In particular, the changes may have been in the pattern of temperature and rainfall over the year rather than in the averages. Different organisms will respond in different ways to these changes, depending on their need for summer rain or warmth, or the duration of the growing season, their frost-sensitivity, or requirement for winter cold.

York Archaeological Trust's excavations are also providing records of mammal, amphibian, fish and bird bones from the city. While proportions and types vary considerably with time, the altered patterns of hunting, domestication and stock preference outweigh other considerations, including climatic ones, in explaining the changes.

Evidence from plant sub-fossils

The study of sub-fossil plant material in Britain has demonstrated quite considerable changes in the past vegetation, making inferences possible about the associated climate. Most sites used in such studies have been natural deposits vastly different, both in nature and origin, from the complex occupation layers of urban archaeological sites. Urban deposits are restricted both in the species and the types of habitat represented. They are often dominated by cultivated crops, their associated weed floras and the common ruderals of disturbed nitrogen-rich areas so prevalent in the vicinity of human habitation. In this respect they are better suited to supply information about man's activities rather than about the environment and climate. Plant species from natural habitats represented in urban deposits have so far been uninformative in climatic terms. The limited chance of the occurrence of 'indicator' species such as *Viscum album* L. (Mistletoe) in these deposits would largely be invalidated by the possibility of their transportation by man. With the relatively small climatic changes likely in Roman and post-Roman times, the influence of man on urban deposits makes it improbable that climatic trends would readily be recognized. Pollen analysis of these deposits might give a more representative indication of the surrounding vegetation. This is particularly so in the case of the trees where the selection for oak timber, and its resistance to decay, make wood remains unrepresentative of the surrounding woodlands. Pollen in urban deposits, however, may well have been reworked or transported, and consequently is of doubtful value, unless the evidence is exceptionally clear.

The study of the plant sub-fossils at York has, therefore, so far only produced the merest hints of climatic events, which will have to be followed up in later work. A striking example comes from the timbers extracted from a third-century Roman well excavated at Skeldergate, York. The growth rings of the oak planks and posts lining the well are considerably wider than those of modern oak trees and suggest a much better growing season than at present. Conceivably, of course, the timber may have been imported; comparison with future finds should settle the point. Urban deposits are rich in cultivated crops, and introduced exotic species are well represented in the Roman period both at York and elsewhere (Godwin 1975: 480, table 46).

It has been suggested that some of these species were cultivated in Britain at that time, as well as being introduced as dried foods. The former still needs substantiation but would, if shown to be correct, indicate better climatic conditions than at the present day. The evidence is still too limited to be conclusive, even for such crops as the vine and fig. The recent finds of Roman grape seeds in York (Greig n.d.), the first record in the north of England, and similar finds from Doncaster and Winterton Villa, Lincolnshire, are unlikely to represent local viticulture (Williams n.d.), if only because of the marked rarity of the seeds. This is possibly substantiated by the tentative evidence for a vineyard of short duration in the late third century at North Thoresby, Lincs., which probably failed due to the unsuitability of soil and climate (Webster *et al.* 1967). Lamb's (1965a) criteria for a good grape harvest would suggest that Britain was completely unsuitable for vineyards except in sheltered spots and walled gardens. However, there is fairly conclusive evidence for Roman viticulture at the villa of Boxmoor, Hertfordshire (Collingwood 1937), and in Gloucester (Medland 1894–5). The former, where vine stems were found on a sheltered south slope, might confirm Lamb's hypothesis, while the Gloucester discovery may be no more than a reflection of the establishment in the area of a colony of ex-soldiers, some doubtlessly of Mediterranean origin (Applebaum 1972) immediately after the demise of Domitian. The flourishing of estates in the south of England towards the close of the Roman period does however suggest a warming up of the climate (Lamb 1972).

There are marked differences in the cereals and other crops (flax and hemp in particular) and their weed floras at different periods. *Anthemis cotula* L. (Stinking Mayweed) is very characteristic of post-Roman to medieval agriculture. Although it is tempting to attribute a climatic cause to these changes, it is probably no more than a reflection of differences in cultures and the areas and soil on which crops were grown. Some crops may even have been imported from a distance, particularly in the Roman period when the Car Dyke system may have given ready contact, for a time at least, with south-east Britain, and when marine transports evidently also reached York.

Published evidence for the medieval period is scarce. There is documentary evidence for a flourishing wine industry in the south of England, particularly in Gloucestershire (Applebaum 1972) and even of a vineyard in York from the Domesday Book (Lamb 1965a). There are many possible reasons for the existence of these vineyards, but one suspects a more suitable climate did exist than during the Romano-British period.

Pollen analysis from Tregaron bog has shown a standstill in the peat formation for the period A.D. 473 to 1182 (Turner 1965). In Europe this hiatus spans A.D. 400 to 700 only (Frenzel 1966). The climatic deterioration of the thirteenth century, associated with the restart of the bogs, also accords with documentary evidence for increasing storms and floods (Manley 1962). Medieval ridge and furrow cultivation above present agricultural limits does not always indicate the climatic optimum; for example nineteenth-century cultivation in Ireland above the present agricultural limits was a result of famine conditions.

Evidence from insect remains

The remains of insects probably are the greatest potential source of evidence of minor climatic fluctuations. A large number of species have their northern or southern limits in the British Isles, in many cases around the level of Lincolnshire or Yorkshire. Many other species become very much rarer in Northern England. The difference in mean July temperature between the areas where a species can be seen to be well established and its known northern limits is often only a degree or so. This means that relatively small changes in climate may cause comparatively great extensions or contractions of range. There is also strong evidence that insects respond more rapidly to climatic events than do plants (Coope *et al.* 1971).

About a dozen species of beetle whose northern limits are now south of Yorkshire have been found in early medieval deposits from York. These records at first sight suggest that present day temperatures are considerably lower than those in, for example, the tenth and eleventh centuries, but this evidence needs scrutinizing with the greatest care. Several of the species are now rare and have scattered populations even in southern England. These insects may be limited in the north by problems of colonization or be present, perhaps in outlyers of the main range, but have been overlooked by insect collectors. We have no knowledge of the exact distribution of most species. In addition we know almost nothing of the pattern of distributional change of insects during the 'Little Ice Age'. Many insects may not have re-colonized the northern parts of their modern potential ranges following this episode due to fragmentation and isolation of their habitat.

Some other beetles recorded from medieval York, like the fen-dwelling Carabid *Dromius longiceps* (Dej.), now present only as far north as Lincolnshire (Lindroth 1974; Moore 1957), may have become extinct in Yorkshire as a result of the destruction of their habitats. Forest species may also be limited by ecological as well as climatic events (Buckland and Kenward 1973). Archaeological records based on single specimens may be of stray individuals, since insects may fly or be carried over considerable distances (Kenward 1975b, 1976, n.d. a).

The artificial habitats of the medieval urban environment may have permitted the occurrence of northern populations of species otherwise limited to warmer climates. The abundance of the beetle *Aglenus brunneus* (Gyll.) in the medieval period of York (Kenward 1975a) and other towns including Durham (Kenward n.d. b) may have been at least in part due to the existence of extensive deposits of rotting vegetation, now absent. This would have reduced problems of colonization, perhaps a major cause of its present day rarity, for this wingless species. It may also have been accidentally transported by man from town to town. The decay of the organic matter may also have contributed to a generally higher temperature regime in the towns, favouring this and other species, but climatic change has probably also had its effect on *A. brunneus*.

Buckland (1975) provides a detailed critique of the evidence for climatic change provided by the death watch beetle *Xestobium rufivillosum* (Deg.), concluding that it was severely curtailed in the sixteenth–seventeenth centuries. He suggests that the medieval infestations may have originated from relict natural populations, but it is possible that early medieval temperatures were high enough for the beetle to disperse by flight; its existence in the northern parts of its range is now mainly due to man since it probably succumbed to the 'Little Ice Age' in the wild (Buckland 1974).

Many species of insect are dependent on locally available ecological conditions and therefore may be limited ecologically rather than climatically. This is well exemplified by the difficulty of determining the factors involved in the changes in distribution and abundance of *Aglenus brunneus* and *Xestobium rufivillosum*. The bug *Heterogaster urticae* (F.) is free of such limitations and provides by far the best evidence for temperatures above those of the present day during the Roman as well as early medieval periods. It is a phytophage, with the stinging nettle *Urtica dioica* L. as its principal host (Southwood and Leston 1959), and it is occasionally found on other related plants (Davis and Lawrence 1974). The bug shows a strong preference for nettlebeds in open sunny places, especially towards the northern limits of its range (Davis 1973). Nettle is found in abundance throughout Britain (Greig-Smith 1948) and its seeds are extremely common in archaeological deposits both in York and elsewhere (e.g. Godwin 1975). The bug is now common only in southern England, with a few records from the north of East Anglia and Lincolnshire, and old, unconfirmed, ones from Yorkshire and Cheshire (Southwood and Leston 1959; Massee 1955). It is extremely rare north of Huntingdonshire where it is local but may be abundant when found (Davis 1973, 1975). *H. urticae* is, however, regularly encountered in early medieval deposits in York, for example at the Lloyd's Bank and Coppergate sites (Buckland *et al.* 1974; Kenward, unpublished), and there is no reason to doubt that it was a common insect at that time. Several specimens have been taken from the fill of a well of the Roman period at the Skeldergate site, York (Kenward, unpublished). This change in distribution and abundance is undoubtedly a real one and can only be attributed to a climatic deterioration since the early medieval period. Problems of colonization following the 'Little Ice Age' cannot be involved, as the bug is a ready flyer (Kenward unpublished) and its host has always been available. We are left to conclude that early medieval temperatures were higher than those of the present day. The bug's preference for high insolation and its mainly southern and eastern distribution hint that the climate may have been more continental.

The insects probably offer the best potential source of this kind of climatic information, being of little interest to man and so not deliberately imported. Accidental transportation may occur, especially of stored products insects, or those associated with artefacts, for example the southern European longhorn beetle *Hesperophanes fasciculatus* recorded by Osborne (1971) from Alcester, Warwickshire. However, this will normally be detected by association with the imported materials. Some species generally found in grain stores are known from natural conditions in southern Britain. Occurrences in grain associations in York (e.g. Hall and Kenward, in press) are of course in no way indicative of climatic changes; on the other hand, conclusive evidence that these species occurred in natural assemblages in the north in the past would be meaningful.

Studies of urban insect assemblages seem likely to provide a wealth of hints about past climates. However, only by a systematic study of faunas from a long time-span and a wide geographical area can we hope to obtain enough reliable data. Such work, including studies of natural assemblages, may be expected to provide a very precise picture both of gross climatic changes and of the average annual pattern of weather in each period.

Evidence from artefacts

Occasionally attempts have been made to use certain archaeological artefacts as indicators of past climate: the presence of large numbers of worn and polished bone skates in deposits of Anglo-Scandinavian date in York was taken by Radley (1971) to imply 'at least fairly frequent long, hard winters during which the river was frozen for long periods'. Such a winter is rare indeed nowadays. Moreover, research on contemporary biological remains from York (Buckland 1974; Buckland *et al.* 1974), although still in its preliminary stages, tends to suggest, if anything, not a deterioration of the climate at this period, but rather the reverse. Indeed it has been accepted in the past that there was a general amelioration following the fifth century, culminating in a warm epoch or secondary climatic optimum for two or three centuries from about A.D. 1000, before a deterioration set in once again in the later middle ages (Lamb 1972). The apparently contradictory evidence provided by the skates could be reconciled by postulating an episode of increased continentality, a concept which is already beginning to find favour with palaeoclimatologists (Lamb, *in lit.*). Continentality, in this instance, chiefly implies a notable frequency of anticyclones and light winds both in summer and winter.

There can be no doubt that the comparatively inefficient land drainage systems of the period and the general absence of arrangements for the regulation of river floodwaters meant that large areas of low-lying countryside spent at least part of the winter under shallow water. These were certainly the conditions which provided opportunities for skating in early medieval London, where the well-known description by William fitz Stephen of *c.* A.D. 1170–83 begins 'When the great marsh that washes the north wall of the city is frozen over, swarms of young men issue forth to play games on the ice . . .' (Douglas and Greenaway 1953: 961) and according to Stow (1603) it was not until the sixteenth century that it was finally drained. In the Vale of York, where widespread gley soils and a low elevation make the natural drainage rather poor (Palmer 1966), evidence has been offered for extensive and repeated flooding from the late Roman period until about the twelfth century (Radley and Simms 1970). These low-lying flooded areas would clearly have been much more prone to freezing than the main river channels, and so it may not be necessary to postulate unduly extreme conditions to explain away the repeated freezing suggested by the skates.

It is rare that artefacts themselves can so clearly suggest altered climatic conditions, though they more often suggest changed environmental conditions. There is, for instance, a series of changes, in retrospect seemingly rapid, in methods of making house foundations between *c.* A.D. 850 and 1500. The earliest in the series are horizontal foundation beams set in shallow trenches. They seem to be succeeded later in Anglo-Scandinavian times by houses based on post and wattle, often of two thicknesses with packing materials in the cavity between. The change may have a cultural cause, the result of Scandinavian or even Irish influence, for similar houses are known from contemporary levels at Dublin. It is possible, however, that the new style represents at least as much a reaction to the colder winters of a more continental climate. The frequency with which timber piles are employed below the foundations of buildings of twelfth to fourteenth century date probably reflects nothing more than unhappy previous experience of building on the spongy Anglo-Scandinavian deposits below. There is a temptation to make climatic correlations later, when timber-framed buildings in York are set on low stone or brick walls instead of directly on to the ground. The coincidence of this development with the general fourteenth century climatic deterioration is as likely as not to be fortuitous, even though the trend seems to be a country-wide one, and the correlation has been suggested before by vernacular building specialists. Clearly such speculative correlations must now await the detailed reconstructions of the changing environment which can come from study of the biological evidence both at York and elsewhere.

Evidence from sediments

There are few natural soils in York, but the accumulated materials below the city are themselves evidence for changing environmental conditions. Many of the Roman levels are now waterlogged, though most were clearly not in Roman times. By contrast many of the Anglo-Scandinavian levels were evidently quite damp, and perhaps odoriferous, even at the time of occupation (Buckland 1974). The explanation of the change is, however, likely to be in human activity rather than in environmental factors.

The York area is still regularly subject to flooding. There is no evidence from the excavations, however, to suggest that this was so in Roman times. An extensive and developed soil profile below Roman deposits near the riverside at Skeldergate, for instance, although on biological evidence representing damp pasture, showed no evidence of flooding, though modern floods regularly reach much higher absolute levels. By contrast, Ramm's suggestion that immediately post-Roman flooding restricted the area then available for occupation implies flood levels even higher than those at present. The evidence for such post-Roman flooding is by no means consistent from one part of York to another, many recent excavations below the assumed flood levels having shown no sign of the 'lacustrine clays' noted by early observers. Whether or not the post-Roman floods prove to have taken place, there is evidence for flooding in the thirteenth and fourteenth centuries, with silt layers in deposits of this date in riverside excavations. The regime of the river must have changed more than once since the establishment of the Roman settlement.

The interpretation of the York soils, and particularly the flood and alluvial deposits, depends on an interrelation of three factors: climatic change, fluctuation in sea levels and water-tables (Buckland 1974) and human activity. Of these, human activity is without doubt the most important, itself perhaps having to some extent influenced local climate. The apparent flood deposits over Roman occupation levels, for instance, might have been the result of a rise in river levels due to soil erosion from intensive agriculture rather than an increase in precipitation. Such soil erosion was evidently going on in the higher Pennines in post-Viking times, as settlement excavations at Ribblehead have recently shown. Deforestation of the river Ouse catchment area would also increase the possibility of flash floods and flood plain deposition. Progressive reclamation of the margins of the river Ouse took place from Roman times onwards, narrowing the channel itself and restricting the flood plain. This may indeed have been the main cause of the late medieval floods, for by that time the river had been constricted between walls to almost its present position.

Accumulation of archaeological deposits in York probably caused a gradual rise in the water table, a process no doubt accentuated by inadequate drainage systems in post-Roman York, and by the breakdown of Roman systems. Overgrazing and cultivation also increase deposition of loess (wind blown soil) (Radley and Simms 1967), an additional factor in soil build-up on urban sites. By far the most important agency in deposition, however, is simply the activities of town life: building, road construction, the digging of industrial installations and wells, and the disposal of rubbish. Such activities account in large part for the great depths of deposits in English urban sites, besides which the subtle influences of minor climatic change pale into insignificance.

Conclusions

Studies of the kind discussed in this paper have an important potential as a source of palaeoclimatic data. This is especially true at York, where the investigation of the biological, artefactual and excavational evidence over two millennia can be closely co-ordinated. Work of this nature will probably be the main source of evidence confirming the history of climatic change indicated by studies based on documentary sources and meteorological theory.

The factors determining the presence and absence, or relative abundance, of plant and animal species are a complex of climatic and ecological ones. In urban situations, which are likely to remain the principal source of material for a while, human behaviour will have had a dominant influence. There will often be some difficulty in separating the various influences, especially as there is a serious deficiency of experimental data about the temperature and other climatic requirements of most living organisms. The microclimate acting on the plant or animal, especially on a small insect living in a protected situation, may be highly localized and occur in an area where the gross climate appears unfavourable. Insects are comparatively independent of man and show a rapid response to climatic change. This suggests that the insects, especially the beetles, will be the most reliable indicators of past climate and also, in towns at least, of ecological conditions. A cautious approach in distinguishing the effects of ecological from climatic changes will, however, be necessary if false deductions are to be avoided.

Climates vary in the pattern of weather throughout the year as well as in the annual averages of their components. The pattern will have been more important than averages in affecting living organisms. This is probably equally true of the effect of climate on the economy of man. Different organisms may be indicators of different aspects of the pattern of climate, through for example their frost sensitivity, intolerance of mild winters, water requirements or need for sustained or high summer temperatures. Combining the evidence of the palaeo-environmental clues from a variety of organisms with the results of meteorological research may allow us to begin to quantify the climatic changes in the past and speculate about the future. On a broader geographical scale such work may lead to a better understanding of past land use and of the distribution and movements of populations.

23.iv.1976

York Archaeological Trust for Excavation and Research
47 Aldwark, York
and *Environmental Archaeology Unit*
University of York

References

Addyman, P. V. 1975. Excavations in York, 1972–73. First Interim Report. *Antiquaries Journal.* 55:201–31.

Addyman, P. V. n.d. *Excavations in York, 1973–74. Second Interim Report.* London: Council for British Archaeology. In press.

Applebaum, S. 1972. *Roman Britain.* In H. P. R. Finberg (ed.), *The Agrarian History of England and Wales A.D. 43–1042*, I, ii:118. Cambridge University Press.

Buckland, P. C. 1974. Environment and Archaeology in York. *Journal of Archaeological Science.* 1:303–16.

Buckland, P. C. 1975. Synanthropy and the death-watch; a discussion. *The Naturalist.* 1975:37–42.

Buckland, P. C., Greig, J. R. A. and Kenward H. K. 1974. York; an Early Medieval site. *Antiquity.* 47:25–33.

Buckland, P. C. and Kenward, H. K. 1973. Thorne Moor; a paleo-ecological study of a Bronze Age site. *Nature.* 241:405–6.

Collingwood, R. G. 1937. Roman Britain. In T. Frank (ed.), *Economic Survey of Ancient Rome.* III:78. Baltimore: Johns Hopkins Press.

Coope, G. R., Morgan, A. and Osborne, P. J. 1971. Fossil Coleoptera as indicators of climatic fluctuations during the Last Glaciation in Britain. *Palaeogeography, Palaeoclimatology, Palaeoecology.* 10:87–101.

Davis, B. K. N. 1973. The Hemiptera and Coleoptera of stinging nettle (*Urtica dioica* L.) in East Anglia. *Journal of Applied Ecology.* 10:213–37.

Davis, B. K. N. 1975. The colonisation of isolated patches of nettles (*Urtica dioica* L.) by insects. *Journal of Applied Ecology.* 12:1–14.

Davis, B. K. N. and Lawrence, C. E. 1974. Insects collected from *Parietaria diffusa* Mert. and Koch and *Urtica urens* L. in Huntingdonshire. *Entomologist's Monthly Magazine.* 109:252–4.

Douglas, D. C. and Greenaway, G. W. (eds) 1953. *English Historical Documents* 2:961 London: Eyre and Spottiswoode.

Frenzel, B. 1966. Climatic change in the Atlantic Sub-boreal transition on the Northern Hemisphere: botanical evidence. In *World Climate from 8000 to 0 B.C.*: 99–123. London: Royal Meteorological Society.

Godwin, H. 1975. *History of the British Flora. A Basis for Phytogeography.* 2nd ed. Cambridge University Press.

Greig, J. R. A. n.d. The plant remains. In P. C. Buckland, The environmental evidence from the Church Street Roman sewer system. *The Archaeology of York* 14, fascicule 1. London: Council for British Archaeology. In press.

Greig-Smith, P. 1948. Biological flora of the British Isles; *Urtica dioica* L. *Journal of Ecology.* 36:343–55.

Heighway, C. 1972. *The Erosion of History.* London: Council for British Archaeology.

Hall, R. A. and Kenward, H. K. n.d. Biological evidence for the usage of Roman riverside warehouses at York. *Britannia.* In press.

Kenward, H. K. 1975a. The biological and archaeological implications of the beetle *Aglenus brunneus* (Gyllenhal) in ancient faunas. *Journal of Archaeological Science.* 2:63–9.

Kenward, H. K. 1975b. Pitfalls in the environmental interpretation of insect death assemblages. *Journal of Archaeological Science.* 2:85–94.

Kenward, H. K. 1976. Reconstructing ancient ecological conditions from insect remains; some problems and an experimental approach. *Ecological Entomology.* 1:7–17.

Kenward, H. K. n.d.a. *Helophorus tuberculatus* Gyll. (Coleoptera-Hydrophilidae) in the City of York. *Entomologist's Monthly Magazine.* In press.

Kenward, H. K. n.d.b. Further archaeological records of *Aglenus brunneus* (Gyllenhal) in Britain and Ireland, including confirmation of its presence in the Roman period. *Journal of Archaeological Science.* In press.

Lamb, H. H. 1964. Trees and climatic history in Scotland: a radiocarbon test and other evidence. *Quarterly Journal of the Royal Meteorological Society.* 90:382–94.

Lamb, H. H. 1965a. The Early Medieval warm epoch and its sequel. *Palaeogeography, Palaeoclimatology, Palaeoecology.* 1:13–37.

Lamb, H. H. 1965b. Britain's changing climate. In C. G. Johnson and L. P. Smith (eds), *The Biological Significance of Climatic Changes in Britain.* 3–31. London: Institute of Biology and Academic Press.

Lamb, H. H. 1972. Our changing climate, past and present. In *The Changing Climate. Selected Papers*. London: Methuen.

Lamb, H. H. *in lit.* A. MacGregor: I am grateful to Professor Lamb for this information in advance of publication in *Climate: Past, Present and Future*, Vol. 2. London: Methuen. In press.

Lindroth, C. H. 1974. *Handbooks for the Identification of British Insects*, vol. IV, pt. 2, *Coleoptera, Carabidae*. London: Royal Entomological Society.

Manley, G. 1962. *Climate and the British Scene*. London: Collins.

Massee, A. M. 1955. The county distribution of the British Hemiptera-Heteroptera, 2nd edn. *Entomologist's Monthly Magazine*. 91:7–27.

Medland, M. H. 1894–95. An account of Roman and Medieval remains found in the site of the Tolsey at Gloucester in 1893–94. *Transactions of the Bristol and Gloucestershire Archaeological Society*. 19:155.

Moore, B. P. 1957. The British Carabidae (Coleoptera), Part II, the county distribution of the species. *Entomologist's Gazette*. 8:171–80..

Osborne, P. J. 1971. An insect fauna from the Roman site at Alcester, Warwickshire. *Britannia*. 2:156–65.

Palmer, J. 1966. Landforms, drainage and settlement in the Vale of York. In S. R. Eyre and G. R. J. Jones (eds), *Geography as Human Ecology*. London: Arnold.

Radley, J. 1971. Economic aspects of Anglo-Danish York. *Medieval Archaeology*. 15:37–57.

Radley, J. and Simms, C. 1967. Wind erosion in east Yorkshire. *Nature*. 216:20–2.

Radley, J. and Simms, C. 1970. *Yorkshire Flooding*. York.

Ramm, H. G. 1971. The end of Roman York. In R. M. Butler (ed.), *Soldier and Civilian in Roman Yorkshire*. Leicester University Press.

RCHM 1975. Royal Commission on Historical Monuments, *City of York IV. Outside the City Walls East of the Ouse*. 1975.

Southwood, T. R. E. and Leston, D. 1959. *Land and Water Bugs of the British Isles*. London: Warne.

Stow, J. 1603. *A Survey of London* (ed. C. L. Kingsford, 1908). Oxford University Press.

Turner, J. 1965. A contribution to the history of forest clearance. *Proceedings of the Royal Society of London*. B 161:343–53.

Webster, D. and H. and Petch, D. F. 1967. A possible vineyard of the Romano-British period at North Thoresby, Lincolnshire. *Lincolnshire History and Archaeology*. 2:55–61.

Williams, D. n.d. A consideration of the sub-fossil remains of *Vitis vinifera* L. as evidence for viticulture in Roman Britain. *Britannia*. In press.

Abstract

Addyman, P. V., Hood, J. S. R., Kenward, H. K., MacGregor, A. and Williams, D.

Palaeoclimate in urban environmental archaeology at York, England: problems and potential

Recent excavations at York, which has a continuous history from Roman times to the present, have produced much biological evidence for early environmental conditions. Climate seems to have had only a minor role in causing the observed changes though it is difficult to separate its effect from that of other factors. Insects appear to offer the best hope of demonstrating minor climatic fluctuations, though artefacts may also provide evidence. Human activity seems to have been the most important factor in environmental change, causing flooding and the build-up of the thick archaeological deposits found in the city.

Contributors

P. V. Addyman has been Director of York Archaeological Trust for Excavation and Research since its inception in 1972, before which he was lecturer in Archaeology at Southampton University. His special interests lie in Anglo-Saxon and Medieval archaeology.

Pat Carter has done fieldwork in Ghana, the Sudan, Ethiopia and Uganda. Formerly Curator of the National Museum of Tanzania, he is now a Fellow of Downing College, Cambridge, and an Assistant Curator in the University Museum of Archaeology and Ethnology.

Richard W. Casteel took his Ph.D. at the University of California, Davis, and now teaches in the Archaeological Department at Simon Fraser University. His previous posts have been in the field of environmental archaeology, and his research interests are climatic change, zooarchaeology, palaeontology and human ecology.

E. R. Eaton received her Ph.D. in Mediterranean archaeology from Brown University in 1975, and since then has been a Research Fellow in the National Museum, Edinburgh.

J. S. R. Hood is a botanist by training. He gained archaeological experience in Dublin and is now Director of the Environmental Archaeology Unit, University of York, where he specializes in soils and animal bones.

R. N. L. B. Hubbard is a Ph.D. student at the Institute of Archaeology, London, where he is carrying out palynological research on the chronology of the British Palaeolithic and studying the economy and environment of early farming communities.

H. K. Kenward is a research Fellow in the Environmental Archaeology Unit, University of York, specializing in invertebrate fauna, principally insects. He previously worked in the Department of Entomology, British Museum (Natural History), after research in the Department of Geology at Birmingham University.

Hugh McKerrell is Principal Scientific Officer in charge of the Research Laboratory of the National Museum, Edinburgh.

A. MacGregor has been Finds Researcher for the York Archaeological Trust since 1972. His archaeological training was at the University of Edinburgh and he is engaged on research into the utilization of bone and antler in post-Roman Britain.

P. J. Osborne is Curator of the teaching museum of the Department of Geological Sciences at the University of Birmingham. His research interests are Quaternary insect faunas and the history of the present-day British insect fauna.

Allison C. Paulsen received her Ph.D. from Columbia University in 1970. She has carried out fieldwork in Ecuador, and her principal research interests include socio-cultural evolution and the archaeology of the Andes and of the Intermediate Area.

T. W. Potter took his Ph.D. at Cambridge and is now Lecturer in Archaeology at Lancaster University. He has carried out fieldwork in the Cambridgeshire Fenland and in central Italy. He is now extensively involved in rescue archaeology of north-west England.

Brent D. Shaw is completing a Cambridge Ph.D. on the ancient history of the Maghrib. The subject of his research is the indigenous society and economy of North Africa under the Roman Empire.

D. Williams is a Research Fellow of the Environmental Archaeology Unit, University of York, specializing in plant sub-fossils. He came to York after research in the Department of Botany, University of Bradford.

Notes to contributors

Manuscripts should not normally exceed 5,000 words in length. They should be typed on good quality A4 paper (i.e. approx. $11\frac{3}{4}$ in. × $8\frac{1}{4}$ in., or 30 cm. × 21 cm.), using double spacing throughout. Two copies of the manuscript should be submitted, the author retaining another. Unsolicited contributions and related correspondence should be addressed to the Executive Editor – Martin Biddle, Winchester Research Unit, Winchester.

Referencing should follow the modern scientific convention. Footnotes, wherever possible, should be avoided. Bibliographic references, to be included in the text, should list the author's last name, date of publication, and number of page, e.g. (Clark 1952: 211). Where an author's name has been cited already in the text, references need only be made to the date of publication and page, e.g. (1952: 211). Extended references should be listed alphabetically at the end of the paper, e.g.

Bouard, M. de 1965. La mesure de la résistivité électrique des sols en archéologie. *Annales de Normandie*. 15:461–77.
Clark, J. G. D. 1952. *Prehistoric Europe: the economic basis*. London: Methuen.
Wace, A. J. B. 1958. Aegean prehistory: a review. *Antiquity*. 32:30–4.
Woodburn, J. 1968. An introduction to Hazda ecology. *Man the hunter*, pp. 49–55 (eds R. B. Lee and I. DeVore). Chicago: Aldine Publishing Company.

Text figures, site plans and distribution maps should be drawn on strong paper, white card, or good quality tracing film. The lettering on diagrams should be in the type face Univers (medium weight). This is obtainable on transfer sheets (e.g. 'Letraset'). They should measure approximately twice the intended final size (i.e. a published full-page illustration may not exceed 8 in. × $5\frac{15}{16}$ in., or 20·5 cm. × 15·5 cm.). Plates should be printed on glossy paper and should be mounted on thin card. Figures, maps and plates should be titled and numbered; originals should be numbered in pencil only. A list of captions to figures and plates must be provided on a separate sheet.

Each contribution should be accompanied by a brief abstract (100–150 words) summarizing its contents. A short note on individual contributions should also be supplied.

It is important that authors should submit accurate, well-prepared copy ready for the printer. Re-drawing of maps or figures cannot be undertaken by the editors, who may return sub-standard work to contributors for re-presentation in an improved form. Galley proofs of all articles will be sent to authors, who are reminded that these are intended for checking, not re-writing. Failure to return proofs by the required date may lead to the executive editor's sending his own corrected proofs to the printer without further reference to the author.

Twenty-five offprints and a voucher copy of the journal will be supplied to authors on publication of a paper. Additional offprints may be purchased at cost price, and should be ordered not later than on the return of corrected proofs. The free allocation must be shared between joint authors.

World Archaeology

ISSN 0043-8243
Volume 8 No 3
February 1977

This issue: Human biogeography

World Archaeology

Volume 8 No. 3 February 1977

Published thrice yearly by the proprietors
Routledge & Kegan Paul Ltd
Newtown Road, Henley-on-Thames, Oxon RG9 1EN

Single copies £3 ($8.00)
Annual subscription £7·50 ($20.00)

ISSN 0043-8243

Printed in Great Britain by
The Camelot Press Ltd, Southampton

Issues of *World Archaeology* now in preparation cover the themes:

'Island archaeology' (June 1977. Editor: I.C.G.)
'Architecture and archaeology' (October 1977. Editor: M.B.)
'Landscape archaeology' (February 1978. Editor: B.W.C.)
'Field techniques and research design' (June 1978. Editor: I.H.L.)
'Archaeology and religion' (October 1978. Editor: C.P.S.P.)

The editors welcome suggestions for contributions to any of the projected issues, and would be glad at all times to consider important new work for immediate publication, whether or not it coincides with an announced theme.

It is not current editorial policy to publish book reviews as a regular feature of the journal. Review articles will cover literature in particular fields, and a list of books received will be printed from time to time.

Editorial note

All of the human biogeography papers in this issue, with the exception of the contributions by Dr Terrell and Dr Slobodkin, are based on papers initially prepared for a conference on 'the application of models in population biology and animal biogeography to the archaeological study of similarities and differences among human populations' which was held at the Smithsonian Institution and at the 39th Annual Meeting of the Society for American Archaeology in 1974. This interdisciplinary conference of archaeologists, anthropologists, biologists, geographers and others was organized by John Terrell and William Fitzhugh, and was funded by the Wenner-Gren Foundation for Anthropological Research, Inc. and the Smithsonian Institution, Washington, D.C. Primary editing and preparation of papers for this issue were undertaken by John Terrell and Marilyn Miller at Field Museum of Natural History.

Human biogeography

Errata

World Archaeology Volume 6 Number 3, February 1975
Ottaway and Strahm, 'Swiss Neolithic copper beads: currency, ornament or prestige items?'
p. 313 line 24 *for* plate 8 *read* plate 7;
p. 317 line 14 *for* figure 14 *read* plate 8

Contents

page

237 Biology, biogeography and man
John Terrell

249 Colonization cycles in man and beast
Jared M. Diamond

262 Long term hunter-gatherer adaptation to desert environments: a biogeographical perspective
John E. Yellen

275 Some implications for hunter-gatherer ecology derived from the spatial structure of resources
Henry Harpending and Herbert Davis

287 Vegetational fluctuation and prehistoric cultural adaptation in Amazonia: some tentative correlations
Betty J. Meggers

304 Adaptive strategies in western Panama
Olga F. Linares

320 Biogeographical theory and cultural analogies
Jonathan D. Sauer

332 Evolution is no help
Lawrence B. Slobodkin

---

344 An Acheulian occupation site at Hunsgi, Peninsular India: a summary of the results of two seasons of excavation (1975–6)
K. Paddayya

359 Index to Volume 8

Cover

'Trucanini, the last aboriginal Tasmanian woman' (by courtesy of the Field Museum of Natural History, Chicago, Section of Photography).

[Editors' Note: This is a portrait of the famed Truganina, the 'last Tasmanian,' who died a hundred years ago at an age of about 70 years. She was instrumental in the final pacification of the few surviving natives. Her image symbolizes many of the themes in this issue of *World Archaeology*: the role of human determination and self-image in directing human evolution, the importance of processes of migration, colonization, competition, reproduction, and extinction in human biogeography, as in the biogeography of all species.]

Theme titles of past issues of *World Archaeology*

Volume	Number	
1	1	Recent work and new approaches
1	2	Techniques of chronology and excavation
1	3	Analysis
2	1	Early man
2	2	Urban archaeology
2	3	Subsistence
3	1	Technological innovations
3	2	Archaeology and ethnography
3	3	Art and design
4	1	Population
4	2	Nomads
4	3	Theories and assumptions
5	1	Colonization
5	2	Trade
5	3	Stone Age studies
6	1	Political systems
6	2	Miscellany
6	3	Currency
7	1	Burial
7	2	Dating
7	3	Archaeology and history
8	1	Archaeology and linguistics
8	2	Climatic change

Biology, biogeography and man

John Terrell

Introduction

In this essay I argue that biogeographical thinking in archaeology and anthropology permits social scientists to consider questions about the size, distribution, ecology and population structure of human groups without succumbing to the fallacies of biological determinism or the similarly naive and deterministic presumption that man is unique and beyond scientific scrutiny. Because biogeographical thinking is probabilistic rather than deterministic, and because biogeography stresses relationships between species and the real complexities of their environments, a biogeographer's approach to ancient and modern man furthers investigation of events and environmental circumstances, natural and man-made, that play a role in the evolution of similarities and differences among human populations and their cultures.

In developing my argument I first examine the claim that man is unique. After pointing out how this claim is ambiguous and ultimately of little scientific interest, I suggest that the study of similarities and differences among human groups and between man and other species is fundamental to social science. Then I consider the part played by biology in determining human similarities and differences. I comment on the present controversy within the biological sciences about the extension of ethological and sociobiological research to include the human species. If human sociobiology is defined as the search for the biological basis of human societies, it is unlikely that sociobiology will contribute much to social science. The surprising fact about man is not the similarities among human populations which may be due to man's common genetic inheritance but rather the diversity of man's cultures. Instead of a sociobiological model of man, social scientists need a model which accommodates human biology while allowing for cultural diversity. I examine briefly one possible model which has been devised by the psychologist Herbert A. Simon and define human biogeography in terms of it. My argument concludes with the observation that a biogeographical approach to human diversity aids the search for regularities in the connections between man's behavior and the specifics of the human situation.

A scientist's paradox

Franz Boas, the father of professional anthropology in the United States, was eloquent in framing the scientific reasons why we must be opposed to biological determinism, including its manifestation as racism. One of the lasting achievements of modern anthropology is his analysis of the relationships between race and culture, nature and nurture, genetic inheritance and learning in his classic *The Mind of Primitive Man* (1911, 1938). Here Boas 'set forth his conviction that there is no fundamental difference between the mind of primitive man and that of civilized man' (Bidney 1953: 54). Differences among the achievements of the races of man are to be accounted for 'on historical grounds rather than in terms of innate biological differences' (*ibid.*).

In *The Mind of Primitive Man*, nonetheless, Boas in a sense contributed to naive biological determinism. In the first edition he notes: 'For the purposes of our investigation, we do not need to enter deeply into a discussion of . . . the differences between the minds of the animal and of man. The differences are so striking that little or no diversity of opinion exists' (1911: 96). In the second edition he remarks:

> If we were to define culture by observing behavior alone there is little in the fundamental elements of human behavior that has not some kind of parallel in the animal world.
>
> Peculiar to man is the great variability of behavior in regard to his relations to nature and to his fellow men. While among animals the behavior of the whole species is stereotyped, or as we say, instinctive, not learned, and only to a very slight extent variable and dependent on local tradition, human behavior is not stereotyped in the same sense, and cannot be called instinctive. It depends on local tradition and is learned (1938: 152).

Most anthropologists and other social scientists persist in the belief that man is unique in the evolutionary history of the world. 'Man is unique: he is the only living species that has a culture,' wrote Leslie White. 'In the course of the evolution of primates *man* appeared when the ability to symbol had been developed and become capable of expression' (1959: 3).

Of course man is unique. As Jared Diamond comments in the next essay, however, every species is different from every other species, just as every individual is somehow unique. 'Each species of animals,' for example, 'has its own method of food quest' (Boas 1938: 150). It may be true that no other animal species has that elusive thing called 'culture' because no other species has the neurogenic ability to use symbols and 'the consequent ability to produce culture' (White 1959: 3). But no other species looks or acts quite like man, either.

Studying similarities and differences among individuals or things, among local populations or entire species may seem elementary and of little consequence. Yet the existence of variation or diversity in nature and in man's cultures reveals the fundamental paradox examined by all the sciences which lies at the heart of scientific epistemology. How a scientist approaches the dilemma posed by the fact that things are at once unique and not unique, individual but similar, determines his expectations for his science, his methods of study and his final results.

If a scientist believes that things or individuals are more dissimilar than similar, more complex than simple, more capricious than predictable, then he is likely to believe also that descriptions of the world must be complex, detailed and historical in character. If he is more inclined to believe that variation is in itself variable – i.e. that differences are neither limitless nor inevitable, then the degree of variability or redundancy within a particular system or set of things is the first problem of science and the measurement and description of similarities and differences is one of its greatest challenges.

If this point of view is acknowledged, then the claim that man is unique, if taken literally, is true and pointless. Such a claim, however, rests on a traditional dichotomy in Western Thought between man and the rest of creation which is today no longer scientifically defensible. There are several reasons for saying this so strongly.

First, if we do not accept the belief that God created man unique in His own image on the Sixth Day, then man evolved. As White has implied, man's uniqueness must have gradually come to be. If anthropologists and archaeologists are to study man's biological and social evolution, they dare not simplify matters to the degree that the problem seems to be one of nature versus culture, animals versus man, instinct versus learning. Yet it has taken archaeologists a long time to understand that evolution is a process, not an event: i.e. a series of steps or events. Many still write as if domestication was 'discovered' in the Middle East, as if the Neolithic was a 'revolution', as if some man-ape in Africa through an Act of Grace, suddenly 'became capable of expression'.

Second, archaeologists and other scientists interested in the past are engaged in research which partakes both of history and of generality. Few archaeologists would claim they are studying unique thoughts, deeds and motivations of individual men. But only the most naive would deny that the evidence they gather concerns historical, evolutionary systems and that therefore the generality of their conclusions must be in itself variable. After all, it was no less a generalist than Alfred Lotka who once observed along with Dollo that '*evolution is the history of a system undergoing irreversible changes*' (Lotka 1956: 24).

Third, as Edward Wilson has documented in his controversial book, *Sociobiology: The New Synthesis* (1975), when we speak presumptuously of 'animals' as if we were not animals, and suggest, as Boas did, that animal behavior 'is stereotyped, or as we say, instinctive, not learned, and only to a very slight extent variable and dependent on local tradition,' we are merely displaying our particular species' ignorance of the rest of creation.

Man then is not unique, at least not unique in any scientifically interesting way. Yet surely man's possession of culture, nonetheless, makes him unique in a manner which far overshadows any of the similarities we can find between man and the apes, between man and the herring-gull, or man and dog. Here archaeologists and anthropologists seem on firmer ground than their biological counterparts who appear only now – during the current debate on the extension of sociobiology into the realm of the humanities – to be discovering truths long ago made dogma in social science (e.g. Gould 1976).

Sociobiology

According to Wilson and other sociobiologists, one of the aims of their new synthesis of evolutionary genetics, population biology, ecology, ethology, psychology and anthropology is to place the social sciences within a biological framework:

> While being aware of the possible dangers of analogy, sociobiology puts heavy emphasis on the comparison of societies of different kinds of animals and of Man. The aim is to construct and test theories about the underlying hereditary basis of social behaviour (Wilson 1976: 342).

This aim is obviously one of concern to a comparative zoologist. It is not one of great interest to most social scientists. There is little danger, in spite of the claims of some, that social science is about to be swallowed up by sociobiology. Wilson and others have been criticized for being advocates of biological determinism. Without taking sides in the debate, I do want to note a few points which are germane to the present discussion.

According to Wilson, sociobiology may some day help us understand the basics of human behavior and the fundamental rules governing human potential (1976: 345). He accepts the notion of human social evolution, a notion with a notoriously long history of contrary speculations and dispute. Personally, however, I think it unlikely that infraspecific diversity within the genus *Homo* owes very much to infraspecific kin selection, a point with which Wilson apparently has no disagreement (1976: 343). If this is correct, then I find it improbable that sociobiology will have much to say of interest to social scientists.

Also I am not enthusiastically impressed by extreme old-fashioned counter-arguments that man, unlike all the other animals, is controlled by 'cultural selection' instead of natural selection. Adaptation – i.e. the Darwinian fitness of genes or the 'cultural fitness' of social and economic traits – is something easy to think about in the abstract. Because adaptation is, however, a time phenomenon observed for aggregates of individuals, while selection acts upon individuals and perhaps upon kindreds or groups of genetically-related individuals, demonstration of the mechanisms of adaptation is difficult and the measurement of fitness is even more difficult. Often arguments about adaptation seem to be little more than a variety of argument *post hoc, ergo propter hoc.*

For example, if when two species are raised through several generations in the same laboratory environment one is found to increase in numbers while the other declines, it could be said that the first is better adapted to that environment. If this change in numbers is not simply accidental, this statement is true. But why is the first better adapted?

The mechanisms involved could be many. Perhaps species A matures earlier and is able to eat many of the eggs of species B before they hatch. Perhaps the eating parts of species A are larger and more appropriately shaped to eat the standard laboratory food. Perhaps species A produces more eggs each generation than species B. And so on.

It may be possible to sort out the important factors in laboratory situations, but could it be done in the field, under natural conditions? One suspects that many arguments derived in the field must be 'after this, therefore, because of this,' e.g. ducks are better adapted to water than pigs. Why? Because ducks have evolved webbed feet and pigs have not.

An apt example of the tautology of many 'adaptive' arguments comes from one of Wilson's most informed critics. 'Adaptation is the hallmark of Darwinian processes. Natural selection operates continuously and relentlessly to fit organisms to their environments' (Gould 1976: 19). This statement is an exaggeration, but it does sound like Darwinism as popularly conceived. 'Disadvantageous social structures, like poorly designed morphological structures, will not survive for long.' Since survival over generational time is the sole criterion of adaptive success, failure to do so obviously means – after the fact – that a social structure was apparently 'disadvantageous.' What does not follow is the next remark: 'Human social practices are clearly adaptive.' Nonsense.

Social practices may be entirely neutral in the Darwinian Struggle, something I would have thought this particular critic wanted to argue for in the first place. At least when thinking about man, there is no reason to agree with the notion that 'social systems thus evolve to maximise the genetic fitness of individuals in specific environments' (May 1976: 392; also: Wilson 1975: 560).

What we do may have genetic consequences, but not necessarily. The stereotyped, physiologically expressed social systems of the social insects may be under direct selection by Darwinian forces. The range of diversity of human social systems, nevertheless, implies only that 'sociability,' not particular social systems, is under genetic 'control.'

Wilson argues that behaviors found to be nearly universal in man are likely to have an underlying genetic component (Wilson 1975: 548–551). Human universals of an interesting sort, however, are difficult to agree upon (Kluckhohn 1953). An anthropologist can speak for hours about the problems of 'cross-cultural comparison'. Surely here is an important clue to the limited significance of heredity in human diversity.

The famous incest taboo is about as universal a phenomenon as we can identify for man. Genetically, this taboo may have the 'merit of minimising the occurrence of crippling genetic malformations' (May 1976: 391; also: Wilson 1975: 553). If there is a biological component to the near universal incest taboo in human societies, however, we can speculate that this basis may be a side-effect of selection for something else. Instead of arguing that some form of 'genetic clairvoyance' has been programmed into man by natural selection which lets us behave as if we knew intuitively that mating with a parent or a sib is dangerous to our distant progeny, it makes sense to try to discover some explanation for the incest taboo where advantages are reaped by individuals in their own lifetime. For instance, perhaps the taboo is a side-effect of aggressive behavior responses, as has long been argued. Consider the following:

1 As described by Slobodkin in a later essay in this volume, organisms respond to threat situations with a series of short- and long-term physiological and behavioral responses useful in meeting dangerous intrusions by strangers, etc.; individuals having these responses in good order are thus more likely to be 'fit' to survive and pass on their genes than individuals which do not. Thus the general set of abilities needed to respond to danger is encouraged by natural selection.

2 Physiological responses seen in threat situations occur also during sexual arousal and may similarly be encouraged by natural selection.

3 Therefore, unfamiliar situations, strangers and dangers can be, in a sense, both threatening and sexual.

4 As a consequence, organisms may act as if 'familiarity breeds contempt.' That is, sex is more fun outside the family.

In a fine old anecdotal fashion this sociobiological account was inspired by my dogs. My oldest bitch will have nothing to do with her resident son until well into her heat, long after she has been observed to run after every stray male she happens to lay eyes on or nose near. This sequence of consequences, nonetheless, argues that aggression and sexuality both contribute to the selection of a general class of physiological responses of direct adaptive usefulness. Perhaps human customs labeled 'incest taboos' are not merely avoidances and may thus be seen as cultural elaborations on a biologically-based proclivity everyone has.

Biological potential and biological determination

This last example suggests more than simply that thinking sociobiologically is intriguing. It indicates the kind of model which may explain what Wilson, his adherents, and his detractors mean when they say that biology governs only man's potential, his possibilities, and not his behaviors. 'Humans are animals and everything we do lies within our biological potential,' remarks the critic we have already heard from before. 'But – and here comes the biggest *but* I can muster – the statement that humans are animals does not imply that our specific patterns of behavior and social arrangements are in any way directly determined by our genes. *Potential* and *determination* are different concepts' (Gould 1976: 15).

In 1952 the renowned anthropologist Clyde Kluckhohn said much the same thing: 'Human biology sets limits, supplies potentialities and drives, provides clues which cultures neglect or elaborate. This is standard anthropological doctrine at present, and it may turn out that this is about all there is to it' (Kluckhohn 1953: 513). I should add, however, that Kluckhohn went on to say: 'Yet when one learns that the introduction of an electric needle into a certain cortical area of one species of monkey results in these monkeys thereafter defecating upon their own kind, whereas previously they would defecate only upon strangers, one wonders if, after all, there may not be specific biological bases for certain of our social habits' (*ibid.*: 513–14). His own suspicion was that invariant or universal categories of culture for the description and comparison of particular cultures do exist:

> Valid cross-cultural comparison could best proceed from the invariant points of reference supplied by the biological, psychological, and sociosituational 'givens' of human life. These and their interrelations determine the likenesses in the broad categories and general assumptions that pervade all cultures because the 'givens' provide foci around which and within which the patterns of every culture crystallize. Hence comparison can escape from the bias of any distinct culture by taking as its frame of reference natural limits, conditions, clues, and pressures (1953: 521).

In short, 'all cultures constitute so many somewhat distinct answers to essentially the same questions posed by human biology and by the generalities of the human situation' (1953: 520).

The phrase 'and by the generalities of the human situation' is one which I think must be emphasized here. It hints at the kind of model I have in mind. Let me explain with an example first. In the final chapter of *Sociobiology*, which concerns the biological basis of human societies that has created such contention among biologists and others, Wilson observes that certain characteristics of contemporary hunter-gatherer societies (such as the !Kung described in an essay to follow by John Yellen) are shared with primate societies. He infers that such traits were probably also displayed by early man. Thus he thinks it likely that ancient hominids lived in local groups of 100 or fewer individuals. They were probably territorial in some undetermined fashion. Males were dominant over females. Game-playing was a feature of daily life. There was prolonged maternal care, pronounced socialization of young, and extended relationships between mother and child – especially between mothers and daughters.

Much can be said for this comparative approach by which Wilson (and others) arrives at inferences about the social life of early man. His deductions sound immediately plausible. It is uncertain, nonetheless, how suggestions or speculations such as these refer in any direct fashion to the biology of early man.

Wilson has written on several occasions recently that 'we can be sure that our innate social responses have been fashioned largely through this life style' (e.g. 1976: 344). What innate social responses? Living in groups of 100 or fewer individuals? Some degree of aggressive territorial behavior? Male dominance? Motherhood? Wilson's argument is not clear, although he seems confident that similarities in human social organization and behavior should be attributed to man's biology, not man's condition. He has stated several times, for example, that the sexual division of labor in society – men hunt while women stay at home or at base camp – has 'a genetic origin.' Unfortunately, he has presented no critical tests by means of which the truth or falsehood of his contentions might be weighed. For the most part, he begs the issue: are these 'universals' because of man's biology and 'social evolution,' or because of the generalities of the human situation? Make no mistake. This is not simply a case of 'nature or nurture.' This is the critical issue.

Most social scientists are aware of the implications of their preoccupation with a single, remarkable species: there *must* be similarities among people everywhere due to their common genetic foundations. There must also be resemblances due to inevitable similarities in the human life style, i.e. in human ecology and social existence. The surprising fact, then, is not that men may usually dominate over women everywhere, etc. There is obvious dimorphism in the human species considered by some to inspire such male dominance. Instead, the surprising fact is that there is so much diversity among human groups. Racists and snobs may explain class and ethnic differences with biology, but most social scientists know better. The model we require, therefore, must be one which accommodates human biology while allowing plenty of room for human cultural diversity. Such a model has been built by the psychologist and computer specialist Herbert A. Simon (1969, 1973) to describe all kinds of complex systems. In brief, his model suggests why an organism behaves *with* its body, but not necessarily *because* of its physiology. Biologists who favor explanations for animal and human behavior couched in terms of biochemistry and the physiology of bodily functions probably reject Simon's model, some at least without thinking about its logical appropriateness. A model of this kind, nonetheless, is needed to avoid the excesses of extreme behaviorism, on one hand, and extreme biological reductionism, on the other.

Near-decomposability of complex systems

Human beings, when they are communicating with each other, interacting with their surroundings or sitting quietly and thinking, do not need to know – and rarely care about – what their bodies are doing, i.e. how their biological systems are functioning. In Simon's terminology, our behavior is 'nearly decomposable' from our internal biology, for our behavior is nearly independent of the details of physiology (Simon 1973: 9–11).

Similarly, how the digestive system works is of no 'concern' to the muscular system as long as the circulatory system delivers needed oxygen and nutrients. How one system works is nearly independent of the details of the other systems. Therefore, biological systems (or any 'subsystems' at the same hierarchic level within a complex system, real or artificial) are also nearly decomposable.

Simon's treatment of the organization of complex systems is more involved and useful than these few remarks I have given may indicate. He should be consulted by anyone interested in the problems of nature and nurture, instinct and learning, etc. It suffices here to jump at once to one of the major implications of near-decomposability.

'To a Platonic mind, everything in the world is connected with everything else – and perhaps it is. Everything is connected, but some things are more connected than others' (Simon 1973: 23). In short, complex systems tend to be hierarchic systems, because hierarchies allow for efficiency and stability. Hierarchic systems evolve by processes of natural selection more rapidly than non-hierarchic systems. 'By virtue of hierarchy, the several components on any given level can preserve a measure of independence to adapt to their special aspects of the environment without destroying their usefulness to the system' (*ibid.*: 23–4).

If Simon's view of the hierarchical organization of complex systems is correct, it would seem that there is no *a priori* reason why human social behavior must be connected to human biology. As long as our bodies work, our behavior may in fact be relatively independent of the details of physiology and the genetic programs for cell growth and differentiation.

Near-decomposability has another implication. Simon phrases this one first as a hypothesis:

> A thinking human being is an adaptive system; his goals define the interface between his inner and outer environments. To the extent that he is effectively adaptive, his behavior will reflect characteristics largely of the outer environment (in the light of his goals) and will reveal only a few limiting properties of his inner environment – of the physiological machinery that enables him to think (1969: 25–6).

I cannot review his fascinating discussion in support of this elegant suggestion. But I do want to repeat the lesson he finds in it: 'we should not look for great complexity in the laws governing human behavior, in situations where the behavior is truly simple and only its environment is complex' (1969: 41).

May I remind you that earlier I said I did not want to take sides in the current debate between sociobiologists and anti-sociobiologists. It may be apparent why I have not: there is no need to do so. Both sides are right. Of course there is a biological basis and genetic origin for social behavior. Of course too, biology and genetics are probably incapable of telling us much that is important about human behavior. Along with many of Wilson's critics, I am willing to bet that the biological program in man is to have few preconceived programs.

Human biogeography

What about biogeography? Is it useful to think about human biogeography? I believe the answer is affirmative, because what I mean by biogeography directs us to consider 'the outer environment' and to ask if there are any 'laws governing human behavior.'

Remember what Kluckhohn once said: 'All cultures constitute so many somewhat distinct answers to essentially the same questions posed by human biology and by the generalities of the human situation.' If this statement is correct, why are the answers many and somewhat distinct? Are all human answers, i.e. cultural answers, equally 'adaptive' to these same questions of human biology and the human situation? If human biology is much the same everywhere, as is likely, is it also true that the human situation is everywhere much the same?

I think the answer to this last question must be a qualified *no*. In so far as man's environment is structured and composed of other human beings interacting with each other in various ways, at various times, in groups of varying size and complexity, it is probable that the human situation everywhere displays common themes and characteristics. But man's environment is not limited to human social groupings. People are elements in a far more complex system, at best only partly of man's design, which I have elsewhere defined as the 'geographic system': the functional configuration between the size, distribution and interaction structure of a population, and the elements and interaction structure of the area of that population's occurrence, analyzed as a complex of intercommunicating elements within which a change in any one element or relationship is likely to effect changes, of a greater or lesser degree, in all the others (Terrell 1972; 1976b: 80).

An important phrase in this formal, decidedly Platonic, definition of what I mean by a geographic system is the expression 'of a greater or lesser degree.' Human populations and social systems are 'nearly-decomposable' from situational or ecological systems, just as man's thinking apparatus is nearly independent of the details of man's stomach. We know this to be true. As long as the trains in Italy run on time, for example, the citizenry may not care why it is they do so.

Thus I think human biogeography can be defined as comparative human ecology. The aim of human biogeography is to study the similarities and differences among human populations and social systems throughout the world. At least one purpose is to study the connections between man and the specifics of the human situation, in order to discover precisely how nearly-decomposable human adaptive behavior is from man's natural and cultural environment. Elsewhere again I have offered this formal definition:

> human biogeography can be described as the study of the size, distribution and population structure of and the interactions among human populations and of the conditions and events leading to similarities and differences among human communities. Thus defined, human

biogeography involves more than human ecology. Also of concern is the history, distribution, characteristics and interrelationships of human groups on a regional and global scale (Terrell 1976a: 2).

Laws of human behavior

The question '*How* nearly-decomposable is human adaptive behavior from man's natural and cultural environment?' raises the ultimate aim of most sciences. Are there any laws governing observed phenomena? If we are asking for probabilistic regularities and not deterministic laws, the answer surely is 'there must be'.

Recall Simon's hypothesis about a thinking human being as an adaptive system. He proposes that human behavior reflects characteristics largely of the outer environment *because of human goals*. If human goals are not wholly capricious and maladaptive, there must be direct connections between behavior and situation.

In *The Sciences of the Artificial* Simon does not initially phrase his hypothesis about thinking man in the form I quoted earlier. Just as the entomologist Edward Wilson has done so often, Simon asks us first to consider the ant:

> *An ant, viewed as a behaving system, is quite simple. The apparent complexity of its behavior over time is largely a reflection of the complexity of the environment in which it finds itself* (Simon 1969: 24).

As Simon demonstrates, it is possible to simulate ant behavior with a relatively small number of adaptive capabilities. In keeping with what he concludes elsewhere, he observes: 'At the level of cells or molecules, ants are demonstrably complex; but these microscopic details of the inner environment may be largely irrelevant to the ant's behavior in relation to the outer environment' (1969: 25).

Simon then presents the first phrasing of his hypothesis. In keeping with his world view, I also suspect that man's social behavior is not incomprehensible. Elsewhere I have presented my reasons for thinking so in detail and by example (Terrell 1974; 1976a and in press). The following papers in this issue of *World Archaeology* explore the pros and cons of biogeographical thinking about man in broad spectrum. This introduction, therefore, is best closed by quoting Simon's hypothesis as he substitutes the word 'man' for 'ant':

> *A man, viewed as a behaving system, is quite simple. The apparent complexity of his behavior over time is largely a reflection of the complexity of the environment in which he finds himself* (1969: 25).

Acknowledgements

I thank Julie Castrop, Kathleen Fine, Nina Green, Carol Jones, Marilyn Miller and John Stowe for comments on the original draft of this paper.

1.viii.1976

Department of Anthropology
Field Museum of Natural History, Chicago

References

Bidney, D. 1953. *Theoretical Anthropology* (2nd ed.). New York: Columbia University Press (Schocken paperback, 1967).

Boas, F. 1911. *The Mind of Primitive Man.* New York: The Macmillan Company.

Boas, F. 1938. *The Mind of Primitive Man* (revised ed.). New York: The Macmillan Company (Free Press paperback, 1965).

Gould, S. J. 1976. Biological potential vs. biological determinism. *Natural History.* 85:12–22.

Kluckhohn, C. 1953. Universal categories of culture. In *Anthropology Today: an encyclopedic inventory*, pp. 507–23 (ed. A. L. Kroeber). Chicago: University of Chicago Press.

Lotka, A. J. 1956. *Elements of Mathematical Biology.* New York: Dover Publications, Inc.

May, R. M. 1976. Sociobiology: a new synthesis and an old quarrel. *Nature.* 260:390–2.

Simon, H. A. 1969. *The Sciences of the Artificial.* Cambridge, Mass.: The M.I.T. Press.

Simon, H. A. 1973. The organization of complex systems. In *Hierarchy Theory: the challenge of complex systems*, pp. 1–27 (ed. H. H. Pattee). New York: George Braziller.

Terrell, J. 1972. Geographic systems and human diversity in the northern Solomons. *Reports of the Bougainville Archaeological Survey.* 5 (Department of Anthropology, Field Museum of Natural History).

Terrell, J. 1974. Comparative human and lower animal biogeography in the Solomon Islands. *Solomon Island Studies in Human Biogeography.* 3 (Department of Anthropology, Field Museum of Natural History).

Terrell, J. 1976a. Island biogeography and man in Melanesia. *Archaeology and Physical Anthropology in Oceania.* 11:1–17.

Terrell, J. 1976b. *Perspectives on the Prehistory of Bougainville Island, Papua New Guinea: a study in the human biogeography of the southwestern Pacific.* Doctoral dissertation, Harvard University (unpublished).

Terrell, J. (in press). Human biogeography in the Solomon Islands. *Fieldiana: Anthropology.* Chicago: Field Museum of Natural History.

White, L. A. 1959. *The Evolution of Culture: the development of civilization to the fall of Rome.* New York: McGraw-Hill Book Company, Inc. (paperback ed.)

Wilson, E. O. 1975. *Sociobiology: the new synthesis.* Cambridge, Mass.: Harvard University Press.

Wilson, E. O. 1976. Sociobiology: a new approach to understanding the basis of human nature. *New Scientist.* 70:342–5.

Abstract

Terrell, John

Biology, biogeography and man

Biogeographical thinking in archaeology and anthropology permits social scientists to consider questions about the size, distribution, ecology and population structure of human groups without succumbing to the fallacies of biological determinism or the similarly naive and deterministic presumption that man is unique and beyond scientific scrutiny. A biogeographer's approach to ancient and modern man furthers investigation of the events and environmental circumstances, natural and man-made, that play a role in the evolution of similarities and differences among human populations and among their cultures.

Colonization cycles in man and beast

Jared M. Diamond

Introduction

In this article I shall compare the colonization cycles of pre-industrial man and other animals – i.e. the cycles of population expansion and contraction that provide the historical basis for instantaneous patterns of biological distribution. Understanding of these cycles in animals has been stimulated by recent advances in biogeography stemming from the work of Robert MacArthur and Edward Wilson (e.g. MacArthur and Wilson 1967, MacArthur 1972, Wilson 1975). Ingredients in these advances have included: realistic mathematical modelling, quantitative field observations, search for ways to describe complex communities in terms of measurable parameters permitting intercommunity comparisons, and emphasis on adaptive strategies. As discussed elsewhere (Diamond 1976), the seemingly teleological language of 'strategic analyses' actually serves as a shorthand description of underlying evolutionary mechanisms.

'But man is basically different from other animals.' So one is often warned when the possible relevance of animal findings to understanding man is suggested. In fact, however, every animal species is basically different from other animal species. Faced with this diversity, biogeography has developed a common framework for understanding such unlike distributions as those of giraffes, rose-breasted grosbeaks, cockroaches and oak trees, by seeking relations among key variables or processes. These variables or processes are ones that are relevant to understanding any species. Like other species, man reproduces, dies, disperses, exploits environments of varying stability and productivity, adapts phenotypically and genetically, is subject to intraspecific competition, and (still like other species) differs from other species in particular characteristics of each of these processes. These are the processes that provide the ingredients for biogeographic analysis.

In this spirit let us proceed as biogeographers and inquire in what particular ways man is unique as a colonist.

Colonization cycles

Gathering the evidence

What do we know about colonization cycles in animals? We have three main sources of information. First, modern cases of rapid progress through colonization cycles have been witnessed directly. Examples famous to the biologist include: the expansion and subsequent partial retreat of the Azure Tit across Russia in the 19th century (Vaurie 1957); the westward expansion of the Serin Finch and Collared Turtle-Dove across Europe in this century, possibly facilitated by a climatic change and by genetic changes in a peripheral population (Mayr 1926; 1942: 238; 1963: 564); and the southward expansion of the Fulmar from the 18th century, possibly triggered by genetic changes in a particular colony and by increased food availability due to man's activities. Nowak (1975) has reviewed 28 examples of modern expansions in animal species of Europe.

A second source of information comes from the present distributions of several species which may each suggest successive stages in a colonization cycle; a source that is like reconstructing a motion picture from scrambled individual frames by arranging them in presumed sequence. There is an extensive literature on so-called 'taxon cycles,' i.e. colonization cycles deduced from sequences of such 'snapshots' (e.g. Wilson 1961, Greenslade 1968, Ricklefs and Cox 1972). For instance, one may guess that the Tahiti Imperial Pigeon came to be confined to the mountain forests of Tahiti, 4,000 miles east of related species on New Guinea, by a cycle of immigrations and extinctions, earlier stages of which are illustrated by distributions of the following species: Mueller's Imperial Pigeon (only New Guinea): Superb Fruit Dove (New Guinea east 1,000 miles to the Bismarcks and Solomons): Reef Heron (New Guinea east to most of the Society Islands, including Tahiti); Grey-green Fruit Dove (six Society islands including Tahiti, with a closely related species on Fiji and Samoa).

A third source of information is the fossil record, from which some colonization cycles can be deduced, although with coarse time resolution. For example, several radiations and retreats of horses in North America (mainly) and Eurasia (secondarily) culminated in their late-Pleistocene extinction in North America and their present confinement in the natural wild state to the Old World.

Colonization cycles in human populations are attested by three corresponding types of evidence. First, parts of some cycles have been witnessed in recorded history, such as the expansion of Europeans to the New World, the expansion of Vikings to Iceland and Greenland and coastal Europe in the 9th and 10th centuries, the westward expansion of Mongols across Eurasia in the 14th century, and the southward expansion of Bantu in Africa associated with the virtual disappearance of Bushmen. Other cycles have been reconstructed from present-day distributions aided initially by only limited historical or archaeological evidence, such as the eastward expansion of Polynesians across the Pacific, the range fragmentation of Finno-Ugric speakers in Eurasia, and the eastward expansion of Australoids to the Sahul Shelf together with the range fragmentation of related populations in southeast Asia and the Philippines. Finally much evidence for colonization cycles in man comes from the archaeological record: for example, the occupation of the New World by Amerindians and of the Nearctic by Eskimos.

There is no other species for which population shifts, especially at the detailed infraspecific level, are documented in anything remotely approaching the detail available for man. Thus studies of man by the methods of animal biogeography, besides placing human distributional patterns in a wider context, may also stimulate and enrich the study of biogeography generally. For example, some readers may be disturbed that in the following discussions I take infraspecific groups as units in considering man but take species as the units in considering animals. This apparent difference may be an artifact of available information: if animal biogeographers had as much information about infraspecific variation in their favourite species, it might be possible to illustrate strikingly different distributional strategies by various populations of the same species, as can be done for man. In fact, examples of intraspecific variation in distributional strategy are known for intensively studied bird species of the New Guinea region, such as the flycatchers *Rhipidura rufifrons* and *Pachycephala pectoralis*.

Cycles, stages and strategies

Colonization cycles in animal species involve changes not only in distribution but also in reproductive strategy, dispersal strategy, resource-harvesting strategy, niche breadth and competitive dominance. While we do not yet fully understand the triggers that drive a species through successive stages of a cycle, we can formulate a general description of the stages in such a cycle. Bear in mind, however, that there are myriads of exceptions to the following generalizations, especially for the reasons discussed in the last two paragraphs of this paper.

1 *Stage 1: expanding phase* In some cases it is clear that the initial trigger setting off a cycle consists of increased availability of resources to a species or population, but this increased availability may be due to one or more of numerous reasons: a change in climate, habitat, or food supply, a change in the population itself (e.g. a genetic change or, especially in man, a cultural or technological change), or decrease in a competitor or predator. In many other cases the trigger is still unknown: the start of the cycle appears sudden and mysterious. This trigger, whatever it is, sets in motion a set of simultaneous changes that initially are mutually stimulatory and autocatalytic: selection for increased dispersal, in order to reach the newly available resources; selection for increased reproductive rate, in order to generate new colonists and build up populations rapidly before potentially competing harvesters of the same resources arrive; and expansion of niche breadth.

2 *Stage 2: local adaptation phase* The colonist populations begin to adapt by genetic as well as purely phenotypic responses to the new environment in which they find themselves. Since the available new territory was 'saturated' with colonists in the expansion phase, selection for dispersal declines to a level just necessary to replace local deaths and extinctions. Selection for high reproductive rate similarly declines, and selection for self-regulation of abundance to conserve local resources increases. Saturated habitats place a premium on enhancing competitive ability, either by increased resource harvesting efficiency or else by aggression directed at potential competitors.

3 *Stage 3: retreating phase* Continued competitive pressure from newly arriving invaders from other populations or species causes the older colonists to specialize ecologically and to narrow their niches. With passage of time, the older colonists retreat to the most stable or most extensive habitats or areas, or to the least easily invadable habitats, where they have an advantage over newer invaders. The colonists' dispersal and reproductive rates are too low to replace local populations that disappear in other areas. Their distributional range begins to contract and take on a relict pattern of disjunct populations. Their retreat proceeds either until the descendants of the colonist wave finally disappear, or until a new trigger sets in motion another colonization wave.

Because immigration rates, local extinction rates and habitat preference vary from stage to stage in this cycle, new and old colonists are likely to be concentrated in somewhat different habitats and geographical areas. For example, among ant species on Pacific islands one often finds new colonists concentrated in the readily invadable coastal habitats and second-growth, as well as on small islands where extinctions are frequent; old colonists tend to be concentrated in the rainforest or mountains (Wilson 1961). In Australia the modest areas of tropical rainforest in Queensland contain mainly species that recently invaded from New Guinea, while older colonists have accumulated in the extensive deserts to which new colonists are ill-adapted.

Let us now consider in more detail four population characteristics which change through a colonization cycle: dispersal strategy, reproductive strategy, niche breadth and strategy for coping with the risk of extinction.

Dispersal strategy Species, or populations of the same species, differ enormously in how many colonists they send out and how far these colonists disperse. Part of this variation is for anatomical reasons: birds generally disperse farther over water than do snakes, flying birds travel farther than flightless birds, long-winged birds farther than short-winged birds, birds that store energy as thick deposits of subcutaneous fat farther than birds with slight fat deposits, etc. Less often appreciated is the major contribution of behavioral or psychological differences to differences in dispersal. For example, out of the known 513 breeding species of New Guinea birds, 509 can fly, yet for only about 210 of these is there evidence that they have ever crossed water gaps more than a few miles wide. Anatomically similar and taxonomically related species may differ greatly in this respect. For instance, the New Guinea Harpy Eagle, which flies dozens of miles overland daily in the course of its normal foraging, has reached no island off New Guinea, not even large islands 2 miles offshore, while the White-bellied Sea Eagle has reached virtually every island within hundreds of miles of New Guinea. Evidently the Harpy Eagle and about 300 other New Guinea bird species have insuperable psychological barriers to flying across water.

What evolutionary forces mold a population's anatomical or psychological ability to disperse? Dispersal involves costs and potential benefits. The costs are the energy expenditure and risk of death in dispersing. The potential benefits are the possibility of finding more available resources than at the point of departure. The trade-off between these costs and benefits determines, and natural selection may produce, an optimal dispersal strategy. If, for instance, Harpy Eagle populations had for any reason lower long-term reproductive success on islands other than on New Guinea itself, and if individual Harpy Eagles initially differed in their willingness to disperse across water, those that did have this willingness would leave fewer descendants, and the genetic basis for this willingness would eventually be selected out of the source population.

We must ask therefore what factors affect the costs and benefits of dispersal: when are an individual's chances of leaving descendants increased by going far from the place of birth before seeking a site to reproduce? Examples of such factors are as follows. Dispersal is favored if local population extinctions occur frequently and create vacant habitat: for instance, among species in highly fluctuating environments (such as the famous Arctic lemmings which plunge *en masse* into water), or among species whose habitat occurs in small patches where demographic extinction must be frequent, or among species in regions where defaunation by volcanic explosions occurs frequently. Dispersal is also favored by poor temporal autocorrelation of habitat rank, i.e. if the best piece of habitat one year is likely not to be the best piece of habitat a few years hence. Again dispersal is favored by high variance in quality of occupied habitat, such that an individual in poor habitat can significantly improve its circumstances by going elsewhere. Conversely, dispersal will be selected against if a species would be a poor colonist for other reasons, such as low reproductive potential or ecological inflexibility. Thus many rainforest bird species are reluctant to disperse over water, and this is linked to the fact that their low reproductive potential would reduce chances of colonizing success even if they reached an island with much underexploited rainforest.

Among communities of populations or species there is great diversity in intra-community variance in dispersal ability. For example, there is greater variance (among species) in dispersal ability within tropical than within temperate bird communities, and within a tree than a fern community. Where this variance is great, only a small fraction of a community contributes to colonization. The few colonizing species must then regenerate, by behavioral niche shifts and evolutionary change, many new taxa to replace the missing populations from the original source community. Colonization, in other words, proceeds through a narrow funnel.

For primitive man, the overwater colonization funnel is narrow. Virtually all colonization is probably by coastal people. Mountain peoples of the Melanesian islands had to be independently rederived from initially coastal invaders. Even coastal peoples must have varied greatly in dispersal ability, ranging for example from the Tasmanians and Bentinck Islanders, who ventured only short distances from land, to the Polynesians. Some of this variation has a technological basis, such as the Polynesians' acquired navigational knowledge, ability to prepare food for long journeys and superior watercraft. There may also have been some anatomical basis in the tendency of Polynesians (like migrant bird species) to store body fat, possibly the result of extreme selection for survival on the long overwater journeys that founded populations on the Polynesian islands. A psychological basis may be illustrated by the situation in aboriginal Tasmania, where watercraft were strikingly absent from the northeast coast opposite the Furneaux islands, which are visible from Tasmania but somewhat beyond the range of the canoe-rafts used on the south and west coasts. A history of deaths or no-returns in attempts to reach these islands may have led to taboos against watercraft on the northeast coast (Jones 1976). For the Polynesians, the evolution of the technology, knowledge and attitudes necessary for water-crossing was probably an autocatalytic process in which the opportunities presented by vacant islands played an essential role, as with expanding animal populations generally. This conclusion is suggested by the fact that, at the time of European discovery of Polynesia, virtually all available islands had been colonized and long-distance inter-island voyaging had virtually ceased.

Reproductive strategy I mentioned that reproductive rate increases, then decreases during a colonization cycle. What determines how much energy should be allocated to reproductive effort?

Biologists discuss this problem in terms introduced by MacArthur and Wilson (1967), who contrasted selection regimes called *K*-selection and *r*-selection. In the growth equations of population biology, *K* represents carrying capacity, *r* growth rate. Consider at the one extreme (*K*-selection) a stable environment in which populations remain relatively constant, individuals are long-lived and vacant territories rarely become available. Populations can saturate the environment's carrying capacity, competition (or predation) rather than environmental harshness becomes limiting, and most energy must be allocated to competing (or avoiding predators). Since new areas rarely become available for colonization, each individual needs on the average to leave barely more than the one descendant necessary to replace itself and it has a long lifetime in which to do this. Producing many offspring is not only unnecessary but dangerous, as it would lead to overharvesting of local resources and hence self-induced population crashes. The absence of an emigration safety valve for excess young means that population density must be closely regulated. As a result, reproductive effort is modest. Tropical birds often lay only one-egg clutches and nest only once a year or less often. Their stable environment does not provide occasional, seasonally-predictable bursts of resource plenty that can be channeled into reproduction, as in spring in the temperate zones. Instead, birds may skip breeding entirely in some years and wait for a productive time to attempt nesting. Since adults have many oppportunities to breed over a long life-time and they need replace only themselves and not whole depleted populations, they do not risk their lives to defend a nest against predators: tropical birds are notorious for deserting nests at a slight disturbance. Once a nestling is fledged, there follows a long period of parental care, during which the adult teaches the juvenile to deal with complex anti-predator devices (mimicry, camouflage, poisons, etc.) employed by the diverse insect prey of the tropics, before the juvenile becomes independent.

At the opposite extreme (*r*-selection), consider a rapidly fluctuating environment in which areas frequently become vacant as a result of populations being wiped out and few populations have time to saturate an environment's carrying capacity before such a crash. Since population densities are usually below carrying capacity, competition is unimportant. Adults must leave more than one descendant, to replace not only themselves but also whole populations that are wiped out. To do this, adults have only a short life-time and must defend nests tenaciously: if they do not die today while fighting off a nest predator, they may die tomorrow from an environmental disaster. These disasters, and the numerous opportunities they create for surviving young, make self-regulation of population density irrelevant. Instead, the premium is on producing many young as quickly as possible. Such *r*-selected tropical bird species may produce several clutches a year; the record is held by a pair of New Guinea flycatchers that is known to have reared six broods in six months. The young disperse, and most die; a few strike it rich and find a large vacant area. For example, those individuals of Sclater's Honeyeater, an extremely *r*-selected 'supertramp' bird species of the New Guinea region, that recolonized Long Island, a large volcano recently defaunated by an explosion, succeeded in founding a population several times larger than all other populations of their species combined.

The possible adaptive significance of our human reproductive strategy poses major unsolved problems of theoretical and practical interest. Human populations, like other animal populations, vary greatly in their reproductive strategies. Humans employ numerous techniques that directly regulate reproductive rate: infanticide, abortion, contraception, child-spacing through abstinence from intercourse, and child-spacing through lactation-induced suppression of ovulation. Further social practices that may regulate reproductive rate indirectly, because their frequency may vary with population density, include warfare and overseas voyaging or other forms of emigration. Are such devices commoner among people in stable, saturated environments than among those living in unpredictably fluctuating environments? (In seeking test cases for comparison, we should not confuse stability with productivity: a desert may be more stable and predictable than a savanna or monsoon forest.) Are such devices commoner among people on small atolls than on large islands, or among coastal people than interior people on Pacific islands? What is the significance of differing reproductive strategies among different sub-groups sharing the same geographical area? Some discussion of these and related questions will be found in Vayda and Rappaport (1963) and in Wagley (1969).

Niche breadth It was mentioned earlier that populations often first expand, then contract, their niche breadth as a colonization cycle proceeds. In more detail, if all populations from a source island establish themselves on a target island, then each population can preserve its original niche breadth and position. Actually, as discussed, dispersal ability and reproductive potential as well as niche characteristics contribute to colonizing success, so that there is always likely to be some mismatch between the habitats that a target island offers to successful colonists and the habitats that these populations occupied on their source island. Thus successful colonists may expand their niches to take advantage of resources that would have been consumed on their source island by species that fail to reach a target island.

The earliest component of niche shifts is an immediate behavioral response of colonizing individuals to altered resource levels. In birds, whose foraging strategies are rather rigidly programmed genetically, this behavioral response consists mainly of foraging in a wider range of habitats than on a source island (Crowell 1962, Diamond 1970). Common shifts are that birds of the coast or of second growth on a source island expand into the rainforest interior on a target island, and that lowland birds expand into the mountains. The reason for this pattern is that coastal, second-growth, or lowland birds disperse better and are more likely to be among successful colonists than are rainforest or montane species.

After this prompt behavioral response there may be slower niche shifts requiring genetic changes in the colonists as they adapt to the opportunities of their new environment. These genetic changes have produced the famous examples of insular adaptive radiation cited in any textbook of evolution: the radiation of marsupials in Australia in the absence of placental mammals, producing ecological equivalents of moles, mice, dogs, deer and flying squirrels; the radiation of Darwin's finches on the Galapagos, and of honeycreepers on Hawaii, in the near absence of other songbirds; and the radiation of shrubs to produce tree-sized plants on many islands in the near absence of mainland tree species (Carlquist 1974). Given unexploited resources and strong selective pressures, such genetic changes can be rapid, as illustrated by the evolution of brown-breasted finches from white-breasted ancestors within a decade in New Guinea's Karimui Basin (Diamond 1972: 411), the adaptation of House Sparrows in size and color to local rainfall and temperature conditions within a century after reaching North America (Johnson and Selander 1964), the size divergence of two honey-eater species within two centuries after colonizing New Guinea's Long Island (Diamond 1977), and the evolution of endemic moth species dependent on bananas about a millennium after bananas reached Hawaii (Zimmerman 1960).

We know little about the rapidity of evolutionary adaptation in man. As an example of a situation where this question arises, it is sometimes claimed that the similarity of the Tasmanians to Melanesians, and their lack of similarity to most Australian Aborigines in hair form, must indicate genetic relationship because such hair form could not have evolved convergently in 10,000 years. In fact, given our ignorance of the genetic basis and selective value of human hair form, we simply have no way of guessing whether the Tasmanian hair form evolved genetically in three centuries or 100,000 years, or even whether it was partly determined non-genetically by diet in the first two years of life.

Finally, niches may contract again as old colonists retreat to stable or extensive or invasion-proof habitats, such as mountains of Pacific islands or deserts of Australia. Partly because of the colonists' small population sizes and their impoverished gene pools, partly because of reduced interspecific competition, colonists may eventually become less efficient at harvesting resources and at competing, ecologically less adaptable in the face of change, and likely to succumb quickly to competition from a new invader. Thus a disproportionate fraction of the bird populations that have become extinct in the past century have been insular populations.

Because the overwater colonization funnel is narrow for human populations, human history provides abundant examples of niche shifts and adaptive radiation: the derivation of mountain peoples on New Guinea, New Britain, Bougainville, Guadalcanal, Espiritu Santo and Viti Levu from coastal peoples rather than from mountain peoples on other islands; the success of Polynesian horticulturalists and fishermen from the tropics at exploiting fern roots, seals and moas in the cold conditions of New Zealand's South Island; the radiation of ancestral Australian Aborigines, initially selected by the filter of coastal tropical rainforest and savanna on the Lesser Sunda Islands, to adapt variously to desert, temperate rainforest and cold maritime environments; and the radiation of ancestral Amerindians, initially selected by the cold lowland tundra filter of Beringia, to produce the high-altitude-adapted peoples of the Altiplano as well as peoples of Amazonian lowland rainforest and a wide spectrum of other habitats. Niche contraction in small isolated populations is strikingly exemplified by the Tasmanians, who lost the arts of fishing, hafting, use of bone tools and use of boomerangs by about four millennia after the drowning of the Bass Straits land bridge severed Tasmania from Australia (Jones 1976); and by technologically impoverished 'pigmy' populations in the mountains of the Philippines, Southeast Asia and New Guinea.

Strategy for coping with the risk of extinction Any isolated or local population runs a finite risk of extinction. This risk increases with decreasing population size, for obvious demographic reasons: even if birth rates on the average equal death rates, the deaths of all adults of the same sex might occur consecutively by chance in the sequence of demographic events in a small population (MacArthur and Wilson 1967). The minimum safe population size, below which extinction probability is very high, may be only a few pairs for species holding non-overlapping pair territories, but consists of many individuals for species that utilize spatially and temporally patchy food supplies and that therefore must hold group territories. Such species include flower-feeding lories, African hunting dogs and man. Among such social species, the mechanism of local extinction may not be the death of the last individual but instead a conscious abandonment of a territory when the territory or the population is perceived as too small. For example, extinction of a pelican population blown to Santa Anna Island in the Solomons by a cyclone in 1952 occurred when the seven surviving individuals all flew off on the same day in 1955. Finally, for populations for which the time-averaged abundance is sufficiently high that the risk of demographic extinction at that abundance is slight, the risk of extinction varies as the temporal coefficient of variation of abundance: i.e. extinction probability depends mainly on the frequency and magnitude of population crashes. These patterns are well illustrated by studies of turnover of bird populations on islands (Mayr 1965). Because of high extinction rates, turnover is most rapid on small islands, where most populations are short-lived and few populations survive long enough to adapt genetically to special local conditions.

Given the omnipresent risk of local extinction, what can a species do about it? Briefly there are two types of strategies: either to concentrate on preventing it from happening, or else to let it happen and concentrate on reversing it by recolonization. The former is the strategy of old colonists, which have lost much of their dispersal ability, can rarely reverse local extinctions by recolonization and become restricted to stable or extensive habitats where extinction is rare. The latter is the strategy of expanding colonists, which have high dispersal rates and can therefore occupy small and unstable habitats, recolonizing as extinctions occur.

There is increasing evidence of the role of local extinctions in human history. Examples of extinctions that could be reversed by recolonization, because they befell groups capable of dispersal, include: extinction of the first settlement of Anuta Island, a Polynesian outlier in the Santa Cruz group, around A.D. 500, to be recolonized about a millennium later (Yen and Gordon 1973); extinction of the first Polynesian settlement of Pitcairn Island at some unknown time before the arrival of the Bounty mutineers; extinction of at least four pre-Columbian groups from Peru or Ecuador on the Galapagos Islands (Black n.d.); and repeated extinctions and refoundings of Eskimo populations in several areas at the southern edge of the Eskimo range (W. W. Fitzhugh, pers. comm.). Other examples involve so-called land-bridge islands, where human populations incapable of efficient overwater dispersal were faced with stranding by rising sea-level at the end of the Pleistocene and survived only on islands large enough to support more than about 500 people. Thus aboriginal Australian populations survived as post-Pleistocene relicts on Tasmania and possibly on Bentinck and Bathurst/Melville, but disappeared on smaller islands (Kangaroo, King, the Furneaux group, and the eastern islands of Torres Straits) (Golson 1972, Jones 1976, Tindale 1976). At least for Kangaroo, King, the Furneaux group and Hunter, archaeological evidence shows the disappearance to have occurred around the time of land-bridge severance, suggesting either that the population crashed rapidly or else abandoned the island like the Santa Anna pelicans. Jersey, off the coast of France, is a further case of a land-bridge island which was too small to retain its Pleistocene human population.

Like these human populations, numerous birds and mammals incapable of overwater dispersal were stranded on land-bridge islands by the post-Pleistocene rise in sea-level and have disappeared from smaller islands. In Bass Straits the Spotted Quail-thrush, the Grey Kangaroo and the rat *Mastacomys fuscus* ended up with the same distribution as man, surviving only on Tasmania and the Australian mainland (Hope 1973). On land-bridge islands elsewhere in the world, such as the Japanese archipelago, Greater Sundas, Taiwan, Ceylon and Ireland, archaeologists should be alert to the possibility of real gaps in the human fossil record corresponding to extinctions during high-sea-level Pleistocene phases.

The opposite strategy for coping with extinction, i.e. rapidly reversing it, reaches its extreme development in so-called supertramp species (Diamond 1974, 1975). These are species that have made a maximum investment in dispersal, reproduction and ecological flexibility. Consequently they can reach, and if necessary repeatedly recolonize, small or remote islands, but are excluded from large or close islands by more sedentary species. For example, the supertramp bird species of the Pacific occur on virtually all islands, including large ones, of remote archipelagoes, but are confined to small or outlying islands of more accessible archipelagoes, such as Tikopia and Anuta in the Santa Cruz group, or Rennell, Bellona, Sikaiana and Ongtong Java in the Solomons (Diamond and Marshall 1976). The supreme human supertramps are the Polynesians, who successfully colonized as diverse remote islands as Hawaii, New Zealand and Easter, but were confined by the presence of Melanesians in the Santa Cruz group and Solomons to the same small or outlying islands as the supertramp bird species. The colonizing ability that enabled Polynesians to reach remote islands such as Hawaii, where they could found large and extinction-proof populations, also enabled them to maintain populations on the tiny and scattered Tuamotus, where extinctions and recolonizations must have been frequent. Other examples of supertramp patterns are these: man and a *Ninox* hawk-owl colonized Madagascar from Indonesia by long-distance dispersal but were prevented from settling on the nearby African continent by more sedentary people and owls; Papuan seafarers and the white-eye *Zosterops citrinella* colonized small, isolated islands in eastern Torres Straits but could not settle on the larger and more accessible western islands, where more sedentary people and songbirds were established.

Conclusion: human adaptations

We have discussed in broad outline the selective value of biological properties that tend to shift through colonization cycles. To place this simplified sketch in perspective, let us conclude with caveats and exceptions. What difficulties should we expect in analyzing the adaptive value of human diversity? I suspect that there will be at least two main sources of difficulty: those associated with adaptive complexes, and with accuracy of tracking the environment.

If adaptive traits were independent of each other, we might hope to find neat correlations between traits and environment. But traits actually exist as adaptive complexes, in which selection acts on the whole complex and the value of one trait depends on other traits present. In addition, several alternative adaptive complexes that differ greatly in individual traits may be of nearly equal selective value in a given environment. For example, the bird species in the montane forests of New Guinea or Bougainville include not only old, distinctive, endemic forms that have low reproductive potential and have ceased to colonize over water, but also recent invaders that are still colonizing islands. Thus we cannot expect to find unique correlations between certain environmental conditions and either a particular trait or a given constellation of traits.

Given a certain optimal solution to an environmental problem, natural selection may eventually be able to produce that solution. This begs the question of a system's 'response time': how soon will selection produce that solution and how rapidly and closely can selection track a fluctuating environment? A system with a rapid response time can adapt quickly to a new maintained set of environmental conditions and can also follow rapid environmental fluctuations. But a rapidly responding system is also 'noisy' and fluctuates itself even in a constant environment. Thus, except for a sluggish system in a very constant environment, the correlation between population traits and immediate local conditions is bound to be imperfect. Perhaps man's rapid behavioral response capability offsets his slow genetic responses imposed by his long generation times and lets his social systems track the environment rapidly but also very 'noisily' (i.e. with much non-adaptive variation). For example, the Polynesians are now many generations past their peak expanding phase; do they still retain traits that were adaptive in this earlier phase? Again man exhibits great linguistic and genetic diversity on Bougainville for which we cannot discern correlated environmental gradients that could offer adaptive explanations (Friedlaender 1975). Is it just that we are too ignorant of the fine adaptive significance of the traits studied or is much of this human diversity just 'noise'?

Acknowledgements

I thank Ernst Mayr for discussions of colonization cycles, and Jim Allen, Rhys Jones, Sharon Kaufman-Diamond and John Terrell for discussions of human distributions.

1.viii.1976

Department of Physiology
University of California at Los Angeles

References

Black, S. n.d. Immigration and extinction: prehistoric populations on the Galapagos Islands. (Unpublished manuscript.)

Carlquist, S. 1974. *Island Biology*. New York: Columbia University Press.

Crowell, K. 1962. Reduced interspecific competition among the birds of Bermuda. *Ecology*. 43:75–88.

Darlington, P. J., Jr. 1971. Carabidae on tropical islands, especially the West Indies. In *Adaptive Aspects of Insular Evolution*, pp. 7–15 (ed. W. L. Stern). Pullman: Washington State University Press.

Diamond, J. M. 1970. Ecological consequences of island colonization by southwest Pacific birds. I. Types of niche shifts. *Proc. Nat. Acad. Sci. USA*. 67:529–36.

Diamond, J. M. 1972. *Avifauna of the Eastern Highlands of New Guinea.* Cambridge, Mass.: Nuttall Ornithological Club.

Diamond, J. M. 1974. Colonization of exploded volcanic islands by birds: the supertramp strategy. *Science.* 179:759–69.

Diamond, J. M. 1975. Assembly of species communities. In *Ecology and Evolution of Communities*, pp. 342–444 (eds M. L. Cody and J. M. Diamond). Cambridge, Mass.: Harvard University Press.

Diamond, J. M. 1976. Distributional strategies. *Sunda and Sahul* (eds J. Golson, R. Jones and J. Allen), in press. London: Academic Press.

Diamond, J. M. 1977. Reconstitution of bird community structure on Long Island, New Guinea, after a volcanic explosion. *Nat. Geog. Soc. Research Reports*, in press.

Diamond, J. M., and Marshall, A. G. 1976. Origin of the New Hebridean avifauna. *Emu.* 76, in press.

Friedlaender, J. S. 1975. *Patterns of Human Variation: the demography, genetics, and phenetics of Bougainville islanders.* Cambridge, Mass.: Harvard University Press.

Golson, J. 1972. Land connections, sea barriers and the relationship of Australian and New Guinea prehistory. In *Bridge and Barrier: the natural and cultural history of Torres Strait*, pp. 375–97 (ed. D. Walker). Canberra: Australian National University.

Greenslade, P. J. M. 1968. Island patterns in the Solomon Islands bird fauna. *Evolution.* 22:751–61.

Hope, J. H. 1973. Mammals of the Bass Strait Islands. *Proc. Roy. Soc. Victoria.* 85:163–96.

Johnston, R. F., and Selander, R. K. 1964. House sparrows: rapid evolution of races in North America. *Science.* 144:548–50.

Jones, R. 1976. Man as an element of a continental fauna: the sundering of the Bassian Bridge. In *Sunda and Sahul* (eds J. Golson, R. Jones and J. Allen), in press. London: Academic Press.

MacArthur, R. H. 1972. *Geographical Ecology.* New York: Harper and Row.

MacArthur, R. H., and Wilson, E. O. 1967. *The Theory of Island Biogeography.* Princeton: Princeton University Press.

Mayr, E. 1926. Die Ausbreitung des Girlitz. *J. Ornithol.* 74:571–671.

Mayr, E. 1942. *Systematics and the Origin of Species.* New York: Columbia University Press.

Mayr, E. 1963. *Animal Species and Evolution.* Cambridge, Mass.: Harvard University Press.

Mayr, E. 1965. Avifauna: turnover on islands. *Science.* 150:1587–8.

Nowak, E. 1975. *The Range Expansion of Animals and its Causes.* Springfield, Virginia: National Technical Information Service (translation of *Zeszytg Naukowe* no. 3, 1971, from Polish).

Ricklefs, R. E., and Cox, G. W. 1972. Taxon cycles in the West Indian avifauna. *Amer. Natur.* 106:195–219.

Tindale, N. 1976. Second report on the Kaiadilt people of Bentinck, Ireland, Gulf of Carpentaria, Queensland. In *Sunda and Sahul* (eds J. Golson, R. Jones and J. Allen), in press. London: Academic Press.

Vaurie, C. 1957. Systematic notes on palearctic birds. No. 26. Paridae: the *Paris caeruleus* complex. *Amer. Mus. Novitates.* No. 1833.

Vayda, A. P., and Rappaport, R. A. 1963. Island cultures. In *Man's Place in the Island Ecosystem*, pp. 133–42 (ed. F. R. Fosberg). Honolulu: Bishop Museum Press.

Wagley, C. 1969. Cultural influences on population: a comparison of two Tupi tribes. In *Environment and Cultural Behavior* (ed. A. P. Vayda). Garden City, N.Y.: Natural History Press.

Wilson, E. O. 1961. The nature of the taxon cycle in the Melanesian ant fauna. *Amer. Natur.* 95:169–93.

Wilson, E. O. 1975. *Sociobiology: the new synthesis.* Cambridge, Mass: Harvard University Press.

Yen, D. E., and Gordon, J. 1973. Anuta: a Polynesian outlier in the Solomon Islands. *Pac. Anthrop. Rec.* No. 21.

Zimmerman, E. C. 1960. Possible evidence of rapid evolution in Hawaiian moths. *Evolution.* 14:137–8.

Abstract

Diamond, J. M.

Colonization cycles in man and beast

Pre-industrial man and other animal species are compared with respect to colonization cycles, i.e. the cycles of population expansion and contraction that provide the historical basis for instantaneous biological distribution patterns. Because every species is basically different from every other species, biogeography has developed a common framework for understanding such unlike distributions as those of giraffes, oak trees and man by seeking relations among key variables or processes relevant to any species. Like other species, man reproduces, dies, disperses, exploits environments of varying stability and productivity, adapts phenotypically and genetically, is subject to intraspecific competition and – still like other species – differs from other species in particular characteristics of each of these processes. These key ingredients for biogeographic analysis are discussed to inquire in what ways man is unique as a colonist.

Long term hunter-gatherer adaptation to desert environments: a biogeographical perspective

John E. Yellen

Introduction

Writing in the 1940's, Taylor (1948) claimed that archaeologists must turn to disciplines other than their own for frameworks within which to interpret archaeological data. Today this necessity is an accepted fact of archaeological scholarship. The further afield one goes in quest for frameworks, however, the more the question of relevance, of square pegs in round holes, comes to the fore. In this article I will turn to a far from harmonious body of theory conveniently lumped under the heading 'biogeography,' in order to show how past and present hunter-gatherer adaptations to desert environments can be given new interpretation within a biogeographical framework.

Although my examples will be drawn from an admittedly limited and carefully selected body of archaeological and ethnographic information, these specific details will serve as an appropriate illustration pointing out the following basic questions which must be considered in any effort of this kind. To what extent are general principles drawn from observations on tropical birds, spruce budworms, various small creatures living in ocean sediments, and so forth, applicable to man? To what extent do biogeographical principles allow us to say something new about man, rather than just something old but in a different jargon? Does biogeography provide a framework for asking questions that may be answered with data obtainable for human societies? Does biogeography offer techniques for analyzing information about man?

In traditional ecology, emphasis is usually placed on the 'vertical' exchange of energy between different trophic or energy levels and on the problem of defining the different links in this food chain. Biogeographers, on the other hand, concentrate on a complementary yet more 'horizontal' view of the world. Their central concern is the distribution of species in time and space. Why, biogeographers want to know, are the tropics relatively species-rich and the temperate zones species-poor? Why do some islands show great diversity in bird life and others little? Why does the range of a particular species end where it does? Why are patchy distributions of birds uncommon in temperate zones but common in the tropics? Obvious answers – such as the assumption that richer or more benign environments have more species than poorer, harsh environments – are not often sufficient explanations. Nutrient-poor deep ocean sediments, for example, generally show a greater variety of species per unit area than their richer estuary counterparts.

Two questions of special interest to biogeographers may indicate where biogeography may be most relevant to anthropology and archaeology. First, what makes one species a more successful competitor than another? Second, what is it that a successful species is adapted to within its particular geographic range and how has it achieved that beneficial relationship? To tackle problems such as these, biogeographers are developing analytical methods and concepts designed to factor out the environmental features essential to a given species and to identify the specific adaptations that have been developed in response to those features. In my opinion it is this effort by modern biogeographers which is most amenable to adoption by anthropologists and archaeologists.

In what follows I will turn to a particular body of biogeographical theory dealing with the mechanics of adaptation to environments varying in their stability and predictability. A stability-time hypothesis will be presented, first in its most general form. Then I will consider the application of this hypothesis to human societies, taking a simple case study as an example. Finally I will review past and present hunter-gatherer adaptations to desert environments, to see if new insights can be gained from such a biogeographical approach to human societies.

The stability-time hypothesis and its application to man

Some nutrient-rich areas contain fewer species than their poorer counterparts. This seemingly anomalous finding suggests a stability-time hypothesis. Sanders (1968, 1969) has analyzed the polychaete-bivalve fraction of marine infauna (i.e. animals found within marine sediments, rather than on top of them) and notes that 'richer' waters of tropical estuaries contain fewer species than their deep sea counterparts. As a group, boreal waters are relatively species-poor, yet boreal waters also contain fewer species than their off-shore counterparts. To explain this pattern, Sanders and Slobodkin (Sanders 1968, 1969; Slobodkin and Sanders 1969) introduce the concept of stability: with all else held constant, the more stable and unchanging an environment, the greater the number of species it will contain. Thus, ocean depths which maintain a nearly constant temperature, salinity and level of absorbed oxygen have relatively more species than their estuary counterparts, which are affected by storm tides and varying amounts of rainfall. Note that this hypothesis says nothing about total biomass, only about number of different species.

The operative concept in this proposition is stress. While nutrient-poor environments provide more stressful conditions than nutrient-rich ones, it is equally important that stress is directly related to environmental fluctuation. Slobodkin (Slobodkin and Sanders 1969) among others notes that some kinds of temporal variability have greater biological effects than other kinds. Certainly amplitude is important: temperate climates, for instance, experience relatively great annual temperature fluctuations and are less stable than their tropical counterparts. Of equal and probably greater significance is the regularity and predictability of environmental fluctuations: when such changes are both regular and predictable, an organism can develop genetic, physiological or behavioral ways of dealing with them. In temperate climates, where the seasons follow each other in a regular and predictable fashion every year, organisms can develop stereotyped mechanisms to adapt to this kind of change. Birds migrate, squirrels store nuts, and woodchucks store up fat and go underground during the winter.

Desert environments, on the other hand, exemplify an opposite extreme. The amount of rainfall from year to year is not predictable. Similarly, its temporal and spatial distribution during a single year may also have a highly random quality. In situations like this one, stress is great.

The stability-time hypothesis relates the properties of both species and entire communities of species to stress in the following way:

> Where physiological stresses have been historically low, biologically accommodated communities have evolved. As the gradient of physiological stress increases, resulting from increasing physical fluctuations or by increasingly unfavorable physical conditions *regardless* [Sanders' emphasis] of fluctuations, the nature of the community gradually changes from a predominantly biologically accommodated to a predominantly physically controlled community. Finally, when the stress conditions become greater than the adaptive abilities of the organism, an abiotic condition is reached. The numbers of species present diminish continuously along the stress gradient. [Sanders 1969: 71–2].

Three consequences arising from this hypothesis are these:

1 More stable environments are conducive to biological accommodation and hence large numbers of species; when fluctuation is limited, it pays for a species to concentrate on utilizing a limited range of resources as effectively as possible and to adapt tightly to a specific and relatively small habitat niche from which it may be able to exclude other species successfully. In overall effect, such a strategy limits the amount of time and energy which must be expended in interspecific competition. If species can adapt to small niches within an environment, it is possible to pack more species into an area than otherwise. In variable and less predictable environments, this kind of specialization is not possible because the underlying base permitting the development of finely-tuned niches is lacking. Since the availability of a particular resource may vary dramatically and abruptly, niches must be wide and the corresponding number of species that can be accommodated within a given environment is fewer than otherwise.

2 Holling (1973) draws the useful distinction between stability and resilience. Stable systems are those which tend to return quickly to equilibrium after a temporary disturbance and can be best described with equilibrium models. In resilient systems, there may be no single point of equilibrium. Individual components may be subject to rapid, unpredictable change; however, basic relationships between components or populations remain the same. Holling argues that stable systems are characteristic of relatively constant, biologically-controlled environments, while resilient systems are a rule in more variable, physically-controlled situations. Elements or species in resilient systems persist, although their numbers and distributions may alter dramatically over time. Their more finely-tuned, stable counterparts are inherently more fragile and less tenacious.

3 The last consequence of the stability-time hypothesis to be noted concerns the question of how species adapt to the 'biologically' and 'physically' controlled ends of the spectrum. Slobodkin and Sanders (1969: 85) attribute stenotrophy, 'low maximum intrinsic rates of increase, narrow physiological tolerance limits and a high ability to resist competition from other species', to species attuned to a biologically-controlled

environment. Alternatively, physically-controlled environments tend to select for eurytopy – broad physiological toleration, a high intrinsic rate of increase and a failure to specialize on the consumption of narrow energy sources.

As a general rule, the greater the variability of an environment, the greater the advantage of behavioral plasticity. For example, birds which breed in temperate regions and migrate during the winter to the tropics shift their niches as well as their geography in the process. Such species face different competitors at different times in the year. They are successful because they are able to modify their behavior to suit each niche situation. Species which defend territories in the temperate regions of the world, for instance, may make no attempt to do so when in the tropics. As Jared Diamond has observed (pers. comm.), studies on temperate, tropical and desert bird species indicate that when resources are abundant, constant and reliable, the maintenance of discrete, intraspecifically defended territories is the rule. As the temporal and spatial patchiness and unpredictability of habitat circumstances increase, however, looser forms of territoriality are to be found, as well as inter- and intraspecific flocking. Many desert bird species in the Kalahari (Maclean 1970) and the western United States (Cody 1971) exhibit such flocking behavior which permits them to make best use of brief, unpredictable but locally superabundant resources. In the northeastern United States, food sources are reliable and usually superabundant during the spring and summer months. Almost all land birds in the northeast maintain territories of one kind or another while they are there.

Karr's (1971) study of bird communities in tropical Panama and in Illinois is quite instructive. Karr found that species inhabiting an extremely limited area of central Panama varied between those which were highly territorial and those which seemed to maintain no territories at all. While more than one factor may be responsible, he has demonstrated that the degree of patchiness and unpredictability of food resources is highly correlated with different types of territorial behavior. A significant finding is his observation that for some non-territorial species while the number of individuals per unit area appears relatively constant over time, the rate of individual turnover is remarkably high, and may involve constant replacement in some instances (1971: 217).

It does not seem unreasonable to assume that factors such as resource abundance, variability and predictability influence human behavior and social organization and also the ways in which human societies change over time. Before examining a particular case in point, I want to emphasize the likelihood that the *predictability* of resources, rather than abundance or variability, may play a central and determining role in adaptation. Karr's own summary of this possibility is as follows:

> When discussing food resources it is important to distinguish between the predictably unreliable food resources in the temperate winter and the reliable but locally unpredictable food resources in the tropical forest. In the tropical grasslands food is predictable at all seasons, but not available throughout the year. Hence birds defend territories to assure themselves of food during the reliable time and leave the habitat when food will be predictably scarce. In the forest food is more or less reliable throughout the year, but locally unpredictable. In this situation territories are not maintained by many species. . . . Food resources probably exert the greatest influence on spacing systems (Karr 1971: 225).

Hunter-gatherer adaptation to desert environments

The more closely one examines the concept of a 'desert,' the fuzzier it becomes. Within the limits of what most people think of as desert environments, rainfall may vary from less than 60 mm average per year in extremely arid regions to as much as 500 mm in areas termed 'semi-arid' by McGinnies *et al.* (1968). In some deserts, rain tends to fall during the winter, in others during the summer. In some, precipitation is spread randomly throughout the year. Some deserts have marked seasons; some do not. In the long run, study of variable behavioral responses within different kinds of desert may prove to be more interesting than studies contrasting deserts and non-deserts.

In spite of their real diversity, nonetheless, all deserts do exhibit a number of significant characteristics in common. All tend to be relatively poor environments, both in terms of biomass and in species diversity. They are also 'water controlled'. The flow of energy from the sun through desert ecosystems is so mediated by water availability that traditional energy-flow models in ecology can be replaced by a water-flow model when discussing deserts. Since water moves in a single direction through desert ecosystems and is not locally recycled, the links in such a water model may be few and straightforward. Finally, as Noy-Meir (1973: 26) comments, 'precipitation is highly variable through the year and occurs in infrequent and discrete events; . . . variation in precipitation has a large random (unpredictable) component' which manifests itself not only during the yearly cycle, but also from year to year and from place to place. Rainfall is patchy and unpredictable from both a spatial and temporal point of view.

Following Noy-Meir, therefore, all deserts may be considered 'water-controlled ecosystems with infrequent, discrete, and largely unpredictable water inputs' (1973: 26). Obviously, any desert species must deal with these facts of life, including plant species (Koller 1972). How have human societies adapted culturally to deserts?

Hunting and gathering societies have survived until recently in desert environments throughout the world. There is, as a result, a large literature available on them. Information on specific desert peoples differs, however, in quality and in kind. Quite detailed records and published descriptions exist for the !Kung speaking peoples of the Kalahari.

The !Kung live in northwestern Botswana and adjacent portions of Namibia and Angola. This region of southern Africa experiences rains coming from the north during the summer. As a result, rainfall decreases regularly on a north to south axis. Changes in plant and animal distributions are clearly related to this geographical pattern. Lee's (1972) analysis of nearly 30 years of precipitation records indicates, as one would expect, that the Kalahari experiences extremely high yearly variation in rainfall, with swings of up to 250% being not uncommon, and a finer-grained pattern of patchy and highly irregular local distribution over the course of a single rainy season. Geological evidence shows that major drier and wetter periods have occurred alternately since late Pleistocene times (Grove 1969). During at least one of the drier periods, Stone Age peoples are known to have inhabited the region.

While many plant and animal resources in the Kalahari are distributed in regular ways and their availability may be seasonally predicted, many others are not. Some of the major plant foods exhibit extremely patchy distributions. The large herbivores, which are highly mobile have movements which are predictable in only the most general fashion. The subsistence strategy of the !Kung hunter-gatherers reflects these facts of life in the desert.

During the dry season, !Kung congregate about water sources which are termed 'permanent' but which may go dry in exceptionally bad years. From these bases, they range out on daily hunting and gathering trips. Over the course of the dry season, they gradually deplete readily available resources. They then turn to less desirable kinds of food. When the rains come, filling temporary pans and tree hollows, the large dry season groups break down into smaller bands which disperse into the hinterland to utilize the comparatively abundant resources there. As the water pans dry up one after another, regrouping gradually occurs once again around the permanent water sources. !Kung informants recognize areas or territories which include a permanent water source and surrounding hinterland. The boundaries of such regions, however, are not carefully or precisely demarcated; these areas are not defended and they overlap considerably in places.

This description of !Kung subsistence strategy is generally agreed upon by observers. Interpretations of their group structure differ markedly. Marshall, an astute observer who has spent extended periods among the !Kung, states:

> Each band, according to !Kung social structure, owns and lives within what we call a territory. The band, through its headman . . . owns the veldkos and water resources within its territory. . . . The headman of the band has the authority and the duty, according to !Kung social regulations, to plan the band's movements, to say to which veldkos area they will go and when. . . . The !Kung have no named, structured patrilineages, but they have a patrilineal emphasis. Inheritance passes from father to eldest son, as does the succession in headmanship (1965: 248, 249, 260).

Lee, working several years later than Marshall at Dobe, an area adjacent to the Nyae Nyae !Kung among whom she had done most of her work, paints quite a different picture. He emphasizes the flexible nature of band structure:

> The basic local grouping is a camp (Marshall's band), which is a noncorporate, bilaterally organized group of people who live in a single settlement and who move together for at least a part of the year. At the core of each of these camps are two, three, or more siblings and/or cousins, both male and female, who are generally acknowledged to be the owners (K''ausi) of the waterhole. . . . Lorna Marshall (1960: 344ff.) has argued that the ownership of each waterhole resides in the person of a band headman who is always male and who inherits his position patrilineally, but my own research indicates that no headman existed among either the Dobe or Nyae Nyae !Kung Bushmen. Instead the sibling-cousin group of K''ausi collectively held the waterhole (1972: 129).

Yellen and Harpending (1972) carry the concept of fluidity of band organization to its logical extreme. They argue that the !Kung band or local group may be regarded as a temporary and unstable aggregation of individuals and nuclear families which, over the long run, may be viewed as moving randomly over the landscape. Changes of personnel of over 50% have been noted in the course of a few years. While the band-territory concept is acceptable from one point of view, it predicts very little about the movement of individuals and families over time.

When one examines hunting and gathering adaptations to desert environments described for other peoples, similar interpretative disagreements may be discovered. In his studies on the Great Basin Shoshone, Steward notes the close connection between environmental fluctuation and group organization:

> All of the plant and animal foods had in common the extremely important characteristic that the place and quantity of their occurrence from year to year were unpredictable, owing largely to variations in rainfall. A locality might be very fertile one year and attract large numbers of families, but offer little food for several years thereafter (1955: 105).

He states that the family in Shoshone society served as the basic social unit and families moved from place to place in reaction to environmental changes. Aggregation into larger social groupings took place in times of plenty when resources in a local area could support a greater number of people. During other times of the year, smaller, highly mobile groups were the rule. Such a description of the Shoshone fits the Yellen–Harpending model of long-term !Kung group fluidity quite well.

Steward's interpretation has been challenged by Service. He argues that pre-contact Shoshone were organized into patrilineal, exogamous bands. Service points to John Wesley Powell's early description of the Shoshone as being divided into 31 tribes, each ruled by a single chief and each being highly territorial. Service also views customs among them currently, such as sororate and levirate, as cultural remnants indicating an earlier patrilineal band organization which was destroyed, he argues, by post-contact influences.

An overview of Australian social organization and land-use is an impossible task, because of the environmental and cultural diversity to be found there. Following Hiatt (1968), it is possible to point out one similarity with the !Kung and Shoshone. Radcliffe-Brown (1931) has described three types of social groups in Australia. The largest of these is what he called the tribe. Since this unit is defined on linguistic criteria, it is not of interest here. Tribes, however, may be said to be composed of patriclans, land-owning units each of which may be associated with a particular territory. Every individual belongs to a specific patriclan, and if asked, can state the one to which he belongs. Although there is general agreement among field researchers that patriclans exist for the Australians, a basic disagreement has arisen concerning the relationship between patriclans and Radcliffe-Brown's third level of organization, the horde. This social unit refers to the actual composition of any group in a given territory at a single moment in time. Radcliffe-Brown argued that the patriclan and the horde are, for the most part, equivalent. Hiatt notes, on the other hand, that many observers have described 'more or less stable communities that included members of from two to twelve patriclans'. Hiatt himself describes a Gidjingali community containing members of six different patriclans; the majority was composed of individuals who were living outside their own patriclan areas.

Thus in these three ethnographic examples the same dichotomy can be seen: from a normative point of view, social organization can be described as circumscribed and rigidly defined. From the historical or observer's point of view, group structure and composition is depicted as extremely loose and fluid.

From an archaeological point of view, the striking thing about desert cultures is their long historical continuity. This phenomenon has been recognized in North America (Jennings and Norbeck 1955) and in western Australia (Gould 1971). Scanty data from the Kalahari indicate that the concept of 'desert traditions' is applicable there, as well. In part, long and unbroken histories in such areas may be explained by the fact that regions of low and unpredictable rainfall offer little inducement for expansion and utilization by competing or differing groups of hunter-gatherers or by peoples adapted to agricultural or pastoral ways of life. Such an explanation, needless to say, is not sufficient, because if deserts are to be seen as refuge areas – as they are often held to be – then one would expect to find successive peoples taking sanctuary in them: a pattern of sequential changes not found to typify desert culture areas.

A second characteristic of desert cultures, in addition to their longevity, is their conservatism, i.e. their resistance to rapid or drastic change. Borrowed culture elements may be added one by one to a basically stable culture core; actual people, individuals who speak foreign languages, may travel through them without inducing sharp discontinuities or changes in the established tradition.

The concept of a 'desert tradition' in the western United States was first formally proposed by Jennings and Norbeck (1955), largely on the basis of Jennings' excavations at Danger Cave, Utah. These authors proposed an unbroken cultural tradition there, the origins of which could be traced back with certainty as far as the 9th millennium B.C., and which might have begun a thousand years earlier than that. They suggested that the core of this tradition encompassed the Great Basin physiographic area including most of Nevada, southeastern Oregon, southern Idaho, western Utah and adjacent portions of California and Baja California. In their reconstruction, the tradition at times seems to have reached beyond the Basin into parts of Arizona and New Mexico, as well as northwestern and central Mexico. In these 'marginal' areas, however, it was succeeded by other culture traditions. The historic occupants of the Great Basin, the Uto-Aztecan Utes, Paiutes and Shoshone are most likely descendants of this desert tradition. Since the original formulation of the Great Basin Desert Tradition, excavations at a number of stratified cave sites have further clarified and developed our understanding of its major archaeological characteristics, as summarized by Willey (1966).

The archaeology of the Western Desert of Australia is far from completely known, but it is possible to note similarities to the Great Basin. Indeed, Gould (1971) draws a direct comparison between Puntutjarpa Rock Shelter (located in the Warburton Range in Western Australia, and excavated by him from 1967–70) and Danger Cave, Utah. According to Gould, the Puntutjarpa shelter was occupied intermittently for at least 10,000 years by peoples within a continuous cultural tradition that culminated with the Ngatatjara aborigines who inhabit the vicinity today. Gould notes the lack of comparable excavated material from other desert areas of Australia, but comments:

> On the basis of extensive surveys and archaeological testing it is thought that this same culture pattern may have been present from early post-Pleistocene times to the present throughout all or most of the roughly 200,000 square-mile area of Australia's Western Desert and in the Central and Simpson Deserts as well (1973: 15).

In southern Africa comparable evidence is generally lacking and no dated, stratified sites similar to Danger Cave and Puntutjarpa have been excavated within the Kalahari itself. In western Botswana, a series of as yet undated Late Stone Age (microlithic) sites have been excavated (Yellen 1971), but analysis of the finds is still in progress. At /kai/kai, an open-air site, over six feet of stratified finds were discovered. The lithic assemblages in these deposits show minimal change from top to bottom. Introduced pottery and bits of iron, obtained through trade, occur at different times during the occupation of the site. In the general region, the distribution of numerous Late Stone Age surface scatters conforms to the historic Bushman camp distribution pattern. While it is almost certain that Bushman peoples were responsible for these Late Stone Age assemblages, no terminal dates for these finds are available yet: continuity between historic and prehistoric populations is at present only a likely hypothesis.

A date of 5,200 B.P. (Deacon 1966) has been obtained for similar finds from a site near Windhoek, in adjacent Namibia (South West Africa) and recent developments in southern African archaeology suggest that the beginning of the Late Stone Age, usually placed about 8,000 to 9,000 years ago, may have been much earlier. Thus, the presence of a desert tradition in the Kalahari region of southern Africa, likely though it may be, is by no means yet a proven fact. It can be stated, nonetheless, that Late Stone Age traditions as a group exhibit little change over time.

Desert adaptations: an explanation in biogeographical perspective

If these ethnographic and archaeological observations on hunter-gatherers in Australia, Africa and the United States are set in a biogeographical framework, the fit is obvious and good. In relatively severe, variable environments of low predictability, populations exhibit resilience and the ability to persist over time. Desert cultural traditions also display such characteristics. Organisms adapted to desert environments generally lack stereotyped behavior response patterns. If discrepancies between ethnographic accounts from the same desert regions are not the result of faulty fieldwork but real complexity in the social organization of the peoples being studied, then the biogeographer's 'behavioral flexibility criterion' is also met by such groups. Finally, like many desert species, individuals and families in the Kalahari, the Great Basin and the Australian desert are mobile.

While hunter-gatherers may fit into a biogeographical framework, does such a framework shed new light on their adaptations as such? I think the answer here is: yes, such a perspective can do just that. Consider the apparently anomalous observation that the composition or personnel of hunter-gatherer bands or groups changes far more readily than it should, given the normative beliefs of the peoples being studied. This observation makes perfect sense in biogeographical perspective: in an environment subject to severe and unpredictable change, it is obviously advantageous for a population to be able to alter its distribution rapidly in order to put the most people in the places where the most resources are available. Among the !Kung, for example, the ability for rapid movement in a number of possible directions is provided primarily through kin ties and the obligations generated through them. Following Lee's (1972) interpretation that the sib group is the basic !Kung residential group, it can be shown that the number of *possible* alternative residences is quite large for any set of married sibs: each person has the choice of staying with one of two parental couples or of residing with any of his or her other sibs who may be living with their own in-laws elsewhere. Since the sibs of these brothers- and sisters-in-law may be even more dispersed, the choices available to a single nuclear family in !Kung society are usually large. Other social patterns such as the belief that people with the same name have special obligations toward each other, and their system of inheritance in which individuals may have rights in scattered places, also increase the number of possible residence locales and permit rapid changes in residence, if need be. Further, as Rose (1968) and others have argued, the highly complicated Australian section and marriage systems perform an identical function in Australian hunter-gatherer society.

But why have some writers described hunter-gatherers as rigidly circumscribed in their social relations? The answer that such statements are normative rather than statistical only begs the issue: why then should such an extreme dichotomy between belief and practice exist among these peoples? From a biogeographical perspective, a close tie between an individual and a particular living site is advantageous if resources are stable and dependable. The seeming contrary normative descriptions written for desert peoples all imply limited freedom of movement, i.e. social patterns working in such a direction. I think it possible to suggest that such descriptions reflect native beliefs which are advantageous when seen in long-term perspective. Although over the short-run practice and belief among these groups of hunter-gatherers may be discordant and contradictory, over the long-run their beliefs may be adaptive to long-range climatic change.

Holling has argued that the use of equilibrium models in ecology may be inappropriate when analyzing natural systems which change continuously and which do not exhibit narrow ranges of variation around equilibria. He suggests:

> Different and useful insight might be obtained, therefore, by viewing the behavior of ecological systems in terms of the probability of extinction of their elements, and by shifting emphasis from the equilibrium states to the conditions for persistence.
>
> An equilibrium centered view is essentially static and provides little insight into the transient behavior of systems that are not near the equilibrium (1973: 2).

It is suggested here that the social organization of desert-adapted peoples might also be better understood in such a fashion.

Consider finally what is often called the conservatism of desert cultures. Why do they exhibit such continuity and persistence over time? The persistence of their ways of life may be explained as a reflection of the adaptive success of these peoples. Those who have learned to survive in deserts at all, are probably effective competitors for any peoples trying to invade such regions. Yet the idea of conservatism is not only hard to define closely, but also probably *not* applicable to desert cultures. In all the traditions I have noted above one can see the appearance and adoption of new culture elements at one time or another. In short, desert traditions are not static; they do change in content.

If it is assumed, however, that cultural divergence, like speciation, is favored by conditions of isolation, then this may be one possible reason for the temporal and areal cohesiveness of desert traditions. The fluidity of movement within hunter-gatherer society, while variable in degree partly because of external circumstance, has the effect over the long run of keeping internal barriers to a minimum.

Conclusion

Can a biogeographical perspective contribute to future research on hunter-gatherers? The greatest potential of such a point of view may be that this approach leads to testable predictions of a widely-applicable form. One can predict, for example, what effects increased environmental unpredictability and severity may have on cultural practices. Perhaps more significant, such an approach allows the direct comparison of divergent cultures in different environments. For example, societies which rely on predictable tropical resources may be conceived as biologically-controlled communities. They should, paradoxically enough, show some of the same characteristics of their desert counterparts: they should exhibit similar long-term stability; yet when change does occur among tropical groups, one may anticipate that the magnitude of the alteration will be greater, the effects more abrupt, and the pattern observed will be replacement rather than gradual alteration. On the other hand, one would expect ethnic areas in the tropics to be smaller than in desert environments, because a more constant environment permits greater specialization to particular aspects of that environment and finer distributions, leading to greater linguistic diversity per unit area, more constraint on mobility and less dissonance between beliefs and practices. Moreover, tropical groups may, as a result, be more susceptible to 'equilibrium' analysis. Since many environments inhabited by man are neither tropical nor desert habitats, it is at very least a fascinating exercise to try to predict the combinations of variability and predictability most conducive not only to stability or instability, but also to rapid and pronounced internal adjustments and change.

Even with the best geological, faunal and palynological data, exact reconstructions of past environments are notoriously difficult to achieve. It is also difficult to document change over time and to determine how an individual group exploited the varied resources available to it. It is possible, however, to talk about long-term rates of change in different geographical regions, to gain some idea about the amplitude, frequency and regularity of change and to compare regions on that basis. In this light, the major significance of the stability-time hypothesis rests in the fact that it focuses attention on the ways in which organisms react to fluctuations and periodicities. The hypothesis allows archaeologists to use as independent variables in their models just those kinds of data most readily available to them.

1.viii.1976

Department of Anthropology
Smithsonian Institution, Washington D.C.

References

Cody, M. L. 1971. Finch flocks in the Mohave desert. *Theoretical Population Biology*. 2:142–58.

Deacon, J. 1966. An annotated list of radiocarbon dates for sub-Saharan Africa. *Ann. Cape Prov. Mus.* 5:5–84.

Gould, R. 1971. The archaeologist as ethnographer: a case from the Western Desert of Australia. *World Archaeology*. 3(2):143–77.

Gould, R. 1973. Australian archaeology in ecological and ethnographic perspective. *Warner Modular Publications*. 7.

Grove, A. 1969. Landforms and climatic change in the Kalahari and Ngamiland. *Geographical Journal*. 135:191–212.

Hiatt, L. R. 1968. Ownership and use of land among the Australian aborigines. In *Man the Hunter*, pp. 99–110 (eds R. B. Lee and I. DeVore). Chicago: Aldine.

Holling, C. S. 1973. Resilience and stability of ecological systems. *Annual Review of Ecology and Systematics*. 4:1–23.

Jennings, J. D. and Norbeck, E. 1955. Great Basin prehistory: a review. *American Antiquity*. 21:1–11.

Karr, J. R. 1971. Structure of avian communities in selected Panama and Illinois habitats. *Ecological Monographs*. 3:207–33.

Koller, D. 1972. Environmental control of seed germination. In *Seed Biology*, pp. 1–101 (ed. T. T. Kozlowski). New York: Academic.

Lee, R. B. 1972. !Kung spatial organization: an ecological and historical perspective. *Human Ecology*. 1(2):125–47.

Maclean, G. L. 1970. The biology of the larks (Alavidae) of the Kalahari sandveld. *Zool. Afr.* 5:7–39.

Marshall, L. 1965. The !Kung Bushmen of the Kalahari Desert. In *Peoples of Africa*, pp. 241–78 (ed. J. L. Gibbs, Jr.). New York: Holt, Rinehart and Winston.

McGinnies, W. G., Goldman, B. J. and Paylore, P. (eds). 1968. *Deserts of the World*. Tucson: Univ. Arizona Press.

Noy-Meir, I. 1973. Desert ecosystems: environment and producers. *Annual Review of Ecology and Systematics*. 4:25–51.

Radcliffe-Brown, A. R. 1931. Social organization of Australian tribes. *Oceanic Monographs*. 1.

Rose, F. G. 1968. Australian marriage, land-owning groups and initiations. In *Man the Hunter*, pp. 200–8 (eds R. B. Lee and I. DeVore). Chicago: Aldine.

Sanders, H. L. 1968. Marine benthic diversity: a comparative study. *American Naturalist*. 102:243-82.

Sanders, H. L. 1969. Benthic marine diversity and the stability-time hypothesis. In *Diversity and Stability in Ecological Systems*, pp. 71-80 (eds G. M. Woodwell and H. H. Smith). Brookhaven Symp. Biol. 22.

Slobodkin, L. B. and Sanders, H. L. 1969. On the contribution of environmental predictability to species diversity. In *Diversity and Stability in Ecological Systems*, pp. 82-95 (eds G. M. Woodwell and H. H. Smith). Brookhaven Symp. Biol. 22.

Steward J. H. 1955. *Theory of Culture Change: the methodology of multilinear evolution*. Urbana: Univ. of Illinois.

Taylor, W. W. 1948. A study of archaeology. *Mem. Am. Anth. Assn.* 69.

Willey, G. R. 1966. *An Introduction to American Archaeology*, Vol. I. Englewood Cliffs, N. J.: Prentice-Hall Inc.

Yellen, J. E. 1971. Archaeological investigations in western Ngamiland. *Botswana Notes and Records.* 3:276.

Yellen, J. E. and Harpending, H. 1972. Hunter gatherer populations and archaeological inference. *World Archaeology.* 4(4):244-53.

Abstract

Yellen, J. E.

Long term hunter-gatherer adaptations to desert environments: a biogeographical perspective

Hunter-gatherer adaptations can be given new interpretation within a biogeographical framework. Emphasizing theories dealing with the mechanics of adaptation to environments varying in their stability and predictability, the author discusses a stability-time hypothesis. Stable environments are conducive to biological adaptation and hence large numbers of species, because concentration upon specific resources limits the amount of time and energy expended through interspecific competition. In variable and less predictable environments, specialization is not a wise adaptive strategy, because the underlying base permitting finely-tuned niches is missing. When resources are subject to rapid, unexpected changes, ecosystems are likely to be resilient rather than stable, i.e. species types do persist but population numbers and distributions alter dramatically over time. It is reasonable to assume that conditions such as resource abundance, variability and especially predictability influence human behavior adaptations and social organization, as well as the ways in which societies change over time. Survey of desert cultural traditions reveals a close fit between biogeographical prediction and ethnographic and archaeological observation.

Some implications for hunter-gatherer ecology derived from the spatial structure of resources

Henry Harpending and Herbert Davis

Introduction

In this paper we discuss the effects of spatial heterogeneity in the resources used by hunter-gatherers and possible consequences in the organization of their subsistence behavior. The underlying premise is: in an environment where resources are distributed evenly and are of many different species, a hunter-gatherer group minimizes energy expenditure by being sedentary and possibly territorial; alternatively, if resources are widely scattered and only locally abundant, then group mobility is necessary in order to exploit the full range of available resources.

Regional variation in subsistence among !Kung Bushmen in northwest Botswana provides a good example of how settlement and land-use respond to the spatial structure of resources (Patricia Draper, unpublished field notes). In the northern part of the area occupied by !Kung, resources are richly concentrated on forested dunes spaced several kilometers apart. This has led to a pattern of sedentary !Kung villages on the dune edges, with relatively low inter-village mobility of individuals and families. A recent recensus of the region showed almost no change, except for births and deaths, from a census six years previously. In the south, on the other hand, hunting of mobile ungulates is a primary subsistence activity while sessile resources are scarce and scattered. Here there is little coherent local occupation of the land for families constantly move over thousands of square kilometers.

We will develop one possible way of studying spatial heterogeneity in the environment of a foraging group. We do not consider temporal variation explicitly, although the theory we discuss is directly applicable to temporal, rather than spatial, variation if 'food storage' is substituted for 'range size'. Further, for simplicity we consider a one-dimensional environment, such as a lake or river shore. The theory presented carries over directly to two dimensions, but the algebra becomes unwieldy.

Our aim is first to develop models for the analysis of real data, and second to use these abstractions for deductive purposes. Currently we are collecting information on plant and animal resources exploited by several groups of Bushman hunter-gatherers along transects in northeast Botswana. The theory we present here will allow us to relate resources conveniently to observed patterns of land-use among these people. In addition, there are some interesting consequences of such a formal consideration of space use, which we will also mention below.

Model

Our model consists of a one-dimensional environment along which we measure the abundance of a variety of natural resources. We will assume that the abundance of a resource can be thought of as a continuous function or variable (such as altitude or temperature) which may be graphed and analyzed as a continuous line, i.e. as a sum of *sinusoids*, expressing the abundance of the resource being measured in a single direction away from some starting point on the ground (fig. 1). In fact, of course, resources occur discretely in the environment: e.g. Bushman hunter-gatherers collect nuts from *mongongo* trees and not from some universal tree producing variable quantities of nuts at different locations in Botswana. The same kinds of models can be applied to both ways of seeing the world. Models for discrete functions, however, have the disadvantage of looking more complicated.

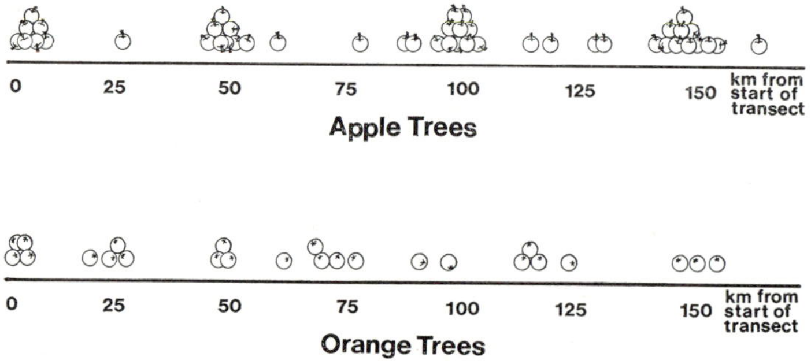

Figure 1 These represent orange trees and apple trees along a hypothetical transect. The apples show a regular sinusoidal variation with a frequency of roughly one cycle per fifty kilometers. The oranges show no clear periodicity. The former case corresponds to a peak in the graph of the power spectral density of apple tree abundance at one cycle per fifty kilometers; the latter implies a more diffuse distribution of power over all frequencies

Imagine that we have measured two resources, such as apple and orange trees found along a transect (fig. 1). Apple trees are discovered to occur in clumps at regular intervals spaced about fifty kilometers apart: that is, the abundance of apple trees is rather periodic. Orange trees, on the other hand, seem to be distributed at random along the transect.

To analyze our model transect, we view the sequence of abundance of apple and orange trees as composed of fourier components; that is, the random functions giving the caloric values of oranges and apples seen as functions of distance from the start of the transect are assumed to be composed of mixtures of sine waves added together. For every frequency, a sinusoid may contribute to the observed series of data values and its amplitude and phase (relative to the start of the transect) can be estimated.

In our model, much of the variation in the calories available from apples along the transect can be accounted for by a sinusoid with a frequency of one cycle per fifty kilometers (fig. 1). We use the phrase 'accounted for' in the same way that a statistician uses this expression when he says that soil type, for instance, accounts for a certain percentage of the variance in crop yield. In time-series analysis, the statistician's term 'variance' and the engineer's term 'power' have the same meaning. Thus we can say that most of the power or variance in apple tree abundance along the transect is at one cycle every fifty kilometers. Further, if this sinusoid were removed, there would be substantially less variation from place to place in the abundance of apple trees.

Orange trees along the transect have no such clear periodicity, a situation implying that power or variance here is much more uniformly distributed over the range of frequencies or abundances possible. In nature we can rarely expect to find clear-cut periodicities such as that set up for apple trees in our figure. Real data often look more like the distribution of orange trees, although characteristically some frequencies or frequency bands contribute more to an actual distribution than others.

A random function of time or space – such as those here represented by sequences of apple and orange tree abundances – for which the mean and variance (average squared deviation from the mean) do not change over time, is called *weakly stationary*. Such a function can be most easily understood in terms of its power spectral density function, which may be written as $f(\omega)$. For a series $X_i(t)$, the spectral density function $f_{ii}(\omega)$ is the amount of the total variance in $X_i(t)$ which is accounted for by variation at frequency ω. The total area under the spectral density is the total variance of $X_i(t)$, i.e.:

$$\int_{-\infty}^{\infty} f_{ii}(\omega)d\omega = \text{variance of } X_i(t)$$

There is value in thinking in terms of power or variance at various frequencies, even when clear-cut sinusoids cannot be drawn for a set of data values. It is useful, for example, to think about the range of frequencies of relevance to human subsistence ecology. At the upper end of the spectrum, very high frequency phenomena are not relevant: spacing between apple trees on the order of tens or hundreds of meters is easily covered in a few minutes' walk, for instance, and thus frequencies higher than, say, one cycle per kilometer are not interesting. At the low end of the spectrum, spatial variation on the order of several hundred kilometers is also irrelevant in the absence of complex social organization and long-distance trade. Therefore, the frequency range of one cycle per kilometer to one cycle per five hundred kilometers is the range of interest for a study of hunter-gatherer mobility. We can design our sampling procedures to ignore both higher and lower frequencies.

The representation of relations between two resources in the frequency domain has an added complication. For example, an ordinary correlation coefficient between apples and oranges in our model could be completely misleading for at least two reasons; one series might lag or lead the other, and correlations between the series may be different at different frequencies. Imagine that the abundance of orange trees was determined mainly by two phenomena: local competition from apricot trees and soil fertility (fig. 2). Then the high frequency, short distance changes or variance in orange tree abundance would reflect competition while the low frequency, large distance variation would reflect changing soil fertility. In this case there would be correlation between soil fertility and the abundance of orange trees *only at low frequencies*, and we would have to look at the correlations separately for different frequency bands in order to detect this.

In order to study the structure of the relationship between two resources, we estimate two functions of frequency, the coherence spectrum and the phase spectrum. Coherence at a frequency ω, $P_{ij}(\omega)$, is a number between zero and one, analogous to a correlation coefficient, which measures the strength of the association between resource i and resource j. The phase at frequency ω, $\theta_{ij}(\omega)$, measures the angle in radians by which resource i leads or lags resource j. Using the example in the above paragraph, we would say that there is low frequency coherence between orange trees and soil fertility and that they are in phase: that is, θ is close to zero. On the other hand, there is high frequency coherence between orange trees and apricots, but here the phase is close to π radians, or 180 degrees, since they are competing with each other (see fig. 2).

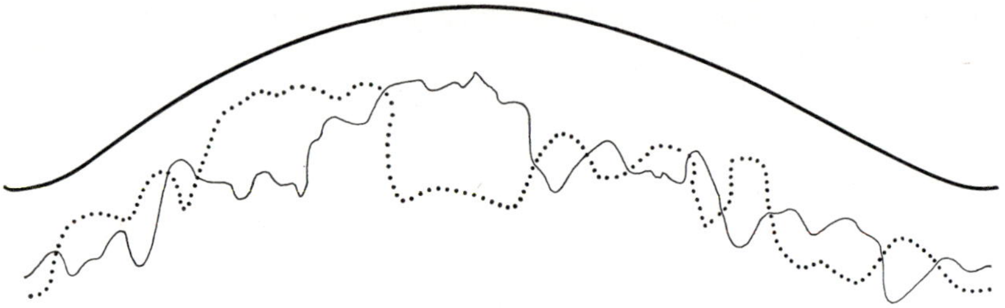

Figure 2 Hypothetical relations along a transect between orange trees (light line), apricot trees (dotted) and soil fertility (bold). Orange trees and soil fertility are coherent at low frequency and in phase; orange trees and apple trees are coherent at high frequencies and out of phase. Orange trees and apricot trees are also coherent and in phase at low frequencies

Space use

A minimal subsistence unit such as a nuclear family or a band uses the resources within a segment of the habitat τ kilometers in length. We will assume population density is constant, so changing range length does not change the total numbers of calories available, since the number of people with whom the range is shared also changes proportionately. In particular, the calories (or whatever the units) available from the i'th resource from a range τ kilometers long, $C_i(t)$, is simply the average over a segment

$$C_i(t)=\frac{1}{\tau}\int_{t-\tau}^{t} X_i(s)ds.$$

The only benefits to be gained from a larger range would be to smooth out local spatial variation, increasing the reliability of the range, and to encompass a larger fraction of the potential resource diversity within the environment. But there are energy and other costs and constraints associated with exploiting a larger territory. We hope, then, that patterns of territoriality and land use may be related, with this kind of theory, to the spatial structure of resources in the environment. We will consider two consequences of changing range size: the variation in total calories available from one range to the next, which should predict uniformity of occupation of the land and perhaps population clustering, and available diversity of foodstuffs within a range of a given size.

Variation in total calories

For a range of length t, we will write the total food available as

$$T(t) = \sum_{i=I}^{k} C_i(t).$$

The mean of all ranges of length τ is simply the sum of the means of each of the resources $X(t)$ and does not depend upon the range size τ. But the amount of variation from one range to another depends directly upon τ and this is the effect we wish to investigate. If the variance of $T(t)$ is large, people should be clumped at particularly rich spots in large groups; if the variance is small, people should be uniformly distributed over the environmental space and local group size should be small.

Recall that variance of X_i from place to place is given by the integral of the spectral density over all positive and negative frequencies:

$$\text{var } X_i = \int_{-\infty}^{\infty} f_{ii}(\omega) d\omega.$$

The variance of C_i, the amount of X_i in a segment of range of length τ kilometers, is closely related; it is the integral over all frequencies of the spectral density of C_i, but this spectral density is simply the spectral density of X_i multiplied at each frequency by the squared gain of the filter

$$\text{squared gain at } \omega = \frac{2(1 - \cos \omega\tau)}{\omega^2\tau^2},$$

so

$$\text{var } C_i = \int_{-\infty}^{\infty} \frac{2(1 - \cos \omega\tau)}{\omega^2\tau^2} f_{ii}(\omega)\, d\omega.$$

This then is the most important reason for working with power spectra and other frequency domain parameters. Subsistence behavior can be modelled as a filter operating on the environment, and the consequences of that behavior can be deduced very conveniently. This filter expresses the smoothing effect in the frequency domain of averaging resources over a range of τ kilometers in the time domain. Thus, very low frequency variation ($\omega \sim 0$) is not attenuated, while, at a frequency equal to $1/\tau$ cycles per kilometer, variation at this and higher frequencies is effectively removed (see fig. 3).

If oak groves are spaced five kilometers apart, a range of twenty kilometers would always include oak groves and the variation between oak groves and whatever intervenes would not contribute to variation between ranges. If, on the other hand, oak groves were spaced fifty kilometers apart, then some twenty kilometer ranges would have oak groves, some would not, and the spatial variation in oak density would contribute to between-range differences. The above algebra formalizes this common sense reasoning.

When we consider several resources simultaneously, there are several extreme cases:

(*a*) Low or no coherence: the resources are effectively independent of each other and the variance of the total caloric supply is simply the sum of the variances of the component series. Thus with a large number of effective food sources we expect the variance to be smaller and land occupation more uniform.

(*b*) The real parts of the off-diagonal spectral coefficients are large and positive. This means that there are correlations over space between the resources and that they are generally in phase, i.e. when one is high the others will be high. Hence the variability from place to place in total resource availability will be great and populations should be aggregated.

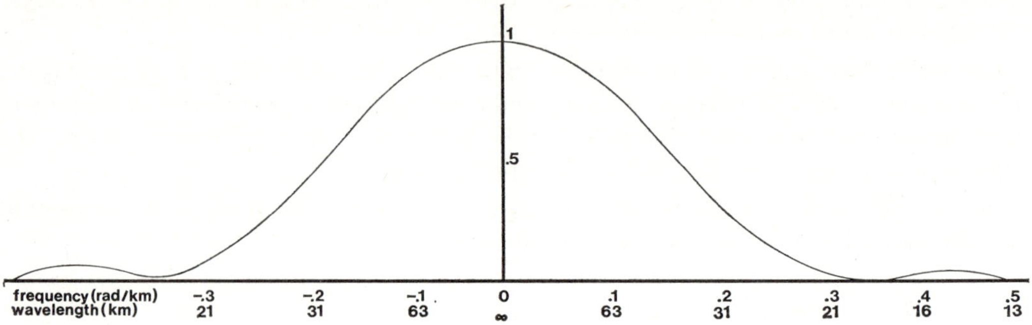

Figure 3 Filter characteristic in frequency domain for $\tau = 20$ kilometers. Variation at frequencies higher than $\frac{2\pi}{20} = \cdot 31$ radians per kilometer is mostly removed.

(*c*) The real parts of the off-diagonal spectral coefficients large (in absolute value) are negative numbers. This implies that resources are out of phase; when one is abundant the others tend to be scanty at a particular place. Here the variation from place to place in total food availability will be small, and more uniform occupation of the space is expected, with very large foraging ranges.

In general one might expect resources to be in phase when they depend upon a common abiotic factor such as water or soil fertility. They might be out of phase if they are competing with each other. For example, berry bushes and oak trees should be out of phase in an eastern woodland subject to periodic burning. Note that only low frequencies, in particular those lower than $1/\tau$ cycles per kilometer, enter into these expressions. The higher frequency spectral densities and phase relations do not matter.

Diversity

We believe that considerations of dietary diversity are more important for many foraging groups than are considerations of total caloric supply. For example, Yellen and Harpending (1972) showed that a !Kung Bushman family in northwest Botswana may live at various places within an area of several thousand square miles over the course of a year. The stated motivation of the !Kung for this chronic mobility over the landscape is dietary diversity. Dobe is a location rich in *mangetti* nuts, for example, while !Ubi, fifteen miles south, has many *tsin* beans, and Hwenasi, twenty miles north, is regularly frequented by large ungulates. A family could simply live at Dobe eating mangetti nuts in caloric bliss if energy capture were the only link between man and the resource base.

We take as a measure of resource diversity the 'effective number of resources'. If there are k resources, and the abundance C_i of each is measured in calories or some meaningful unit, such as essential amino acid content, or utility, then the diversity is

$$H = \frac{(\sum C_i)^2}{\sum C_i^2}$$

This is derived by considering the proportion of all the resources available which is the i'th resource

$$P_i = \frac{C_i}{\sum C_i^2}$$

and by measuring diversity by

$$H = \frac{1}{\sum P_i^2} = \frac{(\sum_i C_i)^2}{\sum C_i^2}$$

If all k resources are available in equal proportions, this is equal to k and the diversity is a maximum; otherwise the effective number of resources will be less than k.

When there is no spatial variation in the resources, all of the spectral coefficients are zero and diversity is

$$H = \frac{(\sum u_i)^2}{\sum u_i^2}$$

where u_i is the mean of x_i or of C_i. This is identical to the diversity when spatial variation is not considered. Spatial variation always decreases diversity. When variation exists, there are several cases to consider:

(*a*) Low or no coherence, in which case the cross spectral terms f_{ij} are zero when i is different from j. The expected diversity becomes

$$H \cong \frac{(\sum u_i)^2 + \sum_i \text{var } C_i}{\sum_i u_i^2 + \sum_i \text{var } C_i}$$

Hence for resources which vary independently of each other at low frequencies, diversity is of the form

$$\frac{a+x}{b+x}$$

where x is positive and increases with increasing spatial variation. Since a is always greater than b, $\frac{a+x}{b+x}$ is always less than $\frac{a}{b}$ so that variation decreases diversity. If most of the variation is at high frequencies, a range size τ large enough to encompass this will minimize the effect.

(*b*) Appreciable in-phase coherence, in which case the real parts of the $f_{ij}(\omega)$ will be positive, and the variance term in the numerator will be greater than the variance term in the denominator. If coherence is very high, and if the resources are all in phase, the diversity approximates

$$H \cong \frac{(\sum_i u_i)^2 + [\sum_i (\text{var } C_i)^{\frac{1}{2}}]^2}{\sum_i u_i^2 + \sum_i [(\text{var } C_i)^{\frac{1}{2}}]^2}$$

and, if the means and variances are all equal for all resources this becomes

$$H \cong \frac{k^2}{k} = k$$

Any deviation from these ideal conditions will mean that diversity is less than k.

In this case of appreciable in-phase coherence, the effects of spatial variation on diversity are minimized and the benefit from increased range size is minimized. An example would be a group depending only on resources in a river valley. There is then little to be gained by extending exploitation to nearby dry lands or to another river valley purely for considerations of diversity.

(*c*) Appreciable out of phase coherence, in which case the integrals in the numerator for which i is different from j are negative, and diversity is drastically decreased by spatial variation. Hence there is great benefit from increasing range size to encompass the significant parts of the resource spectra. If coherence is very high and if the resources are maximally out of phase in the relevant (low frequency) parts of the spectra, diversity approaches

$$H \cong \frac{(\sum_i u_i)^2}{\sum_i u_i^2 + \sum \text{var } C_i}.$$

Conclusions

There is always some benefit from increasing range size unless the environment is absolutely constant in space. This benefit is least when all the resources occur together at discrete locations. Maximum benefit from increased exploitation area occurs when resources are out of phase over the relevant frequencies, which are those between approximately one cycle per kilometer and one cycle per 100 kilometers for man.

The expression for diversity (equation 1) is of the form

$$\frac{f_1 \text{ (means)} + f_2 \text{ (variances and covariances)}}{f_3 \text{ (means)} + f_4 \text{ (variances)}}$$

where the f's are positive increasing functions of the arguments, and this will be true for any reasonable pattern of territory exploitation, not just for uniform exploitation as we have used, since any such pattern will be a low-pass filter in the frequency domain. Thus in environments where the variances of the resources are large, compared to the squared means, the effects of spatial variation and the benefits from increased range size will be greater than in environments where squared mean resource densities are greater than the variances.

We expect maximum range size in poor environments where there are few resources, all of which are maximally out of phase with each other over distances of ten to 100 kilometers. We expect minimum range size either when resources show very little spatial variation or when their variation is exactly in phase, so that population and exploitation are concentrated at particularly rich locations. People such as Bushmen, interior Eskimo, and Shoshone are examples of the former situation and people such as the northwest coast Indians (in-phase resources) or many tropical swiddening groups (little variation) exemplify the latter.

Group size should be small when there is little spatial variation in resources. The effects of high spatial variation depend upon the phase relations among the resources; large groups should aggregate when resources are in phase, as on the American northwest coast, while resources out of phase should lead to hyper-mobility and poorly defined local groups as among !Kung in the southern part of their range.

Population density

We have been examining optimum exploitation range for a minimal subsistence unit, and we have ignored interactions between these units and other effects of population density.

In the kind of environment where the effects of the mean resource densities are greater than the effects of the variances and where resources are in general out of phase there is little payoff in extensive land use. Here the effect of high population density would be caloric scarcity, which might lead in turn to chronic warfare among territorial units. This is the kind of pattern seen in many tropical and rich temperate areas, for example in South America, New Guinea or among California Indians.

In an environment where spatial variation is very large compared to the squared means of the resource densities, and where resources are in general in phase or incoherent, the effect of high population density would be to restrict mobility and to cause a reduction in dietary diversity and reliability. Here, a likely consequence would be inter-regional movement of resources and the development of broader scale social organization to mediate resource use. Increasing dependence upon agriculture would occur in both circumstances, but the spatial distribution of resources in the latter case should lead to larger-scale and more complex types of social systems.

1.viii.1976

Department of Anthropology
and Department of Mathematics
University of New Mexico

References

Koopmans, L. H. 1974. *The Spectral Analysis of Time Series.* New York: Academic Press.

Papoulis, A. 1965. *Probability, Random Variables, and Stochastic Processes.* New York: McGraw-Hill.

Yellen, J. and Harpending, H. 1972. Hunter-gatherer populations and archaeological inference. *World Archaeology.* 4:244–53.

Appendix

Cross-spectral densities

For any frequency ω the cross-spectral density between resources i and j is a complex number $f_{ij}(\omega)$. It is most useful to think of a complex number as a number with the two properties of magnitude and angle or phase. When we write $f_{ij}(\omega)$ in polar form:

$$f_{ij}(\omega)=r_{ij}(\omega)e^{i\theta_{ij}(\omega)}$$

r_{ij} is the magnitude of the cross-spectral density at frequency ω and is completely analogous to the covariance in statistics. One ordinarily estimates coherence, which is

$$P_{ij}(\omega)=\frac{r_{ij}(\omega)}{[f_{ii}(\omega)f_{jj}(\omega)]^{\frac{1}{2}}}$$

where $f_{ii}(\omega)$ is the power in $X_i(t)$ at frequency ω. This is a number between zero and one and is analogous to a correlation coefficient between the two series at frequency ω.

The $\theta_{ij}(\omega)$ in the exponent of (1) is called the phase lead of X_j over X_i at frequency ω. It is like the average lead of X_i over X_j in radians at frequency ω.

Both of these coefficients can be plotted as functions of frequency ω. These plots are called the coherency spectrum and the phase spectrum respectively. Together they provide the most useful graphical representation of the relations between the two series.

The spectral densities are fourier transforms of the auto and cross-correlations of the series. For a single series the autocorrelation at lag s, $R_{ii}(s)$, is the average value of

$$(X_i(t)-u_i)\ (X_i(t+s)-u_i)$$

where u_i is the mean of the X_i. We assume that the mean and the autocovariance of the series are constant, that is, that the series is weakly stationary. When $s=0$, this expression is simply the variance or power of the series $X_i(t)$. The power spectrum of $X_i(t)$ is given by the fourier transform:

$$f_{ii}(\omega)=\frac{1}{2\pi}\int_{-\infty}^{\infty} e^{i\omega t}\, R_{ii}(t)\, dt.$$

The cross-covariance between resource i and resource j is:

$$R_{ij}(s)=\text{average of }[(X_i(t)-u_i)(X_j(t-s)-u_j)].$$

It is not generally true that $R_{ij}(s)=R_{ji}(s)$. The cross-spectral density of the series $X_i(t)$ and $X_j(t)$ is the fourier transform of the cross-covariance:

$$f_{ij}(\omega)=\frac{1}{2\pi}\int_{-\infty}^{\infty} e^{i\omega t}\, R_{ij}(t)\, dt.$$

The cross-spectral density between X_i and X_j is conjugate symmetric; that is the magnitude of $f_{ij}(\omega)$ is the same as the magnitude of $f_{ji}(\omega)$ while the phase angle of $f_{ij}(\omega)$ is the negative of the phase of $f_{ji}(\omega)$. This is a statement of the obvious; if X_i leads X_j by some angle θ, then X_j lags X_i by the same angle.

A clear exposition of frequency domain methods for handling space and time series can be found in Koopmans (1974).

Variance of T

The variance of $T(t)$ will be given by

$$\text{var } T(t) = \sum_{i=1}^{k} \sum_{j=1}^{k} \int_0^\tau \int_0^\tau R_{ij}(t-s)dtds \times \frac{1}{\tau^2}$$

and in the frequency domain this becomes

$$\text{var } T(t) = \frac{2}{\tau^2} \sum_i \sum_j \int_{-\infty}^{\infty} \frac{(1 - \cos \omega\tau)}{\omega^2} f_{ij}(\omega)\, d\omega$$

(see Papoulis, 1965: 351). This expression says simply that the variance of a sum T is the sum of the variances plus twice the sum of the covariances of its components. The components of T are the total amounts C_i of each of the resources within a range τ. The variance of C_i is

$$\text{var } C_i(t) = \int_{-\infty}^{\infty} \frac{2(1 \cos \omega t)}{\omega^2 \tau^2} f_{ij}(\omega)\, d\omega.$$

Note first that this integral depends only on the real parts of the cross-spectral densities $f_{ij}(\omega)$. When the real part of a cross-spectral density is positive it means that the two series $X_i(t)$ and $X_j(t)$ are closer than 90° ($\pi/2$ radians) in phase. If the imaginary part is zero they are exactly in phase and if the real part is

$$Re f_{ij}(\omega) = [f_{ii}(\omega) f_{jj}(\omega)]^{\frac{1}{2}}$$

the coherence is 1; that is, one is the result of applying a deterministic linear operator to the other. When the real part is negative, they are more than 90 degrees out of phase with each other, and if

$$Re f_{ij}(\omega) = -[f_{ii}(\omega) f_{jj}(\omega)]^{\frac{1}{2}}$$

(with zero imaginary part) they are exactly 180 degrees (π radians) out of phase and completely coherent at frequency ω.

These integrals are the area under the spectral densities multiplied at each frequency ω by the squared gain of the filter

$$\frac{2(1 - \cos \omega\tau)}{\tau^2 \omega^2}$$

as shown in fig. 3.

Diversity in range of length τ

Consider a range of length τ kilometers, and write H as the diversity contained in a range of that size. Then the average value of H is approximately the average of the numerator divided by the average of the denominator of the expression for H. Letting E stand for the operation of taking expectation or average:

$$E(\sum_i C_i)^2 = (\sum u_i)^2 + \frac{2}{\tau^2} \sum_i \sum_j \int_{-\infty}^{\infty} f_{ij}(\omega) \frac{(1 - \cos \omega\tau)}{\omega^2}\, d\omega.$$

The expected value of the denominator is

$$E \sum_i C_i^2 = \sum u_i^2 + \frac{2}{\tau^2} \sum_i \int_{-\infty}^{\infty} f_{ii}(\omega) \frac{(1 - \cos \omega\tau)}{\omega^2}\, d\omega.$$

Thus a measure of diversity for a range size of τ kilometers is

$$(1)\quad H \cong \frac{(\sum u_i)^2 + \frac{2}{\tau^2} \sum_i \sum_j \int_{-\infty}^{\infty} f_{ij}(\omega) \frac{(1 - \cos \omega\tau)}{\omega^2} d\omega}{\sum u_i^2 + \frac{2}{\tau^2} \sum_i \int_{-\infty}^{\infty} f_{ii}(\omega) \frac{(1 - \cos \omega\tau)}{\omega^2} d\omega}$$

Abstract

Harpending, H. and Davis, H.

Some implications for hunter-gatherer ecology derived from the spatial structure of resources

Frequency-domain methods for analyzing data on the spatial structure of resources are discussed. The effects of spatial variation on reliability and diversity are high when the variance of resource abundance is greater than the squared mean abundance. Mobility of foragers should be high in poor environments with few resources, all maximally out of phase with each other. Mobility should be low when resources show either little spatial variation or when they vary in phase.

Vegetational fluctuation and prehistoric cultural adaptation in Amazonia: some tentative correlations

Betty J. Meggers

Introduction

The great rain forest that extends from eastern Bolivia, Peru, Ecuador and Colombia across southern Venezuela to the Atlantic and over most of the Amazon river network in Brazil has fascinated Europeans and their descendants since its discovery. Initially explorers and settlers were lured by the prospect that untapped riches lay concealed beneath the magnificent vegetation, and this quest continues despite centuries of disillusionment. More recently, biologists have been intrigued by the problem of reconciling the great diversity of plant and animal life with the absence of natural barriers to interbreeding and dispersal. Archaeological and linguistic evidence also exhibit greater heterogeneity than seems warranted, given the multitude of waterways facilitating communication throughout the lowlands.

A solution to the biological paradox was proposed by Haffer (1969), who postulated that several times during the Quaternary the forest was reduced to 'refugia' or enclaves separated by savanna or parkland. Formerly interacting populations of forest fauna were isolated long enough to differentiate into races, sub-species or full species. Each time the vegetation coalesced, the flora and fauna of the refugia were brought into contact and competition. There were some extinctions, but the more common outcome was adaptation to different niches, permitting coexistence of increasing numbers of taxa. For non-forest plants and animals, the opposite occurred: they were able to invade Amazonia as corridors opened in the rain forest and were isolated, altered or exterminated when their habitat was diminished or destroyed.

This refugia model, developed by Haffer from analysis of the present distributions of forest birds, has been successful in accounting for the geographical patterning of other organisms. When the sizes and locations of the hypothesized forest remnants are compared, they differ less than might be expected given the indirect, incomplete and varied nature of the evidence. Dating is tentative, but Carbon-14 results obtained so far indicate that the two most recent periods of fragmentation impinge upon or postdate man's arrival in South America. It is unlikely that environmental changes of the magnitude inferred by the biologists would have affected human beings and examination of the linguistic, archaeological and ethnographic data reveals several features suggestive of environmental stress. A summary of the biological model will serve as a basis for interpreting the cultural evidence.

Forest refuges reconstructed from animal and plant distributions

Forest birds Haffer (1969: fig. 5) combined inferences derived from modern patterns of avian distribution, variations in rainfall and data on paleoclimate to reconstruct nine locations where forest appeared to have persisted during arid intervals in the Quaternary. Subsequently, more detailed analysis of two families, toucans (Ramphastidae) and jacamars (Galbulidae), led him to add five small regions in Venezuela and eastern Brazil, and to adjust the size or shape of some of those previously proposed (fig. 4; Haffer 1974). He also postulated survival of gallery forest along major waterways. Shrinkage of the

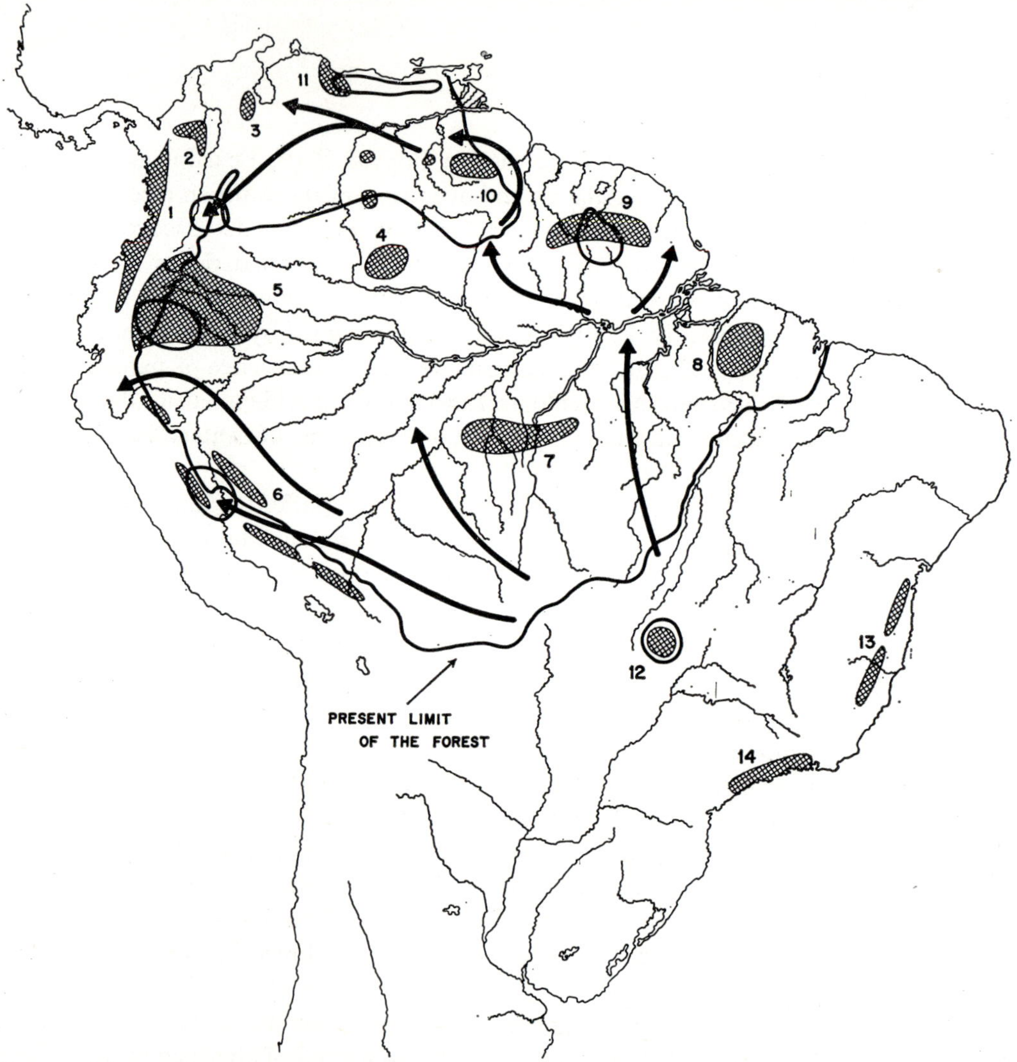

Figure 4 The present extent of the tropical rain forest (Amazonia), compared with the locations of the refugia postulated from modern distributions of birds (cross-hatch) and lizards (outline). The arrows indicate routes of intrusion of non-forest fauna from open habitats to the south during the period of reduction of the forest. (After Haffer 1969: fig. 5; 1974: fig. 13:1; Vanzolini 1970: map 7; Meggers 1971: fig. 6.)

forest not only affected the composition of species in this biome; it also provided opportunities for non-forest fauna to expand into and across the lowlands from the south. Relict populations in isolated patches of savanna, especially in the interior of the Guianas and between some of the southern tributaries of the Amazon, testify to the former continuity of open vegetation and provide a basis for postulating routes of dispersal (fig. 4; Haffner 1969: 134).

These refugia are generalizations of repeated ebbs and flows during the Quaternary. Haffer (1969: 135; 1974: 171) observes that birds with rapid reproductive rates may require no more than 20,000 to 30,000 years, and perhaps only a few thousand years, to achieve speciation. At the opposite extreme, slow-breeding species may require several hundred thousand years. With regard to Amazonia, he concludes that 'some of the more strongly differentiated species probably originated in early Pleistocene refuges, while most other species and semi-species may date back to the late Pleistocene or, in the case of the latter, to the post-Pleistocene only' (1969: 135–6).

Forest Lizards While Haffer was developing a model of climatic fluctuation and vegetational change from patterns of bird distribution, Vanzolini (1970) was arriving at similar conclusions from analysis of the ranges and degrees of differentiation exhibited by two genera of forest lizards: *Coleodactylus* and *Anolis*. His refugia are fewer and smaller than those proposed by Haffer; they are also peripheral to the lowlands and more closely correlated with relief (fig. 4; Vanzolini 43 and Map 7). The biogeographical evidence led him to infer two or three periods of forest fragmentation. The most recent, during which *Anolis chrysolepis* diverted into four well defined sub-species, is estimated to have occurred some 2,700 years ago (1970: 42).

Vanzoloni considers that this model 'explains perfectly why patterns of differentiation in the center of the basin are generally complicated and confused. This area reflects the fusion of numerous stocks differentiated on the periphery and brought into contact during a period of ecological complexity, such as the reconstitution of the forest' (1970: 44; also 1973).

Woody plants When Prance (1973) analyzed the distribution of genera and species of four families of woody plants that occur over most of northern lowland South America, he found them compatible with the model of past climatic change. The inability of many primary trees to survive in habitats that have been significantly reduced in size, or to recolonize areas that have been extensively disturbed, led him to conclude, however, that the refugia must have been larger and more numerous than those postulated by the zoologists. He proposed sixteen enclaves, which include most of those inferred by Haffer (1974) plus a large expanse east of the junction between the Negro and the Amazon (fig. 2, area 13) and smaller ones in western Amazonia between the Solimões and the Juruá (fig. 5, areas 11-12; Prance 1973: fig. 24).

Other botanists have expressed similar reservations about the ability of rain-forest vegetation to survive in refugia as small as those suggested by Haffer and Vanzolini, or to expand as rapidly as would be necessary for coalescence within the span of time available (e.g. Gómez-Pompa, *et al.* 1972; Langenheim, *et al.* 1973: 33).

Heliconius butterflies Butterflies of the genus *Heliconius* are remarkable for their ability to mimic the colors and patterns of other Lepidoptera, with the result that a species may be composed of several races that differ markedly in appearance. The most satisfactory explanation for such striking phenotypical diversification is the isolation of populations of *Heliconius*, followed by natural selection that 'encouraged' survival of individuals most similar to the commonest distasteful species confined to the same refuge (Brown *et al.* 1974; Brown and Benson 1974: 226).

The refugia reconstructed from the present ranges of the species and races of *Heliconius* and other butterflies are more comparable to those proposed by Prance than to the extreme reductions hypothesized by the other zoologists, but are even more numerous

Figure 5 Forest refugia, reconstructed from the present distributions of four families of woody plants (hachure) and several races and species of butterflies (outline). (After Prance 1973: fig. 24; Brown, Sheppard and Turner 1974: fig. 3.)

(fig. 5; Brown *et al.* 1974: fig. 3). Although the entomologists do not suggest a time scale, the fact that they are often dealing with races rather than species or even sub-species may imply a relatively short period of isolation.

Direct evidence for Quaternary climatic change

Geology and palynology Although information is scattered, it is sufficient to demonstrate that alternations between forest and savanna occurred repeatedly over much of the lowlands during the Quaternary. Lateritic horizons and paleopavements have been observed in the following regions: Belém-Marajó, Santarem (two strata), lower Rio Tocantins, Roraima, Amapá (two strata), Cuiabá and Brasília. The geomorphology of the Rio Caroni valley in eastern Venezuela and of valleys in eastern Peru testifies to recurring dry episodes (Vanzolini 1970: 41; Haffer 1974: 137). Pollen profiles from forested portions of coastal Guyana and Surinam, southwestern Guyana, the Colombian llanos and Rondônia in southwestern Brazil reveal that savanna prevailed during one or more periods of increased aridity (Van der Hammen 1972; Haffer 1974; 137-8, 140-1). By contrast, the Maranhão highlands of northeastern Brazil, the Mato Grosso de Goiás on the eastern margin of Amazonia and the Tumuc-Humac range dividing Brazil from the Guianas appear to have remained permanently forested (Vanzolini 1970: 42-3). As yet, these data are insufficient to define the boundaries of the refugia or to identify the episode represented.

Chronology A few Carbon-14 dates provide a general time framework for the two most recent disruptions of the forest. In southern Brazil, the last period began between about 3,500 and 3,280 years ago and ended about 2,680 years ago. In eastern Colombia, the corresponding ages are 3,095 and 1,990 years ago (Vanzolini 1970: 42). On the basis of geomorphical evidence from several parts of Brazil, this episode has been bracketed between about 4000 and 2500 B.P. (Haffer 1974: 142). Consideration of sea-level change and geological data suggests a slightly earlier inception and longer duration, between 5,000 and 2,300 years ago (Müller 1973: 189). These differences in age estimates reflect the paucity of evidence, unequal precision of methods of dating, local variations in rates of change, discrepancies in the portions of the cycle being dated and other variables.

The chronological boundaries of the preceding period are even more uncertain. Study of ocean sediments originating in the Guyana and Brazilian shields suggests that arid conditions prevailed about 11,000 years ago (Vanzolini 1970: 42). Palynological data from the eastern cordillera of the Colombian Andes indicate that 'the interval between *ca.* 21 000 and *ca.* 13 000 B.P. was considerably drier than . . . the periods just before or after that interval' (Van der Hammen 1972: 641). Evidence that the climate was more moist 9000 to 10,000 years ago than at present provides a terminal date for this episode (Haffer 1974: 140-1).

The biological model

Comparison of the refugia postulated from the present distributions of several types of organisms reveals that they fall into two general categories. One is composed of small and widely separated remnants (fig. 4); the other of larger, more numerous and less isolated areas (fig. 5). Even when the incompleteness of the data, differences in rates of evolution, hazards of inferring past distributions from existing ones and other potential sources of distortion are taken into consideration, the discrepancies seem sufficiently great to imply that different episodes of forest fragmentation may be represented. This interpretation is compatible with the nature of the biological evidence: the small and peripheral areas proposed by Haffner and Vanzolini are based on the analysis of higher categories of taxa, which suggest greater antiquity of separation than the sub-species and races studied by the entomologists.

Allocation of the two types of refugia reconstructions to different episodes also seems warranted by the existing dates. The earlier period seems to have been about five times longer than the later one (about 10,000 versus about 2,000 years' duration) and ten thousand years of lowered rainfall would have permitted (or caused) more extreme alteration in the vegetation than is likely to have been achieved in 2,000 years. Thus, the smaller enclaves can be tentatively equated with the earlier, longer episode and the larger ones with the more recent, briefer disruption.

In employing this dichotomy as a working hypothesis, it is essential to keep in mind that the refugia reconstructions presumably depict climax situations. The retreat and advance of the forest is likely to have been gradual, but we do not know how much time it consumed. Was the rate constant or variable? Was it faster in some parts of Amazonia than in others? When was the climax reached and how long did it endure? These are among the uncertainties that affect an attempt to correlate cultural distributions with the refugia model.

Application of the refugia model to cultural distributions

Anthropologists possess three categories of data potentially useful for reconstructing the past: linguistic, archaeological and ethnographic. Their inherent limitations as indicators of prehistoric events are enhanced in Amazonia by the small amount of systematic investigation. Large parts of the lowlands are unknown archaeologically; numerous languages are represented by only a few words; many indigenous groups are acculturated or extinct. Furthermore, the fact that language and culture are independent variables prevents automatic transfer of reconstructions based on either type of data to the other. In spite of these handicaps, some of the characteristics observed by biogeographers can be discerned, among them localized heterogeneity, disjunct distributions and widespread dispersals. Examples of these phenomena provide a basis for judging the relevance of the refugia model to the reconstruction of Amazonian prehistory.

Linguistic distributions At first glance, linguistic maps of northern lowland South America appear hopelessly confused (fig. 6). The two best known are by Mason (1950) and Loukotka (1967). They differ in detail, but exhibit several general similarities. First, both classifications include numerous small relict families, which tend to be concentrated around the margins of Amazonia. Second, some families have disjunct or discontinuous distributions, implying interference with formerly continuous ranges. Third, each of the three major families (Arawakan, Tupí-Guaranian, and Cariban) contains at least one language that is spoken over an extensive area. These kinds of phenomena are interpreted by biogeographers as indicating past disruptions of the habitat and it is reasonable to attribute their linguistic occurrence to the same cause.

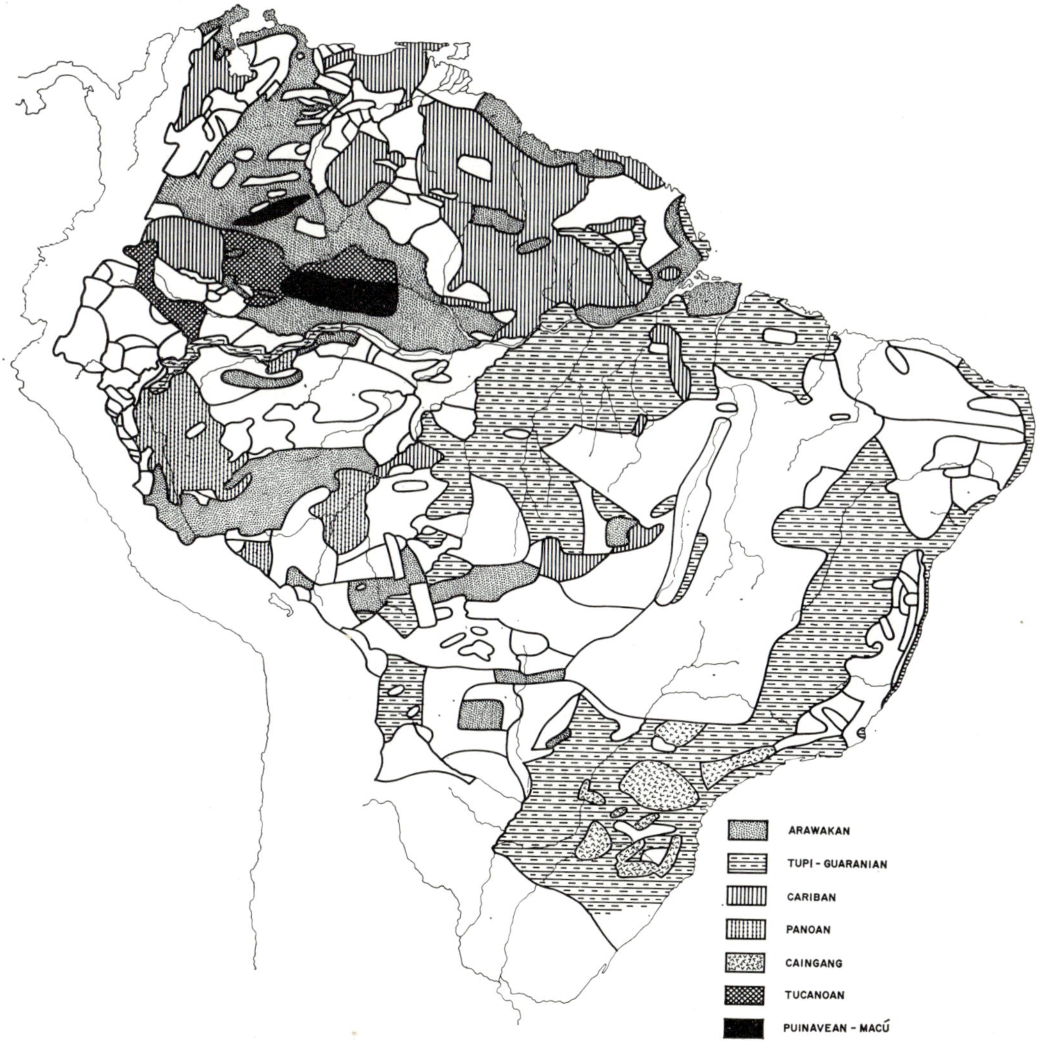

Figure 6 Locations of the principal languages of lowland South America, based on the classification by Mason. Noteworthy are the concentration of isolated languages or relict families on the periphery of Amazonia, the disjunct distributions of languages belonging to four minor families (Caingang, Panoan, Tucanoan, Puinavean-Macú), and the widespread dispersal of the three largest families (Arawakan, Tupí-Guaranian, Cariban). (After Mason 1950: map.)

A more general classification that combines all South American languages into four ancestral stocks has been proposed by Greenberg (1960). Two are insignificant in Amazonia, but the other two display some intriguing patterns of distribution. When the locations of groups assigned to Ge-Pano-Carib are compared with the refugia maps, they suggest that dispersal occurred during the earlier episode of forest reduction. In fact, the routes postulated by Haffer for the intrusion of non-forest fauna into and across Amazonia from open habitats to the south lead toward, or pass through, most of the areas occupied by speakers of languages belonging to this stock (fig. 7). If this correlation is valid, it implies that reconstitution of the forest around ten thousand years ago injected an ecological wedge into central Amazonia that isolated groups to the north from those

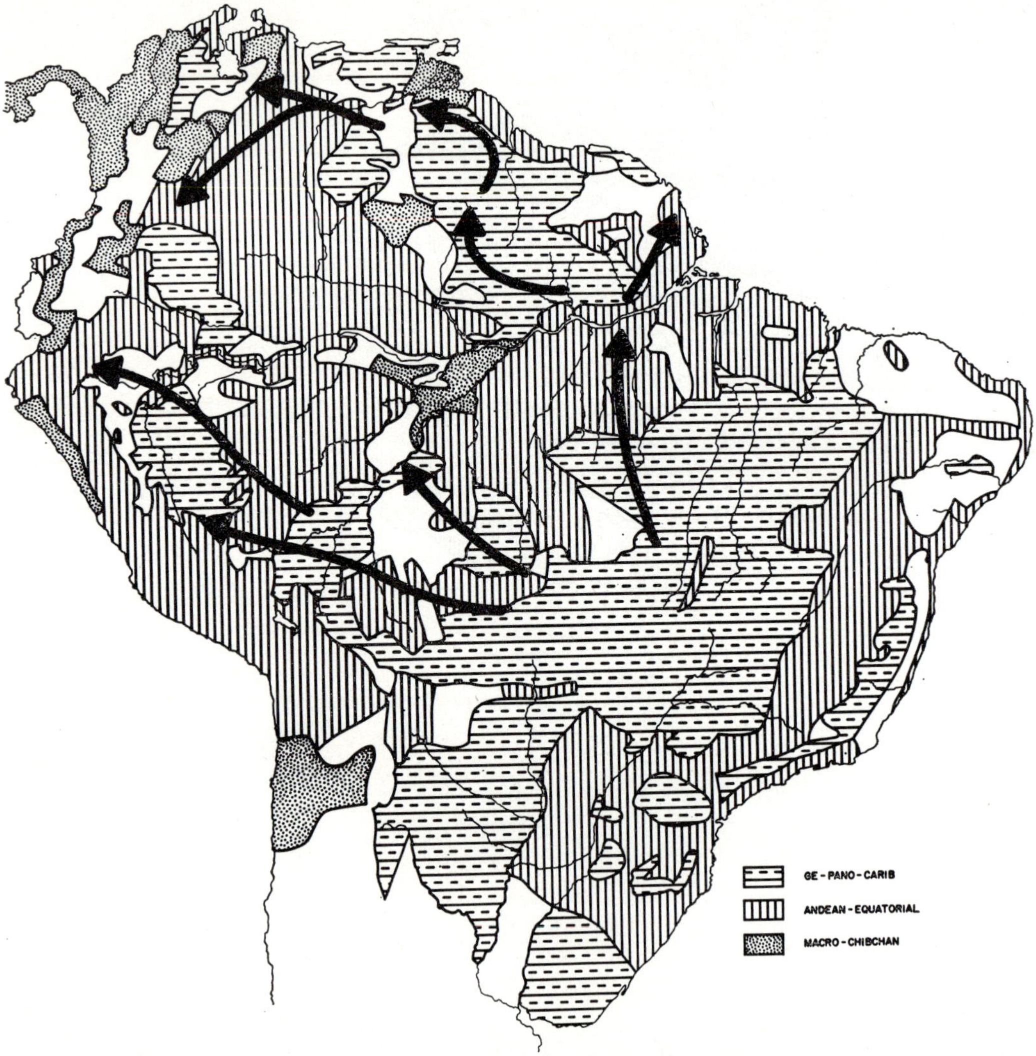

Figure 7 Distribution of the primary linguistic stocks, reconstructed by Greenberg (1960) for northern South America. The correlation between the areas assigned to Ge-Pano-Carib and the routes of faunal dispersal proposed by Haffer is extremely close. (After Steward and Faron 1959: 23; Mason 1950: map; Haffer 1969: fig. 5.)

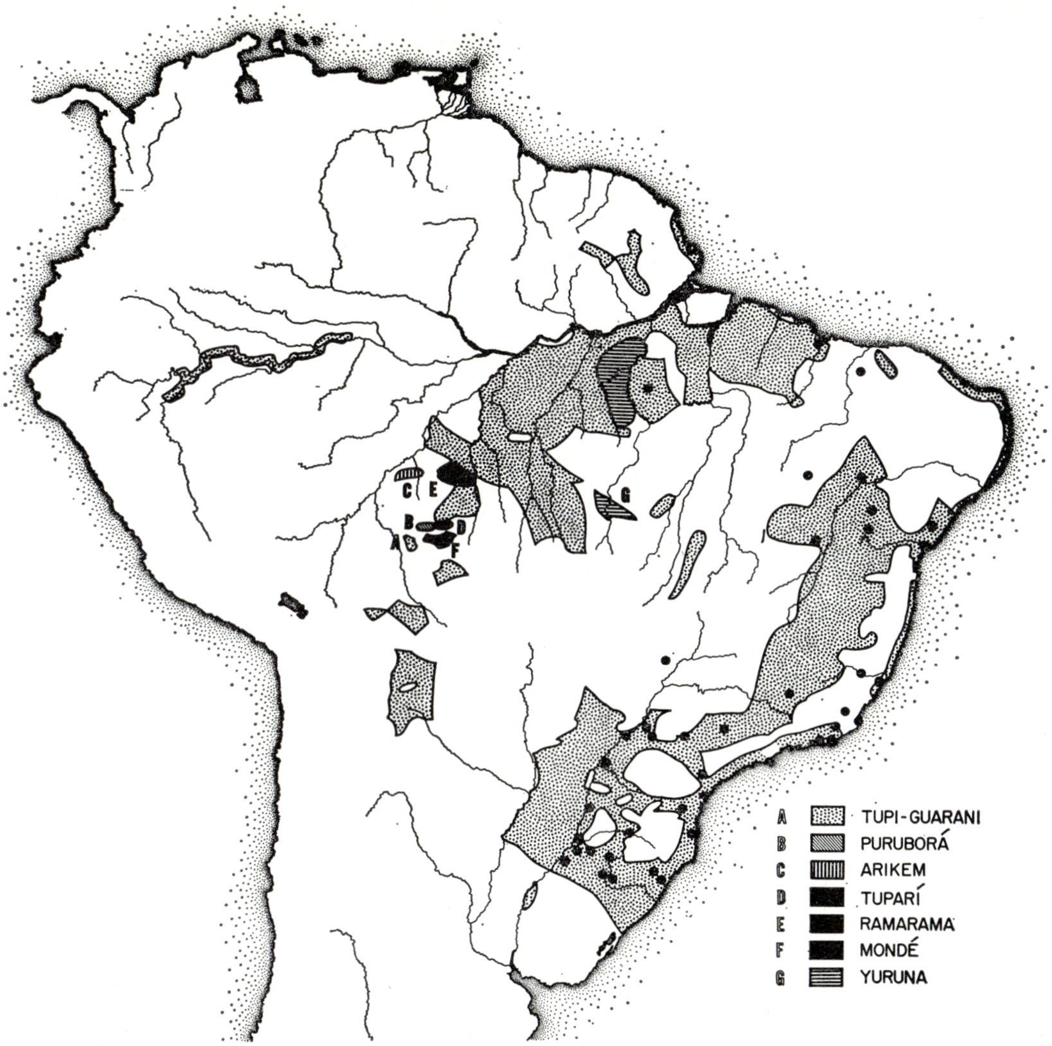

Figure 8 Correlation between the archaeological phases assigned to the Tupiguaraní tradition (circles) and the distribution of speakers of coastal Tupí-Guaranian at the time of first reporting. Glottochronological and Carbon-14 estimates place the arrival of this population on the Brazilian coast about 1,200 years ago. Concentration of representatives of six of the Tupian families in southwestern Amazonia makes it the probable homeland. (After Meggers and Evans 1973.)

to the south long enough to permit differentiation of Ge-Pano-Carib into subfamilies (fig. 9).

Evaluation of the role of the refugia in subsequent linguistic diversification is facilitated by detailed information on Tupian and Arawakan, which belong to the Equatorial division of Greenberg's Andean-Equatorial stock. Rodrigues (1955, 1958a: 234) has assigned to Tupian all languages that share at least 12 percent of their standard vocabularies. He recognizes seven families, the largest (Tupí-Guaraní) composed of six subfamilies, twenty languages and numerous dialects. At the opposite extreme are five families containing no subfamilies and only one to five languages. The presence of representatives of six of the seven families in southwestern Amazonia suggests this region was the center of origin and dispersal (fig. 8). Glottochronological estimates place the separation of Tupian from other members of the Equatorial division about five thousand years ago, the origin of the widespread Tupí-Guaraní family about 2,500 years ago, and differentiation of the latter into subfamilies about 1,200 years ago (fig. 9; Rodrigues 1958b: 684).

The emergence of Proto-Arawakan has been estimated by Noble (1965: 107) to have occurred between 5,000 and 3,500 years ago in southeastern Peru. This agrees with Rodrigues' reconstruction of the time and place of origin of Tupian and indirectly supports Greenberg's assignment of these languages to a common ancestor in the Equatorial division. Differentiation of Proto-Maipuran into six subgroups appears to have been

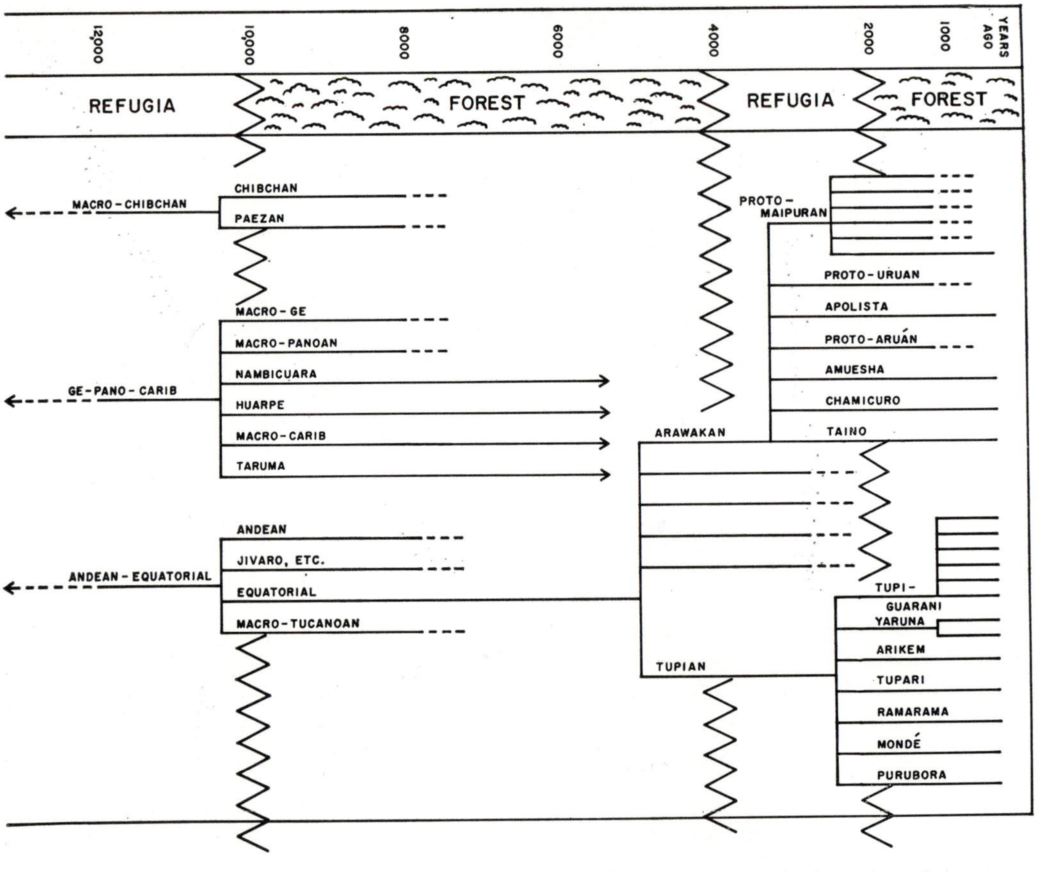

Figure 9 Correlation between periods of major diversification in South American languages estimated by glottochronology, and the durations of the two most recent episodes of forest fragmentation, dated by Carbon-14. Families in the Equatorial division of Andean-Equatorial seem to have diverged a little before the onset of the last arid period; Tupian and the Proto-Maipuran branch of Arawakan, as it was drawing to a close. Arawakan separated into seven segments about the climax of the episode. (After Greenberg 1960; Noble 1965; Rodrigues 1958a.)

generally contemporary with the divergence of Tupian into seven families, since both classifications define these categories by the possession of about thirty-six percent cognates. Noble (1965: 108, 110), however, recognizes an earlier episode of Arawakan divergence, when Taino (spoken in the Greater Antilles at the time of European contact), Proto-Uruan (spoken in the Titicaca area of highland Peru-Bolivia), and four other Arawakan groups separated form Proto-Maipuran. Glottochronology places this event about 3,300 years ago (*ibid*: 111).

Assuming that their origin has been reconstructed correctly, it is of interest to see whether the differentiations and dispersals of Arawakan and Tupian can be attributed to the most recent episode of forest fragmentation, tentatively dated by Carbon-14 between about 4,000 and 2,000 years ago. At first glance, the correlation appears poor (fig. 9). Arawakan and Tupian separated about a millennium before its inception; Arawakan began differentiating prior to the middle of the period; Proto-Maipuran and Tupian were diverging half a millennium before it ended. These dates are all tenuous, however, and some authorities place the onset of fragmentation around 5,000 years ago and reconstitution of the forest about 2,500 to 2,300 years ago. Better agreement with the glottochronological estimates is not necessarily an indication of greater accuracy however, because the rate of linguistic change may be in error. Furthermore, local conditions probably accelerated or decelerated the climatic and vegetational transitions, which in turn increased or reduced the adaptive pressures of human populations. The uncorrected nature of the Carbon-14 results is another potential source of error when comparisons are made with dates obtained by different methods. Given these and other uncertainties, the correlation between periods of major linguistic and environmental change is good enough to warrant the suspicion that they are related.

Archaeological distributions Prior to European contact most Amazonian tools, weapons and other kinds of objects were made from perishable materials. The possibility is consequently slight of encountering sites belonging to the period prior to the introduction of pottery making about 3,000 years ago. The Zoned Hachure tradition of Amazonia is known mainly from the island of Marajó, where it has a terminal age of about 2,900 years. The diagnostic decorative technique, broad-line incision, was employed to create geometric patterns or to outline zones filled with fine cross-hachure. The presence of similar ornamentation on earlier pottery from Ecuador and Colombia suggests an intrusion from the northwest (Meggers 1975: 156-7). Pottery of the Barrancoid tradition, which was being made in the delta of the Orinoco about 2,800 years ago, is also decorated by incision, but motifs and vessel shapes are different. The antecedents of this tradition appear to be on the Caribbean coast of Colombia (Sanoja 1976).

The inceptions of the Zoned Hachure and Barrancoid ceramic traditions fall within the most recent period of forest fragmentation. This, added to their affiliations with northern Andean complexes, suggests that settlement of Amazonia by groups adapted to more open habitats was facilitated by the presence of 'corridors' of parkland. This hypothesis also accounts for the lag of about a millennium between adoption of pottery making throughout the Andean area and its spread into the lowlands.

One widely disseminated language that can be traced archaeologically is the coastal branch of Tupí-Guaraní (fig. 8). Historical information and association with objects of

European origin indicate that pottery decorated principally by polychrome painting and corrugation is associated with speakers of Tupí-Guaraní. Extensive archaeological survey has permitted establishment of numerous localized relative sequences, identification of about a hundred Tupí-Guaraní archaeological phases, and verification via Carbon-14 dating of a dispersal from south to north (Meggers and Evans 1973: 54-56). Dates from several sites in southern Brazil place the arrival of this ceramic tradition about 1300 years ago, which agrees with the glottochronological estimate of about 1200 years ago for the differentiation of Tupí-Guaranian. Although the region between the Brazilian coast and the base of the Andes is too little known as yet to follow the trail toward the west, the fact that both painting and corrugation occur several centuries earlier in the Andean area supports the linguistic evidence for intrusion from this direction. Where and when the language and the ceramic tradition joined remain to be established.

Ethnographic distributions No obvious correlation exists between the refugia and any of the culture areas that have been defined in Amazonia (e.g. Murdock 1951: fig. 1; Steward 1948: map 8; Galvão 1967: map 4). An indication that this lack of agreement reflects emphasis on traits susceptible to adaptive pressures is provided by the combination of cultural homogeneity and linguistic diversity along the upper Rio Uaupés in northwestern Amazonia (Sorensen 1967: 670; Galvão 1967: 181). The existence of more than twenty-five distinct languages representing several families implies cultural convergence by groups with heterogeneous ancestry. The possibility that patterns more in keeping with linguistic and archaeological evidence for past mobility can be obtained from analysis of other kinds of ethnographic traits is provided by the distributions of pole snares and simple nooses for trapping game. Confinement of the former to the northern and southern periphery suggests they were displaced in the interviewing lowlands by users of simple nooses (Rydén 1950: fig. 25; see also Meggers 1975: 155–6). Although there is no direct means of estimating antiquity, it seems reasonable to equate the introduction of simple nooses with the coalescence of the forest some ten thousand years ago.

The refugia model offers a new perspective for interpreting other puzzling ethnographic patterns. Within the Amazon Basin, Steward distinguished six varieties of Tropical Forest culture and five disjunct enclaves occupied by groups that made little or no use of domesticated plants (fig. 10). The best explanation he could propose was that the latter regions were 'difficult of access in pre-Columbian times no less than in modern times to essentially riparian peoples'; inventions and discoveries associated with agricultural subsistence 'flowed along the coast and up the main waterways, stopping where streams were less navigable and leaving the hinterland tribes on a more primitive level' (1948: 883). He also commented that 'more advanced technologies were absent to a surprising degree, even among the tribes who adjoined or formed enclaves within the Tropical Forest peoples and would seem to have had considerable opportunity for borrowing' (1949: 691). The fact that a negative correlation seems to exist between regions occupied by hunter-gatherers and the postulated locations of the most recent refugia (fig. 5) suggests a different hypothesis; namely, when the forest was replaced by savanna, the inhabitants abandoned agriculture (if they had begun to practice it) for an economy based on wild foods, which they retained when the forest returned. From this perspective, their failure

Figure 10 Subdivisions of the Tropical Forest culture area recognized by Steward (numbered), showing the patchwork created by regions dominated by hunter-gatherers (hachure) and incipient agriculturalists (stipple). The negative correlation between the locations of hunter-gatherers and the postulated refugia (cf. fig. 5) may be significant. (After Steward 1948: map 8.)

to adopt 'more advanced technologies' indicates achievement of an efficient adaptation to the environment.

Areas dominated by incipient agriculture tend to overlap with refugia. Did greater environmental stability encourage the development and persistence of their subsistence orientation? The distribution of slash-and-burn agriculturalists has no apparent relation to previous vegetational patterns. Does this imply that the Tropical Forest type of culture spread over the lowlands during the two millennia since the last coalescence of the forest? The combination of widespread distribution of the diagnostic traits – cultivation of tropical root crops, effective watercraft, hammocks and manufacture of pottery (Lowie 1948: 1) – with regional or tribal diversity in dress, ornaments, featherwork and other cultural elements (Steward 1948: 885-6) becomes understandable if the Tropical Forest life style is a recent development. The archaeological evidence that pottery making is a relatively late introduction also supports this hypothesis.

Conclusions

The recognition that Amazonia has suffered successive episodes of fragmentation of the forest during and since the Pleistocene provides biologists with a mechanism for explaining the extensive speciation, disjunct distributions of taxa, and other biogeographical features that could not be accounted for in the absence of natural barriers to interbreeding and dispersal. The same kinds of patterns are discernible in linguistic, archaeological and ethnographic data, implying that human beings were similarly affected by the ebb and flow of the forest. Although geological, palynological, biogeographical and cultural types of evidence are all limited and often tenuous, the correspondences in patterning and chronology are too close to be coincidental.

Comparison of the manner in which the refugia model has been applied to biological and cultural phenomena reveals an interesting difference. Perhaps because the overriding problem for biologists has been explaining the diversity of the tropical forest biome, they have emphasized the role of refugia in isolating populations and inhibiting dispersal. Linguistic and archaeological data suggest, however, that *Homo sapiens* often became more mobile as the forest disappeared. Culture may be a significant variable here, since it provides human beings with the capacity to store and transport food while searching for more productive habitats, and to switch readily from one type of diet to another. The existence of ethnohistorical reports that coastal Tupian speakers were migrating in search of an earthly paradise at the time of European contact raises the possibility that some earlier dispersals may also have been purposeful and of long duration. Other groups probably adapted to changing conditions or followed the plants and animals upon which they depended for subsistence. While human beings were strongly affected by fluctuations in their environment, the 'choice' between surviving in a forest remnant or becoming extinct was mitigated by the possession of culture.

The occurrence of several episodes of reduction and coalescence of the lowland tropical forest during and since the Pleistocene provides a new and exciting context for analyzing prehistoric cultural development. In addition to offering an explanation for several puzzling features of the linguistic and archaeological data, this model calls attention to the potential significance of less obtrusive phenomena. For example, do the differences in degree of emphasis on wild foods that characterize Tropical Forest agriculturalists reflect differences in the length of time since they adopted domesticated plants? What impact did the oscillating environment have on the process of domestication? On population density? On migration into and out of Amazonia? Two things are clear:

(1) given the differential shortcomings of linguistic, archaeological and ethnographic evidence, finding the answers to these questions will require collaboration between specialists in all three disciplines.

(2) given the immensity of Amazonia, tribal and regional studies are unlikely to provide a sufficiently broad perspective. As Vanzolini once observed: 'The phenomena of differentiation can only be understood in their totality' (1970: 44).

1.viii.1976

Department of Anthropology
Smithsonian Institute, Washington D.C.

References

Brown, K. S., Jr. and Benson W. W. 1974. Adaptive polymorphism associated with multiple Müllerian mimicry in *Heliconius numata* (Lepid. Nymph.). *Biotropica.* 4:205–28.

Brown, K. S., Jr., Sheppard, P. M. and Turner, J. R. G. 1974. Quaternary refugia in tropical America: evidence from race formation in *Heliconius* butterflies. *Proc. Roy. Soc.* 187:369–78.

Galvão, E. 1967. Indigenous culture areas of Brazil, 1900–1959. In *Indians of Brazil in the Twentieth Century*, pp. 169–205 (ed. and trans. Janice H. Hopper). Washington: Institute for Cross-Cultural Research.

Gómez-Pompa, A., Vázquez-Yanes, C. and Guevara, S. 1972. The tropical rain forest: a nonrenewable resource. *Science.* 177:762–5.

Greenberg, J. 1960. The general classification of Central and South American languages. *Selected Papers of the 5th International Congress of Anthropological Sciences, Philadelphia*, 1956, pp. 791–4.

Haffer, J. 1969. Specification in Amazonian forest birds. *Science.* 165:131–7.

Haffer, J. 1974. *Avian Speciation in Tropical South America.* (Publs. of the Nuttall Ornithological Club No. 14.) Cambridge, Mass.

Langenheim, J. H., Lee, Y-T. and Martin, S. S. 1973. An evolutionary and ecological perspective of Amazonian Hylaea species of Hymeneae (Leguminosae: Caesalpinioideae). *Acta Amazônica.* 3(1):5–38.

Loukotka, C. 1967. Ethno-linguistic distribution of South American Indians. *Ann. Ass. Am. Geogr.* 57(2): map supplement 8.

Lowie, R. H. 1948. The tropical forests: an introduction. *Bureau of American Ethnology Bull.* 143(3):1–56.

Mason, J. A. 1950. The languages of South American Indians. *Bureau of American Ethnology Bull.* 143(6):157–317 and map.

Meggers, B. J. 1971. *Amazonia: Man and Culture in a Counterfeit Paradise.* Chicago: Aldine Publishing Company.

Meggers, B. J. 1975. Application of the biological model of diversification to cultural distributions in tropical lowland South America. *Biotropica.* 7:141–61.

Meggers, B. J. and Evans, C. 1973. A reconstituição da pré-história amazônica; algumas considerações teóricas. *Museu Paraense Emílio Goeldi, Publs. Avulsas.* 20:51–69.

Müller, P. 1973. *The Dispersal Centres of Terrestrial Vertebrates in the Neotropical Realm.* The Hague: W. Junk B.V.

Murdock, G. P. 1951. South American culture areas. *Southwestern Journal of Anthropology.* 7:415–36.

Noble, G. K. 1965. Proto-Arawakan and its descendants. *International Journal of American Linguistics.* 31(3): part II.

Prance, G. T. 1973. Phytogeographic support for the theory of Pleistocene forest refuges in the Amazon Basin, based on evidence from distribution patterns in Caryocaraceae, Chrysobalanaceae, Dichapetelaceae and Lecythidaceae. *Acta. Amazônica.* 3(3):5–28.

Rodrigues, A. D. 1955. As línguas 'impuras' da família Tupí-Guaraní. *31mo Congresso Internacional de Americanistas, Anais.* 2:1055–71. São Paulo.

Rodrigues, A. D. 1958a. Classification of Tupí-Guaraní. *International Journal of American Linguistics.* 24:231–4.

Rodrigues, A. D. 1958b. Die Klassifikation des Tupí-Sprachstammes. *Proceedings of the 32nd International Congress of Americanists*, pp. 679–84. Copenhagen.

Rydén, S. 1950. A study of South American Indian hunting traps. *Revista do Museu Paulista.* 4:247–352.

Sanoja, M. 1976. *Las culturas formativas del oriente de Venezuela: la tradición Barrancoide.* Caracas: Universidad Central de Venezuela.

Sorensen, A. P., Jr. 1967. Multilingualism in the northwest Amazon. *American Anthropologist.* 69:670–84.

Steward, J. H. 1948. Culture areas of the tropical forests. *Bureau of American Ethnology Bull.* 143(3):883–99.

Steward, J. H. 1949. South American cultures; an interpretative summary. *Bureau of American Ethnology Bull.* 143(5):669–772.

Steward, J. H. and Faron, L. C. 1959. *Native Peoples of South America.* New York: McGraw-Hill.

Van der Hammen, T. C. 1972. Changes in vegetation and climate in the Amazon basin and surrounding areas during the Pleistocene. *Geologie en Mijnbouw.* 51:641–3.

Vanzolini, P. E. 1970. *Zoologia sistemática, geografia e a origem das espécies.* Instituto de Geografia, Universidade de São Paulo, Teses e Monografias 3.

Vanzolini, P. E. 1973. Paleoclimates, relief, and species multiplication in equatorial forests. In *Tropical Forest Ecosystems in Africa and South America: a comparative review*, pp. 255–8 (eds B. J. Meggers, E. S. Ayensu and W. D. Duckworth). Washington: Smithsonian Institution Press.

Abstract

Meggers, B. J.

Vegetational fluctuation and prehistoric cultural adaptation in Amazonia: some tentative correlations

Biogeographical studies have generated the hypothesis that the remarkably large number of plant and animal species inhabiting Amazonia are a consequence of several episodes of forest fragmentation and coalescence, in which periods of isolation that permitted biological differentiation alternated with periods of renewed interaction. Geological and palynological evidence support this reconstruction, but data are insufficient to permit definition of the dimensions and locations of the refugia, or to separate one episode from another. Dating is tentative, but the two most recent episodes appear to fall within the span of human occupation of the continent. Examination of linguistic, archaeological and ethnographic data reveals widespread dispersals, disjunct distributions and other patterns of the kinds observed by biogeographers. Glottochronological and Carbon-14 dates correlate well enough with estimates for the durations of the forest refugia to suggest that the biogeographical model is useful for interpreting prehistoric cultural adaptation to Amazonia.

Adaptive strategies in western Panama

Olga F. Linares

Introduction

This paper considers an example of prehistoric 'adaptive radiation' in western Panama. Two allotropic types of tropical forest agriculturalists, with distinct subsistence and settlement patterns, have occupied different parts of this region for the last 1,000 years. I shall attempt to present, and then evaluate as critically as possible, the evidence for divergence from a common origin with dispersal and colonization of two areas.

At the risk of sounding provincial, I have restricted my discussion to the archaeology of a tiny area (fig. 11) within which I have followed G. Cowgill's observation (1975: 517) that 'it is much better to try to formulate the right questions than to offer the wrong answers.' This is necessary in the case of ongoing research to maintain a healthy perspective on the limitations of our archaeology and the differences that exist between it and biogeography. If biologists are aware of the difficulties involved in the study of adaptive diversity (e.g. MacArthur and Wilson 1967: 4–5), even when they can distinguish between species, how much more cautious we, as archaeologists, should be. We are dealing exclusively with one species, whose distribution is nearly universal, but whose range of cultural variation is enormous and must be reconstructed from partial evidence.

The approach used in the Panamanian research combines the 'method of controlled comparison' (Eggan 1954) with the notion of 'adaptive radiation' in biology (Hamilton 1967: 66). Several studies of divergent adaptations to new environments by historically related groups exist in social anthropology (e.g. Sahlins 1958; Kottak 1971, 1972). Using archaeological evidence I shall explore the possible effects of two agricultural systems known as vegeculture and seed culture (Harris 1971, 1972, 1973; Linares *et al.*, 1975) on the social and political arrangements of related prehistoric peoples. Paralleling a biogeographer's model (Diamond 1973) I will be touching upon the evidence for migration, colonization, population divergence and adaptation in the humid versus the seasonal tropics of western Panama.

The setting: formulation of a hypothesis

The prehistory of lower Central America – that is, the area south of the Maya and north of the Andes – was 'characterized by intensive sociopolitical fragmentation and great variability, both in ecological adaptation and in specific cultural style' (Sanders and Marino 1970: 84). In Panama itself, a type of society which has been called a chiefdom was encountered by the Spanish along the rivers of the Pacific coastal plains including Chiriquí province. 'Chieftainship involves control over a social group by one man; but chiefs lack the regular institutionalized administrative staffs typical of states' (Lewis

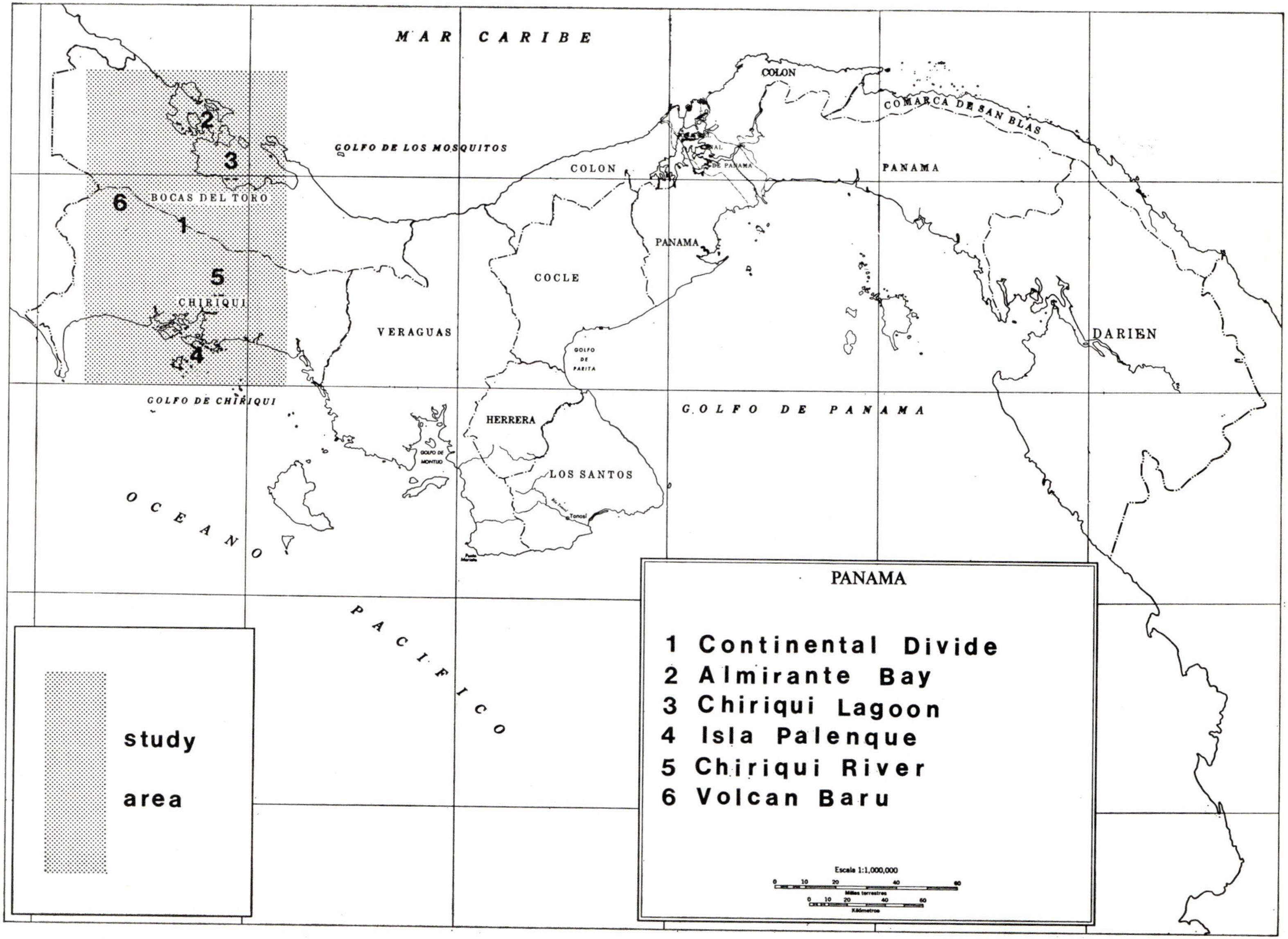

Figure 11 Panama: location map for the area studied

1968: 105). Although the chroniclers' accounts are sometimes unreliable and often incomplete, they suggest that chiefly societies were largely absent from the adjacent Panamanian province of Bocas del Toro (abbreviated Bocas), on the Atlantic or Caribbean side.

Several factors make Bocas and Chiriquí (see fig. 11) an ideal setting for a comparison through time emphasizing cultural-evolutionary divergence and differential adaptations within a tropical setting:

(*a*) The same or closely related groups lived in both provinces during the Conquest, at which time several chroniclers produced works which can be used as references for current archaeological research. Today one single ethnic group, speaking the same dialect variant of Guaymí (a Macro-Chibchan language), inhabit the forested ridges of Bocas and the eroded highlands of Chiriquí on the southern side of the Continental Divide (also known as the Talamancan Range). Guaymí social organization is basically cognatic or bilateral (i.e. there are no unilineal descent groups such as lineages: Young 1971). Hamlets, made up of matrilocal extended polygynous households, vary in composition according to the developmental cycle of the domestic group. Indications are that the Guaymí economy – based on swidden cultivation, with hunting and fishing still important – remains at the subsistence level, even after the introduction of European animals and crops (Young 1971).

(*b*) Despite 400 years of disruption following the Conquest, the modern Guaymí of the two provinces display important differences in their subsistence and settlement patterns. The 8,000 Bocas Guaymí grow tree crops and root crops in a slash and mulch (i.e. shifting agriculture without burning) long forest-fallow system (Gordon 1969). The maize that is grown is a type of *flint* corn used for fermented chicha (i.e. corn beer) and to feed pigs. Except for a few mission settlements, the majority of Bocas Guaymí still live in scattered extended-family hamlets, which are moved continuously.

The 28,000 or so Guaymí living on the Pacific or Chiriquí side are maize and rice agriculturalists. Little game remains in the deforested hills where they practice shifting cultivation. Extensive burning of the land for clearing, and short fallow-periods due to land shortage, are characteristic. Although many Chiriquí Guaymí live in dispersed hamlets, multiple cognatic-group hamlets, including several generations, are common (Young 1971), and some mixed ladino-Guaymí towns, such as Tolé, have several thousand residents.

(*c*) Sixteenth-century sources corroborate the ethnographic situation. At the time of the Conquest, basic socio-political differences seem to have been reflected in the societies inhabiting either province. A numerous but dispersed population, living in small communities near streams and modest rivers, characterized the central Bocas area around Almirante Bay (Sauer 1969). On the coastal plains of the Pacific, however, early accounts by Espinosa, Andagoya and Oviedo y Valdés mention the presence of politically federated tribes, what we have loosely called chiefdoms, centered in large villages with power vested in chiefs and all sorts of status differences expressed in burial customs, wealth and ritual. Best known among these chiefdoms are the ones in the central provinces of Panama (Cooke 1972; Linares 1975). Although Chiriquí is poor in ethnohistoric accounts, the chroniclers frequently mention chiefs such as Urracá, who twice drove out the Spaniards from the southwestern corner of the Isthmus.

(*d*) Ecological contrasts parallel the ethnohistoric and ethnographic situation (fig. 12). Bocas del Toro is in the *Af* tropics (humid with no pronounced dry season, in Köppen's classification). Rainfall in Bocas averages 3,500 mm. and is distributed fairly evenly throughout the year. As a result of the climate and sparse population, a dense 'mature' forest covers much of the land. Since the Continental Divide extends its northern ridges nearly to the ocean edge, Bocas has no extensive coastal plains. Tidal fluctuations are at a minimum and much of the coast is covered by mangrove vegetation. Except for two large rivers, most of the province is traversed by only small streams. Prehispanic, as well as present-day, Bocas Guaymí have tended to settle on the ridges in back of the central embayments formed by the Bahía de Almirante and the Laguna de Chiriquí.

Unlike Bocas, the Province of Chiriquí is in the *Aw* tropics (tropical climates with a pronounced dry-season). Rainfall averages on the extensive coastal plains between 1,800 and 2,200 mm., of which only one-fourth falls during the night, encouraging rapid evaporation. A marked dry season lasts from mid-December to mid-April. The best lands to farm are the riverine zones where alluvial resources and groundwater often permit year-round cultivation without irrigation. Prehistoric settlements are usually found along these rivers traversing the Chiriquí plains.

In an effort to isolate ecological and social-historical factors that may help explain why, within western Panama, chiefdoms developed in some areas and not in others, we designed a research project comparing archaeological developments in Bocas and Chiriquí (NSF-Gr-2846; for details see the acknowledgements at the end of this paper). A number of linked propositions were formulated at the beginning of the fieldwork and subsequently measured against the archaeological evidence. These propositions can be stated as follows:

(*a*) ethnographic and ethnohistorical differences in settlement and subsistence between Bocas and Chiriquí societies were (were not) corroborated by the archaeological evidence;

(*b*) these differences were (were not) manifested by groups sharing the same material culture and sociopolitical system;

(*c*) these differences can be attributed to the following factors, or to none of the following factors:

(i) unequal resource distribution in either province,

(ii) to the presence of trade on one coast and not the other,

(iii) to the frequency with which these areas were invaded from outside.

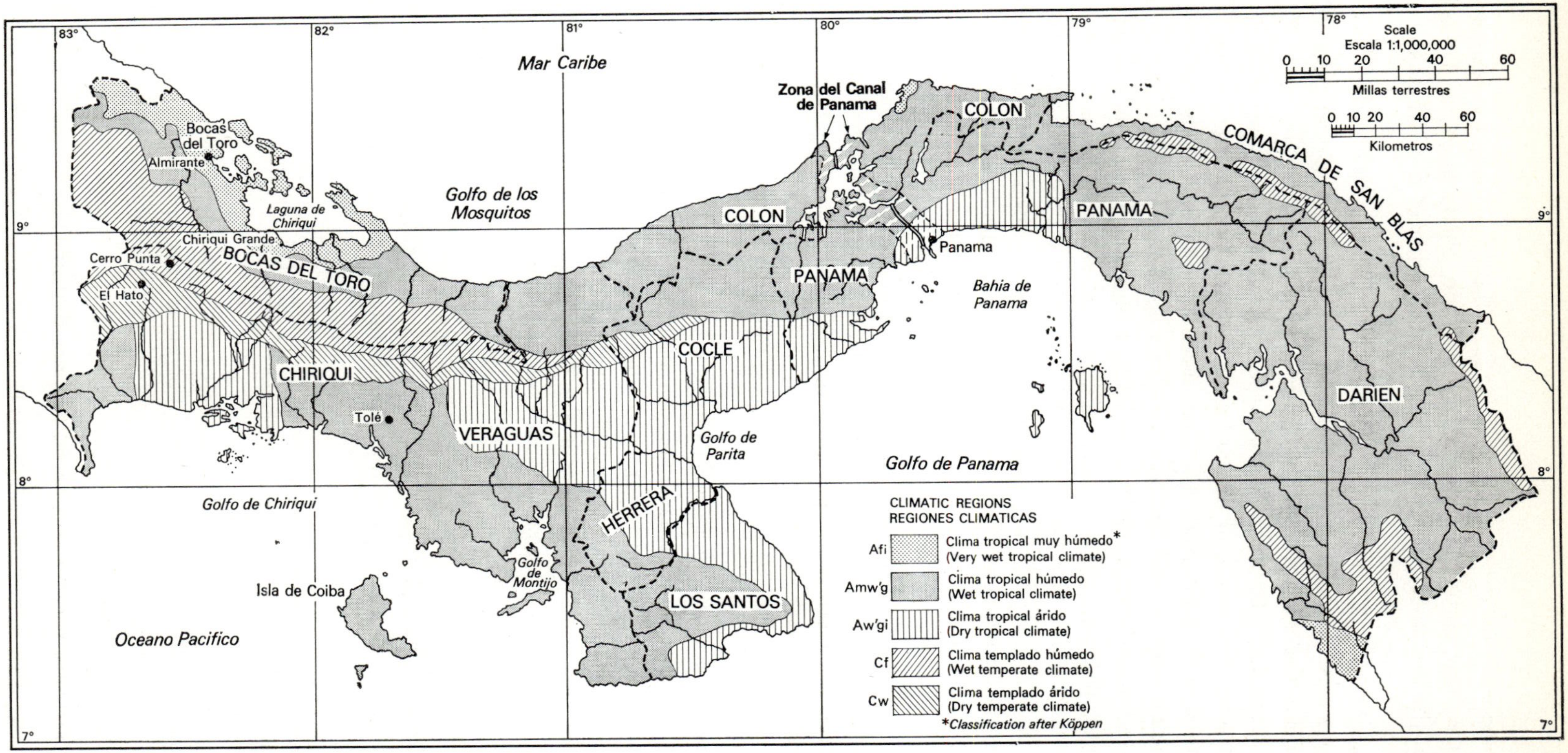

Figure 12 Panama: climatic regions. (After Köppen.)

The prehistory of Bocas and Chiriquí: a comparison of two archaeological sites

Bocas del Toro An intensive survey of the Aguacate Peninsula separating Almirante Bay and the Chiriquí Lagoon (fig. 11) revealed only four very similar widely dispersed archaeological sites in an area 2 × 10 kilometers. Although the possibility that larger sites occur elsewhere in the province cannot be discarded, this peninsula was most definitely sparsely populated.

In 1971 we began excavation at one of the sites called Cerro Brujo (CA-3) on the Aguacate Peninsula. These investigations revealed that the site was once a small hamlet comprised of dwelling localities dispersed along the crest of a ridge, 140 meters above sea level and 3 kilometers inland (Linares and Ranere 1971; Linares 1971). The central part of the Cerro Brujo site was tiny (22 × 36 meters), with smaller middens probably belonging to houses in the same hamlet-unit scattered over a one-kilometer radius. The most recent of the two occupations at Cerro Brujo and related hamlets dated from A.D. 900 (see Appendix) and were also separated by large tracts of uninhabited territory. Overall population density was low; no more than 20 adults per hamlet and an average of 2·5 persons per Km^2 (Linares 1974).

The accumulation of shell in trash middens marking dwelling localities, plus the constant humidity, ensured the preservation of faunal and artefactual remains at Cerro Brujo. These permitted the reconstruction of subsistence patterns based on hunting, fishing and shellfish gathering, in addition to agriculture. Evidence for the restriction of hunting to areas near hamlets and cultivated fields is provided by a large mammalian collection where Agouti (*Dasyprocta punctata*), Paca (*Cuniculus paca*) and Nine-Banded Armadillo (*Dasypus novemcintus*) predominate (Grayson 1973). These are mammals which live in disturbed habitats and eat cultivated crops (Linares 1974). Likewise, the predominant marine fauna represented at the site, with the exception of the green turtle (or *Chelonia*), consisted of species, such as snook (*Centropomus*), grouper or sea bass (*Serranidae*) and snapper (*Lutjanus*), which can be found inshore, near rocky outcrops or on shallow-water reefs. (E. Wing, pers. comm.). Added proof of marine dependence was provided by the mollusk material (Borgogno 1971). All five of the most common shellfish species found at CA-3 are pelecypods with an intertidal shallow-water distribution.

The entire collection of stone artefacts from Cerro Brujo (Rosenthal 1970) show that blades and other hide and woodworking tools predominate in the chipped-stone category. Among the groundstone tools, adzes and celts used for deforestation were most abundant. No maize-processing tools (i.e. manos and metates) came out of 140 meters of excavation. However, a few large mortars were found on the surface of several Aguacate sites. Perhaps these were communal grinding stones.

Chiriquí An intensive survey ot the Chiriquí coast conducted more than a decade ago (Linares 1968) revealed a total of 63 sites. One of these, La Pitahaya (also known as Palenque, or IS-3) was re-excavated more intensively in 1972 in order to obtain information comparable to that from the Cerro Brujo site. Although La Pitahaya is now part of an island (Isla Boca Brava), it was either connected with the mainland 1,000 years ago, or separated from it by a very narrow and protected estuary channel. Hence its geographical location is very similar to that of the Cerro Brujo site. The total surface of both these peninsulas is also comparable (see fig. 11).

La Pitahaya (IS-3) is a very large site, larger than most of the Chiriquí coastal sites, but well within the mean size for occupations on that coast around A.D. 900. Unlike the small and discrete shell-middens that constitute the Cerro Brujo site, those that make up IS-3 are large mounds, seven in total, averaging 20 × 40 meters in size, and rising at least 4 meters in height. Between these mounds, we found a continuous surface spread of cultural materials covering an area 300 by 500 meters. Apparently, every so often this material was swept up, and together with angular rocks and large boulders, was used to construct these artificial mounds. At the site of these mounds special activities, associated with the carved basalt columns on top and the burials at the bottom, were probably conducted. Other activity areas consisted of flat living areas covered by refuse, stone circles with more carved basalt columns, and a cemetery which was not excavated.

In La Pitahaya we have a large, residentially concentrated community, ten to fifteen times larger and internally more complex than Cerro Brujo. The main occupation spanned the centuries between A.D. 760 and A.D. 1075 (see Appendix). A conservative estimate for the population living at any one time in the half-kilometer area covered by refuse remains would be around 500 persons. Widespread trade connections with the Nicoya Peninsula in Costa Rica, and with the Azuero-Parita Bay zone in the Central Panamanian provinces, is suggested by foreign ceramics.

The large quantity of celts and adzes that came out of the nearly 100 cubic meters excavated at IS-3 leave little doubt that this was a predominantly agricultural society. Although more precise knowledge of the swidden-system awaits further palynological evidence, the agricultural practices represented probably involved kitchen-gardens near the households, with milpa fields on the rest of Isla Brava, and possibly also on the mainland. Preliminary pollen analysis of a core from near the site 'shows changes in relative pollen frequencies of grasses, chenoams, composites, and forest elements that suggest extensive human-induced vegetational changes' (West ms. 1972). The abundance of *manos* and *metates*, the classic maize-processing tools of the New World, suggests that this crop was probably grown for tribute and for trade, in addition to being the most important food consumed.

Other subsistence activities besides agriculture appear to have been secondary at La Pitahaya. Shellfish remains at the entire site amounted to less than 5 kilograms (compared with hundreds of kilograms per excavation level at CA-3), and mammal bones to less than 100 specimens (compared with 1,400 at CA-3). A very different marine fauna from that of Cerro Brujo is also represented at IS-3 (E. Wing, pers. comm.). The occupants of La Pitahaya were therefore predominantly agriculturalists, with marine fishing as their main source of animal protein.

To conclude this brief description, we should reiterate the fact that important differences in size, type, and complexity distinguish archaeological sites in Bocas del Toro from those in Chiriquí province. We cannot, of course, exclude the possibility that larger sites, in addition to the four sites encountered in Bocas and the 63 surveyed in Chiriquí, exist in either province. The available evidence, however, does indicate that Cerro Brujo and Isla Palenque were fairly typical of settlement and subsistence patterns in both lagoon-estuary systems between A.D. 900 and A.D. 1000. The Cerro Brujo inhabitants grew root crops and relied heavily on hunting and marine fishing for their animal protein supply. The occupants of La Pitahaya were intensive maize cultivators with less fishing and very little hunting.

Besides differences in subsistence, there were obvious contrasts in settlement patterns between Bocas and Chiriquí. These have already been discussed, so they need no further mention, except to note that dissimilar social and political systems may have been represented by groups on the two coasts. The archaeological settlements of Bocas province appear to represent marginal populations organized on the basis of small family (?) groups, without status differentiation or political centralization of any recognizable kind. In contrast, the whole of La Pitahaya appears to have been a paramount chief's village, also serving as a ceremonial and trading center.

Determining the preceramic and formative origins of western Panamanian cultures

The oldest archaeological occupations in western Panama are found on the highlands separating Bocas and Chiriquí provinces (see fig. 11). Here, at elevations between 800 and 1,000 meters on the southern slope of the Continental Divide, Ranere (1972, 1975, 1976) has excavated a number of rock shelters in the canyon of the Chiriquí River (Linares and Ranere 1971). From the beginning of the fifth millennium B.C. to the beginning of the third millennium B.C. hunting-and-gathering appears to have been the most important adaptation. Agriculture, probably based on root and tree crops and processed by cobble edge-grinders and boulder milling stones, came in gradually around 3000 B.C. A third adaptive pattern, one based on maize agriculture and accompanied by pottery, had replaced the previous system by 350 B.C. This pottery, which is fairly sophisticated in its modeled-incised decoration, duplicates many (though by no means all) of the ceramic types that characterize the numerous agricultural villages nearby in the Volcán Barú area (Linares, Sheets and Rosenthal 1975).

The Volcán Barú occupations consist of 45 single-component village sites within a 62 km^2 area encompassing two highland basins, El Hato and Cerro Punta (Linares, Sheets and Rosenthal 1975). Thirteen radiocarbon dates place the Volcán occupations between 600 B.C. and A.D. 600, with some continuity before and after. A coherent stylistic tradition, employing decorative plastic motifs in the pottery, is represented at all these sites.

The oldest occupations found in the sites of the Atlantic and Pacific sectors of western Panama, including Cerro Brujo and La Pitahaya, are characterized by ceramics that are very similar to those from Volcán Barú. These ceramics occur in comparable circumstances on both coasts: they are always found in the lowest levels of habitation sites; they are not associated with shellfish remains, such as characterize the latter occupations; they duplicate the specific decorative techniques and clear-cut shapes represented in Volcán ceramics (negative painting, zone bichroming, excision with white paint, 'Venus' tripods, etc.); they are assumed to date from A.D. 300 to A.D. 600; and finally, they are separated from the Volcán sites by very short distances. However, some dissimilarities, actual or potential, are also encountered: some, but not *all*, of the specific decorative motifs found in the Volcán pottery are found in Chiriquí and Bocas sites; other ceramics, besides the ones described, occur in the oldest levels of the Chiriquí sites; the artefactual inventory accompanying the ceramics was very poor, forcing these comparisons to rest solely on pottery; even the pottery occurs in small quantities (i.e. the sample-size rarely exceeds 100 sherds per excavation unit).

Furthermore, the Volcán sites are not isolated. They form part of a widespread Middle to Late Formative tradition with a fairly wide geographical distribution: from southeastern Nicaragua (Snarskis 1975), to the Nicoya Peninsula of Costa Rica (Coe and Baudez 1961), to the central and southeastern Costa Rican highlands (Aguilar 1972, Haberland 1969), and finally to the central provinces of Panama (Stirling and Stirling 1964b). In all these areas the ceramics share indisputable and close similarities. This can be explained either by a spread of techniques over a distance of 700 Km in the period between 300 B.C. and A.D. 600, or by a migration of peoples.

Comments on a model of 'adaptive radiation' in western Panama

The idea of a common origin for the coastal Chiriquí and Bocas populations rests on evidence that is suggestive, but also inconclusive and difficult to evaluate. In favor of the 'common heritage' hypothesis are similar ceramics, similar stratigraphic contexts for these ceramics, good chronological overlap, clear-cut antecedents in the highlands, mid-way between both areas and a few days walking from each. In addition, the oldest Chiriquí and Bocas occupations appear to represent the remains of swidden agriculturalists who had not yet begun to exploit littoral resources. The limitations of our data, however, are equally inescapable. There is almost exclusive reliance on ceramics during the earlier periods which are usually characterized by poor preservation and/or absence of accompanying cultural materials. Also, the presence of other pottery types in the oldest Chiriquí occupation suggests that other groups, besides our supposed migrants from the highlands, may have been present from the beginning. This is important in view of competition theory. Moreover, the Volcán ceramics, as well as those from the Bocas and Chiriquí coastal sites, have widespread counterparts elsewhere, so their area of origin cannot be really pin-pointed with exactitude. Finally, intermediate settlements have been located in the areas between highlands and coast on the Chiriquí, but not the Bocas, side.

Assuming for the moment that we can prove beyond reasonable doubt the fact of colonization by migrants from the nearby highlands, we are still confronted with numerous questions. What, indeed, were the circumstances surrounding this event? Were social causes (crowding, conflict), natural factors (volcanic activity, soil depletion), or a combination of these, reponsible for the moves? Did a massive migration take place suddenly, or did families 'trickle off' to the coast? What were the social and ecological conditions in the areas of migration at that time? These questions are crucial to an understanding of adaptive strategies, human or otherwise, anywhere at anytime. Unfortunately, very few of them can be answered by quantitative archaeological evidence alone. In the last analysis, informed qualitative judgement, being recognized for what it is, must prevail in some instances.

To take up our Panamanian example once again, the evidence for purposeful group-migration looks very doubtful indeed, especially on the Chiriquí side where a number of other sites containing early Volcán-like materials have been found on the plains half-way between mountains and coastal edge. These cover a long period (300 B.C. to A.D. 600), and suggested that people spent a long time moving down, assuming that the prevailing movement was from highland to coast. On the Bocas side, a very wet cloud-forest separates the highlands from the coastal ridges. No archaeological sites have been reported from this mid-way area. Here it looks as if small groups did, indeed, move down purposefully to colonize the area around the central embayment. This area offered splendid opportunities for the utilization of marine resources, but obvious drawbacks to some types of agriculture (discussed later). Their movement appears late (after A.D. 500) and deliberate. They seem to have encountered at least a partially vacant area.

As to the causes of the movements outlined above we must rely on the fact that warring chiefdoms and crowded villages characterized the Basin of El Hato by A.D. 300 (Linares, Sheets and Rosenthal 1975). Population densities, however, had by no means reached the maximum carrying capacity of Cerro Punta, the closest highland valley to the Atlantic or Bocas side, before depopulation had occurred. Unpalatable as I have always found most 'catastrophic' explanations for migration, the possibility that Bocas was settled by refugees from volcanic activities cannot be discarded. On the other hand, population pressures on scarce resources, or all of these factors are equally satisfactory (or equally unsatisfactory) as explanations for the Chiriquí migrations. Indeed, if we want to be slightly perverse and unrelentingly contrary we may say that such migrations did not take place at all, and that the highlands and coast of Panama were populated gradually and simultaneously by people from Nicaragua and Costa Rica. This would mean ignoring all radiocarbon dates and getting people to come into the Isthmus from far away, rather than near at hand. As a hypothesis it may be uneconomical, but it is by no means impossible.

In fact, for those archaeologists who may be more inclined than I to see ecology as the overriding force in all human adaptations, our attempts to establish migration and divergence from a common culture may seem a sterile exercise. All that matters, they would say, is that both areas differed in ecology as well as in cultural content (a comment made by William T. Sanders during the oral presentation of this paper). Perhaps such an objection can be met by making a distinction between adaptive *variation* and adaptive *radiation*. The former concentrates on the end-products of evolution, the latter on the processes. If processes of culture change are to be gauged, evaluated or even described, the initial state of the culture must be known. This seems obvious, but it is often ignored by archaeologists.

Now, if one were willing to gloss over some of the difficulties, to close one's eyes and arrange the data here and there, it would indeed be possible to come up with a more or less elegant model of 'adaptive radiation' in western Panama. One would initially compare the ecologies of both areas in times past, and then evaluate the changes that had to be made by migrants to either coast. The model, or explanation, would proceed as follows:

To begin with, going to the coast meant a different shift in ecology for each group. From the small, fertile, cold and mountainous highland valleys, where animal protein may have been the limiting factor, the Bocas migrants entered an area of unlimited marine and terrestrial protein, but of restricted agricultural opportunities. The migrants that opted for the Chiriquí coast encountered *both* rich estuarine resources and good farming land. The shift in habitat for the Bocas migrants also meant going from an area of moderate habitat diversity (Volcán), to an area with few differences in resource distribution due to the even climate and the absence of alluvial areas. The Chiriquí groups in turn encountered an area with extreme contrast and marked seasonal oscillations in rains and tides.

These differences in ecologies and resource distribution encouraged the development of two different agricultural systems. The first, known as vegeculture, or root-crop agriculture, is based on the cultivation of tubers and rhizome-bearing plants (manioc, sweet potatoes, *Xanthossoma*, the *Discoreas*). The second, a seed-culture, was based principally on maize, and secondarily on beans and squash. The limitations of both systems have been discussed by Harris (1972, 1973). In Bocas, where the rainforest still prevails, the restrictions imposed by burning, and conversely the ease with which the soil may be turned and plowed in the vegetative planting process, may have encouraged the adoption of a root crop system to the detriment of maize agriculture. The reverse may have happened in Chiriquí, with the intensification of seed-culture at the expense of other subsistence techniques.

Not only do vegeculture and seed culture have different ecological requirements, but they also have different ecological impacts. To quote Harris (1973: 403), vegeculture has 'greater ecological stability, and this tendency is accentuated by the fact that opportunities for soil erosion are reduced because the soil is more completely and continuously shielded by plant cover.' Seed-cultural systems have the quality of being unstable, leading to ecosystem breakdowns by encouraging open canopy structures that accelerate weed invasion and erosion. 'Seed crop swidden systems, which are ecologically less stable and dietetically more self-sufficient than vegecultural systems are likely to have expanded territorially and gradually gained spatial ascendancy over vegeculture' (*ibid.*: 405). Hence, we may have here an explanation for the expansion of peoples, or of techniques, in western Panama.

Further, one could add to the explanation, or model, by observing that if maize agriculture permitted a greater degree of intensification and increased production than would be possible with most root crops alone, it also facilitated unequal distribution of resources. For maize could only be grown successfully the year round along the moist and fertile edges of large and meandering coastal rivers. In these well-endowed areas, competition over prime riverine areas increased with the population. Crowded conditions encouraged nucleated settlements, the evolution of social differences, trade and war. La Pitahaya may be taken as an example of the kind of society that resulted when these positive feedbacks were set in motion.

Finally, the model I have just put together from the writings of Carneiro (1960, 1961), Chagnon (1968) and Harris (1973) can also accommodate some competition theory. People could be said to have moved from an area of much intraethnic competition (in Volcán between Cerro Punta and El Hato societies), to a vacant area with less competition in one direction (Bocas), and to an area of intense competition between chiefdoms in another direction (Chiriquí). Other shifts that could be reconstructed, if one were willing to speculate endlessly, would involve moving from areas of respectively more and less resource concentration, more and less isolation, more and less trading opportunities, more and less agricultural possibilities, and perhaps more and less disease vectors.

Summary remarks

This essay has considered an example of human adaptive radiation in western Panama. It began with the current ethnography of the Guaymí, an Indian population of the Isthmus, living in two ecologically contrastive provinces of Bocas del Toro on the Atlantic side, and Chiriquí on the Pacific. Differences in settlement-subsistence adaptations between the rainforest-dwelling Bocas Guaymí and the Guaymí on the drier Pacific slope of Chiriquí were traced back to ethnohistoric and late prehistoric (e.g. after A.D. 600) times. The following explanation for differential adaptations was advanced:

(*a*) different segments of the same prehistoric population migrated from the intervening highlands to either of the two coastal lowlands;

(*b*) in the process of migration and adaptation, each of these groups developed contrasting adaptations in accordance with existing differences in the geography and ecology of Bocas versus Chiriquí;

(*c*) vegeculture, the agriculture system developed by the Bocas groups, encouraged population displacement, small group-size and outside reliance on hunting and fishing;

(*d*) seed-culture, as adopted by the Chiriquí Guaymí, permitted intensification, independence from other protein sources and a greater degree of sociopolitical elaboration.

Although there is good evidence to show that contrasting adaptive strategies were developed a long time ago by groups inhabiting either coast of western Panama, the ecological explanation offered for the evolution of sociopolitical differences is felt to be oversimplified. Certainly, natural factors could not be separated from social factors in this example of adaptive processes. Warfare, trade, the lure of perceived possibilities, sheer human resourcefulness, all may have been involved in the evolution of social differences in western Panama. Generally speaking, by emphasizing external circumstances, we may be ignoring just those elements that have made the human species capable of invading every conceivable habitat: our capacity to symbolize, and the intellectual systems (religious and political) that we have developed to cope with each other. At the same time, archaeology may have received the uneasy task of describing obvious events in human history, while leaving the more subtle – and often the more interesting – aspects of human behavior to social anthropologists, psychologists and other social scientists.

Acknowledgements

The research project, which has provided much of the basic information in this article, was entitled 'Archaeological Investigations in Panama: A Comparison of Settlement and Subsistence in Bocas and Chiriquí', and was financed by the National Science Foundation (Gr-2846) for three years (1970–2). The Smithsonian Tropical Research Institute financed the 1973 survey of Bocas conducted by the author. A large number of colleagues and graduate students have participated in the project through the years. Involved in the excavations during one or several seasons were: Anthony J. Ranere (field director, 1970 and 1971), Irene Borgogno (1970–1) E. Jane Rosenthal (1970, 1971, 1972), Máximo Miranda (1970), John Alden (1971), Payson Sheets (field director, 1972), Francine Sheets, Bruce Dahlin, Sara Spang, Robert McNealy (all 1972).

C. Earle Smith (botany), Philip D. Young (ethnography), Donald K. Grayson (faunal analysis) and James West (palynology) served as consultants. While in Panama we received the kind cooperation of Reina Torres de Araúz, Directora del Patrimonio Histórico, Marcela Camargo, Directora del Museo Nacional and her staff, and Martin H. Moynihan and Ira Rubinoff of the Smithsonian Tropical Research Institute.

1.viii.1976

Smithsonian Tropical Research Institute
Balbao, Canal Zone

References

Aguilar, C. H. 1972. *Guayabo de Turrialba: arqueología de un sitio indígena prehispánico*. San José: Editorial Costa Rica.

Andagoya, P. de. 1829. Relación de los sucesos de Pedrarias Davila en las provincias de Tierra Firme o Castilla del Oro. *Fernández de Navarrete*. 3. Madrid.

Borgogno, I. 1971. Mollusk remains from Cerro Brujo. (Mimeographed report.) Philadelphia: University of Pennyslvania.

Carneiro, R. L. 1960. Slash and burn cultivation: a closer look at its implications for settlement patterns. *Men and Cultures*, pp. 229–43 (ed. A. F. C. Wallace). In Philadelphia: Selected Papers of the Fifth International Congress of Anthropological and Ethnological Sciences.

Carneiro, R. L. 1961. Slash-and-burn cultivation among the Kuikuru and its implications for cultural development in the Amazon Basin. In *The Evolution of Horticultural Systems in Native South America: causes and consequences: a symposium*, pp. 47–67 (ed. J. Wilbert). Caracas: Antropológica, Supplement Publicat. No. 2.

Chagnon, N. 1968. The culture-ecology of shifting (pioneering) cultivation among the Yanömamo Indians. *Proceedings of the VIIth International Congress of Anthropological and Ethnological Sciences*. Reprinted 1973 in *Peoples and Cultures of South America*, pp. 126–42 (ed. D. R. Gross.) Garden City, New York: The Natural History Press.

Coe, M. D. and Baudez, C. F. 1961. The zoned bichrome period in northwestern Costa Rica. *American Antiquity*. 26:505–15.

Cowgill, G. 1975. On causes and consequences of ancient and modern population changes. *American Anthropologist*. 77:505–25.

Cooke, R. G. 1972. *The Archaeology of Western Coclé Province, Panamá.* Unpublished PhD dissertation, University of London.

Diamond, J. M. 1973. Distributional ecology of New Guinea birds. *Science.* 179:259–69.

Eggan, F. 1954. Social anthropology and the method of controlled comparison. *American Anthropologist.* 56:743–63.

Espinosa, G. de. 1864. Relación hecha por Gaspar de Espinosa, Alcalde Mayor de Castilla del Oro, dada a Pedrarias de Avila. *Colección de documentos inéditos del archivo de Indias*, p. 467 (ed. D. F. Pacheco and Cárdenas, and Mendoza, imprenta de B. Quirós, Tomo 2). Madrid. 1873, second expedition, 1519. *Colección de documentos inéditos de Indias*, Tomo XX. Madrid.

Gordon, B. Leroy. 1969. *Anthropogeography and Rainforest Ecology in Bocas del Toro Province, Panamá.* Berkeley: Department of Geography, University of California.

Grayson, D. K. 1973. On the methodology of faunal analysis. *American Antiquity.* 38.

Haberland, W. 1969. Early phases and their relationship in southern Central America. *38th International Congress of Americanists.* I:229–42. Stuttgart and Munich.

Hamilton, T. 1967. *Process and Pattern in Evolution.* New York: Macmillan.

Harris, D. R. 1971. The ecology of swidden cultivation in the upper Orinoco rain forest, Venezuela. *The Geographical Review.* 61:475–95.

Harris, D. R. 1972. Swidden systems and settlement. In *Man, Settlement and Urbanism*, pp. 245–62 (eds P. J. Ucko, R. Tringham and G. W. Dimbleby). London: Gerald Duckworth & Co.

Harris, D. R. 1972. The origin of agriculture in the tropics. *American Scientist.* 60:180–93.

Harris, D. R. 1973. The prehistory of tropical agriculture: an ethnoecological model. In *The Explanation of Culture Change*, pp. 391–417 (ed. C. Renfrew). London: G. Duckworth & Co. Ltd.

Kottak, C. P. 1971. Cultural adaptation, kinship and descent in Madagascar. *Southwestern Journal of Anthropology.* 27:129–47.

Kottak, C. P. 1972. A cultural adaptive approach to Malagasy political organization. In *Social Exchange and Interaction*, pp. 107–47 (ed. E. N. Wilmsen). Anthropological Papers no. 46. University of Michigan: Museum of Anthropology.

Lewis, H. S. 1968. Typology and process in political evolution. *Essays on the Problem of Tribe: Proceedings of the 1967 Annual Spring Meeting of the American Ethnological Society*, pp. 101–10. Seattle: University of Washington Press.

Linares, O. F. 1968. Cultural chronology of the Gulf of Chiriquí, Panamá. *Smithsonian Contributions in Anthropology.* 8:1–119.

Linares, O. F. 1971. Cerro Brujo, a tiny Guaymí hamlet of the past. *Expedition.* 13:27–35.

Linares, O. F. in press (*a*). Garden-hunting in the American tropics. *Human Ecology.*

Linares, O. F. in press (*b*). *Ecology and the Arts in Central Panamá: on the development of social rank and symbolism in the central provinces.* Studies in Pre-Columbian Art and Archaeology. 17. Dumbarton-Oaks, Washington D.C.

Linares, O. F. and Ranere, A. J. 1971. Human adaptations to the tropical forests of western Panamá. *Archaeology*. 24:346–55.

Linares, O. F., Sheets, P. and Rosenthal, E. J. 1975. Prehistoric agriculture in tropical highlands. *Science*. 187:137–45.

MacArthur, R. H. and Wilson, E. O. 1967. *The Theory of Island Biogeography*. Princeton, N.J.: Princeton University Press.

Oviedo y Valdés, G. F. de. 1944. *Historia general y natural de las Indias, 1526*. 7: Capítulo XXVI. Urguay: Editorial Guarania.

Ranere, A. J. 1972. *Early Human Adaptations to the New World Tropical Forest: the view from Panamá*. Unpublished PhD dissertation, University of California (Davis).

Ranere, A. J. 1975. Toolmaking and tool use among the preceramic peoples of Panamá. In *Lithic Technology: making and using stone tools*, pp. 173–209 (ed. E. Swanson). The Hague: Mouton.

Ranere, A. J. 1976. The preceramic of Panamá: the view from the interior. In *Proceedings of the first Puerto Rican Symposium on Archaeology*, report No. 1, pp. 103–37 (ed. L. S. Robinson). San Juan: Fundación Arqueológica, Antropológica e Histórica de Puerto Rico.

Rosenthal, E. J. 1970. *Preliminary Analysis of the Stone Artifacts of Cerro Brujo, Site CA-3, Bocas del Toro, Panamá*. Unpublished senior thesis, pp. 1–51. University of Pennsylvania (Anthropology Department).

Sahlins, M. D. 1958. *Social Stratification in Polynesia*. Seattle: University of Washington Press.

Sanders, W. T. and Marino, J. 1970. *New World Prehistory: archaeology of the American Indian*. Englewood Cliffs, N.J.: Prentice-Hall, Inc.

Sauer, C. O. 1969. *The Early Spanish Main*. Berkeley and Los Angeles: University of California Press.

Snarskis, M. J. 1975. Work noted in Current research report for Central America (ed. O. Linares). *American Antiquity*. 40:2:1:239–40.

Stirling, M. and Stirling, M. 1964a. Archaeological notes on Almirante Bay, Bocas del Toro, Panamá. *Anthropological Papers No. 72, B.A.E. Bulletin*, pp. 255–85. Washington, D.C.: U.S. Government Printing Office.

Stirling, M. and Stirling, M. 1964b. El Limon, an early tomb site in Cocle Province, Panamá. *Anthropological Papers No. 71, B.A.E. Bulletin*, pp. 247–54. Washington, D.C.: U.S. Government Printing Office.

West, J. G. 1972. Sediment analysis of a core from Isla Palenque, Panamá. (Mimeographed paper.) University of California, Berkeley: Geology (218).

Young, P. D. 1971. Ngawbe: tradition and change among the western Guaymí of Panamá. *Illinois Studies in Anthropology, No. 7*. Urbana, Chicago and London: University of Illinois Press.

Appendix

Radiocarbon dates for the most recent of the two occupations at Cerro Brujo and La Pitahaya

(*a*) *Cerro Brujo* (CA-3)

970 ± 90 radiocarbon years B.P.: A.D. 980 (I–5326)
965 ± 90 radiocarbon years B.P.: A.D. 985 (I–5327)
990 ± 90 radiocarbon years B.P.: A.D. 960 (I–5328)
990 ± 90 radiocarbon years B.P.: A.D. 960 (I–5329)
990 ± 90 radiocarbon years B.P.: A.D. 960 (I–5330)

(*b*) *La Pitahaya* (IS-3)

1190 ± 100 radiocarbon years B.P.: A.D. 760 (M–1470)
1120 ± 150 radiocarbon years B.P.: A.D. 830 (I–5767)
1120 ± 170 radiocarbon years B.P.: A.D. 830 (I–5879)
875 ± 90 radiocarbon years B.P.: A.D. 1075 (I–5766)

Abstract

Olga F. Linares

Adaptive strategies in western Panama

An example of prehistoric 'adaptive radiation' in western Panama is explored by comparing two allotropic types of tropical forest agriculturalists: those occupying the Bocas del Toro province on the Atlantic side of the isthmus and those living in Chiriquí province on the Pacific side. The two populations appear to be descended from common ancestors who once settled the highlands separating these two coastal provinces. Using the method of controlled comparison and the biological concept of radiation, the possible effects of the vegeculture and seed culture agricultural systems of these peoples on their social and political arrangements are explored. The model developed during the course of discussion is parallel to models built by biogeographers to deal with processes of migration, colonization, population change, divergence and adaptation in the humid versus the seasonal tropics.

Biogeographical theory and cultural analogies

Jonathan D. Sauer

Introduction

As an animal species, *Homo sapiens* fits readily under general biogeographical theory. Since Darwin, physical anthropologists and zoologists have freely exchanged ideas about genetic adaptation, competition, resource exploitation and demographic processes. Such pooling of biological theory based on homologies between species scarcely needs to be promoted here. The purpose of the conference for which this paper was written, as I understand it, was rather to examine biogeographical theory for possible provocative cultural analogies. For example, concepts of species migration may suggest a new slant on cultural diffusion; ideas about ecosystems and regional associations of species may offer parallels with economic systems or culture complexes. As a biogeographer I wish I could offer here a body of elegant and stimulating theory. My role instead will be to warn readers against treating our conceptual models – many of which are very weak – with more respect than they deserve.

The weaknesses of modern biogeographical theory are several. There are, for instance, only a handful of academics primarily concerned with biotic distributions. While many taxonomists and ecologists have geographical interests, they also have hundreds of thousands of species with which to cope. Plant geography, my own speciality, resembles the study of anthropology back when large regions of the world were the domain of individual ethnologists and archaeologists. Most biogeographers are still too absorbed in field exploration to have much time for general theory. Separate scholarly traditions within biogeography have not yet been integrated into a coherent body of thought, even though individual scholars commonly use several traditional approaches in their own work. Specifically, museum and mathematical biogeography each have different sets of concepts which have little connection with those used in field biogeography. Moreover, some schools of biogeography are still in the primitive state of confusing *a priori* assumptions with tested theory and of accepting deductive explanations without investigating the presumed processes involved.

The picture I will sketch of biogeography, however will not be all dark. An increasing emphasis on ecology is enabling field biogeographers, like modern archaeologists, to elucidate evolutionary and migrational processes. In the discussions to follow, however, I shall save the best for last.

Museum biogeography

Distributional knowledge of most species depends on expert identifications of collections accumulated in the world's herbaria and zoological museums. As a rule, specimen collections comprise a sample too spotty to be of use in detecting anything more than broad geographical patterns and major species migrations. Like the 'ethnographic present,' collections spanning decades or even centuries are commonly treated as if they were contemporaneous. Habitat data are usually scanty and unstandardized. It is no wonder that biogeographical patterns perceived from such evidence are often accounted for by simplistic, deductive explanations. In particular, museum biogeographers have tended to postulate grand causes in the dim past: tectonic and macro-climatic changes have been especially favored by many scholars. Little thought has been given to the likelihood that species distributions might be related to ordinary, current processes.

The concept of Pleistocene refugia is a case in point. This concept rests on the assumption that present biotic distributions can be used to deduce ancient distributions. Such an assumption, however, is only reasonable if modern distributions are mystically controlled by past, not present, environmental circumstances. Yet postulating Pleistocene refugia is an old and still active academic tradition (e.g. Lindroth 1970, Meggers 1975, Müller, 1973 Seddon 1971, Vuilleumier 1971).

Deducing Glacial Age refugia is a special case of what may be termed the 'distribution cycle model,' which asserts that species are supposed to spread gradually and coherently outward from a point of origin until they reach a limit at which some gross environmental change forces them to retreat – usually to disjunct relic areas and ultimately to extinction. In the primitive 'age-area' version of this model, the earth is treated as a nearly featureless plain. Hedged with qualifications and complications, such a model has been taught in standard textbooks for decades (e.g. Cain 1944, Good 1947, Seddon 1971).

The assumption that species with similar present distributions have had similar migrational histories is the basis of the voluminous literature on floristic and faunistic 'elements'. In the absence of historical or fossil evidence, such an assumption may be the most plausible one we can make. When such evidence is present, nevertheless, it seldom turns out that this assumption is correct. For example, fossil floras of the Tertiary in western North America indicate that species with similar ranges at a given time level commonly had derived from quite different source regions and in later times they commonly went separate ways (Axelrod 1973). Need it be added that, as for cultural analogies, the primitive concept of deducing origins and past diffusion routes for culture traits solely from present distributions is surely of little interest to anthropologists, least of all to archaeologists?

Multiple, independent origins for a species, unlike a culture trait, are not ordinarily considered a serious possibility. When a species is found to have a disjunct distribution, the normal assumption made is that the fragmentation in its range is due either to retreat or long-range dispersal. Many authors (e.g. Seddon 1971, Tivy 1971) discount the importance of long-range dispersal in biogeographical distributions and regard disjunct patterns as relictual survivals of once coherent ranges. As Polunin (1960) notes, however, either retreat or long-range dispersal may be the most plausible hypothesis in a specific case and historically documented species migrations show innumerable examples of both processes.

Advocacy of a single model, to the exclusion of alternatives, has also hindered investigation of the process of speciation. A hundred years after Darwin many biologists still do not regard the origin of species as a normal consequence of adaptation to diverse environments. Instead they invoke fortuitous, extrinsic events to initiate divergence of related species from their common ancestor when its range became fragmented, or when long-range dispersal led to the isolation of colonists from their parental range. In other words, many biologists believe that spatial barriers dividing a species into non-interbreeding populations are necessary to cause speciation; divergent evolution due to ecological factors is secondary (MacArthur and Wilson 1967; Mayr 1966). This so-called allopatric or geographic speciation model is still the most widely held concept of speciation. An analogy in the study of man would be the belief that spatial isolation and cessation of all contact are essential for the evolution of different languages. Alternative hypotheses about speciation, however, do exist; they have been developed by biogeographers outside museums.

Mathematical biogeography

As museum collections accumulated, regional contrasts in species richness or 'diversity' became apparent. Various mathematical indices have been proposed to compare such geographic diversity, but most of these measures require data that are rarely obtained (Krebs 1972; Peet 1974). Thus comparative studies are generally based on simple counts of species lists from conveniently defined regions, often islands or political units. Areas with high diversity commonly have been assumed to be ancient evolutionary centers. The relatively high diversity of tropical biotas has elicited many explanations (Baker 1970; Krebs 1972; Pianka 1966).

Species counts for islands have long attracted special attention from biogeographers. When the number of species observed is plotted logarithmically as a function of island area, the regression obtained often approaches a straight line – provided the islands are similar enough in climate, topography and location. Fresh interest in this familiar species-area curve has been generated by the hypothesis that, given enough time, the number of species on an island will become constant due to a dynamic equilibrium between species immigration and extinction. The immigration rate is assumed to be an inverse function of distance from the source of immigrants, and the extinction rate is assumed to be an inverse function of island size (MacArthur and Wilson 1967). In original formulations of this idea, island area was offered as a poor but easily measured surrogate for habitat diversity. More recently area has been proposed as actually controlling species numbers directly (Simberloff 1974).

This so-called theory is often credited with starting a revolution in biogeography. To me, however, it seems more like a counter-revolution, a reversion to the time before serious study of ecological and evolutionary processes. I believe this equilibrium model would be taken less seriously if its assumptions were fully recognized. It stipulates a fixed cast of characters, i.e. a constant pool of species capable of reaching a given island. No new species may enter the system either by evolution or inter-regional migration. No species may become extinct in the region as a whole. Immigration and extinction are defined in terms of islands as census sampling-tracts. Immigration is interpreted as local absence in one census and presence in another; extinction is the reverse. In other words, the model predicts the consequences of temporary fluctuations in distribution and abundance within a system in which nothing new is happening. The model was obviously suggested by patterns of continuous species turnover revealed by successive bird counts in the same areas or on the same islands. Beyond the study of ornithology, biogeography generally lacks the manpower needed to keep track of such ephemeral changes. In other fields of biogeography, the terms 'immigration' and 'extinction' are reserved for more consequential events, precisely those that are excluded from the equilibrium model.

An analogous model in anthropology might be one predicting that the number of different kinds of artifacts to be found within a village should equilibrate at a number that is a function of the size and isolation of the village in question. A smaller, more remote village would have fewer kinds of artefacts. In such a model it would be assumed that the villages being compared all were located within a homogeneous region that was tied together internally by regular trade but was sealed off from the world outside. It would also be stipulated that there was no invention or loss of traits within the region as a whole. The lists of kinds of artefacts in each village would vary among the censuses because of vagaries of trade and consumption; however, the total number would remain constant.

I should think that the last thing culture historians could use is an equilibrium model of a self-regulating system with negative feedbacks from any increases in diversity. By definition, such a model is incapable of explaining any important change over time.

Plant and animal ecologists use many mathematical models in dealing with species and habitat patterns. They have developed rigorous methods for population sampling, quantitative analysis, and for inferring relations among variables. So far, however, the results have been like an accumulation of bricks of odd shapes and sizes that have not been cemented together into an architecture. Statistical methods are used to generate *ad hoc* hypotheses rather than to test broad theory. As a consequence, empirical findings apply only within the populations sampled – which are usually delimited arbitrarily – and there is no justification for extrapolation to other geographic regions or to other groups of organisms. Eventually it may be that accretion of such studies will lead to inductive generalizations, but this outcome will require more comparability and less virtuosity in methodology than currently prevails. The present situation within biogeography is analogous to those archaeological endeavors based on quantitative analyses of artefacts which are done without the specification of any theory to be evaluated.

Ecosystem classification

Most ecologists and biogeographers are concerned not only with indices of diversity and other mathematical abstractions, but also with the actual distribution patterns of organisms and habitats. The traditional approach to these patterns has involved classification of ecosystems on the basis of a combination of vegetational and environmental criteria which are usually vague to begin with. Major units, commonly called formations or biomes, are taken from folk usage: e.g. selva, chaparral, mangrove swamp, boreal forest and tundra. These units are usually subdivided on the basis of conspicuous or abundant plant taxa: e.g. pinyon-juniper woodland, palm savanna and cattail marsh. Animal associations seldom enter into definitions of ecosystem types, except in benthic marine communities. More formal ecosystem classifications have been proposed but these are as bewilderingly complicated as Christian sects and heresies (Whittaker 1962). I doubt that these offer much of theoretical interest to anthropology. Such formal classifications are more concerned with the definition of types than with the processes shaping them.

The classical, informal classification of so-called natural vegetation formations remains the standard introduction to world ecosystems (e.g. Colinvaux 1973, Walter 1973, Whittaker 1975). This classification is accompanied by a coherent theory: the distribution of ecosystem types is thought to be controlled by a hierarchy of physical environmental factors, with climate being given top rank in the governance of terrestrial biomes (Billings 1970; Watts 1971). Convergent evolution is credited with producing physiognomically similar formations in similar climates anywhere on earth, regardless of the geographical origins or migrational pathways of the biotas. Geology and topography are assigned the role of producing relatively local patterns which tend to be smoothed out as plant succession, erosion and deposition proceed and as zonal soils mature. Disturbances by storms, fires, or any other natural or human agencies are treated as temporary setbacks after which succession resumes its inexorable march toward the final climax: the single equilibrium biome typical for a given climate.

The theory of organic succession toward a climatic climax has proved to be a powerful tool in explaining some gross biotic patterns. Its shortcomings, however, are obvious. Its simplistic climatic determinism denies any lasting effects attributable to other independent variables. The presumed fixed end-point, the climax type, excludes *a priori* any change in the climax itself through time. Yet ecosystem types are no more timeless than such classical anthropological types as pastoral nomads or shifting cultivators. Even in an imaginary natural world without man, the lack of any historical dimension makes the theory of succession incomplete.

MacArthur (1972) once drew a perceptive distinction between scientists who describe the machinery of a phenomenon and scientists who unravel its history. He thought ecologists like himself tended to be machinery oriented, while biogeographers tended to be history-oriented. Harvey (1969) has recognized the same cleavage within geography: functional-ecological analysis leads to systems analysis while cause-and-effect analysis leads to temporal or historical explanation. This distinction, however, is artificial when applied to cultural and natural systems alike, because such systems are not normally static.

Fixation on equilibrium models has led to the common presumption that stable systems resist change by negative feedback. In truth, however, stable natural systems defined as ones which survive through time may be ones that are flexible and change when perturbed (Holling 1973; Slobodkin and Rapoport 1974). How much systems work and how they develop are really parts of the same question, one that can never be answered finally as long as they continue to evolve. I suppose that this is an idea that culture historians take for granted. Biologists often forget, nonetheless, that the systems they work with are transitory stages in an endless process of evolution and migration. They commonly assume that the organisms comprising a natural community have had a shared history in the habitat type they now occupy. This thought is like assuming that all the elements of a given culture evolved together serving their present functions. Moreover, in plant ecology it is still provocative to suggest that an existing community comprises species of diverse evolutionary histories from diverse environments and that the members of the current biotic assemblage might have been preadapted to, rather than shaped by, the environment which they now occupy together (Axelrod 1975; Whittaker and Woodwell 1972).

Biogeographers have less justification than culture historians for treating the species found in an area as a functional unit. This is so because there is no integrating mechanism among non-interbreeding species comparable to communication among people. A biotic community has no central control system. There is no genetic message for whole communities. Community evolution is a consequence of individual species evolution and individual species migrations, which together result in loose, changeable associations among species at any given place or within any specified habitat (Whittaker 1975).

This view of biotic communities is not shared by all ecologists. Some have attempted to find laws of community development applicable to types of ecosystems or even to ecosystems in general. Consistent quantitative relationships have been sought among abstract properties of communities such as: stability, homeostasis, diversity, productivity and efficiency of energy conversion (as a function of community maturity) (Margalef 1968; Odum 1969).

Unfortunately, testing such hypotheses about community evolution has been hampered because the abstract concepts involved have proved so ambiguous that attempts to define them have led to a semantic jungle. There is enough empirical evidence, however, to say that these abstract properties do not follow consistent trends during succession and to conclude that a universal and unifying theory is a fanciful goal (Horn 1974).

The basic dilemma

Biogeography, like the rest of science, seeks general laws, not unique bits of anecdotal information. The broader the generalization, however, the more we are reduced to least common denominators. A biology based on universal properties of living organisms ends with the origin of life and accounts only for the early pre-Cambrian world. The more kinds of organisms with which we must deal, the less generalization is possible. It is axiomatic that each living species is in some significant way unique in its environmental requirements and thus in its spatial distribution. Normative constructs are used to deduce phylogenies and mutual characteristics of related species are attributed to their common derivation from the postulated primitive ancestor. Yet if we go forward rather than backward in time, we cannot filter out deviations around the generic norm as random noise: the deviations are the message explaining a species' *raison d'être*. I believe that attempts to reach grand syntheses by ignoring species differences are bound to be time-wasting detours, not shortcuts to understanding.

Comparative field study of species distributions

Models and concepts

Between the universal and the unique there is the possibility for limited, but significant, generalization achieved by dealing both with similarities and with differences among species living within geographically restricted areas. Such an approach, indeed, is almost inescapable when distribution patterns are being studied in the field. A good field observer automatically seeks whatever intelligible patterns he can find in the occurrences of organisms and habitats within his study region. Comparisons of such patterns may suggest to him innumerable hypotheses about ecological and evolutionary processes. It is historical fact that hypotheses derived in this fashion have survived critical testing and have become important theory.

For example, the theory of primary succession was established on Kerner's (1863) observations on the spatial relationships among plant species and habitats in the Danube basin, rather than on studies tracing this process over time. Similarly, it was geographic patterns that Darwin saw while on the voyage of the *Beagle*, not direct evidence of evolutionary change. Patterns, not processes, first suggested to him the natural explanation that speciation is a result of migration and selection in unlike habitats (Darwin 1839).

Since Darwin, biogeography has had a basic model of the mechanism of evolution and of migration that has survived with some tinkering and elaboration. There remains much to be learned about variations in the behavior of this mechanism, but the general functioning of its components seems clear. Mutation and genetic recombination in every generation tend to increase the hereditary diversity of species. At the same time, dispersal of progeny tends to increase the geographic range of every species. Both these positive, centrifugal forces are opposed by selective elimination. In a stable environment, the positive and negative forces may equilibrate. Individuals with novel gene combinations or novel locations may be eliminated. In stable environments, in other words, evolution and migration may cease while the biotic machine is idling, a situation analogous to one in which a particular type of artefact within a culture area is being used and replaced without its modification or diffusion into new territory. Equilibrium, however, may be upset – and evolution and migration initiated – by any change in genetic, dispersal or selective forces, due either to spontaneous innovation or external causes.

Evolution and migration are inseparable, because success or failure of the individuals within any species is contingent upon both their heredity and their location. Moreover, individual success or failure simultaneously affects the genetics and geography of the species to which an individual belongs. The evolutionary mechanism, in short, is full of feedbacks.

Dispersibility is itself an adaptive trait, subject to evolutionary change while a species migrates into new physical or biotic environments (Carlquist 1974). Migration may entail evolution of both immigrants and members of the invaded communities, because of changes brought about in competitive, predatory and symbiotic interactions. That is, the repercussions of species dispersal may be extensive in a fashion comparable to the effects of the diffusion of foreign culture traits into new contexts. Migration and evolution need not lead to convergence or homogenization of biotic associations. Rather, both may increase diversity (Whittaker 1975). Perhaps it is here where the closest analogy between biogeographical and cultural processes is to be found.

The concept of allopatric speciation, previously mentioned, is a special case in the workings of the biotic machine in which migration resulting in absolute geographic isolation is completed before the evolution of divergent adaptations or isolating genetic mechanisms has occurred. I doubt that this is the usual sequence. A growing body of speciation theory treats geographic and genetic isolation as matters of degree rather than as absolutes, for it is now recognized that both kinds of isolation may develop gradually along with adaptive divergence (e.g. Grant 1971; Ross 1962; Snaydon 1973; Sokal 1974; Solbrig 1970). Local adaptive divergence can be expected to develop between parts of a continuous species population subjected to differing environmental selection pressures. To the extent that interbreeding among such local races is random, gene exchange tends to maintain genetic similarity within the species. This centripetal tendency, however, is weakened with increasing ecological and geographical segregation. Selective elimination of hybrids poorly adapted to the habitats of either parent protects the divergent ecological adaptations of geographical races, but the cost is lowered reproductive capacity. In such a situation, selection favors the evolution of isolating mechanisms which reduce this cost by promoting non-random mating among parents with similar ecological adaptations.

Whether or not selection can lead to complete reproductive isolation among diverging populations is controversial. Partial isolation may adequately protect different genetic adaptations without shutting off gene exchange entirely. Introgression, i.e. limited hybridization among interfertile but ecologically divergent populations, is a rich source of variation that may be advantageous, especially in rapidly changing environments. Experts disagree, however, on its significance (e.g. Anderson and Stebbins 1954; Heiser 1973; Williams 1966). Most of these concepts and arguments must seem familiar to anthropologists concerned with cultural differentiation among groups having a shared heritage but varying in their isolation from each other.

The Darwinian model of evolution does not postulate deterministic or unilinear finite processes. Each part of the evolutionary mechanism – gene mutation and recombination, dispersal, selection – functions loosely and unpredictably, except in terms of frequency distributions, at least according to our limited perception. We can only hope to formulate probabilistic rules which will be inevitably weaker and vaguer as the range of organisms, habitats, regions and generations that are encompassed becomes broader.

Some current work

In plant geography today, the most interesting results, I believe, are coming out of middle-scale studies of areas and time spans that contain enough biotic and habitat diversity to be challenging without being overwhelming. Among the innumerable fine examples are these studies: Gill (1972, 1973) in the Northwest Territories, Canada, has related dynamic sequences of vegetational succession to shifting river channels, beaver activity and permafrost levels; Thom (1967) in Tabasco, Mexico, has related the patterns of colonization by swamp and marsh species to geomorphic processes operating in an uncontrolled delta; Byrne (in press) in the Bahamas has used recorded changes in vegetation under shifting cultivation to evaluate the vulnerability of an island biota. These studies evade the pitfalls of ecosystem classification by taking all the ecological diversity within a study region as it comes. Actual distributions of species and habitats are plotted along transects and on detailed maps of sample areas. This standard geographic approach often reveals relationships that would be obscured if data were tabulated and pooled without regard to location. Archaeologists surely know the value of dealing directly with spatial patterns rather than with objects of unknown provenience.

Even with an efficient and powerful field approach such as this one, biogeographic studies face very strict limitations on the cast of characters that can be pursued, the kinds of actions that can be observed, and their scope in space and time. In the first place, a field worker can never cope with all the kinds of organisms to be found in even a moderately complex biotic community. Usually he can deal professionally only with a particular group of organisms, such as birds or ants or woody plants. The rest he can observe only superficially. In anthropology, comparable studies would be ones which focus only on kinship or ceremonials or agriculture. Even within his chosen group of organisms, a field biogeographer can observe only certain kinds of things. Important periodic or episodic events surely often occur when he is somewhere else. Many interactions are mediated by flows of matter and energy in quantities too infinitesimal to be detected, or in ways too subtle to be recognized by a field observer. Moreover, some crucial processes cannot be observed without being perturbed. I am sure all of these problems are familiar to anthropological researchers. Biogeographers, however, are in the unfortunate position of being unable to communicate with their subjects, much like an ethnologist who cannot speak the language of the people among whom he has taken up residence.

Each biogeographer's field studies are subject to severe and arbitary limitations on space and time. I suspect a biogeographer learns more if he chooses several moderately different, medium-sized regions than if he sticks to a single large region or hops between many very different small ones. A biogeographer probably learns least by studying many very small and very similar regions. As for the value of knowledge about biotas at different time levels, I would say that in plant geography some of the freshest insights into processes have originated with people working both with living species in the field and also with fossil or archaeological material. These people have revolutionized the study of Pleistocene and post-glacial vegetation by replacing the climatic determinism of earlier studies with complex hypotheses concerning the processes of succession, migration and intervention by prehistoric man (e.g. Davis 1965; Pennington 1974).

This composite approach illuminates the present as well as the past. For example, studies of post-glacial fossil deposits have led to a re-evaluation of the classical model of hydroseral succession as applied to existing marsh vegetation (Walker 1970). On quite a different time scale, Axelrod has used his wide firsthand knowledge of present vegetation to deduce environments for fossil faunas of western North America (e.g. Axelrod 1966). He has also used his knowledge of Tertiary paleobotany to question accepted dogma on the role of climate in shaping modern vegetation (Axelrod 1975).

Conclusion

In sum, I believe that good theory in biogeography is theory that can account for spatial distributions which continuously change and diversify through time. If there is a plan overlying these distributions directing them to reach a final static or cyclic state, we have not yet seen it. Like man, other species are still experimenting with arrangements of matter and energy that have not been tried before and the potentialities of which are still emerging.

1.viii.1976

Department of Geography
University of California at Los Angeles

References

Anderson, E., and Stebbins, G. L., Jr. 1954. Hybridization as an evolutionary stimulus. *Evolution.* 8:378–89.

Axelrod, D. I. 1966. The Eocene Copper Basin flora of northeastern Nevada. *University of California Publications in Geological Sciences.* 59:1–83.

Axelrod, D. I. 1973. History of the Mediterranean ecosystem in California. In *Mediterranean-type Ecosystems – origin and structure*, pp. 225–77 (eds F. di Castri and H. A. Mooney). Berlin: Springer Verlag.

Axelrod, D. I. 1975. Evolution and biogeography of Madrean-Tethyan sclerophyll vegetation. *Missouri Botanical Garden Annals.* 62:280–334.

Baker, H. G. 1970. Evolution in the tropics. *Biotropica.* 2:101–11.

Billings, W. D. 1970. *Plants, Man, and the Ecosystem.* Belmont, California: Wadsworth.

Byrne, A. R. In press. Man and the variable vulnerability of island life: a study of recent vegetation change in the Bahamas. *Atoll Research Bulletin.*

Cain, S. A. 1944. *Foundations of Plant Geography.* New York and London: Harper & Brothers.

Carlquist, S. 1974. *Island Biology.* New York and London: Columbia University Press.

Colinvaux, P. A. 1973. *Introduction to Ecology.* New York: John Wiley & Sons.

Darwin, C. R. 1839. *Journal of Researches into the Geology and Natural History of the Various Countries visited by H.M.S. Beagle.* London: Colburn.

Davis, M. B. 1965. Phytogeography and palynology of northeastern United States. In *The Quaternary of the United States*, pp. 377–401 (eds H. E. Wright, Jr. and David G. Frey). Princeton: Princeton University Press.

Gill, D. 1972. The evolution of a discrete beaver habitat in the Mackenzie River delta, Northwest Territories. *Canadian Field Naturalist.* 86:233–9.

Gill, D. 1973. Floristics of plant succession sequence in the Mackenzie Delta, Northwest Territories. *Polarforschung.* 43:55–65.

Good, R. 1947. *The Geography of the Flowering Plants.* London: Longmans, Green, and Company.

Grant, V. 1971. *Plant Speciation.* New York and London: Columbia University Press.

Harvey, D. 1969. *Explanation in Geography.* New York: St Martin's Press.

Heiser, C. B., Jr. 1973. Introgression re-examined. *Botanical Review.* 39:347–66.

Holling, C. S. 1973. Resilience and stability of ecological systems. *Annual Review of Ecology and Systematics.* 4:1–23.

Horn, H. S. 1974. The ecology of secondary succession. *Annual Review of Ecology and Systematics.* 5:25–37.

Kerner, A. J. 1863. *Das Pflanzenleben der Donaulaender.* Innsbruck: Verlag der Wagner'schen Universität.

Krebs, C. J. 1972. *Ecology: the Experimental Analysis of Distribution and Abundance.* New York: Harper & Row.

Lindroth, C. H. 1970. Survival of animals and plants on ice-free refugia during the Pleistocene glaciations. *Endeavour.* 29:129–34.

MacArthur, R. H. 1972. *Geographical Ecology.* New York: Harper & Row.

MacArthur, R. H., and Wilson, E. O. 1967. *The Theory of Island Biogeography.* Princeton: Princeton University Press.

Margalef, R. 1968. *Perspectives in Ecological Theory.* Chicago: University of Chicago Press.

Mayr, E. 1966. *Animal Species and Evolution.* Cambridge, Mass.: Harvard University Press.

Meggers, B. J. 1975. Application of the biological model of diversification to cultural distributions in tropical lowland South America. *Biotropica.* 7:141–61.

Müller, P. 1973. *The Dispersal Centres of Terrestrial Vertebrates in the Neotropical Realm.* The Hague: W. Junk.

Odum, E. P. 1969. The strategy of ecosystem development. *Science.* 164:262–70.

Peet, R. K. 1974. The measurement of species diversity. *Annual Review of Ecology and Systematics.* 5:285–307.

Pennington, W. 1964. *The History of British Vegetation.* London: English Universities Press.

Pianka, E. R. 1966. Latitudinal gradients in species diversity: a review of concepts. *American Naturalist.* 100:33–46.

Polunin, N. 1960. *Introduction to Plant Geography.* New York: McGraw-Hill.

Ross, H. H. 1962. *A Synthesis of Evolutionary Theory.* Englewood Cliffs, N.J.: Prentice-Hall.

Seddon, B. 1971. *Introduction to Biogeography.* London: Duckworth.

Simberloff, D. S. 1974. Equilibrium theory of island biogeography and ecology. *Annual Review of Ecology and Systematics.* 5:161–82.

Slobodkin, L. B. and Rapoport, A. 1974. An optimal strategy of evolution. *Quarterly Review of Biology.* 49:181–200.

Snaydon, R. W. 1973. Ecological factors, genetic variation and speciation in plants. In *Taxonomy and Ecology*, pp. 1–29 (ed. V. H. Heywood). London and New York: Academic Press.

Sokal, R. R. 1974. The species problem reconsidered. *Systematic Zoology.* 22:360–74.

Solbrig, O. T. 1970. *Principles and Methods of Plant Biosystematics.* London: Collier-Macmillan.

Thom, B. G. 1967. Mangrove ecology and deltaic geomorphology: Tabasco, Mexico. *Journal of Ecology*. 55:301–43.

Tivy, J. 1971. *Biogeography: a Study of Plants in the Ecosphere*. Edinburgh: Oliver & Boyd.

Vuilleumier, B. S. 1971. Pleistocene changes in the fauna and flora of South America. *Science*. 173:771–80.

Walker, D. 1970. Direction and rate in some British Post-glacial hydroseres. In *Studies in the Vegetational History of the British Isles*, pp. 117–39 (eds D. Walker and R. G. West). Cambridge: Cambridge University Press.

Walter, H. 1973. *Vegetation of the Earth in relation to Climate and the Eco-physiological Conditions*. London: English Universities Press.

Watts, D. 1971. *Principles of Biogeography*. New York: McGraw-Hill.

Whittaker, R. H. 1962. Classification of natural communities. *Botanical Review*. 28:1–239.

Whittaker, R. H. 1975. *Communities and Ecosystems*. New York: Macmillan.

Whittaker, R. H. and Woodwell, G. M. 1972. Evolution of natural communities. In *Ecosystem Structure and Function*, pp. 137–56 (ed. John A. Wiens). Corvallis: Oregon State University Press.

Williams, G. C. 1966. *Adaptation and Natural Selection: a critique of some current evolutionary thought*. Princeton: Princeton University Press.

Abstract

Sauer, J. D.

Biogeographical theory and cultural analogies

This article is intended as a warning against giving biogeographical models more respect than they deserve. Few academics are primarily concerned with biotic distributions. Many taxonomists and ecologists have geographical interests, but they must cope with hundreds of thousands of species. Most biogeographers are too absorbed in field exploration to have much time for general theory. The separate scholarly traditions of museum and mathematical biogeography each have sets of concepts having little connection with concepts used in field biogeography. Moreover, some schools of thought are in the primitive state of confusing *a priori* assumptions with tested theory and of accepting deductive explanations without investigating the processes involved. An increasing emphasis on ecology, however, is enabling field biogeographers, like modern archaeologists, to elucidate evolutionary and migrational processes by working on middle-scale studies of areas and time spans that contain enough biotic and habitat diversity to be challenging without being overwhelming. On the other hand, attempts to reach grand syntheses by ignoring species differences are bound to be time-wasting detours, not shortcuts to understanding.

Evolution is no help

Lawrence B. Slobodkin

Introduction

In comparing causality in history and in evolution, I will show that in both cases causality consists of defining a class of possible outcomes from a series of events, rather than defining either a unique event or a stochastic array of events. Then, I consider and reject two hypotheses:

(1) there are trends in the evolutionary process;

(2) since history can be thought of as a sequence of evolutionary events we may be able to infer trends in history from trends in evolution.

The distinction between history as written by Braudel (1972) on the one hand and by Spengler (1934) on the other is the central issue. Braudel provides a recital of historical events placed in an ecological, economic and social context. Generalities are drawn, such as that the occupation of flat plains involves a stronger central government and stronger control of behavior than the occupation of mountains. Braudel does not, however, infer any relation between inevitable sequences of historical events, nor does he consider that historical events are bound by the biological evolutionary properties of man.

By contrast, there is a long intellectual tradition that human history is an inevitable consequence of either a supernatural or a natural destiny. From the Greek concept of human history as an incidental consequence of the destined history of the gods, to the Christian concept of God as free of destiny, that in turn placed the inevitability of human history in abeyance (Jan Kott, personal communication),[1] we come to the nineteenth century theory of evolution. Here, historical inevitability hinges on biology and its assertion of inevitability in the evolutionary process.

I will show that there is no way to infer from the inevitability of biological evolution that there is inevitability in historical events, since there are no inevitable trends in evolution, other than an ongoing, unchanging tendency toward conservative behavior (in an evolutionary, not political sense). In this assertion, I will show that there is no reason, based on evolutionary theory, to consider either the course of human history or the decisions made by individual decision-makers to be limited by evolutionary events (in the sense of Alexander 1974, 1975; Trivers 1971; Wilson 1975).

We will subsequently return to causality to point out that the class of possible evolu-

[1] It is an oversimplification of medieval theological thought to consider that God was made free of destiny. In both Judaism and Christianity there is a strong element of God sharing in the historical process and the historical process somehow being confined in its possible paths.

tionary futures is highly restricted by the properties of the evolutionary present and the conservatism of evolution. Not only is there a tendency to do nothing, but if anything does occur, it does so in the smallest possible steps.

Then I will indicate the biological peculiarities of man which are likely to influence a class of historical events. Men, and at least their close primate relatives, have a biological need for a self-image. This concept of themselves becomes a powerful causal factor in determining their actions and broadens the possible future events that will result from any social, historical, or environmental perturbations. Evolution occurs only in response to perturbation and has no momentum of its own. Since men respond to their self-image as well as to their environment, a new level of looseness enters the relation between the magnitude of a response to an environmental change and the magnitude of the change itself.

I will demonstrate that while the self-image directed nature of man and the higher primates opens up historical possibilities and magnitudes of response that would not otherwise be available, man is not yet immune to elementary biological evolutionary changes. How he responds to them becomes a question, the answer to which lies in the imagination of man and poses more problems than it solves.

From these arguments, I will conclude that the theory of the evolutionist can only be of help to the historian in freeing him of the need to look for biological analogues. Decisions as to morality, as to what is or is not desirable about a political system, must be made by men without the help of evolution. However, one of the factors that must be considered in their decisions is the evolutionary effect of each decision. Human decisions mold the evolutionary process, but human decision-makers cannot rely on evolutionary events or theories to provide them with rectitude, safety or sanctity.

On a different level, however, it will be apparent that beliefs about the evolutionary process are historically significant in the sense that what men believe about the 'laws' that govern history is itself a force in history. Beliefs about the biological nature of man strongly influence practical behavior, aside from the specific problems of evolutionary theory itself. There is a persistent appeal to the idea that since man is in the grip of evolutionary law, politically, socially and historically significant action must be taken to regulate the evolution of man (cf. Wilson's (1976) review of R. Ardrey's *The Hunting Hypothesis*).

Causality in evolution and history

When we look at the narrative of biological evolution or of the events of history, the apparent sequence of events is dependent on how the events are classified. Using a biological example, in the class of animals that swim we find that the ancestors of some members consist of animals that have always been able to swim (fish, protozoa, some crustacea). In addition we find other animals, the early ancestors of which could swim, the less remote ancestors of which could not, but the most immediate ancestor of which returned to swimming again. Tortoises that returned from the land swim by an adaptation of a tortoise walking gait. Whales swim by something that closely resembles wagging their tails. The ancestors of the whales were apparently carnivorous, terrestrial animals.

One group of swimming birds, the penguins, adapted a flying motion to aquatic purposes, while the duck-like birds swim with their feet rather than their wings.

The problems of adapting to water, with their array of possible solutions, may be viewed as a convergence of causal pathways to the development of swimming. We are talking of a many-to-one relationship in time. However, if I could make up a series of words, each representing a type of swimming behaviour, I would then restore the appearance of a one-to-one causality, since the groups that developed swimming will have come to it by their own method and come to their own sub-categories of the general event of swimming. That is, I can alter the apparent nature of the causal relation by altering my classification process. In short, while evolutionary events do not transpire at random, the definition of the kind of causality becomes contingent on the classification of the events being considered.

We can, however, proceed as if the problem of classification did not exist, since a particular evolving system, when acted on by an external stress or when responding to readjustments within its own structure, has a large class of impossible future states and another class of more or less equivalently possible states. The evolutionary process forbids certain futures to evolving units, but does not uniquely determine which of the non-forbidden states will actually arise. There are also certain historical transitions which will probably not occur: for example, the probability of the Kalahari bushmen taking charge of West Africa is so small as to be set at zero, but the extinction (either cultural or physical) of the Kalahari bushmen is within the class of possible events.

So far, we have loosened the notion of strict causality as applied to evolutionary events and to historical events. A qualification is required before the similarity receives too much attention.

In evolution, the fundamental laws of gene frequency change (given certain kinds of natural selection and certain kinds of distribution of populations) are amenable to detailed analysis. More difficulty is created by what the meaning of those gene changes will be in terms of such things as swimming or hiding, becoming intelligent or stupid and so forth. It is the functional consequences of a gene frequency change which have a causality that is analogous to historical causality (Lewontin 1974; Slobodkin and Rapoport 1974). It may, perhaps, be the case that the biological properties of individual men participate as the biological properties of individual genes do, in evolutionary events, but this is dubious.

There has been no general trend in the evolutionary process which can be of historical significance in the sense of producing implications that might guide analyses of history. On a paleontological level, there is no indication of any major trends for the evolutionary process as a whole for the last billion or so years. Most evolutionary lines have not maintained consistent directions of evolutionary change. For most postulated consistent directions of change there is at least one evolutionary line which changes in an opposite sense. For instance, individual evolutionary lines may show an increase in body size for several millions of years, but then may decrease in size.

Certainly, increased control over the environment and increased neural capacity are not general evolutionary trends. Most living organisms have survived beautifully with minimal intellectual accomplishments.

The idea persists, nonetheless, that complexity has increased during the course of evolution. The meaning of this assertion is not very clear. Morphological, biochemical, behavioral, neurological and physiological complexity are each separately definable and may lead to contradictory assertions. The geometric complexity of the genital apparatus of free-living flat worms is enormous (Hyman 1951), as is the capacity of Hawaiian fruitflies to produce new species (Carson *et al.* 1970).

Xenophanes, at the dawn of philosophy, noted: 'If the Thracians made gods they would have red hair and snub noses,' thereby pointing out the dangers of viewing the world from our own preconception of our own importance. There is no more evidence that man has a focal or teleological role in evolutionary history than that man's planet Earth is in a geographically central location in the cosmos. Ayala (1974) has discussed this question and noted the impossibility of assigning any internal, biological criterion of progress to evolution.

Once a decision has been made, however, giving us a criterion of what we will consider progressive, we can ask whether or not individual evolutionary lines, or the average of some assemblage of evolutionary lines, have been progressive. If we were to find some criterion of progress which would permit us to assert that all, or even most, evolutionary lines have been progressive, we could then ask if there is some mechanism responsible for this progress. If we found such a mechanism, we could assert the existence of a trend. To my knowledge no such criterion has been found.

There is some room for question in this area, nonetheless, because evolutionary events share with historical events the property that certain changes have definite prerequisites. It is impossible to modify a wing until a wing has evolved, just as it is impossible to depose a monarch in the absence of a monarchy.

Evolution considered as an existential game

That trends in the evolutionary process must be generally absent becomes apparent when we consider an analogy with game playing. If there were a trend in the evolutionary process universally to maximize a biological aspect, it would be possible to build a theoretical game model in which the organisms would be the players against nature. The organisms should be acting as if the maximization of whatever it is that was involved in the trend is the payoff (Rapoport 1975; Slobodkin 1975; Slobodkin and Rapoport 1974), but one property of most games tells us why this cannot be the case.

A payoff in a game is something that has value away from the place where the game is being played (except in a rather peculiar case, see below). Money won at a dice game is primarily of value because it can purchase things some place away from the crap table. The implication is that if organisms are maximizing something as a universal evolutionary trend, they should be acting as if they had some place to spend their winnings. Yet they do not have any such place. That is, there is no way for evolutionary units to withdraw from the evolutionary game to spend what they have won.

Let us look at the implication of the fact that organisms cannot cash in their chips. There exists a class of existential games that is at least as numerous as the class of payoff games. The existential games are defined as those in which the payoff must be used in the game itself and cannot be cashed in. The way such a game is played turns out to correspond very closely with what evolutionary units seem to do. The optimal strategy in an existential game in which chips cannot be cashed is to minimize the stakes played at each hand. That is, if you cannot win, what you try to do is to persist – because you can lose. Extinction is equivalent to completely losing. Trying to persist means to risk as little as possible, and organisms seem to be playing a minimum-risk strategy.

When the environment shifts and some disturbance occurs in an evolutionary unit, unless it is completely novel, a series of simultaneously initiated responses take place, each one of which can deal with the kind of problem which the environment has presented. The elements in the series may be characterized by the relative rates at which they are activated and the degree to which they are activated and the degree to which they represent a major commitment of the organism's resources, in the sense of altering its capacity to deal with other environmental problems that are likely to arise.

If we rank the responses in terms of how much of a commitment they represent, we will find that those representing the greater commitment take longer to be fully activated. This provides an opportunity for those response procedures which represent a minimal commitment to deal with the environmental problem. To the degree that minimal, fast responses succeed in dealing with the problems appropriately, the full activation of the major commitments need not and does not occur.

We might note that a certain kind of predictability has become available. Those environmental events which occur very rapidly and are highly transitory are optimally responded to by the development of a behavioral response mechanism. Those events which take longer time periods should be responded to by deeper mechanisms. We have defined, therefore, the class of evolutionary solutions which should transpire given any particular environmental event.

The quickest way to get a sense of this is to consider a pedagogic device which I have used: throwing chalk at a student during a lecture. The responses, depending on the age, sex and character of the student may be summarized: there is an eye-blink and a sudden head movement. Despite the fact that the problem has passed, the students typically show signs of some anxiety, an alertness in attitude and they may show signs of circulatory change. As long as 30 minutes after the chalk throwing, the student has a heart rate, an adrenal level and a vasoconstriction pattern that is modified and an attention set that is distinct from a student who has not been the target of thrown chalk. The problem, however, was solved before most of the mechanisms listed really got started. Major possible responses did not occur. In short, a minor disturbance has been handled by a minor response. A lot of back-up machinery was activated but did not have time, between the occurrence of the disturbance and the solution of the resulting problem, to be fully activated in such a way as to alter the life of the organism in any serious fashion.

In the evolutionary process, to the degree that an organism's response mechanisms are inadequate to cope with a particular disturbance the individual either dies or fails to reproduce, and this would quite probably constitute a change in the genetic characteristics of the population from which the individual was drawn.

The anatomy, physiology and behavior of organisms can be thought of as the genes' way of avoiding having to change. Therefore, we have a set of more or less universal properties of organisms in evolution which will mediate the path that evolutionary events take and will give us certain choice criteria for telling what an organism or population of organisms is likely to do under a given perturbation. This does not set any definitive trend other than a minimization of the disruption of the organisms' existing genetic structure. In those evolutionary lines in which learning capacity has developed, however, the story becomes more complicated. This is discussed in the next section.

The peculiar evolutionary strategy of man

I am going to contend that man and at least some other animals have a biological property of possessing an image of themselves to which they respond. That is, in addition to the normal family of environmental responses, people have a set of internal properties that dictate their responses. Obviously all animals have this to some extent. What I am referring to is an elaboration of this property so that the sensory machinery itself is looking inward.

Conscious, normative and introspective self-images are a property of men set by their biology, and this seriously alters their response to evolutionary problems (Slobodkin 1976). When we say 'set by their biology,' we mean that the tendency or propensity to develop a sense of self-awareness is biologically set. The content of the images that a man carries under the heading of self-awareness are almost certainly not biologically determined, but are determined by his cultural milieu. It may be the case that not only is there a propensity to maintain a self-image, but also, if circumstances make it impossible to develop an internally consistent self-image, behavioral pathology may result.

The evolutionary background of this peculiarity of man seems to extend to the social mammals. Arboreal social mammals rely heavily on learned behavior to move through their habitat in an effective way. Such organisms respond to present disturbances in terms of their own histories of the outcomes of responding to past disturbances. The efficacy of learning and the level of intelligence of animals may be defined by their capacity to respond to an intellectual construct of the world and accept information from the world as signals rather than perturbations. This reaches its epitome in man and some of the higher apes, in which the intellectual construct is such that the animal can visualize itself as an object (Gallup 1969, 1974).

Note that I have described a sequence of evolutionary developments in the history of man which, when seen from the present, look like a directional trend. This in no way implies that there existed any force requiring that trend to have occurred – other than the fact that each existing adaptation determines the class of possible further adaptations. Learning capacity may be prerequisite to the possibility of the development of the capacity for self-image, given appropriate selective forces, but it will not be *inevitably* followed by development of the capacity for self-image: witness the abundance of kinds of modern aboreal mammals that have not developed this capacity.

What I am referring to are specific experiments in which chimpanzees (Gallup 1969) and Orang-utans (Lethmate and Dücker 1973) are shown a mirror and respond to the mirror in the same way that a man does. They groom themselves and adjust their own appearance, and do not treat the mirror image as other than a reflection of themselves. Once an animal sees itself as an object, its own ideas or fantasies about itself enter into the complex of forces that act on it in an evolutionary way. The self-image of men, chimps and Orang-utans has a normative component, which is how we can tell that they have a self-image. Using a mirror, a chimpanzee will wipe off flecks of color that have been placed on its skin. The flecks do not correspond to the chimpanzee's own image of what it *ought* to be, which is an implication of the normative.

I am suggesting that men have a propensity, determined genetically, to develop a self-image. The self-image, once developed, acts as a normative standard. The development of the self-image content, one would think, must be a matter of upbringing. That is, you can raise a child in a context in which he develops for himself a self-image. Once this has been developed, that image becomes a major force in his behavior, and to the degree that the public representation of these images in speech and description are common to a culture or a time, they can become major historical and political forces.

I am making the strong statement that the biological nature of man is to have fantasies, images and dreams. There is no evidence that the content of these mental constructs is biologically determined by genetic differences between individuals or between groups of humans, or that there is any fantasy that is impossible to mankind as a whole. This is in contradistinction to the various statements of the assumed innate behavioral propensities of man, aside from those that are immediately tied to biological function (e.g. the innate propensity to yawn when sleepy). The innate behaviors seem to derive from the fantasies of their authors and seem to be descriptive of the publicly shared fantasies of certain cultures. The fact that the north Europeans have prided themselves for centuries on their warriors, toughness and ability to drink says nothing about the biological propensities of the northern Europeans compared to, say, Bushmen. The northern Europeans have been sharing one fantasy, while the Bushmen have been sharing another.

Fantasy has at least the role of a partial molder of history. The ability to fantasize comes out of the evolutionary process, but there is no present evidence that the content of fantasies derives directly from evolutionary laws. I am saying that the common sense feeling that major historical events are initiated by ideas as well as by economic and perhaps ecological events is perfectly consonant with all known biological fact. One cannot consider most major historical events to be pushed or to have been directed by biological laws, but rather by the intellectual activities of men in their most private and poetic form, acting in a social and ecological context.

This is not a new discovery. The Soviet Union has been imprisoning poets for years, and Plato made it clear that the forms of music and art are critical to the functioning of the state. All I have added is the clarification of how this kind of fantasy relates to the biological nature of man. I have denied the spate of recent speculations by Ardrey (1966), Lorenz (1966), Morris (1967), and others, asserting that the content of man's self-image is biologically determined. All we can say is that man's need or at least capacity to have a self-image is biologically determined. There is no evidence of biological restriction of the content of that image, nor of genetic differences between individuals affecting differences in the content of their self-images.

What does this do to history and evolution? It says that it is impossible to assign major historical events to causes resident in biological evolutionary laws. We cannot deduce the laws of history, if they exist, from the laws of evolution. This does not deny the possibility of constructing similes between historical events and evolutionary events or 'laws.' These have empirical meaning only in a most attenuated sense (Koenig 1975). For example, just as evolutionary modification of wings is only possible in winged animals, the historical modification of wheels is only possible after the invention and adoption of the wheel.

In review, I have shown that the evolutionary process is momentum-free and is driven by external perturbations to which organisms respond in minimal fashion. People and some of the higher apes have interposed a rather complex set of mental images between themselves, their response machinery and their environment. They respond to environmental disturbances so as to minimize the effect on their mental image as well as to minimize the effect on their physiology. This tendency is probably so pronounced that the fantasies men have about mankind are themselves a major historical force. Certainly, the behavioral propensities of man derive as much from his ideas about man as they do from any innate tendency to behave in certain modes.

We must distinguish between the biological behavioral responses and those responses related to such things as motivation. The biological responses we share with the bulk of animals: blinking, eating, sweating, and so on. The more interesting behavior about which some controversy can exist are behaviors involving values, motives, goals – all those things which are embodied in man's image of himself. The reasonable biological position, then, is that the image is completely determined by culture and is not biologically given.

This makes the historian unable to rely on biology to help him look at human historical trends. Once the self-image capacity and communication about images and fantasies were fully established (in at least the last half million years), intellectual constructs become more important than evolution in determining history. On the other hand, however, the consequences of human dreams and human motives can have major evolutionary effects. We cannot abrogate our personal responsibilities and avoid problems by saying it is the nature of man.

Residual evolutionary problems

In general, evolution is conservative. A gene frequency change is a response to an environmental change, and there are certain dangers to future survival associated with any change severe enough to result in such a response. Certain human activities, however, cause gene frequency changes in human populations and administrative decisions have to be made in conjunction with these changes.

Gene frequency change is the response to an adaptive failure and, in that sense, is to be avoided under most circumstances. This is not equivalent to saying that one deliberately avoids evolutionary change, but that biological solutions can be very unpleasant indeed. For example, imagine a human society in which there is always high infant mortality, war and misery, but the society is in an ecological and evolutionary steady state. Then, if one avoids the death of children, eliminates war and alters the general state of misery, it is almost certain that one will cause gene frequency changes. Therefore, if one is going to be on the side of evolution, one will be on the side of the *status quo*, for to make a change in the life pattern of any group of people will result in evolutionary shifts. At that point it matters very much whether one believes that the 'naturalness' of evolution is a good to be maintained. One's belief is part of one's mental world; it does not come from the evolutionary process itself. The future evolution of man, to some degree, will grow out of his fantasy of man.

A modern case in which biological evolution of man is now occurring is in a famous genetic abnormality called the sickle-cell gene, which produces abnormal hemoglobin. I will provide an over-simplified description for purposes of argument and the more technical literature should be consulted for a sense of the complexities involved (Rucknagel and Neel 1961). Individuals hybrid for this gene are immune to certain kinds of malaria. A double dose of this gene results in early death from sickle-cell anemia. If malaria is widespread and sufficiently virulent, the majority of people that grow up to reproduce will have a single sickle-cell gene and a single normal gene. If they marry persons sharing their genotype with regard to the sickle-cell gene they will have one quarter of their children dying of anemia and almost one quarter dying of malaria. Half of their children, however, will not die of these causes and consequently will live longer. A few individuals not carrying the sickle-cell gene will probably survive the malaria, but the overwhelming majority of their children will die of malaria unless they marry someone carrying a sickle-cell gene, in which case approximately half of their children will die of malaria. All parents, therefore, must be reconciled to the early death of approximately half of their children.

If the malaria is wiped out, or the people are moved to some area where malaria is absent, most of the children of a non-sickle-celled parent will survive. However, the survival of the children of the sickle-cell parent will depend heavily on whether the other parent carries the sickle-cell gene.

Two social attitudes are now possible. One is to rely on the evolutionary process. Those who adopt this position note that, since carriers of sickle-cell genes will be lower in reproductive capacity than other members of the population, each generation will have a smaller proportion of such individuals. When only one percent of the individuals have the sickle-cell gene, only one marriage out of ten thousand will give rise to children that die from sickle-cell disease.

An alternative approach is based on a human ethical image. A person carrying the sickle-cell gene usually has abnormally shaped blood cells, so that they can be warned that they are carriers of the sickle-cell gene and then left with three choices: ignore the problem; marry a person known to be free of sickle-cell (half of the children will be sickle-cell carriers, but none will die of anemia); or marry a person with sickle-cell genes and avoid reproducing. The social implication of this approach is that the frequency of the gene will be slightly reduced in the population in the course of time. Meanwhile, those people who suffer from either sickle-cell anemia or the sociological and psychological consequences of knowing that they are carriers, will just have to accept their role in evolutionary history.

A third possibility is to consider sickle-cell anemia as a hereditary disease that one can attempt to cure. A medical program can be initiated which, if successful, might perhaps transform the sickle-cell anemia condition into one that an individual could deal with in normal life by taking medication, like diabetes. Such a program would give sickle-cell trait parents the same reproductive potential as normal hemoglobin parents, and would also permit individuals with a double dose of sickle-cell gene to reproduce. This would maintain the sickle-cell gene in its present ratio in the population, but would also eliminate a great deal of personal misery.

Therefore, one has to think either of man as an evolving organism subject to the laws of evolution, or of man as having his own image of the world from which he builds his own environment, as far as possible. It is within that environment that we define the notion of fitness and of selective value. We build our definition in terms of the moral values which we have adopted out of the freedom evolution has given us to make our decisions.

The suffering of a parent or the suffering of a baby due to the sickle-cell anemia condition can now be thought of either as a consequence of evolutionary law, or as an inadequacy in human medicine and society. I think my preference is obvious. In fact, I believe that what I have done is to reaffirm, on the basis of the facts of evolution, the curious metaphysical bind in which men are condemned to freedom. We are condemned to deal with moral and aesthetic issues as moral and aesthetic issues and cannot relegate our naturally given responsibility to some kind of natural law.

Acknowledgements

This article was written while the author was supported as a Guggenheim Fellow. Research relevant to this paper has been supported by the National Science Foundation (NSF 31-756A). It is contribution no. 162 of the Ecology and Evolution Program, S.U.N.Y., Stony Brook.

1.viii.1976

Department of Ecology and Evolution
State University of New York at Stony Brook
and Natural History Museum,
Smithsonian Institution,
Washington, D.C.

References

Alexander, R. D. 1974. The evolution of social behavior. *Annual Review of Ecology and Systematics*. 5:325–83.

Alexander, R. D. 1975. The search for a general theory of behavior. *Behavioral Science*. 20:70–100.

Ardrey, R. 1966. *The Territorial Imperative*. New York: Atheneum.

Ayala, F. J. 1974. The concept of biological progress. In *Studies in the Philosophy of Biology* (eds F. J. Ayala and T. Dobzhansky). London: Macmillan Press.

Barzun, J. 1958. *Darwin, Marx, and Wagner: a critique of a heritage*. New York: Doubleday.

Braudel, F. 1972. *The Mediterranean World in the Age of Phillip II* (translated from the French by Sian Reynolds). New York: Harper and Row.

Carson, H., Hardy, D. E., Spieth, H. T. and Stone, W. S. 1970. The evolutionary biology of the Hawaiian Drosophilidae. In *Essays in Evolution and Genetics in honour of Theodosius Dobzhansky*, pp. 437–543 (eds M. K. Hecht and W. C. Steere). New York: Appleton-Century-Crofts.

Cervantes Saavedra, Miguel de. 1968. *El retablo de las maravillas. Entremeses. Prologo y notas de J. A. Franch*. New York: Las Americas Publishing Co.

Gallup, G. G., Jr. 1969. Chimpanzees: self-recognition. *Science.* 167:86–7.

Gallup, G. G., Jr. 1974. Toward an operational definition of self-awareness. In *IXth International Congress of Anthropological and Ethnological Sciences: Primatology Session, subsection D* (ed. R. H. Tuttle). The Hague and Paris: Mouton Press.

Grant, M. 1916. *The Passing of the Great Race or the Racial Basis of European History.* New York: Charles Scribner's Sons.

Huizenga, J. 1950. *Homo ludens: a study of the play element in culture.* Boston: Beacon Press.

Hyman, L. H. 1951. *The Invertebrates: Platyhelminthes and Rhynchocoela. The Acoelomate Bilateria* (Volume II). New York: McGraw-Hill Book Co.

Kamin, L. J. 1974. *The Science and Politics of I.Q.* New York: Halsted Press Division of John Wiley and Sons.

Koenig, O. 1975. Biologie der Uniform. In *Evolution ein Querschnitt der Forschung*, pp. 175–211 (ed. H. V. Ditfurth). Hamburg: Hoffman und Campe.

Lethmate, V. J. and Dücker, G. 1973. Untersuchungen zum Selbsterkennen im Spiegel bei Orang-utans und einigen anderen Affenarten. *Zeitschrift für Tierpsychologie.* 33:248–69.

Lewontin, R. C. 1974. *The Genetic Basis of Evolutionary Change.* New York: Columbia University Press.

Lorenz, K. Z. 1966. *On Aggression.* New York: Harcourt, Brace, and Jovanovich Inc.

Morris, D. (ed.). 1967. *Primate Ethology: essays on the socio-sexual behavior of apes and monkeys.* Chicago: Aldine Publishing Co.

Rapoport, A. (ed.). 1975. Uses of game-theoretic models in biology. *General Systems: Yearbook of the Society for General Systems research.* XX:49–58.

Roth, C. 1964. *The Spanish Inquisition.* New York: W. W. Norton and Co.

Rucknagel, D. L. and Neel, J. V. 1961. The hemoglobinopathies. In *Progress in Medical Genetics.* I:158–260 (eds A. G. Steinberg and A. G. Bearn). New York: Grune Publishing Co.

Slobodkin, L. B. 1975. Die Strategie der Evolution. *Evolution ein Querschnitt der Forschung*, pp. 33–55 (ed. H. V. Ditfurth). Hamburg: Hoffman und Campe.

Slobodkin, L. B. 1976. The peculiar evolutionary strategy of man. *Transactions of the Boston Colloquium of Philosophy of Science.* 31. (In Press.)

Slobodkin, L. B. and Rapoport, A. 1974. An optimal strategy of evolution. *Quart. Rev. Biol.* 49:181–200.

Spengler, O. 1934. *The Decline of the West.* New York: A. A. Knopf.

Trivers, R. L. 1971. The evolution of reciprocal altruism. *Quart. Rev. Biol.* 46:35–57.

Wilson, E. O. 1975. *Sociobiology: the New Synthesis.* Cambridge, Mass.: The Belknap Press of Harvard University Press.

Wilson, E. O. 1976. The lyric poet of evolution. (Review of: *The Hunting Hypothesis: a personal conclusion concerning the evolutionary nature of man* by R. Ardrey). *Saturday Review*, 3 April 1976: 27–8.

Abstract

Slobodkin, L. B.

Evolution is no help

There is no way to infer from the inevitability of biological evolution that there is inevitability behind historical events. There are no trends in evolution other than an ongoing, unchanging evolutionary tendency to do nothing and, if anything does occur, to do something in the smallest possible steps. Likely evolutionary futures are highly restricted by the properties of the evolutionary present and this conservatism of the evolutionary process; evolution occurs only in response to perturbation and has no momentum of its own. Man and at least his nearest primate relatives have a biological need for self-images. Their self-images are a powerful factor in determining their actions. The capacity to have self-images broadens the scope of possible evolutionary futures resulting from social, historical or environmental perturbation. Nonetheless, man is not yet immune to evolutionary biological change. Human decisions mold the evolutionary process, but human decision-makers cannot rely on evolutionary events or theories to provide them with rectitude, safety or sanctity.

An Acheulian occupation site at Hunsgi, Peninsular India: a summary of the results of two seasons of excavation (1975–6)

K. Paddayya

Introduction: the Hunsgi area and its sites

The writer has elsewhere given an account of the results of his first season of excavation at the Acheulian site of Hunsgi, North Karnataka (Paddayya 1975a; n.d.). With a view to obtaining further evidence, the site was excavated for another season during February–March 1976. The report given below is a summary of the results of both seasons of work at the site.

The Acheulian locality at Hunsgi containing the occupation site is one among a group of 13 occurrences explored by the writer in an oval-shaped valley, situated in the Shorapur Taluk of Gulbarga District. This valley, called the Hunsgi valley after the village of Hunsgi, lies about 450 m. above sea level and is enclosed by shale and limestone plateaux rising to a height of 70 m. from the valley floor. It measures 15 km. north–south and 10 km. east–west. Several minor streams originate in the plateaux and cut across the valley in an easterly direction. Excepting one stream which flows throughout the year because of the existence of a few springs in its bed, these streams carry water during the wet season only (July to October). They join at or slightly upstream of the village of Hunsgi, forming a bigger stream popularly known as the Hunsgi nullah. The village of Hunsgi is thus situated at the very outlet for the whole drainage of the valley. The Hunsgi nullah has a breadth of 35 m. and 2 to 3 m. high banks, and joins the river Krishna after an easterly course of about 35 km. Owing to the existence of the springs referred to above, this stream also has a shallow water channel even during dry seasons. The area receives an average annual rainfall of about 70 cm. and is covered with thorn, scrub-forest type of vegetation characteristic of the semi-arid climate. The occurrence of a large number of sites ranging from the Acheulian stage to the Early Historical period proves that the valley formed a very favourable habitat for human habitation in ancient times.

Confining ourselves here to the Acheulian culture, we have four sites, with a total of 13 occurrences comprising workshops, occurrences in river gravel deposits and localities with living or occupation horizons (Paddayya 1975b). The site at Hunsgi (Lat. 16° 27′ North; Long. 76° 31′ East) was discovered in February 1974. To obtain material for the construction of the earthen embankments of a minor irrigation dam that was being built across the Hunsgi nullah, the Public Works Department dug a considerable area on the right bank of the stream. (This area, lying about 200 m. northeast of the village, was later

Plate 1 View of the Acheulian Locality V at Hunsgi, with the Hunsgi stream in the foreground. (Trench 3 containing the occupation floor is indicated by the arrow.)

Plate 2 View (facing west) of the Acheulian occupation floor exposed in 1975 in Trench 3 at Locality V, Hunsgi.

Plate 3 Complete view (facing east) of the Acheulian occupation floor exposed in Trench 3 at Locality V, Hunsgi. (The blank area in the centre delimited by pegs was excavated in 1975.)

designated as Locality III.) The cuttings exposed an implementiferous deposit consisting of rubble and gravel of limestone and granite blocks of various sizes, all set in a matrix of dark brown gruss derived from the weathering of granite. Intensive explorations on either bank of the nullah led to the discovery of four more tool-bearing localities; a sixth locality was discovered in March 1976. These are in the form of oval-shaped concentrations of artefacts (15 to 50 m. across), lying 100 to 450 m. away from one another. The mint-fresh condition of the artefacts, the occurrence of a large number of limestone slabs and granite blocks, and the sub-angular to sub-rounded character of the limestone gravel suggested that the tool-bearing deposits found at these localities are of localized or colluvial origin and hence quite different from alluvial gravels. It was therefore felt that careful excavations at some of these localities might reveal undisturbed archaeological horizons. With this objective in view the writer conducted excavations at Locality V for two seasons in 1975 and 1976, each lasting for about six weeks. This work enabled the writer to expose a complete occupation horizon.

The occupation site

Locality V, situated on the left bank of the Hunsgi nullah, lies half a kilometre northeast of the village (fig. 13; plate 1). It is a horseshoe-shaped piece of land measuring about one hectare in extent, and forms a distinct terrace rising to a height of 5 m. above the bed of the stream. On the eastern and northern sides it is bounded by a feeder stream of the Hunsgi nullah and on the west by a field bund. The eastern part has 50 cm. of thick black soil, which is partly under cultivation, while the western part is a barren patch strewn with tool-bearing deposits. The whole locality is dotted with numerous granite boulders of various sizes, which form part of a low ridge cutting across the Hunsgi nullah in a southeast–northwest direction. Several artefacts in fresh condition were found scattered

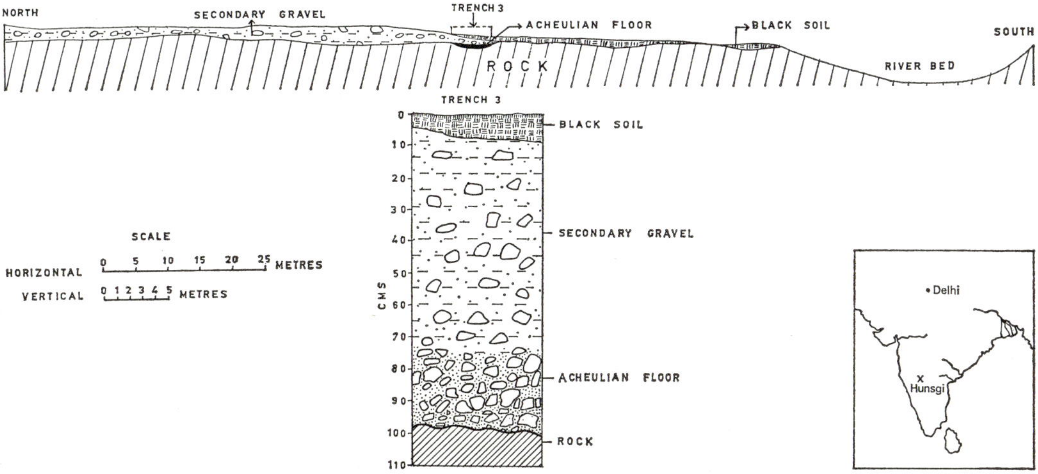

Figure 13 Transverse section at Locality V, Hunsgi, showing the stratigraphical position of the Acheulian occupation floor in relation to other deposits. (*right*) Location of Hunsgi in Peninsular India

in the western part. With these surface scatters serving as the clues, several test pits were dug during February–March 1975 for ascertaining the existence of undisturbed cultural horizons. These pits proved to be very disappointing, inasmuch as they exposed either a 30 cm. thick deposit of black soil or a 30 cm. to 1 m. thick secondary gravel yielding only isolated artefacts, without bearing any evidence of a regular archaeological horizon.

One of the test pits (1 × 1 m.), however, produced entirely different evidence. This pit (later to form grid square A-2 of Trench 3), situated immediately to the east of a cluster of granite boulders, lay 45 m. away from the bank of the Hunsgi stream and 4 m. above its bed. Here a concentration of seven artefacts along with limestone rubble and gravel was encountered below a 70 cm. thickness of secondary gravel. In order to know whether this was only a stray phenomenon or whether it formed part of an undisturbed cultural level, the pit was extended on the northern side to cover another square meter (later to form grid square B-2). This second square yielded a larger number of artefacts at the same depth. It was now fairly certain that we were exposing a cultural horizon preserved in its primary context. Such finds remain rare in the Indian subcontinent. Hence the trench (called Trench 3) was extended to the north, west and east, covering an area of 4 × 4 m. The cultural level was found to spread over the whole area of 16 square meters. In order to verify whether, as on the western side, a natural cluster of granite boulders exists (as suggested by the top portions of a few blocks exposed on the surface), an extension trench was excavated on the eastern part of the main trench. It was L-shaped and covered an area of 6·75 square meters. The total area excavated in 1975 thus measured 22·75 square metres (plate 2). With the exception of the easternmost part of the extension trench, where bedrock was struck immediately below a thin deposit of secondary gravel, the cultural horizon was found to cover the whole excavated area. In short, the 1975 excavation revealed a primary cultural level measuring about 9 m. in length (east–west), with its eastern and western limits marked by natural clusters of granite blocks forming part of the bedrock. With a view to finding out its northern and southern limits, the trench was extended on these sides during the second season. On the north an area of 23 square meters was excavated; on the southern side an area of 17·25 square metres was added to the trench. The final trench was thus rectangular in plan, measuring 9 m. east–west and 7 m. north–south (plate 3).

Stratigraphy and lithology

The stratigraphy of the trench is briefly as follows (from the top downwards):

(*a*) black soil (maximum thickness: 30 cm.);

(*b*) somewhat loose, dark brown secondary gravel with scattered artefacts (maximum thickness: 70 cm.);

(*c*) Acheulian floor (10–35 cm. thick);

(*d*) bedrock (granite) partly weathered into gruss.

Owing to the limited time left at our disposal during the first season of work, it was not possible to keep an account of the various rock pieces found in each square of the floor. This shortcoming was amended in the second season, so that it is now possible to know the lithological composition of the Acheulian horizon in precise terms. Table 1 gives the number of pieces of various categories and their size-ranges found in the area (40·25 square metres in extent) excavated in 1976.

TABLE I

Lithological composition of the Acheulian floor in Trench 3, Hunsgi Locality V

Size (in cm.)	Granite		Limestone gravel		Other rocks		Limestone rubble	
	No.	%	No.	%	No.	%	No.	%
<2	—	—	16	5·0	44	12·7	15	6·8
2·1– 4	53	12·0	163	50·6	165	47·5	81	36·7
4·1– 6	117	26·5	70	21·8	67	19·3	53	24·0
6·1– 8	85	19·2	36	11·2	33	9·5	29	13·1
8·1–10	73	16·5	20	6·2	19	5·5	25	11·3
10·1–12	36	8·3	10	3·1	10	2·8	9	4·1
12·1–14	27	6·1	4	1·2	3	0·9	3	1·3
14·1–16	19	4·3	2	0·6	2	0·6	5	2·3
16·1–18	6	1·3	1	0·3	1	0·3	1	0·4
18·1–20	6	1·3	—	—	—	—	—	—
>20	20	4·5	—	—	3	0·9	—	—
Total	442	100·0	322	100·0	347	100·0	221	100·0

The granite blocks vary greatly in size and form part of the bedrock. They must have provided a hard surface for the Acheulian occupants. In the course of excavation several blocks were found in a disaggregated state, thereby suggesting that originally the level contained a much larger number of pieces which subsequently weathered to give rise to gruss. With regard to the limestone gravel, pieces up to 4 cm. are sub-rounded to rounded, whereas a majority of the pieces above this size-class are only sub-angular. Considering the riverine setting of the site, it is very probable that the former category of pieces form part of a thin gravel spread laid down over the locality prior to Acheulian occupation. The larger pieces, on the other hand, would seem to have been gathered from the immediate vicinity and brought to the camping spot for use as raw material for tool-making. As a proof of this observation we may cite here the case of certain handaxes and other finished tools in which the flaked portions show up fresh edges and corners, while the unworked area still preserves the pebble cortex of the blank (fig. 16, no. 12). As in the case of the limestone gravel, pieces of other rocks (chert, shale, quartzite, quartz, schist, dolerite and sandstone) measuring below 4 cm. show a better degree of rounding and hence may be regarded as natural components of the floor. Those above 4 cm. are angular to sub-angular and must have been introduced by man. As to the limestone rubble, the only source of its origin is the limestone plateaux lying 1 to 2 km. north of the locality or the scree deposits occurring in the foothill region. While some of the smaller pieces may have been derived through natural processes like surface run-off, the larger slabs, more particularly those measuring above 6 cm. in length, were undoubtedly brought to the spot by man for use as raw material. In breadth and thickness they measure up to 9·5 cm. and 4 cm. respectively and hence serve as ideal blanks for fashioning tools (cf. figs 15, no. 7 and 17, no. 14).

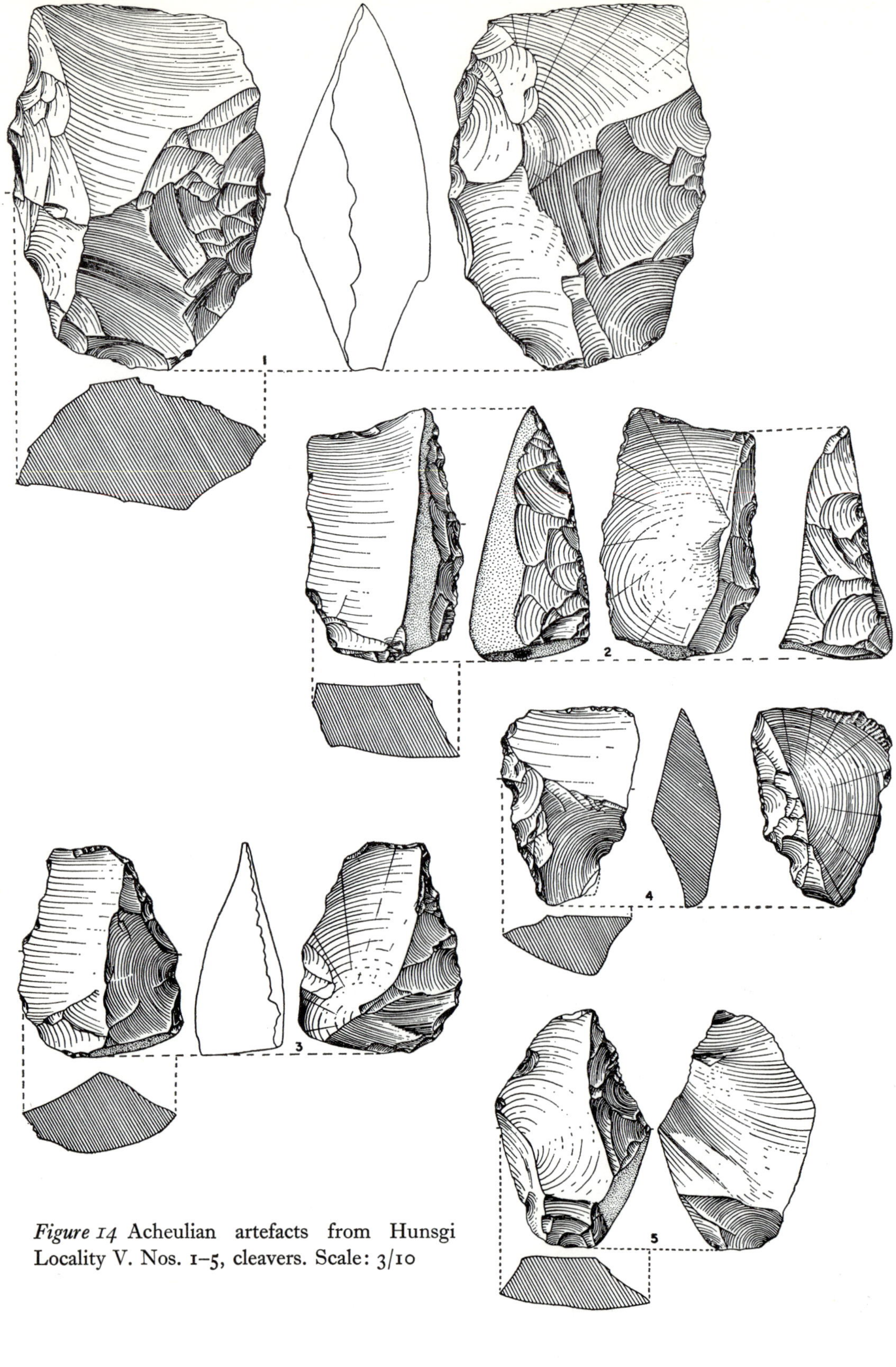

Figure 14 Acheulian artefacts from Hunsgi Locality V. Nos. 1–5, cleavers. Scale: 3/10

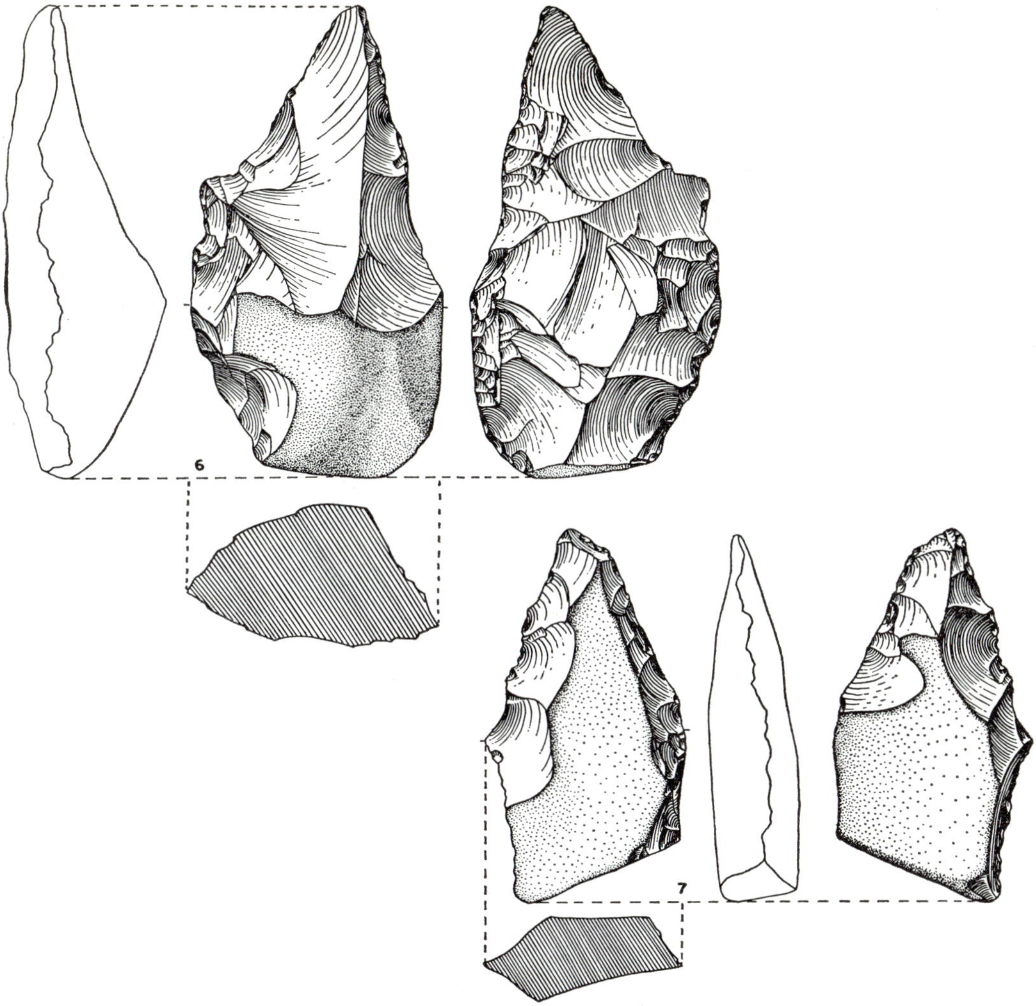

Figure 15 Acheulian artefacts from Hunsgi Locality V. Nos. 6–7, handaxes. Scale: 3/10

The matrix of the floor consists mainly of light brown/whitish gruss and, to a lesser extent, of secondary carbonate accumulated through groundwater percolation. From the fact that a number of granite pieces of the floor occur in a disaggregated state, it would seem that the gruss is by and large derived from the *in situ* weathering of granite. In contrast to the overlying secondary gravel which is only moderately consolidated, this sediment is well cemented and consists of nodules and clods of various sizes.

A noteworthy feature of the floor is that neither the artefacts nor the rock pieces show any preferred orientation or sorting. Likewise, the deposit is also lacking in pebble-to-pebble contact. These features, taken together with the fact that a considerable number of the rock constituents were introduced by man, make it certain that the layer under consideration is not of fluvial origin but an *in situ* accumulation. At the same time it must be admitted that, subsequent to its desertion by man, the spot must have been affected by surface flow and such other hydrological processes, leading to minor changes in the

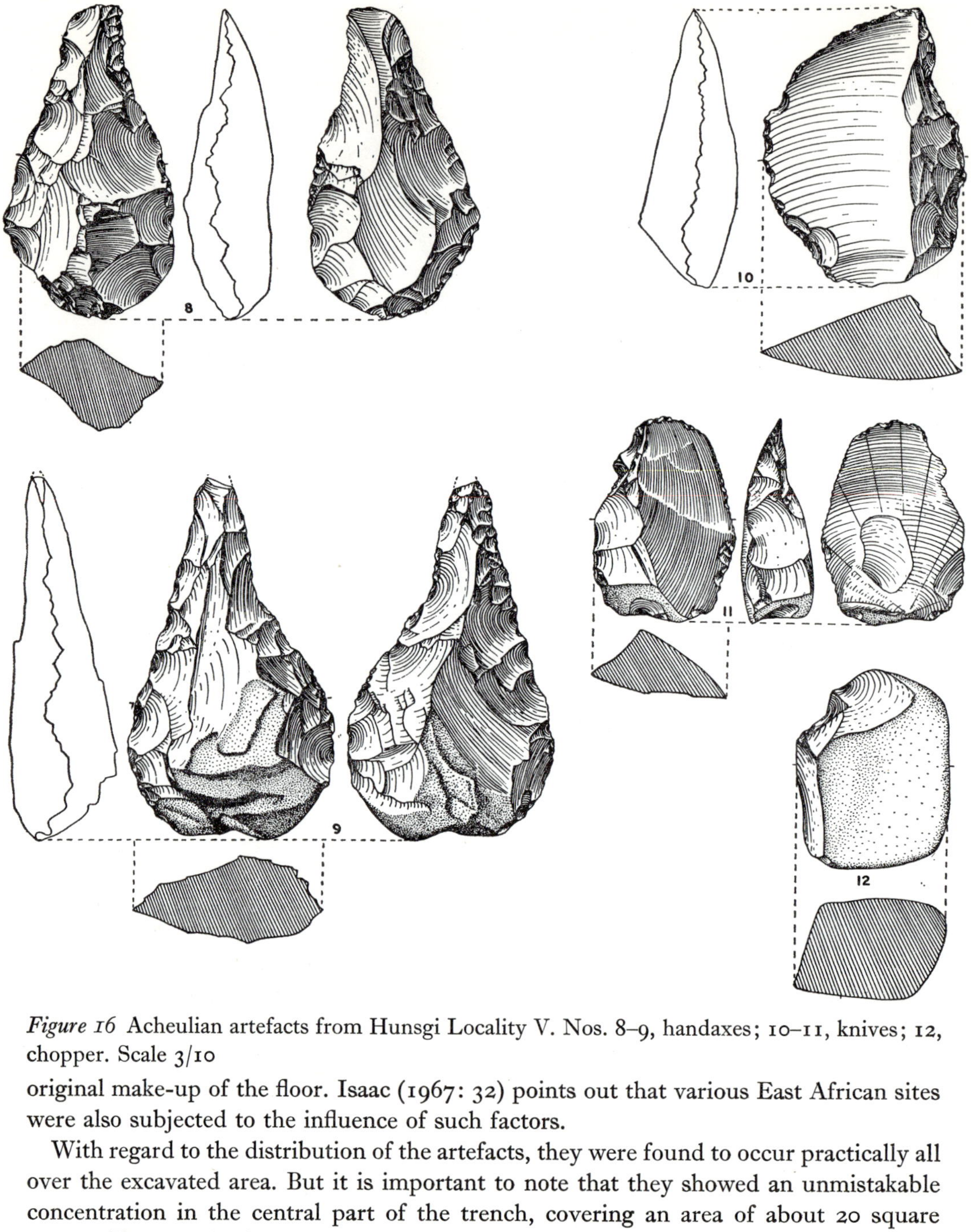

Figure 16 Acheulian artefacts from Hunsgi Locality V. Nos. 8–9, handaxes; 10–11, knives; 12, chopper. Scale 3/10

original make-up of the floor. Isaac (1967: 32) points out that various East African sites were also subjected to the influence of such factors.

With regard to the distribution of the artefacts, they were found to occur practically all over the excavated area. But it is important to note that they showed an unmistakable concentration in the central part of the trench, covering an area of about 20 square meters. Two granite boulders (one now disaggregated), measuring about 50 cm. across, were found associated with this cluster; it is very probable that they served as seats for the Acheulian occupants in their stone-working activities. The number of artefacts decreased considerably towards the northern and southern limits of the area. This was particularly true of the southern side where very few or no artefacts and rock pieces were present in

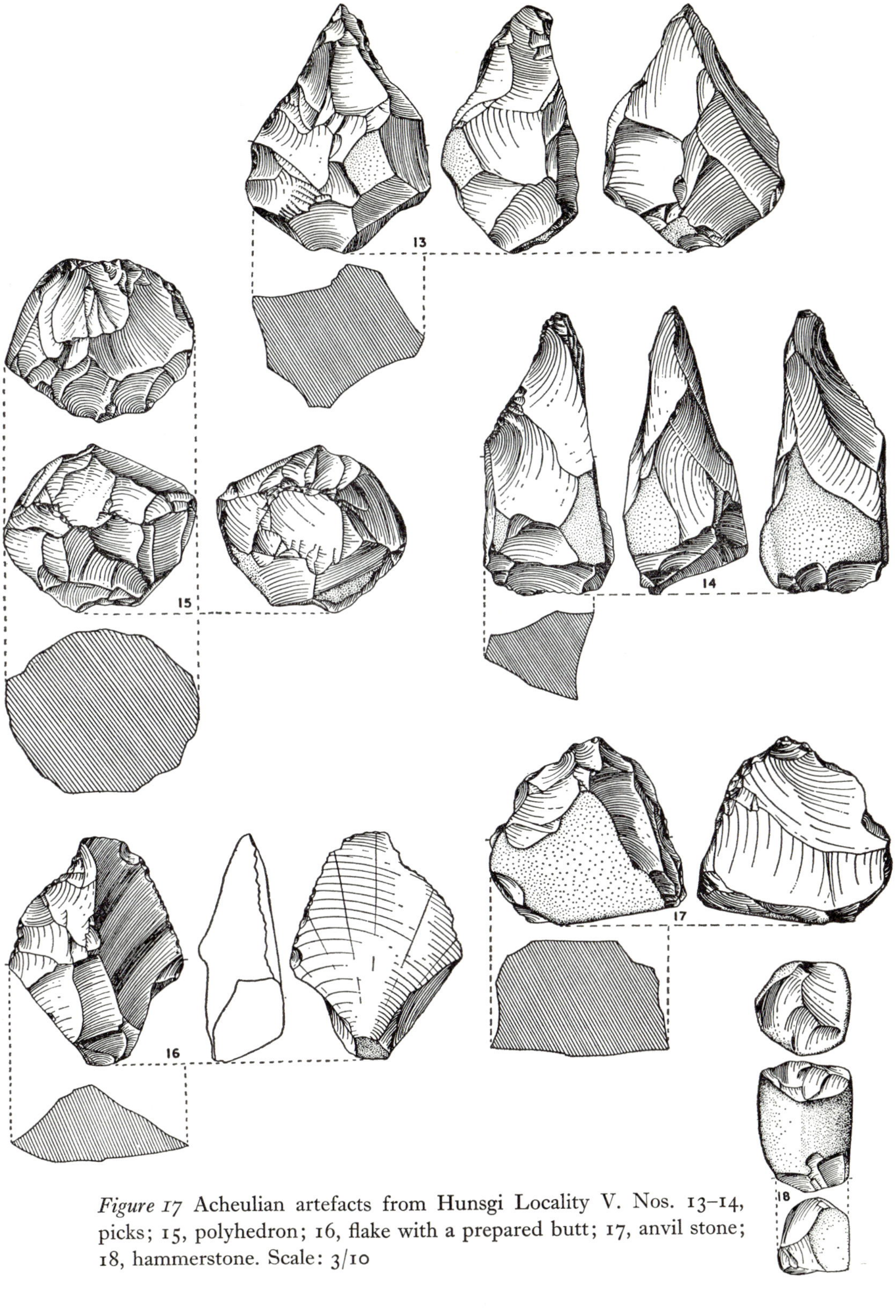

Figure 17 Acheulian artefacts from Hunsgi Locality V. Nos. 13–14, picks; 15, polyhedron; 16, flake with a prepared butt; 17, anvil stone; 18, hammerstone. Scale: 3/10

some of the grid squares. Interestingly enough, one dozen granite boulders were found in the northern part of the trench. These varied between 30 and 80 cm. in size and, unlike the blocks found in other parts of the trench, stood 25 to 50 cm. above the floor. They formed a line, albeit discontinuous, in east–west direction. It seems very likely that they were intentionally arranged by man to serve as an enclosure for the living area. As has been mentioned above, the eastern and western limits of the floor are marked by naturally formed clusters of boulders standing 50 cm. to 1 m. above the level of the floor. In short, the site consists of an oval-shaped open area (over 60 square metres in extent) surrounded by granite boulders on the west, north and east. Strewn as it was with granite pieces of various sizes mixed up with gruss, the spot must have provided a hard surface suitable for camping purposes.

Palaeoenvironment

Dr S. N. Rajaguru, who is making a detailed study of the palaeogeographical setting of the site, observes that the drainage system of the valley was not yet fully organized at the time of Acheulian occupation. The stream ancestral to the present-day Hunsgi nullah was flowing at a higher level (2 to 3 m. above the present bed) and in a much broader channel system (about 200 m.), comprising several shallow braided water courses. It is very probable that the locality containing the living site under study formed a part of this channel system. The site must have been occupied for a temporary period during the dry season; it may be noted that several of the Acheulian living sites in East Africa also lay in or close to channels of shallow seasonal streams (Isaac 1972). Professor W. van Zeist of the Biologisch-Archaeologisch Instituut, Groningen, who has analysed the soil samples from the floor from the palynological point of view, reports (pers. comm.) the presence of pollen of twenty plant species. The samples are dominated by the pollen of *Graminae* (52% to 64%) and *Tubuliflorae compositae* (18% to 26%), thereby suggesting an open grassland type of vegetation. But it must be emphasized that Professor van Zeist is doubtful of the Acheulian age of the pollen grains; he suspects that they may be of a later date and have infiltrated into the Acheulian level. Such a process is not unlikely, because the deposits overlying the floor measure less than one metre in thickness. However that may be, our present knowledge of the Pleistocene period in Pensinsular India does not warrant us to postulate environmental conditions vastly different from those prevailing in the area today. It can therefore be safely assumed that the Hunsgi valley was covered with flora similar to the present-day thorn, scrub-forest type of vegetation.

The industry

The area excavated in 1975 yielded a total of 291 artefacts. They show a density of 13 pieces per square metre. Over 600 artefacts were found during the 1976 excavation. The assemblage from the first season has already been studied in a detailed way; the following comments are confined to this collection (for details, see Paddayya n.d.). The preponderance of simple artefacts over finished tools, the occurrence of anvils and hammerstones, and the fresh *état physique* of the artefacts prove for certain that the manufacture of tools took place on the spot itself. An interesting feature of the industry is that over 90% of the specimens are made of limestone; they are made on both slabs and water-worn pieces. The following artefact types are present in the collection (figs 14–17):

Classification	*No. of examples*
1 *Shaped tools*	
1 Cleavers (fig. 14, nos. 1–5)	28
2 Handaxes (figs 15, nos. 6–7; 16, nos. 8–9)	18
3 Knives (fig. 16, nos. 10–11)	14
4 Choppers (fig. 16, no. 12)	9
5 Picks (fig. 17, nos. 13–14)	8
6 Polyhedrons (fig. 17, no. 15)	10
7 Spheroids	4
8 Scrapers	15
9 Flakes with prepared butts (fig. 17, no. 16)	2
10 Backed tool	1
2 *Utilized pieces*	
1 Anvil stones (fig. 17, no. 17)	3
2 Hammerstones (fig. 17, no. 18)	5
3 Utilized flakes	15
4 Utilized tabular pieces	2
3 *Débitage*	
1 Cores	5
2 Indeterminately worked nuclei	20
3 Flakes	5
4 Waste products	127
Total	291

Cleavers, handaxes, knives, choppers, picks, polyhedrons and scrapers are the principal types among the finished tools. Most of the cleavers are fashioned on flakes and have parallel or convergent sides. Eleven specimens belong to the guillotine type, in which the working edge is inclined at 15° or more to the long axis of the artefact (fig. 14, no. 5). The handaxes are made on both flakes and complete blanks (slabs and cobbles), and belong to the lanceolate, ovate, triangular and cordate types. In the case of the knives (mostly made on elongate flakes) one of the edges is blunt, while the opposite one is sharp and serves as the working edge. Both uni- and bifacially worked specimens occur among the choppers. The picks are made on elongate angular blocks and show bold flaking on the surfaces. Their transverse cross-sections are parallelogram, trapezoidal or triangular. The polyhedrons are sub-spherical artefacts showing flaking all over the body. The flake-scars intersect one another, giving rise to several ridge-like features. The majority of the scrapers are fashioned on flakes. In regard to the quality of secondary working and regularity of shape, these artefacts do not stand comparison with their counterparts in the succeeding Middle Palaeolithic industry.

The frequent employment of stone hammer technique for making handaxes and other heavy-duty tools (as reflected in the irregular outlines and thick cross-sections) and the occurrence of choppers, picks, polyhedrons and knives in fairly large numbers impart an Early Acheulian character to the industry. On the whole it compares quite well with the industries from Chirki (Corvinus 1970; 1973) and Anagwadi (Pappu 1974). As opposed to this group, sites like Gangapur (Sankalia 1952; *IAR* 1965–6: 30–1), Bhimbetka (Misra 1974) and those on the Rallkalava river in Andhra Pradesh (Murty 1966) seem to represent an evolved stage within the Acheulian. But this grouping is based purely on typological and technological criteria and does not carry with it any chronological implications.

Apart from stone artefacts, small pieces of red haematite were found at the site during the second season of excavation. The only known geological source of this material lies about 25 km. northeast of Hunsgi. Hence it would seem that the Acheulian occupants brought larger pieces to the camp site, presumably for use as a colouring material.

Acknowledgements

The present research project was undertaken by the writer under the University Grants Commission's scheme of Special Assistance in Prehistory granted to the Department of Archaeology, Deccan College, Poona. Grateful thanks are due to Mr R. B. Warke for his assistance during the two seasons of excavation and to Dr S. N. Rajaguru and Mr M. D. Kajale for their help in interpreting the past and present environments of the site. Acknowledgement is also due to Professor W. van Zeist for readily undertaking pollen-analytical studies of the soil samples.

11.viii.1976

Deccan College
Poona, India

References

Corvinus, G. 1970. The Acheulian workshop at Chirki-on-Pravara, Maharashtra. *Indian Antiquary*. 4:13–32.

Corvinus, G. 1973. Excavations at an Acheulian site at Chirki-on-Pravara, India. In Hammond, N. (ed.), *South Asian Archaeology*, 13–28. New Jersey: Noyes Press.

IAR. Indian Archaeology – A Review. Annual Bulletin of the Archaeological Survey of India. New Delhi.

Isaac, G. Ll. 1967. Towards the interpretation of occupation debris: some experiments and observations. *Kroeber Anthropological Society Paper*. 37:31–57.

Isaac, G. Ll. 1972. Comparative studies of Pleistocene site locations in East Africa. In *Man, Settlement and Urbanism*, pp. 165–76 (eds P. J. Ucko, R. Tringham and G. W. Dimbleby). London: Duckworth.

Misra, V. N. 1974. The Acheulian industry of Rockshelter IIIF-23 at Bhimbetka, central India: a preliminary analysis. (Unpublished paper read at the *Seminar on Indian Prehistory* held at Poona in June 1974.)

Murty, M. L. K. 1966. *Stone Age Cultures of Chittoor District.* (Unpublished Ph.D. thesis, Poona University.)

Paddayya, K. 1975a. Acheulian occupation site at Hungsi, Gulbarga district, Karnataka – a preliminary report. *Bulletin of the Deccan College Research Institute.* 35:87–93.

Paddayya, K. 1975b. Investigations into the Acheulian phase in the Shorapur Doab, Peninsular India – a preliminary report. *Quartär.* 26:5–11.

Paddayya, K. n.d. The Acheulian culture of the Hunsgi valley (Shorapur Doab), Peninsular India. *Anthropos* (in press).

Pappu, R. S. 1974. *Pleistocene Studies in the Upper Krishna Basin.* Poona: Deccan College.

Sankalia, H. D. 1952. *The Godavari Palaeolithic Industry.* Poona: Deccan College.

Abstract

Paddayya, K.

An Acheulian occupation site at Hunsgi, Peninsular India: a summary of the results of two seasons of excavation (1975–6)

Several Acheulian sites have been discovered recently in the vicinity of Hunsgi, North Karnataka, and one of them (Hunsgi Locality V) appears to be an occupation site in primary context. Such finds are still rare in the Indian sub-continent. A preliminary report is given, based on the excavation so far carried out. The stratigraphy and lithology of the Acheulian floor are described. The occupation area, of some 60 square metres, was bounded on two sides by natural accumulations of granite boulders and on a third side by a discontinuous line of boulders which is likely to have been artificially arranged. Palaeoenvironmental evidence is at present under study. The industry is described and a selection of the artefacts figured. The industry seems to resemble the earlier Acheulian of Peninsular India, rather than the evolved Acheulian, as these are known at present, though no clear dating evidence is yet available from the Hunsgi site.

Contributors

John Terrell, Assistant Curator of Oceanic Archaeology and Ethnology at the Field Museum of Natural History in Chicago, is especially interested in the prehistory and human diversity of Melanesia. A Fulbright Fellow to New Zealand in 1965 after gaining his B.A. from Harvard College, he received his graduate education at the University of Pennsylvania and at Harvard.

Jared M. Diamond is Professor of Physiology at the University of California, Los Angeles. He took his B.A. in biochemical sciences at Harvard and his Ph.D. in physiology at Cambridge University. During 1962–5 he was a Junior Fellow, Society of Fellows, Harvard University. At this time he began to specialize also in his second research area, ecology and evolutionary biology. He has studied and written on the bird faunas of New Guinea and other south-western Pacific islands.

John E. Yellen is currently working again in Botswana among the !Kung hunter-gatherers. He gained his Ph.D. at Harvard.

Henry C. Harpending is Assistant Professor of Anthropology at the University of New Mexico. He has a B.A. from Hamilton College and a Ph.D. from Harvard. He is working in the areas of human population genetics and demography.

Herbert Davis is Assistant Professor of Mathematics and Statistics in the Department of Mathematics at the University of New Mexico. He obtained his Ph.D. from Johns Hopkins University. His special interests are in time series analysis, stochastic processes, radiation biology and analysis of large data sets.

Betty J. Meggers is Research Associate in the Department of Anthropology, National Museum of Natural History, Smithsonian Institution. She received her B.A. from the University of Pennsylvania, her M.A. from the University of Michigan and her Ph.D. from Columbia University. She is especially well-known for her studies on the prehistory and human ecology of South America.

Olga F. Linares is Research Scientist at the Smithsonian Tropical Research Institute in Balboa, Panama Canal Zone. A B.A. from Vassar College, she took her Ph.D. at Harvard. She is also Associate Curator of Central American Archaeology at the Peabody Museum of American Archaeology and Ethnology, Harvard University.

Jonathan D. Sauer is Professor of Geography within the Department of Geography and Director of the Botanical Gardens-Herbarium, Biology Department, at the University of California, Los Angeles. He has a Ph.D. from Washington University and is interested in recent plant migration and evolution.

Lawrence B. Slobodkin has a Ph.D. in zoology from Yale. He is Professor of Biology in the Department of Ecology and Evolution at the State University of New York, Stony Brook. His principal work is in theoretical and experimental population ecology, evolutionary strategy and environmental management.

K. Paddayya received his Ph.D. in 1968 from the University of Poona. His main interests are in the prehistory and protohistory of Peninsular India. He has also carried out research for some time on the late Palaeolithic cultures of northern Europe at the Biologisch-Archaeologisch Instituut, Groningen. He is now a Lecturer in prehistory at the Deccan College, Poona.

Notes to contributors

Manuscripts should not normally exceed 5,000 words in length. They should be typed on good quality A4 paper (i.e. approx. $11\frac{3}{4}$ in. × $8\frac{1}{4}$ in., or 30 cm. × 21 cm.), using double spacing throughout. Two copies of the manuscript should be submitted, the author retaining another. Unsolicited contributions and related correspondence should be addressed to the Executive Editor – Ian Glover, Institute of Archaeology, 31–4 Gordon Square, London WC1H 0PY.

Referencing should follow the modern scientific convention. Footnotes, wherever possible, should be avoided. Bibliographic references, to be included in the text, should list the author's last name, date of publication, and number of page, e.g. (Clark 1952: 211). Where an author's name has been cited already in the text, references need only be made to the date of publication and page, e.g. (1952: 211). Extended references should be listed alphabetically at the end of the paper, e.g.

Bouard, M. de. 1965. La mesure de la résistivité électrique des sols en archéologie. *Annales de Normandie*. 15:461–77.
Clark, J. G. D. 1952. *Prehistoric Europe: the economic basis*. London: Methuen.
Wace, A. J. B. 1958. Aegean prehistory: a review. *Antiquity*. 32:30–4.
Woodburn, J. 1968. An introduction to Hazda ecology. In *Man the hunter*, pp. 49–55 (eds R. B. Lee and I. DeVore). Chicago: Aldine Publishing Company.

Text figures, site plans and distribution maps should be drawn on strong paper, white card, or good quality tracing film. The lettering on diagrams should be in the type face Univers (medium weight). This is obtainable on transfer sheets (e.g. 'Letraset'). They should measure approximately twice the intended final size. A published full-page illustration may not exceed 8 in. × $5\frac{15}{16}$ in., or 20·5 cm. × 15·5 cm. Plates should be printed on glossy paper and should be mounted on thin card. Figures, maps and plates should be titled and numbered; originals should be numbered in pencil only. A list of captions to figures and plates must be provided on a separate sheet.

Each contribution should be accompanied by a brief abstract (100–150 words) summarizing its contents. A short note on individual contributors should also be supplied.

It is important that authors should submit accurate, well-prepared copy ready for the printer. Re-drawing of maps or figures cannot be undertaken by the editors, who may return sub-standard work to contributors for re-presentation in an improved form. Galley proofs of all articles will be sent to authors, who are reminded that these are intended for checking, not re-writing. Failure to return proofs by the required date may lead to the editor of the issue sending his own corrected proofs to the printer without further reference to the author.

Twenty-five offprints and a voucher copy of the journal will be supplied to authors on publication of a paper. Additional offprints may be purchased at cost price, and should be ordered not later than on the return of corrected proofs. The free allocation must be shared between joint authors.

Index to Volume Eight

Index of Contributors

Addyman, P. V. 220
Blust, Robert 19
Carter, P. L. 197
Casteel, Richard W. 192
Davis, Herbert 275
Diamond, Jared M. 249
Eaton, E. R. 169
Ehret, Christopher 5
Harpending, Henry 275
Hood, J. S. R. 220
Hubbard, R. N. L. B. 159
Kaufman, Terrence 101
Kenward, H. K. 220
Kinkade, M. Dale 83
Linares, Olga F. 304
MacGregor, A. 224
McKerrell, Hugh 169
Mallory, J. P. 44
Meggers, Betty J. 287
Osborne, P. J. 150
Paddayya, K. 344
Paulsen, Allison C. 121
Phillipson, D. W. 65
Potter, T. W. 207
Powell, J. V. 83
Sauer, Jonathan D. 320
Shaw, Brent D. 133
Slobodkin, Lawrence B. 332
Terrell, John 237
Wild, John Peter 57
Williams, D. 220
Yellen, John E. 262

Index of Articles

Acheulian occupation site at Hunsgi, Peninsular India: a summary of the results of two seasons of excavation (1975–6) (Paddayya) 344

Adaptive strategies in western Panama (Linares) 304

Archaeological and linguistic correlations in Mayaland and associated areas of Meso-America (Kaufman) 101

Archaeology and Bantu linguistics (Phillipson) 65

Austronesian culture history: some linguistic inferences and their relations to the archaeological record (Blust) 19

Biogeographical theory and cultural analogies (Sauer) 320

Biology, biogeography and man (Terrell) 237

Climate, environment and prehistory in the Sahara (Shaw) 133

Climatic change on settlement in Eastern Lesotho during the Middle and Later Stone Age, The effects of (Carter) 197

Climatic variation during the Flandrian period: a preliminary note, Evidence from the insects (Osborne) 150

Colonization cycles in man and beast (Diamond) 249

Column and whole unit samples for recovering fish remains, Comparison of (Casteel) 192

Crops and climate in prehistoric Europe (Hubbard) 159

Environment and empire: climatic factors in prehistoric Andean culture change (Paulsen) 121

Evolution is no help (Slobodkin) 332

Hunter-gatherer ecology derived from the spatial structure of resources, Some implications for (Harpending and Davis) 275

Language and the prehistory of North America (Kinkade and Powell) 83

Linguistic evidence and its correlation with archaeology (Ehret) 5

Loanwords and Roman expansion in north-west Europe (Wild) 57

Long term hunter-gatherer adaptation to desert environments: a biogeographical perspective (Yellen) 262

Near Eastern alloying and some textual evidence for the early use of arsenical copper (Eaton and McKerrell) 169

Palaeoclimate in urban environmental archaeology at York, England: problems and potential (Addyman *et al.*) 220

Time perspective and proto-Indo-European culture (Mallory) 44

Valleys and settlement: some new evidence (Potter) 207

Vegetational fluctuation and prehistoric cultural adaptation in Amazonia: some tentative correlations (Meggers) 287